America
Goes Hawaiian

ALSO BY GEOFF ALEXANDER
AND FROM MCFARLAND

*The Nonprofit Survival Guide:
A Strategy for Sustainability* (2015)

*Films You Saw in School: A Critical Review
of 1,153 Classroom Educational Films (1958–1985)
in 74 Subject Categories* (2014)

Academic Films for the Classroom: A History (2010)

America Goes Hawaiian

The Influence of Pacific Island Culture on the Mainland

GEOFF ALEXANDER

Foreword by DESOTO BROWN

McFarland & Company, Inc., Publishers
Jefferson, North Carolina

LIBRARY OF CONGRESS CATALOGUING-IN-PUBLICATION DATA

Names: Alexander, Geoff, 1952– author.
Title: America goes Hawaiian : the influence of Pacific Island culture on the mainland / Geoff Alexander ; foreword by DeSoto Brown.
Description: Jefferson, North Carolina : McFarland & Company, Inc., Publishers, 2019 | Includes bibliographical references and index.
Identifiers: LCCN 2018056959 | ISBN 9781476669496 (softcover : acid free paper) ∞
Subjects: LCSH: Hawaii—In popular culture. | Popular culture—United States—History—20th century. | Hawaii—Civilization—20th century. | United States—Social life and customs—1945–1970. | Hawaii—Social life and customs—20th century. | Art, Polynesian—Influence. | Cultural appropriation—United States—History 20th century. | National characteristics, Hawaiian. | Hawaii—Relations—United States. | United States—Relations—Hawaii.
Classification: LCC DU624.5 .A529 2019 | DDC 303.48/2730969—dc23
LC record available at https://lccn.loc.gov/2018056959

BRITISH LIBRARY CATALOGUING DATA ARE AVAILABLE

ISBN (print) 978-1-4766-6949-6
ISBN (ebook) 978-1-4766-3356-5

© 2019 Geoff Alexander. All rights reserved

No part of this book may be reproduced or transmitted in any form or by any means, electronic or mechanical, including photocopying or recording, or by any information storage and retrieval system, without permission in writing from the publisher.

Front cover art by Mike Rangner

Printed in the United States of America

*McFarland & Company, Inc., Publishers
Box 611, Jefferson, North Carolina 28640
www.mcfarlandpub.com*

For Alec Alexander (1925–2017)
and Olive Gwendoline Freeman Leskovsky (1916–2014),
who gave their boy a thirst for Far Away
and the resolve to find it

Table of Contents

Acknowledgments	viii
Foreword by DeSoto Brown	1
Preface	3
Of Hawaiian Words and a Note on Money	7
Introduction	8
One—Sailing to Paradise	17
Two—Flying Air Paradise: The Evolution of Flight to Hawaii	33
Three—The Hula: Taking America by Dance	51
Four—Sliding into Paradise: The Hawaiian Steel Guitar	81
Five—Ring My Bell: Music from the Paradise of Exotica	95
Six—Passing the Tiki Torch	121
Between pages 142 and 143 are 8 color plates with 12 photographs	
Seven—A Twisted Tale: The Emergence of Rattan Furniture	143
Eight—The Shirt Heard Round the World	157
Nine—If It Swells, Ride It: A Surfin' Tsunami Surges to the California Coast	193
Ten—Breeding a Hope for the Future: Interracial Romance Embarks for the Mainland	210
Afterword	224
Appendix A—Bigger, Better and Braver: Why the World's Largest Flying Boat Ever Made Never Flew a Commercial Route to Hawaii	225
Appendix B—The Zenith Trans-Oceanic: Bringing Hawaii to Your Living Room via Shortwave	228
Chapter Notes	230
Bibliography	256
Index	265

Acknowledgments

The joy I experienced in writing this book was tempered by the loss of two people who contributed generously, were important in the annals of Hawaii, and were dear friends of mine.

Jerry Hopkins was an old Asia hand and the noted author of some forty books, translated into 16 languages, and selling some four million copies. One of these was his definitive monograph *The Hula*. He was also the editor of the Hawaiian Music Foundation's *Hailono Mele* newsletter, an important resource cited several times in this book. Jerry provided me with critical back-stories that didn't make it into print in either of the two editions of his hula book, the first edition of which he considered definitive (he was highly critical of the edits and omissions in its second edition, which was unsupervised by him). His involvement in my book included insightful questions, pertinent criticisms, and suggestions leading to additional resources that proved to be extraordinarily valuable. Getting around by wheelchair in his last few months, Jerry was a rolling encyclopedia of many of the hidden corners of Asia and the Pacific and pointed me to some important areas I would have not seen without his insight. Jerry and I had been Bangkok buddies for a number of years, and our forays into that city's back corners were fine fodder for another book that might have been written by either of us. Jerry, who was in ill health, passed away fewer than four months after he painstakingly pored over my manuscript. He desperately wanted to write another book on the subject of ladyboys, another passion of his. Sadly, it will never be written. After reading my chapter on exotica music, he wrote in its margins, "You are as obsessed by exotica as I am by ladyboys; I bet my fantasies are better than yours." He was probably right. Sensing the narrowing of time, he asked me to take him on an evening excursion to his favorite bars in Bangkok, a soiree I will forever treasure. As mutual friends Jason Schoonover and Susan Hattori wrote, "the long vigil is over ... what a life lived."

Surfing, art, and publishing legend John Severson enthusiastically provided an abundance of minutiae regarding the process of making his art ready to produce onto aloha shirts. Although he had a reputation for being resistant to interviews, he was enthusiastic about this book, and was always available and happy to share his passion and aloha. John passed away before this book went to print, and I'll always remember him for his generosity.

I was a thorn in the side to many people while in the process of writing this book. Tim McCullough unlocked the mysteries of Hawaiian shirt-making, spent hours being interviewed and working with me to ensure I got everything right, and never failed to respond to email requests for yet additional information. As was the case with a number of individuals interviewed for this book, some of his behind-the-scenes insights were spoken off the record, but provided confirmation to stories that remain in the text. Tim also provided access to his wonderful collection of surfing photos. Dale Hope, who knows more about the history of Hawaiian shirts than anyone alive, was stoked on the idea of the book, and proved to be a source of important information as well as allowing me to use a stunning photograph he made of John Severson. Camille Shaheen and Bill Tunberg patiently answered my questions about Camille's father, Alfred Shaheen. Shirt designer Eddy Y took the brave step of mailing me his personal history portfolio in order for me to gain a better insight into his work. I deeply appreciate his trust. Miles M. Mason invited me into his studio, and artists Guy Buffet, Mike Field, Naoki Hayashi, and Robert Lyn Nelson were kind enough to call me to discuss their art and their Reyn Spooner shirt designs. Ron Anderson, Nicholas "Nicky" Black, and Avi and Keytoe Kiriaty provided valuable insight into their designs used in making Kahala aloha shirts. Additional thanks on the aloha shirt chapter to Josh Feldman and Jason Zaputo of Tori Richard. Thanks to Go-Go Jane Wiedlin for providing a welcoming place to stay while I conducted interviews on the Big Island.

Kaui Isa-Kahaku generously gave me her time and resources for the chapter on hula. Tony Gualtieri read the complete manuscript and found a number of those tiny but important pieces of erratic minutiae that writers often overlook when reading their own words.

Harvey Schwartz graciously opened up his unique and all-encompassing rattan warehouse to me and gave me an entire afternoon on his day off to answer my questions. Grateful thanks to Tobi Smith of the California Heritage Museum for sharing a number of Harvey Schwartz stories. Alberto Guerrero of Miami's Iconic Design Gallery provided valuable information regarding lesser-known but historically important rattan furniture designers. Stephen Siebert graciously shared data on the state of contemporary rattan harvesting practices. Lisa Kocab Meade enthusiastically participated in sharing the story of her former husband Al Kocab and his days of designing numerous elements that were a significant part of the success of Fort Lauderdale's Mai-Kai Restaurant. Lisa generously provided ephemera created by Kocab that today is largely unobtainable. Jeff Chenault, through his writings, emails, and conversations, was an important resource of information for exotica music (chapter five) and tiki culture (chapter six). Jim Spencer, Les Baxter's biographer, provided additional contacts and important behind-the-scenes stories of the composer. Matt Warshaw's book *The History of Surfing* proved to be an invaluable resource for the chapter on surfing. Mike Rangner generously provided the artwork for the cover of the book, a wonderfully graphic depiction of America going Hawaiian. A special shout-out to Phil Dirt, who introduced me to instrumental surf music through his long-running (and lamentably gone) Saturday night surf music program on KFJC/FM in Los Altos Hills, California. Many of my friends are expat writers in Bangkok and I thank them all for their continued interest in and suggestions pertaining to whatever I'm writing about at the moment, Dean Barrett, James Fuss, and Harold Stephens in particular.

I was honored that author and archivist DeSoto Brown graciously agreed to write the foreword. I admire his writing and have enjoyed his books on Hawaii, several of which have been cited as resource material in the manuscript. I have done my best to find and credit those whose photographs and illustrations appear in the book. If I've missed any, please contact me so I'll have the opportunity to make corrections in future editions.

My San Jose support team was a great help in never tiring of hearing my Hawaiian anecdotes and stories throughout the three years it took to write this book. Thank you Don Campau, Jenny Do, Cevan Forristt, Rhonda Lackmann, Victoria Robledo, and Barinda Samra.

This is my fourth book working with editor David Alff at McFarland & Company. Our conversations are wonderful and we spend way too much time talking baseball, sharing our love for last place teams and the minor leagues. You've always been a joy to work with, David.

Foreword
by DeSoto Brown

The Hawaiian Islands do not occupy much total space compared to the expanses of the world's continents, even accounting for the immensity of just Mauna Kea by itself, the largest single mountain on earth. The Hawaiian Islands are far, far away from everything else in the world as well, perhaps the most distant of any inhabited lands anywhere. The Hawaiian Islands today have a population of about a million and a half people, which could be dropped into some immense cities without much of an effect.

And yet—the Hawaiian Islands managed to somehow capture the minds and hearts of millions and millions of people in the United States and internationally. A group of comparatively small islands, extremely isolated and without a large population, affected the world far beyond what could ever have been imagined. How? And why?

Perhaps "why" is unanswerable. All the usual clichés apply; people do have a tendency to want what they don't have, or to desire the different and exotic. But Hawaii does have undeniable beauty in abundance, overlaid with a nearly perfect climate, and it also boasts an intriguing culture based on its indigenous one that's been blended with many others in the last two centuries. The lengthy journey to travel there perhaps adds to the allure of being far away from everyday responsibilities, which can be abandoned and forgotten for the duration of a vacation.

"How" all those millions fell in love with a fantasy of Hawaii and the South Seas is easier to describe. The story is complex—probably more complicated than most people would think—and it was a process that evolved through the work and efforts of changing generations that built on what had occurred previously. It was dependent on the growth of technology as well, in communications and transportation. An unexpected innovation or fad would push the awareness of the public, and in turn influence a clever person to take things further. And so it went.

This latter aspect of the story is what Geoff Alexander covers so well here: the people. Some were just participants, occasionally unplanned; others were planners and movers who saw the potential for making money, and worked to achieve it. A few of these people became famous, often by creating an imaginative new persona for themselves that they played out against a background of some real or imagined South Seas experiences. Both native people (usually Hawaiian) and non-natives mixed together in the often-embellished and dream-inducing world that their audiences admired and wished to experience. This book will introduce you to many of them, and will acknowledge what they did and how they did it.

No one individual worked entirely by himself or herself. Political, social, recreational and technological forces had a great deal to do with how the exotification process happened. Nobody could force something like Hawaiian music or surfing to become popular internationally; nobody could even anticipate that such a thing could happen at all. No one could stop World War II in the Pacific from occurring; no one could anticipate in turn how it could affect American popular culture in the decades afterwards. If you'd told people in the United States in 1945 that they'd be dressing up in silly outfits and staging a "luau" in their basements fifteen years later, they wouldn't have believed you—but it really happened, and often.

Looking back from the vantage point of the twenty-first century, we can pass judgment with hindsight. Was all this merely fun, or was it exploitive? Each reader can decide, but having the story laid out for you, as this book does, will give you the knowledge to be able to do so. I guarantee that even if you think you know all this history, you're going to read about things you either didn't know before, or didn't fully understand. Better yet, just go along for the ride and let yourself fantasize about the exotification of America, because that's what it's all about—a fantasy world. Go native, get primitive, sail away to your special island, or however you want to do it. Enjoy it.

DeSoto Brown is the historian at the Bernice Pauahi Bishop Museum in Honolulu, Hawaii. A native of Honolulu, he has spent much of his personal life collecting and studying printed material pertaining to the promotion of Hawaii for tourism and the fantasy image of Hawaii and Hawaiian culture. He has written or coauthored several books and articles, including Hawaii Recalls: Selling Romance to America, 1910–1950 *(1982).*

Preface

This book attempts to explain how the arts, culture, and society of Hawaii specifically and Polynesia in general influenced the arts, culture, and society of the mainland United States and Canada in the 20th century and continue to do so in the 21st. It provides a painted landscape, rather than a linear historical reading, its brushstrokes overlapping into other spaces, colors changing and melding into one another. A few white spots in the canvas may still show through, although I made every attempt to isolate and investigate them. No author, upon re-reading his or her recently published work, fails to see something left out, something further that could have been expanded upon or better explained, and then still something else that should have been deleted. We learn as we write, continuing to obtain additional information, and thus exposing ourselves to "feature creep," a high-tech term that aptly describes a situation that, remaining unchecked, will result in the product never being finished. The information curve escalates as the manuscript is proofread by peers, goes to the publisher, is edited and proofed again, and then printed. The experience can be frustrating, and remains one of the reasons a number of fellow authors refuse to re-read their own books after they've arrived on the bookshelves: they're more confounded by their errors and omissions than they are overjoyed that the book is finished. My own editor paid the price of my series of delays in getting the manuscript to him. New ideas and topics kept popping up, new resources unveiled themselves, and I swore on a stack of Oxford English Dictionaries that the book would be so much the poorer without them. It's fashionable these days for writers to issue an apology for errors and omissions as necessary in their prefaces, but you won't get that from me. When I find them, I'll be beating myself up worse than you could ever do.

All books are intensely personal for their authors, increasingly more so as the story evolves. It soon became apparent to me that I'd been "writing" this book since I was an adolescent. I look today at my high school yearbook from 1970. It reflects a culture about as "whitebread" as you can get. The graduating class of 400 boasted a mere 10 individuals who would have been classified in the day as people of color, one African, two Asian American, seven Latino. The remaining 390 of the seniors, as well as the entire faculty, were white. There were, among the boys, three generally agreed upon social classifications: you were a jock, a surfer, or a greaser. Girls typically fell into the same roles, depending on who they were dating or hung out with. The aspirations of the senior class fell along the lines of the professions of their parents. They would be Silicon Valley engineers, middle-class working stiffs, and homemakers. Just like their parents (my dad was a grocery clerk who somehow missed the high-tech call; mom stayed home taking care of five kids until they somehow managed to make it into high school). Two or three of the senior kids in my high school class were headed off to prestigious universities, their applications proudly vetted by the counseling staff before being signed, submitted, and approved. But if any of those 400 seniors were weird or different, they pretty much kept it to themselves. Fitting in was the major pastime of a student body that was terrorized of being socially ostracized.

In such a non-diversified school, there wasn't much of an opportunity for anyone to become exposed to anything that might be considered "worldly," or perish the thought, "exotic." Unless there was a family like the Clydes in the neighborhood. The Clydes, like all of us, were in that neighborhood full of inexpensive new houses because the barrier to own a home was so low. The homes were built in 1961. A 1,300 square foot four-bedroom two-bath house cost $19,000. The down payment was $600, with a forty-year loan. One of the reasons there were so few Latino families in the neighborhood was that in San Jose's east side, traditionally Mexican American, houses were even more affordable, being built and sold for zero down, again with a forty-year mortgage. My neighborhood, responsible for contributing so many members of my graduating class, was primarily working class. A more upscale housing development was built simultaneously next to it, with a different postal code, too. That's where the white collar folks lived.

The Clydes somehow landed in our neighborhood like a spaceship that missed a turn and hit the wrong planet. And when you visited their house, you really did walk into a different world. While the rest of the homes in the neighborhood reflected the sports-and-sitcom culture of their owners, the Clydes had tons of exotic stuff you never saw anywhere else. In the dining room, next to a tiny TV, there was a hi-fi system with a jazz music library. You'd amble into the house to the music of Miles Davis instead of Mitch Miller, whose *Sing Along with Mitch* television program seemed to be all the rage in every other neighborhood home. The Clydes' TV would rarely be on, but when it was, the channel selector was welded to National Educational Television. Buddha images and books were the keynotes of the living room. In fact, there were books in every room in the house. Their hallway, lacking the extended family photographs that graced the walls of typical neighborhood homes, instead sported a long three-tiered bookshelf that extended weight-wise as far as the studs and drywall would allow, ensuring that one had to crab along sideways to avoid getting nailed in the head or on the shoulder by some protruding hardback. Instead of bookends, the stacks were shored up by smaller pyramids of paperbacks that went all over the place when anything or anyone jarred them just a bit. To fix things, the offender scooped up psychology, history, philosophy, art, literature, and anthropology, hoisted them back on the shelf, straightened out the other books that were now keeling precariously over the edge, and tried to square all corners and make things look neat. Neither the Clyde children nor I tried to put them back in any order. There didn't appear to be one to begin with.

The backyard was equally at odds with our working class barrio, having a Japanese motif bamboo garden instead of a lawn. There weren't American cars in the garage, either, the two-car space being taken up by a monstrous and magnificent black Jaguar Mark VII sedan. It resided hard by the tool bench and a tall stack of *Playboy* magazines, over which hung a wooden caricature of an Indian with a tomahawk. When you moved his loincloth aside, the space underneath said "Howdy!" The Clydes' second car, a cute powder blue Morris Minor convertible, was usually parked in the driveway. Stating what should now be fairly obvious, the Clydes didn't go to church, either.

A visit to the Clydes' house represented an excursion into the unfamiliar, visually, auditorily, conversationally. They were wildly but stoically unconventional for the times and that little neighborhood of ours. Robin Clyde was a professor of psychology at San Jose State College, working in the counseling department. Shirley Clyde taught high school English. Under their breaths, the neighbors called them oddballs. Unlike their neighbors, Dr. Clyde wore a beard, and Shirley cared more about reading beat poetry than straightening up the kitchen. Without a doubt, they were the weirdoes of the neighborhood. For neighborhood kids who stumbled in to play with their children, that house was the only hint, clue, or latchkey that promised that there just might be a big, beautiful, magnificent, exotic fairytale world out there, somewhere in the clouds, ensconced in a rain forest, beyond gilded gates, heretofore hidden from us except in encyclopedias and *National Geographic* magazines. And for the few of us neighborhood kids privileged enough to visit that house, it was an insight into what "exotic" looked like, encased in a cottage-cheese ceilinged ranch style home. The Clyde experience broke down some mighty high psychological walls, in terms of possibilities of one day building our own Xanadus, incorporating foreign cultures into our own lives and living spaces. The Clydes were the first exotics many of us had ever met. And we adolescents, along with our parents, wondered just how they got that way.

Those of us privileged enough to be bought into this exciting, exotic, multicultural, and optimistic world were transported there before we had finished elementary school. It was a fairytale that we could see, hear, touch, smell, and feel, and in one way, it was even better. Even at that young age, we knew that it was attainable.

Although leisure travel to places like Hawaii and the Pacific islands became increasingly easy and affordable, people having the tastes of the Clydes really didn't have to visit there to get a dose of exoticism. A person could live in a distant, magic world at home, right after the workday ended and on the weekends, surrounding oneself with the trappings of exotica, whether sitting on it, listening to it, wearing it, imbibing it, or even cohabitating with it, and remain ensconced in a tropical cocoon thousands of miles away. All one needed was a Hawaiian shirt, rattan furniture, some exotica music on the hi-fi, and a few tropical drinks. Anyone could even be exotic in the car on the way to work in the morning, with a magnetic hula girl on the dashboard sway-dancing to Arthur Lyman's music playing on the AM radio.

The dream of exotica doesn't have to be based on reality, either, which is, after all, the fundamental nature of reverie. The dream can be fed by the noble rivers of art, literature, and music, or arrive as the flotsam of advertisers and press agents. The dream is shaped by the perspectives of the dreamer via information living in long-term memory, subjectively reshaped by romantic desires, notions of longing for a Better Place, and perhaps a drive to create a more concrete concept of individuality. The subjectivity of the dream, while ignoring or not seeing the often uncomfortable truths and realities surrounding it, is why it's so enchanting. What became apparent to me as, I wrote this book, was that the imagined exotica of armchair travelers was just as true to them as the varied realties of those residing in those far-off islands were to those inhabitants.

In proofreading the chapters for the final time, it occurred to me how many dreamers I interviewed for this book whom could just as well be called geniuses. What they had in common was an aspiration, a sense of hustle, and a business savvy that allowed them to achieve a vision and be financially successful—defined in their own terms—in doing so. Generally, these people had multiple careers, at times simultaneously, had the knack for bouncing back when hard times hit or the economy slowed, and then had the foresight or fortitude to reinvent themselves anew. There was not one second of boredom in writing this book and I hope the reader will enjoy reading about these colorful characters as much as I did writing about them. I remain in touch with many of these folks and it's an honor to bask in their brilliance a bit as I continue to uncover stories told to me after a certain amount of trust had been established and alcohol consumed, with assurances that what was confessed in confidence will stay off the record. The reader won't be cheated. What's documented in the book is fascinating enough.

There's another side to this book as well. Embracing the exotic fantasy world embodied in Hawaii and the Pacific means experiencing the joy of interacting with its population, whether face-to-face or through fantasies of the ideal of distant lands. It's decidedly a mixed-race fantasyland, where people of different cultures and skin colors live together, work together, and intermarry. It's a working model of inclusion and diversity, honed decades before those commonly used terms were popular. Hawaii's biggest influence on the mainland was, ultimately, her people.

This book presents an overview of influential Hawaiian people, causes, art forms, and objects, most—but not all—of Hawaiian or Polynesian origin. Nevertheless, they are associated in most Western minds with Hawaii or the Pacific islands. To a very large extent, it's an opinionated pastiche, an interpretation of a series of social and cultural waves that hit the mainland and never ebbed. This book will no doubt provoke differing opinions from readers, critics, and scholars. Ethno-sensitive people of all races at times express the belief that while it's appropriate for individuals of their particular ethnicity to write about their own world as well as everyone else's, the same right doesn't apply to "outsiders" writing about cultures other than the one with which they're most familiar. Some elements of this book, particularly those in the final chapter, will prove to be provocative and perhaps uncomfortable. *America Goes Hawaiian* reflects on a number of different cultures that, like a family, embrace each other, argue, fight, kiss and make up, fight some more, then somehow figure out how to live together. Refusing to be provocative just spoils the fun.

Of Hawaiian Words and a Note on Money

Hawaiian is a language incorporating glottal stops, called 'okina, which are formally indicated with an apostrophe inserted at the appropriate place within the word and before a vowel, but never before a consonant. The sound is the same as when pronouncing the word "uh-oh." The Hawaiian pronunciation of the name of Hawaiian steel guitarist Sol Ho'opi'i, for example, is radically different when written on the mainland as Sol Hoopii, without the diacritical marks. The Hawaiian language also includes the kahakō, a stress mark known as a macron that appears over vowels as a hyphen, used to indicate a slightly longer pronunciation of the vowel sound. As in David Kalākaua.

For the sake of consistency as well as a means to better facilitate internet searches, I have elected not to use them in this book. Other factors that went into this decision included the inadequacy of the Western keyboard in generating Hawaiian diacritical marks, and the lack of conformance with older texts that don't use them at all. Then there's the very real possibility of misspelling a word Hawaiian-wise, even when using diacritical marks. When possible, to avoid the ambiguity of alternative spellings, I have included life span dates, in parentheses, with the first mention of the names of native Hawaiians. I've done this as well as for a number of mainlanders and others making an impact on Hawaii.

A number of Hawaiian words commonly appear throughout the text. The word "haole" is one of them. That term is used in Hawaii most commonly to refer to Caucasian non-natives, but may also—but not always—be used as a pejorative to describe residents or visitors of Western extraction who are considered ignorant of or in disagreement with native concerns and traditions. In the broadest sense, it refers to any person or element foreign to Hawaii. I have used this word in the book with its sense defined by the context in which it's used.

Many references cited in this book list the historical costs related to salaries, fees, fines, transportation passage, and you name it. Without an explanation of what these figures would amount to today, their meaning is inconsequential. I've therefore, when possible, used Alan Eliasen's historical currency converter keyed to the years 2017 and 2018, when this book was written. It's an inexact science, as Eliasen suggests, particularly prior to 1912, when the algorithm is based, to a large degree, on economists' estimates. Nevertheless, it's better, I think, than simple non-referenced price data.[1]

Introduction

Particularly when compared to the final tumultuous four decades of the 20th century, it's easy to see why many in the United States today view the 1950s as being—with the exception of the rock and roll boom—something of a drab and colorless ten-year span. Many elements of The Eisenhower Years, however, were far from dull. They were the days when U.S. Secretary of State John Foster Dulles and his brother Allen, head of the CIA, rode roughshod over democracies deemed unhealthy to American business interests (Guatemala and Iran are two examples), replacing them with puppet governments.[1] It was the time of Joseph McCarthy, whose mania for seeking out and terminating the careers of alleged communists, ruined the lives of thousands. The decade also brought into being a de facto state religion, culminating with the words "under God" added to the pledge of allegiance, and "In God We Trust" printed onto cash money.[2]

Drab and colorless, however, are apt and ironic terms to describe the 1950s world of anyone of color living in the United States. These were times of segregation, discrimination, and fear. It was a primal fear: many whites were afraid that integration would ultimately lead to men of color impregnating white women and producing mixed-race children. The fear was two-sided: people of color knew just one tiny step in the wrong direction could lead to incarceration or death. The United States was engaging in the fitful, trying, and painful early stages of the process of coming to grips with equalizing and embracing its multicultural, multi-ethnic population. The words "diversity" and "inclusion" would wait more than half a century to be included in discussions of the county's inexorably flowing, bubbling, simmering, and cooling melting pot. Behind the scenes, though, was a socio-economic force that was silently but assuredly eroding the walls of racism and fear, winding its way into the minds and living rooms of immediate post-war America. That force is embedded in the meaning of the word exotica, a term that embraces other cultures, originally applied to describe a genre of music, but also relating to clothing, furniture, lifestyle, philosophy, and numerous other elements. Exotica has no racial boundaries.

Hawaii is ground zero for exotica and *America Goes Hawaiian* reflects its role in exporting an exotic, sensual, tropical raincloud that showered its culture over the mainland. I've described it as the "exotification of America." From a historical perspective, I've examined exotica's origins, its pervasiveness and longevity, and looking forward, offer a discussion of its continuing influence. The roots of this phenomenon predate the 20th century, but it had its greatest impact as a post–World War II cultural and social force. Mainland-based GIs and war workers traveling to Hawaii for the war effort were a big part of the story. To paraphrase Caesar, they came, they saw, and the tropics conquered *them*.

How many GIs from the United States were active in the Pacific Theater of World War II? Figuring a grand total of U.S. military personnel serving in the Pacific is a challenge. An estimated 16.1 million GIs were involved in the global U.S. war effort in World War II. U.S. naval records indicate that by August 1945, there were 1,366,716 U.S. naval personnel serving ashore and afloat in the Pacific Theater alone. Of all U.S. personnel serving in the Pacific, an estimated 108,504 were killed. In terms of naval personnel alone, therefore, more than one million of those serving returned to the United States after the war.[3]

GIs and war workers went into battle, served in support operations, did R&R time or lived in Hawaii and the Pacific, then brought back to the mainland new perspectives on everything from social and racial relations to furniture, clothing, the arts, music, restaurants and bars, and water sports. Many of these men and women came originally from places that didn't have year-round summers. It seems natural for humans to lust for far-off places that have the promise of being more enticing, more enchanting, more bountiful. Almost invariably, these places are warmer, climate-wise, as well. The lust for warmth dates back to the emergence of the first humans, still etched in our collective memories in forms as varied as warming pits for cave-dwellers, hearths in middle-age castles, fireplaces and patio fire pits in modern ranch-style suburban homes. The mindscape of exotica is similarly imbued with palm trees, beaches, warm waters, and bamboo huts.

The magic that was—and is—exotica took place on a mass scale in the 1950s as a wide-ranging social phenomenon that colored the post-war generation with a tropical palette that extended through the ensuing decades, involving culture, dress, social attitudes, and subsequent generations. It's the latter concept—the effect on later generations—that drives the impulse to look at it further, to determine what led up to it as well as to what it, in turn, influenced. And it begs the question of how much it might affect cultural attitudes moving into the future.

Inherent in the term "exotica" are the notions of exoticism, primitivism, and—to a degree and with a caveat—orientalism, three concepts that defined Hawaii and the Pacific for ex–GIs, suburban armchair adventurers, and stateside bohemians. It's therefore valuable to explore the definitions of these terms and calculate deeper meanings, not only as they relate to the world of today, but also with an eye looking backward through the time machine, to investigate how they might have combined to impact the America of more than 60 years ago.

"Exoticism" can be defined as "the quality of being exotic." *Webster's* online dictionary lists 10 entries that define "exotic" as an adjective.[4] The first five offer a broad brushstroke pertinent to the use of the word in this book:

1. Being or from or characteristic of another place or part of the world; "exotic plants in a greenhouse"; "exotic cuisine."
2. Strikingly strange or unusual; "an exotic hair style"; "protons, neutrons, electrons and all their exotic variants"; "the exotic landscape of a dead planet."
3. Introduced from a foreign country; not native; extraneous; foreign; as, an exotic plant; an exotic term or word.
4. Being strange, outlandish, odd, alien or unaccustomed.
5. Being foreign, extraneous, extrinsic or external.

"Primitivism" may be defined as "a wild or unrefined state." Primitive, as an adjective, has six particularly instructive definitions:

1. Belonging to an early stage of technical development; characterized by simplicity and (often) crudeness; "primitive movies of the 1890s"; "primitive living conditions in the Appalachian mountains."
2. Little evolved from or characteristic of an earlier ancestral type; "primitive mammals"; "the okapi is a short-necked primitive cousin of the giraffe."
3. Used of preliterate or tribal or nonindustrial societies; "primitive societies."
4. Of or created by one without formal training; simple or naive in style...
5. Of or pertaining to the beginning or origin, or to early times; original; primordial; primeval; first; as, primitive innocence; the primitive church.
6. Of or pertaining to a former time; old-fashioned; characterized by simplicity; as, a primitive style of dress.

Taken together and viewed as a whole, the twin terms of "exotic" and "primitive" could very well pertain to cultural elements found just about anywhere in the world at virtually any time in the past. To define the world of mid–20th century exotica as it relates to the impact of an American vision of Hawaii and the tropics, therefore, an additional term is needed. That word is "Orientalism." As with the other two terms, it comes with its own caveats that require clarification. But does the term offer a meaningful insight and contribution to the world of exotica as a musical, cultural, or lifestyle construct? It's classified as a noun, and defined as:

1. The scholarly knowledge of Asian cultures and languages and people.
2. The quality or customs or mannerisms characteristic of Asian civilizations; "orientalisms can be found in Mozart's operas."
3. Any system, doctrine, custom, expression, etc., peculiar to Oriental people.
4. Knowledge or use of Oriental languages, history, literature, etc.

From the perspective of its contribution to the world of exotica, none of these definitions truly fits. To perhaps the majority of Americans "the Orient" evokes the countries of East Asia. For much of the rest of the Western world, particularly during most of the last several centuries, it was indicative of the Near East. Many Lebanese still use the word to describe elements particular to their own country.[5] The word can torch a tinderbox: referencing an Asian American with whom one is conversing as being "Oriental" is to invite a corrective rebuff. In social discourse, the "O word" is considered politically incorrect unless describing a carpet.

Orientalism, however also speaks of a world decidedly non-Western. It hints at a mindscape of fantasy, of imagined worlds as fleeting as "Xanadu," "Eden," or "Utopia." It suggests a wishful place of escape, a fantastical venue encompassing and triggering all five senses, of sights, sounds, smells, tastes, and touches. Orientalism, seen from this perspective, therefore, isn't necessarily solely Asian, but it certainly is non–Western. Unlike exoticism and primitivism, the construct of Orientalism is more abstract than concrete. At the same time, it's as real as the first peal of a temple gong, unleashing a sensory bombardment of imagined memories, powerfully evocative of a time and place that, one might imagine, probably never was, but just as equally probable, could be. Or perhaps better stated, one wishes it *would* be.

In her discussion of Edward W. Said's landmark book *Orientalism*, Rebecca Laydon, writing in the anthology *Widening the Horizon: Exoticism in Post War Popular Music*, suggests that "In the West, the 'exotic' and the 'primitive' are closely related qualities that have been mapped onto a monolithic non-western Other.... Independent of any particularities of geography or language or culture, the Orient is a collection of knowledges of the East.... The purpose of the Orient is to act as a repository of the West's own repressed desires and fantasies; the Orient thus becomes a reservoir for all that must be excluded from the definition of the western self."[6]

Said himself, although writing specifically about Europe's relationship with the Near East, underscores the elements of fantasy and imagination imbued in the concept of Orientalism: "The idea of representation is a theatrical one: the Orient is the stage on which the whole East is confined. On this stage will appear figures whose role it is to represent the larger whole from which they emanate.... In the depths of this Oriental stage stands a prodigious cultural repertoire whose individual items evoke a fabulously rich world: the Sphinx, Cleopatra, Eden ... Sodom and Gomorrah ... Babylon, the Genii ... and dozens more; settings, in some cases names only, half-imagined, half-known: monsters, devils, heroes; terrors, pleasures, desires."[7]

Substituting the Javanese temple of Borobudur, the headhunters of Borneo, the voyages of Captain James Cook, Polynesian seafaring canoeists, and lush tropical islands for Said's people and places provides an additional global element to the concept of Orientalism as a stage of fantasy and dream. It represents a driving force that propels Westerners to seek a utopia fueled by a desire to escape the realities of nine-to-five jobs, cold weather, homogenous racial relationships, and inherited—and perhaps undesired—social responsibilities.

Mainland visitors to Hawaii today, especially first-timers, have some pretty specific expectations. They arrive expecting to be exoticized almost as soon as they step off the plane. Perpetuating this powerful and long-lived cultural flow, they return home with pieces of Hawaii, from leis to shirts to pineapples.

The search for the lost Eden remains as American a concept as Manifest Destiny. Writer Orvar Lofgren pins it down nicely when he remarks that such imaginative territories represent "imagined nostalgia," where you learn to miss things you never really had.[8] In the United States, the storied land of imagination, where comparatively little can be defined as impossible, people have been seemingly forever creating their own exotic mini-worlds that have nothing to do with the reality of what lies around the corner and down the street. Such locally conceived and crafted Edens could be as grandiose as the Hearst Castle or John Ringling's Ca D'Zan in Sarasota, Florida, or as small as Uncle Joe's backyard lanai, where friends gather for mai-tais under the stars every Saturday night. The foundation of exoticism is practically biblical, where everyone gets to create a personal Garden of Eden, with the requisite music, clothes, and furniture in place to make it convincing.

As opposed to the notion of exotica representing a cultural attempt to re-enter Eden, a contrarian view may be to view exotica as merely a passing fad. The United States has a history of embracing fads, from raccoon coats, to Hula Hoops, to Rubik's Cubes, to thumbing a smart phone with eyes cast downward, imperiling people and objects. So what made exotica more than a fad? A primary reason lies in its interdisciplinary aspect. It encompassed music, dance, furniture, and clothing, on a mass scale, spiced with the sport of surfing, flamboyant drinks, tiki art, and tropical-themed businesses exemplified by the Don the Beachcomber and Trader Vic's restaurants. By its very definition, a fad is a fleeting enterprise lasting perhaps two or three years (think again, this time of Beanie Babies). Exotica, on the other hand, is still with us, more than 100 years after the first needle was dropped onto a Hawaiian music 78 rpm record. The influence of Hawaiian exoticism on the mainland has had staying power. Men and women today still sport Hawaiian shirts, rattan furniture remains an element of interior and patio design, and mainland cities and towns continue to have tiki lounges, Hawaiian-inspired events, and Pacific-themed restaurants. Hundreds of hula schools proliferate throughout North America. There has been resurgence in the interest of the music of Hawaii, from traditional songs and hapa haole music, to the exotica music recorded and performed by artists including Les Baxter, Martin Denny, and Arthur Lyman. Hawaiian culture has been exported to the mainland in the form of almost 237,000 people of Hawaiian origin and ancestry who resided on the mainland as of the 2010 census, nearly 75,000 of them in California alone.[9]

Exotica, as with any successful social trend, had to meet three criteria to achieve that success: it had to be notorious, it had to be accessible, and it had to be affordable. These important and interrelated objectives were critical factors in Hawaii's march to becoming the influence on the mainland that it came to be. A discussion of the importance and evolution of these criteria make up much of the first two chapters of this book. They belong at the beginning as a reminder of how challenging traveling to the Pacific islands once was, technologically and economically.

Chapter One discusses the impact of the shipping business on Hawaii and Polynesia, from the early days of contact forward. Initially, ship passengers were mainly a sideline to the business of carrying freight. Adventurer writers including Mark Twain, Jack London, and Robert Louis Stevenson braved unpredictably angry seas to visit the islands and told their stories in newspapers and books, whetting Americans' thirst for the island paradise. Paul Gauguin and other artists focused on Polynesia as a theme, bringing the tropics to the world's art galleries and museums. It was Gauguin, also, who helped create Western enthusiasm for languorous, beautiful Polynesian women, an interest that remains unabated, and has inspired and untold number of artists. Mainland businesses, driven by moguls including sugar king Claus Spreckels and shipping magnate William Matson, derived increasing profits from their interests in the steamship business and Waikiki hotels. Selling Hawaii to Americans was the objective of the tourist bureau and advertising done by shipping and hotel interests. By the first decades of the 20th century, these public relations machines had succeeded in making Hawaii a popular destination for those who could afford it. Noted illustrators including Frank McIntosh and Eugene Savage created menu covers and other ephemera that travelers on Matson's white-hulled ships *Lurline, Malolo, Mariposa,* and *Monterey* were encouraged to take home, show to friends, and frame for the library walls. For those who couldn't afford the passage, sheet music covers illustrated with Hawaiian themes painted by popular artists graced parlor pianos from coast to coast. The heyday of luxurious steamship travel effectively continued to the mid–1950s.

Ship travel to Hawaii was eventually replaced by trans-Pacific airlines, the subject of Chapter Two. Air travel had made tremendous leaps in the three decades since the Ford Tri-Motor was introduced in the late 1920s. Trans-Pacific air passenger travel began with the iconographic Pan American Clippers, and eventually eclipsed the steamship era with low-cost fares to the islands, first on the massive piston-driven Boeing 377 Stratocruiser, and then by passenger jets. By 1960, the conquest of long sea distances by nonstop aircraft had ushered in the era of low-cost travel to Hawaii, making the islands financially accessible to mainland middle class visitors for the first time. In this chapter, I trace the evolution of passenger aircraft from the days of the land-based Ford Tri-Motor through the jet age.

With low-cost airfares soon bringing record numbers of visitors to the islands, what did visitors expect to see? The hula, the subject of Chapter Three, seemed to be at the top of just about everyone's list. As early as the 19th century, it had been introduced on the mainland through traveling shows and was a "must see" for visitors to America's great international fairs and expositions. Hula schools were initiated all over the mainland. In Hawaii, conversely, the hula was problematic. The hula and the chanting of mele were the means by which native Hawaiians had conveyed the history of their gods, nobles, and history, but they were banned and taken underground in the 19th century, victims of Calvinist morality. Their resurgence under King David Kalakaua reestablished their popularity as an art form and hula today has an extraordinarily large presence in the continental United States with more than 600 schools on the mainland. This chapter includes passages relating to notable dancers including Kini Kapahu and Pualani Mossman, who were responsible for popularizing hula on the mainland. Hapa haole music, a song form typically with English words and Hawaiian themes accompanied by Hawaiian instruments, often served as the accompaniment for hula, was performed in tourist venues in Waikiki and on the mainland in showrooms, of which New York's Hawaiian Room in the Hotel Lexington was the most notable. The importance of hula as an element in USO entertainment was important to its increasing popularity, as untold numbers of GIs and war workers—estimated to be as many as 70 million—were introduced to it in this way. Today, hula culture in Hawaii is not without controversy, surrounding everything from hybrid forms to hula festivals, and it remains a vital and ever-evolving art form.

Chapter Four, "Sliding into Paradise: The Hawaiian Steel Guitar" is the first of two chapters discussing the influence of Hawaiian music on the mainland. Ukulele playing was a craze on the mainland in the first decades of the 20th century, but it never had the impact on American popular music that the Hawaiian steel guitar did, particularly on western swing and country music, exemplified in its earliest days by steel players Bob Dunn and Leon McAuliffe. They were directly influenced by Sol Hoopii and other players from the islands, who toured the mainland, wrote instruction books, and recorded on disc. The popularity of Hawaiian music increased seemingly unabated, broadcast all over the world on shortwave radio via the *Hawaii Calls* radio program.

Chapter Five, "Ring My Bell: Music from the Paradise of Exotica," is the second chapter on the subject of Hawaiian musical influences on the mainland. The music we now call "exotica" was popularized by artists including Les Baxter, Martin Denny, and Arthur Lyman. It was a hybrid of jazz and Latin music, featured exotic instruments, and in its heyday was often punctuated by bird calls and animal cries. It is most associated with Hawaii, where it was featured in clubs including the Shell Room on Waikiki, and on television shows, *Hawaiian Eye* among them. The sound of exotica was transformed into contemporary jazz, most notably in the work of McCoy Tyner and Bobby Hutcherson. The vibraphone was a key instrument in the sound of exotica, and I trace its history as well as its bell-like timbre back to Chinese instruments in the Bronze Age. I suggest that the vibes are but the latest and most successful attempt humankind has made to master the art of tuning and playing bells. It's a luxury to write about music in these days of the proliferation of the internet. I have chosen a number of musical examples along with their URLs and embedded them in the text to underscore the importance of the music and musicians. They also allow for the pleasure of listening to the music under discussion while reading about it. Some of the URLs will undoubtedly change, owing to the ever-changing character of the internet. Those that no longer remain in force will serve as an indicator that someone took the trouble of uploading them at one point and therefore may well upload them to another site. If a music link has vanished, search again. My experience is that if it was uploaded once, it will reappear somewhere else almost immediately.

Tiki culture, a mass movement that has extended far beyond the United States, is the subject of Chapter Six. Deriving from carved images of gods, royalty, and supernatural beings found all over Polynesia and reaching into Borneo, the Western world of tiki was spawned by countless restaurants and bars. It embraced noted architects including Pete Wimberly, interior/exterior designers exemplified by Eli Hedley and Stephen Crane, and countless other artists and artisans who crafted furniture, massive tiki heads, tiki mugs, tiki calendars, and other ephemera. Tiki bars and restaurants, serving rum drinks and mostly Chinese food sporting Polynesian names, still proliferate through North America, including the massive Mai-Kai Restaurant in Fort Lauderdale, Florida. Tiki culture and its elements pervade the sets of Hawaiian-based television dramas, providing something of a moving catalogue of decorative ideas that ultimately end up in mainland homes. The power of tiki today is underscored by the large number of websites and blogs dedicated to the celebration of its ongoing popularity.

Any tiki venue is expected to focus its interior décor on rattan furniture, the subject of Chapter Seven. Here we visit what is estimated to be the world's largest warehouse of vintage rattan furniture, explore several of the companies known for making it, and discuss the role of the Philippines in the creation of many the earliest 20th century rattan pieces. Rattan furniture was never made in Hawaii, but Hawaii was where most GIs and war workers were exposed to it.

Although rattan furniture had been sold in high-end mainland showrooms in the 1930s, it blossomed in popularity in the post-war years. Designer Paul T. Frankl is credited with bringing rattan furniture out of the patio and into the living room. The crafting of rattan furniture, from the selecting of the stalks to the manufacture of the finished product, is a fascinating story. Rattan furniture is known for its beauty, lightness, and resiliency, the latter of which is a direct result of the exacting rigors of what's known as the Philippine Standard, established in 1976. A perusal of the elements of the standard is particularly enlightening to an estimated millions who own rattan furniture and marvel in its rugged serviceability.

Anyone owning rattan furniture will probably look better sitting in it when wearing a Hawaiian aloha shirt, the subject of Chapter Eight. The shirt has a fascinating history and has historically represented a significant element of Hawaii's economy. I include a brief history of the aloha shirt and have invited author and former Kahala executive Dale Hope, surfing legend and artist John Severson, and former Reyn Spooner executive Tim McCullough to unveil a number of their secrets surrounding the making of these garments. Hope and McCullough spearheaded efforts to bring island-based artists, including, among others, Guy Buffet, Robert Lyn Nelson, and Eddy Y, into the shirt design process, creating collections named for the artists. Tim McCullough takes us behind the scenes in describing the manufacture of a shirt, a process involving a surprising 44 separate operations. McCullough's discussion of manufacturing includes fascinating and little-known details that unveil the manner in which the shirts are costed out and eventually priced for retail sale.

In the islands, Hawaiian shirts are often worn by surfers. The sport and culture of surfing is discussed in Chapter Nine. Wave-riding was first described to Westerners in Joseph Banks' diary, written for Captain James Cook's voyage of 1768. It made its North American debut in 1885 when three Hawaiian princes, attending school in California, fashioned boards out of redwood and surfed in Santa Cruz. Writer Jack London surfed in Hawaii in 1907, and a number of others, including Hawaiian Olympian Duke Kahanamoku, soon became key individuals in popularizing the sport on the mainland. An entire culture grew up around riding the waves in southern California and spread to the Eastern Seaboard, fueled by post-war teens with discretionary income and automobiles that allowed them to travel to remote beaches. Surfing engendered an abundance of new businesses, including magazines, board manufacturing, clothing, wetsuits, music, and films. The influence of Hawaii on mainland board-riding engendered a cultural U-turn, in which surfers born in the continental states moved to Hawaii and became innovators themselves in technique, especially as it applied to riding large waves. This chapter also addresses instrumental surf music. Considering the ethnic origins of its creator, the Lebanese American guitarist Dick Dale, the music can be said to owe more to the Middle East than Hawaii, but the music, directly inspired by Dale's wave-riding exploits, has been adopted by the surfing world.

Perhaps Hawaii's most significant contribution to the mainland has been through its integrated interracial society, as is discussed in Chapter Ten. During the war years, millions of GIs and war workers were exposed for the first time to a world in which people of different ethnicities worked, played, and married together. Many mainlanders had experienced little or no socialization with people of color back at home, and they found themselves suddenly thrust into an environment consisting of a racially, economically, and socially mixed society. In those times, many of the states on the mainland had laws on the books preventing interracial marriage. Interracial dating there was socially, if not legally, taboo. Through USO dances, military men could interact with Hawaiian women of native, Chinese, Filipino, Japanese, and Korean extraction. In brothels, GIs could have sex with women of different races. Many of these GIs and war workers came home with changed attitudes about race mixing, then raised children with even more liberal attitudes on integration. Still other GIs and war workers stayed in Hawaii and married local women. I argue that the exposure to racial mixing in the islands changed the mind-set of a significant number of mainlanders, contributing to the increasing involvement of European Americans in the racial struggles taking part in the mainland during the 1960s. I provide several statistical analyses that indicate a significant and soaring forward movement of interracial marriages in the United States today, a trend which I suggest was much influenced by the Hawaiian experience. This chapter includes references to various anti-miscegenation and anti-ethnicity laws on the books in 20th century America, and provides a history of the struggle in Hawaii to build a successfully integrated interracial society.

Two appendices discuss technological inventions tangential to Hawaii. Howard Hughes' "Spruce Goose," if it had ever flown beyond its maiden voyage, would have been the largest flying boat ever to fly commercial passengers. The war in the Pacific nixed that idea, but the notion of the first jumbo aircraft to carry passengers to Hawaii, and its impact on Pacific travel in general, remains a compelling fantasy. For years, the *Hawaii Calls* radio program could only be heard on shortwave radio, a technology which today exists as not much more than a footnote in the history of radio and television entertainment. In its time, the Zenith Transoceanic radio, profiled here, represented a revolution for its ruggedness and portability, uniquely bringing the romance of Hawaii and its music to the most far-flung corners of the globe.

This book's 10 chapters document what I feel to be the most significant Hawaiian and Pacific island contributions to the culture of mainland United States. The edenic dream called Hawaii became a state of mind well before it became a state in the union. How that lotus land in the middle of the Pacific, along with several of its sister islands, influenced a far away continent is a fascinating tale of a number of disparate forces that managed to combine in a powerful wave continually surging toward, then enveloping North America. Like the tail wagging the dog, the elements of Pacific tropical island lifestyles powered significant cultural and social trends that warmly washed over a massive continent to the east, and a people seeking a return to paradise.

ONE

Sailing to Paradise

The exotification of American in the Post–World War II years was driven to a great extent by GIs and merchant seamen returned home after the war from tropical Pacific ports. They were imbued with the cultural trappings of island groups all over the Pacific, including the contiguous geographical areas of Oceania, Polynesia, Melanesia, and Micronesia. Where U.S. military personnel didn't do any actual fighting (Australia, for example), they nevertheless maintained a powerful military presence. They and the Allies were supplied by U.S liberty ships manned by non–GI merchant marine crews. Prior to leaving for the Pacific Theater, though, many may conceivably been introduced to South Seas imagery through illustrated sheet music title pages or tropical Art Deco passenger ship menu covers, created by Frank McIntosh for Matson Navigation, that they'd seen framed on a wall in the kitchen or dining room of a well-traveled friend's home.

Early 20th century ocean liner passengers weren't the first Americans to arrive in tropical Pacific ports. Whalers, merchant seamen, traders, and missionaries were among those who preceded them, arriving as workers before the era of promotional schemes, public relations flacks, and advertising campaigns. Aided by an increasingly well-funded series of promotional campaigns by island tourism promoters, the Matson Navigation Company made a profitable business of taking travelers to Hawaii in the pre–World War II years in its white-hulled luxury steamers. Its own advertising did much to create a mental picture of the exotic fantasy paradise that awaited visitors, even those who could only afford to travel there through magazine advertisements read in the comfort of their armchairs. It was a distant eden, accessible only by ship, and an expensive proposition. To make people go to Hawaii, they all reasoned, you had to make them *want* to go there first.

Selling Paradise: Packaging the Lure of Polynesia

Decades before middle class Americans could afford to go to the Pacific islands, the public relations dream machine was hard at work convincing them of Hawaii's value as a destination of paradise. It was an ingenious and prescient effort that successfully primed the mainland public with a desire to engage in all the redolence, promises of passion, and comparative safety Hawaii had to offer.

The design movement known today as Art Deco was embraced in the 1920s and 1930s by artists engaged in promoting the exotic milieu of Hawaii. Elements of Deco found their

Alii on the Shore Greeting Tall-Masted Ship, **painted by Arman Tateos Manookian, c. 1927 (Honolulu Museum of Art, gift of the Estate of Aneliese Lermann, 1998 [26469]).**

ways into advertising campaigns by companies including the Hawaiian (later Dole) Pineapple Company, the Los Angeles Steamship Company, Matson Navigation, and, of course, the Hawaii Tourist Bureau.[1] Dole Pineapple was particularly active in the 1930s, promoting the islands with full-page magazine ads designed by notable artists, including Georgia O'Keeffe (1887–1986), Miguel Covarrubias (1904–1957), and surrealist Pierre Roy (1880–1950).[2]

Artists and writers extolling the paradise of Hawaii did their best to involve all five senses of the potential visitor. If Americans could visually imagine the appeal of such a paradise, they might also engage their sense of smell in the far-off wonder of tropical flowers. They could thrill to the touch of powdery white sand running through their fingers and imagine plunging into the warm, azure surf. They could practically taste the pineapple and savor the roasted pork of a luau. And the sounds! The breeze rustled warmly through the palms, bowing in the breeze on a beach where the music of the crashing surf could be lazily enjoyed for hours, minus the arctic cold, sand-blasted offshore winds or tormenting, biting insects one often experienced in North American climes. There was real—or real sounding, at least—

tropical music, too, easily accessible, first by phonograph records and then radio programs, providing an instant soundtrack to a vision of hula girls and ukulele boys playing and lazily dozing on Waikiki Beach. The romantically inspired sheet music covers of Hawaiian melodies, sold in shops all over the mainland, proved it (the "hula girls," of course, were portrayed as being Caucasian). And how could one not be swayed by the friendly, ethnically diverse population, where service would always be accompanied by a smile and a softly spoken and sincere "aloha"?[3]

It was, of course, a fantasy. Author Theresa Papanikolas refers to the imaged Hawaii as a "safe and accessible paradise on Earth, where history lived on, where time was suspended, and where the experience and lifestyle, though designed for modern comfort, were also presented as uniquely Hawaiian."[4] Remaking the story of Hawaii was a public relations writer's dream, an ongoing and ever-building formulaic myth that worked so well that it was eventually copied by tourism and visitors bureaus from other countries *ad infinitum*, from Thailand to Tahiti. The myth, inculcated rigorously and religiously by powerful commercial forces within Hawaii, and adopted by political and military interests on the mainland, was, in no small part, greatly responsible for the United States annexing Hawaii, first as a territory, and then a state. Fantasy had become fact. Or so it seemed.

Hawaii was, above all, "picturesque," a term that author Orvar Lofgren describes as a way of seeing a landscape, faming it with a sensibility of beauty and paintability that embodied atmosphere, colors, and perhaps even a sense of nostalgia.[5] The campaign to forge Hawaii as a destination spot had longevity. Even today, in a post-millennial world, mainlanders can view themselves and Hawaii in their minds' eyes, emblazoned at the end of a selfie stick, Diamond Head in the background wrapped by a deep blue whitecapped surf, a scene suddenly transformed by the tropical nightfall, where silhouetted palms sway to breezes enveloped by a fierce orange and red sunset. And it's close. Hawaii has become so accessible for many Americans, especially those living on or near the West Coast, that it seems just a bit farther away than the corner mom and pop. It's been that way for less than a century, however.

East of the Sun and West of the Moon: Island Dreamlands and Nightmarish Voyages

For much of the 19th century, Hawaii was, to a large extent, the embodiment of an exotic but still distant Eden for Americans. It wasn't, in realistic terms, considered a travel destination for U.S.–based vacationers on par with Europe. It wasn't easy to get to, and for the first 60 years or so of that century, was visited primarily by American merchant seamen, workers on whaling vessels, and occasional intrepid sailors. But that didn't mean that state-siders weren't already dreaming of island paradises. The popularity of Daniel Defoe's *Robinson Crusoe*, first published in 1719, introduced New World armchair adventurers to the flora, fauna, and climate to be found in a sub-tropical island. Defoe's tale was loosely based on the exploits of Alexander Selkirk, an irascible seaman left to his own devices on an island off the coast of Chile with no human inhabitants. It was populated with goats, had adequate edible vegetation and sea life, and access to potable water, which he collected during rainstorms. Selkirk lived there for 52 months until picked up by a British ship. Initially, he was viewed by the astonished public as a heroic figure, an intrepid Odyssean romanticized by the mind and pen of the imaginative

Defoe. Contemporary reports state that Selkirk's reality wasn't quite utopian. His rescuers reported that his hair and beard were matted and he was unwashed, smelling of the untanned goatskins that served as his vestment. Later reports described his sport of having intercourse with goats, notching the ear of each of his conquests to ensure that he'd never involve the same goat twice.[6]

Captain James Cook (1728–1779) is credited with being the first European to visit Hawaii, which he named the Sandwich Islands on his second Pacific voyage of 1772–1776, chosen in honor of John Montagu, the Fourth Earl of Sandwich, and First Lord of the Admiralty. Cook was famously killed there on his trip of 1779. His voyages opened up the Pacific to British trade and colonialization. One of the most notable of these later Pacific colonists was the "White Rajah" of Sarawak in north Borneo, James Brooke (1803–1868). A wealthy adventurer who owned his own ship, Brooke, who was born in India, arrived in northern Borneo in 1838, assisted the Sultan of Brunei in putting down a rebellion, and was rewarded with the governorship of the state of Sarawak. He was granted the title of Rajah of Sarawak in 1841 and died there in 1868. His concerns over mercantile colonialism mirrored those of the Hawaiian monarchy of the same era. Mindful of the designs powerful British businessmen had on the potential profits to be gleaned from Borneo's resources, Brooke wrote disparagingly of them: "The pollution of lucre takes possession of them. It is the devil's own go-cart, with four or five other pet vices as lackeys hanging on behind.... I will become no party to a bubble.... Really, the mania for an El Dorado is so universal that I should not be astonished if such a place was discovered—a mountain of gold with nothing wanting but pickaxes.... Everything distant seems to attract the imagination; distance leads to enchantment of the view—distance of time softens down the crimes and errors of the dead."[7]

Brooke's views on mercantilism as it related to its potential impact on his Paradise would be echoed by countless others in the ensuing decades throughout the entire Pacific region. It was a path to economic paradise fraught with dangers, to be sure. Cook had been killed in a skirmish with the native Hawaiian population, and Brooke's Sarawak, where Dayaks controlled most of the country, was rife with an active headhunting culture, which Brooke strove to eradicate, although unsuccessfully. In the 20th century, Dayaks were, in fact, encouraged by the allied forces of World War II to employ any means necessary to fight Japanese troops in Borneo, even if it involved, surreptitiously, the taking of heads.[8] Even today, heads of past enemies are prominently displayed in the Iban longhouses of Sarawak as sources of pride, culture, power, and good fortune.[9]

A more fetching element of this exotic world, for many male visitors to Borneo, was the Dayak female presence in Sarawak. British sailor, author, and artist Frank Marryat (1826–1855) stayed at Brooke's house, along with the remainder of the crew, while his ship, the *Semarang*, was being repaired. In his journal he made special note of the attractiveness of the women: "It was a beautiful starry night and, strolling through the village, I soon made acquaintance with a native Dyak, who requested me to enter his house. He introduced me to his family, consisting of several fine girls and a young lad. The former were naked from the shoulders to below the breasts, where a pair of stays, composed of several circles of whalebone, with brass fastenings were secured round their waists; and to the stays was attached a cotton petticoat, reaching to below their knees. This was the whole of their attire. They were much shorter than European women, but well made; very interesting in their appearance, and affable and friendly in their manners. Their eyes were dark and piercing, and I may say there was something wicked in their furtive glances; their noses were but slightly flattened; the mouth rather large; but when I beheld the magnificent teeth which required all its size to display, I thought this rather an advantage. Their hair was superlatively beautiful, and would have been envied by many a courtly dame. It was jet black, and of the finest texture and hung in graceful masses down the back, nearly reaching to the ground. A mountain Dyak girl, if not a beauty, has many most beautiful points; and, at all events, is very interesting and, I may say, pretty. They have good eyes, good teeth, and good hair;—more than good: I may say splendid;—and they have good manners, and know how to make use of their eyes.... As it was late I bade my new friends farewell by shaking hands all round. The girls laughed immoderately at this way of bidding goodbye which, of course, was to them quite novel. I regretted afterwards that I had not attempted the more agreeable way of bidding ladies farewell which, I presume they would have understood better; as I believe kissing is a universal language, perfectly understood from the equator to the pole."[10]

Tahiti was yet another island increasingly fabled for its beautiful women. Painter, sculptor, and woodcut artist Paul Gauguin (1848–1903) was one of its most notable visitors. He made his first trip to Tahiti in 1891, spending the greater part of 10 years in French Polynesia and writing a book of memoirs and myths, *Noa Noa*, published in 1901. He married his 13-year-old bride Tehaamana there, who became the subject of several of his paintings. He conceived a child by her, then returned to France. Upon his return to Tahiti in 1895, began living with Pauura, a girl of nearly 15, who bore him two children, one of whom died in infancy. He relocated to the island of Hiva-Oa in the Marquesas, where he began cohabitating with Vaeoho, known as Marie-Rose, who was 14 years old. She became pregnant then left the painter to have her child in the presence of her family in a neighboring valley. Paul Gauguin died on Hiva-Oa and was buried there.[11] His images of the women of French Polynesia are among his most famous and recognized works, and he has been cited as an influence by a number of other artists well-known for their paintings of beautiful Pacific island women.

Primitive artist Henri Rousseau (1844–1910) was a contemporary of Gauguin. His painting *The Dream* (1910), with its nude woman reclining amid iridescent, exotic tropical foliage, would serve as an inspiration for painters working in the South Seas who painted along similar thematic lines. In addition to Tahiti, Bali was a haven for Western painters focusing on native women amid lavish or traditional tropical surroundings. The best-known of these painters would include Rudolf Bonnet (1895–1978), Miguel Covarrubias (1904–1957), Theo Meier (1908–1982), and Antonio Blanco (1912–1999). Meier is especially memorable for his statement that he was incapable of painting a female nude body without having an erection.[12]

The attraction of Polynesian women for Western males, particularly in press stories generated by newspapermen, was not limited by the class or social standing of the women. Perhaps the most notable Polynesian beauty of her day was Hawaii's Victoria Kaiulani Kalaninuiahilapalapa Kawekiu i Lunalilo Cleghorn, better known in the west as Crown Princess Kaiulani (1875–1899), heir to the Hawaiian throne. She was the daughter of a Western man, Archibald Scott Cleghorn, and Princess Likelike (1851–1887), sister of King David Kalakaua. Kaiulani's aunt was Queen Liliuokalani (1838–1917), the last royal ruler of Hawaii.[13] Kaiulani deserves more than a simple footnote. Her poise, education, and beauty were celebrated by Western writers of the day. An arranged marriage with Prince Komatsu of Japan had been discussed by both Kalakaua and Liliuokalani. Kaiulani, in a letter to her aunt, suggested that she prefer to marry for love, "unless it is absolutely necessary."[14] It has been surmised that if she had married the Prince, Hawaii could conceivably been a Japanese protectorate in December 1941. She famously visited Washington D.C., where in 1893 she subtly and unofficially lobbied for Hawaii to remain a monarchy, rather than be either absorbed as a U.S. territory or declared a republic run by a cadre of Western businessmen. She returned to Hawaii and lived in her father's royal estate at Ainahau. She died there in 1899 at the young age of 23, never having married. After her death, her father wanted to will Ainahu to the people of Hawaii as a public park. The fate of this offering is told by authors Nancy and Jean Francis Webb: "In accordance with this last tender hope, the old man in his will directed his trustees to offer his premises at Ainahau to the government, with the proviso that they be forever kept a public tropical park named Kaiulani Park, and closed to visitors (who might damage the botanical specimens) from sunset to sunrise. A near riot broke out in the Territorial Legislature over Cleghorn's bequest. Various interests stirred up opposition to its acceptance, crying that appropriations for such a park's upkeep would be excessive and that the restrictions placed upon its use were 'unfulfillable' and 'insulting.' Although the chief spokesman against the park was a legislator of colorful political reputation, 'Too Bad' Jack Kalakiela, it was understood that at the core of the opposition stood heirs to Kaiulani's half-sisters, who had hopes of inheritance. After several stormy sessions, the offer was rejected. Thus left unprotected, the acres of Ainahau passed through a variety of fortunes until, no longer a vista of rare beauty or a beloved private retreat, they were cleared for the construction of the tallest ... of the many new hotels that a growing tourist boom brought to Waikiki."[15]

Princess Kaiulani in 1897 at the age of 23, two years before her death (Hawaii State Archives).

Whether through the paintings of Gauguin, the photographs of Kaiulani, sheet music covers of Hawaiian songs, traveling hula troupes, or the smiling hibiscus-coiffed maidens gracing the advertisements of passenger ship lines, Western men were drawn by the siren song of exotic women waiting for them across the seas. The allure of Hawaiian women and their easy availability was noted as long ago as the 18th century, in one of Captain James Cook's diaries: "No women I ever met were less reserved. Indeed it appeared to me that they visited us with no other view than to make a surrender of their persons."[16] The Hawaiian Islands were also, increasingly, seen as a land primed for adventure, as well as adventurers.

By the mid–19th century, Hawaii was beginning to attract adventurous travelers including Mark Twain (1835–1910), who visited in 1866, stayed for several months, and published his reports as letters in the *Sacramento Union*. He also delivered approximately one hundred lectures in the States and England on the topic of Hawaii. One of his more descriptive quotes on Hawaii, made in 1899, was this: "No alien land in all the world has any deep, strong charm for me but that one; no other land could so longingly and beseechingly haunt me, sleeping and waking, through half a lifetime, as that one has done. Other things leave me, but it abides; other things change, but it remains the same. For me its balmy airs are always blowing, its summer seas flashing in the sun; the pulsing of its surf-beat in my ear; I can see its garlanded crags, its leaping cascades, its plumy palms drowsing by the shore; its remote summits floating like islands above the cloud rack; I can feel the spirit of its wooded solitudes; I can hear the splash of its brooks; in my nostrils still lives the breath of flowers that perished twenty years ago."[17]

Based on three voyages made between 1888 and 1890, Robert Louis Stevenson's (1850–1894) tales from the South Seas also whetted the appetites of those yearning for an opportunity to experience balmy breezes, tropical palms, and a world of romance. The yacht *Casco* brought him to Honolulu in 1889 where, living on the estate of Frank Brown, he worked on the novel that became *The Master of Ballantrae*. He called on King David Kalakaua at the Iolani Palace and at the Cleghorn residence at Ainahau, where he met the 13-year-old Princess Kaiulani, serving as hostess after the death of her mother, Princess Likelike.[18]

American businessmen had already for some time been enjoying the tropical life and making profitable trade from Hawaii, most notably in the sugar and ship provisioning industries. A number of Western businessmen had engineered a coup that overthrew Queen Liliuokalani in 1893, and after her failed effort to take back her country, the Republic of Hawaii was formed in 1894. Hawaii was eventually incorporated as a territory of the United States in 1898.

Leisure travel to Hawaii wasn't much of an option for casual visitors prior to the end of the 19th century. The advent of luxury steamship travel, for those that had the time and money, made Hawaii accessible to the leisure class. Nineteenth century travel statistics unveil only part of the story. More than 1,600 ships visited Honolulu from 1823 to 1837, an average of 114 per year, or roughly one every three days. These consisted primarily of merchant and whaling ships, and occasional foreign naval vessels. For the adventurous and well-heeled traveler, clipper ship travel from San Francisco to Honolulu required a significant amount of time and financial resources in the mid–19th century, requiring up to two weeks at sea traveling from San Francisco.[19] Prior to the advent of the transcontinental railroad in 1869, comparatively few travelers from the eastern U.S. would even consider Hawaii as a viable destination, as it would require an at-best uncomfortable voyage "around the Horn" (the Panama Canal wouldn't open until 1914).[20] By the end of the century, steamship travel, becoming increasingly popular as a means to getting to Hawaii, had dramatically diminished the time needed to travel there from western ports.[21] In 1881, for example, the Pacific Mail Steamship vessel *China* made the trip from San Francisco to Honolulu in five days and eight hours, half the time of a sailing ship.[22] Pacific Mail had been operating profitably on its Honolulu run because of a mail subsidy from the U.S. government, but ceased making the voyage after the contract expired in 1885. The mail contract was taken on by the Oceanic Steamship Company, incorporated in 1881 and led by sugar king Claus Spreckels' sons John Dietrich (1853–1926) and Adolph Bernard Spreckels (1857–1924).[23] Hawaii, however, was not the end destination for many Pacific route ships of the era, which stopped in Honolulu primarily for provisions, water, and fuel. For the majority, it was simply an intriguing stopover on their final destinations to Asian ports, Australia or New Zealand.[24]

Claus Spreckels' (1828–1908) prime concern was sugar. With the signing in 1876 of the Treaty of Reciprocity between the Kingdom of Hawaii and the United States, the major trade barrier to Hawaii's raw sugar industry and its largest potential market was broken. Spreckels therefore made a concerted effort to corner the Hawaiian sugar market, buying up more than half of the 1877 sugar production in Hawaii. He also leased or bought thousands of acres of land on the islands of Hawaii and Maui, and in 1879, began building a fleet of nine sailing ships to carry the raw material to his refinery in the States. Independent businessman William Matson (1849–1917) began chartering one of those ships in 1882, the *Emma Claudina*. He incorporated the Matson Navigation Company that year and began his shipping business, running inter-island and trans-Pacific cargo.[25]

Seeking a faster way to move product to the States, the Spreckels' Oceanic line launched its new steamship, the *Mariposa*, in 1883. In addition to cargo, it began taking passengers from San Francisco to Honolulu for vacations. Soon after, it added the ports of Auckland and Sydney to its itinerary. For the typical U.S. passenger, the price of Pacific Ocean travel was expensive. In 1884, the estimated cost for a trip to Hawaii, allowing for three weeks there and two weeks' travel by ship, was $270, at a time when the average individual yearly earning for a U.S. citizen was less than $500 (those figures represent $6,570 and $12,167, respectively, in 2017 money).[26]

Ocean travel by sail could be both beautiful and terrifying, as contrasted by two very different voyager's tales. Palm Langdon, writing in 1913 in the magazine *Forest & Steam*, described refreshing baths in which a bucket of seawater was hauled on board and splashed over the head, while for evening entertainment they watched the stars and danced to music played on the captain's phonograph. A year later, a Honolulu newspaper related a voyage somewhat less enchanting on the sailing ship *Andrew Welch*, westbound to Hawaii, skippered by Captain Kelly: "There was no way of running away from the storm. Fourteen days after leaving San Francisco, they were not far south of that port. The seas were mountainous. The deck cargo suffered and some of the sails were blown away ... drums of distillate were lifted out of their lashings by the water that poured over the ... side as the ship wallowed in the swirling waves. Most of the drums of distillate went overboard of their own accord but others had to be jettisoned in order to save the ship. Altogether, 150 drums were lost ... two topsails were torn right out of place by winds which must have reached 95 miles an hour, according to the calculations of the officers."[27]

Even considering the travails of sailing vessels, William Matson, after the founding of his company, continued to add more ships as a means to increase the size and scope of his fleet. He sold his interest in the *Emma Claudina* and bought a quarter-share in the larger brigantine *Lurline* in 1887. He had his eye on innovation, acquiring the British ship *Roderick Dhu* in 1896 and outfitted her with cold storage and electric lights, a first for the Pacific. His first steamer, the *Enterprise*, was acquired in 1901, which he soon converted from coal power to oil, the first such vessel in the Pacific to be propelled by that means. Matson's brand new steamship, the *Lurline* (the second of several Matson ships to bear that name) was launched in 1908, with a carrying capacity of 51 passengers in addition to 8,000 tons of cargo, more than doubling the load and passenger potential of any other ship in Matson's fleet.[28]

At the start of the 1930s, Matson Navigation began having a significant influence on the way Americans would be introduced to Hawaii as a holiday destination in the form of magazine advertisements and take-home paper items from her voyages. These items featured palm trees, moonlight, Waikiki and Diamond Head and above all, her "white ships," the most prominent of which was the *Lurline*, now in its third iteration.[29] Matson hired first rate artists, first Frank McIntosh, then Eugene Savage, to design everything from luggage tags to shipboard menus, reaching an apogee with the massive murals painted by Savage (unfortunately never destined to be displayed a on ship due to the advent of the Pacific war). These images created both an idealized exotic world of the wonders that were promised to be seen at destination, as well as a lasting—if not entirely true—mental picture of what the visitor had experienced. Or could have. Matson also hired noted photographer Edward Steichen (1879–1973) to create photographs of the luxurious on-board experience for its magazine advertisements, and printmaker John Melville Kelly to design menu covers to be used in its Royal Hawaiian Hotel on Waikiki Beach in Honolulu. Beginning in 1937, Matson featured Honolulu dancer and model Pualani Mossman in its ads. With a red hibiscus flower in her hair, she became known as the "Matson Girl." The photographs of yet another "Matson Girl," dancer Tootsie Notley, were featured in 36 Matson advertisements. Both she and Pualani Mossman shared the reputation of being "the most photographed hula girl in the islands."[30] Matson's onboard entertainment included noted performers that included hula dancer Pauline Kekahuna.[31]

The Artists of Matson's Hawaii

As author DeSoto Brown notes, from the 20th century onward, publicity-focused artwork played an increasingly significant part in creating the image of Hawaii as a proto-tropical, romantic, and safe destination. "Palm Trees, a distant mountain (frequently a smoking volcano), and a hula maiden, all surmounted by a splendid full moon, usually summed up the ideal."[32] Artists working for Matson Lines concentrated on evoking this romantic ideal, whether or not a ship was actually part of the seascape or included in the image. The artists most often associated with Matson were John Kelly, Eldridge Logan, Louis Macouillard, Frank McIntosh, Richard C. Moore, and Eugene Savage.[33]

Louis Macouillard (1913–1987), a San Francisco–like painter and illustrator, specialized in posters mostly detailing South Pacific ports of call for the *Mariposa* and *Monterey*. An illustration focusing on the ships' New Zealand route features a stylized Maori maiden sitting next to a carved divinity sculpture in the foreground, while the white-hulled liner lulls in the harbor beneath a snow-capped volcano.

Richard C. Moore (b. 1932), a well-regarded artist of ships and seascapes, made two commissioned paintings for Matson in the early 1980s: "The Matson art director insisted that the Royal Hawaiian and Moana hotels be included in the *Lurline* painting, since Matson apparently owned them at the time. I was paid to do it—so I did it—but seem to recall that if the ship had been that close to the coastline, *Lurline* would probably have been aground! 'Hawaiian Merchant' was painted coming out of San Francisco, so I didn't have that worry about grounding that ship."[34]

Oakland, California born printmaker **John Melville Kelly** (1879–1962, also said to be born in 1878 in Phoenix, Arizona) designed menu covers for the Royal Hawaiian Hotel in the 1930s. After several years studying art, he spent 14 years as an illustrator for the *San Francisco Examiner*. Sometime in the early 1920s he, his wife, sculptor Katherine "Kate" Harland Kelly, and young son John Jr. traveled to Hawaii, invited by developer Charles Frazier, who offered Kelly an opportunity to draw a "futurama" to illustrate Frazier's Lanikai real estate development. The Kellys fell in love with Hawaii and stayed. Kelly worked in several media, including etching, drypoint, and aquatint. He would often work from photographs, many of them taken by Kate, of native Hawaiians, including local tennis star Litheia Hall, and Marion, the wife of their son John, Jr.[35] He was noted for his "ravishing depictions of Polynesians," many of whom were undoubtedly Marion, who was described as "languorously lovely."[36] Kelly focused much of his work on cross-cultural and native themes and dress. He was influenced by many schools of painting, his work at times reminiscent of the water prints of Hokusai, the sunlight-dappled garments of Joaquin Sorolla, the angularity of Modigliani, the palette, spatial planes, native and subject matter of Gauguin. Favorite themes included native women clothed in colorful native garb placed against or framed in lavish vegetation.

Frank H. McIntosh was born in Portland, Oregon on July 17, 1901. He graduated from the California School of Fine Arts, studied in Paris, and operated a studio in San Francisco 1923–1924. In 1924, he studied with designer Norman Bel Geddes in New York. He illustrated three children's books that were published between 1927 and 1929 and approximately 125 colorful Art Deco, orientalist covers for *Asia* magazine from 1924 through 1937.[37] These, as well as the illustrations he made for other publications (the magazine *Women's Home Companion* was one) are reflective of his interest in stage design and display an influence of the work of Aubrey Beardsley. He habitually spent nine months each year in New York and three in California, the latter of which he would devote to experimenting with new ideas in art. In the early 1930s, McIntosh taught in Los Angeles and was on the faculty at the Chouinard Art Institute. He began providing illustrations for covers of *Asia* magazine, which would eventually number approximately 125.[38] During this period, he began producing illustrated designs for Matson. He produced items ranging from luggage tags to ticket envelopes. His covers for Matson's "Travel Offerings" brochures, published from 1935 to 1940, display the vibrantly colored airbrush designs that stylistically defined his work of that era. From a Matson perspective, he was best-known for the series of six menu covers that were featured in dining rooms on the Matson ships *Lurline*, *Malolo*, *Mariposa*, *Matsonia*, and *Monterey*. The themes were resplendent with colorful Hawaiian iconography: fruits and lavish botanical specimens, fish, luau, ukulele, and stylized interpretations of Hawaiian women. Matson encouraged these to be kept as souvenirs and many were framed and graced the homes of returning passengers (McIntosh's menu covers were replaced by those designed by Eugene Savage when Matson resumed passenger service in 1948). In 1940 McIntosh had a studio in New York City, but returned to Los Angeles in the 1960s, where he owned a gallery specializing in Oriental paintings and artifacts. He died in Santa Cruz, California on May 29, 1985.

Eugene Francis Savage's (1883–1978) murals, completed in 1938 and depicting scenes relating to the culture and history of Hawaii, today represent the best-known art pieces commissioned by Matson. Born in Covington, Indiana, he studied at the Art Institute of Chicago. While there, his painting *Morning* won the Rome Prize, enabling him to further his studies at the American Academy in Rome, where he received his Bachelor's Degree in Fine Arts. The studies of large classical art paintings he made while living in Europe would have a direct influence on his later murals in the United States. Savage taught art at Yale after returning to the U.S., and went on to earn another BA and an MFA. He was also engaged in the Works Progress Administration (WPA) federal art program. From 1935, he created a series of paintings on the subject of Florida's Seminole Indians that contained elements of the style Savage used in his subsequent Hawaiian-themed work. His painting of 1936, *Biscayne Holiday*, for example, although comparatively small at 36 × 36 inches, celebrated native dress and featured multiple human figures layered geometrically upon each other. While Savage's images are reminiscent of the work of Thomas Hart Benton, they were, in fact, contemporaries.

In 1935, he was hired by Matson Lines to create a series of paintings that would eventually be used as menu covers. Electing to portray the pageantry of Hawaii as a theme, he spent three months making sketches on location and two years completing the paintings, each of which were eight feet wide by four feet high. Although the original intention may have been to place them aboard her passenger liners, the conversion of her passenger liners to troop transport ships postponed the idea. They were never installed when the ships were re-converted to passenger use after the war and were instead placed in storage. Matson, however, created lithographs of them, which were used as menu covers for shipboard dining rooms from 1947 through approximately 1955. Eventually, more than 250,000 of them were either given to passengers or sold as mementos. Thematically, they range from scenes depicting elements surrounding the exaltation of Hawaiian royalty ("Aloha … the Universal Word," "Festival of the Sea," "Island Feast," "Pomp and Circumstance") to the arrival and triumph of colonial interests ("A God Appears," "Hawaii's Decisive Hour").

Savage's Hawaiian designs were converted to fabric in 1950 by the Mallinson Company and textile designer John Keoni Meigs, and were fashioned into Hawaiian shirts by the Kamehameha Garment Company.[39] As of this writing, two of Savage's Matson mural designs ("Pomp and Circumstance" and "Boat Day Aloha") can still be purchased as shirts made by garment manufacturer Tori Richard. Savage, whose murals and paintings appear in many public buildings and museums in the United States, retired from his position as art professor at Yale in 1951, and died in 1978. His Matson murals were unveiled publicly for the first time in an exhibition at the Honolulu Museum of Art that ran from July 2014 through August 2015.[40]

Matson's Luxury Liners

Matson did have its challenges in the 1930s and 1940s. The Great Depression arrived, but nevertheless many of its well-heeled target travelers could still afford first class fares. The trans-Pacific airplane made its appearance as well, although Matson, in the initial stages, saw these handsome but comparatively small craft as supplements to its passenger business, rather than competitors. World War II presented a larger challenge, with Matson losing its ships and its luxury passenger income along with them.

Matson's major push for luxury passenger travel can be said to have really begun in the era of its president, Edward Davies Tenney (1859–1934), who took over after William Matson's death in 1917 and served until May 1927. But it positively bloomed under the presidency of Matson's grandson, William Philip Roth (1879–1963), who served until March 1945. Tenney's era was one of acquisition, of ships as well as an erstwhile competitor. The Spreckels' Oceanic Steamship Company had been absorbed under the Matson umbrella in 1926. Another competitor, the Pacific Mail Steamship Company, had gone out of business in 1925, with several of its ships acquired by the ill-fated Dollar Line.[41] Tenney, along with Matson Vice President William P. Roth, also saw the need to create a destination hotel/resort that reflected the increasing elegance of her passenger liners. A new company was formed, with

Matson's SS *Lurline* leaves San Francisco for Hawaii, April 1941 (Bill Regan/author's collection).

the charter of building what was to become the Royal Hawaiian Hotel, which opened in 1927.[42] The Royal Hawaiian's 12 acres of lavish tropical grounds featuring 800 palm trees, were designed by R.T. Stevens. The hotel itself had 400 richly furnished guest rooms, many with lanais resplendent with bronze furniture. Public spaces were extravagant, the ballroom decorated with murals of Nile barges, its massive ceiling beams covered with bird motifs and ornate floral medallions. Noted hula dancer, choreographer, and producer Louise Akeo Silva and her Royal Hawaiian Girls Glee Club, were brought in as the resident vocal and hula group, staying there until 1958. In 1934, Hawaiian bandleader Johnny Noble became the entertainment director.[43]

Matson's first modern luxury passenger liner to sail its Hawaiian route was the *Malolo*, making its first landfall trip to Honolulu in late 1927. Author William L. Worden describes the impact of the iconoclastic vessel on luxury Pacific travel: "The ship was 582 feet long, with seven decks, a Pompeian-Etruscan swimming pool ... a veranda cafe, a ballroom lounge, two theaters, a gymnasium, and room for 650 first-class passengers in 480 beds, each with a telephone beside it, and 170 Pullman berths. No ship afloat could match the *Malolo's* 100 complete private baths and 50 private showers with toilets. Hot and cold fresh and saltwater taps were in each bathroom, and a ventilating system changed the air in the staterooms every three minutes. With 25,000 horsepower, she could cruise at 21 knots and cross from San Francisco to Honolulu in four and one-half days."[44]

A Matson liner's arrival in Honolulu must have seemed like something out of a tropical fairytale for its passengers. The ship was welcomed by Hawaiians in outrigger canoes and passengers were festooned in leis to music played by the Royal Hawaiian Orchestra. They were welcomed at the hotel by the haole general manager and immediately served drinks by Japanese American "geisha" girls dressed in kimono. Their trunks were quickly hauled off by Chinese American attendants in "Cathayan costume" to the guests' rooms, where they were quickly unpacked by the passengers' servants or hotel staff. The guests soon learned that the geishas and baggage handlers were in actuality upwardly mobile U.S. citizens who spoke textbook English.[45]

The *Malolo* also introduced the Matson tradition of beautifully designed menu covers. A menu for a Royal Hawaiian Hotel celebration of her arrival was illustrated by the talented and ill-fated local artist Arman Tateos Manookian (1904–1931). It featured a red-hulled steamship set against muted green and blue sky and brilliant yellow clouds, heralded by a school of flying fish swimming atop mountains of white-capped emerald and violet seas. Born in Constantinople of Armenian parents, Manookian served as an illustrator for the *Honolulu Star-Bulletin* and contributed work to *Paradise of the Pacific Magazine*. His best-known work is a mural he created for the Green Mill Grill in Honolulu, *Men in an Outrigger Canoe Headed for Shore*, a study of two Hawaiians in a fruit-laden canoe, heading toward a stylized group of hills banded in three shades of green. His career was cut short by his suicide a few days prior to his 27th birthday. A memorial exhibit of his work was held at the Academy of Arts in Honolulu in 1933.[46]

In 1932, Matson added the newly built *Lurline* (chronologically the third Matson ship of that name) to the Hawaiian route. Advertisements touted the Lurline as "a sea-going night-

The Matson Line's passenger liner SS *Lurline* approaching Pier 10 at Honolulu in the 1930s, under the Aloha Tower (National Park Service).

club that strikes joy to the toes of those who love to dance. Tropical nights blend into carefree days." A year earlier, the single-stacked sister ships, *Mariposa* and *Monterey* had been built for her more extensive South Pacific routes, which sailed from the West Coast and included stops in Tahiti, New Zealand, and Australia, as well as Hawaii. All four luxury ships were painted in white, part of the new Matson passenger liner branding and beginning in 1937 carried Polynesian-themed menu covers designed by Art Deco illustrator Frank McIntosh. McIntosh's menu covers were in use on Matson liners until World War II, when her ships were converted to use for military transport.

Luxury ship travel was put on hiatus with the United States' entry into World War II. For the war effort, the federal government commandeered all U.S. merchant ships, including 38 of Matson's. In addition, all four Matson passenger liners were painted gray and refitted for troop and cargo transport. They carried "ammunition, bombs, battle casualties, Japanese prisoners, war brides, and children."[47] At a speed of 22 knots, they could outrun any submarine, and therefore often sailed without armed escort in areas free of axis aircraft. They were exceptional military ships. In addition to their speed, their large fuel tanks allowed for greater range than standard troop transport ships, an estimated 21,000 nautical miles without refueling. They were better armed than freighters, sporting 22mm and Bren anti-aircraft guns on their decks.[48]

Profits were out of the picture for companies with passenger liners during the war. But the war wasn't the only threat to that particular part of the travel business. Air travel to remote destinations was right around the corner. And Matson was interested. The concept of Hawaiian air travel had begun innocently enough, with the incorporation of the Inter-Island Airways Ltd. company in 1929.[49] Its first aircraft purchases were two Sikorsky S-38 flying boats for travel to and from other Hawaiian destinations, an idea welcomed by Matson. By 1934, though, the small idea had expanded. Pan-American Airways was determined to repeat her Caribbean successes by adding trans-Pacific routes. Both Martin and Boeing were building flying boasts with enough range for Hawaii and points east, made possible via fuel stops on Midway and Wake islands. Matson and Inter-Island each invested $500,000 in Pan American, which agreed to the concept of the three companies forming a new corporation to serve West Coast-to-Hawaii travelers. The idea, though, was ended by the Civil Aeronautics Board (CAB) in a decision made in 1941. Matson sold its Pan American stock in response.[50]

Matson wasn't completely done, though, with the thought of adding air routes to its travel network. As part of the war effort, the U.S. Navy contracted with the firm to operate an airplane repair facility at the Oakland airport, which was operational in 1943. Among other aircraft, it serviced and modified 38 DC-4 passenger aircraft, converting them to R5D military transports or specialized aircraft for officers, prompting Matson to again apply to the CAB for commercial air routes from the West Coast to Hawaii.

Matson eventually had approximately 700 personnel on the ground at its Oakland airport facility, which remained in operation after the war, re-converting military transport planes for commercial and passenger use for a number of companies. It began servicing United Air Lines flights as well, as it continued to present its case to begin regularly scheduled air service to Hawaii, citing its experience and investment in the civilian transportation and hotel business. It also began non-scheduled flights between the West Coast and Hawaii aboard four-engine DC-4 aircraft, which did not require CAB route approval. Matson's air plans called for eight DC-4 aircraft, each with 24 overnight berths, and 25 operating crews. The planes were outfitted with mahogany trim and served meals on linen tablecloths, provided by two stewardesses and a steward. Food was prepared under the same chef that served the passenger steamships, and fare might include squab with wild rice, a whole pig with an apple in its mouth, and baked Alaska. The CAB, however, was reluctant to allow a shipping company to manage both regularly scheduled ocean and flight departures, despite Matson's argument that not allowing it to adopt formal air service would eventually have a negative financial impact on its passenger liner business. The final CAB rebuff came in 1946. Both Pan American Airways and United Air Lines were flying regularly scheduled trips to Honolulu via San Francisco, and although Matson continued non-scheduled, non-advertised flights, it could not compete profitably, especially when Pan American and United began engaging in a fare war for Hawaiian traffic. Matson was therefore out of the air passenger business for good by the end of 1947.[51]

In all probability, concerns of Matson having a potential monopoly on visitor traffic to Hawaii contributed to the decision to deny its potential air routes. An economic middle class was rapidly gaining power in Hawaii, and with the traditional influence of the "Big Five" sugar monopolies fresh in their minds (Matson's interests and those of Castle & Cooke were virtually inseparable), it's not difficult to conclude that input from Hawaiian anti-monopolists was a factor in the decision.[52]

From a tourism perspective, Matson continued to focus on its hotel and passenger liner business, while uncomfortable in the knowledge that air transport might soon be eroding its market share in tourism transportation. It therefore dedicated its marketing and advertising budgets to emphasize the luxury, fun, and social advantages of multi-day ocean holidays. By 1948, the *Lurline* had been returned from war duty and completely refurbished for passenger travel, an effort that took two years and $20 million. Her staterooms were crafted by star industrial designer Raymond Loewy (1893–1986), her public rooms festooned with Polynesian décor, and she now boasted an on-board shopping center.

This third version of the ship named *Lurline* sailed the Hawaiian route until 1963 when she sustained turbine damage sufficient enough for Matson to sell her. In December 1963, the former *Matsonia* (which had begun life as the *Monterey* in 1931), was re-christened the *Lurline*, the fourth and final Matson passenger ship to use that name.

From the early 1950s, low-cost air travel began to eat away at Matson's Hawaiian passenger business. Why take four and a half days each way to Hawaii, air passengers felt, when one could get there and back in two days and spend the rest of the time in the islands? Matson's answer was to begin selling the cruise as a destination in itself, with games, Captain's dinners, music and dancing, and various Hawaiian-themed events. Matson found that voyagers could be fussy, based on a survey it took of some of its passengers in 1958. It found, among other things, that cabin-class passengers wanted first-class options at no additional fees. While some loved the idea of free champagne, others complained that it should be a chargeable item because it was running up the bar prices, included in the overall price of passage, for everyone else. Others complained about the two seating times for dinner: early diners missed the cocktail hour, while later diners missed the evening on-board movie. Lines at the beauty parlor were a problem. Why? Of the passengers, 60 percent were female, 70 percent of them aged 60 and over. Clearly, younger travelers, single males, and families were in the minority.[53]

From today's perspective, it's easy to see that the passenger capacity of the ship itself was part of the problem. The *Lurline* #3, which sailed until 1963, had room for 715 passengers, 475 in First class, 240 in Tourist class, with a crew of 369. The *Lurline* #4, which operated as a Matson ship until 1970, held approximately the same number of passengers (by 1967, all passage was first class). In comparison, today's cruise ships are massive: the *Carnival Legend*, as of this writing, sails to Hawaii with a guest capacity of 2,124 and a crew of 930.

In 1970, when the proliferation of airline travel had made luxury ocean liner unprofitable for Matson, the company discontinued *Lurline* service, and the last passenger ship of that name was sold. She lived on for a few more years, sailing as the *Britanis* for Chandris Lines until 1996, was sold again to A.G. Belofin Investments of Lichtenstein, but never again took on cruise passengers. After several failed attempts to repurpose her as a hotel in San Francisco, now rusty and forlorn, she was towed across the Atlantic, took on water, and sank near Cape Town in 2000, on the way to being scrapped.[54]

Artist Gordon Grant's painting *Yankee Clippers Sail Again*, contrasting two majestic means of crossing the ocean, was used for promotional postcards and posters by Pan American Airways (author's collection).

The demise of the classic passenger steamships leaves quite a dent in the bulkhead of maritime history. One reads about the Matson ships and reflects that they were actually well-appointed cities afloat. Period photographs provide a provocative teaser for those looking for historically accurate representations of high-fashion interiors by Raymond Loewy and other well-known designers. One wonders as well how much of that went down with the ship, as was the case of the last *Lurline*.

These quintessential floating palaces were put out of business by the airlines, but they did get, in a twisted sort of way, the ultimate revenge on the first "flying palaces" that heralded the end of ultra-luxury steamship travel. In terms of the fading ships, at least people got to say goodbye and wish a fond, perhaps tearful farewell. The last days of the early Pan American Clipper flying boats wasn't nearly as ceremonial.

Two

Flying Air Paradise
The Evolution of Flight to Hawaii

I've come here to Foynes, a small city near Shannon, Ireland, to see the Boeing 314 Pan American Clipper, the most iconic of all historical flying boats, the one most typically seen in photos, travel posters, advertisements, and numerous other ephemera depicting the romance of early air transoceanic travel. In one of its best-known photos, it flies over the San Francisco Bay, the Bay Bridge in the background below, on its way to making its last westward turn on the way to Honolulu. She was the largest passenger aircraft of her day, the absolute last word in luxury air travel. She served gourmet meals, had cocktail lounges, sleeping berths, first class tableware, and was reputed to have the most attentive cabin crew in the business. She was so big that her deck crew could walk standing up inside her wings, performing periodic in flight maintenance checks. Her massive tail consisted of three vertical stabilizers. Those are the first things I see as I walk up to the Foynes Flying Boat Museum. Reflected in the water in which she reposes, towering some 30 feet over the museum's main building, her tail proudly affirms that she's registered as the NC18603, the *Yankee Clipper*. Her inaugural flight was in 1939, and her route was the Atlantic. Not a Pacific Clipper, of course, but then again, Foynes was the *Yankee Clipper's* European terminal. I'm excited to see her anyway.

I pay my admission and head right for the 314, past her massive stainless steel nose, walk up the ramp, and steal reverentially into the cockpit. I study the rudder pedals that connect to nothing, glance at the instruments with needles that have never moved, and attempt to peer out the windows that have been forever blind. It's the only full sized Boeing 314 in the world, but nothing works. Most every surface inside the fuselage is bare, although the Foynes folks have done a great job at adding period seating, berths, and elements. The Foynes Flying Boat Museum's Boeing 314 Pan Am Clipper, is, after all, only a model. Of the 12 Boeing 314s that were made, the last remaining craft was scrapped in 1951. For more than 60 years, she has lived the life of a ghost, a fata morgana, a will-o'-the-wisp, strewn upon the killing fields of forgotten fuselages, waylaid wings, lamented landing gears, crucified cockpits. Of the original fleet of 314s, not even a skeleton remains. She is lost to time, without even so much as a death mask to show how gracefully she might have aged. For those of us who are still enthralled with the beauty and romance of this iconic airplane, the Foynes mock-up is the best thing we've got.

These massive flying boats were built by Boeing from 1938 to 1941. Their mission was to fly Pacific and Atlantic routes faster, more comfortably, and with more passengers than their Martin M-130 and Sikorsky S-42 predecessors. Like the Boeing 377 Stratocruiser, which eventually replaced her as the Pan American flagship, the 314 had a military pedigree, inheriting, in this case, the wing of Boeing's XB-15 bomber prototype.

She revolutionized Pacific travel, making the 2400 mile San Francisco to Honolulu leg in 19 hours, flying at approximately 140 mph and carrying 25 seated passengers, with available sleeping berths (on shorter legs, with more modest fuel requirements, she could carry up to 74 passengers and fly at 188 mph). Seeing her circle the San Francisco Bay before heading west or watching her glide lazily into the azure waters of Oahu was as close as most people would ever get to her. With a one-way ticket of $278 (the approximate equivalent of $4,500 in today's money), she was unaffordable to all but the wealthy who could pay her first class-only airfare.[1]

To illustrate how rapidly the technology of passenger air travel had progressed in the 1930s, both within the United States and transoceanically, it's worth considering several of the Boeing 314's predecessors. In considering these early passenger airplanes, the concept of flying range alone is sobering. The distance from San Francisco to Honolulu is 2,393 miles, and there's no runway to touch down upon along the way. It took years to develop a passenger plane that could traverse the continent alone without refueling (the distance from New York to San Francisco, by comparison, is 2,572 miles). If an emergency situation developed when flying over land, there might be a number of landing strip options somewhere below. Over the Pacific, you only had deep, blue water. The Pan American 314 began its regularly scheduled flights to Honolulu on March 29, 1939, but it wasn't the first to handle that non-stop route. That had occurred several years earlier, when Pan American's Martin M-130 flying boat made the first commercial passenger flight to Honolulu on Nov. 23, 1935. It carried 36 passengers and boasted a range of 3,200 miles.[2]

The Martin M-130—discussed below—was, along with the Boeing 314, a marvel of technology and innovation. These Pan American *Clippers* instilled, through photographs and travel posters, the romance of travel to the exotic Pacific islands and the Orient. They were a far cry from the land-based passenger airliners that preceded them. The story of the airline path to Hawaii is perhaps best begun by attempting to understand what air passenger travel looked like prior to the advent of the transoceanic flying boats. By today's standards, it was primitive. Some would use the word quaint. To conquer the Pacific by air, it took a series of jumps, rather than one gigantic leap. What never fails to impress is how short a period of time it took, from the days of the Ford Tri-Motors to the air conquest of the oceans. What is most poignant, however, is how short the age of the transoceanic passenger-carrying flying boat actually was.

To gain a better understanding of the chasm between early land-based passenger airliners and these astounding flying boats, there's nothing like starting by going back in time and climbing aboard a Ford Tri-Motor….

The weather's lovely this late October morning in the year 2016, the sun beaming on the tarmac of a tiny airport lazing on the eastern side of San Francisco Bay. The object of my visit glows aluminum blue and silver in the morning light. I squint to make out the details tattooed onto her skin. *City of Wichita*, she calls herself. The controls are attached to the rudder by external wires extended to below the cockpit. Her engines are polished a gleaming silver. Ten of us, this morning's payload, stoop as we enter the door at the right rear. The cabin has lovely metal and leather seats, and above each are a reading light and an air valve.

I sit in the left rear seat but don't have to elbow my way to getting a window. Every seat is a window seat. The pilot and co-pilot sit in the front of the cabin, starting the engines, then running up the RPMs as streams of blue exhaust alternately cough and purr, then settle in to a deafening roar. Our 1928 Ford Tri-Motor 5-AT-B, designated NC9645, climbs over strip malls and cookie cutter post-war ranch home subdivisions on her way to the old Leslie Salt flats, reclaimed baylands now, and populated by Wandering Tattler, Marbled Godwit, and Semipalmated Sandpiper, who heed the noise and power of the Tri-Motor, staying well below the mighty propellers of her three Pratt & Whitney Wasp engines, growling proudly in the afterdawn. Below, in the multicolored shallows, we suspect there might be Prickly Sculpin, Threespine Sticklebacks, and Threadfin Shad, basking below the surface in the early light, wary of winged predators, the most formidable of which—as well as the least deadly—wears blue and silver steel-clad livery.

We pitch and yaw with the morning breezes as we bank west, rolling as if on a sideways swing set moored a few thousand feet above the tide. Along with the ever-present roar of the engines, we're reminded of their proximity by a faint smell of exhaust ever-present in the cabin. And, we ask ourselves, flying thousands of feet higher, rocking like crazy, with the perfume of the mighty exhaust pipes never quite far, how did people brave a transcontinental multi-stop flight on these lovely and primitive aircraft?[3]

In 1929, the fastest form of transcontinental travel in the United States was by coast-to-coast train, a trip taking between three and four days. At the time, the Ford Tri-Motor was the most significant commercial passenger aircraft flying American skies, the first passenger airliner to be mass-produced. It was incapable of non-stop continental or transoceanic flight. The Ford 4-AT and 5-AT Tri-Motors have a capacity of 10 to 17 passengers, depending on the interior specifications. On July 8–9, 1929, the first combination air-rail route was inaugurated by Transcontinental Air Transport (TAT) on a transcontinental route from New York to Los Angeles. It encompassed 13 cities, four railway stations, and 11 air terminals. Eleven Tri-Motors were put in service for the trip, which took an exhausting 48 hours to complete. Notable passengers on the inaugural flights (two were made simultaneously) included Amelia Earhart, and pilots included Charles Lindbergh.[4]

It was an arduous trip for both airline personnel and passengers. The one lavatory, which included a washbasin, towel rack, soap dispenser, and first aid kit, was located at the rear of the plane between the main cabin and the mail storage area. The engines were loud, the aircraft rocked and rolled, its passengers assaulted by airsickness and later fatigue as they were rushed from air terminals to train stations. One New York to Los Angeles passenger noted, "It took me over a week to recover. Besides being quite deaf from the roar of the motors, and dizzy from the constant rolling and yawing, as well as a little queasy from the more gentle motion of the trains at night, I ended up just plain tired from all the hectic rushing from one moving object to another. It saved thirty-six hours, and I was glad that I'd done it once, but never again."[5]

Faint traces of engine exhaust would make their way into the cabin, but attempts were made to make the flight as comfortable as possible, given the technology. Passengers were given a small packet before each flight, containing chewing gum and a wad of cotton. As writer F. Robert van der Linden noted, "The contents were not peculiar souvenirs ... passengers sat on thinly padded seats of wicker or metal and needed the chewing gum to help soothe stomachs distressed by the continual bouncing of an all-day flight. With one engine in the nose, the vibration and sound echoing throughout the thinly insulated cabin was often unbearable without the cotton wadding for the ears deadening the deafening roar."[6]

The Tri-Motor served multiple commercial enterprises, included the carrying of mail, which had to be sorted in a tiny enclave, entered through the rear door of the restroom. In one legendary story, the co-pilot began sorting the mail shortly before landing, and a few moments later a passenger entered the lavatory. As the Tri-Motor began its descent, the co-pilot tried to enter the cabin on the way to his seat, but found the door blocked and slammed shut by the passenger in the restroom. He pushed on the door, saying, "I've got to get to the cockpit. I'm one of the pilots." The passenger replied, "What have you got, a pilot on each end?"[7]

In 1930, TAT combined with several other airlines to form Transcontinental and Western Air, Inc. (TWA). The new airline commenced flying an all-air transcontinental route on Oct. 25 of that year, advertising a trip time of 36 hours at a price of $200, equivalent to roughly $2,750 in 2016.[8] The Ford Tri-Motor 5-AT had a maximum speed of 150 mph, less than the top speed of many of today's sports cars, with a cruising speed of up to 100 mph and a top speed of 135 mph. It had a range of 550 miles, operating at a maximum ceiling of 18,500 feet. Designed prior to the advent of sophisticated electronic navigation instruments, it could not fly at night.[9]

It was apparent to the industry that in order for air travel to be more acceptable to paying passengers, aircraft would have to be more comfortable, fly faster, and have a greater range between refueling stops. The Tri-Motor wasn't the answer; its most aggressive iteration, the 40-seat Model 14A, built in 1932, never carried paying passengers, and the project was essentially scrapped after its non-steerable rear wheel broke through the fuselage during taxi tests.[10]

The challenges in building a better aircraft involved speed and payload requirements as well as consideration as to the costs of building and flying the airliner. Improved ground logistics were also part of the equation. Over the ensuing decades, these factors would drive aircraft manufacturers' decisions on everything from engine, wing, fuselage, and propeller design, to the amount of space dedicated to passengers versus cargo. This rapidly developing revolution in airplane design resulted in new technologies continually leapfrogging each other in a highly competitive and expensive manufacturing environment. In terms of passenger travel, the primary goal was to extend the speed, range, and carrying capacity of the aircraft. The secondary goal was to fly the passengers at a price point that would prove to be profitable. What that meant, in realistic terms, was that for most of the three decades to follow, air travel would be financially feasible for only business travelers and the wealthy. The story underscores the difficulties that lay ahead in getting significant numbers of visitors to Hawaii. For working-class Americans prior to the days of low-cost air travel, visiting the tropical paradise in the Pacific would remain little more than a distant dream for the foreseeable future.

Several notable radical new designs in passenger aircraft took to the skies in the immediate years following the heyday of the Ford Tri-Motor. The Boeing 247, introduced in 1933 with great fanfare, was a revolutionary aircraft and is considered the first modern passenger airliner. With a streamlined all-metal monocoque fuselage integrating the chassis with the body of the craft, innovative aerodynamics, and two powerful Pratt & Whitney Wasp engines, it flew at a top speed of 182 mph with a cruising speed of 161 mph, 50 percent faster than the Tri-Motor. It carried 10 passengers up to 482 miles without refueling, less than the Tri-Motor's 550-mile range, but still dramatically reducing transcontinental travel time due to the increased speed. It flew from New York to San Francisco in 21 hours, seven hours faster than any other passenger aircraft. "Across the continent in a single night," boasted United Air Lines advertisements. The Boeing 247's passenger comforts included plush seating and a soundproofed cabin that reduced engine noise and eliminated exhaust fumes. Its streamlined construction dramatically reduced the pitch and yaw associated with the boxy Tri-Motor. Front wheels were partially retracted into the undercarriage, a critical factor in reducing wind resistance. Technical innovations included a cantilevered lower wing, autopilot, and two-way radio, which allowed it to fly at night. It was the first twin-engine passenger aircraft able to fly on one engine alone. One-way coast-to-coast passage was $160, the equivalent of $2,926 in today's money.

The Boeing 247's remarkable capacity to take off and land on short runways, as well as its outstanding reliability, gave it additional utility when flying in demanding geographical conditions. It flew well into the 1950s in the challenging environment of Alaska and was a mainstay in foreign countries including Colombia, where it successfully tackled the high Andean range and short airfields in the llanos. It was also repurposed to fly in non-commercial applications including crop-dusting. Its last commercial flight was made in the early 1960s. Today, four Boeing 247s are housed in air museums, including one, hanging appropriately next to a DC-3, in Washington's National Air and Space Museum.[11]

The next revolution in commercial air travel began when the Douglas Aircraft Company rolled out the new DST (Douglas Sleeper Transport) in 1935. It was placed in service on June 25, 1936, flying from Glendale (Los Angeles) to Newark in 17.5 hours with three intermediate stops, topping the previous commercial passenger-carrying speed record, held by the Boeing 247, by six hours.[12] The DST was a hybrid of sorts, with 14 double seats that could be folded down to make seven sleeping berths. On day flights, it accommodated 28 passengers, although the most common configuration had 21 seats. The 21-seat aircraft soon became the DC-3, which lacked the upper "eyebrow" windows provided for sleepers in upper berths. By 1942, 80 percent of scheduled commercial flights in the United States were by DC-3. Eventually, more than 16,000 DC-3s were sold, either in the passenger configuration or as the military outfitted C-47 and RAF Dakota II.[13] Today, it's estimated that more than 200 DC-3s (many with Basler BT-67 turboprop and cabin conversions) are still flying, carrying passengers and freight, and used for a wide range of purposes, among which are smoke-jumping, pest control, scientific duties, private "air-limos," and general military.[14]

Although the Boeing 247 and Douglas DC-3 represented a quantum leap over the Ford Tri-Motor in terms of range, speed, and passenger comfort, they weren't capable of carrying passengers over the Pacific to Hawaii. In the pre–World War II years, there was only one way to fly to Hawaii. It was by flying boat.

The Age of the Clipper: The Luxurious Pacific Flying Boats

A 2,400 mile-ocean crossing was required to fly non-stop between California and Hawaii, and the story of the arduous steps it took to successfully carry passengers is a reminder of how important the route was perceived to be, by aircraft companies, airlines, tourism authorities, and travelers. The first attempt to cross this distance by air was a military effort involving two Navy PN-9 flying boats that left San Francisco for Maui on Aug. 31, 1925. These two-engine aircraft, fitted with additional fuel capacity, were specified to carry five crewmembers and one ton of cargo. One PN-9 experienced engine failure 300 miles west of San Francisco, leaving the remaining PN-9, piloted by Lieutenant B.J. Connell and navigated by Flight Commander John Rodgers (1881–1926), alone on the quest to conquer the Pacific route. Rodgers was an aviation pioneer, an expert in air navigation, and the second Navy pilot to earn his wings. Connell's and Rogers' arduous but ultimately successful attempt to reach Hawaii resulted in one of the more legendary stories of early flight. The fact that it was completed under sail remains one of the great survival tales of any ocean crossing.[15]

Rodgers' PN-9 flew its Pacific route over a series of naval ships that served both as beacons and as potential refueling or rescue vessels. As he passed over the aircraft carrier *Langley*, 1,200 miles out of San Francisco, Rodgers realized that the tailwinds were of less strength than anticipated and he'd be forced to make a water landing and refuel from one of the station ships. At 1,400 miles out, he requested radio compass bearings from the seaplane tender and minelayer *Aroostook*. These proved to be in error, and, compounded by a series of squalls that diminished visibility, the PN-9 was forced to cut her engines and glide into the water in heavy swells. She touched down at 4:15 p.m. on Sept. 1, virtually out of fuel at an unknown distance from the *Aroostook*. Rodgers and crew were some 300 miles away from Maui and 365 miles off Honolulu. The PN-9 had flown 2,155 land miles and established a world flying boat distance record.[16]

The PN-9's transmitting radio receiver was powered by a wind-driven generator mounted on the wing, inoperative when the plane wasn't flying. The radio could, however, receive transmissions powered by a battery. The crew monitored ship transmission, knowing the search for them was a priority. Within the next few days, at least 23 ships and a number of scouting planes searched for her, between the 21st and 23rd parallels, and the 153rd to 155th meridians. There was no trace of her. After three days, with diminishing food and water supplies, fabric was cut from the bottom wing, fastened to the upper wing, and became a sail. Steering by compass course and a keel improvised from floorboards, the crew headed toward Hawaii. At a rate of 2 knots, they were sailing 50 miles a day toward their destination. On the eighth day, the radio confirmed that the search for them was called off. They'd have to make it by improvised sail. Their course took them through the Kauai channel and they headed toward Ahukini Harbor. Ten miles off shore, she was intercepted by the *R-4* submarine. On Sept. 12, the plane and her bearded, tired, hungry and thirsty crew, wearing torn clothing, were towed into the harbor, arriving at nine in the evening. After flying 1,870 air miles, they'd sailed an additional 450 miles in nine days.[17] It remains one of the most amazing adventures in the history of flight. But Hawaii remained unreached by air alone.

Like the rest of the world, James Drummond Dole (1877–1958), founder and president of the Hawaiian Pineapple Company, was impressed by Charles Lindbergh's solo flight over the Atlantic, landing his Ryan monoplane in Paris on May 21, 1927, covering 3,600 miles. Hearing that Lindbergh had received a reward of $25,000 from a New York hotel owner, Dole initiated a prize reward himself. The first person to fly non-stop between the mainland and Hawaii would receive that amount from Dole. As an incentive to increase the number of contestants, he also offered $10,000 to the pilot who came in second (these figures represent approximately $352,000 and $141,000, respectively, in today's money). Not one plane succeeded. Behind the scenes, the Army Air Corps was planning an attempt on its own.[18]

The army had successfully tested the new Fokker C-2-3 sporting a Wright 220 engine, and had selected Lieutenants Lester James Maitland (1899–1990) as pilot and Albert Francis Hegenberger (1895–1983) as navigator. Their plane, the *Bird of Paradise*, lifted off from Oakland on June 28, 1927, headed for Honolulu. Halfway through the flight, the engines balked, resulting from carburetor icing. Dropping to a lower altitude, they made the rest of the trip without mishap. At 3:20 a.m., they arrived over Kauai, deciding to circle in until daybreak, when they would land in Oahu. They touched down at Wheeler Field at 6:29 a.m. on June 29, 1927, having logged 2,425 miles over 23 hours to Kauai, with an additional three hours to circle Kauai and land at Oahu. It was the first successful non-stop flight from the mainland to Hawaii.[19]

Pan American's founder and President Juan Terry Trippe (1899–1981) had begun exploring the possibility of trans-Pacific routes in 1931, but early plans to fly via the northern Great Circle route were stymied by Russia, which refused to allow U.S. carriers to use bases in Siberia. After securing rights to land in Hong Kong and Shanghai, Trippe determined that using the U.S. territorial islands of Hawaii, Midway Island, Wake Island, Guam, and the Philippines would allow him to develop an air bridge spanning the Pacific, provided that he could find an aircraft with acceptable range and develop bases along the route. A Sikorsky S-42 flying boat was utilized as a test aircraft, stripped of her passenger seats and refitted to accommodate greater fuel capacity. Now having an increased range of a little less than 3,000 miles, she was test flown successfully on March 23, 1935, on a 2,500 round trip flight from Miami to the Virgin Islands. She was then ferried to Alameda on the eastern shore of San Francisco Bay to reside at Pan American's new Pacific Divisional headquarters. Trippe had secured rights to land in the Pacific islands from the U.S. Navy, and soon laded the freighter *North Haven* with enough material to outfit Pan American's new Pacific outposts. She left the San Francisco Bay on March 27, 1935, a scant four days after the S-42's successful flight to the Virgin Islands. Aboard the ship was essentially the entirety of Pan American's new Pacific operations. It included two complete villages, five air bases, 250,000 gallons of fuel, 44 aircraft technicians, 74 construction staff, motor launches, landing barges, generators, windmills, and water and fuel tanks. Within 55 days, bases were fully operational at the islands of Midway, Wake, and Guam, and fully completed at the existing facilities at Honolulu and Manila.[20]

The Sikorsky S-42 had already made its first survey flight to Honolulu on April 16, 1935, piloted by chief Pan Am pilot Edwin Charles Musick (1894–1938). The crew included navigator Frederick Joseph Noonan (1893–1937, whose most famous flight was to be his last, accompanying Amelia Earhart on her ill-fated flight over the Pacific).[21] Pan Am's test flights to Midway, Wake, and Guam were completed on Oct. 5, 1935. Shortly thereafter, Pan American shortly secured the trans-Pacific mail concession from the U.S. government. On June 20 of that year, Pan Am reached cooperative agreements with the Matson Navigation and Inter-Island Steam Navigation companies for its new air service to the Pacific. Pan American agreed to provide meteorological data to Matson and contracted to haul passenger baggage on Matson's ships. Hawaii-based carrier, Inter-Island Airways Ltd., had been founded in 1929, named after the steamship company, which put up 76 percent of the common stock. By Oct. 11 of that year, it was flying its two eight-passenger Sikorsky S-38 amphibious flying boats on regularly scheduled inter-island flights, serving Maui, Hilo, and Kauai, with flights to Molokai and Lanai on request. In 1934, it finalized it agreement to carry mail within the islands, and soon added more powerful Sikorsky S-43 amphibious craft to its fleet. Inter-Island changed its name to Hawaiian Airlines on Oct. 1, 1941.[22]

Pan American's Sikorsky S-42 Clipper was a popular subject of postcards, noting that they were "The world's largest aircraft, 40 passengers [and] wider than a Pullman car."

Pan American now had the infrastructure to allow her to take passengers to Hawaii, the first leg on the Far East route. But the S-42, with its range severely limited when its additional fuel tanks were replaced with passengers, wouldn't be the plane to do it.

Pan American's Martin M-130 was the first aircraft to fly commercial passengers from the United States to Hawaii and the Far East. Its range capability of 3,200 statute miles was greater than the S-42, and its gross takeoff weight of 52,000 pounds was 20 percent more than the Sikorsky. Its cruising speed, at 130mph, was similar to that of the S-42. At $417,000 fully equipped, the M-130 cost nearly twice as much as the S-42 (also considerably more than the $78,000 DC-2, the largest contemporary land-based passenger airliner).[23] Its first trans-Pacific passenger flight to Hawaii left California on Oct. 21, 1936, eventually bound for Manila. Initially, it flew only once per week on the Manila run, with a stopover in Honolulu, and then typically carried only eight or nine passengers on the Hawaii leg, the rest of the space taken up by mail and cargo. It was capable of seating up to 52 passengers if mail and cargo were absent, but the weight needed for fuel on the California to Hawaii segment severely limited the number of passengers. It was a flight of luxury, with first-class meals served to passengers on fine bone china, using utensils of sterling silver, atop linen tablecloths. Upon landing, passengers were regaled with island entertainment and greeted by star hula dancer Tootsie Notley.[24] Only the wealthiest or those on business accounts could afford the $720 round trip fare ($12,489 in today's dollars) on the 18–20 hour flight from San Francisco to Hawaii. Despite the hefty fare, each passenger's baggage allowance was a mere 55 lbs.[25]

Due to the subsequent emergence of the Boeing 314 flying boat, only three Martin M-130s were made, none of which survived the war years. On July 28, 1938, the *Hawaii Clipper* was lost at sea, east of the Philippines. No trace of her nine crewmembers, six passengers, or the plane itself was ever found. The *Philippine Clipper* crashed into a mountainside near Ukiah, California, on Jan. 21, 1943 in poor weather, carrying military personnel from Honolulu. Among the 10 crewmembers and 10 passengers who perished was Rear Admiral Robert Henry English (1888–1943), commander of the U.S. Pacific Submarine fleet. The last of the M-130s, the *China Clipper*, met her fate in January 1945, striking an obstacle in the waters of Port-of-Spain, Trinidad, rupturing her hull, and resulting in the deaths of 20 of the 30 people on board.[26]

Pan American's Juan Trippe realized the limitations of his M-130s, in terms of both speed and capacity. In 1935, he made specifications available for potential manufacturers of a new flying boat. Glenn Luther Martin (1886–1955) couldn't meet the specs with his new M-156 design, and Donald Douglas was focused on building land-based craft. Boeing was chosen as the designer of the new flying boat, designated the model 314. The first of an initial order of six was delivered on June 7, 1938. At the time, it was the most luxurious passenger aircraft ever built, as well as the largest and most technically advanced. It was rated to carry 74 seated passengers, or 30 to 40 in sleeper configuration, had a crew of 10, and had almost twice the power of the M-130. It had seven split-level compartments, allowing for the slope of the hull,

Pan American Airways' Boeing 314 "Yankee Clipper" (Library of Congress).

and 65 windows. Its gross takeoff weight was 82,500 pounds (30,000 more than the Martin). Its range was 3,500 miles, (300 more than the M-130) with a cruising speed of 183 mph (more than 50 mph faster than the Martin). Passengers enjoyed formal table settings for meals, which were prepared in the sizeable forward galley, and included French wines, champagne, and a host of other drinks. Her lavatories had twin-lighted make-up mirrors and she was the first passenger airliner with toilets that could be emptied over the ocean. The 314 had lounge armchairs covered in wool tapestry, a bar, and a private suite in the rear of the craft. Passengers sleeping in berths would find their shoes shined when they awoke. In terms of safety, the cabin upholstery was fireproofed and she carried eight 10-person life rafts, emergency radios, signal flares, and life jackets for all. The enormous size of the craft allowed for more individual passenger luggage as well. She was the epitome of luxury air travel was considered the first true wide-bodied passenger airliner.[27]

Taking into consideration the fact that her first scheduled Honolulu flight occurred on March 29, 1939, her glory days in the Pacific lasted fewer than three years. The effective life of this, one of the most storied, legendary, illustrated and photographed, and romanticized passenger aircraft ever built, ended on morning of Dec. 7, 1941, with the events occurring over the skies of Pearl Harbor.

The nine Boeing 314s in service at the beginning of the Pacific War were hurriedly pulled out of scheduled flights hours after the Japanese attack, and were requisitioned by the U.S. Army and Navy. As her engine design was considered a top military secret, the military took enormous strides to ensure that no Boeing 314 fell into axis hands. The story of the return of the *Pacific Clipper* underscores the military's concern. En route to New Zealand when Hawaii was attacked, she was ordered to continue to Auckland, New Zealand, maintaining radio silence the entire way, and upon arrival await further military instructions. The orders arrived in two weeks. She was mandated to have all identifiable markings stripped and then immediately fly west to the United States' Eastern Seaboard. Since radio silence was critical, she navigated solely by sun, stars, and compass. On Jan. 6, 1942, having flown over Australia, India, Africa, and the Atlantic, on an improvised route taking six weeks and encompassing more than 31,500 miles, the *Pacific Clipper* finally reached New York City.[28]

With the end of the war, several Boeing 314 Clippers continued to fly Pan American routes, but by now she was considered an outmoded aircraft in view of the fact that airstrips capable of serving heavy land-based aircraft were now all over the Pacific. Without the necessity of providing a hull capable of landing on water, aircraft manufacturers could now prioritize creating streamlined fuselages that would provide better speed and carrying capacity. The last Pan American Boeing 314 flight serving Hawaii was made on April 8, 1946. A month earlier, the 314's final Atlantic crossing had occurred in BOAC livery. Pan Am's Clippers were sold off to charter carriers or parted out. The last Boeing 314 in service, the *Anzac Clipper*, met her end in a Baltimore chop yard in 1951. The era of massive flying boats as flagships of international overseas travel was over. The Boeing 314 was born in 1939 and died in 1951, never seeing its 13th birthday.[29]

The Pan American flying boats experienced a second life as a graphical icon of tropical travel, serving as a reminder of the romance of the Pacific more than 60 years after the Clipper flew its last flight. Today's artists and illustrators continue to use the exotic flying boats of the past in contemporary designs. Artist Mike Rangner, for example, in his tropically exotic print *Pacific Flyways*, places a Martin M-130 clipper in front of cascading mountaintops, flying over water and a thatched roof landing pier, in a scene framed by palm trees, exotic flowers, and a bird of paradise.[30] A number of companies making Hawaiian shirts, Tori Richard and Reyn Spooner among them, conjure up the romance of flying boat travel to Hawaii and the islands with fabrics featuring the larger Boeing 314, Martin M-130, and Sikorsky S-42 flying boats, as well as smaller amphibious craft, including the Consolidated PBY Catalina and the Sikorsky S-41. Along with Matson's white-hulled passenger liners, Pan American's huge flying boats remain today the most recognizable icons of romanticized travel to the Pacific. The fact that only the wealthy could partake of the experience has never dulled their historical luster; in fact, it probably enhances it. They remain a particularly poignant memory. As with Matson's passenger ships, not one example of those grand Martin M-130 and Boeing 314 flying boats survives today.

The end of the war heralded the era of low-cost air travel to Hawaii. Thanks to the war, tarmacs were everywhere and massive transoceanic flying boats were relegated to history. The first post-war commercial routes from the mainland to Hawaii were flown by the four-engine, pressurized Douglas DC-6, which began flying to Hawaii in 1947 on United Airlines routes, with a round trip fare, as announced in 1948, of $270 (about $2,731 in today's money). The DC-6 flight to Hawaii was heavily publicized by United, and significant shots of the exterior, interior, cockpit, and cabin food service were shown in the feature film *Million Dollar Weekend* (1948, dir. Gene Raymond).[31] The advent of the faster and larger Boeing 377 Stratocruiser essentially ended the days of the DC-6 as a carrier to Hawaii, and later, with scheduled airlines converting to jet aircraft, DC-6s were increasingly repurposed as air freighters, a number of which remain in use today.[32]

Swords into Plowshares: The Massive Boeing 377 Stratocruiser

The war in the Pacific changed the concept of travel to Hawaii to such a radical extent that it begs the question of how things might have been if there had been no war. There might not have been tarmac landing strips on every island in the Pacific with a significant population. Flying boats were handling air travel nicely, if expensively, without them. With new technologies continually emerging, seaplanes were bound to carry more passengers faster and more economically. A peaceful Pacific might possibly have resulted in a new age of flying boats. Instead, as practical overseas carriers of large numbers of passengers, they were outmoded by the end of the war.

It can also be argued that flying boats were already being perceived as potential dinosaurs, even in the pre–World War II years. Charles Lindbergh, in a consulting capacity for Pan American, stated in a letter to Pan Am President Juan Trippe dated Oct. 28, 1936, that continuing to invest heavily in flying boat technology could have negative financial ramifications: "I believe it is probable that the landplane will replace the flying boat on all important routes in the future…. Pan American will otherwise be vulnerable to competition by companies … who operate landplanes of considerable higher performance than the Boeing flying boats."[33]

With the end of the war, there were landing strips, airports, terminals and baggage depots, and significant fuel storage facilities throughout the Pacific. Some of the smaller airports might have consisted mainly of Quonset huts, but the era of land-based, propeller-driven, long distance aircraft had begun. It would be yet another decade before the jet engine would again revolutionize travel. The issue now at hand was how to move increasingly larger groups of visitors to Hawaii in propeller planes big enough to handle a greater capacity than the Boeing 314 flying boat or the Douglas DC-6. The answer arrived in the form of the mighty Boeing B-29 Superfortress bomber, modified into its new role as a passenger airliner. It was called the Boeing 377 Stratocruiser. At 110 feet long, 38 feet high at the top of the tail, and with a wingspan of 141 feet, it was the biggest passenger airliner the world had ever seen. It was so massive that scheduled maintenance necessitated the creation of a jack that would lower its three-story high tail enough that it could fit into a hangar for maintenance.[34]

Juan Trippe considered the yet-to be built Stratocruiser to be such a potential competitive advantage that he persuaded Boeing, with his initial order of 20 aircraft, that no U.S. carrier other than the U.S. government would receive any Stratocruisers until Pan Am received its first. Furthermore, no other carrier would receive more than six Stratocruisers until Pan American had received all 20 in its charter order.[35]

The Stratocruiser was based on a variation of the B-29 bomber, a proposed cargo plane called the XC-97. It had a large figure-eight fuselage that would carry a significant payload and Boeing designed it so it could be modified into a post-war passenger aircraft (the lower part of the fuselage is where the cocktail lounge would eventually be located). Boeing boasted of the craft's significant revenue potential to prospective buyers. Its capacity of 80 passengers plus mail and freight was enormous, with a maximum take-off weight of 142,500 pounds. With a distance range of up to 4,600 miles and a top speed of 375mph, it was optimized for the speed and capacity needed by carriers wishing to improve revenues on long distance trans-continental and overseas flights. It would cut the air travel time to Hawaii from 14 to eight hours. And it would shorten the time from the West Coast to the Eastern Seaboard to six hours.[36] In fact, after the Stratocruiser's introduction into the Pan American fleet, with its inaugural flight on April 1, 1949 (San Francisco to Honolulu), it set passenger plane speed records to every one of its destinations.

The Stratocruiser, with its 19 cockpit windows and four Pratt & Whitney R-4360 turbocharged engines, was a marvel and it was beautiful. The revolutionary new interior was designed by a team led by Frank J. Del Giudice (1916?–1977) of Walter Dorwin Teague Associates. Among the passenger cabin innovations introduced on the 377 were overhead panels containing reading lights and oxygen masks, call buttons for flight attendants, and vinyl cladding on finished surfaces that could be easily washed. Del Giudice also placed emphasis on color coordination, eschewing red and green clashing colors that he felt were conducive to motion sickness, and using a dark-to light vertical color scheme. Seats were vertically striped to make them seem wider than they actually were.[37]

United Airlines hired Zay Smith (1902?–1995) & Associates to design the 377's cabins specifically for Hawaiian routes, including the use of richly patterned Avodire blond hardwood (also known as white mahogany) paneling for bulkhead walls, the entrance, and the stairwell.[38]

Depending on the configuration mandated by a given airline (Northwest, Pan American, and United all flew them nonstop to Hawaii), the Stratocruiser could seat more than 80 passengers. There were sleeping berths, a lounge that could seat 14 people comfortably, and a honeymoon suite. Its service ceiling was a record for a passenger plane, 33,000 feet. The Stratocruiser was instantly famous, appearing in everything from travel posters to magazine ads, and rendered as a graphic on at least two Hawaiian aloha shirts, one made for Pan American

World Airways, the other commemorating United Airlines' "Highway to Hawaii" in 1951.[39] United Airlines heavily promoted Stratocruiser travel to Hawaii, resulting in two exceptional travel posters created by Hawaii-based artist Joseph Feher (1908–1987). In one, a stunning hula dancer offers a lei to the viewer, encircling images of Diamond Head, Waikiki, and a seagoing outrigger. A Stratocruiser flies in front of the sun, located between the dancer's orchid bejeweled hair and raised left hand. The other poster depicts a giant hula girl dancing on an island platform, surrounded by exotic fish, volcanic mountains, and iconic cultural motifs. The Stratocruiser soars parallel to her outstretched right arm, mirroring an animated sun caressing her left elbow.[40]

The Stratocruiser of course was advertised to passengers as being perfectly safe. But as is the case with many initial rollouts of innovative transportation technology, it had some serious flaws that still needed to be worked out after commercial deployment. And until they were, booking airline passage on the 377 Stratocruiser bought a number of its early patrons a ticket to disaster.

Before the first year of Stratocruiser service had elapsed, fatalities attributed to her airworthiness had made headlines. The main cabin door of Pan Am's *Clipper Mayflower* flew open on Jan. 11, 1950, while over Long Island, and a cabin steward was ejected from the craft and fell to his death. Two years later, a similar event on Pan Am's *Clipper Southern Cross* caused a female passenger to be sucked out of the aircraft at 12,000 feet over Brazil. On Sept. 12, 1951, United lost Stratocruiser N31230 on a training mission approach to San Francisco's airport, which killed all three crewmembers on board. On April 29, 1952, Pan Am's *Clipper Good Hope* went down in a mountainous area of Brazil, killing all 41 passengers and a crew of nine.[41]

Significantly, of the total of 56 Stratocruisers built, 10 went down in crashes or openwater ditches, taking a toll of 135 individuals. There were two significant technical issues that led to the downed aircraft, related to the engine cowling flaps and her Hamilton Standard propellers. It was determined that open cowl flaps combined with retracting wing flaps caused a loss of control, and was ultimately considered to be resolved through improved flight personnel training. The Stratocruiser's original hollow-core aluminum Hamilton Standard 2J17B3–8W propellers had a tendency form cracks and separate from their rubber cores, causing vibrations that could tear the engine apart and separate from the aircraft, the cause of the fatal flight in Brazil. Ultimately, they were successfully replaced with Hamilton's new Duralumin blades.[42]

On the heels of Pan American, two other carriers scheduled their inaugural Stratocruiser flights to Hawaii, Northwest on Nov. 6, 1949, and United on Jan. 15, 1950. United set its fares at $160 one way, $288 round trip, with an additional $25 surcharge for berths on night flights ($1,554, $2,797, and $243, respectively, in today's currency).[43] It's worth considering how much had changed in the 14 years since the first California to Hawaii passenger flight on the Martin M-130 took place in 1936. The M-130's 1936 ticket fare of $720 for a round trip fare represents an effective buying power of $12,489 today. In contrast, the Stratocruiser had lowered its fare to Hawaii in 1950 to $288 ($2,797 today), a difference in today's monetary terms of almost $10,000.

But what did those figures really mean, subjectively, to the visitors of the day? It helps to compare airfares and domestic statistics from 1940, as census charts are easily available. Although finding the price of a round trip ticket from California to Honolulu that year can be challenging, the one-way fare was $278. Pan Am charged double price for the round trip on the M-130 in 1936, so figure the 1940 round trip cost double, or $556.[44] According to the U.S. census, the median price of a home in 1940 was $2,938. $2,729 was the average household income in 1940. A round trip flight to Hawaii, therefore, would have cost roughly 20 percent of either the price of a new home or of the entire yearly income of the average family.

The statistics of 1950, in comparison, tell a fascinating story of how much airfares to Hawaii had dropped, relative to the average individual's buying power. In 1950, that family was making $3,376 per year. The median price for a house was $7,354. The Stratocruiser's round trip fare of $288 now represented less than 9 percent of a household's yearly income and less than 4 percent of the price of a home.[45]

The End of the Stratocruiser?

On Dec. 18, 1960, a Pan American Stratocruiser made final flight from Hawaii, ending the effective life of the craft on passenger routes flown by major carriers. Pan Am mothballed her remaining Stratocruisers and parked them in San Francisco and Miami, traded a number of them to Boeing as a down payment for new Boeing 707 jets, and put the rest up for sale.[46]

Unlike the fate of the romantically exotic Boeing 314 flying boat, however, the Stratocruiser wasn't condemned to eternal oblivion. Instead, she was eviscerated, vivisected, and implanted. Once the jet age arrived, major carriers no longer had use for a gargantuan, pistoned, four-prop passenger plane. Some 377s were traded to Boeing as partial payment for a fleet of Boeing 707 jets or to Lockheed for L188 Electra Turboprops. Some were acquired by non-scheduled carriers. Others, including a couple of South American companies and the Israeli Air Force, valued her lifting power and substantial interior area, and acquired the powerful Stratocruisers for bargain basement prices, then adapted interior spaces and cargo doors to fit their needs. The Israelis went as far as to modify the tail section to swing open to allow more efficient loading from a newly designed rear cargo bay.[47]

Her most significantly unorthodox second life, however, involved her adaptation into the Super Guppy, an unwieldy looking but remarkably serviceable air freighter, capable of carrying rocket stages, airplane fuselages, helicopters and other large and heavy cargo over great distances. That particular vision belonged to John M. "Jack" Conroy (1920–1979) co-founder of AeroSpacelines, Inc. The Apollo space program was in full force by 1960, and the massive Saturn IV rocket stages, 40 feet long and 18 feet high, too big to travel by truck or rail, had to be freighted by sea from Huntington Beach to Cape Canaveral via the Panama Canal. Conroy and AeroSpacelines co-founder Lee Mansdorf (d. 2003) determined that modified Supercruisers could do the job faster and hired On Mark Engineering of Burbank to amalgamate two of the aircraft into one huge superplane.[48] An extra section was added behind the trailing edge of the wings, the craft was modified to swing open aft of the wing, and additional 19-foot-tall "bubble" was created over the length of the craft, resulting in an air behemoth. Designated the B-377PG, it was aptly nicknamed the "Pregnant Guppy," and flew its maiden flight on Sept. 19, 1962, piloted by Conroy and Clay Lacy (b. 1932). Recognizing the need for a craft that could handle even bigger payloads, Conroy began surreptitiously to buy up any remaining Stratocruisers he could find in order to build more super-sized air freighters. The resulting aircraft, a further modification of the 377PG, became known as the Super Guppy, designated the B-377SG. It required parts from three different Stratocruisers to build her. Compared to the earlier Guppy, it was further lengthened, the tail and wing surfaces increased, more powerful engines added, and cargo was now introduced through the opening created by the swing-out front nose section. With a 94-foot-long cargo bay and a total height of a little over 46 feet, it was the biggest aircraft in the world when it flew its maiden voyage on Aug. 31, 1965.[49]

Today, there are no "stock" B-377 Stratocruisers to be seen in museums or airfields anywhere. The Pregnant Guppy, though, can be seen at the Tillamook Air Museum in Oregon, and the enormous Super Guppy sits in the collection at the Pima Air and Space Museum in Tucson.

The Jet Age Comes to Hawaii

By the end of World War II, it was apparent to just about everyone in the industry that jet passenger travel was on the near horizon. Travel time to Hawaii was more than 12 hours and it was anticipated that faster aircraft would lower it significantly. And the British, with the dramatically streamlined de Havilland Comet, stood first in line to get the business. The story of the star-crossed Comet is fascinating and tragic, emblematic of the perils involved in developing a technology that would challenge and eventually overcome the physical of high speed air travel. It was the first step in the aircraft revolution that would allow its successors, the Douglas DC-8 and Boeing 707 to succeed in safely bringing significant numbers of visitors to Hawaii quickly and safely.

The genesis for what was to be the world's first passenger jet was an outcome of a study made by the Brabazon Committee, chaired by early British air pioneer Lord John Theodore Cuthbert Moore-Brabazon, First Baron Brabazon of Tara (1884–1964). Its charter was to determine potential aircraft types that would make an impact on the marketplace and prove competitive to the near monopoly held by American aircraft designers. The decision was made in favor of the development of a passenger jet that would fly higher and faster than any other passenger craft, and prove to be comfortable for passengers, with particular attention to temperature and humidity. Sir Geoffrey de Havilland (1882–1965), a committee member, strongly advocated the manufacture of a commercial jet, which would involve designing an airframe capable of high speeds as well as building its engine. De Havilland's company was given the contract to build it. A number of engines and airframe prototypes were evaluated, and the new aircraft would be introduced with a swept-wing design and one iconic streamlined, dual engine nacelle located under each wing.

The maiden flight of prototype D.H. 106, upon which the Comet would be based, took place on July 27, 1949.[50] Based on the success of the prototype, BOAC ordered eight airliners. Before the first delivery took place on April 2, 1951, and additional eight planes were ordered by Canadian Pacific and two French carriers, UAT and Air France.[51]

The Comet's first commercial flight occurred on May 2, 1952, from Heathrow to Johannesburg with five stops, carrying 36 passengers on the 6,724-mile trip.[52] She flew at 460 miles per hour, more than 100 miles faster than any propeller-driven passenger airliner, at a cruising height of 35,000 feet. Based on the early commercial success of the Comet, Pan American announced on Oct. 20, 1952, that it had ordered three of the new Comet 3s for delivery in 1956, with options for seven more to be delivered the following year. It was the first time a

U.S.–based passenger carrier had ordered a British aircraft. After one year of service, Comets were flying 370 hours a week for more than 122,000 miles. Far East, Southeast Asia, and Pacific routes included Rangoon, Bangkok, Singapore, Manila, and Tokyo.[53] Eddie Rickenbacker of Eastern Airlines was so entranced with the aircraft that he planned to order 35 to 50 Comets, provided they were delivered within two years of the date of the signed contract.[54]

Three spectacular mid-air explosions doomed further use of the Comet on commercial air routes flown by U.S. carriers. On May 2, 1953, one year after its successful maiden flight, BOAC flight 783 exploded six miles after takeoff from Calcutta at approximately 7,500 feet. All 37 passengers and six crewmembers were killed. Indian authorities determined that the crash was caused by structural failure of the airframe during a thunderstorm. On Jan. 10, 1954, BOAC flight 781, flying from Rome to London broke up at 27,000 feet near the island of Elba, killing 29 passengers and six crew members. Two weeks later, on April 8, 1954, South African Airlines flight 201, chartered through BOAC and flying from Rome to Cairo, exploded at approximately 35,000 feet, killing all aboard. BOAC immediately grounded all flights and the Comet's Certificate of Airworthiness was revoked.

Stress tests soon determined a structural failure point at the corner of the craft's square windows, leading to the decision to standardize on rounded windows on all jet aircraft from that point forward. It was also determined that repeated cycles of pressurization had fatally fatigued the rivets holding the skin together, leading to more thorough pressurization testing for all future jet aircraft.[55] In October 1952, in light of the technological failings of the Comet, the ATA (Air Transport Association), to which all U.S. scheduled carriers belonged, issued design recommendations for future passenger jet development. Pointedly, it recommended that, unlike the Comet, jet engines be separated from each other in individual pods, so that a fire in one engine would not put both out of commission. It further recommended that the design prevent engine fire from jeopardizing the aircraft's primary structure or controls; fuel would now be carried outside the fuselage, either in wings, in pods, or both; tire wells were to be reinforced to contain fire damage should a tire explosion occur; and aircraft would necessarily be able to travel at low speeds with the loss of one engine on a two or three-engine jet, or two engines on a four or five-engine jet.[56] These recommendations were heeded by the designers of the Douglas DC-8 and Boeing 707, the two successful jet passenger craft that followed the Comet. The most visual changes were the physically separate engines being attached to wing pylons, rather than integrated with the wing itself, as had been the case with the Comet.

The Comet experienced a number of design changes and iterations, and would not fly again commercially until April 1, 1959, when the Comet 4 was introduced by BOAC on European and Asian routes. The new Comet 4 series, which ultimately carried 101 passengers, was deemed a success, but none were ever purchased by a U.S. carrier. A total of 76 Comet 4s were produced from 1958 through 1964, when the last of the series rolled off the assembly line. The last de Havilland Comet 4 passenger flight occurred on Nov. 9, 1980. Today, ten Comets may be seen in museums, only one of which has the original square windows of the Comet 1. Registered F-BGNX, it consists of the original fuselage and replicated cockpit, and can be seen at the de Havilland Aircraft Museum in Hertfordshire, England.[57]

In the United States, the race was on between Boeing and Douglas to create a viable jet passenger aircraft. Two significant reasons for the United States jumping into the jet area as it did were the surplus of aeronautical engineers after the war and the willingness of manufacturers to take large financial risks in an attempt to stave off the competition. Airline companies were in the forefront of the surge, especially after Pan American placed orders for 20 Boeing 707 and 25 DC-8 jets on Oct. 13, 1955. The threat of Pan American dominance in the commercial airline business was seen as an immediate and critical threat, to both domestic and international carriers. From an economic perspective, the productivity of jet aircraft, measured in seat-miles or ton-miles (for cargo) was four to five times greater than that for Douglas or Lockheed propeller planes.[58]

The Boeing 367–80 demonstrator, a design based on the B-47 turbojet bomber, made its maiden flight on July 15, 1954. Able to match the speed of that bomber as well as the B-52, it was marketed to the U.S. Air Force as an in-air refueling tanker. In March 1955, the Air Force ordered a number of craft, and Boeing created a commercial version, the Boeing 707.[59] The first Boeing 707 to enter passenger service flew its inaugural commercial flight, in Pan American livery, on Oct. 26, 1958. Boeing sold 763 Model 707s to commercial airlines, government and military customers. Its last delivery of a new aircraft occurred on Jan. 30, 1978.[60]

Douglas DC-8s were introduced to commercial service on Sept. 18, 1959, initially by Delta Air Lines and soon after by United Air Lines.[61] On Aug. 24, 1959, Pan American initiated the first mainland-based jet service to Hawaii. United Airlines followed suit in March 1960, introducing service from the mainland on Douglas DC-8 aircraft.[62] The DC-8 was the first commercial passenger plane to have electro-mechanical flush toilets, replacing the old chemical types. Since the Civil Aeronautics Administration mandated that cockpit windows withstand a bird strike at 391 mph, a series of four-pound chicken carcasses were fired at the DC-8's front windows from a "chicken gun" at 460 mph to ensure window integrity. The DC-8 was the fastest passenger aircraft of its era. On Aug. 21, 1961, the craft flew an experimental test run in Canadian Pacific colors, reaching a record passenger craft altitude of 52,090 feet, and breaking the sound barrier, flying up to 662.5 mph, the first passenger jet to do so. On Nov. 6 of that year, Alitalia broke that speed record, at 691 mph, on a delivery flight from Long Beach to Rome.[63]

Perhaps the most wildly improbable story surrounding the DC-8 occurred on June 19, 1976, when it was "ridden bareback" in flight by a daredevil. Known as "The Human Fly," the masked, anonymous stuntman strapped himself in standing position atop his own DC-8, flown by Captain Clay Lacy, and made several low altitude passes at 250 mph over the crowd at the California National Air Races in Mojave, California. He was later revealed to be Canadian Rick Rojatt.[64] Perhaps the most famous of all DC-8s also represented one of the largest paintings ever made. Braniff Airlines, in an effort to publicize its South American routes, hired artist Alexander Calder to design the paint scheme for its "Flying Colors" DC-8. It debuted on Nov. 3, 1973, reportedly just a few hours after Calder himself painted the finishing touches on the nacelles.[65] Boeing sold 556 DC-8s prior to its final commercial jet delivery on May 17, 1972.[66]

The Impact of Low-Cost Air Travel on Hawaiian Travel

The 707 and DC-8, precursors to the jumbo jet era, revolutionized travel to Hawaii, from both a time and cost per ticket perspective. The number of total visitors to Hawaii as a final destination had arisen dramatically in fewer than ten years during the pre-jet era due to a large extent on the introduction of the Boeing Stratocruiser, jumping from approximately 25,000 in 1941 to more than 57,000 in 1950. Westbound air and sea Hawaiian visitors, a statistic first kept in 1951, totaled 43,426 that year, doubling to 89,772 in 1955 (one-way mainland to Hawaii fares had been dropped to $125–$1,141 in today's money—a year earlier, in 1954).[67] Hawaiian visitors doubled again in 1960, to 213,670, a rise attributable to the advent of the Boeing 707 and Douglas DC-8 jet aircraft, and reached the million mark in 1969, with 1,008,802. By 1976, the number had increased exponentially, to 2,245,252.[68]

The percentages of those arriving by air versus sea in those years make a compelling argument for the impact of low-cost air travel on the increasing numbers of visitors coming to Hawaii from the mainland. In 1951, air arrivals represented 56.4 percent of Hawaii's visitors, and it rose to 76.7 percent in 1955. By 1976 the figure had jumped to 99.9 percent.[69]

Hawaii's cultural impact on the mainland had actually begun in the 19th century, when the first hula dancers arrived in the United States. The craze for Hawaiian music followed, but most Americans had to admire Hawaii from afar due to the high cost of getting there. World War II brought GIs and war workers, but it was for duty, rather than pleasure. The evolution of passenger aircraft and low-cost fares allowed middle-class mainlanders to see it for themselves on vacation and bring aloha back home with them. The pull of the islands represented a desire that could be instantly gratified by the airlines, whose constant marketing efforts ensured that "America Goes Hawaiian" was attainable, hulaed into the minds of millions of mainlanders through radio, television, and print advertising. While the days of an incoming aircraft being met by a troupe of hula dancers probably ended during the early days of the 377 Stratocruiser, millions of annual visitors coming from the mainland by air could now see and hear the hula in person, right on the beach. For many of them, experiencing the hula in Hawaii represented their most quintessential island experience.

THREE

The Hula
Taking America by Dance

Dozens of hula dancers, from ages three to 73, gracefully tell Hawaiian stories old and new, arms and hands in constant, choreographed movement, bare feet moving in rhythm to songs played by a Hawaiian string trio. The musicians have their own amplifiers and from somewhere in the distance the music is being echoed back to us, ever so slightly. Each dance and song lasts three minutes or so. There is constant shifting and rustling in the background as the next group of dancers, male, female, younger or older, waits its turn at the side of the stage. There's evidence of a luau nearby, the aroma of roasting pork gently perfuming the dancers and audience. Looking down, I can't help but wonder how those bare feet will hold up. The stage, after all, is asphalt.

The 80 or so dancers of Halau Na Wai Ola, also known as Island Moves, are performing neither on a wooden platform nor an earthen floor, and there's not a thatched roof to be seen. There's no waterfall nearby, not a palm tree in sight, and the tiki torches are missing. Those have been replaced by beckoning beer taps, forty-foot tall light towers, painted murals of old baseball players on concrete walls, and the beginnings of what promises to be an amazing sunset. The hula dancers are here, as they have been, one night each year for the past ten years, at 73-year-old San Jose (California) Municipal Stadium, performing for fans, friends, and family. Tonight's the minor league baseball San Jose Giants' Hawaiian Night. The dance stage is the tiny parking lot at the entrance to the ballpark, more often the temporary home of bobtail beer and food trucks unloading hot dogs, hamburgers, and lager. Tonight, Hawaiian-clad Giants' employees ensure that each fan is given a lei upon entering the ballpark along with a smile and an "aloha." The dancers and musicians are already performing as the gates open, welcoming the brand new citizens of the two-minute old territory of San Jose, Hawaii. In 90 minutes, the event will be official, proclaimed by both the national and the Hawaiian state anthems sung a cappella. The theme carries into the game itself, where Giants players sport specially designed Hawaiian-themed uniforms—different for each year Hawaiian Night has taken place—for nine innings of baseball. Tonight, everyone in this neck of the woods either is Hawaiian or has gone Hawaiian.

Kaui Isa-Kahaku is the director of Halau Na Wai Ola, and doesn't seem too concerned about performing on the asphalt in front of the ticket office at an old-fashioned baseball stadium. In fact, judging by the smile on her face, there aren't too many places she'd rather be right now. She founded her halau, or hula school, in 1995, and introducing Hawaiian traditional dance to newcomers is part of her mission, the first two elements of which read, "To Make A Positive Impact on ... people's lives through the Hawaiian art of the Hula, and the spirit of Aloha; To Share Knowledge unconditionally in order to continue to perpetuate the Hawaiian culture." Tonight, she and her dancers are doing both.

The breadth of hula's impact on the continental United States culture is tough to measure, but one fact is indisputable: today on the mainland there are an astounding 627 hula schools, providing regularly scheduled weekly hula classes (about one for every 50,00 people in the continental United States). There are 24 in Canada (roughly one for every 1.45 million people).[1] No corner is too remote: five hula schools are in Alaska (the 2010 U.S. census reports that there are 3,006 individuals in Alaska with some degree of Hawaiian ancestry).[2] Kaui's school averages between 180 and 250 dancers each year, and hers is one of 10 halau in San Jose alone. Judging by the number of schools in the continental U.S., it's indisputable that a significant number of people are hula-ing today on the mainland. And 4,000 people at San Jose Municipal Stadium tonight are joining them.

An event like tonight's could not have occurred 150 years ago, even in Hawaii. It would have been banned. The concept of tourism, as we regard it today, didn't exist in the Hawaii of that era, either. The story of what's going on in this ballpark tonight is yet another chapter in the resurgence of the art form of hula, which began as the pride of the Sandwich Islands, fell to official shame, and then returned, larger, and stronger than ever, to become perhaps the most definitive embodiment of Hawaii's people and culture. The physical representation of Hawaii's aloha spirit is to be discovered in her dance.

The Trouble with Hula

Ever since the Hawaiian tourism industry began heavily promoting the island paradise in the late 19th century, the enchantments to be found in the islands have been described in a fascinating array of descriptive terms. Advertisements were placed in numerous magazines and travel brochures, inviting visitors to the islands in a flowery, romantic, and fantasy-inspiring style, coupled with romantically inspired illustrations, densely packed with vibrant colors. The Hawaii Bureau of Information, founded by local Publisher Lorrin Andrews Thurston (1858–1931) in 1892, and a successor, the Hawaiian Promotion Committee (HPC) founded in 1903, were planting images in mainland minds of palm trees bending gracefully under balmy moonlit nights, outriggers and surfers braving crashing azure waves under the watchful eye of Diamond Head, and grass-skirted hula girls enthusiastically welcoming each visitor with a lei while their sisters strummed the ukulele.[3] In words that art historian Russell Lynes would later apply to advertisers several decades into the future, early 20th century Hawaiian publicity flacks were selling Hawaii using "the emotional pipe organ ... with stops for envy, greed, fear, and lust."[4] The resulting spiel, imaginatively paraphrased to suggest how advertising targets were supposed to decode it, might have been interpreted by potential visitors as: "Your friends visited Hawaii and you didn't? You should go too, and come back with stories that your friends can't top! You wouldn't want to be seen as a fuddy-duddy, would you? The hula is a naughtier dance that anything you'll see back home, and in the balmy Hawaiian weather, it doesn't make sense for hula girls to wear many clothes, does it?" Hawaiian themes crafted by graphic artists in the early 20th century were replete with the standard tropical images and fired the imaginations of mainlanders. The hula was undeniably a draw. But Americans visiting Hawaii weren't privileged to see the hula during most of the 19th century. Ironically, neither were native Hawaiians.

The hula was historically performed by both men and women, naked from the waist up and tattooed with traditional designs. It was also danced by mahu, "transgendered or effeminate men who embodied both genders," notes Adria Imada in her book *Aloha America: Hula Circuits Through the U.S. Empire*. Clothing was made up of kapa cloth derived from pounded tree fibers; grass skirts didn't exist. In a culture lacking a formal written language, hula conveyed both historical lore and contemporary tales via hand and body movements, accompanied in performance by chanting, percussion instruments, or both. Imada writes, "Its practitioners were guardians of Native historiography, cosmogony, and genealogies, undergoing ritual training to reproduce and transmit knowledge for high-ranking chiefs. Some religious forms of hula honored akua (gods), having survived the repression of Christian missionaries who arrived in 1820. Bridging the sacred and secular, hula also provided entertainment for both chiefs and commoners."[5]

Hula was a danceable oral tradition and the performers were essentially living archivists of Hawaiian culture. Themes included stories of creation, nature, history, native religion and beliefs, celebrations and events, and royal accession and activities. Fully integrated into traditional society, it was performed by both amateurs and professional court dancers. Western visitors from the early contact years were often enchanted by the hula, as evidenced by the exquisitely beautiful illustrations documenting the art form, made by visiting Westerners including Jacques Arago and Louis Choris, in the early 19th century.[6]

Artist Nicolas Eustache Maurin, working from a sketch by Jacques Arago, in 1822 depicted a sitting dancer from Maui with particular attention to indigenous tattoos.

The hula, which captured the imaginations of hosts of mainlanders, was first presented to American audiences in the 1850s, when promoter Charles Derby's "Hula! Hula!" show presented "wahines" and "kanaka dancing girls," direct from the Sandwich Islands, to California audiences. Women were prohibited from attending, lending a salacious tone to the advertising posters. The price was 50 cents, a little more

Female dancers performing before a mixed Native and European audience, as depicted by Louis Choris and published in 1822.

than $15 in today's money.[7] It would be fascinating to know more about the performers. A number of Hawaiians came to California to participate in the Gold Rush. Did members of an existing Hawaiian troupe come to California to make their fortunes in gold, and then discover a promoter who could help them make some side money? Or instead, did Derby bring them over from Hawaii specifically to perform? Or was it perhaps more haphazard, the group a newly assembled one, formed in California by Hawaiian workers whose fellow performers they may have met for the first time on the mainland? In any of those scenarios, did the performers remain on the mainland or return home?

The hula, in particular the swaying hips and limited clothing worn by female dancers, had been problematic for Hawaii's missionaries since the time of their arrival, who saw in the hula a shocking reflection of the biblical times of Sodom and Gomorrah. To a very great extent, the missionaries were responsible for the banning of its public performance over several decades of the mid–19th century. The missionary movement in Hawaii is said to have formally begun with the arrival, in 1820, of a boatload of Protestant Christians from Boston's Sandwich Islands Mission. The passengers included two ministers, Hiram Bingham I (1789–1869) and Asa Thurston (1787–1876). After meeting with King Liholiho (1797–1824, known as Kamehameha II) and his chiefs, permission was granted for Bingham and Thurston to establish missions on Oahu, at Kailua and Honolulu. These early Christian setters were determined to print biblical excerpts and tracts in the native language, which had never been codified in Roman script. They immediately began learning the language and creating a Western alphabet for it, containing eight consonants and five vowels. In 1822, they published the first books written in the Hawaiian language. The Christian movement grew rapidly with the support, conversion, and ultimate baptism of Queen Kaahumanu (1678–1832), consort of Kamehameha I (1758?–1819), and co-reigning regent of Kamehameha II and Kamehameha III (Kauikeaouli, 1813–1854). By 1853, the census noted 56,840 Protestants out of a total islands population of 73,138.[8]

Missionaries were vehement in their opposition to the hula, and the social and political influence of Christian morality on the Hawaiian royal family finally succeeded in driving the hula underground when regent Kaahumanu banned public performances of the dance in 1830. For the ensuing two decades, it was kept alive through clandestine hula schools, in performances at private parties, and for selected royal gatherings. Mahu, third gender persons who filled a traditional spiritual and social role within Hawaiian culture, also helped keep the hula tradition from vanishing, through dancing as well as preserving chants, many of which, in the Pele cycle, described aikane (pre-contact gay or bisexual) relationships with alii (the heredity line of Hawaiian rulers).[9]

For the occasional hula performed for royals, the strict dress code of the missionaries prevailed. In 1851, public performance of the hula was allowed on a limited basis, and then only in Honolulu and Lahaina. Each performance was licensed for a fee of $10 ($310 in today's money), a ridiculously steep charge. Failure to obtain a license was punishable by a fine of $500 ($15,507 in the currency of today) or a six-month imprisonment at hard labor.[10]

In a plea written by a dozen missionaries, and submitted to Kamehameha IV (Alexander Liholiho, 1834–1863,) in 1858, the hula was denounced as "a very great and public evil, tending, as we believe, to demoralize the people very rapidly and very generally … [diverting] them from all industrial and intellectual pursuits … [fostering] idleness, dissipation, and licentiousness." Writing in the newspaper *Pacific Commercial Advertiser* in 1857, Publisher Henry Martyn Whitney (1824–1904), son of Hawaiian missionary Samuel Whitney (1793–1845), noted that "a hundred young females are now under daily training … unless some measure is taken to check the evil … soon, its consequences will be felt in every household, and on every farm and plantation, for so infatuated do males and females become under it, that it will be in vain to urge them in industry or to any efforts to raise themselves above brutes."[11]

Mark Twain, who visited Hawaii in 1866 as a correspondent for the *Sacramento Union*, although noting the sexuality of the dance, saw the hula in a different light than the missionaries, recognizing the art inherent in its performance: "the girls danced the lascivious hula hula—a dance that is said to exhibit the very perfection of educated motion of limb and arm, hand, head and body, and the exactest uniformity of movement and accuracy of 'time.' It was performed by a circle of girls with no raiment on them to speak of, who went through an infinite variety of motions and figures without prompting, and yet so true was their 'time,' and in such perfect concert did they move that when they were placed in a straight line, hands, arms, bodies, limbs and heads waved, swayed, gesticulated, bowed, stooped, whirled, squirmed, twisted and undulated as if they were part and parcel of a single individual; and it was difficult to believe they were not moved in a body by some exquisite piece of mechanism."[12]

When King Kamehameha V (Lot Kapuaiwa, 1830–1872) died without naming an heir, an election brought Prince William Charles Lunalilo (1835–1874) to the throne. He soon passed away in February 1874, also heirless. David Kalakaua (1836–1891) was then elected king, besting Queen Emma (1836–1885), widow of Kamehameha IV. The queen's supporters rioted at hearing the election results, and Kalakaua therefore decided to begin his reign without the pomp ordinarily accompanying ascension of such importance. It was a diplomatic pause on his part, as his reign was the more radically progressive, from a cultural standpoint, than those of the several monarchs who preceded him.

Kalakaua was a curious, well-read, and worldly leader. In 1881, he became the first head of state in the world to circumnavigate the globe. His goals of the trip were to secure immigration agreements, familiarize himself with the practices of other leaders, and perhaps above all, to legitimize his monarchy in the eyes of the world. The agreements with other countries would broaden Hawaii's global reach. By engaging in such agreements, Kalakaua hoped to bring other countries into Hawaii's sphere of influence, and thus counter efforts to annex the islands to the United States. In addition to preserving tradition, he was an advocate for modernizing the country: his Iolani Place had electric lighting prior to its installation at the White House or Buckingham Palace.[13]

His coronation of 1883 was meant to be his personal statement to the world's nations, the United States, haole interests in Hawaii, and his own people, as to the legitimacy of his throne and the sovereignty of his nation.[14] For his own people, the message included a call for a cultural renaissance, of which hula would play a significant part. He determined that the decades-long territorial kapu (taboo) on the performance of hula would be brought to an end, and it was an integral part of his 1883 coronation as well as his jubilee celebration of 1886. Known as the "Merrie Monarch," Kalakaua favored traditional Hawaiian entertainment, which included mele oli (plain chanting), mele hula (chanting accompanied by hula), drumming, and magnificent luaus. "Merrie" was an apt sobriquet. He was the antithesis of a teetotaler. His ability to consume liquor at an extraordinary rate during the day while appearing sober as a schoolmarm in official receptions at night was noted by Robert Louis Stevenson, an occasional visitor to Kalakaua's dining table. Free flowing liquor at his Iolani Palace was a good part of the reason his reign was known as the "Champagne Dynasty."[15]

At Kalākaua's coronation in 1883, the hula was performed during a high state affair for the first time in more than 50 years. Prior to the festivities, he'd brought noted kumu hula (hula teachers) to Honolulu, established them as court retainers, and allowed them to live on the grounds of the palace while preparing performances for the coronation, held on Feb. 12 of that year, as well as other festivities which took place over the following two weeks. At his 50th jubilee celebration in 1886, more than 260 chants and dances were performed, featuring seven different teachers (or chanters) and approximately 50 dancers. For the occasion, a new genre was produced called hula kui, combining aspects of Hawaiian and Western music and dance.[16] Yet another dance performed for the occasion, the hula mai, celebrating the genitals of the chief, was considered deviant

King David Kalakaua (1836–1891), circa 1882 (Hawaii State Archives).

Kini Kapahu and fellow hula dancer at the Midway Plaisance at the World's Columbian Exhibition, Chicago, 1893 (Hawaii State Archives).

behavior by a number of influential individuals of Western origin, sparking particular outrage among various haole business leaders.[17]

One of Kalakaua's favorite dancers was the 16-year-old Kini Kapahu (1872–1962, born Ana Kini Kapahukulaokamamalu Kuululani McColgan Huhu), who joined his troupe as a court dancer in 1888, and whose importance and influence would last until her death in 1962.

She was hanaied to a hula teacher (hula kumu) by her mother at the age of four in a practice known as hula kapu, a sacred ritual in which a child at the age of approximately four years is informally adopted (hanai) by a hula teacher until the age of eight. The kumu also serves as a mentor and guardian. For most of her waking hours, the young girl is engaged in learning chants, dance, and traditional comportment. During this time, the child cannot play with other children and receives no other outside formal education. The young dancer's life is dedicated to a Hawaiian deity, often Laka or Pele. Laka is the deity of dance, vines, and wildwood plants. She has been compared to Terpsichore, Greek goddess of music, song, and dance. Pele is the Hawaiian goddess of volcanoes, fire, wind, and lightning, believed to be the force behind all volcanic eruptions on the Big Island. She is thought to take on the human form of a beautiful young woman or an old crone, asking for rides or cigarettes on the highway. To refuse her, or to take lava rocks as souvenirs, it is said, is to invite misfortune.[18]

At the age of 14, Kini Kapahu was invited by David Kalakaua to join his court dancers. Her mother initially refused until convinced by Queen Kapiolani (1834–1899). In addition to dancing the hula, she played the ukulele, sang with his Hui Lei Mamo (also known as the Kawaihau Glee Club), and learned ballroom dancing in order to act as a hostess at the king's parties. This group consisted of eight young women, under the age of 20, who sang choral music and danced the hula and non-traditional dances at least once a week at Kalakaua's Healani boathouse. They entertained the king and his guests, among whom occasionally included Robert Louis Stevenson. Three of the group's members, including Kini, would form the core of a Hawaiian troupe that would tour North America and Europe from 1892 to 1896.[19] Over the ensuing 15 years, she, along with the dancers and musicians that accompanied her, would introduce traditional Hawaiian dancing to thousands worldwide.

Kalakaua's reign ended with his passing in 1891. Several years earlier, a rebellious faction of businessmen and politicians had forced him to sign the "Bayonet Constitution," which severely limited his powers and signaled the beginning of the end for Hawaiian autonomy. But with his jubilee celebration, as well as other deeds and edicts, David Kalakaua had initiated a renaissance of Hawaiian tradition, history and culture, rebelling against much of the Euro-American philosophies adopted by Hawaiian rulers in the previous decades. Kalakaua's emphasis on the importance of documenting traditional history was underscored by his establishment of two societies, Ka Papa Kuauhau Alii O Na Alii Hawaii—Board of Genealogy—Hawaiian Chiefs, and Hale Naua. The former codified Hawaiian royal lineage through the Kumulipo, a genealogical document that linked alii (the heredity line of Hawaiian rulers) to the gods and the beginning of the world. The latter was a royal secret society, open only to men of native ancestry, chartered with the purpose of "the revival of Ancient Sciences of Hawaii in combination with the promotion and advancement of Modern Sciences, Art, Literature, and Philanthropy."[20] His emphasis on restoring hula to open practice was critical to its history and survival. It has never again been relegated to being solely an underground art form since his reign. His legacy remains strong. In 1964, the Merrie Monarch Festival was begun in the city of Hilo on the Big Island. Held annually, it features as its keynote event the pre-eminent Hawaiian dance competition in the islands. Portraits of the king and his Queen, Kapiolani flank the stage, and men and women are chosen to represent members of his court.[21]

With her monarch's passing in 1891, however, Kini Kapahu's years as an international ambassador of Hawaiian dance were only just beginning. She began learning the sacred, traditional dance forms of hula pahu and hula alaapapa. A visitor from San Francisco, jeweler Harry W. Foster, heard the sounds of hula coming from Kini's home, and returned a day later with the idea of bringing her and her troupe to the mainland. Three of her fellow dancers decided to join her, along with drummers, chanters, and brothers Kanuku and Kamuku. After performing in San Francisco, they toured the western states and British Columbia. The troupe wasn't highly paid, and the adventure of travel probably factored into their decision to go. Foster paid the performers five dollars a week (roughly $132 in today's money) plus all their expenses for six months. While it was more than the three dollars a week they'd make back home working plantation fields, it was less than the $25 a week ($660 today) minimum generally paid to dime museum entertainers.[22]

With the seeds of hula interest sewn in the west, the troupe opened at the World's Columbian Exposition in Chicago, which operated from May 1 to Oct. 30, 1893, performing there for six months. Following that, they toured the southern vaudeville circuit.[23] Although the troupe missed the Eastern and Midwestern states (they would finally tour the Northeast a year or so later), a strong argument can be made that the genesis of hula teachers and schools on the mainland began with Kini's performances and the publicity they received.

Kini "Jennie" Kapahu Wilson (1872–1962), circa 1890s, hula dancer, musician, and singer, recognized as Hawaii's "Honorary First Lady."

The Chicago fair was huge, built over 600 acres and containing 200 buildings. The landscaping was laid out by Frederick Law Olmsted and architect Daniel Burnham supervised the construction of the Beaux-Arts buildings, most of which were temporary. It was a boon for commercial enterprises as well as the entertainment industry: Wrigley's gum and George Ferris' huge, rotating observation wheel were introduced to the world there. The mile-long Midway Plaisance at the Chicago fair was replete with cultural "villages" from around the world featuring native performers. Forty-six nations participated in it. The Chicago fair was the national entertainment event of the year, with attendance estimates as high as 27 million out of a national population of 62 million. On one day alone, Oct. 9, designated as "Chicago Day," 751,026 individuals attended. Among the thrills was the "hootchy-kootchy" dance, famously performed by Fahreda Mazar Spyropoulos (1871?–1937), better known as Little Egypt.[24]

The success of Little Egypt couldn't have been far from Kini's mind. Recognizing that their exoticism engendered an interest in the sexual content of their dances, Kini and the troupe used it as a marketing ploy, promising "naughtiness" to those paying to see the show. Kini served as her own barker, playing the ukulele and ballyhooing the following verses, written for her by a haole man:

> On the Midway, Midway, Midway Plaisance
> Where the naughty girls from Honolulu do the naughty hula dance
> The married men with their wives cast about a glance
> At the naughty naughty doings at the Midway Plaisance[25]

The troupe's 10-minute show included vocal, ukulele pieces, and the following dances:

- hula alaapapa: hula performed with a double gourd (ipu heke), often dedicated to deities
- hula kui: a hybrid hula, combining aspects of Hawaiian and Western music and dance
- hula olapa: hula performed with a double gourd (ipu heke), often dedicated to alii, but not considered sacred
- hula puili: hula accompanied by the puili, a bamboo rattle
- hula uliuli: hula accompanied by the uliuli, a gourd rattle[26]

The troupe filled the 300-seat theater five times a day. Given the six-month run of the fair, it's not out of the question to suggest that it was seen by a quarter of a million people. And Kini remembered her barker's spiel well enough that she was able to recite it some 60 years later. She was fully aware, given the nature of the male fair-goers, that the female sexuality intimated by their performance would represent a bigger potential draw than the notion of a sacred ritualistic dance from the Islands. At the age of 20 (she was born in 1872), she was already an astute enough businesswoman to understand the value of using marketing as a way to introduce Americans to Hawaii's culture. She experienced the drawbacks of that philosophy as well, as men would continually goad the dancers to remove their clothes while dancing, and, without a doubt, promising lucrative financial rewards for doing so in the process. Many men, expecting the dancers to be bare-breasted, walked away somewhat disappointed. The dancing costumes for the girls consisted of a cotton blouse, cotton pantaloons, and a dried grass skirt.[27]

From the Fair, Kini took home body adornments that would be attached to her for the rest of her life. She'd made friends with the Egyptian dancers who presented her with a dozen metal bracelets like theirs. These were measured to her wrists and soldered together. She refused to have them removed, even later in life when they no longer fit as well, reveling in their role of reminding her of her early friends and adventures.[28]

In 1894 Kini's troupe toured Europe, appearing in London, at the Folies Bergère in Paris, and dancing before Kaiser Wilhelm II in Germany and Czar Nicholas II in Russia. She returned to Chicago in 1895, toured the Northeast, and went on the vaudeville and "dime museum" circuits. For the latter, the troupers were advertised as novelties from the Sandwich Islands, sharing the billing with curiosities including peoples from other lands, human oddities, magicians, sword-swallowers, and other sideshow performers. Kini returned to Hawaii with the three remaining members of the troupe (the brothers had already left for other lands) in 1896.

She had a keen understanding of the differences between the sacred and profane, dancing traditionally for Hawaiians and "tourist hula" for the rest of the world. She insisted that her performances be held only in theaters, royal palaces and other proper venues and never on the streets. "We don't go down to the wharf and dance to ... every Tom, Dick, and Harry, oh no!" she said. Not all native Hawaiians were enamored of her role as hula ambassador. She was spit at on the streets of Honolulu and called shameful. "You go to mainland and dance the hula," she was told, "You disgrace the Hawaiians. You disgrace yourself." This was not an uncommon feeling in the islands, despite the efforts of Kalakaua and other proponents who followed into the 20th century. This sentiment continued to linger until the 1920s and 1930s, when it was considered financially expedient to utilize the hula as a tourist draw to the islands.[29]

Kini Kapahu was a consummate show woman who refused to succumb to an unwritten code propagated by Hawaiians steeped in Western religion who demanded and tried to enforce a restrictively conservative manner for Island females comporting themselves in public. Her performance and demeanor called for a bold new approach to individuality for island women. The fact that many considered her an extremist is a tribute to her impact. Considering that she was making her own choices, career-wise and internationally, when she was in her early twenties, and more emphatically, before the turn of the century, it's undeniable that she was charting her own future, regardless of criticism. It's not out of the question to consider her to be the first world famous non-alii Hawaiian woman to be liberated and empowered, and, defined by her own terms, successful.

Kini returned to North America in subsequent years, serving as hula stage manager and producer at the Trans-Mississippi Exposition, held in Omaha, Nebraska, from June 1 to Nov. 1, 1898, and the Pan-American Exposition, held in Buffalo from May 1 through Nov. 2, 1901.[30] The musicians and dancers in the Omaha and Buffalo fairs were managed by Kini's childhood friend Johnny Wilson. He was also her lover.

With a grant of $10,000 (nearly $286,000 in today's money), the Honolulu Chamber of Commerce developed a 4,000-square-foot pavilion at the Omaha fair. The aim was to showcase Hawaii's business environment and temperate climate as a means to entice white emigration from the mainland. Hawaii's amiable population was represented by students from her Christian schools, demonstrating their industrious capabilities through carpentry, tailoring, and blacksmithing exhibits. There was little doubt that the aim was to increase the haole population to counter the growing influence of native and Asian Hawaiians. The Chamber, however, wasn't quite ready for the activities at the rival Hawaiian village nearby on the midway, which provided a lively alternative to the whitewashed view favored by the haole businessmen who funded the pavilion. The Hawaiian village was a private concession that featured hula dancers, lively musicians, and exhibits featuring diving children. In what would serve as a model for an almost identical village at the Buffalo fair two years later, visitors would pay 25 cents (about $7 today) to enter the village. There, they were entertained by approximately 44 hula dancers and musicians, could buy newly woven Hawaiian hats and machine-sewn kapa mats, eat poi and other Hawaiian fare, and drink Hawaiian coffee. It offered a significant counterpoint to the staid Chamber pavilion, much to the chagrin of its funders. The Buffalo Exposition Hawaiian village of two years later also offered the amazing Kilauea Volcano Cyclorama. Cycloramas were a phenomenon at the turn of the century, consisting of a circular 16-sided building with interior walls holding the world's largest paintings, 50 feet high and 400 feet long, encircling the space in a 360-degree arc.[31] The cyclorama depicted an angry Kilauea. Patrons walked past lava tubes and experienced volcanic eruptions augmented by lighting and mechanical effects, culminating with Hawaiian kahuna (priests) appeasing Pele, the fire goddess.[32]

Hawaiian villages in Omaha and Buffalo were not affiliated with the exhibitions produced by the Honolulu Chamber of Commerce, but instead were concessions funded by local businesspeople as an investment. They hired an experienced showman to manage the concessions. He, in turn, hired a native Hawaiian middleman to manage the labor and sales and serve as a communication link between the investors, the management, and the performers. That man was Johnny Wilson. In return, he received a guarantee and a percentage of the profits. The performers in Buffalo worked a six-day week and were paid $12 to $25 a month ($365 to $760 in today's money), based on a six-month contract. Writer Adria Imada surmises that transportation costs to and from Hawaii as well as daily expenses were part of the contract.[33]

Stung by Hawaiian criticism of her interpretation of the hula for mainland audiences, Kini apparently stopped performing until 1922, concentrating instead on giving private hula lessons and managing her farm in the Pelekenu Valley on Molokai. In 1920, she moved back to Honolulu, occupying the mayor's residence and serving as the first lady, under her Anglicized first name and married surname, Jennie Wilson.[34]

Also known as Keoni Wilisona in the Hawaiian press, John Henry Nalanieha Tuaori Tamarii "Johnny" Wilson (1871–1956), like Kini, was linked socially to Hawaiian royalty. Johnny's father, Charles Wilson, was born in Tahiti, the son of a Scottish trader and a high-ranking Tahitian woman. Moving to Hawaii after the death of his father, he was eventually appointed by King David Kalakaua to the posts of fire chief and water works supervisor. Later, he became Queen Liliuokalani's (1838–1917) Marshal of the Kingdom and a member of her privy council. Johnny Wilson's mother served as the queen's lady-in-waiting.[35] Kini's background was far more humble. She was born in a seaside grass hut to an Irish tailor, John N. McColgan and a "pureblood" Hawaiian mother. Kini was her 14th child. She was given away (hanaied) at birth to a Hawaiian woman, Kapahu Kula O Kamamalu, who was walking by the hut, heard the baby cry, and took the child to raise, a gift from her birth mother. Her new mother lived in a home adjacent to that of David Kalakaua.[36]

Johnny Wilson was on the fast track to success practically from birth. The queen sponsored his education at Stanford University, where he began studying engineering in 1891. One of his guardians there was sugar baron Claus Spreckels. Wilson also formed a friendship with classmate and future U.S. President Herbert Hoover. Losing his patroness in 1894 after the overthrow of the Hawaiian monarchy, he was forced to withdraw from the university. While at Stanford, however, he had met a number of influential people, including showman E.W. McConnell, who had a working arrangement with the Hawaiian Village concession at San Francisco's MidWinter Fair of 1894. Upon leaving Stanford, he had hoped to secure an engineering job on sugar magnate Claus Spreckels' Hawaiian railroad, but instead, Spreckels arranged for him to manage the Bana Lahui (Hawaiian National Band, also known as Puali Puhiohe Lahui), a post which coincided with the band's tour of the mainland in 1895–1896. It was in Chicago in 1895 that Kini and Johnny, traveling on separate tours, renewed acquaintance and began a relationship. His mother forbade him to marry her, primarily due to choice of careers. He married a haole woman in 1899, the relationship soon failed, and Kini and Johnny renewed their relationship. They toured together on mainland hula circuits frequently for the next several years. By staying away from Hawaii, they removed themselves from social scrutiny and criticism. They married in 1908 or 1909.[37]

Johnny Wilson was a serial entrepreneur who always managed to have more than one business iron in the fire. He distanced himself from the ruling oligarchy in the islands and forged relationships with mainland businesspeople and politicians, including Norman Edward Mack (1855–1932), a powerful Democratic Party leader and editor of the *Buffalo Times*. Eventually, Wilson was elected as Hawaii's representative to the Democratic National Committee and attended his first Democratic convention in Baltimore in 1912. Mack introduced him to a number of influential party members, and Wilson was soon viewed in the islands and on the mainland as a person of growing influence.

Wilson was elected mayor of Honolulu in 1920 and served until 1927. He was re-elected again in 1929, serving until 1931. He was elected again in 1946 and occupied the seat until 1954, serving as mayor a total of 19 years.[38] He served with great humor, and when Honolulu city and county employees were allowed to wear aloha shirts to work in August 1947, he stated that "I don't think the mayor should be so informally dressed. As to the others in the city government, they can come to work in malos (loincloths) if they want to."[39]

After her marriage, Kini became known by the name Jennie Wilson, her first name being an English derivation of Kini. She championed women's suffrage, convening the first meeting in the islands, in 1920, to discuss the impact of the 19th Amendment, giving women the right to vote.[40] She served as an advocate for traditional Hawaiian arts, and was designated "Hawaii's First Lady" by the Hawaiian legislature in 1959.[41]

Hapa Haole Music and the Hula Craze Hits the Mainland

Writer Jerry Hopkins has suggested that the emerging popularity of the hula on mainland America in 20th century may have derived from a series of hapa haole, or "half-foreign" songs written by Hawaiian musician Albert Richard "Sonny" Cunha 1879–1933) beginning in 1903. His "My Waikiki Mermaid"—said to be the first hapa haole song ever written—was sung in English, accompanied by ragtime piano. "My Honolulu Girl" and "Hula Blues" (co-written by Johnny Noble) were choreographed as hula tunes, prompting the beginning of an Americanized song and dance interpretation that left little—or nothing—remaining in the way of the traditional Hawaiian art form.

Another legendary "hula girl" of the era was Hannah Toots Jones Whitford (b. 1871?), a Broadway performer of Indian heritage, who broke her foot while on tour in San Francisco in 1899. There, she met Hawaiian steel guitarist July Kealoha Paka (1874–1943). They were soon married.[42] Paka, who had arrived in San Francisco in 1899 with four other Hawaiian musicians, had made, on Edison beeswax cylinders, what are believed to be the first-ever Hawaiian recordings.[43] Never having been to Hawaii, Toots learned some hula steps and a few Hawaiian words from July and his band mates. She designed a daring—for the era—ankle-baring skirt, began performing, and in 1902 found a New York booking agent and then took her show, Toots Paka's Hawaiians, on the vaudeville circuit. By 1916, she was headlining an act that included Ethel and Lionel Barrymore, the Dolly Sisters, and Charles Dana Gibson. Toots Paka was one of the first to dance what is now known as the hula auana, the westernized form of the dance, with melodies containing English, or hapa haole lyrics, accompanied by stringed instruments. Chances are she never danced hula kahiko, the traditional dance accompanied by chanting, alone, or with drums and gourds.

On the mainland, the hula, regardless of any questions as to its authenticity to traditional island dance, was a hot commodity. What's more, its popularity seemed to heighten interest in Hawaii as well, to the dismay of Hawaii's white power structure. Mainland visitors now coming to Hawaii increasingly insisted, to the chagrin of Hawaii's conservative puritanical press, on seeing a hula performance, even if they had to pay top dollar to do it. In 1911, the standard price charged to visitors from the mainland wanting to see a hula performance was five dollars ($134 in today's currency).[44]

With a semi-hysteria that can be likened to the folksong-hootenanny craze of the 1950s-1960s, hula and its accouterments became a rage on the mainland. Hawaiian tin-pan alley songs, many with kooky, mock-pidgin words and titles (e.g., "Yaaka Hula Hickey Dula"), flooded the market, while their iridescently colored sheet music covers depicted Anglo-looking hula girls cavorting or sighing under the palms on a moonlit night, with Diamond Head posing for the backdrop.[45]

Another major Hawaiian entertainment that rocked the mainland began with the 1912 Broadway debut of *The Bird of Paradise,* a show featuring a melodramatic story line involving the romance between a Hawaiian princess and a doctor who saves the islanders from leprosy. Hawaiian songs were performed in the show by the Hawaiian Quintette, comprising five native singers and island musicians, including noted steel guitarist Walter Kolomoku and fiery vocalist A. Kiwala. The Quintette's version of "Tomi Tomi" (https://www.youtube.com/watch?v=28DPLvY1wuE) is a vocal tour de force for Kiwala, whose trills, burrs, grunts, screams, and tightly punctuated Hawaiian words drive the spirited call-and-response song.[46] The show's music was augmented by a haole chorus line of 100, dancing what writer Christine Skwiot refers to as "a New York choreographer's interpretation of the hula." It was successful enough that it toured America and the world until 1924, providing audiences a particular vision of the exotic joys and tropical languor to be found in the islands. Somewhat surprisingly, the show was partially funded by the Hawaiian Promotion Committee, which just a few short years earlier had vigorously supported a ban of the hula in Hawaii. The show would result in at least one future benefit for the islands. One audience member in Kansas City was the 21-year-old Donald Benson "Don" Blanding (1894–1957), who, inspired by the show, moved to Hawaii in 1915, and became noted for his poetry, painting, and founding of Lei Day in Honolulu in 1927, which still occurs on the first of May every year.[47]

San Francisco had been exposed to the hula as early as the 1850s and beginning in the early weeks of 1915 was again a prime mainland venue. From Feb. 20 through Dec. 4 of that year, more than 18 million people poured through San Francisco's 635-acre Panama-Pacific International Exposition, many of whom were captivated by the activities taking place in the Hawaiian Pavilion. A year earlier, the territorial legislature appropriated $100,000—nearly $2 million in today's money—to establish a Hawaiian presence there as a means to promote tourism. At the Exposition, it was anticipated that one could see hula dancers. As author David Stannard notes, "Flower bedecked, grass-skirted hula dancers of both pure and mixed-race ancestry enthralled San Francisco fairgoers … as did the Hawaiian musicians' delightfully dexterous plucking and strumming on a variety of stringed instruments, including one which appeared to be a tiny guitar." This fed into the emerging national craze for the ukulele, which ultimately resulted in hundreds of thousands of facsimiles made and sold on the mainland, many of them falsely stamped "Made in Hawaii."⁴⁸ The popularity of the Hawaiian Pavilion stoked the interest of recording companies as well, who introduced a groundswell of Hawaiian recordings to be enjoyed in the home and used as accompaniment for hula schools and private instructors.

In the islands, the hula was being fiercely perpetuated by members of the native population despite the histrionics voiced in periodicals including as the *Hawaiian Annual* of 1918, in which Publisher Thomas George Thrum (1842–1932), referring to the hula, warned "in modern times it has wandered so far and fallen so low that foreign and critical esteem has come to associate it with the riotous and passionate ebullitions of Polynesian kings and the amorous posturings of their voluptuaries." Each island had significant individuals who learned the hula from youth and were renowned for sharing their knowledge with future dancers.

On Oahu, Katherine "Keaka" Keakaokala Kanahele (1860?–1940) was raised as a dancer and inherited her grandmother's hula school, training a number of other noted teachers along the way. On Maui, the life of Emma Kapiolani Farden Sharpe (1904–1991) followed in a similar vein. From the Big Island came Harriet Daisy Kawaiala Kaoionapuapiilani "Napua" Stevens (1918–1990), noted for her dancing, singing, promotion of the hula in festivals, and as a writer and later television host of native culture programming. Iolani Luahine (b. Harriet Lanihau Makekau, 1877–1937), from Kauai, became one of Hawaii's premier dancers, and the subject of two noted documentary films. Renowned dancer Ted Shawn, after seeing Luahine in 1946, noted, "She alone could change the false impression now almost universal—that the hula is a cheap, sexy, superficial dance suitable for a supper club. Iolani can and does show the world that the hula is a noble art, rich, beautiful and with great dignity, and a fitting expression of a noble race."⁴⁹

The legacy of Toots Paka's dancing on the mainland had direct bearing on a number of other Hawaiian dancers who toured America and/or performed in films in subsequent years. Beginning in the 1920s, Agnes (Aggie) Kaonohimakaokalani Auld (1905–1983) performed on the Orpheum circuit, vaudeville's best-known venues, and eventually married and toured with Prince Leilani (b. Edwin Kaumualiiokamokuokalani Rose, 1887–1971) into the 1940s. She danced in numerous hotel showrooms on the mainland, including San Francisco's St. Francis, the Adolphus Hotel in Dallas, the Broadmore in Colorado Springs, and the Beverly Wilshire in Beverly Hills. She was credited with choreographing a hula for ice skater Sonja Henie and taught hula lessons in Los Angeles during the World War II years. She made appearances with Bette Davis, Bing Crosby, and Dorothy Lamour in feature films including *Hawaii Calls* (1938, dir. Edward F. Cline), and *The Moon of Mona Koora* (1945, dir. Josef Berne).⁵⁰ She also appeared in *Around the World in Eighty Days* (1956, dir. Michael Anderson).⁵¹

Another notable hula luminary was Winona Nancy Love (1911–1981), a descendant of the niece of the regent Kaahumanu, who began dancing at age four and debuted professionally at age 14. She danced at the opening of the Royal Hawaiian Hotel in 1927, appeared with Johnny Noble's orchestras at both the Royal Hawaiian and Moana hotels, and danced on the mainland in San Francisco, Los Angeles, and Portland. Love can be seen in two travelogues, *Aloha Hawaii* (1930) and *The Blonde Captive* (1931, prod. William M. Pizor) and the feature film *Picture Island* (1933, dir. Roy Mack). She was hired as a consultant by David O. Selznick and King Vidor to teach the hula to Dolores Del Rio for the feature film *Bird of Paradise* (1932, dir. King Vidor), the first full-length Hawaiian talkie. In Hawaii, she was also noted for her long-standing relationship with politician, sportsman, and bon vivant Francis Hyde Ii Brown (1892–1976).⁵²

Although she was better known as a dancing, singing, and acting comedian, Clarissa "Hilo Hattie" Haili (1901–1979, also known by her married name, Clara Inter) belongs in the hula conversation. Born in Honolulu in 1901, she was the most recognized female Hawaiian performer of the 20th century. She had been a teacher at Waipahu Elementary School from 1923 through 1939 when the school administration asked her to decide between performing and teaching. She chose the former. Her trademark song was "When Hilo Hattie Does the Hula Hop," first performed on a ship taking her to a mainland teachers' conference in 1936. Hattie was also noted for "The Cockeyed Mayor of Kaunakakai."[53] She appeared in her first film, *Song of the Islands* (1942, dir. Walter Lang), dancing the "Hawaiian War Chant" and singing and dancing along with Betty Grable on the song "Down on Ami Ami Oni Oni Isle."[54] Her introduction to the film world was facilitated by her friend, bandleader Harry Owens, who suggested she legally change her name to Hilo Hattie, the professional name she would use for the rest of her life. Her performance costume was instantly recognizable, consisting of a wide-brimmed hat, a muumuu that appeared several sizes too big, cinched up with the help of a bandana, and a lei. She made liberal use of her mobile face muscles and rolling eyes, and appeared in nine feature films, including Elvis Presley's *Blue Hawaii*. Her acting credits include at least two episodes of the television series *Hawaii Five-O*. In 1969, a hybrid orchid was named after her, and she became the namesake for a popular brand of Hawaiian clothing.[55] In the islands, she was also known as Auntie Clara Nelson, a beloved figure who passed away in 1979. She was the subject of a biography by Millie Singletary, *Hilo Hattie: A Legend in Our Time* (1979).[56]

Haole Hula Meets Hollywood

Hollywood was on the hula—or at least the grass skirt—bandwagon long before Auld (1938), Love (1933), and Hilo Hattie (1942) appeared in feature films. Enid Markey may have been the first actress to wear a grass skirt and a sarong in a Hollywood film, appearing as the female protagonist in producer Thomas Ince's *Aloha Oe* of 1915.[57] Other Hawaiian films followed mostly featuring female haole dancers, in films that included *Passion Fruit* (1921, dir. John Ince, with dancer Doraldina), *The White Flower* (1923, dir. Julia Crawford Ivers, with dancer Betty Compson), *Aloma of the South Seas* (1926, dir. Maurice Tourneur, with dancer Gilda Gray). Even Clara Bow, the famous vamp of the 1920s, joined the fun, in her film *Hula* (1927, dir. Victor Fleming), based on well-known author of Hawaiian subjects Armine Von Tempski's (1892–1943) novel *Hula: A Romance of Hawaii*. On the Bow film, writer Jerry Hopkins notes that the dancers included a team of girls from Honolulu's Territorial Normal School led by Dorothy M. Kahananui (1895–1984). Hawaiian hula performers and teachers were often hired as performers or consultants to provide some degree of verisimilitude to the dances, although never achieving star billing.[58]

The 1930s and early 1940s were replete with Hawaiian-themed Hollywood films featuring major stars, often including Hawaiian musicians and dancers. As mentioned above, Winona Love served in a consulting capacity for the 1932 feature film *Bird of Paradise*, with Isabella Desha (1864–1949), Helen Desha Beamer (1882–1952), and Harriet Beamer (1905–1965) all appearing as dancers. Shirley Temple danced the hula in *Curly Top* (1935, dir. Irving Cummings), as did Dorothy Lamour in *Road to Singapore* (1940, dir. Victor Schertzinger),

Lupe Velez in *Honolulu Lu* (1941, dir. Charles Barton), and Betty Grable in *Song of the Islands* (1942, dir. Walter Lang). Writer Jerry Hopkins notes that Eleanor Powell's "jazzy hula" in *Honolulu* (1939, dir. Edward Buzzell) elicited protests from a number angry Hawaiians who demanded the dance be removed from the film. The film, of course, was never intended to be a documentary, its producers choosing instead to make a light, unrealistic, romantic fantasy, similar in scope to many Hollywood films of that genre and era. The film was notable, beyond Powell's "Hula" and "Hula Tap" dances for featuring music played by Andy Iona and His Islanders, with Lani McIntire on steel guitar.[59] In 1938, MGM and the Consolidated Amusement Company of Hawaii cooperated to hold a hugely popular inter-island hula contest. The grand prize was a trip to Hollywood and a screen test at MGM. Nearly 500 contestants entered, and with preliminary rounds held on each island, resulting in an island finalist. On Sept. 6, 1938, the Hula Nui Night Grand Final was held at the before a packed house at the 1,400-seat Hawaii Theater in Honolulu. The winner, chosen from a field of five finalists, each from a different island, was crowned the Hula Queen by a panel of judges, one of whom was Jennie Wilson (Kini Kapahu). The winner was Alice Kealoha Pauole Holt (1919–2010), from Kauai. She went to the mainland for three months, passed her screen test, and appeared in a brief role in *Honolulu*, an MGM production.[60]

Haole Hula Greets New York

With the popularity of hula and Hawaiian music at its peak on the mainland, entrepreneurs saw an opportunity to provide Hawaiian entertainment at a fixed venue and at an ongoing basis. Hotel nightclubs were the answer. Patrons could pay to see Hawaiian performers and hula dancers, buy dinner as well as drinks, and perhaps stay in the hotel as well. The first formally designed Hawaiian showroom in a United States hotel was the Hawaiian Room in New York City's Hotel Lexington. Located at the corner of 49th Street and Lexington Avenue, the Hawaiian Room opened on June 23, 1937, the brainchild of Charles E. Rochester, Vice President and Managing Director of the hotel.[61] It was an oval basement room with two rows of tables, a supper club, bandstand, and dance floor all in one, decorated with murals of Waikiki and Diamond Head, kapa cloth on the walls, palm trees, and rattan furniture. Effects included a tropical rainfall, presumably accompanied by lightning and thunder provided by the audio-visual system. Exotic food and drink were served in hollowed coconuts by lei-adorned servers.[62] Hawaiian orchestra leader, composer, and singer Ray Kinney (1900–1972) was brought in to lead the band and choose additional Hawaiian talent. Lani McIntire (1904–1951) and Andy Iona (1902–1966) were among the first musicians hired, and it is said that Kinney named the house band "Andy Iona and His Twelve Hawaiians" because "McIntire and Kinney" sounded too Irish. One of Kinney's most famous vocalists was famed falsetto singer George Kainapau (1905–1992).[63] Kinney's musicians were all men, sporting white jackets, and the dancers all light-skinned hapa haole Hawaiian women, thought to be more acceptable to the largely white audiences (in keeping with the racial discrimination of the era, blacks were not admitted as patrons). Kinney hired his first hula team, the Aloha Maids, in Honolulu, whose charter group included solo dancer Meymo Ululani Holt (1915–1995, Kinney was married to her older sister, Dawn), and line dancers Pualani Mossman (1916–2006), Mapuana Mossman Bishaw (Pualani's cousin), and Jennie Hanaialii (Napua) Woodd

(1912–2003).⁶⁴ Patrons paid a $1.25 cover charge (about $20 in today's money). For the dancers, the pay was preferable to most work available to young women in the islands. They were paid between $60 and $100 ($1,044 and $1,740 today) per week in those pre-war days, while pineapple cannery workers earned $4 to $10 a week ($70 to $174 today). The stay in New York offered material temptations that were all too easy to afford. "I wore my salary on my back, spent it on furniture and clothes," noted dancer Leilehua (Lei) Becker (b.1927), "I didn't save any money." It was a common complaint, apparently, as most of the Aloha Maids had to work side jobs to make ends meet.⁶⁵

Charles Rochester eschewed Tin Pan Alley Hawaiian novelty songs, and had his own idea of what the pure Hawaiian sound represented to him. In an interview with the *Honolulu Star-Bulletin* in 1940, he stated, "Don't let Hawaiian music go modern! Keep your music to its present lilting and languorous tempo ... [otherwise] there'll be no place for Hawaiian musicians on the mainland. Over there the patrons want the real thing, not imitation jazz and swing."⁶⁶ Rochester, however, eventually modified his ideas, as exemplified by Lani McIntire's Hawaiian Room ensemble of the late 1940s.

The number of dancers in the Hawaiian Room show could change at any given moment, depending on who was available. Two films made in the late 1940s featuring Lani McIntire's performances at the Hawaiian Room, for example, show different numbers of dancers and staging configurations. Each film is named for the song performed. In *King Kamehameha*, four line dancers perform as four others sway to the music behind them. In *Holo Holo Kaa*, the background dancers are absent.⁶⁷ In short order, showmen in other major cities attempted to copy the Hawaiian hotel supper club experience, including San Francisco's St. Francis Hotel (and later, the Fairmont Hotel's Tonga Room), Chicago's Roosevelt Hotel, Buffalo's Statler Hotel, and New Orleans' Roosevelt Hotel. Cleveland's El Dorado Club was yet another venue hosting Hawaiian shows. These clubs drew from wide geographical regions, as out of town visitors often made it a point to see an exotic Hawaiian show when traveling to a larger city. Not all the dancers came to New York or other cities with formal dance training in their backgrounds. Overall attractiveness no doubt factored into the hiring decision, and these women were expected to learn the requisite steps and hand, arm, and torso movements from their veteran colleagues.⁶⁸

Each member of the Aloha Maids had her own agenda, whether determined in advance or realized after her introduction to New York. Pualani Mossman, for example, danced for a few months and then opened a hula school with her sister Piilani. She eventually married Hotel Lexington's accountant Randy Avon, had a child, and then moved to Florida, where she resumed teaching hula and ran several shops selling island goods and apparel.⁶⁹ Meymo Holt got her bachelor's degree in New York, married, had a child, and moved to Michigan, eventually ending up a an executive assistant at a manufacturing company. Napua Woodd, one of the original Aloha Maids, had a life that was somewhat more flamboyant. She married for a third time to trumpeter and slide guitarist Lloyd Gilliom, played with the Sammy Kaye and the Dorsey Brothers orchestras, and appeared in the Broadway musical *Helzapoppin'* (1938). She traveled extensively, opening hula shows in Cleveland's El Dorado Club, Reno, and Los Angeles. Woodd appeared in two short films, *Oni Oni E* (1944, dir. Joseph Berne) and *Isle of Tabu* (1944, dir. Josef Berne). She moved to Hollywood in the early 1950s, opening a hula studio and appearing in television shows including *Adventures in Paradise, Hawaiian Eye, My Three Sons,* and *Family Affair*. She married a total of six times, the last to a man 40 years her junior. Lei Becker toured the mainland with steel guitarist Hal Aloma, and spent two years in the Hotel Lexington's Hawaiian Room as producer, emcee, choreographer, hula dancer, costume designer and lead vocalist. Later, she toured with big band leader Claude Thornhill under the stage name Paula Martin.[70] What's remarkable about these—and other— Aloha Maids is their far-reaching trek through the world of mainland entertainment, opening their own hula studios, appearing on film and television, and performing with touring bands, touching millions of people in the process.

From the 1930s through the 1950s, New York was the mecca for Hawaiian entertainers on the mainland, and in being so, created an environment conducive to the furthering of this genetic or career-related extended family. This informal but powerful ohana family dynamic included every musician and dancer. It also enveloped Hawaiians working in blue collar and service industries, sometimes—but not always—related by kinship. Performers tend to consider themselves a separate breed, particularly those on the stage performing erotica or— like the hula girls and their musicians—what may be perceived as others to be erotica. In a case of entertainment role-reversal, they often view their audiences as exhibits in themselves, where the performers take on the role of the audience. To entertain themselves, stage performers will follow the gazes of their customers, watch their body language, note their vocalisms, and view their interactions with adjacent audience members. Performers will single out individuals and then discuss them backstage or over after-show cast dinners. It is a source of prime amusement for the performers, who by reversing the roles of audience and performer, view themselves in a dominant, rather than submissive position.

Although island hula dancers and musicians seemed to be on a never-ending conga line to New York, the art form was far from dormant in Hawaii. In the islands of the pre-war era, there was one particularly significant tourist venture that employed hula dancers and musicians, some of whom eventually left for the mainland to appear in hula shows. The venue was George Paele Mossman's (1891–1955) Lalani Hawaiian Village (named after Mossman's wife), a combined school and tourist attraction located adjacent to Waikiki Beach. Mossman founded the village with a mission to preserve Hawaiian traditional culture and language through performance. "The old people with the knowledge of the old Hawaiian customs are rapidly dying; and their knowledge is dying with them. Our task now is to preserve everything we can," he noted. Mossman himself was steeped in Hawaiian culture. He'd been a ukulele builder since 1915, and in 1928, founded a school that taught Hawaiian language and chanting.[71] One of his first efforts in building the village was to convince 95-year-old chanter James Pihanui Kuluwaimaka Palea to serve as his kumu. Kukuwaimaka was renowned for his phenomenal memory, repeating up to 1,700 lines at a time, describing Hawaiian rulers, genealogies, and events, always in monotone (recordings of him are in the Bishop Museum archives). He performed chants at the village at least once per day.[72]

The mission of the village was to educate and entertain, and Mossman's family was heavily involved in the day-to-day operations and attractions. Pualani Mossman, who was 16 years old in 1932, when her father founded his venture, performed the featured volcano dance in the early years of the Lalani Village. She was one of a number of Waikiki dancers that would springboard to New York, and gained additional fame as the face of many of Matson Navigation's advertisements for island travel.

The village was designed to emulate a pre-contact Hawaiian environment, and structures built for the village included seven hale pili (grass huts), built by master craftsman versed in traditional building techniques. In front of the huts, craftspeople in traditional dress would carve canoes, make leis, pound poi, and make kapa cloth. Important elder hula dancers and chanters from rural districts came to live at the village, performing as well as teaching their arts to others. Locals and nearby hotel visitors alike could see a show, eat traditional Hawaiian food, and take hula lessons from notables that might include Eleanor Leilehua Hiram (1918–1983).[73] Military personnel also visited the village: a photograph from 1935 shows Pualani Mossman performing at the village before an audience of U.S. sailors. The entertainment was a hybrid of traditional and hapa haole music, dance, and costuming. At village luaus, the Mossman family dressed as alii, with George wearing the royal ahuula (feathered cape), his wife sitting next to him as consort, and his daughters Pualani, Piilani, and Leilani standing above him, holding the regal kahili (staff).[74] Today, Mossman's Lalani Hawaiian Village is viewed nostalgically, with an appreciation for the effort made by him and his family to preserve traditional culture. The village supported elder performers, thus enabling them to pass their crafts along to others, and introduced Hawaiian culture to untold numbers of visitors. By the early 1950s, the village was evidencing a decline in popularity. Mossman was developing plans to redesign it when he passed away at the age of 64, and the land was subsequently sold. Those old enough to remember the village and wish to make a return visit will today instead walk into the lobby of the Waikiki Beach Marriott Hotel, where George Mossman's Lalani Hawaiian Village once stood.[75]

Religion Embraces Hula: The LDS Church and Traditional Hawaiian Culture

Considering the strong animosity toward the hula on the part of Western organized religion, a somewhat surprising development in the 20th century was its eventual support and promotion by at least one organized religious organization, a 180-degree turn from the prevalent Calvinist philosophy.[76] A major player in the emerging movement for the social acceptance of the hula in the Hawaii of the 20th century was the Church of Jesus Christ of Latter-day Saints (LDS). Mormons had made a significant enough advance in the islands that by 1913, LDS missionaries were estimating that 22 percent of all islanders were of that faith.[77] Hawaiian belief in the importance of ancestral relations meshed well with the teachings of the Mormon religion. Mormons believed that Polynesians were the lost tribe of Israel, and beginning in the 19th century, developed a deep interest in Hawaiian cultural history and practices.[78] Hawaiians were drawn to this Western religion that embraced their spiritual customs, the antithesis of the Calvinist philosophies of the protestant missionaries that preceded them. While Mormon practice forbade rituals involving prayers and tributes to traditional Hawaiian gods, it encouraged the preservation and practice of Hawaiian music and dance. In all probability, native Hawaiian teachers subscribing to the Mormon belief system continued to teach traditional chants to their students, under the noses of church authorities.[79]

In the 1930s, George Mossman had learned the essentials of hula traditions from Sam Pua Haaheo (1886–1953), like himself, a member of the LDS church. Born on Oahu, Haaheo, an elder in the church and a policeman by profession, was a hula dancer and teacher whose memorable and influential Mormon students included kahuna and entertainer "Daddy" Bray (1889–1968) and his wife, Lydia "Mama" Bray (1890–1957).[80] Other important early dancers that were church members in the Haaheo era included, Katie Kekaula (also known as Kakalina Nakaula), Keaka Kanahele (1860?–1940), Lucy Logan Munson, and teacher and scholar Mary Kawena Pukui (1895–1986). Later notable dancers who were also church members included Edith Kanakaole (1913–1979), Eleanor Leilehua Hiram, Alice Namakelua (1892–1987), Iolani Luahine, Napua Stevens, singer and songwriter William Lionel Kalanialiiloa "Bill" Lincoln (1911–1989), and Sally Moanikeala Naluai Wood (1909–2000, b. Julia Tong Lock, Hawaiian name Moanikealaonapuamakahikina).[81]

Much of the hula activity on Oahu occurred in the town of Laie, home of the Mormon temple as well as a branch of Brigham Young University. According to hula teacher Mary Kawena Pukui, "art, singing, dancing, composing, weaving, carving and painting … reminded man of his interrelationship with the universe and the gods … [demonstrating] to men the kind of god-like behavior they should emulate." This philosophical approach was embraced by the LDS church in Hawaii culminated in the annual church-sponsored Laie Day, which featured statewide hula and song contests. The church also founded the Polynesian Cultural Center, a popular tourist attraction, in 1963, which today includes cultural exhibitions about the islands of Aotearoa (New Zealand), Fiji, Samoa, Tahiti, and Tonga, in addition to Hawaii.[82] The LDS church led the way for other churches to follow in promoting hula as a cultural institution worth preserving. Margaret "Maiki" Aiu (1925–1984), for example, began teaching ancient hula classes in her Catholic church 1n 1948.[83]

Teaching Hula on the Mainland

Through recordings, radio, films, hotel showrooms, national exposition fairs, and traveling shows on the hula circuit, Hawaiian dance had become a significant force in entertainment world in pre–World War II America, and thousands of mainlanders were inspired to learn it. A growing number of mainland-based hula instructors taught both privately and in public institutions, many of whom were professional performers looking to secure an additional source of income. The appearance of hula as a dance form taught on campuses added strength to its burgeoning reputation as a critically important element of traditional Pacific culture.

One of the better-known early haole hula teachers on the mainland was Vivienne "Huapala" Mader (1901–1972). Born in Brooklyn, she formally studied dance with Ted Shawn and Ruth St. Denis, among others. She was exposed to hula in 1929 at the Royal Hawaiian Hotel in Honolulu, where she saw performances by the Bray family and Winona Love. She remained in Hawaii to study with Helen Desha Beamer, eventually living with the Beamer family in Hilo. She also recorded phonograph records of her own mele hula, and made films, now archived at the Bishop Museum, of a number of Hawaiian chanters, singers, musicians, and dancers. She returned to live on the mainland and taught kahiko hula for more than 40 years, both privately and New York institutions including Adelphi College and the New School for Social Research.[84] Dancer Aggie Auld chose to stay in Los Angeles during World War II and taught hula privately during the war years. In the post-war years, Winona Kapuailohiamanonokalani Beamer (1923–2008) joined the faculties of Sacramento State College and Mills College, introducing hula in an academic environment. Sally Wood taught hula at Monterey Peninsula College.[85]

Hula Goes to War

War in the Pacific Theater enabled most GIs and war workers to see hula in person for the first time, primarily through USO shows. The United Service Organizations (USO) was a cooperative venture including six service organizations: the Salvation Army, Young Men's Christian Association (YMCA), Young Women's Christian Association (YWCA), National Catholic Community Service, National Travelers Aid Association and the National Jewish Welfare Board. Founded in 1941, the overall goal of the organization was to boost morale by providing activities and entertainment to troops on leave or otherwise unengaged in active operations. The USO's aim was similar to that of the Hawaii Tourist Bureau, to provide its visitors with the Aloha Experience. An informational tract given to GIs stated, "A lot of things have changed in these islands since December 7th . We can't take you back home, but we can give you the next best thing while you're here.... And most of all, we can give you Aloha."[86]

Hawaii rapidly mobilized its USO organization. Entertainment included music, home parties, social dances, tours, luaus, and hula. Professional as well as amateur hula dancers joined the USO circuit, performing everywhere they were needed, including Honolulu, remote island military installations, and aboard ships. Prominent hula dancers working with the USO included Sally Wood and Emma Sharpe, who was the director of the hula troupes that entertained in camps on Maui. Sharpe would spend late nights with dancers, their friends, and families stringing together fresh flower leis for the GIs that would attend the next day's performance. Another dancer taught hapa haole hula to military women on Oahu, in classes that occasionally numbered up to 500 participants.[87] By the end of 1942, its first year of operation, the USO had operations on the five main islands, 400 camp show entertainers, and 2,000 volunteers working in 51 clubs and units. The camp show unit, which was organized one month after the beginning of the war, produced 25 variety shows, cooperated with Army Special Services on another five, and gave a total of 12,228 performances for more than six million persons. During 1943, the Army Special Services Department began generating its own entertainment programs, freeing the USO camp show department to concentrate on naval personnel and war workers.[88]

Fort DeRussy was one popular USO venue on Oahu, having the largest recreation center of the Mid–Pacific Command. Its ballroom seated 1,200 and its grounds could accommodate 10,000 servicemen and women. The USO Rainbow Club, which opened in Honolulu in April 1945, became a hub for African American GIs, although everyone was welcome in this interracial environment. More than 186,000 men attended events there, which included music, sports, and sightseeing tours. USO entertainers traveled everywhere they could, under sometimes arduous conditions. One hula troupe spread the spirit of aloha by traveling 12 miles over a rocky, narrow trail to do a show at a small outpost at an elevation of 1,700 feet. Another group donned riding apparel and rode for three hours by horse to a mountain camp. Other groups performing under the USO banner catered to specific ethnic groups serving the war effort. One such group was the Hana Like club, formed by girls of Chinese ancestry, who entertained Chinese American GIs and war workers from the mainland.[89]

One notable USO hula dancer at Fort DeRussy was Tootsie Notley (b. Doveline Imakalani, 1915–1998). As a high school student, she had begun dancing at the Royal Hawaiian Hotel in 1929, and by the mid–1930s, was serving as a model for Matson Navigation's passenger ship advertisements. At Fort DeRussy in 1940, she met Col. Frank Steer, who became provost marshal of Hawaii during the days of martial law in World War II. Notley was 25 years old and he was 39. They were soon married. According to reporter Bob Krauss, Steer "established a reputation for fairness to and consideration for local people. His wife may have had something to do with that." They remained married until her death in 1998.[90]

By the end of the war, a staggering number of 67 million servicemen, servicewomen, and war workers had been entertained in Hawaii. For many, the effort put forth by the Hawaiian volunteers at USO shows would not be forgotten, and the spirit of aloha would remain a lasting mark. The GIs were in Hawaii to fight a war and no doubt spent much of their time in the Pacific wondering if they'd ever see their homeland again. The Hawaiian shows at the USO brought fun into their lives, a precious commodity in uncertain times. As hula scholar Adria Imada notes, "When they went back to their American homes, they took the memories of the luau and hula with them."[91]

Hula in the Post-War Years

On the mainland, the impact of hula remained undiminished. The Hawaiian Room at the Hotel Lexington was still packing them in, hula girls were traveling to the mainland to make money in other hula venues, and hula schools were thriving. Popular entertainers like Arthur Godfrey and Bing Crosby kept Hawaii and the hula in the public eye via radio, television, and film (Godfrey stayed at the Hotel Lexington during the week, and occasionally broadcast his shows from the Hawaiian Room). The film *Bird of Paradise* was remade in 1951. Director Delmer Daves insisted on emphasizing the dignity of the Hawaiian people and hired a number of well-known Hawaiians for music and chanting, including David K. "Daddy" Bray, Rosalie Lokalia Lovelle Montgomery (1903–1978), Soloman Pa, and George Tautu Archer. Nose flutes, gourd rattles, and snakeskin drums were provided by Lokalia's husband Tim Montgomery. Iolani Luahine, one of kumu Lokalia's former students, choreographed the dances.[92] Elvis Presley took notice of the groundswell of mainland interest in Hawaii, making his film *Blue Hawaii*, released in 1961, on location in Hawaii in 1959.[93]

While there remained the usual anti-hula (or anti haole-hula) pockets in the islands, the post–World War II era in Hawaii was a beneficial one for hula, whose popularity continued increasing on the mainland and in the islands. In one sense, it went sky-high, becoming an important element in Trans-Pacific Airlines' (later re-named Aloha Airlines) inter-island DC-3 service as soon as it received its charter in 1946. Its in-flight entertainment consisted of performances by its hula dancing, singing, and ukulele playing flight attendants.[94] The tourist business was rapidly becoming the biggest moneymaker in the islands.

United Airlines was now competing with Pan American on flights from the mainland to the islands, and new hotels were being built to accommodate the influx in tourist traffic. Each hotel, it seemed, had a hula troupe, providing constant work for the island's dancers. Nightclubs, notably Queen's Surf, Club Pago Pago, and La Hula Rhumba reveled in their hula shows. When Donn Beach opened his Don the Beachcomber restaurant in Honolulu in 1947, his troupe of hula girls would wind their way up Kalkaua Avenue, handing out orchids to passersby every "Aloha Wednesday."[95]

Aloha Week, described as the "Mardi Gras of the Pacific," began in 1947, an idea cobbled together by Honolulu businesspeople looking for a way to keep the culture alive and generate profits from tourism. They won the endorsement of Princess Abigail Kawananakoa (b. 1926), which engendered participation from numerous civic and cultural groups. It was held in October, the traditional month of the makahiki harvest festival. For its initial year, a royal court was convened and a hula festival was held in Ala Moana Park. Katie Kekaula, a legendary hula kumu, opened the proceedings with a chant. In the ensuing years, major hula pageants were held and numerous side stages set up with even more hula performers, many of them teenagers from halau based on other islands. A notable and ongoing participant was San Francisco–born Domingo "Kent Ghirard" Ghirardelli (1918–2011), a noteworthy example of a mainlander so impacted by his youthful experiences in Hawaii that he returned and made a significant contribution to the international popularity of Hawaiian dance.[96]

Ghirard's father, who, along with his two brothers, owned San Francisco's renowned Ghirardelli Chocolate Company, took a family vacation to Hawaii in 1932 that included the 11-year-old Kent.[97] They stayed at the Royal Hawaiian Hotel, where Kent was introduced to hula through the performance of the Bray family. He returned five years later, and a year after that enrolled for a music appreciation summer course at University of Hawaii. He cut classes on Monday nights to see the Kodak Hula Show. During the war years, he attended Polynesian clubs in the Bay Area, came out of the audience to dance at the Seven Seas club, and took hula lessons from Marguerite Duane.[98] He moved to Hawaii permanently after graduating from Stanford University in 1947, his friend Marguerite joining him shortly thereafter, and they both began teaching at the Betty Lei Hula Studio. Kent cobbled together a hula team and entered them in a hula show at Kapiolani Park, which led to a gig for him and three of his best students at the Niumalu Hotel. In 1950, he set up a formal studio. He had a reputation for being strict, insisting that the girls wore long hair, wore no makeup, and performed precisely choreographed steps. His Hula Nani Girls, which included dancer Pauline Kekahuna (1920–1978) among others, became one of the most popular troupes in Honolulu, dancing at the Moana and Royal Hawaiian hotels, greeting celebrities for the Hawaiian Visitors Bureau, and performing at clubs including Don the Beachcomber. The Hula Nani Girls appeared in at least two films, *Big Jim McLain* (1952, dir. Edward Ludwig) and *Hell's Half Acre* (1954, dir. John H. Auer). Ghirard's trip to Japan in 1955—they were the first Hawaiian performers to visit there in the post-war era—contributed significantly to the rising enthusiasm for hula in that country. Although Ghirard's troupe was denigrated in some circles as being overly tourist-oriented, Jerry Hopkins points out that his significance lay in the fact that he was a Westerner teaching traditional hula to Hawaiians, a case of the Hawaiian influence on the mainland returning full circle.[99]

Kent Ghirard ended his run with the Hula Nani Girls in 1961. In the late 1950s, the American Guild of Variety Artists began organizing musicians in Hawaii, and hula girls were encouraged to join. Those joining the union were now receiving musicians' scale pay. In response, many hotels fired their dancers rather than incur this new cost. A significant number of dancing jobs were lost, and the situation worsened when the Honolulu branch manager of the union was convicted of embezzling initiation fees and dues. "Putting it simply," Ghirard stated, "the jobs dried up. It was one of the reasons I folded the Hula Nani Girls and retired."[100]

In 1964, the Merrie Monarch Festival was launched in Hilo. The idea had been initiated by activities promoter, kumu hula, chanter, and preservationist George Lanakilakekiahialii Naope (1928–2009). Helene Hale, the Chairman of the County of Hawaii, had been searching for a way to bring income to the Big Island, recently damaged by a tsunami and suffering from an economic downturn. She dispatched Administrative Assistant Gene Wilhelm, and her Promoter of Activities, Naope, to the Lahaina Whaling Spree on Maui to see what could be learned. They returned with an armload of ideas and their Hilo event became a reality in 1964. The inaugural festival didn't include the hula contest, for which today it's best known. Among the events were a King Kalakaua beard look-alike contest, a barbershop quartet contest, a relay race, a re-creation of King Kalakaua's coronation, and a Holoku (the long dress introduced in Hawaii in the 19th century) Ball. The hula contest was added in 1971 and featured nine wahine (women) halau teams. The judges consisted of many of the most significant kumus and dancers in Hawaii. It was in 1976, when male hula dancers were allowed to compete, that the festival began gaining international attention. Since then, the hula contest has been the prime focus of the festival committee, which states, "The major purpose of the festival is the perpetuation, preservation, and promotion of the art of hula and the Hawaiian culture through education." In addition to the halau competition, individual contestants vie for the title of Miss Aloha Hula, performing hula kahiko, hula auana and oli (chanting). The 2017 contest featured 23 competing halau and 10 contestants in the Miss Aloha Hula competition.[101]

Not all qualified individuals and halau choose to compete, however. For some, the competitiveness is seen as counter to the aloha philosophy. Others say that the words of the mele are too often ignored. Still others suggest that the act of losing defeats the whole purpose of the event, which is, after all, to celebrate Hawaiian tradition and island culture. Controversies continued to surround the festival. In 1974, nearly all the halau prizes were carried away by adorable kids dancing hula. Cuteness stole the show, angering many of the other participants. In response, for the next year's competition, each contestant had to be at least 13 years old. Another year, the controversies were over what properly constituted hula kahiko, the appearance of modern props, the incorporation of martial arts steps into hula, and the lack of native tongue fluency among the dancers.[102]

Cute kids have been stealing the hula show long before the Merrie Monarch contest. Millions of Western mainland television watchers of the 1960s will never forget the super-catchy C&H Sugar jingle ("mommy uses it to bake her cakes") which made up the entire commercial for the sugar cooperative, featuring island kids munching on cane and a little girl hulaing the story at 36 seconds into the 50 second spot (https://www.youtube.com/watch?v=nH_eKDZdoZk).

Hawaii's Cultural Renaissance

The success of the male dancers in the Merrie Monarch Festival of 1976 was part of a resurgence in the popularity of Hawaiian arts and culture, documented in the 1970s, that today may be called the Hawaiian Renaissance. This cultural groundswell was defined, defended, and celebrated in an influential lecture by Hawaiian Music Foundation president Dr. George S. Kanahele at Kamehameha School's Culture Lecture Series in 1979. He had first written about it in *Honolulu Magazine* in 1977, and the entire text of which, encompassing nine pages, was printed in the Foundation's *Hailono Mele* newsletter of July 1979. Likening the renaissance to similar cultural breakthroughs made by various marginalized ethnic groups on the mainland, Kanahele discussed a number of nearly forgotten Hawaiian traditional elements that hade made a successful comeback, engendered by both natives and non-ethnic Hawaiians, the latter of whom he noted "have come to identify themselves culturally, psychologically, and spiritually with Hawaiianness." Among the resurgent elements he celebrated were male hula dancing, the revival of the Hawaiian music industry, traditional arts and crafts including featherwork, canoe racing, surfing, literature, and the Hawaiian language itself. He noted that the language was comprehensively documented in a new dictionary, and courses were now taught in schools and university.[103]

Kanahele made particular note of the voyage of the *Hokulea*, which he celebrated as the greatest symbol of the Hawaiian Renaissance. This twin-hulled seafaring canoe made the arduous voyage from Hawaii to Tahiti and back in 1976, using traditional Polynesian navigation techniques. An important objective of the voyage was to prove that long distance Polynesian travel was purposeful, rather than a matter of simply drifting with the currents. She made numerous other voyages, including a round the world trip from 2014 to 2017.[104]

"Hawaiians have finally retaken hula from the tourists," Kanahele said, pointedly returning to the new popularity of male dancers. "I remember as a kid in the not too remote past no local boy would be caught dead doing the hula for fear of being called a sissy.... Perhaps the most forceful evidence of how far we've come is the picture of Russ Francis, Arnold Morgado, and other football players who did the hula during the half time show at last year's Hula Bowl."[105]

Hula Today

Hula today thrives in the continental United States. The 627 mainland hula schools with thousands of dancers attest to its impact on the mainland alone. It continues to evolve in Hawaii. Hula kue, hula that resists or opposes, represents hula as an element of social activism, advocating for traditional Kanaka Maoli (Native Hawaiian) practices. Led by activist-performers including Vicky Holt Takamine, the performance is used to protest against proposed laws requiring permits to gather various forms of flora for use in traditional practices, a right considered necessary to the continuation of traditional native culture. And hapa haole music and hula, denigrated by purists for decades, has experienced a resurgence on the islands. The annual Hapa Haole Hula Festival debuted on Waikiki in 2003. Sponsored by Takamine's PAI foundation, its mission is to bring back the lost era of high-style shows, comic hula, and glitz and glamour.[106] The concept, to no surprise, migrated to the mainland in 2006, at the Bally Hotel in Las Vegas.[107] It's gone north of the border as well. Vancouver's Hapa Haole Hula Competition was held on July 28, 2017, with the following proviso: "In keeping with the hapa haole tradition, all songs within each category must be sung in English and the theme of the performance must be about Hawaii. The era of music must be from the 1900 to 1959 period when classic Hapa Haole music was at its prime."[108]

Writing in 1982, Jerry Hopkins, who interviewed dozens of kumu, dancers, and chanters, noted a growing alarm with the hula's slide toward pandering to commercial tastes. "If the eyes of the dancer do not follow their hands," said Napua Stevens, "they're not telling the story ... they're so busy being gorgeous that they say absolutely nothing."[109] Ti-leaf skirts, worn traditionally below the knee, were now cut high on the thigh on many dancers working at Waikiki. "They aren't going topless yet, but watch for someone to come along ... with only a flower lei pasted down strategically to hide the offending nipples," noted one commentator.

Like every other art form, hula was going through growing pains, internecine squabbles and major disagreements, and accusations flung back and forth between strict traditionalists and modernists attempting to find new ways to evolve the dance. There were always those in the middle, as well, ducking the arrows coming from both directions. In a way, it was reminiscent of the time on the mainland when Bebop produced a shockwave that ran roughshod over the New Orleans and Swing jazz forms that preceded it, confounding, pleasing, or annoying jazz enthusiasts and critics.[110]

In common with art forms embracing cultural traditions, hula can be heavily politicized, and there are many who feel that a haole has no business writing about it in the first place. Jerry Hopkins, a haole from the mainland, was, at age 39, a relative latecomer to the islands when first introduced to the hula scene. The first edition of his book *The Hula*, published in 1982, remains a valuable reference. He wrote by adhering to the perspective of an enthusiastic but politically disinterested observer, attempting to avoid taking editorial positions that a Hawaiian may have felt an obligation to either embrace or denigrate. Nevertheless, he was still sued by a performer who took issue with a statement in the book.[111] Like Mark Twain, who wrote of the Hawaii of a century earlier, Hopkins had the advantage of writing as an outsider, beholden to neither family pressures nor social and political concerns. He summed up the art of hula succinctly, critically, and optimistically: "The hula is a mass of contradiction and paradox, anachronism and idiosyncrasy. It is eccentric. It is alive. It is growing still."[112]

Back to the Ballgame

Kaui Isa-Kahaku descends on her father's side from a Polynesian lineage so old that it's mentioned in the Kumulipo, the 18th century Hawaiian creation chant that provides a genealogy of the royalty of the islands. She and I are sitting in a café in San Jose's Japantown, a neighborhood that's been here so long that photographs exist of its baseball team in the 1890s. Her school, one block away, has its own unique characteristics, but also shares a fundamental philosophical approach not all that different from many—if not all—of the others. I'm initially puzzled as to the reason, considering her ancestry, she isn't honing her craft and teaching it to others back in the islands. Why San Jose? I ask. It turns out that she was her family's first mainland import. "I was inside my mother on the flight to the mainland," she says, "and a few months later, I was born in Santa Clara." Her mother, a third generation Japanese-Hawaiian whose parents arrived in the islands in the early 20th century, was also a dancer. She encouraged her daughter, who began dancing at age three, the same age as many of the girls Kaui now teaches, to pursue the art form. Kaui began giving lessons in her home at the age of 13, on Tuesday and Thursday nights, after the school day had finished. Other nights, she was practicing martial arts, another passion of hers. She founded Halau Na Wai Ola in 1995 and began teaching in conjunction with the county adult education system at a 7,000 square-foot facility in nearby Sunnyvale. Shortly thereafter, she was occupying her own space on Sixth Street in Japantown. She's been there ever since. From the start, she was teaching traditional kahiko, modern auana, carefree hapa haole, the ori (traditional Tahitian dance) and hybrid dances, including hula versions of the rhumba and cha cha.[113] She refers to an early hybrid song, Lena Machado's "E Kuu Baby Hot Cha Cha" (https://www.youtube.com/watch?v=OwEHrT1UjlY), featuring Sol Hoopii on steel guitar, from the pre–World War II years. Lena Kaulumau Waialeale Machado (1903–1974), dubbed "Hawaii's Songbird," had picked up the cha cha from Latin performers she met while performing at San Francisco's Golden Gate International Exposition on Treasure Island in 1939. "Anything we see," Kaui says, "we can hula on it." Like other enduring art forms, hula evolves with the times.

Her hula school, like many others on the mainland, has noticeably long arms, embracing dancers from different ages and backgrounds. She averages 180 to 250 students at any one time, ranging from three years old to dancers old enough that you wouldn't want to be impolite by asking. They are 50 percent Japanese or Japanese American, 35 percent mixed Hawaiian, 15 percent everybody else. Ninety-eight percent of her dancers are women ("We're always looking for men," she says, an invitation and a statement rolled into one). She divides dancers into four formal age groups, corresponding to divisions in hula competitions, ages six to 12, 13 to 35, 36 to 54, and 55 plus. Competition season begins each summer, and Kaui's dancers attend several every year. They're constantly working up to performances and they dance at public or private events more than 20 times annually.

The figure of 50 percent Japanese or Japanese Americans in kumu Kaui's halau might seem surprisingly high, but hula has always been popular with Japanese Americans. A photograph taken in 1942 at the Santa Anita Assembly Center shows five female dancers performing hula before an audience of fellow detainees.[114]

Hula has impacted Japan itself, which has 46 hula schools offering scheduled classes occurring at least once per week, 22 of them in Tokyo alone.[115] There are an estimated 400,000

Halau Na Wai Ola dancers perform at San Jose Municipal Stadium, August 2014 (author's photograph).

hula fans in Japan, and there is always a large contingent from that country traveling to Hilo's Merrie Monarch Festival each year.[116]

Kaui's Halau Na Wai Ola opens up to new students twice a year. Requirements to enroll aren't rigid, but students are expected to take their roles and responsibilities seriously. "They must commit to coming to classes once they enroll, and to focus on their dancing every moment they're here," she says. "They must respect the school. Everything they do, how they behave, whether they're at classes or away from the halau, reflects on the school. Above all, they can't be 'mahaoi.'" That's a word which has no exact translation in English, but which encompasses rudeness, brazenness, nosiness, and disrespect for elders. It's not surprising that many Asian cultures have a similar word for it, but English doesn't (in Thai, for instance, it might be translated as "mariat mai dee"). Often, the behaviors associated with mahaoi are valued or rewarded in Western cultures. Kaui provides an example. "One of my young dancers wanted to know why she hadn't moved up to the next level. 'You can't ask that,' I told her, 'it's an honor when it happens, and you'll be told at the right time.'"

Kaui's background in the discipline associated with martial arts is never far away, and neither is the tremendous responsibility she feels toward her students and her culture. "The

Japanese-American women performing the hula before fellow internees, Santa Anita Assembly Center, 1942 (Flaherty Collection, Japanese Internment Records, MSS-2006-02, San Jose State University, Special Collections & Archives).

hula itself has responsibilities associated with its performance, to our elders and ancestors, and to future generations as well," she says. The majority of students in her halau aren't native Hawaiian. At least not during the day. But at night, in the halau, or when performing on one of their many other stages, they are "locals" in the Hawaiian sense of the word, evoking the aloha spirit and Hawaiian culture, past, present, and future, sharing it among themselves and with those experiencing their performances.

Kaui Isa-Kahaku's dancers always perform in public to music. Music, whether consisting of chants, drums, or ensembles, was traditionally an essential part of the hula performance. For Hawaiian musicians traveling to perform on the mainland in the first part of the 20th century, accompanying hula dancers provided instant access to audiences larger than they would have attained through music alone. Hawaiian music however has always been more than accompaniment to dance. It transformed 20th century American music and branched out to new hybrid forms that sold millions of records in a post–World War II America that seemed to be aching for anything Hawaiian.

Four

Sliding into Paradise
The Hawaiian Steel Guitar

In terms of its impact on mainland audiences, the two most significant Hawaiian musical influences on the music of the 20th century mainland were the Hawaiian steel guitar and the musical genre that has become known as *exotica*.

First introduced to the mainland in the final year of the 19th century, the acoustic Hawaiian slide steel guitar influenced mainland music ranging from Western swing to Delta blues. The world's first successfully marketed electric guitar was, in fact, invented by a guitarist wishing to amplify his Hawaiian steel laptop guitar. The electric steel guitar, along with its Hawaiian technique and phrasing became a vital element in the "sound" that defined western swing in the 1930s, exemplified by Bob Dunn playing with Milton Brown's Musical Brownies, Leon McAuliffe with Bob Wills' Texas Playboys, and Andrew Schroder and Wilson "Lefty" Perkins, both of whom played for Bill Boyd and His Cowboy Ramblers.[1] A further development, the electric pedal steel guitar, became a critical factor in the development of modern country music.

Exotica music, with its instrumental combination of vibes, piano, and Latin percussion, augmented by bird cries and animal calls, soared on the music popularity charts from the mid–1950s through the 1960s. By the 1970s, it had pretty much been given up for dead as rock music pushed "easy listening" instrumentals off the charts. And yet today, it's undergoing a revival, as elements of exotica music continue to crop up in contemporary musical settings, most commonly in jazz and "ambient music" recordings. People continue to write about and enthuse over exotica on websites. Collectors and music fans enthusiastically buy older exotica albums, either by haunting shops and websites selling used vinyl, or buying it reformatted onto newer media. Its cachet of being retro chic attracts younger generations as they are introduced to it via tiki bars, whether newly minted or old enough that their parents might have dated there.

The "long tail" of steel guitar and exotica music is exemplified by the viral manner in which they've crept into different musical forms, separating them, influence-wise, from the ukulele. The emergence of the ukulele was a craze, a social phenomenon, and a musical instrument rolled into one, but it never had a strong influence on non–Hawaiian musical forms. Its tonal limitation, which impeded its potential as a musical influence, was at the same time a large part of its charm. As a picking instrument, it lacks the range of the guitar, and as a strummed rhythmic instrument, particularly in pre–World War II mainland recordings, it was used in much the same way as the banjo. The sub-genre of hapa haole music, with English, pidgin, or nonsensical lyrics, contributed highly to the mass interest in ukulele ownership in the North America. Part of the uke's attraction was that unlike the guitar or vibraphone (a key instrument in later exotica combos), the ukulele was easy enough to play that just about anyone could quickly become musically functional enough to enjoy playing with similarly minded friends. In the islands, of course, its popularity has never waned, and lessons today remain easily available in Hawaii and the mainland.

Hawaiian music was introduced to the mainland on a large scale in the late 19th century, in tours and fair appearances that were primarily driven by interest in the hula. Its mainland popularity surged in the first several decades of the 20th century. Pre radio-era recordings of Hawaiian music proliferated, and Hawaiian touring groups—with or without hula dancers—played in venues all over the U.S. and Canada. The emergence of the *Hawaii Calls* radio program in the 1930s increased mainlanders' access to Hawaii's music and musicians, and fed the increasing interest of Americans to visit the islands themselves. Hawaiian music's clarion call and signature instrumental sound was the Hawaiian steel guitar.

The Hawaiian Steel Guitar: Early Hawaiian Popular Music and Its Antecedents

Hawaiian steel guitar technique is defined by a combination of picking and sliding a metal or glass object along the strings of a steel-bodied guitar to produce "bent" notes and glissando effects. Initially, these techniques were performed on wooden acoustic guitars held across the lap. By the 1920s, metal-bodied resonator guitars, which increased acoustic amplification and provided additional metallic tonal effects in the higher registers, were manufactured by the National String Instrument Corporation and the Dobro Manufacturing Company.

There is some disagreement among scholars as to how the Hawaiian steel guitar sound began in the first place. One theory is that Hawaiian cowboys, known as paniolos, began dragging the back edge of a jackknife along the fret board and strings of a Spanish guitar.[2] More commonly, Joseph Kekuku (1874–1932) is credited as being the original innovator of the Hawaiian slide guitar style and sound, which he developed while a student at the Kamehameha Boys School in Oahu. As far back as 1894, he was using a comb, knife, or a steel bar to bend notes and forge glissandi, gliding from one pitch to another.[3]

The first Hawaiian slide guitarists to arrive on the mainland were July Kealoha Paka (1874–1943) and Tom Hennessy, brought over in 1899 by William Kalii Sumner Ellis (b. 1874) as members of Dr. Kanahele's Hawaiian Music and Musicians to record music on Edison beeswax cylinders.[4] Joseph Kekuku followed in 1904. Other transplanted slide guitarists included Palakiko "Frank Ferera" Ferreira (1885–1951), Walter Kolomoku (b. 1899), and Pale Kealakuhilima Lua (1895–1917). All became prolific performers and recording artists, Ferera with his wife Helen Louise, Kolomoku with the Hawaiian Quintette, Lua with his fellow musician David Kahanamoku Kaili (1897–1998), and July Paka with his wife's Toots Paka's Hawaiians.[5] Another early Hawaiian steel guitarist, Samuel Kalunahelu Nainoa (1877–1954), toured extensively in the Vaudeville circuit after arriving on the mainland in 1912 along with his wife Eugenia. He was a cousin of Joseph Kekuku and played violin with him in their early years in Hawaii. Samuel, Eugenia, and the Nainoa children moved to Los Angeles in the late 1920s, where they played in local venues and he began teaching guitar, steel guitar, and voice at his Nainoa Hawaiian Music Foundation School and Studios. They were involved in several films, including *Mutiny on the Bounty* (1935, dir. Frank Lloyd), *Hurricane* (1937, dir. John Ford), and *South of Pago Pago* (1940, dir. Alfred E. Green).[6]

Frank Ferera was a Portuguese Hawaiian, born in Honolulu, who arrived on the mainland in 1902. He is credited with inventing the triple picking style using a third finger along with a thumb pick. He recorded and toured with his wife Helen Louise (nee Geenus), playing Hawaiian and Mexican music, and popular dances. He was a member of George "Keoki" Elama Kaelemakule Awai's (1891?–1981) Royal Hawaiian Quartet, who performed before many of the estimated 17 million people who entered the Hawaiian Pavilion at San Francisco's Panama-Pacific International Exposition in 1915. It is believed that he and Helen Louise first performed as a guitar duo there. In 1916, their recording of "Drowsy Waters," made for Victor as the Hawaiian Guitar Duet, sold more than 300,000 copies (https://archive.org/details/78_drowsy-waters__gbia0000219b/Drowsy+Waters.flac). Helen Louise, originally from Seattle, was washed overboard in a never-solved mystery, on a voyage from Los Angeles to Seattle aboard the Pacific Steamship Company ship *President* in 1919.[7] Following Louise's death, Frank brought on Anthony J. Franchini as a partner, performing as Franchini and Ferera. He also performed under the name Hilo Hawaiian Orchestra and is estimated to have performed on a quarter of all Hawaiian recordings made between 1915 and 1930. Ferera's impact was so great that his recordings were licensed in 20 countries in an amazing breadth of diverse cultures: Argentina, Australia, Belgium, Canada, China, Croatia, Czechoslovakia, Denmark, France, Germany, Great Britain, Greece, India, Italy, Japan, Mexico, Poland, Spain, Sweden, and Switzerland.[8]

Pale Lua was born on Oahu and began his musical career as a violinist with the Royal Hawaiian Glee Club. He began playing the steel guitar in Hawaii, moved to Cleveland, Ohio in 1910 and embarked on a successful recording and touring career with guitarist David Kaili, who he had met when touring with the Irene West Royal Hawaiians. Lua is thought to be the first steel guitarist to have recorded with Spanish guitar accompaniment.[9]

The Hawaiian Quintette was also known as the Hawaiian Quintette of the Bird of Paradise Company, which may have been the musical group accompanying the famous musical that opened in New York in 1912. Walter Kolomoku was its steel guitarist (Joseph Kekuku joined the performers after the group was reorganized for its European tour in 1919). The Quintette recorded 24 discs for Victor in 1913.[10] San Francisco's Panama-Pacific International Exposition of 1915 featured a Hawaiian Pavilion, whose band, the Royal Hawaiian Quartette, featured steel guitar player Keoki Awai and other Hawaiian steel guests, among them Joseph Kekuku, Frank Ferera, and Pale Lua. The exposition was credited with helping to jump-start the steel guitar and ukulele craze on the mainland.[11]

As the nascent recording industry blossomed throughout the decade, the market was rife with recordings featuring Hawaiian acoustic steel guitar. The Victor Talking Machine Company (and presumably other recording companies as well) placed ads in major newspapers promoting their Hawaiian music catalogues, with flowery descriptions of the romantic idylls to be enjoyed by listening to the sounds of the islands. Such splendor could be acquired by buying a Victor Hawaiian recording, which sold for 75 cents (more than 13 dollars, in today's money). The following description is from an advertisement published in the Feb. 21, 1917, issue of the *New York Tribune*:

All the Fascination of Hawaiian Music Is in These Victor Records

There's a quaint and dreamy beauty to the music of Hawaii as it comes like a whispering breeze from the mid–Pacific. It breathes the lightsome spirit of this land of sunshine. Its languorous rhythm is typical of Hawaiian life, of the swaying trees, the beating surf, of the joys and sorrows of this interesting, music-loving people. All the enrichment of Hawaiian music, all the charm of their quaint instruments, all the peculiar beauties of their light voices are brought to you on Victor Records. You are in fancy transported to the islands.[12]

Hawaiian Steel Guitar: The Second Wave

The second wave of Hawaiian steel guitar players arrived on the mainland between 1920 and 1940, and featured Hal Aloma, Sol K. Bright, Sol Hoopii, Andy Iona, Dick and Lani McIntire, "King Bennie" Nawahi, and Sam Ku West.

Sol Hoopii (Solomon Hoopii Kaaiai, 1902–1979) was born in Honolulu. The first of 21 children, he was playing the ukulele by age three, chose the steel guitar in his teenage years, and debuted with Johnny Noble's orchestra at age 17. He stowed away to San Francisco on the Matson ship *Matsonia* in 1919 and began playing for passengers, who ended up paying his fare. He was brought to Hollywood in the early 1920's to play in cowboy actor and champion roper Edmund Richard "Hoot" Gibson's (1892–1962) western band, said to be the first time a Hawaiian ever performed on stage with a country music group.[13] In 1924 or 1925, he formed the Sol Hoopii Trio, with ukulele player Glenwood Leslie and guitarist Lani McIntire (1904–1951). He played both the Martin acoustic as well as a Rickenbacker Bakelite electric guitar, and may have been the first to use the electric steel guitar for an audience, playing a Rickenbacker A-22 "Frying Pan" prototype at a private party to assist in garnering funds for its production (the A-22 was first played in a public performance by Jack Miller in 1932).[14] His style was described by historians George Kanahele and John Berger as "forceful, sophisticated, suave, and at times flamboyant—as when he used the hollow body of the guitar as a drum and his fingerpicks as the drumstick to fill in a four-beat break."[15]

Hoopii appeared in several films, including *His Jazz Bride* (1926, dir. Herman C. Raymaker), *Bird of Paradise* (1932, dir. King Vidor), *Divorced Sweethearts* (1930, dir. Mack Sennett), *Radio Kisses* (1930, dir. Leslie Pearce), *Flirtation Walk* (1934, dir. Frank Borzage), *High Tension* (1936, dir. Allan Dwan), *Waikiki Wedding* (1937, dir. Frank Tuttle), and *Hawaiian Nights* (1939, dir. Albert S. Rogell). His playing is featured in a Betty Boop cartoon, *Betty's Bamboo Isle* (1932, dir. Dave Fleischer).[16] He also appeared in a number of Charlie Chan films, among them *Charlie Chan at Treasure Island* (1939, dir. Norman Foster). In 1938, he began concentrating on religious music and became an evangelist, touring with Aimee Semple McPherson.[17] Evangelism continued to be the main focus of his career until his death in 1953.

The Sol Hoopii Quartet's 1933 version of "Hula Girl" a rag written by Sonny Cunha, is a tour de force of Hawaiian steel guitar. Here, Hoopii's rapid-fire 16th notes, indicative of the jazz influence on his playing, are interspersed with classic bent notes that are unmistakably Hawaiian in phrasing (https://www.youtube.com/watch?v=Ir2Gtg0PdpY). His note-bending and glissando technique is further showcased in *Musical Moments with Sol Hoopii and His Hawaiian Guitar*, a film made in 1942, featuring hymns played on his Rickenbacker electric steel, accompanied by piano.[18]

Solomon Kekipi (Sol K.) Bright (1909–1992) was born in Honolulu and played drums before moving to the mainland in 1928 to play with Sol Hoopii and learn the steel guitar. Sol K. Bright and His Hawaiians played San Francisco's Golden Gate International Exposition in 1939–1940. From 1946 to 1950, he was the entertainment director for the Tonga Room at San Francisco's Fairmont Hotel, featuring a lagoon crafted from the building's swimming pool. Around 1976, he returned to Hawaii. Bright, who was fascinated by music from other countries, bought himself a set of bagpipes in Canada and played them on his song "The Hawaiian Scotsman." His "La Rosita" of 1932 is a tango with marvelous interpretation on lead steel guitar and includes several bars from "St. Louis Blues" (https://www.youtube.com/watch?v=Y5_SfcV3E8E).[19]

Hal Aloma (Harold David Alama, b. 1908) played with Lani McIntire in the Hawaiian Room at New York's Hotel Lexington (https://archive.org/details/KingKamehameha). He later played with Tommy Dorsey. He appeared on television with Arthur Godfrey, Ed Sullivan, and Perry Como, and he and his band opened Disney World's Polynesian Village in 1971.[20]

Steel guitar player Sam Ku West's (1907–1930) original last name has been reported as either Kuanoni or Kulua. Impresaria Irene West probably heard Sam Ku first in Hawaii in 1925, and he soon joined dancer West's protégée Amie Maynard and her Royal Hawaiians on a tour of Asia, which included Penang, Singapore, and Hong Kong. West split from Maynard in Hong Kong and formed her own group, La Belle Irene and the Royal Hawaiians, showcasing Ku's guitar work. The group toured Java, India, and Shanghai then returned to the mainland U.S. in 1926, where Ku began taking harp lessons from San Francisco Symphony musician Kejetan Atti. He began touring with Irene West's Royal Hawaiians in 1926 and adopted her last name at her suggestion.[21] Moving to the East coast, he performed on guitar and harp on several Vaudeville circuits and began making a series of recordings for Gennett and Banner. The remainder of Ku's life was rife with tours and performances on the mainland, in Hawaii, the Far East, and Europe. He began playing the National Tricone steel guitar and made his last recordings in Oakland in 1928 for Victor. In all, he had recorded 27 discs in a 15-month period beginning in June 1927. He was something of an inventor as well, designing an 18-string double steel guitar that he made as a prototype while in Italy.[22] One of the great hypotheticals in the history of Hawaiian music is how his music might have evolved had he not died in 1930, at the age of 23 in Paris, of a liver abscess.

Sam Ku West had a style that more than occasionally evoked the wild abandon of youth—in this case a 21-year-old—in terms of powerful plunges up and down the fretboard, bending notes to an extreme that stop just short of atonality, or muffling the strings and striking them for percussive ornamentation. This last effect could emulate a snare drum, and can be heard at the 1:39 mark of his "Farewell Blues" (https://www.youtube.com/watch?v=fjP3X5a53xA). His phrasing and overall technique is Baroque, in the classic sense of the word, in its use of ornamentation. Ku's "Huehue" is an amazing pastiche of Hawaiian guitar inflections, from harmonics to severe note bending, verging on atonality. The tune represents a pinnacle of Ku's varied phrasings, radically and playfully changing every four bars, highlighting the multiplicity of sounds that the steel guitar could create (https://www.youtube.com/watch?v=R32tR33GbIg).

Benjamin Keakahiawa "King Bennie" Nawahi (1899–1985) was yet another Hawaiian steel guitarist who influenced mainland entertainers. In 1919, he began appearing with his brother Joe's group, the Hawaiian Novelty Five, on the Matson liner *Matsonia*. The group then began touring the mainland on the Orpheum circuit, but Bennie had left to begin performing as a ukulele and steel guitar performer. His act included such crowd-pleasing effects as playing ukulele behind his head and using his foot instead of a metal bar on the fretboard. Promoter Sid Grauman (1879–1950) called him the "King of the Ukulele," and the name stuck. Nawahi, who played a number of string instruments as well as the harmonica, is viewed today as a major influence to mainland steel guitar players. He incorporated jazz, country, blues, and pop in his playing, and recorded prolifically. His instrumental "Hawaiian Capers" of 1929 provides both Hawaiian and country elements, and is a precursor to western swing (https://www.youtube.com/watch?v=S3zK7nrrQAw). He eventually moved to Los Angeles, where his group King Nawahi and His International Cowboys showcased noted singer, guitarist, and future television star Roy Rogers.[23]

Palm Trees in Winnipeg?

The Hawaiian steel guitar made a significant impact in Canada. Its two its most important figures are William Miles (1877–1979) and Ben Hokea (1898–1971). Miles was a child prodigy who mastered mandolin, banjo, and drums by the time he arrived in Honolulu in 1899, playing with the Sun Circus Band. There he was introduced to the steel guitar by Keoki Akea, and later took lessons in Pasadena in 1902 from a Mexican teacher who had also visited Hawaii. Miles moved to Winnipeg in 1903, where he played in the symphony and began teaching Hawaiian steel guitar. According to Miles, no vaudeville bands playing Hawaiian music had arrived there to that point, and the first touring Hawaiian band to appear north of the border may have been Irene West's Royal Hawaiians in 1910. In approximately 1904, Miles organized a Hawaiian band with Spanish and steel guitars, mandolins, banjos, and eventually ukuleles. His ukulele classes promoted by Eaton's Department Store attracted 2,500 students and Miles held massive 500-pupil classes, taught with the aid of a 10-foot-high ukulele mock-up featuring light bulbs blinking on and off to indicate finger positions. Miles was an accomplished composer and singer as well, and drew up steel guitar solos on tunes that included "Pacific Ripple," selling sheet music for it in 1919. He moved to Toronto in 1922 and refused to adopt the electric steel guitar, feeling that it took away the purity inherent in the Spanish guitar. Miles continued playing and teaching until his death in 1979, ending a career of 73 years.[24]

Steel guitarist Ben Hokea arrived in Toronto in 1915 as a member of Clark's Royal Hawaiians. When the band returned to the United States after several successful years in Canada, Hokea elected to stay. In Toronto and later Montreal, he played at night and taught by day, enrolling so many students that approximately 200 of them were featured in a Hawaiian music concert held at Massey Hall. He toured Canada during the winter months, playing at a number of military camps during the World War I years, performed on the radio and made numerous recordings sold in Canada. Miles and Hokea along with Frank Ferera and Pale Lua, who were popular in Canada due to their recordings, influenced a number of Canadian groups playing Hawaiian and hapa haole music, including Al Campbell and Henry Burr, Charles Harrison, and Allan McGuire.

Fred Van Eps' Quartet and Billy Reid and His Hawaiian Serenaders both had xylophones in their groups.[25] Willis Wilfred "Billy" Reid, from Halifax, began playing on radio station CHNS in 1922 on a run that would last more than 20 years.[26] Canadians bought guitars and learned to play in the Hawaiian style through advertisements and promotions. One of these was Maude Marie Hatt "Marie" Snow 1889–1953), a singer and minstrel performer, who, in the 1920s, bought a kit that included a guitar, lessons, and phonograph records. Her son, country singer Hank Snow (1914–1999), learned to play on that guitar.[27]

The Influence of Hawaiian Steel Guitar on Mainland Musicians

Hawaiian musicians and performing groups had been playing in mainland United States venues since the early part of the 20th century, often as part of Chautauqua circuit groups who, from roughly 1903 to 1930, toured mostly smaller towns, pitching tents and performing during the summer months. The music thus spread in popularity from musicians to the public at large well before Hawaiian music was sold on shellac 78 rpm discs.[28]

Hawaiian steel guitar players influenced a wide number of stateside musicians who recorded in an abundance of styles. Lemon Henry "Blind Lemon" Jefferson (1893–1929) is said to be the first mainland musician to record in the Hawaiian slide steel guitar style, with his "Jack O' Diamonds Blues" of 1926 (https://www.youtube.com/watch?v=xhKBbjmpCrE).[29] Cowboy film star Hoot Gibson is credited with being the first country musician to have a Hawaiian in his group. The Nebraska-born Gibson had displayed a rapt interest in the islands, to the extent that he was a co-sponsor of *The Spirit of Los Angeles*, a plane that entered the Dole Air Derby of 1927, his goal to complete the first civilian non-stop flight from California to the Hawaiian Islands. Steel guitarist Sol Hoopii had arrived in San Francisco in 1919. Sometime in the 1920s, he was invited to Hollywood by Gibson, who introduced him to others and put him in his band Hoot Gibson and the Hawaiian Foursome. They recorded in 1929. Unlike much of the vocal Hawaiian hapa haole music appearing on the recordings of the day, Gibson's vocalist contributed hard-charging, glottal-punctuated Hawaiian lyrics to "Mai Giyee (Don't Give it Away)," embellished by Sol Hoopii's steel guitar (https://www.youtube.com/watch?v=og-aHuSkwFU).

Mainland-born guitarists were catching on quickly to Hawaiian steel guitar, and the first steel guitar instruction book, *Superior Collection of Steel Guitar Solos, Volume I*, by Keoki E.K. Awai, was published by Sherman Clay in 1916 or 1917.[30] Pennsylvania-born Roy Smeck (1900–1994) was one of the best-known mainland musicians specializing in Hawaiian music. He was playing on the vaudeville circuit as early as 1923, and recorded on the octachordia, an eight-string lap steel guitar, in 1928. His short film *His Pastimes*, showcasing the multi-instrumentalist playing octachordia, ukulele, and banjo, accompanied the feature film *Don Juan* (1926, dir. Alan Crosland), both of which showcased the Vitaphone sound-on-disc system (https://www.youtube.com/watch?v=g9CaonSO1Ns). He played at Franklin Delano Roosevelt's inaugural ball of 1933 and made many television appearances and more than 500 recordings. His proficiency with the Hawaiian Spanish guitar slide technique was showcased in his version of "Little Grass Shack" from the short film *Club House Party* (dir. Milton Schwarzwald) of 1932 (https://www.youtube.com/watch?v=oFWf1UFU9_w).[31]

Other mainland guitarists influenced by early Hawaiian steel guitar include white country musicians Jimmie Rodgers, Cliff Carlisle, and Pat Patterson's Champion Rep Riders as well as black guitarists Tampa Red, Son House, Cryin' Sam Collins, and Robert Johnson, along with to the aforementioned Jefferson.[32]

The Steel Guitar Becomes Electric

The first commercially successful electric guitar was the Ro-Pat-In Model A-22, nicknamed the "Frying Pan" due to its shape, which more resembled a beefed-up banjo than a traditional guitar."[33] Guitarist George Delmetia Beauchamp (1899–1941) had invented the electromagnetic string pickup as a means of amplifying the Hawaiian music he had been playing on his lap steel guitar, which he had previously attempted to amplify by connecting it to a radio circuit. After successfully testing his device, Beauchamp enlisted craftsman Harry Watson to engineer the neck and cast aluminum body. Beauchamp then made an agreement with Adolph Rickenbacher (1886–1976) to manufacture the guitar. The Rickenbacher Manufacturing Company had started business in the late 1920s, manufacturing metal bodies for the National String Instrument Corporation.[34] Beauchamp and Rickenbacker (who'd changed the spelling of his name to cash in on the name recognition of his distant cousin, flying ace Eddie Rickenbacker) founded the *Ro-Pat-In Corporation* in 1931, and the Model A-22 was commercially introduced.

Jack Miller was reported to be the first guitarist to play the A-22 in public. Records show that he received his A-22 electric steel guitar on Oct. 30, 1932. He played it at his regular gig at Grauman's Chinese Theater, and joined Orville Knapp's (1904–1936) orchestra in May 1934. The band was booked into the Silver Palm Room in Santa Monica's Grand Hotel, where it broadcast a weekly radio program. This and subsequent tours heightened the popularity of Miller and his new instrument.[35] The first known electric steel guitar recording was reported to be made on Feb. 22, 1933, by the Noelani Hawaiian Orchestra on Victor Records featuring an unidentified steel player.[36]

In 1934, Ro-Pat-In's corporate name was changed to the Electro String Instrument Company and their guitars were known as "Rickenbacker Electro" instruments. Their patent for the electric guitar, requested in 1930, was finally approved on Aug. 10, 1937, delayed by the fact that the U.S. patent office had no category for electrified string instruments. Approximately 2,700 "frying pans" had been sold by 1939, when production ceased. By this time, a number of other companies were producing electric guitars, including Fender Guitar, which started production as early as 1938. Clarence Leonidas "Leo" Fender (1909–1991) had become familiar with Electro String's guitar by repairing their amps in his radio repair shop. During World War II, Fender met Clayton Orr "Doc" Kauffman, an inventor, guitar designer, and steel guitar player working for Rickenbacker. In 1944, Fender and Kauffman formed the K & F Manufacturing Corporation to sell lap top steel guitars and amplifiers, which they sold together in kit form beginning in 1945. In 1948, Fender formed a new company, Fender Guitars, a partnership with Francis C. Hall (1908–1999), whose Radio and Television Equipment Company was one of Fender's prime suppliers. In the new company, Fender was responsible for manufacturing and Hall for distribution. Fender and Hall's rocky business relationship led to Hall leaving, then buying Fender's chief competitor, the Electro String Instrument Company, by purchasing Adolph Rickenbacher's stock in 1953. In 1965, Hall changed the company name to Rickenbacker, Inc.[37] Ironically the remains of these two competitors are within hailing distance of each other at the Fairhaven Memorial Park in Santa Ana, California.[38]

Hawaiian steel guitar was a major influence on noted western swing electric steel players Bob Dunn and Leon McAuliffe, and their recordings in turn influenced a new generation of players. Documentarian Ken Sitz relates a story told by Indiana-born steel guitarist Herb

Remington (b. 1926). Remington was one of thousands enrolled in steel guitar classes formed by the Oahu Publishing Company, finding himself in a class of 15–20 other young students. The best players were invited to join a local "professional club" whose players would occasionally meet in gatherings that would amount to more than 200 steel players. An especially memorable event occurred when clubs from a five-state area met to play, comprising some 1,500 players. "We tuned the guitars (probably within a few half-tones) and murdered 'Stars and Stripes Forever,'" remembered Remington, "only this time probably a hundred decimals louder. This event took place at Soldiers Field in Chicago in August 1940—another day that may live in infamy."[39]

Robert Lee "Bob" Dunn (1908–1971) reportedly first heard Hawaiian steel guitar in a performance by touring Hawaiian musicians in Kusa, Oklahoma in 1917, then took correspondence lessons from Walter Kolomoku.[40] Heavily influenced by the technique of Sol Hoopii, Dunn began playing steel guitar with Milton Brown and His Musical Brownies. Dunn played with Brown beginning in 1934 and stayed until Brown's death in 1936. Brown's "You're Tired of Me" features Dunn's Hoopii-inspired phrasing and note bending, in a tune reminiscent of Hawaiian steel recordings of the era, with the banjo taking up the rhythmic backdrop usually played by the ukulele (https://www.youtube.com/watch?v=B3bESwYW9_8). Dunn's steel guitar introduction to "Taking Off" comes directly out of the Hoopii playbook, with rapid-fire staccato notes and emphatically rendered note bending and flirtations with dissonance. His second solo contrasts his single note and chordal approaches (https://www.youtube.com/watch?v=Zxq2WmrE7cE). Hawaiian music heavily influenced a number of other steel guitarists of the era, including Theron Eugene "Tad" Daffan (1912–1966), who led a group called the Blue Islanders and played Hawaiian on radio station KTRH based in Houston.[41]

William Leon McAuliffe (1917–1988) was perhaps the best known of the western swing steel players. He began playing guitar with the Light Crust Doughboys at age 16 and joined Bob Wills' Texas Playboys in 1935 at the age of 18. He was introduced to the steel guitar by Bob Dunn, and Wills bought McAuliffe his first amplified guitar in 1935. Leon McAuliffe soon became a signature player in Wills' band and although his playing had less of a Hawaiian influence than Dunn's, he can be credited with evolving the steel guitar to what can be characterized today as a more traditionally "western" style of steel playing. McAuliffe bridged the gap between the earlier Hoopii-oriented approach of Dunn and the pedal steel western guitar players that would come later, including Speedy West, Bud Isaacs, and Lloyd Green. McAuliffe's "Steel Guitar Rag" of 1936 (https://www.youtube.com/watch?v=hxzxH6wIPCY) displays his emerging western style as well as a touch of Hawaiian-inspired playing midway through his final chorus. His later "Panhandle Rag" (1949) is a pastiche of Hawaiian, Swing, and Jazz, with McAuliffe "comping" chords, in jazz fashion on his steel guitar behind the solos of other band members (https://www.youtube.com/watch?v=pRoZpvBWwHc).[42] Steel guitarists Andrew "Andy" Schroder and Robert Wilson "Lefty" Perkins both appeared with William Lemuel "Bill" Boyd 1910–1977) and his Cowboy Ramblers, one of whom is featured on the Hawaiian-steel inspired "Roadside Rag" (https://www.youtube.com/watch?v=a4bF5Al39aM).

Wesley Webb "Speedy" West (1924–2003) began playing the National steel guitar in approximately 1937. He moved to Los Angeles in 1946 to get session work, bought a Bigsby pedal Steel guitar in 1948, and recorded on more than 6,000 records with 177 singers during a five-year period in the early 1950s. The Hawaiian influences on West are readily apparent is his exuberant version of "Steel Guitar Rag" (https://www.youtube.com/watch?v=PTi7FPfcWEw).[43]

A sub-genre unto itself, the music of yodeling cowboys dates back to the early Jimmie Rodgers (1897–1933) years. Two yodeling singers who incorporated Hawaiian steel guitar their groups were Cliff Carlisle (1904–1983) and Ottis Dewey "Slim" Whitman (1923–2013). Whitman's extraordinary version of "Hawaiian Cowboy" (1957) includes pedal steel guitar (https://www.youtube.com/watch?v=SkPH_n4Devk).

The Hawaiian influence can be heard in the playing of African American electric steel players Muddy Waters (b. McKinley Morganfield, 1913–1983) and Elmore James (1918–1963), the latter of whom recorded "Hawaiian Boogie" in January 1952 with Ike Turner on rhythm guitar, a tune which is as raw and powerful as any Hawaiian-influenced piece ever recorded (https://www.youtube.com/watch?v=i6kRK2Xdkug). Ohio-born Gerald Lester "Jerry" Byrd (1920–2005) became attracted to the Hawaiian steel guitar at an early age, eventually moving to Hawaii in the early 1970s, and is credited with helping to revive the popularity of the instrument in the islands. He taught many Hawaiians the intricacies of the steel guitar, yet another example of haoles returning to the fount.[44]

Today, the pedal steel guitar is a staple of country and western music, played by guitarists still using the picking and sliding methods introduced by early 20th century Hawaiian musicians. A variation of the Hawaiian sliding metal object was the "bottleneck," a piece of glass or metal tubing used to slide across the strings. Bottleneck, also known as "slide" guitar, became particularly popular with the acoustic blues musicians exemplified by Mississippi Fred McDowell, who started by playing a filed-down beef bone, electric blues artists including Elmore James and Hound Dog Taylor, and a large number of rock guitarists, the best-known of whom included Duane Allman, Ry Cooder, Peter Green, Alvin Lee, Johnny Winter, and Ronnie Wood.

Although not influenced per se by Hawaiian music or vocals, a number of mainland singers and musicians flirted with hapa haole music, often utilizing the talents of notable Hawaiian musicians. The Mills Brothers 1933 up-tempo version of "My Little Grass Shack in Kealakekua Hawaii," featured the Brothers singing and doing vocal imitations of jazz trumpets and trombone https://www.youtube.com/watch?v=HavCL3J6Fz8). Louis Armstrong joined Andy Iona (1902–1966) and his Islanders for a recording session in 1936, and one of the results was "On a Little Bamboo Bridge," with a restrained vocal and wonderful muted trumpet solo by Armstrong, accompanied by Iona's steel guitar and band (https://www.youtube.com/watch?v=IZXyggvjtLc). In 1943, Dorothy Lamour covered "My Little Grass Shack in Kealakekua Hawaii," accompanied by Dick McIntire (1900?–1951) and His Harmony Hawaiians (https://www.youtube.com/watch?v=80tzNvVT6Nk). Singer and actress Frances Langford combined with steel guitarist Dick McIntire in 1945 to sing her hit "In Waikiki" (https://www.youtube.com/watch?v=Dnf70FF_A9o). Ethel Merman recorded a cover of "Ukulele Lady" in 1950, made famous by Hilo Hattie in 1940, and Jo Stafford offered a version of "Hawaiian War Chant" in 1951. This small list indicates the impact of Hawaiian music on mainland popular music throughout much of the 20th century, and just barely scratches the surface of the breadth of performers recording at least one hapa haole song.

Hello Haole Hawaiian

Neither the vibraphone, nor jazz, nor the genre of exotica music had much to do with a sub-category of Hawaiian music first identified in print by writer Jerry Hopkins in 1979.

Everyone who bought a Hawaiian music album in the era was familiar with those that performed it and the music was typically either loved or loathed. One found it difficult to be non-committal. Hopkins termed it "Haole Hawaiian," and it consisted of Hawaiian or Hawaiian-influenced songs and melodies recorded by well-known mainland performers that American radio would mostly term MOR (Middle of the Road) artists. Hopkins called it the third wave of Western Hawaiian music, the first beginning with Tin Pan Alley and the second occurring in the late 1930s, with well-known singers including Bing Crosby, singing "Sweet Leilani" and other hapa Haole songs. Hopkins' third wave, haole Hawaiian, was popular from the mid–1950s through the 1970s. In two articles Hopkins wrote for the Hawaiian music publication *Hailono Mele* in 1979, he identified and reviewed 42 haole Hawaiian albums, by popular artists that included Dick Contino, Ray Conniff, Bill (Jose Jimenez) Dana, Burl Ives, 101 Strings, Hugo Winterhalter, and Andy Williams. Hopkins girded for war and really did listen to each album, including *Golden Hawaiian Hits* by The Banjo Barons ("12 medleys ... 36 songs in all, blessedly short").[45]

Indigenous and Derivative Hawaiian Song Forms

Hawaiian music with which most mainlanders were familiar, Tin Pan Alley, hapa haole, and haole Hawaiian songs, had very little in common with traditional island music. In his Ph.D. thesis *The Development of Waikiki, 1900–1949: The Formative Period of an American Resort Paradise*, scholar Masakazu Ejiri notes that there are six forms of music which may be said to be indigenous to Hawaii, each reflective of a historical point in time:

- Mele oli (chanting only), mele hula (chanting with hula dancing), and mele hula kui: The former two are chants related to, but not always deriving from the pre-contact era; the latter represents a chant and dance style with Western influence, developed in the late 19th and early 20th centuries from mele hula.
- Himeni: hymns related to 19th century missionaries.
- Himeni-like songs: non-religious songs related to Hawaiian royalty, based on Western melodies and harmonies.
- Hula songs: folk songs based on hula kui.
- Hapa haole songs: part-white or foreign songs, originally based on hula kui, blending with mainland popular songs.
- "Contemporary Hawaiian" songs: influenced by Western popular music.[46]

It's worth noting that hapa haole songs made Ejiri's list. Untold numbers of mainlanders who were unfamiliar with them before they left for Hawaii soon found out about them when they attended a musical show aboard ship or at a Waikiki hotel.

Johnny Noble's Role in Popularizing Hotel Hapa Haole Music

Hapa haole music was especially popular as hotel musical entertainment, both on Waikiki and on the mainland. The tunes were hummable and the words, largely in English, were intelligible to those who spoke little or no Hawaiian. Its lyrics typically spoke of romantic images associated with Hawaii, including swaying palms, hula girls, and the soft sands of Waikiki. The rhythms were simple, in 4/4 time or 3/4 waltzes. Bandleader John Avery "Johnny" Noble (1892–1944) was a Honolulu-born drummer, pianist, xylophone player, composer, and arranger whose blend of Hawaiian lyrics, ragtime jazz, blues, and hapa haole music introduced "Hawaiian pop" music to large numbers of mainland audiences through recordings, radio broadcasts, and performances. Born in Honolulu, Noble studied music from a young age and performed in a number of musical groups before joining Sonny Cunha's hapa haole band in 1918. In 1919, he joined the Moana Hotel orchestra as a drummer, and then pianist. He took over leadership of the orchestra in 1920, and co-wrote, with Cunha, the "Hula Blues" the same year. When the Royal Hawaiian Hotel opened in 1927, Noble was hired to lead its house orchestra.

Feeling that the complexities of much of the new music coming from the mainland were becoming a significant challenge for his musicians, he disbanded the orchestra in 1931, intending to pursue song writing and other musical endeavors. Mainland musician Harry Robert Owens (1902–1986) was brought in to lead the hotel's orchestra. In 1934, Noble became the Director of Entertainment for the Royal Hawaiian and Moana Hotels, both owned by Matson Navigation. "Johnny Noble Day" was declared on April 23, 1938, celebrating his 25th anniversary in the music business. On that occasion, he performed again with members of his old Moana Hotel orchestra at the Princess Theater. He eventually wrote or co-wrote some 30 hula kui pieces and went on to collect and publish a large number of Hawaiian traditional songs, copyrighting his arrangements in the process. Although reflecting a Westernized approach in performance, he used traditional instruments including the gourd, split bamboo rattles, and iliili stones as percussion accents. His music epitomized the dreams of the mainland tourist resort culture, with heavy emphasis on evoking the usual idylls—whether real or imagined—to be found on the beach at Waikiki. Today, he is perhaps best known for his novelty songs, many of which are still in the repertoire of musicians performing Hawaiian hapa haole music. These include "My Little Grass Shack," "King Kamehameha," and "Moku Kia Kahi" ("One Masted Schooner Hula"), co-written with Lydia Bray, a double-entendre song referring to a sexually aroused male. He is also given credit for popularizing the "Hawaiian War Chant." He died in 1944, at the age of 51.[47]

A classic song in the Noble repertoire was "I Went to Hilo," written and sung by Samuel Ah Sin "Sam" Alama (b. 1898). Its words are sung in English and Hawaiian with falsetto vocal passages, embellished by a short steel guitar break. The song represents something of a geographical and cultural tour of the islands, referring to three islands, two volcanoes, and the Moana Hotel on Waikiki. It also refers to three girls of different and mixed ethnicities as well as items including as leis and ice cream, commonly associated with each island (https://www.youtube.com/watch?v=JlWEth2hsho).[48]

A Johnny Noble and His Hawaiian Music recording, "Kukuna o Ka La," typical of the understated elegance of much of his music, was made in 1935. It opens with several bars of steel guitar, followed by a vocal that soon soars into a falsetto, returns with a steel guitar break, then breaks into a choral section. The pattern is repeated several times, with all words being sung in Hawaiian (https://www.youtube.com/watch?v=tY8TVG87G0w).

A memorable version of Noble's song "'King Kamehameha," performed by Lani McIntire and His Orchestra, was filmed in 1947, during McIntire's residency as the leader of the house band at New York's Hotel Lexington Hawaiian Room (he would remain in that capacity until 1951, the year of his death).[49] McIntire's is a Hawaiian Swing version of the classic song, driven by Hal Aloma's elegantly phrased steel guitar, McIntire's vocals, and a well-choreographed quartet of hula dancers (https://archive.org/details/KingKamehameha).

The song was written by Johnny Noble and Ted Fio Rito and included *"Ua mau ke ea o ka aine i ka pono"* [first spoken by Kamehameha III in 1843, it can be translated as "The sovereignty of the land is perpetuated in righteousness"].[50]

Much of the reason that the popularity of hapa haole music remained unabated for several decades was due to the influence of a radio program emanating from Hawaii. It was called, appropriately, *Hawaii Calls*.

It's Hawaii, Calling You on the Shortwave Radio

"We listened to *Hawaii Calls* on the radio just to hear the surf roll up on the beach. The songs, the romance, the dreams of being there," John Severson recalled.[51]

Perhaps the Hawaiian musical experience most effective in reaching mainland ears in the years bookending World War II was producer and host Webley Edwards' (1902–1977) 30-minute weekly radio program *Hawaii Calls*. Radio had become a mainland entertainment phenomenon for more than a decade prior to Edwards' initial broadcast on July 3, 1935. From its early beginnings in 1920 with KDKA in Pittsburgh, radio listening increased all over the nation. By 1924, 30 percent of mainland furniture budgets were being spent on radio receivers. In 1930, 40 percent of American homes had radios, a figure that jumped to 82 percent by 1938.[52]

Hawaii Calls began broadcasting from the outdoor stage at Matson Navigation's Royal Hawaiian Hotel, later moving to the lanai stage at the Banyan Court of the shipping company's Moana Hotel. The show was beamed to the United States and the rest of the world via shortwave radio. The live audience consisted of 1,000 to 2,000 residents and visitors. Harry Owens (1902–1986, composer of the well-known song "Sweet Leilani," dedicated to his newly born daughter) conducted the 11-piece Royal Hawaiian Orchestra.[53] The program, showcased a number of noteworthy musical guests, including vocalists Alfred Apaka (b. Alfred Aholo Afat Jr., 1919–1960), slack key and steel guitarist Philip Kunia "Gabby" Pahinui (1921–1980), and Al Kealoha Perry's (1901–1979) Singing Surfriders. Dancing was performed by the "Waikiki Girls," and many other soloists, including Louise Akea Silva and Napua Stevens, appeared on the show from 1937 to 1940.[54] The show's longevity resulted in world exposure to two generations of Hawaii's most notable singers and musicians.[55]

Hawaii Calls promoted the new style of Hawaiian music popularized in the 1920s, based on hula kui chants and music, adorned with falsetto vocals and Hawaiian steel guitars. Its repertoire began with of approximately 100 Hawaiian songs, sung mainly in English for the benefit of international radio audiences, with 10 featured on each half-hour broadcast. To avoid repetition, additional songs were collected from archival music resources and villages. Eventually, the program drew from approximately 1,500 compositions. A signature element of the show was a mix of the sound of Waikiki's crashing surf, punctuated by the steel guitar melodies of David Kelii, who was with the show from practically its inception to 1952. Dozens of mainland celebrities and show business people including Al Jolson and Arthur Godfrey made guest appearances on the program, underscoring the romantic magnetism of the islands.[56] Edwards would be remembered as the "voice of Hawaii," closing each show with an invitation: "All of us wish you were here with us—here in Hawaii—on this fine day. Come on over and see us sometime!" *Hawaii Calls* was a key factor in creating a yearning in the minds of its mainland and world audiences to visit Hawaii and experience the islands' edenic qualities for themselves. In the pre-war years, it represented a mythical, romantic dream for most Americans who would never be able to afford the costs for Hawaiian travel in that era. With the proliferation of affordable airfares in the post-war years, the beckoning shores of Waikiki became a reality for middle class mainlanders, who could also now share in the excitement of seeing the show live.[57]

The program lasted for 40 years, with a brief intermission during the war years. At its height in 1952, it was carried by 750 radio stations all over the world. The program would occasionally be broadcast from other islands and venues, including the *Matsonia* passenger liner. Its final broadcast on Aug. 16, 1975 was made from the Cinerama Reef Hotel, the last of 2,083 shows. By then, its popularity having waned, the program was carried by only 10 radio affiliates. Its territorial and state government subsidies, which had sustained the commercial-free program for decades as a promotion for Hawaiian tourism, had finally ended, bringing the close to a barely believable 40-year run. More than 300 of Hawaii's singers and musician had appeared on the program.[58] Edwards also made some 23 record albums of varying vocal and instrumental treatments, including the remarkably strange *Webley Edwards Presents: Hawaii Calls Romantic Instrumentals of the Islands* (1963, Capitol Records), prominently featuring the Hammond organ, swelling behind steel guitars, vibes, and chorus (https://www.youtube.com/watch?v=MQFwuKxRJFs).

With much fanfare, *Hawaii Calls* was re-launched in late 1992 after a hiatus of 17 years. No longer broadcast live, this new iteration was taped at the Hilton Hawaiian Village's beachside Tropics Showroom before an audience numbering 350 (a quarter of them locals, the remainder tourists), then transmitted via satellite to affiliates. Once a month the program was taped on one of the neighboring islands. It was produced by veteran island broadcaster Bill Bigelow and featured, among other performers, steel guitar player Barney Isaacs (1924–1996), who played on the original program from 1960 until its end in 1975. The weekly half-hour show was broadcast by 50 radio stations on the mainland as well as a number of Asia-based stations. The show failed to attract enough advertising to keep it afloat and ended a year after it began.[59]

Entering into the fifth decade of the 20th century, Hawaiian showrooms in America's hotels were still booming, Hawaii was prominent in recorded music and films, and *Hawaii Calls* kept the islands firmly in the minds of radio listeners. The Hawaiian steel guitar had made its mark on country music. In 1951, a new phonograph record would appear that would lead to the next surge in Hawaiian-inspired music on the mainland. Its creator wasn't Hawaiian, and he cited among his main influences Claude Debussy, Maurice Ravel, and Igor Stravinsky.

Five

Ring My Bell
Music from the Paradise of Exotica

> "My music is a combination of the South Pacific and the Orient ... what a lot of people *imagined* the islands to be like. It's pure fantasy, though. A lot of tourists have listened to my records, and when they come to Hawaii they expect some kind of romantic setting like James A. Michener conjured up in *South Pacific*."—Martin Denny[1]

Perhaps the simplest way to describe the music we today call "exotica"—a term coined by producer Si Waronker in 1957—is to call it, in its purest form, a collection of compositions, typically based on minor tonality, driven by an ostinato bass line, played by a musical ensemble often consisting of vibraphone, piano, and Latin percussion. This may be accentuated with animal and birdcalls voiced by the musicians, creating a sound evocative of exotic localities, most generally those associated with the Pacific islands. Exotica eventually encompassed a larger sphere, but this definition describes its fundamental elements. The music developed and thrived thanks to three artists who essentially defined the genre in its formative years; the first provided the playbook, the second created its signature sound, and the third supplied the technique to take it to its artistic summit. The creation of a "book" of tunes that were inherently exotic in themselves, rather than being originally associated with any other genre, is credited by many historians as being an essential element leading to the formation of exotica. The writer of that book was Les Baxter. The genre also needed an ensemble consisting of musical instrumentation and vocal nuances that would be uniquely associated in the minds of listeners with that sound. This was created by Martin Denny. It also needed a "star," technically proficient enough to carry the music to new levels of sophistication and artistry. That man was Arthur Lyman. Although exotica was played by thousands of musicians, solo, in combos, or large orchestras, much of the history of exotica revolves around the personal stories of Baxter, Denny, and Lyman.

Its heyday, in terms of mass popularity, occurred in the brief five-year period spanning approximately 1957 to 1962, and in spite of the waxing and waning interest on the part of music lovers, exotica music never completely disappeared. Musicians recording exotica albums ranged from small combo and orchestra leaders to individuals with histories largely forgotten. At least two musicians recording music included in the exotica genre could be considered ascetics. George Alexander Aberle (1908–1995), known as eden ahbez—he preferred the lower case spelling—recorded his *Eden's Island* album in 1960 on Del-Fi Records, lived a vegetarian lifestyle, and for a time camped under the first "L" on the Hollywood sign in Los Angeles. He is best known composition, "Nature Boy," was a hit for singer Nat King Cole in 1948.[2] Ahbez' peripatetic existence is reminiscent of that of beachcomber/designer Eli Hedley, discussed later.[3] Russell "Russ" Garcia (1916–2011), whose album *Fantastica* (1959, Liberty) combined exotica with themes related to outer space, sold all his possessions in 1966 and sailed in the Pacific for three years, spreading the philosophy of the Baha'i faith, before finally settling in New Zealand.[4]

The exotica genre is almost universally agreed to have begun with Les Baxter's orchestral recording of 1951, *Ritual of the Savage* (https://www.youtube.com/watch?v=XTwwnEggw24). Not only did the album break new ground in creating a sound palette evocative of the exotic and the primitive, it was the source of a number of compositions that represented a series of exotica "standards" that were in the repertoire of every ensemble that made its living by focusing on the genre. The anthemic Baxter composition "Quiet Village," probably the most recorded tune in in the genre, was introduced on Baxter's *Savage* album, although it achieved its greatest fame when recorded by Martin Denny and his combo several years later.

Exotica can be said to be "atmospheric" in the sense that it's evocative of a time and place that is, in all probability, geographically far removed from the immediate environment of the listener. The place in time is the Pacific island region, Polynesia, to be more specific, in the decades that preceded World War II and the two that followed. The music is replete with an edenic quality reflective of the romance, fragrance, balmy breezes, languorous atmosphere, and lush tropical beauty commonly associated with Hawaii and other islands in the Pacific. Without a notion, of course, of the humidity, the mosquitoes, the saline sea air that consumes every metal object one owns, the termites that make meals out of wooden houses, and on the Big Island, the vog.[5] Exotica music evokes Hawaii, to be sure, but just how "Hawaiian" is it?

Critic and musicologist Shuhei Husokawa notes that exotica music never included the ukulele or slack key guitar (or, for that matter, steel guitar) traditionally associated with Hawaiian music in the 20th century.[6] In writing of Martin Denny's ensemble, Husokawa notes: "What exotica represents is not so much Hawaiianness but *paradise-ness*. For Denny, Hawaii is simply one imaginable earthly paradise. What is at stake in his live performance is the ability to associate Hawaii with any sort of paradisiacal fantasy in the minds of tourists visiting the islands—tourists who have just been released from their daily routines into (keenly anticipated) environs such as daiquiri lounges. In this regard, they are no longer 'armchair travellers' but 'cane-chair travellers.'"[7]

Exotica engendered a specific packaging concept particular to a tropical fantasy as well. Album covers featured elements commonly associated with Hawaii, the South Pacific, and the Orient, including bamboo, rattan furniture, grass huts, wooden tikis and masks, jungle foliage, waterfalls, volcanoes, and pyroclastic activity. There was even an exotica "cover girl," Sandy Faye Warner (b.1935), who graced the cover of Martin Denny's first albums (and a total of 16 in all), in different states of dress and undress, hair-color, and jewelry.[8]

Although the three names most commonly associated with exotica, Les Baxter, Martin Denny, and Arthur Lyman, are essentially products of the 1950s, its roots reach back three millennia. It can also be said that it has influenced a number of musicians operating within the framework variously called "world beat" or "world music," catchall terms that broadly encompass music played primarily on non-Western instruments.[9] In terms of jazz, exotica

Sandy Warner, exotica music's "cover girl."

appears to have had a direct influence on a sub-genre of music I'll call "post-exotica," in which classic elements of exotica are used as rhythmic, melodic, and harmonic bases for music that utilizes extended improvisational solos. Two musicians frequently playing within a post-exotic framework are jazz pianist McCoy Tyner and vibes player Bobby Hutcherson, who, playing together or in their own groups, evoke something akin to a highbrow exotica form (two notable examples are "Little Madiba" and "African Village," from the album *Time for Tyner*, recorded in 1968).[10] Post-exotica pervasively includes work by numerous lesser-known musicians. Just one example would be jazz drummer Stix Hooper's "Jasmine Breeze," from the album *The World Within* (1979), which evidences several of the basic elements found in exotica, replacing piano and vibes with Japanese shakuhachi and koto.[11] One could argue that there are also post-exotic elements in non-tropical, but decidedly Eastern albums, for example flautist Herbie Mann's *Gagaku & Beyond* (1976). One element of exotica not commonly found in much of the realm of post-exotica is the use of bird and animal calls, with the caveat that the Brazilian cuica, a percussion instrument capable of a wide range of groans, screeches, and cries, is often substituted instead, resulting in much the same effect.[12] The exotica genre also influenced a number of rock bands, particularly those of the late 1960s–early 1970s, including Peter Green–era Fleetwood Mac, the Dutch group Focus, and England's Jade Warrior.[13]

Elements of Classic Exotica

The elements of classic exotica are all present in Martin Denny's prototypical interpretation of Les Baxter's composition "Quiet Village," released in 1958. The tune, prominent during the heyday of Top 40 radio and long-playing phonograph recordings, remains the most popular example of exotica ever recorded, rising up to number four on the pop hit charts on June 1, 1959, and number 11 on the R&B charts.[14]

Classic Exotica has a signature sound that can be defined, in its most representational form, as having up to seven basic musical elements. Some of the most representative examples of exotica music actually contain all seven, while those evidencing three or more may still be considered definitive to the extent that they easily fall into the genre:

- Instrumentation: lead melodic instruments commonly consist of vibes and piano, often played in unison. These will occasionally be augmented by a flute. The remainder of the ensemble consists of percussion instruments otherwise associated either with Latin music, marimba, bongos, congas, and guiro, for example, or Asian music, consisting of gongs, temple bells, and wind chimes. An exotic ensemble may be rounded out with anything from conch shells to mechanical birdcalls to malleted tom-toms and steel drums.
- Exotica compositions are most commonly written in a minor key.
- An ostinato (repeating) bass line forms the rhythmic basis for much of the music. Any variation of instruments may maintain the ostinato, including malleted drums.
- The main melody is often played in fourths or parallel octaves, typically on piano alone or doubled with vibes and commonly including arpeggiated sequences occurring every 8 or 16 bars.
- Pedal point, a musical technique in which a fundamental bass tone repeats through multiple chord progressions, occurs in a large number of exotica pieces, particularly those of Arthur Lyman, in which pedal point involves the piano and vibes, both solo and in tandem.
- An abundance of rhythmic elements commonly found in Latin music, involving clave rhythm (5/4), reverse clave, and quarter- note triplets reflected in the melodic passages (e.g., "Quiet Village").
- Animal and bird calls, co-created as a musical element by Augie Colón and Arthur Lyman while members of Martin Denny's group, are a fundamental characteristic of many exotica pieces. Not all exotica music features bird and animal calls, but music featuring bird and animal calls is almost always exotica.

The Foundations of Exotica

The roots of exotica were formed by Les Baxter, extended to the quintet led by Martin Denny, and achieved their greatest technical brilliance in the work of Denny alumnus Arthur Lyman. Along the way, numerous other small groups and orchestras performed in lounges and on recordings. Exotica's originator, Les Baxter, was a complex individual who soared to great heights and plunged to significant depths in his career, both artistically and financially.

He gave birth to this new genre, from a recording perspective, in 1950, with assistance from a Peruvian diva.

Les Baxter

Texas-born Leslie Thompson "Les" Baxter (1922–1996) released his recording *Ritual of the Savage (Le Sacre du Sauvage)* in 1951, a foundation work that encoded and cemented the concepts that would lead to the development of exotica music. Of the 12 cuts on the record, six ("Quiet Village," "Bangkok Cockfight," "Busy Port," "Jungle Flower," "Coronation," and "Love Dance") have become exotica standards, recorded as staples of exotica musicians and albums into the 1960s. Baxter intended the album to be a tribute of sorts to Igor Stravinsky, whom he cited as an influence as a composer and orchestrator, while introducing African, South American, and Cuban motifs to the music.[15] *Ritual* was heavily orchestrated, with flutes in the lead for much of the arrangements, accompanied by a variety of woodwinds, over a foundation of Latin rhythm and percussion. Strings, which occasionally took over the melodic lead ("Jungle Flower"), and voices were written into the orchestrations, which utilized brass instruments solely in a supporting role. "Busy Port," the first piece on the disc, establishes several of the musical motifs heard throughout the recording, including an ostinato bass line, a mambo rhythmic beat, and a quarter-note triplet passage.

In the liner notes to the album, Baxter described the music as offering a "tone poem of the sound and the struggle of the jungle." Discussing the album in the book *Widening the Horizon: Exoticism in Post-War Popular Music*, musicologist Rebecca Leydon notes "Baxterisms" recurrent in the music, including a modally flavored ostinato bass pattern, voices in parallel triads, nonfunctional chromaticism, destabilizing syncopations, and "Sonorities that suggest a whole-tone collection.... With the particular registral deployment of melody and accompaniment in [a] three-voice texture, Baxter is employing a surefire technique designed to induce a specific physical response from his listeners." Leydon further provides a transcript of the opening measures of the album's "Quiet Village" as support evidence.[16]

Les Baxter was born in Mexia, Texas. He moved to Detroit in 1928 as a result of his parents' decision to seek an improved economic situation. His formal music studies began at the age of seven in 1929, at the Detroit Conservatory of Music. By the time he was nine, he was playing classical selections on piano and clarinet, and at the age of 10 was accompanying instrumentalists and singers in concerts. He began playing piano between theater matinees in his 12th year. In 1933, he moved with his mother to Los Angeles, and throughout his high school years, played as a tenor, alto, and clarinet sideman in various local dance bands. According to biographer James Spencer, Baxter also took advantage of having the personal freedom to enjoy something of an underground and bohemian lifestyle. Baxter told stories of gas stations that were fronts for prostitution rings where teenage boys could make a quick buck by servicing both women and men. Baxter played in dive bars during his high school years and enjoyed that scene. In later years, he remained cagey about his precise involvement. "It was 1940s Hollywood," he reminisced, "things happened.... I was young and in the land where dreams could come true. I soaked up all the life I could, and this meant the joyous as well as the seedy side. I have no regrets."[17]

Baxter studied at George Pepperdine College in Los Angeles beginning in 1939, but, unhappy with its Christian moral code and frustrated with the music department's emphasis on music of the Classical and Romantic eras, he left before completing his degree. As a requirement for graduation, he composed a chamber piece, "Pan's Merriments," scored for two flutes, oboe, bassoon, clarinet, and piano. It was influenced by Debussy's use of ancient Greek modality, and included sequences based on the Phrygian, Aeolian, Dorian, and Lydian scales. Impressed with Duke Ellington's band of the 1939–1941 years, Baxter became friends with Duke Ellington sidemen Albany Leon "Barney" Bigard (1906–1980) and Benjamin Francis "Ben" Webster (1909–1973), who were playing in small ensembles in the Los Angeles area. Baxter would discuss his arrangements with Webster, who would critique them and offer advice on chord changes and melody. Baxter also listened extensively to the work of tenor saxophonists Lester Young and Coleman Hawkins. Hawkins' famous solo on Johnny Green's "Body and Soul," with its "vertical" interpretation of chord changes, was the most studied jazz solo of the era.[18]

In 1942, Baxter left Pepperdine College to join clarinetist Barney Bigard in his Sextet. Soon, both Baxter and Bigard would join boogie pianist Frederick Charles "Freddie" Slack's (1910–1965) jazz band, a group soon augmented by electric guitarist Aaron Thibeaux "T-Bone" Walker (1910–1975). The band's hit single, "Cow Cow Boogie," sung by 17-year-old Ella Mae Morse (1924–1999), reached number one on the Hit Parade in 1942 as Capitol Records' first gold single.[19] Baxter joined singer Melvin Howard "Mel" Tormé's (1925–1999) singing ensemble, The Mel-Tones, in 1944 as a lower baritone-bass voice. Baxter's value included the fact that he could sight-read, compose, and arrange. Baxter left the group in 1946 and began singing commercials radio shows including *The Maxwell House Hour* and The *Pepsodent Show*, starring Bob Hope. During the next several years, he put together two more singing groups, the Les Baxter Trio and the four-voice Miriam Singing Group.[20]

Baxter's first major recorded effort was the extended play album *Music Out of the Moon: Music Unusual Featuring The Theremin–Themes By Harry Revel*, released in 1947, featuring orchestra, chorus, and theremin, playing Baxter's arrangements of composer Harry Revel's (1905–1958) themes. The individual song titles carried space-related themes, "Lunar Rhapsody" and "Mist O' The Moon" for example, and the recording originated the idea of the "concept album," in which the musical themes, album packaging, and liner notes combined to form a unified marketable musical concept. It was the first album cover to feature a color photograph, and the first to sport a cheesecake model (Virginia Clark).[21] Revel, who had sought out Baxter to score the album, followed it up a year later with the recording *Perfume Set to Music*, again utilizing Baxter's arrangements in a similar musical format.

Baxter's first foray into the world of exotica would occur with the 1950 release of Peruvian singer Yma Sumac's (1922?–2008) *Voice of the Xtabay* (https://www.youtube.com/watch?v=xpfs4vN4lkI), featuring Baxter's compositions and arrangements. Sumac was exotica's first "star," a possessor of a mercurial personality who meticulously managed her "back story" and public image. Born Zoila Augusta Emperatriz Chávarri del Castillo in either Callao or Ichocán, Peru, she marketed herself as a descendant of Inca ruler Atahualpa. Her status as a South American legend at the approximate age of 27 was underscored by the liner notes of the album:

"Small wonder that in the mysterious land of the Incas, Yma assumed an almost deified position as 'the bird who became a woman,' and 'the voice of the earthquake.' No one in the native village of Ichocan, 16,000 feet high in the Andes of Peru, had ever heard such a voice in human form when this 'chosen maiden' sang at their annual festivals to the sun ... when exciting rumors of her rare talent and beauty reached officials of the Peruvian government, they arranged to bring Yma Sumac down to the coastlands ... a decision that almost caused an uprising among some thirty thousand Indians over the loss of their revered ritual singer."

Sumac was renowned for her vocal range and inflections, described by writer Rebecca Leydon as "growling, her vibrato, her gasps and groans ... an unearthly rasping *sprechstimme*, punctuated by husky laughter and breathy gasps."[22] She began performing in South American radio programs in 1942 and recorded her first tracks in Argentina in 1943. She moved to New York City along with her husband, Moisés Vivanco in 1946 and performed along with him in the Inka Taky Trio, heard by Baxter on a visit to New York in 1949. With Baxter's assistance, she was soon signed by Capitol Records. On *Xtabay*, which featured Baxter's original compositions, Latin rhythms and percussion augment Baxter's orchestra and Sumac's voice.[23] He also manipulated her vocals with tape editing. "It was before we had all the buttons we have now," Baxter said. "We simply had her do her phrases until we got what we liked. And there we had a phrase going up high. And then we had her rest—had her sit down—'Hit the high f,' and when she finally hit the high f we'd paste it on the end of the progression. So she's pasted a lot."[24]

In a 1992 interview with biographer James Spencer, Baxter discussed the difficulties of working with Sumac and her husband, Moisés Vivanco. Upon hearing Spencer recite from the liner notes of a later re-release of the album, Baxter unveiled some of the mysteries behind the mystique. Spencer read, "but this beautiful Incan princess displays ... tonal color [resulting] in a unique and spellbinding experience." Baxter replied: "Incan princess my ass, she was a self-fabricated hard-to-work with prima donna from a small, rural working class seaside village, as common as they come, but yes her voice was indeed extraordinary and easily four octaves if not four and a half." Spencer continued reading from the liner notes: "And in a faraway world of her native Ichocan, the natives still regard her as the reincarnation of Xtabay, lovely and mysterious woman of the Inca legend." In reply, Baxter said, "Xtabay is just a pidgin made up jumble of my last name Baxter ... look closely BAXTER ... XTABAY"[25]

The Sumac album is particularly notable for the thematic approach Baxter would employ to even greater effect in his following album, *Ritual of the Savage* (1951). After *Ritual*, Baxter went on to produce several other concept albums with orchestra and chorus that displayed his interest in the exotic, including *Tamboo!* (1956, https://www.youtube.com/watch?v=ppDPLxzLOJU) and *The Sacred Idol* (1960, https://www.youtube.com/watch?v=EDMI7ez0NZo). None of his subsequent albums, however, would have the impact or influence, compositionally, that *Savage* did. Baxter later made a name for himself in film scoring, but also descended to an artistic low by recording pop orchestral schmaltz LPs, including Arthur Murray dance albums and recordings with the 101 Strings, mostly featuring pop-tune warhorses rather than his own compositions.[26] In a sense, he was a victim of his own early success. To support his lavish lifestyle, he had signed agreements that required a continual output of albums to fulfill the terms of the contracts, producing recordings that even he agreed didn't measure up to his once-exacting standards. He eventually made more than 60 albums, yet reportedly owned no vinyl copies of them at the time of his death.[27]

Martin Denny

New York City–born pianist Martin Denny (1911–2005) is credited with being the creator of the classic exotica musical combo, consisting of piano, vibes, bass, and Latin percussion. The animal and bird cries made by group members—for which Denny was also noted—were originated by vibes player Arthur Lyman and percussionist Augie Colón while members of Denny's ensemble. Denny recorded 37 albums with total sales of more than four million copies. His cover of Les Baxter's "Quiet Village," from his album *Exotica*, was number one on the hit charts for 13 consecutive weeks, and instantly created a market for the music today known as *exotica*. "Village" became, within a period of those few weeks, the "anthem" of exotica. By 1999, musicologist Rebecca Leydon had catalogued 38 additional covers of the tune.[28] The album itself sold approximately 400,000 copies. Martin Denny's story reveals a fascinating insight into the era of exotica's greatest popularity and also offers a stark unveiling of the difficulties of managing relationships among club owners, agents, recording companies, and fellow musicians.

Denny's classical piano studies began in approximately 1921 at the age of 10. By 1931, he was playing a six-month gig at the Granada Hotel in Bogota, Colombia, in a musical group led by Don Dean. After the engagement, the band toured South America through 1935, including stops in Lima, Peru, Santiago, Chile, Rio de Janeiro, Brazil, and Buenos Aires, Argentina. Denny's life-long interest in adopting Latin rhythms and percussion instruments in his music dates from this era. After serving for the U.S. Army Air Forces in World War II, he continued his musical education in 1945 studying piano, composition, and orchestration at the Los Angeles Conservatory of Music. Denny was playing piano, solo as well as in ensembles, in 1954 when his friend Bill Howell, who was leaving for another engagement, asked Denny to replace him as a solo pianist in Honolulu at Donn Beach's Don the Beachcomber restaurant. When Denny finished the Honolulu engagement, he returned briefly to the mainland. Missing Hawaii, he soon found another solo piano slot there, playing at the Surf Room at the Royal Hawaiian Hotel. Donn Beach then offered him another gig at the Beachcomber and Denny agreed to it, provided he could put together a second combo. For the next few months, Denny played concurrent gigs at the two venues. Denny's ensemble at Don the Beachcomber was a trio, featuring Hailakalani Hotel desk clerk Arthur Lyman on vibes, and bassist John Kramer. All the musicians doubled on percussion instruments. Denny's model for his small group was the piano and vibes "cocktail jazz" sound made popular by George Shearing (1919–2011) in the early 1950s. Sitting in occasionally was Puerto Rican percussionist Augie Colón (1927–2004).[29] Music historian Rebecca Leydon aptly referred to Denny's group as "the chamber music counterpart to [Les] Baxter's large-ensemble idiom."[30]

After a pay disagreement, Denny amicably left Don the Beachcomber and got a new gig in the Shell Bar at Henry J. Kaiser's new Hawaiian Village Hotel.[31] In 1956, Denny formally added Augie Colón to his group.[32] With a dedicated percussionist, Denny began incorporating percussion instruments he'd collected over the years from South America, Asia, the Pacific, and the Far East. He made friends with airline personnel, who would add to his percussion collection with instruments they brought back from their overseas travels. Denny's biggest break would come a few months later, but it came at the expense of creating a formidable enemy in the process.

His popularity growing, Denny had decided to hire a manager and seek a recording contract. His new manager was Arnold Mills of the firm Grabbe, Lutz, and Heller, who soon signed Denny to a recording contract with Liberty Records. After hearing a tape of the band, Liberty Records' co-founder and producer Simon "Si" Waronker (1915–2005) began searching for a marketing term that would adequately describe the group's music. He came up with the word "exotica," and the band's first recording would be called *Exotica: The Sounds of Martin Denny*. It was recorded in one session at Webley Edwards' studio in Honolulu, in October 1956.[33]

Denny had wanted to include his musicians in any of the band's financial successes. He drew up a contract in which Lyman and Kramer would each get 25 percent of the profits the group made over union wages, with Colón getting 10 percent. When Kaiser found out about the Liberty recording contract, he was outraged, as he'd intended to record the group, minus Denny, on his own, without Denny's permission. "I refused," Denny was to say later, "and the following day was read the 'riot act' in his office in the presence of my group. Henry J. accused me of disloyalty, and showered me with a barrage of intimidation. He demanded I cancel the contract with my new management, telling my boys that he had great plans for the group and that I was ruining their future—that I was an *ingrate*. He carried on this tirade for a half-hour, browbeating and humiliating me. I could not get a word in edgewise." For the final two months of his Shell Bar contract, which ended Dec. 31, 1956, neither entertainment director Alfred Apaka nor any other Hawaiian Village employees would speak to him, on direct orders from Henry J. Kaiser.[34]

At the beginning of 1957, Denny's group toured the western mainland. Hawaiian sportsman Francis Ii Brown and his partner, hula dancer Winona Love, owned a house in Pebble Beach, and arranged to get Denny's group a gig playing at a party at the Crosby Golf Tournament. After that and several gigs in Las Vegas, Denny's returned to Don the Beachcomber in Honolulu. In November 1957, Kaiser hired away Denny's band members Arthur Lyman and John Kramer, and booked them in the Shell Bar. Marimba and vibes player Julius Wechter (1935–1999) then replaced Lyman in Denny's band, while Hilo bassman Harvey Ragsdale (1931?–1990), a Chinese-English-Hawaiian, replaced Kramer.[35] Denny and Lyman were now competitors of a sort, each fronting an exotica group in Waikiki. Denny recorded prolifically, and noted that he had as many as three or four LPs on the *Billboard, Cashbox,* and *Variety* charts when "Quiet Village" rose up singles charts. Even considering the losses resulting from his disagreement with Kaiser, Denny might have had the last laugh. When he left Kaiser in 1956, he was making $4,800 a year (about $45,500 in today's money). In 1959 alone, he earned $250,000 from royalties and appearances (more than $2 million today).[36] Denny's band was constantly on tour, and often appeared at Trader Vic Bergeron's restaurants. Denny's only feature film appearance, as "Marty" in several scenes from director Charles B. Griffith's *Forbidden Island* (1959), was filmed in Trader Vic's Hawaii location.[37] Augie Colón chose to stay with Denny for another eight years after Lyman and Kramer left. Denny later reconciled with Lyman, and the two played together again on Denny's *Exotica '90* CD. From Jan. 11 through 18, 1977, they appeared together at the Latitude 20 restaurant and bar in Torrance, California.[38] They remained friends, and in approximately 2000, Denny arranged a benefit to pay medical costs for Lyman, who would die from cancer in 2002.[39] Bassist John Burnett Kramer (1921–2014) became a stockbroker and eventually ended up handling Martin Denny's accounts.[40]

Denny's *Exotica* (https://www.youtube.com/watch?v=f2dQ3WbcF44), released in May 1957, was an extraordinarily influential album, with a number of tunes that would be included in the repertoire of virtually every successive exotica musical group. The piano, vibes, and percussion foundation was a mainstay of Denny-influenced exotica combos, as were the bird and animal cries. The cries began, it was said, during an alcohol-fueled set. The band was playing the theme from the movie *Vera Cruz* (1954, dir. Robert Aldrich). Lyman admitted to having "a little to drink" along with percussionist Augie Colón, and they began playfully to squawk at each other on stage. "The next thing you know, the audience started to answer me back with all sorts of weird cries. It was great."[41]

Denny remembers the night it happened, in the outdoors setting inn the Hawaiian Village: "There was a pond with bullfrogs next to the bandstand ... we were playing a song and I could hear the frogs going [deep voice], *Rivet! Rivet!* ... as a gag, the guys spontaneously started doing these bird calls.... At the next rehearsal I said, 'Okay, how about if each one of you does a different bird call? I'll do the frog...' by holding [a guiro] up to the microphone and rubbing, it sounded like a frog. We played it next night, and people kept saying, 'We want to hear the one with the frogs and the birds again!'"[42]

The song was "Quiet Village."

The bird calls and animal cries became associated with both Denny and Lyman throughout their careers, becoming perhaps the most noted signature characteristic of exotica music. Denny's album, however, wasn't the first time animal cries would be voiced by humans on a recording evidencing a feel for exotica. *Here's Cugat*, a 1962 10-inch LP recorded by bandleader Xavier Cugat (1900–1990) on the Mercury label featured a vocalization somewhere between a jungle cat and a howler monkey on the tune "Jungle Flute" (https://www.youtube.com/watch?v=XU29DwjVayQ).

Liberty Records chose not to credit the composers of any of the tunes on Denny's seminal *Exotica* album, nor were they put on the disc label. Seven of them were penned by Les Baxter. The liner notes for Denny's the recording were written by film director John Eliot Sturges (1910–1992), who a number of years later would travel to Burma to film his picture *Never So Few* (1959). While doing so, he added to Denny's growing collection of musical instruments. Near a temple atop a sacred mountain where he was filming some background scenes for his film, Sturgis bought what amounted to two large packing cases of Burmese instruments for his friend Denny. These included traditional drums and gongs, the latter of which included a tuned set of eight, which Denny strung together in ascending size, and played like a scale.[43]

Denny's first two albums, *Exotica* and *Exotica II* (both 1957) both feature pieces that are heavily Latin influenced. These included "Bacoa," a mambo (https://www.youtube.com/watch?v=hlLjZDkfRhk), and "Busy Port," ending with a short Latin descarga percussion jam (https://www.youtube.com/watch?v=BnNb5iB_Hsw). Denny also enjoyed what he called "window dressing" well-known tunes, exoticizing standards, "Flamingo" among them, recorded on his *Primitiva* album (1958), with piano, vibes, Latin percussion, and bird calls, over a Latin rhythmic structure (https://www.youtube.com/watch?v=Uj_lCo_Ccqs). In his arrangement of "Sayonara," a Japanese farewell song on his album *Exotica II*, he used the samisen, a Japanese stringed instrument (https://www.youtube.com/watch?v=CZfmSBMAoXQ). In keeping with the multi-cultural feel of his music, he was proud of the fact that his group was ethnically mixed, reflecting the varied population of Hawaii.[44]

Martin Denny's exotica recordings took an artistic plunge from the 1960s onward. At times, in similar fashion to the latter recordings of Les Baxter, they were marred by overly sentimental, lavishly orchestrated string arrangements (*Romantica*, recorded 1961). There were rumors that Denny didn't actually play on many of the later albums that bear his name. The process is known as "ghosting" and Denny eventually owned up to it. He discussed the subject with interviewer Dana Countryman in 1997, mentioning that constant touring and pressure from Liberty Records to produce more albums were two of the main factors in his decision to choose not to play on a number of "Martin Denny" credited albums. He didn't discuss the particulars of the Liberty agreement with Countryman, but in all probability Liberty had signed him to a lucrative multi-record deal, with the stipulation that they be recorded within a specific timeframe, similar to the agreement Les Baxter made with Capitol Records. With Denny's touring schedule as active as it was, he therefore agreed to have his recordings ghosted. The results could be dismal. Denny cited two albums in particular, *Spanish Village* (1965), featuring arrangements he admitted disliking, and *Exotic Moog* (1971), for which he attended some of the recording sessions but did not, in fact, play in them. "I'm not really happy about that part of my career," Denny would later confess.[45]

Arthur Lyman: Great Vibrations

As "exotica" can be said to have signature musical elements, it also has a keynote instrument, the vibraphone, more familiarly known by its shortened plural form, "the vibes." The instrument also had a signature player, Arthur Hunt Lyman (1932–2002), a jazz-influenced musician who made more than 30 recordings. Lyman was a member of Martin Denny's band when Denny's version of "Quiet Village" was recorded, and is credited with being the co-originator of vocalized bird and animal calls.

Lyman's story contains fascinating and tragic elements, unveiling a dilemma that beguiles musical historians attempting to take an unbiased approach to documenting Lyman's highs

Arthur Lyman's group circa 1963.

and lows as a performer. The "classic" sound of small group exotica was codified in Martin Denny's *Exotica* album released in 1957. Lyman was its co-creator, and the genre's most prominent, creative, and technically adroit improviser. The dark side of paradise played a significant role in Lyman's life and it's doubtful whether the classic sound of exotica would ever reached its apex if it hadn't been for the abusive childhood suffered at the hands of his demanding father.

Kauai-born Lyman was one of eight children born to a Hawaiian mother and a father of French, Belgian, and Chinese extraction. Lyman was a mercurial figure, with a personality influenced by a rigid task-master of a father, who, after Arthur's school day was over, habitually locked him in his room with a xylophone and ordered him to play along with Benny Goodman records for the rest of the day.[46] He reportedly was spanked or beaten regularly for complaining about his musical imprisonment. According to the liner notes on his live record *At the Crescendo*, he "hated it ... but I mastered every Lionel Hampton solo."[47]

He was proficient enough that at the age of eight he made his public debut playing the marimba on radio station KGMB's *Listerine Amateur Hour*. He soon joined his father and brother playing USO shows on the bases of at Kaneohe and Pearl Harbor and on navy ships including the *Hornet*. In 1949 at the age of 17, he was playing with a local jazz group, The Gadabouts, at Leroy's, a tiny club in a Honolulu cellar, performing from 9 p.m. until 2 a.m., Monday through Saturday.[48] He was making $45 a week (about $473 in today's money), playing "George Shearing stuff, cool jazz."[49] Somehow, he managed to make it to his morning classes at McKinley High School. After graduating in 1951, he began working behind the desk at the Halekulani Hotel. There, he met pianist Martin Denny, who, having heard of Lyman's prowess, auditioned then offered him a job in his band. It wasn't a difficult decision for Lyman: Denny paid $100 a week (about $935 today), a considerable raise over the $280 a month ($2,600 today) he was making at the hotel. Lyman would stay with Denny's group until the end of 1956, approximately the same time as the release of Denny's landmark *Exotica* album.[50]

Surfing legend and aloha shirt designer John Severson remembers seeing both the Denny and Lyman bands and participating in the call-and-response involving bird and animal cries: "In '57 when I was stationed in Hawaii, a PFC, surfer, and broke, I used to hang out at the Hawaiian Village and soak up the tropical vibes from Martin Denny and Arthur Lyman. We'd gravitate to the Shell Bar pond until the management shooed us away. It wasn't long before I could go inside for a beer. I had some pretty good bird calls."[51]

Angered over a disagreement with Martin Denny regarding a potential recording contract, Henry J. Kaiser made a separate agreement with Lyman to permanently take over the gig at the Shell Bar in Hawaiian Village, and Lyman then formed a new new band. From the Denny band, Kaiser hired away two more of Denny's musicians, bass player John Kramer, who also played percussion, woodwinds, guitar, and ukulele, and percussionist Harold Chang (b. 1928), who played marimba and xylophone as well.[52] Lyman added Alan Soares, who performed on a variety of keyboard instruments, including the celeste, and doubled on virtually any percussion instrument within reach. Lyman was a perfectionist at that stage in his career, and chose to rehearse his group for eight months before they played in public. The result was a completely memorized repertoire of some 300 musical pieces. Sheet music would never appear on Lyman's stage.

All of Lyman's musicians were multi-instrumentalists, and the stage was typically loaded with several dozen instruments. Lyman's signature instrument was the vibraphone, which he played with four, and occasionally five or six mallets.[53] His marimba was within easy reach on stage, as were the dozens of percussion instruments he played, including the steel pan.

By 1962, Lyman had become a force in the musical world. According to writer Otto von Stroheim, he made $120,000 that year (just shy of $1 million in today's money) and produced six albums in 45 days.[54] Harold Chang remembered each show was musically and physically demanding, where changes of instruments might occur as often as every two or three beats.[55]

The Shell Bar series of shows lasted for nine years, after which the band went on the road for an extended tour. Band member Arthur Chang notes that the percussion instruments alone took up 14 cases and weighed 1200 pounds. When they returned, between recording sessions, they played venues in Waikiki including the Canoe House bar at the Illikai Hotel. They continued to tour extensively.[56]

Lyman's group had a hectic tour schedule, typically three months on the road, then back to Hawaii, followed by three months on the road again. The schedule was tough on personal and professional relationships. Over the years, he hired four different piano players and four bass players. He married Marie, a camera girl working at the Shell Bar and a former hula girl greeter on the *Lurine*.[57] She became his manager. Neither that marriage nor two others lasted.[58] Lyman's playing was a magnet for women. Harold Chang remembers Lyman telling him that when he played vibes "I feel like I'm making love to a woman." Chang remembered the effect: "All these women in the front row were out, I mean, seriously ... out!"[59] Dalliances with women imperiled his marriages, which proved to have an impact on his personal finances. In later years, Lyman would ruefully admit, "Wives, they got all my money. I never smelled it."[60]

Lyman's original lineup remained unchanged from 1957 to 1965, recording some 30 albums. In 1965, bassist Archie Grant replaced Kramer, Clem Low replaced Sores on piano, and Lyman's daughter Kapiolani, along with dancer, percussionist, and vocalist Kaipualani joined the group, which stayed intact until 1975.[61]

Lyman's group was at its creative and financial peak during the years 1959–1963, when the weekly *Hawaiian Eye* detective drama was shown on ABC television. Lyman's group appeared in 10 of the episodes, performing in a mocked-up version of the Shell Bar on a Burbank sound stage. Several clips from the series have found their way on to the internet, as parts of a video tribute to Lyman's percussionist, entitled *Tribute to Harold Chang: Harold Chang and Arthur Lyman—18 Years of Making Music Together* (https://www.youtube.com/watch?v=G9PslwssoVk). The video, which may be the earliest footage shot of the Lyman combo, allows the viewer the treat of seeing Lyman's group as they would have performed at the Hawaiian Village, illustrating how each member contributed to the arrangement of the pieces by playing and interchanging a number of different instruments. The group also accompanied singer Connie Stevens, acting in the role of Cricket Blake. In this fascinating and historically significant video, the group, at 2:36, performs "Taboo Tu" and "Return to Paradise," pauses then continues at 3:41 and again at 5:34; Gershwin's "Rhapsody in Blue" is performed at 7:43. Connie Stevens as Cricket Blake appears with Lyman's group at 10:45 with a version of "Indian Summer," followed by a ballad, and then the show's theme song at 14:33. At 16:22, the group appears without Stevens, with Lyman playing a calypso tune on the steel pan. From Lyman's later years comes yet another illustrative performance on video, a marvelously introspective solo version of "Quiet Village" at the Makai Bar, showcasing his four mallet style with a short and subtlety beautiful counterpoint passage beginning at the 2:17 mark (https://www.youtube.com/watch?v=_nrP0GcZRTw).

Lyman's exposure on national television went beyond *Hawaiian Eye*. He appeared on Red Skelton's show on Dec. 12, 1961.[62] WABC produced a half-hour ABC-syndicated program that aired on Oct. 30, 1965, *An Evening With ... Arthur Lyman*. Lyman appeared on NBC's *The Andy Williams Show* on April 18, 1966, a one-hour program that also featured Martha Raye and Red Buttons. He also appeared at least once on a Steve Allen-hosted television program.[63]

Lyman's Early Recordings

There is a degree of conflicting information when it comes to settling on the years of Lyman's recordings and their sequence of release. *Leis of Jazz*, for instance, is listed in different sources as having been produced in both 1957 and 1959. Writer Jeff Chenault discusses the challenge of documenting Lyman's work on record, citing a confusing number of re-releases and changed album titles: "Arthur Lyman's famous *Taboo* album was later released as an Italian import on Vedette Records and spelled *Tabu*. Instead of the active volcano cover it sported an exploding Atom Bomb on the cover! Arthur's albums were also released in Canada on the Sparton label but no cover variations are known to exist. Probably the most famous of cover variations has to be for the *Taboo 2* album, which, when originally released, had the picture of two real shrunken heads on the cover. This proved a little 'too' exotic for 1960 so the cover was toned down and released again with another active volcano scene similar to the original *Taboo* cover. Percussion records during this time period, propagated by musicians including Enoch Light, probably helped in the repackaging of Arthur's *Yellow Bird* album into *Percussion Spectacular* (actions taken by record companies hoping to sell more records by capturing another market trend). Another title change came with Arthur's *I Wish You Love* album. Because of the strong success of the album's single 'Love for Sale' in 1963, it was later re-titled and packaged as *Love for Sale*. HiFi Records wasn't the only label re-titling their records. When Arthur Lyman and the group signed over to GNP Crescendo, they would also repackage a few albums. *Arthur Lyman At The Crescendo* (with a beautiful glossy picture of the Arthur Lyman group on the cover) later became a very cheap and drab looking *Cast Your Fate to the Wind* and the *Paradise* album would later morph into *Pearly Shells*. This was such a common practice for smaller labels that it could get very confusing and frustrating for the record buying public. Another unique Arthur Lyman oddity was a compilation released by Mark 56 Records in Anaheim California. The album was called *Luau Time* and was a promotional tool used by Jan-U-Wine to help promote its chain of Oriental frozen foods."[64]

What is known is that after *Taboo*, which is generally agreed to be his debut recording as a leader, Lyman was never far from a recording studio. *Taboo* (1958) produced by engineer Richard Vaughn for his HiFi label, was recorded inside Henry Kaiser's aluminum dome before the group actually began playing before live audiences at the Shell Bar.[65] Recording it presented a number of challenges. Due to the dome's propensity for picking up exterior sounds, it had to be recorded at 3 a.m., after the outside traffic had subsided. A truck can be heard during Alan Soares' solo on "Misirlou." To create a mock stereophonic effect, musicians carried microphones from one side of the stage to another as the music was being recorded. The album spent 62 weeks on the *Billboard* charts, peaked at number four, and sold more than two million copies.[66] In the book *Widening the Horizon: Exoticism in Post-War Popular Music*, Jon Fitzgerald and Philip Hayward wrote a highly informative, three-page musicologist's view of "Taboo," the title track of the album, delving into key changes, varied time signatures, and the entrances and exits of various instruments, all underscored by musical notation.[67] What remains unclear is whether the arrangement under analysis was by Lyman or Paul Conrad, who Lyman hired to arrange at least several of the pieces on the album.[68]

Lyman's next several albums are representative of much of what he played in live performances over the ensuing decade. They are (with estimated years of release in parentheses) *Bwana A* (1959), *Hawaiian Sunset* (1959), *Bahia* (1959), *Arthur Lyman On Broadway* (1959), *Leis of Jazz* (1959), *The Legend of Pele* (1959), *Taboo 2* (1959), and *Yellow Bird* (1960). The last album featured the title track, becoming Lyman's best-known single recording. It remained on the *Billboard* charts for 10 weeks and peaked at number four, generating enough radio exposure that Lyman's name became known beyond exotica circles.[69]

Lyman's album *The Legend of Pele* was musically his most intriguing, a riot of Latin and Polynesian percussion showcasing the talent of Harold Chang. The recording is introduced by Lyman's arrangement of Manuel De Falla's "Ritual Fire Dance," an album that reflected Lyman's Spanish-influenced music that predated both Miles Davis' *Sketches of Spain* (1960) and John Coltrane's *Olé Coltrane* (1961). *Pele* is a landmark of exotica that also leaves a burning question: why were versions of warhorses "Fascination" and "76 Trombones," thematically at odds with the other pieces on the album, included on the tail end of this otherwise cohesive recording? Was it Lyman's decision or producer Richard Vaughn's? A good guess would be that it was Lyman's. Seemingly incongruous to his mastery of jazz and his established reputation as a performer and arranger of "classic" exotica, Lyman appeared to have a passion for marches as well. These included "Colonel Bogey's March" (better known as the theme for the 1957 film *The Bridge on the River Kwai*, recorded on Lyman's *Bwana A* album) and "Hilo March," from Lyman's *Taboo*, released the same year. Replete with snare drums and policemen's whistles, they offer a jarring and irrelevant contrast to the mood evoked by the remainder of the material on the albums, contributing to the enigmatic aura of Lyman's musical personality.

Pele also had a provocative album cover. Writers delving into exotica music often take great pains to examine the marketing elements and cultural meanings of the genre's album

A detail from Arthur Lyman's controversial *The Legend of Pele* album cover.

covers, and one of the most delicious comments on the *Pele* covers comes from writers Jon Fitzgerald and Philip Hayward, who note the "spectacularly buxom, blonde, pale-skinned female, representing Pele, rising in flames from a pool of molten lava."[70] Methodical investigation studiously reveals that the left breast is completely engulfed by a fiery lava geyser (with a hint of nipple), while the right breast consists of little more than a highlighted outer shadow, leaving inquiring minds to wonder just how many hours the writers spent gazing at the cover before they agreed on the term "spectacularly buxom." Sexually suggestive album covers were a keynote of many exotica albums (the reach-around breast fondle on Marty Wilson's *Jun'gala* was one of the more notable), but overt references to sexuality were generally absent in the music.[71] An exception was percussionist Leon "Chaino" Johnson's (1927–1999) and producer Kirby Allan's (b. Sidney Allen Pittman, 1928–2011) *Jungle Echoes* (1959, Omegadisk), which offered "The Jungle Chase" (https://blacksweat.bandcamp.com/album/jungle-echoes) as an opening tune. With its orgasmic female cries of passion amid primally suggestive male grunting noises, it predated by 10 years the more famous, and frankly less orgasmically enthusiastic hit by Jane Birkin and Serge Gainsbourg, "Je T'aime … Moi Non Plus."

In a critical sense, Lyman's *Leis of Jazz* (1959) represents one of the most satisfying vibes-led jazz recordings of the late 1950s post-bop era, with tight ensemble arrangements that provide a vehicle to showcase Lyman's improvisational expertise. *Leis* is essentially an exotica flavored jazz record, featuring standards including "Body and Soul" and "The Way You Look Tonight," mixed with pieces of classic exotica. The album showcases Lyman's superior jazz chops and his outstanding percussion ensemble (Lyman's virtuosity is apparent in his fiery solo on "How High the Moon" equal to that of any vibes player of his era). The album was influenced to a good degree by drummer Forestorn "Chico" Hamilton's (1921–2013) 1955 album *Spectacular*, a chamber jazz recording.[72] Lyman's rendition of "My Funny Valentine," with its bowed bass guide tone in the final several bars, mirrors the version originally recorded by Hamilton. Lyman also covers Buddy Collette's minor key "Blue Sands," a melding of jazz and the exotic, fueled by Collette's flute and driven by Hamilton's ostinato mallet work in the original. *Leis of Jazz* represents Lyman's only straight ahead jazz recording and contains much of his finest solo work.

The album *Polynesia* (1965) features Lyman's band playing a relatively sedate, straight-ahead version of Mongo Santamaria's composition "Afro-Blue" (mislabeled "Afro Blues"). The first recording of the song was made when Santamaria was a percussionist in vibes player Cal Tjader's band, but its most improvisationally expansive interpretation was done by soprano saxophonist John Coltrane in *Coltrane Live at Birdland*, recorded in 1963. Coltrane's version represented a rhythmic change from the original to ¾ time, and his soloing, featuring altered scales and atonality, would appear not to have influenced Lyman's later version.

One perplexing question is what was Lyman listening to when he wasn't playing? One surmises that he was probably aware of the original Tjader version of "Afro-Blue," yet chose to put it on a recording only after it was popularized in jazz circles by Coltrane. Or perhaps he heard of it via a review in *Downbeat* magazine (the jazz polls often featured Lyman's name in the "Vibes" category). By the end of the 1960s, at least two of Coltrane's sidemen were themselves making inroads into the music of Africa and Asia, making albums that—while not classic exotica—were heavily influenced by non-Western rhythms and instruments.

Trumpeter Don Cherry's *Eternal Rhythm* (1968) explored the far reaches of Balinese music, with instruments that included vibes, gongs, bells, and a gamelan orchestra. Reedman John Tchicai's *Afrodesiaca* (1969) featured the Western African balafon, a wooden xylophone consisting of approximately 27 bars, "afrodrums," and gongs. The recordings were released originally on Germany's MPS label, part of a vanguard of German-made jazz recordings of the era that joined jazz and traditional music from faraway lands. Trombonist Albert Mangelsdorff's *Now, Jazz Ramwong* included variations on the traditional ramwong dance from Thailand as well as "Three Jazz Moods on 'Theme from PatherPanchali'" written by Ravi Shankar.

It's unknown whether Lyman was aware of these or similar recordings, and if so, whether they made any impact on him. The recorded evidence suggests that they did not. Going in the other direction, though, it would be surprising if Coltrane, his sidemen, and Mangelsdorff, considering the explosive presence of exotica on the charts and on radio and television, were unaware of Lyman and his music. In terms of Coltrane's fellow musicians, pianist McCoy Tyner might constitute the most notable link from classic exotica to the post-exotica jazz.

Judging by the overall brief length of the tunes and their relative lack of improvisational inventiveness, Lyman's playing—on albums at least—declined significantly after the release of *Leis of Jazz*. From roughly 1960 onward, Lyman's music took on an increasing emphasis on the nonadventurous and openly commercial, providing more value as bar and patio background music than as a vehicle to showcase Lyman's improvisational virtuosity. At least in terms of recorded evidence, the fire had departed from Lyman's playing, replaced by tepid fare including unimaginative recordings of contemporary pop hits, and, of course, a gratuitous Christmas album.

So what happened to alter Lyman's playing and musical direction so drastically? Given a blindfold test, an astute listener might easily conclude that there were two different players. Perhaps in retrospect, that deduction may not be too far off. As in the cases of both Les Baxter and Martin Denny, success, or perhaps merely the trappings of it, might have resulted in the artistic free-fall. Baxter and Denny both signed recording contracts that forced them to produce albums that had to be released in a timely fashion under the terms of the agreement, regardless of whether the material was adequately "cooked" beforehand. It wouldn't be surprising if Lyman were similarly tempted by such a lucrative agreement, and then fell into the same trap that doomed much of the latter output of Baxter and Denny.

On the other hand, given Lyman's childhood, dominated by a martinet father, his rigorous touring schedule, and the constant late-night scheduling demands of his profession, perhaps he was, by the age of 30 or so, artistically exhausted. Suppositions aside, Lyman clearly no longer saw a reason to progress musically. His work therefore represents a fascinating yet frustrating dilemma. The albums he made through the first five years of his recording career contain many moments of brilliance and virtuosity, displaying fiery mallet work and a talented ear for arrangement. When he was good, he was the equal of just about any vibes player in jazz, reminiscent in many ways of his contemporary Milt Jackson.

In his later years, his recording career was virtually at an end and he had largely stopped touring, choosing instead to remain in Honolulu and playing in venues that included the New Otani Kaimana Beach Hotel.[73] His career can be defined, in its early stages, by what it was and what it promised. What remains, considering, the last four decades of his life and projecting into exotica's future, is the lingering question of what might have been.

Exotica Beyond Baxter, Denny, and Lyman

A number of other musicians made notable forays into the world of exotica, including Gene Rains and Robert Drasnin. Vibraphonist Rains, who made three recordings under his own name, remains the most enigmatic of all exotica musicians. His name has rarely appeared in print, and there is little data on his life and career. Even obscure musicians leave "breadcrumbs" for future historians to stumble over, and in today's world of the internet, seemingly nothing remains hidden. What ultimately became of Gene Rains remains enigmatic and even his beginnings are cloaked in mystery. His name does not appear in any jazz encyclopedia of note.

His known story begins with the armed forces. Rains, a member of the U.S. Air Force on Oahu, played vibes in various military clubs on the island. There, he met 264th Army Band pianist Paul Conrad (b. 1932), who would thereafter join Rains' Air Force band occasionally. Rains left the Air Force in 1959, and inspired by the success of Denny and Lyman, decided to form a band and focus on exotica. He hired Conrad, who had done arrangement for both Denny and Lyman, as a pianist and arranger. The Rains group was soon hired to play in the Shell Bar in the Hawaiian Village Hotel by entertainment director Alfred Apaka. Apaka also introduced Decca Records' Sonny Burke, in town to produce an Apaka recording, to the work of Rains. Rains' first of three Decca albums, *Lotus Land* (1960), featured Conrad on piano (who also provided half the charts), bass and flute player Archie Grant, and percussionist Alan Watanabe. The title cut is a pensive, moody interpretation of a Cyril Scott composition that became an exotica standard, replete with bird calls and subdued interplay between Rains' vibes and Conrad's piano, and a timbre reminiscent of Erik Satie's "Gnossienne 1" (https://www.youtube.com/watch?v=wWHBGlaR95g).

Rains' band went on a mainland tour midway through 1960, which included an engagement, beginning on June 14, at the Polynesian Village at Chicago's Edgewater Beach Hotel. The program, *Rage of the Tropics*, featured a number of other Hawaiian acts, including Kent Ghirard's dancers. Rains' group also performed in Denver and Nevada.[74]

Upon the group's return to Hawaii, pianist Paul Conrad left the group to pursue a series of gigs as a soloist and was replaced in Rains' group by Byron L. Peterson, who appeared on Rains' final two recordings, *Far Across the Sea,* (1961), and *Rains in the Tropics* (1962). A later release on Decca, *The Call of the Tropics*, was a compilation based on his three earlier recordings. Conrad, who co-arranged music on Rains' first recording, eventually released his own disc, *Exotic Paradise* (1963) for Mahalo Records.

While working and recording with his small combo, Rains also made records with Staten Island–born Axel Stordahl (1913–1963), an arranger best known for his work with Frank Sinatra in the 1940s at Columbia Records. Stordahl had become passionate about Hawaii and made several island-themed albums. *Broadway Wears a Lei* was released in 1958 under Alfred Apaka's name on Hawaiian Village Records, and Gene Rains appeared as a sideman on at least two others, *Jasmine and Jade* (1960, Dot Records), and *The Magic Islands Revisited* (1961, Decca).[75]

Rains' recordings have been compared to the early work of both Martin Denny and Arthur Lyman, but his recordings indicate that he was less inspired by pop material than by jazz standards. His approach to exotica is more measured than either, eschewing both Lyman's marches and Denny's increasing reliance on modern pop tunes. What is unknown today is how he fared musically after the early 1960s, or indeed, what he did for a career. In December 2014, Paul Conrad told interviewer Kerry J. Byrnes that the last he'd heard of Rains was that he was "selling Cadillac cars in Seattle."[76]

Robert Drasnin

Robert Drasnin (1927–2015), best known as a composer and orchestrator of film and television soundtracks, created some of exotica's most compelling music. His initial landmark album was *Voodoo!* (1959, Tops Records). With exacting arrangements for small ensemble, it must be considered one of the most sophisticated exotica recordings ever released. It was recorded in two five-hour sessions, and featured Drasnin on piccolo, noted mezzo soprano Salli Terri, two flute players, and three pianists (one of whom was John Williams, later famous for his film scores). Rounding out the group was a harpist and seven percussionists, including multi-instrumentalist and marimba played Milt Holland. All 12 melodies were composed by Drasnin. As a composer, Drasnin was the equal of Baxter, writing haunting, minor key melodies that lent themselves well to his extraordinary chamber ensemble. Unlike Baxter's ubiquitous *Ritual of the Savage* tunes, Drasnin's exotic compositions weren't widely played by other musicians associated with the genre, due to both the relatively late year of their release and the fact that Tops, the album's label, didn't achieve the brand recognition, publicity, or distribution as did albums made by Denny and Lyman.

After gaining notoriety for scoring films, writing incidental music for popular television programs including *Mission: Impossible*, *The Wild, Wild West*, and *Hawaii Five-0*, and acting as music supervisor for a number of CBS television series, his reputation as a creator of exotica enjoyed a resurgence. In 2002, three of his pieces were included in the documentary film *Cinemania* (dir. Angela Christlieb and Stephen Kijak). Drasin appeared at the 2005 *Hukilau* festival at Fort Lauderdale's Mai-Kai restaurant with a 16-piece orchestra, playing tunes from his 1959 album as well as newer compositions. The latter would form the basis for his next release, *VooDoo II*, released in 2007 as a Dionysus Records CD. Drasnin performed at the Hukilau again in 2007.[77]

While exotica became most popular through the recordings of smaller combos, a number of large and small orchestras jumped on the bandwagon in an attempt to mirror the success of Les Baxter's *Ritual of the Savage*, and to a greater or lesser extent, his overall sound as well, Dominic Frontiere's *Pagan Festival* (1959, Columbia) was just one example. Others, including Ted Auletta's *Exotica* (1962, Cameo), attempted to maintain the "quiet jungle" sound, while more tried to co-opt exotica by reframing it with brassy arrangements reminiscent of those from the Big Band era, Morton Gould's *Jungle Drums* (1956, RCA) being one notable example.

Of the many orchestral treatments that hit the record stores in the late 1950s through the early 1960s, three merit special mention. Milt Raskin's (1916–1977) efforts in *Kapu (Forbidden)*, recorded on Crown Records in 1959, was more in keeping with the general mood of exotica, featuring an ensemble of 12 with emphasis on Latin rhythms, minor themes, and a liberal use of quarter-note triplets. Raskin's ensemble arrangements adeptly mimic Baxter's large orchestral sound while using surprisingly few musicians, among whom were notable studio veterans Larry Bunker and Milt Holland (https://www.youtube.com/watch?v=W8ON7NXWgiQ).[78] Marty Wilson's *Jun'gala* (1960, Warner Bros) combined exotic themes with Latin percussion and mambo and rumba dance rhythms, with its racy album cover undoubtedly accounting for a number of impulse sales. Yet another large orchestral interpretation of exotica was Stanley Wilson's *Pagan Love* (1960, Capitol Records), a heavily orchestrated collection of themes dedicated to various non-Western countries. The ill-fated Michel Magne's (1930–1984) *Tropical Fantasy* (1962, Columbia Records) leads the list of bizarrely eclectic exotic albums. Magne took the standard vibes and percussion-based ensemble and included elements of *musique concrète*, which features non-musical sounds in both their original and electrically altered forms. He also included combo organ (a guess would be the Farfisa VIP-500, with its "syntheslalom" feature), brief Stockhausen-like percussion interludes (reminiscent of "Zyklus"), a detached, wordless choir comparable to that of Carl Orff, banshee screams and animal calls, and flamenco guitar. Magne's influences were many and varied, and he surprisingly created a seamless pastiche that may never be equaled, in terms of its orchestral complexity (https://www.youtube.com/watch?v=VfAyTzmo3oc).[79]

The overall influence of exotica on performers the world over is stunning in its variation. It resulted in dozens upon dozens of albums, ranging from relatively straightforward interpretations based on the work of Baxter, Denny, and Lyman to creations eclectic and bizarre, utilizing instruments not usually associated with classic exotica, including wah-wah guitar, combo organ, and synthesizer.[80]

Exotica music experienced a revival in the 1990s, accompanying the retro interest in Tiki culture. It spawned new artists and recordings, some of who are still playing, while others have moved on to other projects. What's notable is that a genre that seemed dead by 1970 has never really gone away, inspiring even more new recordings as this book goes to press.

The Vibraphone and the Bell: Exotica Through Asian Music History

The vibraphone holds bragging rights for forming the basis of the fundamental signature sound of exotica, particularly in a small group setting. In a more visceral vein, the instrument represents the sound of bells, whose sonorous, age-old resonance has granted them a special place in palaces of spiritual philosophy, from European cathedrals to Tibetan monasteries. From a historical perspective, the vibes might be considered the perfect example of tuned bells optimized for music. The human quest for exotica, through its fascination for controlling the sound of bells, is thousands of years old.

For practically as long as it's been in existence, attempts have been made to turn the bell—or an assortment of bells—into a musical instrument. The challenges have been threefold: playability (including attack, sustain, and vibrato), portability, and cost. The vibraphone replicates the sound of the bell (up to four bells, harmonically, when double mallets are used to strike the aluminum bars) and is the apogee of a long line of bell-sounding instruments, activated when struck by mallets, levered keys, hammers, and even fingers.

We might characterize the sound of the bell as primordial, except that bells weren't heard by anyone prior to their invention in the Bronze Age. The earliest known examples of musical bells were those built during China's Anyang period (ca. 1350–1045 BC) They were dramatically improved from both a decorative and sound perspective during the Western Zhou (885–771 BC) era and were further refined during the time of the Eastern Zhou (550–400 BC).[81]

The latter time evidenced the most extraordinary set of chimed bells found to date, those found in the tomb of Zeng Hou Yi, known as the Marquis Yi of Zeng. This tomb, containing what amounted to a full chamber orchestra of instruments including chime-bells, zithers, mouth organs, flutes, drums, and chime stones, was accidentally discovered in 1977 in Hubei province by a unit of the People's Liberation Army, while leveling a hill to establish a factory site. The newly unearthed bronze chime-bells—collectively called bianzhong—numbered 65 in an array of sizes and weighed approximately two-and-half tons in total. In keeping with the custom of the day, 21 attendants—all female—were strangled in order to follow the Marquis to the next world. Some of these, it is surmised, were his musicians.

Presented as a gift to the Marquis in 433 BC, the bells, displayed in three ranks, were fitted to two massive stands and estimated to have been played by five musicians (a further guess is that 24 musicians would have been required to play all the instruments in music written for the full ensemble).[82] Each bell had dual striking points, resulting in either of two tones when struck, thus providing harmonic options that could be considered sophisticated for any succeeding era. This astonishing instrument had an overall range of five octaves, with the capability of playing all 12 notes of the chromatic scale over a range of three octaves. Nobody today, however, has any idea of how the music sounded or was played. When the Marquis' tomb was excavated, it contained no identifiable musical scores.[83]

Bronze bianzhong bells of Marquis Yi of Zeng, circa 433 BCE, Hubei Provincial Museum, Wuhan, P.R.China (ZhengZhou/Wikimedia Commons).

Hammers and large poles of lacquered wood, which struck the bells to create individual tones, were found in Marquis Yi's tomb, but there is nothing to explain whether the issues of precise control of attack and sustain was ever addressed, or even if they were considered to be important. Sustain can be controlled by hand dampening. But how would that be accomplished if all 65 bells were employed in a given work of colossal scope, with the 10 hands of five individuals both striking and dampening? The biggest bell was approximately five feet (152 cm) in length and weighed nearly 450 pounds (203.6 kg), yet another potentially and physically confounding task for a player wishing to dampen its sound. One educated guess suggests that the bells would not have served as the main melodic instrument of Marquis Yi's ensemble, as their lingering beats would not allow them to be dampened quickly enough to follow faster musical passages.[84]

Marquis Yi's tuned bell ensemble is the richest example to date of an early civilization's attempt to harness the sound of bells to make music integrated into an orchestral setting. But it's not the oldest example of an early bell instrument. A set of 10 individually tuned nao bells were unearthed in a tomb in Ningxiang, Hunan province, in the 1990s (nao are played with their mouths in an upward position). They date from the 12th or 11th century BC, hundreds of years before Marquis Yi's were made. As such, these 10 bells represent the earliest evidence for bell music anywhere in the world.

The age-old problem with using the bell itself as a musical instrument, and most particularly with the large casts, was the lack of control over the sound, specifically attack and sustain. In the case of large bells, the note might actually sound fractions of a second after the bell was struck. The length of sustain would need to be controlled by dampening, which during Marquis Yi's day was probably done by hand. Imagining five players simultaneously striking and dampening some 60-odd bells by hand is daunting and the feat fantastical. The existence of written music would have helped to unpin the mystery of attack and sustain that may never be solved.

A number of other bell-related instruments from Asia post-dated Marquis Yi's bells, ranging from the tuned gong gamelan orchestras of Java and Bali that may have originated in the 12th century AD, to several bell-like percussion instruments from Thailand. In the latter country, noted metallophones (instruments with tuned bars) Ranat ek lek and Ranat thum lek, are two nearly identical instruments of alternately high and low musical ranges. "Circle of gongs" instruments Khawng wong yai and Khawng wong lek, along with Khawng mawn, as with the previously mentioned two instruments, were crafted in the 19th century AD (the latter is especially evocative of the sound of the western marimba).[85]

The Emergence of "Vibratone Bells" and the Vibraphone

The vibraphone belongs to a family of instruments called "struck idiophones," as defined by the Hornbostel-Sachs system of musical instrument classification. Erich Moritz von Hornbostel (1877–1935) and Curt Sachs (1881–1959) were musicologists who published their system of musical instrument classification in 1914. It has been used since then, with occasional updates by ethnomusicologists, organologists, and other scholars. The system has five top levels of classification and more than 300 categories in all. Its classification codes are modeled on the Dewey Decimal System. Hornbostel and Sachs weren't the first to attempt a broad classification of musical instruments. Their best-known predecessor was Victor-Charles Mahillon (1841–1924), a collector of more than 1,500 instruments (some of which he built himself) and the curator of musical instruments at the Brussels Conservatory. His classification book, *Éléments d'acoustique musicale & instrumentale*, was published in 1874.[86] Mahillon classified instruments into four broad sound-producing categories, air column, string, membrane, and the instrument body itself. It was a major leap in classification, but focused primarily on European instruments. The Hornbostel-Sachs system broadened the work of Mahillon by including sub-categories that would allow classification for musical instruments of any culture.[87]

The vibraphone lives in Hornbostel-Sachs sub-category 111.222, "Sets of percussion plaques," characterized by instruments that vibrate within their own structures, rather than with the assistance of strings or membranes. A number of other instruments, including the celesta, glockenspiel, metallophone, and toy piano are included in that category as well. The marimba and xylophone appear in category 111.212, "Sets of percussion sticks." Metallophones are defined as instruments having tuned metal bars cross through Hornbostel-Sachs categories and include the glockenspiel, celesta, and vibraphone.[88]

If the vibraphone had never been invented, it's fascinating to imagine how earlier idiophones with metal bars or tuning forks would have sounded in the classic exotica ensemble, along with piano and Latin percussion. Two 19th century inventors created musical instruments that produced notes by striking metal tuning forks via a manual keyboard-engaged mechanism. Victor Mustel's typophone of 1860, created in France, and Thomas Machell's dulcitone, produced in Scotland the same year, essentially used this same technology. Lacking amplification, their volume was considered too limited to be of use in a concert hall. Electric amplification was still decades into the future. In 1886, the celesta, perhaps better known as the celeste, was invented by Auguste Mustel (1842–1919), son of the inventor of the typophone. Unlike the earlier instrument, which utilized metal tuning forks, the celeste produced sounds through a keyboard activated lever and hammer mechanism striking tuned metal bars. The celeste produced more volume than the earlier instrument through a wooden box resonator associated with each tuned plate. Most people's familiarity today with the sound of the celeste is through Peter Ilyich Tchaikovsky's (1840–1893) use of it in "Dance of the Sugarplum Fairy," from his ballet *The Nutcracker* (Op. 71, 1892).

In jazz circles, the celeste is first believed to have been recorded on Louis Armstrong's "Basin Street Blues" (1928, Okeh 402154), played by Earl Hines during the first two choruses and briefly again at the end of the song (https://www.youtube.com/watch?v=ox5F5J9SsZ8). Memphis Slim recorded it with a livelier tempo in his undated version of "Celeste Boogie No. 2" (https://www.youtube.com/watch?v=jT19M6SpUwU). While it was played by a number of jazz luminaries, including Art Tatum, Fats Waller, Thelonious Monk, Oscar Peterson, and even McCoy Tyner, it was most often treated as a novelty.[89] Its most powerful jazz interpreter was Meade "Lux" Lewis, whose "Celestial Express," recorded while a member of clarinetist Edmond Hall's Celeste Quartet (Blue Note, 1941), remains a pinnacle of the instrument's improvisational and comping capabilities (https://www.youtube.com/watch?v=oM9tRRDUwhY). A coda to the idea of the celeste employed as an instrument in exotica music was the fact that Martin Denny did occasionally play it himself on recordings, but used it as an ornament, rather than a lead instrument, on albums including *Forbidden Island* (1958).[90]

In terms of melodic and harmonic range, attack and sustain, volume, portability, and cost, the invention of the vibraphone was the ultimate answer to bringing the sound of tuned bells to fruition. It all started with Herman Winterhoff and his marimba.

Herman E. Winterhoff (1876–1945) began experimenting with the sound of the marimba in about 1916 while working at the Leedy Manufacturing Company of Indianapolis. The company had been founded by Ulysses Grant "Lys" Leedy (1867–1931) in 1898 as a maker of folding, height-adjustable snare drum stands, then soon manufactured instruments including snare drums, xylophones and orchestra bells. It was reportedly the largest percussion instrument manufacturer in the world by 1920.[91] Winterhoff experimented with various means of creating a tremolo effect on the steel bar marimba, finally achieving success in 1922, with the addition of two pulsating shafts, driven by motorized rotating fans in the resonator tubes and under the sound bars.[92] The resulting instrument was first called the Leedy-Vibratone Bells, but at some point early in its life, its name was changed to Vibraphone and was trademarked.[93] Approximately 25 were sold between 1924 and 1929. A pedal-activated damping mechanism was invented by Billy Gladstone (b. William David Goldstein, 1892–1961), who performed on the vibraphone as a band member during Edward "Major" Bowes' (1874–1946) *Capitol Theatre Family Program*, aired by WEAF radio direct from New York City's Capitol Theatre. Gladstone's device was fastened by a clamping mechanism to the vibraphone.[94] In terms of recordings, xylophonist Signor Lou "Friscoe" Chiha was an early adopter and played the Leedy vibes on two Edison recordings released in 1924, "Aloha Oe" and "Gypsy Love Song" (https://www.youtube.com/watch?v=DSL_ky37ySY). Leedy had apparently not adopted the term "vibraphone" yet. The label on "Aloha Oe" lists the instrument as the "Leedy-Vibratone bells."[95]

The increasing popularity of Leedy's Vibratone Bells led John Calhoun Deagan (1853–1934), founder of J.C. Deagan, Inc., primarily known a maker of the xylophone and tuned bells and chimes, to ask his chief tuner Henry J. Schluter (1889–1971), to develop an instrument similar to the Leedy vibraphone.[96] Schluter created an instrument called the Vibraharp, which differed from the Leedy design in several ways, including replacing the steel sound bars with those made of aluminum, adjustments to the dimensions and tuning of the bars, and introducing a built-in, foot-controlled damper. The Deagan Vibraharp model 145 was introduced in 1927. Schluter continued to make changes to the instrument, including brass and chrome resonators, resulting in an additional four models being introduced through 1929. A "King George" model was made for Lionel Hampton in 1930.[97]

Yet another significant name emerged in the business of manufacturing vibraphones. Marimba virtuoso Clair Omar Musser (1901–1998) joined the J. C. Deagan company sometime in the 1927–1930 timeframe, and was said to have been the manager of the mallet instrument division. In addition to making instrument improvements relating to tuning and harmonics, Musser designed new instruments. One of these was the Marimba-Celeste, which featured tonal characteristics of both marimba and vibraphone, with amplification built to aid the volume of the lower bars. Musser toured with the instrument from 1927–1930. Musser also developed marimba orchestras, including the 25-piece "All Girl" girl marimba orchestra that appeared at Chicago's Oriental Theatre in 1929, and a 300-piece marimba orchestra that appeared at the Chicago Fair of 1950.[98] Following World War II, Musser left Deagan to form his Musser Marimba Company, making vibraphones, xylophones, glockenspiels, and chimes, in addition to the marimba. Sometime shortly after 1949, he built the Musser Maestro

Marimba Metron, a percussion sequencer with 13 pre-loaded rhythms, a precursor to the modern-day drum machine.[99]

In approximately 1949, he engaged in his final design project, the Celestaphone, which combined Musser's interests in music, metallurgy, physics, and outer space. The frame, bars, and resonators were built using 678 pounds of meteorites from Musser's own collection, their elemental composition determining how they'd be used in the instrument. It weighed 83 pounds, had 30 bars, and more than 353 parts were machined in order to construct the instrument.[100] After leaving the music business in 1956, Musser, an inveterate tinkerer and inventor, went on to work in astronomical capacities for Hughes Aircraft and NASA. His Musser Copernican Planetrarium, invented while working for the Hughes subsidiary Scientific Space Industries, was placed at both the Griffith Park (California) Observatory and the University of California at San Diego.[101]

Vibraphone and Vibraharp were both trademarked names, but "vibraphone" has become more popular in usage when describing either instrument, as has the catch-all term "vibes." The Deagan, Leedy, and Musser companies did not survive as lone entities. Deagan was sold to the Slingerland Drum Company in 1978 and its trademark and patents are today owned by Yamaha. Musser's company was sold twice before being acquired by the Selmer Company in 1981.[102] According to the Archives Center, National Museum of American History, Smithsonian Institution, Washington, D.C., C.G. Conn Co. Ltd. gained control of Leedy in 1929, and in 1930, Leedy's operations were moved to Elkhart, Indiana. The production of Leedy-branded vibes was discontinued in 1958.[103]

The Vibraphone in Jazz

Lionel Leo Hampton (1908–2002), a jazz player, brought nearly universal popularity to the instrument, introducing it to people who weren't familiar with it as well as many who didn't particularly like jazz. Originally a drummer, he doubled on vibes while in Les Hite's Sebastian's Cotton Club Orchestra. His first recorded vibes solo was said to have been on "Memories of You" (1930, Okeh) with Louis Armstrong & His Sebastian New Cotton Club Orchestra (https://www.youtube.com/watch?v=UWB3fWZIiPY) Hampton's work on the recording barely constitutes a solo, with little improvisational development, serving mainly as an intro. His four-year tenure, beginning in 1936, with Benny Goodman's Quartet featuring drummer Gene Krupa and pianist Teddy Wilson, resulted in what was said at the time to be the first major musical group to have racially integrated players appearing in live settings.[104] Hampton left Goodman in 1940 to form his own orchestra, and recorded his first major hit, "Flying Home," with 19-year old Texas tenorman Illinois Jacquet (1919–2004) introducing his highly emotional "honking" style to raving audiences (https://www.youtube.com/watch?v=cMrvtkfUKaM). As noted by *New York Times* writer Peter Watrous, Hampton's band, featuring Jacquet, "set the emotional atmosphere for rock."[105]

Other notable jazz vibes players included Red Norvo, Milt Jackson, Bobby Hutcherson, and Cal Tjader, known for his use of Latin themes and rhythms. Multi-instrumentalist jazzman Adrian Rollini was memorably filmed in 1948 on "Girl with the Light Blue Hair," soloing on both the vibes and tubular bells in a trio setting, underscoring the musical similarity between the vibraphone and tuned bells (https://www.youtube.com/watch?v=wdNzCNQmGG0).

The link from Lionel Hampton to Arthur Lyman, engendered by the latter's painstaking ordeal in learning Hampton's solos as a youth, underscores the importance of the vibraphone as a key element in exotica combos, from the Martin Denny era forward.

While the mainland's embrace of exotica as a viable musical format waned in the 1970s, the genre remained well-represented in the musical collections of Hawaiiana enthusiasts. By the end of the millennium, though, it was enjoying its revival in popularity, largely driven by what can be best described as a thriving, worldwide tiki culture.

Six

Passing the Tiki Torch

The concept of tiki, originating in Polynesia and then conquering the mainland, has evolved so dramatically over the last century that it has grown from a noun, referring to carved sculptures of Pacific gods and nobles, to an adjective, as in "tiki bars," "tiki restaurants," "tiki drinks," and, of course, "tiki torches." In reality, it is *tiki culture* that describes a phenomenon that seems to be stronger and more prolific today than it has ever been. A surprising number of tiki websites and thousands of other tiki-oriented pages are scattered over the internet. Tiki images represent a significant force in e-commerce: a search for the word "tiki" on eBay reveals nearly 73,000 listings.[1] Tiki bars are all over the world, operating in environments not traditionally associated with the tiki culture. Lucky Lukes's Tiki Bar, for example, holds up the southeast corner of Bangkok's notorious Nana Entertainment Plaza, the go-go girl and lady boy emporium on Sukhumvit Soi Four. Tiki culture seems to be all-enveloping, with references to exotica music, Hawaiian and Polynesian shirts and garments, rattan-filled Polynesian-themed bars and restaurants, and anything else that conceivably might fall under the banner of "Polynesian Pop." Pilgrimages are made to the still-thriving Mai-Kai restaurant in Fort Lauderdale, Florida, and there are a number of well-attended annual tiki festivals, among them *Tiki Oasis* in San Diego, the *Hukilau Festival* in Fort Lauderdale, and *Ohana: The Luau at the Lake* held at Lake George, New York.[2] The Fraternal Order of Moai is a non-profit organization with nine active chapters in various pockets of North America, an untold number of at-large members, and a mission statement that reads "to serve as the premier fraternal organization and social network for all men and women interested in tiki culture and the Polynesian pop era; to spread the aloha spirit."[3]

And those who can't find a locally available tiki venue only have to turn on the television to get a tiki fix via the décor of any of a seemingly endless number of Hawaiian-themed television dramas.

The beginnings of tiki culture can be traced to a small watering hole in Southern California that opened in the 1930s, with a trajectory that soared dramatically upward in the 1950s. Mainland tiki parties of that latter era represented a quasi-Bacchanalian celebration of the end of the war years, which spanned an era running between Pearl Harbor in late 1941 and 1953, the end of the Korean War. Journalist Richard Von Busack quotes author Sven Kirsten's brief but exact analysis of the early post-wars tiki parties: "The generation of our parents, for the first time, were ridding themselves of the Christian heritage of Puritanism. Also, to them, it was as far as they could go with their Puritan upbringing. Tiki style was almost like an alternative lifestyle, like what the hippies wanted to create with drugs and free love. Our parents were dreaming of free love in the South Seas, and their drug was these potent cocktails, their rebellion was dressing in Hawaiian shirts."[4]

Like virtually any other mass social trend, tiki culture had its low points in terms of popularity, but in the late 1980s, it suddenly returned, evolving from being turgidly passé to coolly retro. The movement is historically fascinating and its luminaries exceedingly memorable.

The term "tiki" derives from the Māori language, and refers to the world's first man. By extension, it also applies to carved effigies, which most often were created out of wood or stone. Tiki carvings vary in design from one Polynesian culture to another, graphically detailed by painter Miguel Covarrubias (1904–1957) in a series of maps, *Pageant of the Pacific*, created for San Francisco's Golden Gate International Exposition in 1939.[5] *Art Forms of the Pacific Area* was a Covarrubias map offering details of seven forms of tiki carvings found in Polynesia, including Easter Island, Hawaiian, Maori, Marquesan, Rarotongan, Samoan, and Tubuai carvings. Those in Covarrubias' map representing the New Hebrides (now Vanuatu) and neighboring Melanesia bear comparable human characteristics. Farther west, the *hampatong* carvings of the Borneo Dayaks—particularly those of the Iban—display characteristics similar to those of Polynesian carvings. Carvings made by the seven groups indicated in Covarrubias' map, though, represent the iconographic tiki images most often seen on the mainland, including colossal statues, drinking mugs, and garden decorations.

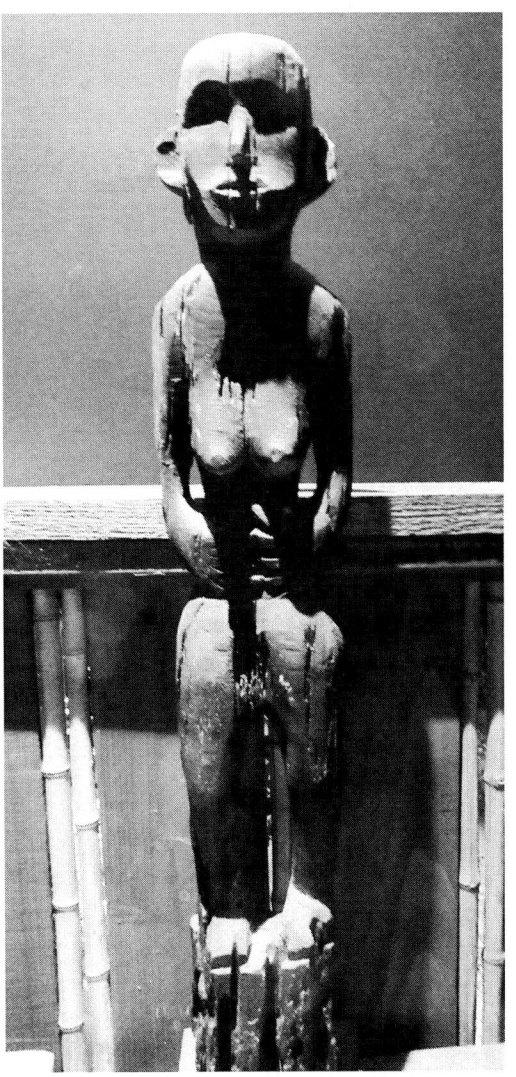

Iban *hampatong* figure from Sarawak, Borneo, used as a guardian over rice stores (author's collection).

In Hawaii, the word kii is used, rather than tiki. Among the better known kii in Hawaii are those located at Puuhonua o Honaunau (City of Refuge) National Park on the Big Island, acting as guardians to the bay and the nearby heiau (temple).

The tiki figure's earliest mass visibility on the mainland seemed to be through Polynesian-themed restaurants and lounges created in the decade of the 1930s. Don the Beachcomber, said to be the first, opened in 1934 and was in full Polynesian regalia by 1937, the same year that the fabled Hawaiian Room in New York's Hotel Lexington began its hula and Hawaiian music shows.

The most distinctive architectural construction associated with the Polynesian style is the massive peaked thatched roof soaring above an A-frame façade. Two representative buildings of the type can be found in another map from Covarribias' *Pageant of the Pacific, Native Dwellings of the Pacific*. The Polynesian architectural style so identified with tropical venues on the mainland is a combination of two Pacific meeting houses, the *Papuan* (New Guinea), with its rakishly angled roof, and the *Pelew* (Palau) with its elaborate multi-level carvings and paintings on the façade of the A-Frame.

Often flanking the entrance to these Polynesian-themed structures on the mainland were huge tiki figures, palm trees, water features, boulders, and any number of large and small devices throwing flames. The interior mirrored much of the iconography found outside. As the style developed, water features became increasingly elaborate and versatile, changing from a trickling, murmuring waterfall to a raging tropical storm, accompanied by audio and lighting effects. Although interior fires were kept to a minimum for safety reasons, there were still tiki torches and table hurricane lamps, along with the occasional fire-dancing stage routine. Interior walls were resplendent with bamboo and tapa cloth, inexpensive and easily imported. Décor was essentially the Polynesian version of a winter ski lodge, including anything that could be found on or around a trading schooner or any wooden craft found in any Pacific port of call. Preserved sea life, from blowfish to sea stars and shells, were commonly suspended from fishing nets. Shields, masks, tribal weapons and hanging lanterns enhanced the effect. In terms of mass exposure, this faux Polynesian version of an imagined Pacific Eden culminated in Walt Disney's Enchanted Tiki Room, built in 1963, in which even the performers, a cast of more than 150, were Audio-Animatronics ersatz.

Patrons in Polynesian bars and restaurants came there to eat and drink in the midst of tropical eye candy, reveling in staged performances at the larger clubs. Tiki would occasionally expand into restaurant gift shops offering a wealth of knick-knacks, from ceramic cups to ashtrays. Like exotica music, aloha shirts, and rattan furniture, tiki had its peak, suffered a decline in popularity, and then a resurgence. Some of the old iconic tiki-themed restaurants and bars have survived and are places of pilgrimage for what might be called the "tiki underground." Tiki culture has cut a broad swath through the Western world, encompassing architecture, interior design, food and drink, and the number of "tiki venues" worldwide today is so vast and ongoing as to be uncountable.

An important reference to this world is Sven A. Kirsten's *The Book of Tiki*. Nearly 20 years old, the material in the book was turned down by a number of publishers before Taschen agreed to publish it. As tends to be the case with art forms in general, tiki had gotten to the point to where it was old enough to be *déclassé*, but not ancient enough to be *antique*. A number of online resources focus on tiki and "Polynesian Pop," one of the largest of which is *Tiki Central* (www.tikiroom.com). Instead of defining precisely what the world of Polynesian Pop is, the site's writers elect instead to characterize it by what it isn't:

- It's not about Jimmy Buffett and Parrotheads
- It's not modern plastic, brightly-colored tiki party decorations
- It's not about the Caribbean/Key West design aesthetic
- It's not about Reggae
- It's not about African-art inspired masks/carvings/design,
- It's not about Margaritas and tequila-based drinks,
- It's not about simply anything that has a tiki on it or in it.[6]

So what, then, is it? To a large extent, the Polynesian pop concept was originated by a man who built a restaurant, came up with the décor, and determined which rum-fueled drinks would have something in common with his vision of paradise. Donn Beach's idea caught fire and then propagated to hundreds of mainland spots, large and small, within a very few years. He was offering a cheap trip to paradise (round-trip airplane tickets to Hawaii in 1936 cost $720, the equivalent of more than $12,000 today). He was also one of two men who vied for the title of inventor of the mai-tai. Vic Bergeron died in 1984 and Donn Beach in 1989, yet their creations, Trader Vic's and Don the Beachcomber respectively, are still household names. The mai-tai, probably the most ubiquitous single invention within the Polynesian Pop sphere of influence, is today savored and slugged down by the millions each year. These are joyously imbibed by people who will neither know nor care that Vic and Donn engaged in one of the best-known spats in the history of the liquor business for the privilege of being called its creator. The drink survived both of them.

The world of Polynesian restaurants, bars, and structures on the mainland was a huge one, involving multiple facets, venues, stories, and memorable individuals. These spanned from large establishments, including the Mai-Kai in Fort Lauderdale and the Kahilki in Columbus, Ohio, to hundreds of smaller venues, Frances Langford's Outrigger in Jensen Beach, Florida among them. The names start with Donn Beach and Vic Bergeron, but include contributors and influencers ranging from designer Steve Crane to architect Pete Wimberly.

The Memorable Restaurateurs

Donn "Don the Beachcomber" Beach (1907–1989), born Ernest Raymond Beaumont Gantt in Texas, opened Don's Beachcomber Café, a Polynesian-themed bar in Hollywood late in 1933, specializing in fruity rum drinks including Missionary's Revenge the Pi Yi (served in an open pineapple), the Sumatra Kula, and the Zombie. Beach's drinks were always potent and never cheap. The Sumatra Kula sold for 75 cents (more than $13 in today's money). The 14-ounce Zombie, made with five different rums, sold for $1.75 (nearly $32 today). He decorated the place with South Seas artifacts he'd picked up over the years, including boat parts, fishing nets, and miscellaneous flotsam. The space was tiny (13 × 30 feet, patrons had to walk next door and up a flight of stairs to use the restroom), but the cozy exotic atmosphere soon became a favored drinking spot for well-known Hollywood denizens, including Charlie Chaplin, Bing Crosby, Marlene Dietrich, Greta Garbo, the Marx Brothers, and Mae West .[7]

Don's tiny Beachcomber was so successful that he leased a spot across the road and moved, opening his 175-seat bar and restaurant, now named Don the Beachcomber, in 1937. The restaurant added to its full-blown Polynesian décor. Against a backdrop of lauhala matting and bamboo, Don the Beachcomber was loaded with anything that added to the Old Pacific Hand mystique, including bunches of pineapples and bananas, fishing nets, Japanese glass floats, Polynesian tribal weaponry, rattan furniture, hurricane lamps, and anything else a beachcomber was likely to put up in his seaside shack. He flew in fresh leis aboard the Pan American Clipper, to the tune of $7,800 worth ($136,351 in today's money) by 1938 alone. These, he would wear himself, sell to patrons, and each night, would present one to the woman who he deemed to be the loveliest in the bar.[8]

Ernest Gantt's passion for all things exotic began at the age of seven, when he sailed the

Caribbean route on his grandfather's yacht, destination Jamaica. Funded by his family's sudden success in the oil business, he decided to sail the Pacific rather than attend college. He crewed on a yacht and then joined the merchant marine. By 1929, he was familiar with Australia, Borneo, Brunei, the Cook Islands, Fiji, Hawaii, Hong Kong, Indonesia, New Guinea, Singapore, Tahiti, Tonga, Japan, China, India, Africa, the Caribbean, and Central and South America. He arrived in Hollywood in 1931 and worked in jobs ranging from Chinese soup kitchens to bootlegging whiskey. The illegal liquor business was partially responsible for his name change. Mafioso and fellow bootlegger Tony Cornero jokingly referred to Gantt as a "Don," and Gantt adopted it first as the name for his bar, and later his own name, when he had it legally changed to "Donn Beach."[9]

Donn Beach had a passion for rum. Rum wasn't exactly the liquor of choice for high-tone imbibers, who generally preferred whiskey or gin, when Beach opened his bar in 1933. He'd spent considerable time in the West Indies and knew his sources. He could find it for as little as 70 cents a quart. The bar was Beach's laboratory, where he'd experiment with dark and light rums, pineapple, papaya, passion fruit, anise, vanilla, almond extract, liqueurs, and flavored brandies. Up to 12 ingredients might be used in a given drink.[10]

As his drinks became more popular, Beach added seven bartenders, each specializing in a different mix of drinks. They were backed by a number of Filipino assistants.[11] Concerned that his employees would leave and take the secrets of Beach's drinks to a competitive bar, he set up a system almost Stalinesque in secrecy. "I went to extreme lengths to preserve the secrets of my drink recipes.... From the beginning, I realized that rivals would try to raid my establishment of employees in an effort to copy the formulae," he noted. "First I removed the labels from all bottles and used a method of codes so employees could not memorize the various ingredients and proportions of my concoctions. Numbers and letters were placed on the bottles. Recipes were written in code for the bartenders, all trained by me, to follow." Falnerum, a syrup of almond, clove, lime, and ginger, was spelled backward on Don's label as "nurenlaf." Individual drinks were assembled assembly line fashion by bar assistant mixers who were capable of fingering three jiggers simultaneously, first pouring their contents into the drinking vessel before handing it over to the next mixer for additional contents. Only Beach knew exactly what went into his mix recipes, which had unexciting names including "Don's Mix #2" and "Don's Spices #7." Every drink had a different glass from which to drink it, and there were more than 50 in all.[12] Beach also maintained a serious collection of exotic rums. Eventually, his restaurants would stock 138 brands of rum, from 16 countries, to go along with some 60 of his own rum concoctions.[13]

Almost immediately, Beach had his imitators, copying his Polynesian-themed establishment and focusing on rum drinks. By 1939, there were 15 of them in the Los Angeles area alone.[14] One competitor, Harry M. Sugarman, did his best to copy Beach's Zombie at his Tropics club, which opened in 1936 in Beverly Hills, calling it a Zulu, with the tag line "One drink, you're important! Two drinks, you're impatient! Three drinks, you're impotent!"[15] Sugarman was a great competitor on promotion and word play as well. He offered a book of matches showing a bare-breasted maiden with molded breasts raised in high relief on the match cover. The text read "Fine Foods Exotic Drinks are a stand-out at the Tropics."[16] Ever the hustler, Donn Beach managed to make money off his competitors. He opened his Trade Winds Trading Company specifically to sell Polynesian décor and artifacts, bamboo, and matting to any and all bar and restaurant operators wishing to sport a Polynesian theme.[17]

Donn Beach had married business partner Cora Irene "Sunny" Sund in 1937. Sund had been with Beach since the beginning, and their first bar was begun with a loan that she had obtained. They divorced in 1940, but maintained their business relationship, opening two more restaurants, in Palm Springs and Chicago.[18] Beach was commissioned as a Captain in the U.S. Army Air Corps in 1942, and thanks to his friend Jimmy Doolittle, took on the job of opening messes and officers' clubs. He then transferred to Europe, where he was charged with requisitioning hotels, villas, and mansions for U.S. service personnel. One of these was the Villa Vismara in Capri, a 14 room, seven-bath estate, which became home to Doolittle, General Carl Spaatz, and Beach himself. He was inventive. Hearing of a secret cache of Scotch whisky in Africa, he commandeered two C-47 aircraft to bring it to Italy. He hired out-of-work Italian chefs, formerly employed by ocean liners and fine hotels. His war annals describe an adventurous time of inventiveness and, when necessary, subterfuge. At least once, the mention of his Chicago underworld friends may have saved his life while in Italy.[19] His efforts during the war earned him a Bronze Star and a Purple Heart.[20]

By the time he returned from the war, Sunny Sund had turned the Beachcomber restaurant operation into a thriving interest with several mainland locations (the number eventually reached 16). As part of their divorce agreement, Donn relinquished all interest in mainland operations, but was free to open up in Hawaii under the same name. He opened two locations in Honolulu, replete with rattan furniture, tikis, and fishing motifs. He gave himself credit for inventing the mai-tai cocktail (a claim also made by restaurateur "Trader Vic" Bergeron), and was described by writer Sven Kirsten as "a 20th century urban beachcomber, an individual somewhere between well-traveled connoisseur, beach beatnik, and marina swinger."[21] Beach's Hawaiian establishments were known for their notable Hawaiian performers, which included singers Alfred Apaka, Haunani Kahalewai and Rosalie Stevenson, musicians Martin Denny and Arthur Lyman, and dancers comprising Kent Ghirard's Hula Nani Girls, Pauline Kekahuna, Iolani Luahine, and Queenie Ventura Dowsett. At his Sunday Feast of the Islands Luau, Beach had an ensemble of more than 40 performers, which included his Beachcomber Serenaders and a 15-piece orchestra.[22]

Although located in Hawaii, Beach was never far from Hollywood. Through his film contacts, he parlayed his knowledge of the Pacific into becoming a technical advisor for the films *Hell's Half Acre* (1954, dir. John H. Auer) and *South Seas Adventure* (1958, dir. Carl Dudley, et al.), in which he also made a brief appearance playing himself. He also appeared in two short films, *Screen Snapshots: Hawaii in Hollywood* (1948) and *Screen Snapshots: Hula from Hollywood* (1954), both directed by Ralph Staub. In 1956, Beach helped launch the International Market Place in Honolulu, a massive project that included more than 40 shops, nine restaurants, tropical gardens, and Polynesian entertainment. A Don the Beachcomber restaurant was there too, along with Beach's two-story banyan tree house.[23] In 1959, he agreed to act as a consultant in the formation of the Aku Aku restaurant at the Stardust Casino in Las Vegas. He brought over a crew of restaurant workers and servers from Hawaii and was paid for each of his two trips with $50,000 cash in a brown paper bag. In 1961, he sold his interest in the restaurant at the International Market Place and moved to Lahaina, Maui, where, among other projects, he worked with architect Pete Wimberly in a successful effort to establish the Lahaina Historic District. The rest of his life was filled with a number of other grand entrepreneurial projects with varying degrees of success. He passed away in Honolulu in 1989.[24]

George J. "Pete" Wimberly (1914–1995) of the architectural firm of Wimberly Allison Tong & Goo (WATG) was noted for his Polynesian-themed tropical resorts and a number of smaller but significant projects which included Honolulu's Don the Beachcomber restaurant (1947). Known for his preference for tropical-themed buildings rather than mainland-derived structures, he favored ocean breezes over air conditioning, and designs that incorporated native elements and geological formations inherent in the locale. He first came to Hawaii in 1940 as a journeyman architect working at Pearl Harbor for the U.S. Navy. When the war ended, he stayed in Hawaii, co-founded a firm with builder Howard Cook, and immediately started on the first project, the rehabilitation of the Royal Hawaiian Hotel, which had been damaged and changed due to its use for R&R naval personnel in World War II. As noted by writer Curt Sanburn, typical elements incorporated into Wimberly's work included:

- local materials: coral stone, lava rock, wood beams, thatch, bamboo, etc.—and glass
- local forms: flowing indoor/outdoor open spaces sheltered by big, dramatic roofs with big eaves
- liberal use of figurations, patterns and motifs derived from the cultures of the Pacific[25]

Many of Wimberly's best known buildings graced Honolulu's Kalakaua Avenue and included Don the Beachcomber, the International Market Place next door, Bishop National Bank (1959), McInerny's department store (1959), and Canlis' Restaurant (1954), which was to serve as an influence on architect Charles F. McKirahan's Mai-Kai restaurant building in Fort Lauderdale, Florida. These one-story structures would all be demolished to make room for high rises and shopping malls. Another well-known building was the Waikikian Hotel (1956), "an unair-conditioned, two-story beachfront hotel on a very narrow lot with lush, tiki torch-lit gardens and a dramatic, hyperparabolic soaring lobby inspired by Melanesian men's-house forms."[26] It was demolished in 2005, "the last structure remaining in Waikiki from the brief postwar era when angular, low-slung modern designs were paired with dark native woods, glass and lava rock to create a new kind of tropical architecture."[27] Wimberly's exotic structures dotted the Pacific and included Tahiti's Hotel Bora Bora (1961), with its thatched huts built on stilts at lagoon's edge, and Tahiti's Taharaa Hotel (1969), "no taller than three-quarters of a coconut palm, spilling down a lush hillside above Matavai Bay."[28]

Honolulu, though, was Wimberly's home. By 1966, with jet-age massive Islands tourism fully established, Wimberly began to take on lucrative high-rise projects, the first of which was the 15-story Bank of Hawaii tower on Kalakaua Avenue. Large projects on Waikiki followed. Wimberly's one-story "tiki architecture" buildings have been demolished, their "footprints" having more value as pieces of real estate than as exotic, one-of-a-kind structures. They were icons of a romantic age of travel now passed, accessible today only through historical photographs. One wonders whether Wimberly's work would have had greater longevity had he designed restaurants for Vic Bergeron, rather than Donn Beach.

Victor Jules "Trader Vic" Bergeron, Jr. (1902–1984), who the *San Francisco Chronicle* called "an irascible, one-legged genius," opened Hinky Dink's, his first Polynesian-themed restaurant in Oakland in 1934. After a trip to Los Angeles in 1937, where he viewed Polynesian restaurants including the South Seas and Don the Beachcomber, Bergeron rebranded himself and his restaurant. Hinky Dink's became Trader Vic's, and Bergeron became The Trader himself (it was his wife's idea, based on the fact that he seemed to always be trading something).²⁹ He decorated his restaurant with more than $8,000 worth of Polynesian items bought from Donn Beach, beginning a friendship based on amiable competition.³⁰ Rather than offering authentic Polynesian food, he gave his Cantonese menu a twist: "I just got Chinese cooks and got them to cook it up my way," he said. "I don't want a fish coming with its eye staring at you or funny cuts of meat. This is adapted to American tastes."³¹

Bergeron invented rum drinks with inventive names including the Sufferin' Bastard.

Trader Vic's menu cover, unidentified year.

Bergeron was a bon vivant who sang, painted, sculpted, wrote cookbooks and bar guides, and invited patrons to stick an ice pick in his wooden leg. He was regularly noted and quoted by Herb Caen in his *San Francisco Chronicle* column, who enjoyed writing about Vic, at one point lauding the restaurant by saying "The best restaurant in San Francisco is in Oakland." Another time, "on a hot night…. I found Vic sitting alone at this bar, trying to adjust his artificial limb to a more comfortable position, and looking thoroughly miserable," Caen once reported. "'Let me tell you something, kid,' he said. 'Don't get one of these unless you really need it.'"[32]

Bergeron's menus featured cartoons or woodcuts of comely, bare-breasted Polynesian women, providing an idealized graphic model for the scantily clad young, dark-haired waitresses who graced many of the mainland Polynesian restaurants that followed in Vic's wake.

Bergeron opened his first franchised restaurant in Seattle in 1940, built another in Hawaii in 1950, and founded his iconic San Francisco location in 1951. By the 1960s, 25 of the restaurants were operating domestically and internationally, including a Havana, Cuba venue, which changed its name to *Polinesio* during the Castro era and remains open today, with much of the same tiki theme intact.[33] Bergeron formed a close working relationship with architect Lloyd Julius Nicholas Lovegren (1906–1989), who designed at least three Trader Vic's restaurants, in Denver (1954), Chicago (1957), and Havana (1958).[34] Vic Bergeron was always happy to credit Donn Beach with inventing the concept of the Polynesian-themed restaurant, as well as originating a host of rum drinks. But not the mai-tai. At one point Beach sued Bergeron, claiming he, not Bergeron, had invented the drink. It was reportedly settled out of court in favor of Bergeron.[35]

The successes of Donn Beach and Vic Bergeron began a wave of Polynesian restaurants on the mainland, founded by dozens of imaginative entrepreneurs, including film and recording artist Frances Langford, and three others, Bob Thornton, Bill Sapp and Lee Henry, who would scale the concept to heights unseen before, or since.

Actress and singer **Frances Langford** (1913–2005) fell in love with the South Pacific in the war years to such an extent that she and then-husband Jon Hall bought land in Jensen Beach, Florida, with the idea of opening a resort and a Polynesian-themed restaurant. After divorcing Hall, she married Ralph Evinrude, of the motorboat engine family, and opened a marina and restaurant, Frances Langford's Outrigger, at 1401 NE Indian River Drive, sometime in the 1960s. Built in Polynesian style, the restaurant had views spanning from the Stuart Causeway all the way up the river to the Jensen Beach Causeway Bridge. The restaurant was designed and managed by Ed Lawrence, a Hollywood set designer and architect who worked on the original Don the Beachcomber restaurants and did the set designs for the feature film *Rain* (1932, dir. Lewis Milestone).[36] After hard economic times, the restaurant was sold and refurbished, with the assistance of Langford. As of this writing it's still serving food and drink as the Dolphin Bar and Shrimp House, and includes a shrine dedicated to Langford.[37]

Fort Lauderdale, Florida's Mai-Kai restaurant was opened by 25-year-old Robert F. "Bob" (1932?–1989) and brother Jack R. Thornton (1929–2008) in 1956. Bob and Jack's father, Fulton, a successful Wilmette, Illinois, businessman, had made it a habit of taking his young sons to the Chicago location of Don the Beachcomber, where they were smitten with the exotic ambience of the tropical-themed restaurant. The boys' mother, Helen "Betty" Schraeder, was the daughter of the owners of the Monarch Brewing Company, and Fulton Thornton's marriage to Betty eventually led to his becoming president of the company. With a family background in business and libations, Bob and Jack attended Stanford University and spent a significant amount of their non-study time in visiting various Polynesian-themed restaurants and bars in the San Francisco Bay Area, picking up ideas that would culminate years later with the formation of the Mai-Kai. They spent spring break of 1951 in Hawaii, further whetting their appetites for Polynesian culture and entertainment. They left college for military service, serving in Fort Lauderdale.[38]

After their military years, Bob and Jack, desiring to learn the business from the inside, hung out or worked in a number of Polynesian restaurants on the mainland and in Hawaii, observing business, entertainment, and food and beverage operations. One of their employers was Donn Beach.[39] They met Robert "Bob" Van Dorpe (b. 1926), a buyer and one of the seating captains for Chicago's Don the Beachcomber, and soon became fast friends, each with a passion for eventually starting their own restaurants. They quickly came to an agreement that the Thorntons would open a Polynesian-themed restaurant and Van Dorpe, as general manager, would take charge of purchasing and personnel. The Thorntons selected Fort Lauderdale as the city of choice for their new restaurant, and hired architect Charles F. McKirahan Sr., (1920?–1964) to build it.[40] McKirahan had been stationed in the Pacific with the Army Corps of Engineers, had an affinity for Polynesia, and took several trips with the Thornton brothers to scout out competitive Polynesian-themed restaurant buildings, including architect Pete Wimberly's Canlis Restaurant in Honolulu. The result was McKirahan's exotic 40-foot-high A-frame façade, built in Fort Lauderdale, with expansive wings, waterways, and an open roof (the building would eventually be added to the National Register for Historic Places). The Mai-Kai was financed with $40,000 each from Bob and Jack, $60,000 from mother Betty, plus additional collateral from her to float a loan.[41] It opened in December 1956. Reportedly costing $1 million to build, it grossed that same amount in its first year of business. Wayne Davidson (1917?–1998) and George Nakashima are two of the people credited with the original décor, which featured an abundance of Polynesian artifacts, including a shrunken head in the Samoa room, a tropical garden, and cascading waterfalls. Much of the Filipino and Chinese kitchen and bar staff at the Mai-Kai came directly from Chicago's Don the Beachcomber facility. As the story goes, while they loved Donn Beach, they were less than enthusiastic about working for his former wife, Sunny Sund, who had taken over the business after the divorce. One of her boyfriends had gotten into a heated argument with head chef Lee Zoun, which led to a three-day staff walkout. The end result was that a number of the staff soon left to begin employment at the Mai-Kai. Several of the Filipinos were already familiar with Florida, having come there for holidays to play the horses. As there was no Chinese community in Fort Lauderdale, the Thorntons bought an apartment building that enabled them to live together.[42]

Beautiful women were a critical element of the Mai-Kai brand, and Bob Thornton was adamant that they kept their figures throughout their employment. In the process of putting the wait staff together, the first 50 women Bob Thornton interviewed for the job didn't meet his expectations, so model, agent, bikini designer, and photographer Linnea Eleanor "Bunny" Yeager (1929–2014) was called in to assist. Her first choice, the legendary Bettie Page (1923–2008), turned down the job because it didn't pay enough. *Playboy* centerfold Myrna Weber was one woman that did make the cut, appearing as the Mai-Kai's Mystery Girl several months after the issue hit the stands. Scantily clad beauties, who often worked second jobs as models, served drinks in the Mai-Kai's 150-seat Molokai Bar. The original dress code mandated dark hair, which blondes achieved by dyeing or wearing wigs. Their revealing costumes were custom-made to their proportions, easier to work in than the stiff tops and stiletto heels mandated by the Playboy Club in Miami, a few miles to the south, which opened in 1961 and competed with the Mai-Kai in hiring the area's beautiful women. Waitresses averaged $300 to $400 a night at the Mai-Kai, roughly $3000 in today's money.[43]

Of the women on the wait staff, the Mystery Girl who presided over the Mystery Drink ceremony was the most prominent. Heralded by the sound of a gong, she would appear barefoot, in a torso-revealing grass skirt and a small strapless top. The drink, consisting of 13 shots of rum, was presented in a specially designed bowl holding four long straws, and the recipient was always a man. The Mystery Girl would enter with an exotic dance, present the flaming bowl, remove her lei, bend close while draping it over his neck, and give him a kiss. She would finish her dance before exiting. Her appearance was considered special enough that she had no other customer-facing duties at the club. Her revealing top, like those of the other female Mai-Kai servers, was a conversation point in the Fort Lauderdale of the day, which still banned bikini tops on beaches.

The Mai-Kai's beauties, clad either in their working wear of sarongs with strapless tops or in bikinis, also appeared in the restaurant's pin-up calendars, which were produced from 1963 through 1990. Those from the 1960s through the early 1970s, designed by Al Kocab, were in a 6 × 9 inch stand-up format. Ideal for desks, the pin-up girl faced the man behind the desk while the calendar graced the view of the visitor on the opposite side of the desk. Kocab's pen-and-ink renderings of restaurant interiors, customers, and employees appeared on the calendar pages. Many of the mid-to-late 1960s calendar photos, taken on the Mai-Kai's interior and grounds, were shot by noted New York photographer Sid Latham.[44] Available by mail or in the Mai-Kai's gift shop for 50 cents (roughly $3.50 in today's money), the calendars were virtual giveaways that probably did little more than pay for their production cost, but they had a promotion value far beyond their revenue.

Mai-Kai girls also figured prominently in the 8mm color film *Mai-Kai*, probably made by James A. "Jaf" Fletcher.[45] Like the calendars and tiki vessels, the film could be purchased by mail order or in the restaurant's gift shop. The movie's box cover displayed a photo of a waitress, adorned in a low-cut strapless top, serving a pineapple, and invited the viewer to watch "Saronged serving girls" and the "Mystery Drink Ritual."[46]

An additional promotional item was the restaurant-produced quarterly mailed *Happy Talk* newsletter, which featured an ongoing column by a Mai-Kai regular who wrote under the name Pahea Ka Piko. He was Leslie Charteris (b. Leslie Charles Bowyer-Yin, 1907–1993), creator of *The Saint* series of books, films, and television programs. Charteris received free food and drink in return for writing the column. Each issue also featured a tongue in-cheek, barely plausible story on one of the Mai-Kai women.[47]

Tahiti-born Mireille Levy had joined the Mai-Kai's in-house dance troupe for its inaugural performance in 1961. She had been discovered in Tahiti by Bob Van Dorpe, who danced with her at a party. Although admitting that she wasn't adept at traditional dances, she was hired by Bob Thornton on Van Dorpe's recommendation. Upon seeing her dance, Thornton fired her, adding that she was also overweight. Dancer Toti Terorotua pleaded with Thornton to keep her, and she was given a two-week reprieve. Given a boot camp in Tahitian dancing by Toti and his wife Sizou, and adopting a harsh training regimen to lose weight, she was reinstated. Sizou also taught her the art of choreography. She became the chief choreographer

Mai-Kai islanders, 1972 calendar designed by Al Kocab (Lisa Kocab Meade).

and costume designer in 1962, traveling regularly to the Pacific to ensure the authenticity of the costumes and dances. In 1971, she and Bob Thornton were married. The Mai-Kai featured as many as three performances per evening, each consisting of 11 production numbers, performed by the likes of Pasefika and Teronga in their Samoan fire and knife dance, and the Tahitian drum dance performed by Kainoa.[48] The staff and performers, wanting some party-time on their own, often departed the Mai-Kai, which closed at 3 or 4 a.m. during the winter months, and continued the revelry up the road at Porky's Hideaway, which stayed open until 5 a.m.[49] At least two prominent Hawaiians known for their careers in entertainment set up island shops in the Mai-Kai. Dancer and model Pualani Mossman Avon (1916–2006), a Florida resident, opened a Hawaiian store there, as did artist and singer-songwriter Kuiokalani "Kui" Lee (1932–1966), who also designed a bowl for the Mystery Drink before returning to Hawaii.[50]

In 1969 Bob Thornton came to the conclusion that the business relationship with brother Jack was becoming a challenge and determined that either he'd buy out his brother's share of the Mai-Kai or sell his share to Jack. It was agreed that Bob would buy Jack out and Bob took full control of the Mai-Kai in 1970. Waiting lines at the Mai-Kai were an ongoing issue, and Bob Thornton answered it with a series of renovations and expansions, done mostly at night to ensure the restaurant would never close. In 1969, it grew from 225 to 600 seats.[51] The same year, the Molokai Bar was reconfigured to resemble a wooden sailing vessel, shored up by old timbers from sunken vessels, and featured cascades of water falling down its windows to simulate a tropical rainstorm. Much of the rattan furniture, lamps, and drinking vessels in the bar were designed by Al Kocab, who also worked with George Nakashima on architectural mockups for the renovations.[52]

The Mai-Kai's lush tropical landscape, which included waterfalls, allegedly 400 varieties of palm trees, tropical plants, and shrubs, had been designed by landscape designer Pat Wells over a ten-year period, reportedly costing $350,000. Greenhouses were added, which housed tropical plants that were rotated back through the Mai-Kai every month, traded for the sun-starved indoor plants which would re-appear in the restaurant when revitalized. The overall indoor-outdoor ambiance led a number of companies to shoot tropical-themed advertisements there, including Eastern Airlines, Hertz, and L&M Cigarettes.[53] By 1981, the 600-seat venue was grossing $7 million in annual revenue, with a staff of 225, including 11 parking valets.[54]

Bob Thornton ran the restaurant until his death at age 57 in 1989, the same year his mentor and old friend Donn Beach passed away. Bob was succeeded by Mireille Thornton, and later by her son David Levy. In addition to its still-thriving entertainment-themed restaurant business, the Mai-Kai restaurant hosts the Hukilau, billed as the world's second largest tiki event, over a four-day period each year.[55]

The **Kahiki Supper Club** was opened in 1961 by Bill Sapp and Leland W. "Lee" Henry, Jr. (1930–2015) in Columbus Ohio, two years after their bar, the Grass Shack, burned to the ground on the same site. The Kahiki would be better protected, spirit-wise, thanks to Philip E. Kientz (1924–2006), who cast two 20-foot-tall Rapa Nui Moai heads in reinforced concrete for the new restaurant.[56] With hair aflame, they guarded the moat, the front door, and the briefly costumed Korean and Japanese cocktail waitresses inside. Sapp and Henry, noting the successes of other mainland Polynesian-themed restaurants during their travels, hired Bernard "Bernie" Altenbach (1927–1998?) as the architect, who based his design on a New Guinea meeting house.[57] When Altenbach's workload became too heavy, the responsibility to finish the Kahiki fell on the shoulders of Coburn Morgan, head of the design division at Tectum Company, responsible for much of the engineering and design, and Ned B. Eller and Ralph Sounik (d. 2012) of Design Associates Architects, who completed the blueprints.[58] At a cost of more than $1 million, the Kahiki, which Bill Sapp named after identifying the word in a Polynesian dictionary (it was defined as "sail to Tahiti"), took seven months to build. It was a classic example of Polynesian mid-century architecture with an upwardly soaring roofline rising to meet the peak of the 50-foot A-Frame facade. It was 150 feet long and 70 feet wide. It was huge, with three bars and seats for 560 guests.[59] Inside were thatched huts, luxuriant tropic flora, and tropical birds patrolling the aviary, where tropical thunderstorms, thunder, and lightning occurred on an ongoing basis, augmenting the water theme established by the South Pacific tropical fish in the wall-sized aquarium. The most arresting icon in the club was a 20-foot high moai fireplace, with open mouth aglow, integrated with a waterfall.[60] Writer Wayne Curtis described the interior: "No surface was unmolested. In and around the dining huts were totems, carved masks, woven grass mats, parts of ersatz shipwrecks, lamps fashioned from seashells, fountains spewing luridly tinted water, adult beverages served in skull-shaped mugs, and an assortment of lavishly varnished blowfish."[61] The Outrigger and Maui bars lined the foyer, and patrons ordered tropical drinks from sculpted Polynesian cups, which they were invited to take home as souvenirs. The exotic choices of food could be problematic, for diners as well as servers. Hot hand towels could be mistaken for egg rolls, and one diner, after adding mustard and sweet-and-sour sauce, took a bite and pronounced that these were the worst egg rolls she'd ever had. They were taken away and discreetly replaced with real egg rolls. Another diner ordered a flaming dessert. Upon tableside ignition, "the flames were about 2 feet high and quickly advanced across the table and engulfed the bread basket." Several waiters rushed in to douse the blaze.[62] Drinks were served in an assortment of 30 different goblets, glasses, and other vessels, culminating with the Mystery Drink for four, heralded by a gong and served by a barely clothed waitress offering the recipient a lei and a kiss. The Kahiki boasted a multi-ethnic workforce. When it opened, the waitresses were predominantly Japanese and Korean wives of former U.S. servicemen, and latter-day Caucasian waitresses either dyed their hair or wore dark-colored wigs as part of the dress-code, "the poofier the better."[63]

The exotica house band was the Beachcomber Trio, led by multi-instrumentalist Marcel "Marsh" Padilla (1918–2010), and included a significant number of other players during the 17 years he served as music director.[64] Columbus was noted as one of the homes of the summer stock Kenley Players, which made liberal use of film and television stars in its productions.[65] Visiting Kenley celebrities who dined and drank at the Kahiki included Milton Berle, Raymond Burr, Zsa Zsa Gabor, Robert Goulet, Paul Lynde, and Andy Williams.

In 1978, Sapp and Henry sold the Kahiki to local businessman Michael M. "Mitch" Boich (d. 2000). In 1980, Michael (1950?–2005) and Alice Tsao were brought in from Trader Vic's in Hollywood to run the club. The Tsaos acquired the Kahiki in 1988. The fact that the Kahiki was placed on National Register of Historic Places in 1997 didn't do much to boost its flagging business. The area had become run-down and well-heeled patrons increasingly disliked its location. The club was showing signs of wear, and the cost of remodeling became daunting to Tsao. Items needing renovation included the dicey rainforest water system, backed up drains, and rotting timbers. Choosing to focus on their growing frozen food business, the Tsaos closed the Kahiki in 2000.[66] The building, purchased by Walgreens, closed on Aug. 25, 2000, and was razed to make way for another structure. Before his death, Michael Tsao had intended to reconstruct the Kahiki on Columbus' riverfront, but he passed away before anything would materialize. Many of the interior and exterior design elements were eventually sold to collectors.[67] Mid-century tiki items, particularly those that can be linked to a specific venue, are getting increasingly hard to come by, even for seasoned tikiers. An added cachet is imparted if the piece can be associated with a particular designer, craftsperson, or architect renowned for working within the tiki environment. They range from the legendary Steve Crane to the barely known Al Kocab, but all of them created work that was memorable and helped to define the tiki world as a culturally and artistic phenomenon.

Polynesian-Themed Designers

There are a number of significant designers that contributed to Polynesian-inspired businesses in the United States. Those who are noted here should be considered to be just a taste of what is ultimately a larger drink of water. A future book written on the subject of the hundreds of individual design contributors to the Polynesian American gestalt would be a large one indeed. Among the most significant designers are Steve Crane, Eli Hedley, Al Kocab, Ed Lawrence, Coburn Morgan, Robert Van Oosting and LeRoy Schmaltz, and William Westenhaver.

Joseph Stephenson "Stephen" Crane (1916–1985) was an iconoclast in the Polynesian-themed restaurant world, a legendary bon vivant on a par with Donn Beach and Vic Bergeron. Born in Indiana, he moved to Hollywood in 1939 to pursue an acting career. While in the process of drumming up acting roles, Crane had found that his true calling was living the high-life, engaging in fine dining and dating Hollywood starlets and A-List actresses, including Ava Gardner, Rita Hayworth, and Lana Turner. He famously entertained each of them individually on successive evenings at *Ciro's* in Hollywood, prompting one of the nightclub's owners to remark: "This town's three top queens, I never saw *anybody* do that." In 1942 he married Turner, with whom he had a daughter. Referring to their tumultuous relationship, Turner asked, "How does it happen that something that makes so much sense in the moonlight doesn't make any sense in the sunlight?"[68]

Crane's first film screen presence occurred in Columbia Pictures' *Cry of the Werewolf* (1944, dir. Henry Levin). Two more Columbia films followed, *Tonight and Every Night* (1945, dir. Victor Saville, co-starring a barely showing yet pregnant Rita Hayworth, a past love interest of Crane's, and *The Crime Doctor's Courage* (1945, dir. George Sherman). Crane's Columbia goose, however, was soon to be cooked. After entertaining a Polish ballerina in his apartment, Columbia mogul Harry Cohn called him into his office, where Crane was summarily fired. The dancer was Cohn's girlfriend. Crane bought his first restaurant, a trendy nightspot called Lucy's, in 1946. Its regulars included Humphrey Bogart, Ava Gardner, and Robert Mitchum. He sold it in the late 1940s, eager to live in Paris. There, he failed to become a Europe-based gossip columnist, but took advantage of his personal charm to live the life of an international playboy on the French Riviera and the North African coast, counting Prince Rainer of Monaco, Egypt's King Faroukh, and Aristotle Onassis among his friends. He was a regular at the casino in Monte Carlo, supporting his gambling losses by smuggling liquor, luxury items, and miscellaneous contraband. He returned to the United States in October 1950.[69]

He opened his 174-seat The Luau restaurant on Rodeo Drive in July 1953, in the space formerly occupied by Harry Sugarman's The Tropics. To attract men to his new venue, daughter Cheryl Crane noted that her father discreetly encouraged failed starlets and high-priced, well-heeled sex workers to mingle with male customers at the bar. Cozy, dimly lit booths were only a few feet away.[70] Embracing the Polynesian theme, he emphasized the importance of the tiki in the text of his menus. Encouraged by the success of his restaurant, he founded the design firm of Stephen Crane Associates (SCA), utilizing the talents of designers that included George Nakashima and Florian Gabriel. In 1958, his firm was hired by Sheraton hotels to design the Polynesian-themed Kon-Tiki restaurant (Crane had licensed the name from adventurer Thor Heyerdahl) for its hotel in Montreal.[71] Crane-designed Sheraton Kon-Tikis soon arrived in Portland, Cincinnati, Cleveland, Dallas, and Honolulu, along with restaurants named Kon-Tiki Ports in Boston and Chicago, and Ports o' Call in Dallas and Toronto. Crane's firm supplied all manner of Polynesian décor and furnishings, along with water features including a waterfall designed into the restaurant in Dallas. He owned and operated each of the restaurants.[72] By 1969, SCA had 200 employees and was bringing in some $10 million a year in licenses and restaurants. By 1978, the revenue had doubled to approximately $20 million a year. Crane sold The Luau that year for $4.1 million, to a consortium that wanted to develop the property, and bulldozed it the following year. It was his last business deal.[73] Stephen Crane died on Feb. 6, 1985, largely a forgotten man. As daughter Cheryl Crane wrote, "Dad knew that his glory days were gone, never to return. The new movie stars were all on diets, didn't drink, and had never heard of him. The studios were now owned by soft-drink conglomerates.... Where the Luau had flourished there now stood a chrome and marble shopper's paradise called "The Rodeo Collection.""[74]

Texas born **Eli Hedley** (1903–1981), failing to make ends meet as a Piggly Wiggly grocer in Depression-era Oklahoma, moved his wife and three daughters (a fourth would come later) to land leased from the military on Whites Point, near San Pedro, California.[75] There, he found a dilapidated home that he soon filled his home with furniture and decorative accents he crafted from driftwood and miscellaneous pieces of flotsam that had washed up on nearby beaches. His daughter Marilyn describes his newfound treasures: "Rusty anchors, crusted with pink barnacles, life preservers gray with the buffeting of the sea and wind, reams of dark brown fishnet, all weaves.... Net needles, slick from lying buried in the sand, fish floats of blue, amber, and amethyst glass, driftwood, beautiful, bizarre, and grotesque, star fishes ... and silvery corks strung on chocolate brown rope."[76]

The family was living a hand-to-mouth existence and Hedley began taking his findings into Los Angeles, his pick-up truck loaded to the gills, trying to sell its contents to various businesses. His first customer was Bullock's Wilshire, whose display managers sought something different and exotic for the department store's windows. Soon, Bullock's made a decision to decorate their entire store for the summer with a beachcomber motif, with everything supplied by Hedley. Emboldened with his success, Hedley then offered his creations to Hollywood studios. Columbia Pictures became his first studio customer, using his décor for the film *Cover Girl* (1944, dir. Charles Vidor). Other studios followed, including MGM, Paramount, and Warner Bros. The Hedley house on White Point was used as a background for at least the first film in Columbia Pictures' *Jungle Jim* series (1948, dir. William Berke).[77] Wishing to solidify control over strategic areas on California's coast, the military took command of Whites Point, whereupon the Hedley family moved to Hollywood, where Hedley opened a shop on La Cienega Boulevard. A customer of the shop, set designer and painter Eugene Berman, soon became a good friend.[78] Hedley's beachcombing locations became further extended each year, running from as far south as Mexico and north as far as Washington State. The excursions were memorable family events. Daughter Marilyn remembered: "We have all reached the status of true vagabondism. We can feel at home anywhere. We go in our station wagon, taking a big trailer for carrying our beachcombings and sleeping bags. We take wool blankets, seven spoons, seven plates, seven breakfast food bowls (somebody might happen to drop in), a big knife, a can opener, an iron pot, an iron skillet, and a big coffee pot. Anything else on a trip is too much.... And too, daddy has a side road complex, really a fixation.... We go joggety jog down a dirt road for miles."[79]

Over the years, Hedley also provided furnishings to a number of mainland Polynesian clubs (Donn Beach was a customer) hotels, apartment buildings, and Polynesian rooms, most notably the Stardust Hotel's Aku Aku in Las Vegas. Hedley became known for his hand-carved tiki figures and opened his Island Trade Store to sell his creations, first in Huntington

Beach and later in Disneyland's Adventureland. In the late 1970s, he retired to the Islander Apartments in Santa Ana, which he had decorated some years earlier.[80]

In the world of Polynesian design, painter, illustrator, and craftsman, **Al Kocab** was primarily known as the creator of much of the furniture and décor of Fort Lauderdale's Mai-Kai Restaurant. Originally from Cleveland, he was an airman stationed at the Amarillo Air Force Base, where he worked with Dave Stevens in the Visual Aids department. In the winter of 1960, he made a trip to Fort Lauderdale to visit Stevens, who owned a sign business and was doing additional work for the Mai-Kai as an artisan, crafting elements that included ersatz rocks and tortoise shells (he was also known for his three-dimensional billboards, including the "winking girl" he created for the Kahiki Supper Club in Columbus, Ohio).[81]

Al Kocab in 1966 (Lisa Kocab Meade).

Kocab began working for Stevens' sign business, and became enamored of Bob Thornton's tiki-inspired themes. Kocab designed a tiki decanter, several of the restaurant's tiki-inspired drinking vessels (including a shrunken head coffee cup), its table lamps, ceiling fixtures, and outside lights, as well as its advertisements, postcards, and pin-up calendars. Along with Leonce Picot (b. 1932), a manager and marketing director at the Mai-Kai, he co-authored several restaurant guides highlighting dining experiences in Puerto Rico, Florida, New York, and San Francisco. The experience of writing the books encouraged them to start their own restaurant in Fort Lauderdale, the Down Under, in 1968. The exterior was crafted by local architect Dan Duckham, with the interior built by Kocab. The restaurant featured a New Orleans-inspired wrought iron balcony, with gaslights and ancient bricks forming the fireplace. Their Casa Vecchia (now Go Fish!) restaurant, also in Fort Lauderdale, opened in 1979 and featured a casual island theme, replete with stained glass and an antique cut glass parrot.[82] Believing art was a necessary accent for just about everything, Kocab hand-painted an individual design on each blade of the ceiling fans. Kocab passed away in 1994 at the age of 64.[83]

Ed Lawrence has seemingly slipped under the radar of biographers. A set designer for the 1932 film version of W. Somerset Maugham's Rain (dir. Lewis Milestone), Lawrence is said to have designed the interior of Don the Beachcomber in Hollywood in the 1930s. He's also credited with designing the Kalua Room in Seattle's Hotel Windsor (approximately 1953), and Frances Langford's Outrigger (1960s), which he also managed.[84]

Coburn Morgan was a prominent restaurant designer from Ohio, noted for engineering and decorating the Kahiki Supper Club in Columbus in 1960. At the time, he was head of the design division for the Tectum Company, which made composite construction materials including pressed wood for roof supports, soundproofing, and decorative wall panels. National

Mai-Kai decanter, shrunken head mug and tiki mug designed by Al Kocab (Lisa Kocab Meade).

Gypsum, which bought the firm in 1963, described the versatility of the panels: "The panels made of shredded wood treated with certain special chemicals [provide] a structural roof deck, insulation, fire resistance, sound proofing, and a decorative, attractive ceiling on the other side—all in one product."[85] After the Kahiki, Morgan went to the design a number of other themed restaurants, including the Thunderbird Restaurant (featuring Aztec motifs) in Lima, Ohio, and the Tangier Restaurant in Akron.[86]

Oceanic Arts was founded in 1956 by college buddies **Robert Van Oosting** and **LeRoy Schmaltz**. They began by carving masks out of palm fronds, and soon met Robert Carter, who was supplying interior items for both Don the Beachcomber and Trader Vic's. Oosting and Schmaltz carved everything from Tahitian support posts to masks and weaponry, selling to Carter and other designers working in Polynesian restaurants. In the early 1960s, after a grand South Pacific tour, they opened a shop in an old horse barn in Whittier, California, moved again in 1964, relocated in the 1980s to a 15,000 square foot facility leased from Southern Pacific, and made their final move in 1990 to a 10,000-square-foot facility on Whittier Boulevard, which included its own railroad spur. They've employed numerous carvers in their 60-plus years of existence. Their customers include the Getty Corporation, Marriott Hotels, and Disney World's Polynesian Village Resort. Unlike many of the companies and people associated with Polynesian-themed tiki culture, this company continues to prosper. Ironically, as native island carvers moved to more lucrative careers, Oceanic Arts began selling its carved-in-California Polynesian sculptures to venues in Hawaii, Samoa, and Tahiti. They also acquired native artifacts from the Asia-Pacific region. After buying a significant number of pieces from a competitor that was going out of business, they began a sideline business, renting décor to the film industry as set material. They've evolved with the times, marketing their décor on their informative website, which includes a photo of one of their most remarkable pieces, the massive 20-foot-high, 5½ ton *#109—Maori Tiki*, carved by Ed Crissman.[87]

William Westenhaver (1925–2016) was born in Washington state and discovered Polynesian culture while serving in the military in World War II. In the Pacific, he found a passion for drawing and witnessed the work of native carvers in the Admiralty Islands. After the war, he enrolled in Los Angeles' Art Center School of Design under the GI bill, and eventually returned with his family to Washington. There, he and cousin Robert Post, Jr., creator of Western International Trading Company (later Witco Decor Inc.), worked together specializing in furnishings with Polynesian accents.[88] Witco produced interior elements that enabled buyers to have Polynesian-inspired décor in their own homes, with carved tribal motifs that included chairs (often sporting faux leopard-skin prints), tables, beds, wall art, statues, and tiki bars.[89] Witco customers included Hugh Hefner, Roy Orbison, and Elvis Presley. By the 1960s, Witco had showrooms in a number of large mainland cities. With the decline of the mass popularity of Polynesian décor, Witco closed its doors in the late 1970s, allowing Westenhaver to concentrate on his own painting and carving pursuits.[90]

Tiki Culture and the Television Experience

How did a mainlander without a nearby tiki venue get a steady dose of tiki culture without having to travel to Hawaii? Via rabbit ears. Beginning in the late 1950s, an ongoing barrage of serial television programming focusing on Hawaii has been beamed into America's living rooms, magnetically pulling the mainland back to the islands. Stateside tiki enthusiasts are among the millions of viewers who bring island culture into their homes each week. Due to its pervasive presence on mainland TV screens, tiki icons, along with Polynesian architecture, aloha shirts, and rattan furniture, allow home viewers to have Hawaiian objects in their living rooms without actually having to pay for them. And if the TV screen is big enough, Hawaii's presence can be enlarged to the extent that an island scene can be transformed into an additional room in the home of the viewer, allowing him or her to be virtually present in the islands.

Although the most common theme of Hawaiian-oriented television programming has been the island-based detective drama, one of the earliest tropical series didn't really have much to do with Hawaii at all, nor was it particularly crime-related.

Running from October 1959 through early April 1962, ABC's 91-episode *Adventures in Paradise*, created by James Michener, followed the exploits of Captain Adam Troy (Gardner McKay) in the South Pacific seas aboard his *Tiki III* schooner. The colors of the tropics had to be supplied by the viewers, as the show was filmed in black and white. *Paradise* was famous for the allure of its beautiful guest stars, which included Barbara Bain, Yvonne DeCarlo, Barbara Eden, Suzanne Pleshette, Inger Stevens. Noted tenor saxophonist Richie Kamuca also appeared as a guest, as did a who's who of male television supporting actors.[91]

The first of the Hawaiian detective crime shows was *Hawaiian Eye*, an ABC series that ran for four seasons, from October 1959 through April 1963, comprising 134 episodes. It was filmed both on Oahu and at the Warner Bros. lot in Burbank and focused on a detective agency and private security firm, initially run by Tracy Steele (Anthony Eisley) and Tom Lopaka (Robert Conrad), assisted occasionally by photographer Cricket Blake (Connie Stevens), who also sang in the Shell Bar in the Hawaiian Village Hotel. The cast included nine regularly appearing characters. Musical guests included Arthur Lyman and Sterling Mossman and his Barefoot Bar Gang. The show was sponsored by Henry J. Kaiser, looking for a novel way to promote his Hawaiian Village Hotel.[92]

Five years later came the CBS *Hawaii Five-O* series, which ran from 1968 to 1980, starring Jack Lord as Detective Captain Steve McGarrett, the head of a fictional special state police task force. Comprising 279 episodes, it was shot in color in various Hawaiian locales as well as several shot in California, and one each in Hong Kong, and Singapore. Up until 2003, it was the longest running crime show on American television. The series focused on Hawaiian and international crime syndicates, and crime bosses were played by actors such as Ross Martin, Gavin MacLeod, and Ricardo Montalbán. Filming was done under hardscrabble conditions during the early years. Honolulu was a long way from Hollywood, and the show's first season was shot from a leaky Quonset hut in Pearl City. Filming conditions were primitive compared to Hollywood. Rats gnawed on the cables and locals on the crew learned their crafts on the job. A studio was eventually built at Diamond Head and was used during the final four seasons.[93] A remake of the series was begun in 2010 and continues to run through 2018, comprising more than 180 episodes, with McGarrett's role played by Alex O'Loughlin. Writer Jerry Hopkins suggested the importance of Hawaii itself in the series, occupying a role as virtually a character in itself. "Never has scenery played such and important series or movie role," he noted.[94]

Magnum, P.I., starring Tom Selleck as private investigator Thomas Sullivan Magnum IV, was launched in 1980, the final year of the original *Hawaii Five-O* series. Filmed in Hawaii, the CBS series comprised 162 episodes over an eight year run, ending in 1988. Selleck's character was known for his Hawaiian shirts, the Ferrari he drove, and the countless numbers of beautiful damsels in distress, available to be rescued from one predicament or another by Magnum. As was the case with the earlier Hawaii-based series, guest stars were an important drawing card, and included James Doohan, Patrick Macnee, Frank Sinatra, Sharon Stone, and Leslie Uggams. Much of the location shooting was done at the Pahonu estate on the shores of eastern Oahu, which has been on the National Register of Historic Places listings in Hawaii since 1978.[95] In an interesting side note, Selleck was chosen by George Lucas and Steven Spielberg to play Indiana Jones for the film that became *Raiders of the Lost Ark*, but had to turn down the role due to his commitment on the Magnum series. The role went to Harrison Ford instead.[96]

The CBS series *Jake and the Fat Man*, starring William Conrad as prosecutor J. L. (Jason Lochinvar) "Fatman" McCabe and Joe Penny as investigator Jake Styles, was a hybrid of sorts. Running from September 1987 to May 1992, the show's first season was filmed in Los Angeles, then moved to Hawaii for its second year, after *Magnum P.I.*'s run ended. Hawaii filming resumed in year three, and half of year four, when it returned to Los Angeles to finish out its run of 106 episodes.[97]

CBS tested the waters with a medical drama set in Hawaii, starring Richard (Dr. Kildaire) Chamberlain in the *Island Son* series, which ran from September 1989 to March 1990, comprising 18 episodes. Chamberlain played the role of Dr. Daniel Kulani, born in Hawaii, who returned to the islands after having practiced for many years on the mainland. One of the show's co-creators was noted National Educational Television documentarist Lane Slate.[98]

Probably even more television shows and films would have been produced in Hawaii if it hadn't been for the expensive employee padding mandates of the islands' Teamsters Union. *Magnum, P.I., Jake and the Fat Man,* and *Island Son* were among the productions plagued by problems associated with the Hawaii Teamsters Union Local 996 production and unit leadership and drivers, and its relationship with the local organized crime syndicate. Founded by Arthur Rutledge in the 1960s, the union was populated by "a rogue's gallery of felons and head-breakers," according to author James Dooley. "Literally dozens of drivers had long, varied, and sometimes very violent criminal careers. Drivers regularly shuttled between film sets and prison, keeping up with their union dues while locked behind bars." Tom Selleck complained that *Magnum* producers were forced by the union to hire twice the necessary drivers and had little say in the matter of who was hired and fired. Union drivers refused to show up during the production of *Fat Man,* and the show's transportation coordinator Leroy Reed complained of daily intimidation by union members. Leo Reed, head of Teamsters Local 399 in Los Angeles, said that there would have been 10 times as many productions in Hawaii if the local union hadn't insisted on hiring unnecessary drivers. Payroll padding wasn't the only problem. In 1991, teamsters George Cambra and Joseph Tavares torched expensive film production vehicles owned by two competitors of George Cambra Movie Production Trucks, Inc., forcing those companies out of business and resulting in Cambra becoming the islands' main film vehicle supplier.[99]

Despite the constant union battles, mainland production companies were drawn by the islands' beauty. CBS was one of them, resuming its Hawaiian detective programming in August 1994 with the *One West Waikiki* series, starring Cheryl Ladd as Dr. Dawn "Holli" Holliday, the state of Hawaii's medical examiner, and Richard Burgi as Honolulu homicide detective Lt. Mack Wolfe. The show comprised 19 episodes and finished its run in May 1996.[100]

The most famous fictional Hawaiian detective in the pre-television era was Charlie Chan, who became increasingly popular to baby boomers when older Chan films began appearing on afternoon and late night television in the 1960s. Ironically, Honolulu's best-known real life detective never appeared on screen, but Chang Apana (1871–1933), famous for arresting 40 gamblers singlehandedly while armed with only his home-made bullwhip, was the model for Charlie Chan. Chan's creator, Earl Derr Biggers, acknowledged Chang as the inspiration for his fictional detective. Chang Apana worked as a paniolo (Hawaiian cowboy) in his youth and carried a bullwhip as one of the tools of his trade. He joined the Honolulu Police Department in as a patrolman in 1898, working the part of Chinatown known as Hell's Half-Acre. He became a detective in 1916, focusing on gambling and opium traffic, and his fluency in multiple languages and use of informants was critical to his success in solving crimes. Biggers either met Chang or read about him (sources vary), but he acknowledged Chang to be Charlie Chan's inspiration in 1932. Biggers wrote a total of six *Charlie Chan* novels, leading to more than four dozen films based on the Chan character, the best-known of which starred Swedish actor Warner Oland. Charlie Chan's place as either a role model or stereotype remains ambiguous, as discussed by writer Jerry Hopkins: "Chan also remained a controversial figure—one side insisting he created respect for Asians in a time when no one else did, the other side arguing that the subservient, cartoonish way the detective was portrayed both in print and on film—and by Caucasian actors in most of the films—made him as much a racial stereotype as Fu Manchu."[101] One writer who viewed Chan's persona as a unique cultural element was Chinese-born writer and professor Yunte Huang. In his book *Charlie Chan: The Untold Story of the Honorable Detective and His Rendezvous with American History*, he likens Chan to legendary fictional detectives Philip Marlowe, Sam Spade, and Hercule Poirot, but with a difference: "The core strength of Chan's character lies in his pseudo-Confucian, aphoristic wisdom. Unlike the Kung Fu movies, which showcase a Chinese penchant for ass-kicking and sword-brandishing, Chan reveals the Chinaman as a sage: a wise, calm, responsible, and commonsensical man who also happens to be a hilarious wisecracker.... Charlie Chan, America's most identifiable Chinaman, epitomizes both the racist heritage and the creative genius of this nation's culture.... Each of these streams is a story in itself, a slice of bona fide Americana."[102]

Tiki culture represents one of the most enduring influences of Polynesia on the mainland. It remains visible in numerous tiki bars and mid-century antique and collectible showrooms, spawned a generation of designers specializing in the craft of creating tiki ambiance in public spaces, and its physical elements occupy an important drawer in the toolbox of every set designer working on a Hawaiian-themed television program. The climax to that ambience might come to full fruition with exotica music on the sound system, where aloha shirted men and saronged women down rum drinks poured into tiki mugs set on a rattan table or bar. Like tiki, rattan furniture was just a little bit Hawaiian, but the isles of aloha were critical to its popularity. Thousands of Hawaiian residences featured rattan furniture, which trended back to the mainland in untold numbers of interiors, patios, homes, and businesses.

Detail from Eugene Savage Matson's mural *Pomp and Circumstance* (New York Public Library).

Frank McIntosh, illustration for Matson menu (New York Public Library).

Hawaiian sheet music cover illustrated by Leland Stanford Morgan (author's collection).

C4

The Mai-Kai Restaurant, illustration by Al Kocab (Lisa Kocab Meade).

Rattan chair and ottoman, Tropical Sun Rattan showroom (photograph by Geoff Alexander).

Betty, Mai-Kai calendar girl, August 1967 (photograph by Sid Latham, design by Al Kocab).

Tim McCullough, left, and artist Eddy Y at McCullough's Waimea studio, fall 2004 (HULA Le'a/ Midori Kitta).

Author and garment executive Dale Hope (photograph by JOSS).

Front panels of Hawaiian shirt featuring Miles Mason design, from the Miles Collection by Reyn Spooner (Miles M. Mason).

Sikorsky S-42 flying boat shirt by Tori Richard (author's collection).

Shirt design by Avi Kiriaty from the Avi Collection by Kahala (author's collection).

Workers in Pineapple plantation, 1914. From *How We Serve Hawaiian Canned Pineapple* (Hawaiian Pineapple Packers' Association).

SEVEN

A Twisted Tale
The Emergence of Rattan Furniture

The appearance of rattan furniture in post-war mainland homes and patios was the most visible proof that from a domestic living perspective, America had been exotified by the Pacific islands. Millions of U.S. military and defense workers saw it or sat in it for the first time in Hawaii (prior to the war, the only mainlanders who could afford it were the well-off). Rattan furniture has been linked to Hawaii for decades, a full, participating member of the gestalt that includes aloha shirts, rum drinks, exotica music, and tiki-themed bars and restaurants. To many, rattan furniture seems as Hawaiian as pineapple upside down cake, which, as most food historians agree, wasn't a Hawaiian invention at all.[1] And neither was rattan furniture, the tropical furniture most evocative of the Hawaiian mystique. For the most part, it was made in the Philippines.

Although its popularity, as with many forms of art and design, waxes and wanes, rattan furniture has never gone out of fashion with those favoring an exotic décor or lifestyle, or others who prefer sturdy, lightweight, attractive furniture. Collectors and antique dealers love it, as premium vintage pieces continue to command top dollar.

The golden rattan furniture that was so popular in the post-war years had been introduced to the U.S. market some years earlier. A photograph in Harvey Schwartz's book *Rattan: Tropical Comfort Throughout the House* features a 1938 showroom rattan living room setting from the Tropical Sun Rattan Company of Pasadena, complete with woven wall hangings and standing screens. Another photo shows the catalogue cover of the *Baughman Furniture Factory* in the Philippines, dated 1940, with a contemporary golden rattan living room chair, split sofa, and table ensemble. The cover text offers "Top Quality Rattan: Tropical Furniture for the Modern Home." Yet another photo from the era provides a view of a gorgeous dining room setting made by the Philippine company Rattan Art & Decorations.[2] It was noted designer Paul Theodor Frankl (1886–1958), however, who is credited as the first to evolve rattan furniture from outdoor and patio use to luxurious indoor decor.[3]

Frankl, originally from Vienna, spent his early career in New York City, where, influenced by the Succession movement and Modernism, he had his first successes with his Skyscraper Furniture, designed to resemble the buildings that were rapidly emerging in the skyline of America's largest city. Moving from one New York location to another, his small gallery dabbled in a number of things to make enough money to stay afloat, including fabrics, exotic wooden furniture, decorative matches, Christmas cards, and assorted curios. Interior design

Pre–World War II living room setting from Rattan Art & Decorations, Philippines (courtesy Harvey Schwartz).

commissions enhanced his reputation as a modernist. He embraced streamlining, his upholstered Speed lounge chair of 1932 being perhaps his most famous example. His future designs involving rattan are hinted at in a table he created in 1929 as part of an outdoor seating group, with bold horizontal lines broken up by large and small spaces.[4] In 1934, fed up with New York on several levels, he moved to Los Angeles, initially lecturing at the Chouinard Art Institute. Soon, he opened a gallery on Wilshire Boulevard and began taking on interior design commissions for wealthy homeowners, which often included exterior elements and outdoor plans as well. From a rattan perspective, the watershed project was the commission for the interior design of a house in Palm Beach, Florida, for Vadim and Elisabeth Harding Makaroff. His plan called for using rattan furniture in the home, but Frankl was disappointed by the examples of rattan pieces available in the marketplace. Recalling seeing a rattan chair made in the Philippines that had been copied from one of his wicker designs, he traveled to the islands in 1936, determined to find a manufacturer that would design rattan furniture to his specifications. In Manila, the American Chamber of Commerce pointed him to Frank H. Hale (1872–1952), who had just built a rattan manufacturing facility.[5]

Today, Frank Hale is viewed historically as a legendary entrepreneur in the Philippines. He was born in the U.S., became a volunteer shoemaker for the Army, and under General

John J. Pershing, set up shop at Fort McKinley in 1898. He soon established his Exchange Shoe Company (ESCO) in the Philippines, acquired machinery from United Shoe Manufacturing in Boston, and imported fine leathers from the U.S., Italy, Argentina, and Australia. He manufactured for leading brands in the United States and Europe, and by the beginning of World War II, it was estimated that he was the largest shoe manufacturer in Asia. His workers were 100 percent Filipino, who were provided housing, medical, and sports facilities. They thrived to the extent that some of them started their own businesses, backed by ESCO resources. Always looking for additional opportunities, he founded the Tropicraft Corporation to manufacture rattan products. There, in his Manila rattan factory, located in the ancient quarter of Santa Ana, he met Paul Frankl.[6]

Frankl had brought a number of full-scale drawings of his rattan furniture to the Philippines, and Hale agreed to build Frankl's designs in return for guaranteeing ongoing orders. Hale's shop foreman immediately began building prototypes under Frankl's direction and within several days, the designer was satisfied that the models met his specifications. The designs were a radical change from rattan furniture that had been previously sold in the U.S. His "square pretzel" shape for chair arm assemblies became a standardized Frankl element, as did stacked and curved rattan poles, used for chair and sofa bases. The stacked poles were reminiscent of the wooden designs, utilizing horizontal wood strips, made by Frankl in the late 1920s. Rather than coating the rattan with dark lacquer as was the custom, he used hand-rubbed beeswax instead, emphasizing the natural golden color that Frankl thought would better lend itself to high-end, modern interiors. His goal was to stock his gallery with the new furniture and create enough pieces to begin wholesaling them on the mainland.

When Frankl returned to the United States, he was faced with disconcerting news. Frank Hale informed him that the shop foreman and prototype-maker had left the company, started his own concern, and was engaged in pirating Frankl's rattan designs. Despite the bad news, Frankl found himself with a profitable rattan furniture business. His designs were being sold in the United States and Europe. In Hollywood, Metro-Goldwyn-Mayer and Paramount placed large orders, using his furniture in motion picture sets. Film stars including Charles Boyer, Charlie Chaplin, Ronald Colman, and Charles Laughton, bought his rattan furnishings for their own homes, having been introduced to them through their work with the studios. By 1939, still working with Hale in the Philippines, he expanded his rattan furniture line to include more than 20 individual pieces, including dining room sets, chaises lounges, and small tables. He made no distinction as to whether his furniture was being used outdoors or indoors, citing his appreciation for the Japanese philosophy of connecting exterior and interior spaces. "Our Western civilization is beginning to comprehend what the Japanese have practiced for centuries ... it is coming to life by opening up and letting life flow from the outside," he noted.[7]

In March 1939, another setback occurred. His shipments had stopped coming from the Philippines, and Hale was not answering Frankl's letters or telegrams. Learning that Hale was experiencing financial challenges, Frankl hopped on a ship that took him directly to Manila. Having no success in reaching Hale by telephone, he went to factory, and found it padlocked and empty. A visit to the American Chamber of Commerce confirmed the problem. Lacking furniture expertise, Hale had relied on a series of managers to supervise the work, none of whom had panned out. Hale had declared bankruptcy. Frankl hastily found another producer, Gonzalo Puyat, but was disappointed with the quality control. Neither the strength of the pieces nor the finish conformed to Frankl's specifications.[8] According to Harvey Schwartz, Frankl's Philippines-manufactured rattan pieces were neither signed nor had an identifying design label. Extant Frankl pieces from the era, therefore, might have been manufactured by Hale, his departed foreman, or by Puyat.[9]

In 1946, Frankl closed his last boutique, then located on Rodeo Drive, and instead concentrated on manufacturing, custom interiors, and designing for large furniture companies. His final rattan pieces may have been those he designed for the Ficks Reed Furniture Company in the early 1950s.[10]

In the pre-war years, rattan furniture in the United States was hardly a national phenomenon, its popularity limited largely to the cognoscenti reading design magazines or living in proximity to showrooms in New York, Los Angeles, and Florida. Designers of Frankl's reputation served the high-end clientele, but large numbers of working-class furniture buyers had never even seen rattan furniture. The war in the Pacific changed everything.

With the advent of the hostilities, millions of servicemen and women operating in the Pacific Theater were now introduced to this strong, durable, lightweight, insect-resistant, serviceable, and, from a social perspective, classless furniture. It graced shore-based military offices, bars, and clubs, and was a staple in military and native homes and businesses. Many servicemen and women stationed in the Pacific were attracted to the exotic, tropical look of rattan furniture, used it at work or play, and—if they were officers—eventually might well have brought it back home with them, transported on Liberty ships after the war.

People coming home from the Pacific War could also go on to acquire additional pieces for their interiors and patios back at home, and their admiring friends could start their own collections as well. Through firms that included Ficks Reed, Ritts, Seven Seas, Tropical Sun, and Vogue, rattan furniture became a thriving business after the war, especially in California, Florida, and any area of the country where warm weather and sunshine graced patios and sunrooms for most of the year. Many of the pieces available for sale avoided having high the price tags associated with designers in Frankl's class, but were nevertheless strong, utilitarian, and evocative of a tropical lifestyle.

Today, untold numbers of interior spaces in America have rattan furniture in them. The influence of designers including Frankl, who championed integrating interior and exterior living spaces, was lasting. Rattan furniture continues to thrive as an iconic element to home exotica. New pieces continue to be made, manufactured in countries ranging from Indonesia to Vietnam. Vintage golden rattan, prized by collectors, can still be found in an astounding range of places, from antique stores to thrift shops and even to sidewalk gutters, waiting for the garbage collector to haul it away.[11] It's a bit more of a challenge for those trying to find a collection of vintage rattan furniture in superior shape, a specific piece to complete a room, or a museum-quality design by Paul Frankl, his contemporaries or successors. To find them, head down to the railroad tracks.

Rattan by the Railroad Tracks: A Tale of Preservation and Persistence

This non-descript warehouse is no different than thousands of others that exist on the side streets of greater Los Angeles. You drive through a maze of auto repair and tire shops on

Harvey Schwartz in the Tropical Sun Rattan warehouse (photograph by Geoff Alexander).

Sepulveda Boulevard, turn right onto Raymer Street, pass the Triple G Grind and Roll Company, then cross over the Pacoima Wash. It's there on the right, across from the railroad tracks, through two locked double gates. On this Sunday, it's so quiet that the only sound to be heard is the bolt sliding through the lock. Harvey Schwartz works the keys to the door of 20th Century Props and then opens the door, shuts off the alarm, and hits the light switch. What has to be the world's largest inventory of vintage rattan furniture is piled, slotted, and neatly stacked on dozens of industrial racks, in the aisles, and against the walls. Some of the furniture, although old, is in terrific original condition; some is waiting to be repaired at his three-person workshop at the far end of the warehouse, near the roll-up door. He's especially proud of the woman who perfectly re-weaves the ancient joints with new *bury* wrappings. I ask if she learned the trade in the Philippines, like most of the early bury weavers did. "She's from Mexico," Schwartz says, "we taught her the fine points, now she's an expert."[12]

Aisle after aisle unfolds new vistas displaying the most collectible tropical grass furniture ever made—rattan is, after all, a grass. "Here's an original Paul Frankl settee," Schwartz says, "just look at that wonderful woven bury pattern on the joints. Frankl was meticulous." He points at a rattan sofa. "That's from *The Golden Girls*," he says. "After they used it on the TV show in 1986, business went crazy." Around the corner, on a second-level tier, sits Claudette Colbert's chair from the 1934 film version of *Cleopatra*. Howard Hughes' own desk, used in the film *The Aviator* (2004), is somewhere inside here too, we know. Art Deco, Schwartz's other passion, is resplendent throughout, punctuating the corridors of rattan. He points to molds he crafted for 17- foot high art deco angels. "We only had four originals, and one set designer wanted more, so we cast them." Spoken like an engineer. Which Harvey Schwartz was.[13]

Schwartz has two businesses. 20th Century Props is one of them, a one-stop shopping mecca for set designers that nearly closed for good in 2009, threatened by the recession. Operating in those days from a 200,000-square-foot facility, it had more than 94,000 items. Then the movie industry fell on tough times, driven by the economic recession. Rapidly running out of money, Schwartz auctioned off what he could and concentrated on his other business, a small boutique. With an upsurge in the fortunes of the film industry, he re-opened 20th Century Props in 2015, but on a smaller scale, in this 18,000-square-foot warehouse, with an inventory pared down to roughly 3,000 props. It's practically unimaginable, envisioning a space ten times this large, filled to capacity with vintage rattan pieces that have become challenging to find *anywhere*. That's why we're here today. Harvey Schwartz isn't the only person in the United States who can sell you golden rattan, made mostly from the 1930s through the 1960s. He's just got more of it than anyone in the United States and wrote the only book on the subject of collecting it.

Schwartz opened his first retail business, a streetside boutique, in the early 1970s. Earlier, his career path had led him to work for a number of marquee aerospace firms, where as an electro-mechanical aerospace engineer, he specialized in making mil-spec drawings for technology that ended up in high places. Like Skylab. "The specification drawings for the military were enormous," he says, discussing an unnamed Lockheed aircraft. "At the end, the drawings, when rolled up, weighted more than the plane itself."[14]

What becomes obvious when talking to Schwartz is that he wears two hats simultaneously, that of an astute collector, and another of a formidable, never-say-die hustler. It's in his genes. His father sold newspapers from a New York street corner, moved to Los Angeles, and opened a newsstand at Beverly and La Brea, dealing the *Los Angeles Mirror*. Harvey himself started selling newspapers on his own LA street corner at age 6, at Melrose and La Cienega, just after the end of World War II. He finished high school, showed an aptitude for mechanical drawing, and was hired to work in the burgeoning defense industry that mushroomed in Southern California in the post-war years. Hughes Aircraft and the Lockheed Corporation were two of several defense contractors for whom he worked. When hard times hit the military-aerospace industry, Schwartz was laid off. Like many who suddenly fall on tough times, he hit the thrift stores, and also began acquiring old things at the Santa Monica swap meet.

"I always liked straight lines, circles, and squares" he says, and there were plenty of those embedded in the discarded rattan furniture he began buying. He soon amassed a large enough collection—of rattan and other items—to hang out a shingle.[15]

His first shop was on Third Street in Los Angeles in the early 1970s, but he soon moved to Beverly Boulevard, across from CBS Television City. Schwartz continued buying up anything from swap meets and flea markets that would fit into the back seat of his 1952 Allard convertible.[16] He loved rattan because of its portability, and soon found himself a regular visitor to Palm Springs. "It was a great place for rattan," he says. "The military moved household goods from officers' houses in the Pacific back to the mainland after the war, and lots of it was rattan furniture. Many of these people retired to Palm Springs, so rattan furniture was all over the place. It was so light that I could carry a houseful of rattan furniture in my car on one drive."[17]

His fortunes changed dramatically one day when someone else's convertible pulled up to his shop, its driver ogling a rattan rocker and chaise longue he had placed on the sidewalk in front of the curb. "Barbra Streisand was behind the wheel. She bought the rocker and the chaise. She was furnishing her house in Malibu, and she started asking me to find things for her." Other celebrities took note, and soon Schwartz found himself moving from one larger shop to another while continuing to increase his stock in rattan and Art Deco pieces. His customers weren't just celebrities, either. Nearby West Hollywood, known for residents with a keen eye for design, became a significant market for Schwartz's vintage rattan and Deco.[18]

In 1977, learning that the Tropical Sun rattan furniture company in Pasadena was planning to go out of business, Schwartz bought their remaining stock. Tropical Sun, along with Ritts Furniture Company (Tropitan) and Vogue Rattan Manufacturing Company, was one of three major suppliers of rattan furniture in the United States in the two post-war decades.[19] Schwartz had been a customer of theirs. "I would go to them whenever I needed a piece to complete a collection or needed something custom-made. There was a guy there known as 'Howard the Sample-Maker,' who could design just about everything. I came to him with an idea, he'd draw it up, and Tropical Sun would build it for me."[20]

Tobi Smith, director and founder of the Santa Monica Heritage Museum (now the California Heritage Museum) saw vintage Bakelite radios in Schwartz's window on his Melrose shop one day in 1989. She was designing an exhibition involving vintage radios and lifted one up to inspect it. "Don't pick that up!" yelled Schwartz, and a friendship was born. Schwartz not only lent radios for the show, "A Radio for Every Room: A Dazzling Collection of Vintage Radios and Memorabilia," but he designed the space as well, which included flamingos, rattan, and other mid-century pieces. The show ran from November 1989 through January 1990. "John Candy came in one day," he remembers, "and bought the whole room and shipped it up to his house in Canada after the exhibition finished."[21]

The friendship with Tobi Smith led to the publishing of Schwartz' book on rattan. "Peter and Nancy Schiffer [of Schiffer Publishing] had been coming to the museum to see the shows," Smith recalls, "and they'd often do a book on it. Ultimately, there were ten of them. We mounted a show called *Aloha Spirit: Hawaii's Influence on California's Lifestyle*, which ran from April through July of 1997. I'd been nagging Harvey to write a book on rattan, so he and the Schiffers finally decided to do one."[22]

The Schiffers were fascinated with Hawaiian art and culture, and Nancy herself had recently authored a book on Hawaiian shirt designs.[23] A few weeks after the initial discussions, photographer Bruce M. Waters came by the shop to shoot Harvey's collection while he and

Nancy Schiffer swapped stories. The resulting book, *Rattan: Tropical Comfort Throughout the House,* was published in 1999, authored by Harvey Schwartz.

Although now nearly 20 years old, the 160-page book remains the most comprehensive book on rattan furniture design and collecting in print. It's replete with rattan furniture photographs taken from Schwartz' collection as well as those taken from manufacturers' catalogues, including those of Tropical Sun, Ralph Stein of Hudson (New York City), and Baughman Furniture Factory in the Philippines, along with manufacturing factory photos. The book contributes information on fabric and color as well as rattan growing, harvesting, and manufacture. It offers a contemporary price guide to many of the pieces and suggests the following features to be found on best quality rattan:

- Intricate bends, the more the better. Pretzel and related variations command the highest prices
- Many poles tightly stacked, ranging from two poles in more common forms to twelve poles, which are nearly impossible to find today ... the most sought-after rattan has six stacked poles
- Few blemishes, such as dark spots or stem nodes
- Well wrapped joints, which add beauty to the pieces
- The older the better[24]

The rattan boom ended for Schwartz in the late 1990s, ironically right around the time the book was published. For the enterprising Schwartz, it resulted in yet another business opportunity. "Rattan furniture had lost its popularity, the market just dried up. I closed my shop and expanded my props business," he remembers. Schwartz had begun renting props in 1984, when 20th Century–Fox decided that the overhead and upkeep of an on-site props department was too much to handle. As was the case with a number of larger studios, Fox needed to free additional space on its lot and the props department, which was essentially "dead space," had to go. Schwartz took over the entire department, rented a warehouse in North Hollywood to give it a home, and began renting the props to television and film companies on a consignment basis for Fox (he would buy out the entire department in 1994). The warehouse was huge, at 113,000 square feet, with another 90,000 feet outside, along with an adjacent parking lot. "Those old set designers were wonderful," he says. "They'd just speed along the rows, 'I need this and this and this,' and there'd be a guy with a clipboard walking behind him, taking down numbers. They could do the whole thing in seconds."[25]

The wheels flew off the cart in 2009. Brooks Barnes told the story in a *New York Times* article on June 17, 2009. "Battered by the surge in out-of-state movie production and the demise of scripted programming on network television, the once-thriving business—one of a handful of its type remaining—is failing. 'I ran out of money three months ago, and I don't know what else to do' [Schwartz] said softly. 'It's terrifying. I've devoted my entire life to something that is over.'"[26]

After liquidating virtually the entire warehouse, Schwartz retreated to his small and manageable boutique, specializing in rattan, Deco, and mid-century. Business was good, the bills were paid, and in 2015, as a result of a series of tax credits directed toward helping to revive the television and film business in California, Schwartz re-opened his props business on a smaller scale.[27] Even today, Schwartz loves to talk rattan, which he does from his boutique Harvey's on Beverly, today located at 20th Century Props in Van Nuys, five days a week. He's a peripatetic LA nomad; as business and rental rates fluctuate, his shop moves with the times (Harvey's is now in its 12th location), filled to the gills with old and new rattan pieces. He still has a number of Tropical Sun vintage pieces in new condition, amounting to roughly 40 standard chairs, 70 arm chairs, 10 settees, and 10 tables, at last count. If a specific rattan piece isn't in the boutique, he's probably got it somewhere in the warehouse. Just ask him. Without even pausing to look at an inventory chart, he'll have memorized its precise location.

Rattan Furniture: The Back Story

In the post–World War II years, the curvilinear forms embodied in golden rattan designs graced thousands of American homes and patios, encompassing all manner of living room, dining, bedroom, bar, and library furniture. Rattan durably withstood the rigors of indoor and outdoor use. It was strong, relatively inexpensive, and could be used in hot and humid southern climates. In keeping with the "form follows function" architectural and design philosophy increasingly fashionable by the 1920s, the rattan frame itself was seen as encompassing an inherent beauty that was previously, in the early part of the 20th century, almost always hidden by thin strips of cane. The rattan joints, or internodes were now preferred visible, evoking beauty and authenticity. Rattan furniture corners, joints, and splices were wrapped, often elaborately, with elaborately woven strands of binding, known as buri. Thinner strips of cane, called sika, provided design accents, whether curvilinear or straight.[28] The natural color of the cane itself had become an important element of the charm of the mid-century rattan pieces, a dramatic change from painted or stained canes that were prevalent in 19th century rattan furniture. And instead of seating made from woven cane, cushions on 20th century rattan furniture were made from bark cloth cotton with striking floral and tropical patterns, floating on fabric-and-spring supports.

The history of "golden rattan" furniture in North America is challenging to document. Most manufacturers never stamped their creations. William S. Rawitzer's (1905?–1968) Vogue Rattan Mfg. Co., founded in Los Angeles before moving to Lexington, Kentucky in 1957, was one of the few that did, boasting at one point that it was the largest rattan furniture manufacturer in the United States.

Although largely anonymous, rattan furniture designers included a number of well-known artisans and designers creating their own collections of rattan. In addition to Paul T. Frankl, another innovator was John Calhoun McGuire (1920–2013) of the McGuire Furniture Company, who patented the use of rawhide to bind the rattan and whose pieces are included in the Smithsonian Collection of the Cooper-Hewitt Museum in New York. After serving in the U.S. Navy in World War II, McGuire found a position with Standard Oil in the Philippines and then returned to the mainland in 1947. Shortly thereafter, he moved to San Francisco and began selling advertising for the *San Francisco Examiner*. He soon encountered an old Navy friend, Dwayne White, who had a warehouse full of furniture that he couldn't sell. McGuire sold the pieces and wanted more, but White declined his offer. McGuire, however, had been bitten by the rattan bug. During his tenure in the Philippines, he made acquaintance with Doña Maria Montenegro-Aboitiz, who founded the Mehitabel Furniture Company, which began as a small backyard furniture business on the island of Cebu, in 1947.[29] In 1948, she agreed to produce rattan furniture for McGuire to design and sell. The McGuire Furniture

Company was launched. John and his wife, Elinor Stevenson McGuire, who had design and engineering experience with Boeing Aircraft, created furniture with unique rawhide wrappings and dyed poles, and eventually expanded their business to include furniture made from redwood, bamboo, teak, and other hardwoods. The McGuire Furniture Company, still in business 65 years after its founding, was acquired by the Kohler Company in 1989.[30]

In Europe, French designer Janine Abraham (1929–2005), and Dirk Jan Rol (b. 1929), born in the Netherlands, collaborated and crafted stunning curvilineal rattan chairs based on modernist metal frames (they also worked in other materials, including bent plywood and aluminum). Abraham and Rol met while employed in the design studio of Jacques Dumond (1906–1988), a pioneer in using non-traditional materials including rattan for home furnishings.[31] Other European designers making extensive use of rattan for home furnishings included Italian architect Franco Albini (1905–1977) and Arne Emil Jacobsen (1902–1971).[32] In terms of newer mid-century designs, the work of Henry Olko (b. 1929) at his Willow and Reed company, is worthy of note. Olko created new rattan pieces for the high-end furniture market, providing a bold new look that remains compelling decades later.

An interesting offshoot deriving from the popularity of rattan was its imitation by manufacturers working with traditional materials made of wood. Heywood Wakefield Furniture's Ashcraft line, for example, featured steam-bent ash in its catalogue of rattan-look pieces, substituting oak veneers for those of mahogany, the wood most often preferred by rattan manufacturers (beginning in the mid-century, a number of rattan furniture manufacturers would replace mahogany with Formica veneers).

The national craze for rattan furniture, primarily made in the Philippines in the immediate pre and post–World War II years, had actually begun in the United States in the mid–19th century, where firms including the Wakefield Rattan Company and the Heywood Bros. & Company produced Victorian wicker pieces built on rattan frames (these outfits would merge in 1897). Compared with 20th century all-rattan furniture, they seem heavy and overly ornamental, in keeping with much of the furniture manufactured in the Victorian era. The term "rattan," incidentally, is often confused with wicker and bamboo. Rattan is a climbing palm belonging to the subfamily of Calamoidae. There are more than 600 species of rattan, approximately 10 percent of which are traded internationally. Only a dozen or so are considered acceptable for furniture making.[33] Bamboo and wicker furniture are often mistaken as being crafted of rattan. The term "wicker" is used to describe furniture utilizing woven strips of cane for seating, backing, and including pieces of furniture completely covered in wicker, a look that was prevalent in chairs and sofas of the 19th century. Bamboo, also a popular product used for furniture, has a hollow core, and thus lacks rattan's solid core tensile strength, making it impractical for load-bearing furniture. In general, therefore, bamboo furniture lacks the durability and longevity of that of rattan. The density of rattan's core also allows for superior joining and bending capability. Rattan has a surprising number of uses beyond furniture manufacturing. These would include basketry and fish traps, food, medicine, resins, dyes, leaves chewed to expel intestinal worms, roots used to treat syphilis, toothbrushes and graters, and poison.[34]

In the Philippines, canes known as Palasan rattan (Calamus merrillii) are harvested from stalks that are typically in their 15th year of growth. They may be as high as 600 feet and are green to yellow in color. The trunks vary in diameter, but are usually two inches or fewer and never bigger than five inches. Larger diameter trunks, four or five inches in diameter, indicate old growth, said to be one hundred years or older, and are rare. When used on rattan furniture, they're often seen on older coffee tables with thick legs and cross pieces. Typically, the cane is initially cut low on the base, at a height of roughly three feet, then left to dry for several days before its removal (new growth will eventually emerge from the root structure, to be harvested again in six or seven years). It is then cut into 13-foot lengths. The leaves are cut, internodes trimmed, and stalks blemished by fungus, scarring, bruising, checks (longitudinal fissuring), or otherwise unusable, are tossed away. The stalks are graded for diameter in five sizes ranging from 1 to 1½ inch or greater, and quality, based on the spacing of the internodes (10 inches or longer is preferred).[35]

They are then shipped to the factory. The Cebu Furniture Industries Foundation describes how the stalks are harvested, then prepared and jigged for furniture manufacturing: "Rattan is ready for harvesting by the 15th year when the stems average 24–30 meters [roughly 80 to 100 feet] in length. Thereafter, selective cutting of the matured canes may be done at three to four year intervals. The canes of the subsequent harvest will be of better quality than those from the previous harvests. Harvesting is usually done in the dry season. While still fresh, big canes are scraped to remove the thin silicious coating and to bring out the yellowish, lustrous color. Rattan poles are dried to not more than 20 percent moisture content based on oven-dry weight to minimize fungal attack. Dipping the canes for at least two minutes in a chemical solution does anti-stain and Stem-borer treatment.[36]

"The bending is done in two ways. The pole is cut into the required sizes and placed in a steam compartment for 10 minutes. The poles are then transferred to wood or metal jigs and clamped in place overnight until formed into the required shapes. The other method is with a blowtorch, heating the part to be bent directly, or by heating a piece of metal and transferring the heat to the rattan pole. Like wood, rattan can easily be given whatever color products made out of it require. It can also be maintained in the natural color inherent to it. Application of color can be done before or after making the product. Dyes and tints can be dissolved into a liquid solution in which rattan is soaked for a certain period. Spraying and topical application for coloring are two methods used after the product is finished."[37]

In the Philippines, veneers for desk and table tops would be cut from Big-leafed mahogany (Swietenia macrophylla), a reddish-colored surface wood that naturally darkened to brown. The underlying sapwood is yellow, which is occasionally seen in vintage mahogany-topped pieces that have been overly sanded.

The factory floor of a rattan furniture making facility featured 12 discrete manufacturing functions: pole preparation, crosscutting, molding, rattan machining, wood machining, framing, checking, sanding, binding, weaving, finishing, and upholstery.[38]

The manufacture of rattan furniture required a number of specialty cutting tools and hardware to make the six standard joints. A cope cutter, for example, was used to machine pole ends in cope joints not concealed by cane binding. The carbide cutter consisted of two turnblade knives with four cutting edges and two regrindable spurs. The joint assembly was then fixed by a special case-hardened steel plastic-coated screw with a thin core and wide threads, resulting in high tear-out resistance.[39]

Once completed, three samples of every design were given a stress test in the Philippines. The fact that vintage rattan furniture lasts through generations of owners is a tribute to the exacting standards exercised in that country. Developed over decades of manufacturing and quality control experience, they were formally codified in 1976 as PS (Philippine Standard) No. 821-09.03. The section on testing is particularly illuminating:

Figure 89. Structural joints

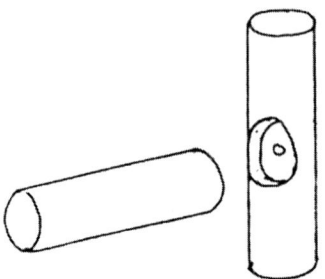

CHUCKING & BORING.

For Structural Joints Boring should not be more than ⅓ diam. deep.

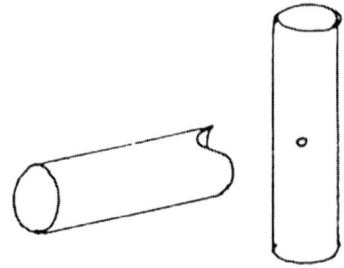

COPING OR SCREWING.

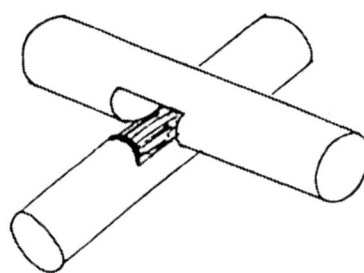

HALVING JOINT.

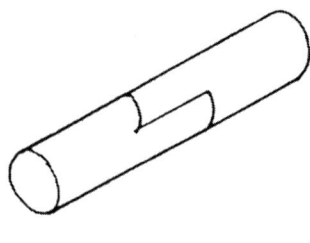

SPLICING JOINT.

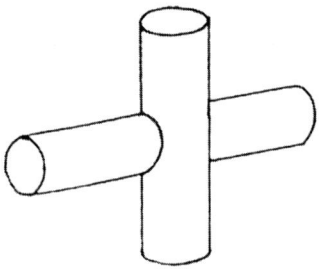

HALF-COPING JOINT.

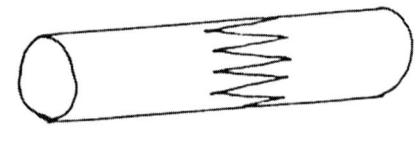

FINGER JOINT.
Straight or Mitred.

Common rattan furniture structural joints (United Nations Industrial Development Organization).

7.4 Tests

a. *Test Samples.* Samples selected at random in accordance with [section] 6.1 shall be tested as specified herein.

b. *Level Test (all items).* Casters or glides shall be removed. Items shall be placed on a flat level surface plate. All legs shall simultaneously rest on the surface plate. Any evidence of rocking when light force is applied at any corner shall be cause for rejection.

c. *Sand Bag Test (chairs and sofa frames).* These items shall withstand six impacts of a 29.5 kg (65 pounds) sand bag, 30.48 cm (12 inches) in diameter at dropped end, a distance of 106.68 cm (3.5 feet) in each of the following locations: (a) directly over a leg, (b) midway between the legs on the side frame members and (c) on front frame rail at midpoint.

d. *Impact Test.* Chairs shall withstand 12 drops from a height of 91.44 cm (3 feet) above a concrete floor. The chair shall be tilted to an angle of 12 degrees diagonally across the plane of the feet to insure that one leg receives the initial impact.

e. *Diagonal Load Test.* Chair shall be laid back in such a way that the front edge of the seat is directly above the feet or the rear legs. Apply a vertical load of 68.04 kg (150 pounds) to the front edge of the seat. The force shall be applied and completely removed steadily during periods of not less than 5 seconds for 20 times.

f. *Static Load Test (chair frame with deck).* A static load of a 68.04 kg (150 pounds) sand bag shall be applied vertically over a 30.48 cm (12 inches) diameter area in the center of the deck and allowed to remain for 15 minutes. Upon removal of the load, there shall be no evidence of breakage or loosening or separation of frame joints.

g. *Static Load Test (tables).* The height of the table shall be measured accurately. A static load of 45.36 kg (100 pounds) shall be applied vertically over a 30.48 cm (12 inches) diameter area in the centre of the table top and allowed to remain for 30 minutes. Upon removal of the load, the height shall not have decreased by more than 0.31 cm (⅛ inch) and there shall be no evidence of breakage or separation of joints.[40]

7.5 Criteria for Success

a. No part of the furniture or its components or fittings shall develop any fracture, or any apparent loosening of a joint intended to be rigid, or any deformations which would adversely affect any of its functions.

c. Each sample tested shall sustain each of the forces described in 7.4.[41]

While each of the tests enforces the integrity of the finished product, one of the more interesting of them is the diagonal load test, which emulates a 150-pound person rocking back and forth on the rear legs of the chair. The Philippine Standard is still applied today in rattan furniture manufacturing operations worldwide, to varying degrees.

    There appear to be neither available data suggesting the total number of pieces of rattan furniture that were sent home to the mainland from the Pacific immediately after the war, nor how much has been sold from that time onward. The fact that rattan furniture remained in demand was underscored by the numbers of individuals on the mainland who were buying raw materials and making rattan furniture themselves, crafting pieces in home workshops. Finished rattan poles came to distributors on the mainland in 15 to 25 or more bundles, lengths cut from 8 to 10 feet. Sika strips and buri wrap arrived in coils. Home-based furniture makers could order everything in different lengths and widths, shipped directly to their addresses by distributors. As of 1979, there were at least ten mainland companies engaged in shipping rattan materials to home craftspeople. Poles (also known as swords) could be ordered in bundles, whole length or pre-cut to lower shipping charges. The same year, the population of home rattan crafters was considered big enough that a book was published for do-it-yourselfers, Max and Charlotte Alth's *Rattan: A Home Craftsman's Guide*. Over its more than 200 pages, it covered everything from selecting and ordering materials to bending, joinery, and wrapping, with numerous photographs. By 1986, *Popular Mechanics* magazine was offering assistance to home crafters, devoting six pages to Neil Barrett's how-to article "Back to Rattan: A Guide to Fabricating Furniture with This Versatile Building Material."[42]

Harvey Schwartz' book on rattan was published in 1999, a confirmation of rattan furniture's remarkable popularity over more than 50 years since the end of World War II. Demand for large diameter canes used for rattan furniture frames dramatically increased after the war years, and by the 1990s, the international rattan furniture industry was valued at $6.5 billion.[43] The presence of rattan in the homes of North Americans continues through the new millennium, and raw rattan material is harvested sustainably in the Philippines and Indonesia, Malaysia, Thailand, and Vietnam, among other countries.[44] Today, in addition to newly designed rattan pieces that appear in a staggering variety of forms, rattan is being used as a sculptural form by artists including Cambodia's Sopheap Pich (b. 1971), who mounted a show at New York's Metropolitan Museum of Art in 2013.[45] Additional modern designers crafting rattan furniture include Santiago Calatrava (b. 1951), Piet Hein Eek (b. 1967), Jaime Hayon (b. 1974), Johannes Foersom (b. 1947) & Peter Hiort-Lorenzen (b. 1943), actress-designer Mette Munk Plum (b. 1956), and Cebu-based Kenneth Cobonpue (b. 1968).[46]

Seekers of mid-century vintage "golden rattan" furniture can still an amazing number of good pieces in antique, used furniture, and thrift stores in the United States. There are at least two companies on the mainland that sell goods to repair old pieces or to build new ones from scratch.[47] Rattan furniture still oozes exoticism. It's a look that remains timeless, durable in construction, evocative of the Pacific and days past, yet so contemporary in its concept that its influence is formidable, and beauty never dated. In an exotic sense, it can be said to dress a house in similar fashion to the manner in which a Hawaiian shirt ornaments its wearer.

Eight

The Shirt Heard Round the World

The popularity on the mainland of the Hawaiian, or aloha shirt, perhaps the garment most evocative of tropical exoticism, has spanned decades. It has transitioned through periods of growth, decline, and resurgence. It remains a staple of men's wardrobes, and its versatility is limitless, worn with khaki slacks and blue jeans, shorts and swimwear. Today, judging by the customers of just about any bar on Waikiki, aloha shirts are worn by nearly as many women as men.[1] For mainlanders, one of the reasons for their appeal is that they've always been relatively inexpensive mementos of a visit to the islands. For those who've never been to Hawaii, wearing a Hawaiian shirt represents a happy reminder to put a check mark next to "Hawaii" on the bucket list. Exotic icons and floral motifs on a well-used Hawaiian shirt give the wearer the benefit of being just a mirror glance away from paradise. Depending on the era, however, it might be debatable whether others in proximity felt the shirt lent the same aura of exoticism to the individual wearing an aloha shirt. Even today, some consider aloha shirts passé, others classify them as kitsch. What's not arguable is the idea that wearing the shirt makes its owner feel exotic. It conveys an emotion and an attitude: "If I'm not there, I'm thinking of being there. Or at least I look like I'm there." For stateside wearers, it offers the twin emotions of *longing* and *belonging*. "Although Paradise is far, far away," a wearer might say to oneself, "it's that much closer because I can touch it, button it, put something in its pocket, caress its fabric, hold it in front of me and admire it, show it off to my friends, flaunt it to the guys at the car wash, or get a compliment from someone else wearing one at the mall or the tractor-pull." Paradise for $50 (if that's what the shirt cost). Costs a little more than a mai-tai at a trendy bar, plus you get to keep it and wear it again. It's Waikiki without the crowds, the Big Island without the vog, Gilligan's Island without the mosquitoes.

In contrast to the expense of actually taking a trip to Hawaii, exotic shirts have always been an affordable way to do a little mind tripping. On the mainland, shops selling used clothing commonly have anywhere from one or two to as many as a few dozen tropical-themed shirts. Outlet shops for major department stores often display deeply discounted name-brand Hawaiian-style shirts, while retailers known for low prices on new goods frequently carry house lines of tropical shirts in season. Increasingly, themed Hawaiian shirts are sold in places ranging from air museums to sports stadiums.[2] They're manufactured in numerous countries, with rayon, cotton, and silk among the most popular fabrics.[3] Traditional Hawaiian shirt images, comprising native flora and fauna, traditional Pacific tapa designs, volcanic landscapes, and Hawaiian lifestyle themes including luau and fishing, have morphed into graphics of wide ranging diversity, from muscle cars to baseball teams.

In her book *The End of Fashion*, Teri Agins discusses the means by which the world of fashion is based on planned obsolescence. Seasons come, seasons go, and people are encouraged to buy new clothes continually to remain in style.[4] The Hawaiian shirt is the antithesis of the concept. The shirt bought today will, in all probability, look just as modern 30 years from now. Granted, Hawaiian shirts made in the 1950s–1970s era have telltale fashion elements, which might include flared collars, horizontal buttonholes, fewer buttons, and labels that indicate sizes that are now one or more sizes too small for today's bigger bodies.[5]

This evolution suggests that the traditional concept of the Hawaiian shirt might be better considered as a sub-genre of an overall *tropical shirt* classification, where large numbers of international manufacturers craft well-made natural fabrics into shirts replete with tropical iconography in representational, stylized, and abstract designs that utilize a staggering rainbow of colors.

The attractiveness of tropical patterns, their representation of exotica, and their affordability have made them among the most enduring of garments. They cross generations, never seem to go out of style, and are consistently re-used as their original owners pass on and the contents of their closets donated to thrift stores, thereby finding new homes with a new generation of enthusiasts. Hawaiian shirts are collectible at a wide variance of price points. Some older vintage shirts easily fetch several thousand dollars in high-end island boutiques, while shirts of the same age and quality are still commonly found by the discerning buyer for well under $50 in mainland shops specializing in retro-look garments.

While the appreciation of specific shirt designs is somewhat elastic, trends do emerge, reflecting the popular culture of a given decade. The Retro movement of the late 20th and early 21st century revived an interest in shirts with tiki motifs, in much the same manner that rattan furniture, exotica music, and tiki décor, having experienced periods of dormancy, were resurrected by the end of the century.

Basic Hawaiian Shirt Classifications and Elements

There are a number of basic Hawaiian shirt print designs, identified by terminology common to the industry. Some shirts are hybrids, featuring an integrated design that encompasses more than one design type. Some designs, including engineered patterns and many border prints, are made to be specifically worn outside the trousers, while others can be worn inside or outside. The following classifications represent the most common patterns:

- **Border print** shirts have a horizontal pattern that runs across the front of the shirt, the motif often duplicated on the reverse. The design typically runs from 10–12 inches and repeats, thus differing from the engineered shirts that consist of a larger pattern of approximately 18 inches. Some border shirts have a strong horizontal pattern across the bottom and are meant to be worn outside to reflect the beauty of the border. A variation of the border print can best be described as a boxed print, consisting of a series of designs set in boxes, symmetrical or staggered. Boxes are often bordered by bamboo or small flower motifs.

- **Chop-suey, hash, all-over, or repeating pattern** shirts feature of a series of replicated images that occur throughout the shirt. They can consist of virtually anything, from flowers to birds to beer bottles and airplanes. Although the pockets often match, the front button panels may not. Post-card shirts are a variation of the chop-suey shirt, featuring real or imagined post cards, and have evolved to including ephemera including luggage tags, repurposed photographs, and travel tickets.
- **Engineered** shirts consist of patterns that begin on the front of the shirt and cross over side seams to the back of the shirt. Images tend to be large, often 18 inches or greater. The image is matched over the front button panels and pocket. The shirt is meant to be worn outside. These are among the priciest shirts, as more fabric is required.
- **Panel** shirts consist of vertical patterns against a single-color background, and may be worn inside or outside. Patterns commonly consist of flowers, leaves, and fruits.
- **Scenery or Scenic** shirts consist of repeating scenic motifs, commonly volcanoes, oceans and beaches, grass huts, sunsets, and surf-related themes. Pockets are generally matched to the pattern, but front panels may not be.

A Short Glossary of Shirt Elements

- **Buttons** are traditionally made of coconut, created from by a special drill jig. They may also be crafted from wood and shell, the latter most commonly found on pricier shirts. Mid-century era shirts often had metal buttons, with Asian character motifs or alii heads. Cloth-covered buttons, wrapped around metal and using the same fabric as the shirt, would still be used into the 1970s.[6] Plastic buttons are found on many of the more affordable shirts, but they're not always mundane. Jams World shirts have sported compelling spray pattern multi-color plastic buttons that enhance the design of its shirts.
- **Fabrics** for Hawaiian shirts most often consist of cotton, silk, rayon (viscose), polyester, poly-cotton blend, and polyester microfiber. Linen will occasionally be used, but is susceptible to wrinkling. Cotton is durable, holds dye capably and breathes well. A variation is "cotton lawn" cloth. More sheer and with a higher thread count than standard cotton, lawn can be semi-transparent or opaque (its name derives from the old linen manufacturing city of Laon in northern France). Silk is somewhat less durable than cotton and can be more susceptible to washing machine damage than cotton. Rayon has a silky finish that is more durable than silk, but doesn't breathe as well as cotton. Poly-cotton is a blend, and while extremely durable, can be uncomfortable in humid tropical climates as it tends to retain body moisture. Polyester microfiber has been praised by some as a tropically comfortable alternative to polyester-cotton, but opinions differ. Many men who make a habit of wearing Hawaiian shirts still prefer cotton or rayon.
- **French seams** are double sewn so that raw edges are enclosed within the seam. They offer greater durability than single-sewn seams which, with repeated wearings and washings, are often the failure point of the garment.

- **Identity apparel** refers to matching pattern Hawaiian garments, generally with a corporate logo, used as stylized work uniforms, primarily for public-facing employees. Reyn Spooner is one company that has found manufacturing identity apparel to be profitable, even occasionally identifying the garment with the Reyn logo along with the customer's corporate name.
- **Jacquard weaves** are created through a mechanical loom that imparts a raised design within the fabric itself. On tropical shirts, it is most often used on silk shirts. Some of the more compelling Jacquard designs consist of garments of one color, where the subtleties of the impressions on raised fabric enhance the pattern as it interacts with light. Tommy Bahama and Jamaica Jaxx are two manufacturers that have created a number of compelling Jacquard garments.
- **Matched panels and pockets** coordinate the design so that front panels and pockets fit the pattern perfectly across the front of the shirt. This requires a more refined sewing technique as well as more fabric. As a result, such shirts cost more to produce, which is typically reflected in the retail price. Matching panels and pockets are somewhat less critical on shirts with extremely busy designs, where the lack of matching may be hardly noticeable.
- **Reverse prints** refer to shirts made from fabric that has been reversed, producing a well-washed and worn "faded" look that is particularly prized by watermen.

A Brief History of the Aloha Shirt

The history of the Hawaiian shirt has inexact beginnings, but the shirts' mass popularity on the mainland arose in the immediate post-war years, fueled by thousands of military personnel returning home with shirts reminding them of the beguiling, exotic side of life that contrasted so deeply with the perils and harsh realities of the Pacific Theater. It made it possible for blue collar Americans, who could never afford trans-Pacific passage on Matson's ships or the Pan American Clipper, to own shirts made by Hawaiian tailors. Prior to the war, wearing a Hawaiian shirt on the mainland carried the cachet of high society, or perhaps better said, high earnings.

While authors DeSoto Brown and Linda Arthur state that the Hawaiian shirt has no definable inventor or date of introduction, historian Dale Hope suggests that, based on a letter appearing in a 1984 issue of the *Honolulu Star-Bulletin*, it very well could have been Gordon S. Young. In 1926, he was said to have introduced his shirt designs to college friends, sewn by his mother's dressmaker from yukata hand-dyed cotton cloth normally used to make work kimonos. The design consisted of blue or black bamboo or geometrical renderings against a field of white. By the end of the decade, Ellery Chun remembers classmates at the Punahou School wearing floral shirt designs.[7] Around the same time, Koichiro Miyamoto (1895–1986), "Musa-Shiya the Shirtmaker," began making shirts from traditional kapa patterns.[8] Shirts from this early era also reflected designs often derived from cotton floral bark cloth material that was also used for upholstery and curtains, silk that is said to have originally been intended to be used to manufacture kimonos, or *kabe crepe*, a variety of silk with a highly textured surface. Author Linda Arthur notes that many of the early Hawaiian shirts from the post-war years didn't resemble earlier pre-war shirts, which often were of the pullover variety, made of white cotton, with three-button plackets (the double layered fabric that holds the buttons and buttonholes on a shirt), and a maximum of two other colors on the print.[9]

Their popularity among island visitors increased with the rise of Honolulu shirt retailers in the 1930s. The first shop to offer a Hawaiian shirt inventory is said to have been that of Ellery Chun (1909–2000), who sold shirts from his King-Smith apparel shop in 1932 or 1933.[10] Although the term "aloha shirt" was apparently first used by Musa-Shiya the Shirt-Maker, it was eventually trademarked by Ellery Chun.[11] By the summer of 1935, mainland-based fashion retailer Gump's and manufacturer Musa-Shiya were running newspaper advertisements for the increasingly popular aloha shirt. Visiting movie stars including John Barrymore, Douglas Fairbanks, and Mary Pickford ordered shirts from Musa-Shiya during their stays in Honolulu. The inaugural flight of the Pan-American Clipper in April 1935 dramatically shortened the time it took to get to Hawaii from the mainland from several days to fewer than 24 hours, increasing the tourist trade to allow for visitors who simply didn't have the time for a lengthy trans-Pacific crossing by sea. By 1936, there were 275 tailors in Honolulu, many of whom were active or specialized in the Hawaiian shirt business.[12] Visitors of the era got off the boat or plane, ordered shirts from a convenient shop near the wharf or hotel, picked them up a day or so later, and wore them during the vacation stays.

A number of legendary Hawaiian shirt manufacturers, whose businesses thrived for decades, began their operations in the pre-war years, including Kamehameha, Royal Hawaiian, Surfriders, and Pacific Sportswear. Another manufacturer, Branfleet/Kahala, worked out a licensing arrangement with Olympian gold medalist Duke Kahanamoku (1890–1968). By the end of the 1930s, Hawaiian shirts were beginning to appear in shops overseas. Herbert "Herb" Briner (d. 1966), founder of Kamehameha, had the cloth printed in California and then designed and manufactured his shirts in Hawaii. A shipping strike in 1936 prevented his fabric from reaching him in time to be sewn for the Christmas season, and because Hawaiian customers weren't buying enough shirts to keep his business profitable, he soon began exporting garments to the U.S, Australia, New Zealand, and Europe. Eventually, 95 percent of Kamehameha's garments were sold overseas.[13]

The Pearl Harbor attack on Dec. 7, 1941 changed the Hawaiian shirt business dramatically. Luxury travel to the islands ended when the Matson ships and Pan Am Clippers were requisitioned by the U.S. military. Tailors were put to work making uniforms, although they still managed to create shirts for the local trade, which now included thousands of GIs on R&R, who would buy shirts from the PX. The paucity of imported fabrics and clothing during the war enhanced the acceptance level among locals for aloha attire, which continued unabated.

With the end of the Pacific war, Hawaiian shirt manufacturers geared up for the return of tourism. Between 1944 and 1953, Dale Hope notes, more than a dozen manufacturers were launched, including such iconic names as Hale Hawaii, Iolani, Lauhala, and Malihini. Another, company, Sun Fashions, was founded by Dale's father Howard Hope. Robert Shizuo Takeshige (1917?–2012), a bartender, changed careers and opened his Holo-Holo shirt company, using an electric cutter to shear 300 shirts at a time, with his wife crafting the designs.[14]

There was a design revolution going on as well. Author Linda Arthur notes that many designers began to use the whole shirt as a canvas, incorporating classic motifs encompassing hula girls, Hawaiian flora, pineapples, Diamond Head, seagoing outriggers, tribal motifs and tikis, splashed with a dizzying array of colors. In the pre–1970 era, coconut buttons were the most prevalent, with a smaller yet significant number made of oyster shell, wood, metal, stamped leather, Chinese braided "frog," and plastic. The metal buttons were among the most intriguing, sporting alii warrior heads, Asian script, basket weave patterns, royal shields, flowers, and images of King Kamehameha.

The button industry itself was a significant contributor to the shirt business, often situated in private homes. Nancy Schiffer quotes a fascinating passage in her book *Hawaiian Shirt Designs*: "Dorothy Shimabukuro ... works late each evening at her modest Emerson Street home making intricate Chinese buttons for Hawaii's garment industry. Daytime she gets her materials ready. She has turned out as many as 600 in a night—10,000 a month ... her feat made all the more remarkable by the fact that Mrs. Shimabukuro is blind. She is one of 24 sightless men and women for whom the work is subcontracted through clothing manufacturers by the State Home Industry Program in the Department of Social Services. [Begun in 1957].... More than 50 percent of the clothing manufacturers have participated in the program since its inception."[15]

In terms of producing traditional Pacific motifs on fabric, the influence of Alfred Shaheen was significant. He and his Alfred Shaheen Ltd. team pored through old books and manuscripts and traveled to far-flung places including Samoa, Tahiti, Hong Kong, and Tokyo to transcribe motifs particular to Pacific cultures. Many of those designs appeared on his prints and garments, influencing a generation of Hawaiian garment makers.[16]

The abundance of exotic images available on Hawaiian shirts resulted in a cornucopia of choices for shirt buyers on the mainland, reflected in soaring sales statistics. Prior to the war, the Hawaiian fashion industry had sales of approximately $50,000 per year. The figure climbed to $2.5 million in 1947. With the advent of *Aloha Week* in that year, Hawaiian garments could now be worn in a business environment in Honolulu, allowing both men and women to eschew—if only for a week each year in October—traditional Western office clothing. By 1951, the Hawaiian fashion industry was a $6 million a year business, with 50 percent of its production sold to retailers in the United States.[17] Thereafter, until 1961, it increased approximately 30 percent annually.[18] Hawaiian shirts were popular among all social strata, which included President Harry S. Truman, photographed wearing one on the cover of *Life Magazine's* Dec. 10, 1951, issue.

In the years bookending World War II, movies both mirrored and augmented the popularity of Hawaiian shirt. Film as a fashion trendsetter was nothing new in the luxury garment world, of course. As writer Dana Thomas notes in her fascinating book *Deluxe: How Luxury Lost its Luster*, Macy's sold half-a-million versions of an Adrian-designed gown worn by Joan Crawford in the 1932 film *Letty Lynton* (dir. Clarence Brown).[19] The Hawaiian shirt, on the other hand, was hardly a *haute-couture* item, selling for as little as 75 cents in the 1930s (roughly $13 today), to $2.50 in the early 1950s (about $22 in today's currency), affordable to both locals and visitors wishing to create collections for their own closets.[20]

The 1953 release of the feature film *From Here to Eternity* (dir. Fred Zinnemann), in which Montgomery Clift and Frank Sinatra were shown wearing bold Hawaiian print shirts, popularized the garments even further. Neither shirts could be said to have been colorful, though, as the film was released in black and white. *Eternity* wasn't the first feature film in which Hawaiian shirts were worn. One of a number that preceded it was *Tahiti Nights* (dir. Will Jason), released in late 1944, in which notable Hawaiian entertainment figures including Hilo Hattie and Harry Owens made appearances. The costuming of the male characters in these two films contrasts the manner in which the shirts were worn. In the later film, Clift wore his shirt outside of his trousers, whereas the characters in the earlier movie wore theirs tucked into their belted pants. With the exception of engineered shirts (discussed above) and those with a specifically designed lower border, both of which are made to be worn "outside," Hawaiian shirts can be worn either way, simply as a matter of preference. They can even be worn tied bare-midriff, as Elvis Presley did when photographed on Matson's *Matsonia* in 1957.

The squared-off tail on the Hawaiian shirt has been attributed to Duke Kahanamoku, who decided that it would be an aesthetic improvement over round cut tails when worn outside trousers.[21] Kahanamoku, a legendary Olympic star, goodwill ambassador, and eventually Honolulu sheriff, lent his name to several lines of shirts made by local manufacturers in return for royalties, which averaged out at about $1,000 from the years 1952–1960.[22] In the 1950s, popular stars including Bing Crosby and Arthur Godfrey kept Hawaiian shirts in the public eye as mainlanders yearned for some exoticism in their lives. Godfrey took the Hawaiian motif one step further by playing the ukulele.

Hawaii became the 50th state in the union on August 21, 1959. The run-up to statehood was underscored by the tremendous increase in tourism, increasing from 50,000 to 250,000 from the years 1950 to 1959. The population of the islands was evolving as well, from 350,000 to 500,000 during the same period. By 1959, the Hawaiian shirt business was grossing $10

Amelia Earhart and Duke Kahanamoku in Hawaii, December 1934 or January 1935 (Matson Navigation Company Archives).

million annually in sales, becoming the third largest industry in Hawaii, behind sugar and pineapple.[23] Every male resident, it seemed, wore Hawaiian shirts, and many visitors who bought them in Hawaii grew their collections by buying from retailers on the mainland when they returned home.

Fabrics and print designs were evolving at the same time. Rayon, which prior to the war was considered unsuitable for shirts because it wasn't dye-fast, was improved after the war and became a fabric of choice, light, breathable, and colorful. Hawaiian-themed prints, often consisting of traditional lifestyle subjects, local flora, and tropical travel themes, increased in popularity as the earlier Japanese themes waned.[24]

In terms of the workers actually making the shirts, the seamstresses were largely *Nisei* (second generation Japanese Hawaiians) whose parents commonly worked in pineapple and sugarcane fields or in canneries. Sewing garments was seen as a step up from toiling in the fields, less strenuous and better paid. In addition, manufacturers including Alfred Shaheen, Iolani, and Kamehameha had profit-sharing programs. Herb Briner, proprietor of Kamehameha, bought a house near the factory in Hilo to house seamstresses, who could choose to live there rather than commuting to work. On weekends they were free to stay there or return home. Cutters were typically men, who used electric knives capable of cutting hundreds of garments at a time. It wasn't exactly a panacea for the workers, however. In the decades leading up to statehood, the industry was not unionized and air-conditioned manufacturing facilities would not come along until later.[25] Although the industry was optimized for efficiency, quality was emphasized over speed. By the 1970s, dozens of Hawaiian-based companies were competing for the business, whether making clothes under their own labels or as manufacturers making garments for other firms. In the latter case, buyers were astute, insisting on flawless garments that would result in fewer returns from customers.

The breadth of the Hawaiian shirt retailing market was reflected through a variety of outlets available to the consumer. Department stores, including Montgomery Ward, J.C. Penney (the Towncraft Hawaiian Holiday label) and Sears (Sears Hawaii and Hoaloha labels) sold significant numbers of shirts direct, either through stateside and island stores or catalogues.[26] Liberty House, a venerable Hawaii-based department store founded in 1849, contracted with a number of local manufacturers for its house label, made by well-known names including Hawaiian Casuals, Iolani, Malihini, Pacific Sportswear, Tori Richard, and Tropicana.[27] Watumull's, owned by brothers Jhamandas and Gobindram J. "Goma" Watumull (1891?–1959), another island-based department store that began its life as the East India Store in 1913, went one step further, purchasing the Royal Hawaiian label from founder Max Lewis in 1955, carrying the brand in its own stores as well as distributing it to other retailers.[28]

Island-based clothing stores, including Andrade, McInerny's, Linn's, and Ross Sutherland, featured store-labeled island fashions along with traditional business and casual clothing. Waltah Clarke (1912–2002), whose first name resulted from the island patois pronunciation of his given name, Walter, moved to Hawaii in 1937 or 1938 and soon became manager for "Trader Vic" Bergeron's Honolulu restaurant. Later, he served as general manager and publicity director for the Don the Beachcomber restaurant chain. Clarke opened his first shop in 1952 at the El Mirador Hotel in Palm Springs, specializing in Hawaiian fashions. Eventually owning 31 shops on the mainland and in Hawaii, he became the largest retailer of Hawaiian shirts in the United States before closing operations in 2001.[29]

Alfred Shaheen

No discourse on the history of the Hawaiian shirt would be complete without a discussion of the creative and manufacturing innovations of Alfred Shaheen. He was born on Jan. 31, 1922 in Cranford, New Jersey. to George, an immigrant from Lebanon, and Mary Shaheen, owners of a silk mill and clothing manufacturing company. They eventually moved their business to Compton, California, where Alfred attended high school. George bought silk for his Compton factory in Guam, where he also owned a department store. Habitually, he stopped for a few days in Honolulu on each trip. In 1938, George and Mary Shaheen and their manufacturing business moved to Hawaii, leaving Alfred in the States to finish high school, where he also took up flying lessons. According to daughter Camille Shaheen Tunberg, George, who was a devotee of physical culturist Bernarr Macfadden (1868–1955), devoted much of his time to health retreats and running his department store, while Mary tended to their clothing store in Hawaii. Mary was a seamstress noted for her wedding and prom dresses, and was able to craft complex dragons onto a fabric with several rapid semi-circular passes on the sewing machine. After his high school years, Alfred decided to remain in California to go to Whittier College, where he received a BA in Aeronautical Engineering. He put the degree to immediate use in World War II, piloting his P-47 Thunderbolt on 84 combat missions for the Army Air Corps in the European Theater.

Alfred moved to Hawaii in 1946. He became active in his parents' dressmaking and clothing manufacturing business. The first items he made were sharkskin shirts and trousers for his father's department store in Guam. He opened his own small shirt manufacturing shop with four sewing machines in 1948, with Mary Shaheen teaching the seamstresses the arts of sewing, pattern cutting, and other critical aspects of the manufacturing process. A crippling dock strike in 1949 and the resulting lack of imported fabric inventory provided him with a revolutionary idea that would transform the Hawaiian garment industry. To avoid the problems of fabric availability, inventory, and high cost, he would manufacture his own fabrics in Hawaii. He had saved a considerable amount of money during his war years, and that, along with his engineering background, enabled him to create a factory that handled all manufacturing processes. He bought his plain fabrics, created his dyes, built his equipment, created textile design and fashion departments, sewed, and distributed. After a number of frustrations, fits, and starts, his printmaking subsidiary, Surf 'n' Sand Hand Prints, was finally fully operational by 1952.[30]

Shaheen's one-stop factory solved a major problem inherent in the Hawaiian shirt industry, namely the lengthy lead times needed by Japanese and U.S.–based textile converters. The arduous process began when the shirt maker sent the design to New York. It took 30 days for it to be engraved on machine rollers. An additional 30 days were needed to approve, print, and finish the design. 30 days later, the finished shirts arrived in Hawaii. Because of the 90-day lead time, Hawaiian shirt makers were forced to carry 60 days' worth of inventory as an insurance policy against any additional unforeseen delays, which might potentially include labor strikes and transportation problems.[31]

In terms of design, Shaheen eschewed the chop-suey, or "hash" shirt, a design featuring small traditional images commonly found on Hawaiian shirts, in favor of cohesive larger designs. His color palette consisted of an inventory of more than a thousand hues. Rather than use the 15-inch print rollers common in the era, he instead painstakingly imbued his three-to-five color designs with dyes squeegeed, rather than rolled, two to four times over the fabric. He invented his own metallic dyes, washable, chlorine and salt-water-resistant, and light-fast. By the mid–1950s, with an output of 4,000 to 6,000 yards per day, he was selling fabric to more than 3,000 establishments on the mainland. He made Hawaiian shirts for retailers including as Andrade, Waltah Clarke, McInerny's, Penney's, and Stetson. He licensed his prints to European clothing manufacturers and set up a factory in Hong Kong to make brocades.

Since aloha shirt sales were largely seasonal, Shaheen began manufacturing women's clothing, enabling his workers to be employed the entire year. Shaheen also had a profit-sharing plan for his workers and hosted a company bowling team, whose members wore Shaheen-designed shirts with a stylized bowling ball on the reverse.[32] As the only printmaker in Hawaii, he promoted his business through numerous fashion shows featuring his men's shirts and women's garments. He was particularly noted for his colorful cocktail dresses, which, like his shirts, often included iconographic ethnic and cultural patterns and imagery that he'd discovered during his travels. These included influences from India, Asia and the Pacific islands, and Hiroshige-inspired Japanese motifs. He pioneered "fusion fashion," blending East and West. He was particularly proud of his prints, telling his daughter Camille on many occasions that he wanted his prints to be remembered. His women's fashions were known for their buttons, resplendent with Asian images carved in ivory, for his After Five silks.[33]

Shaheen was confronted by increasing competition toward the latter part of the 1950s, particularly from Japanese fabric manufacturers. In 1958, he began manufacturing engineered prints in which the design flowed 360 degrees around the garment, a technically challenging and expensive process for other fabric printers to duplicate.[34]

Shaheen never forgot his retail roots, and his empire evolved by creating a significant local market for his shirts by increasing his retail operations in Hawaii, eventually encompassing seven stores in the 1960s, run by his mother Mary. By this time, he was employing 400 people and running a combined retail and manufacturing operation that was grossing more than $4 million annually in worldwide sales.[35]

Shaheen's business model was based heavily on leasing rather than owning, and the company reached a financial crisis when the prime rate shot up past 20 percent by the end of the Jimmy Carter administration in 1981. Shaheen always felt that the creative process was most engaging for him, and increasingly, he was now spending more time engrossed in dealing with ongoing financial challenges in a difficult economy. His mother Mary had passed away in 1975, a loss keenly felt for emotional as well as business reasons, as she was the bedrock of the retail operation. In 1988, Alfred Shaheen sold his machinery, die-forms, and retail shops, by now numbering nine establishments.

In overall terms, Shaheen was proud enough of the family name and reputation that he refused to sell the Shaheen brand to the highest bidder, preferring instead to enjoy his accomplishments in retirement. Although his glory years were from 1948 through the late 1960s, he remained an innovator in design until he closed his company. His design creators produced more than 6,000 pieces of art from 1948 to 1988.[36] Alfred Shaheen passed away in 2008. His designs are licensed today by daughter Camille Shaheen.[37]

Hawaiian Shirts in the Late 20th Century

On the mainland, demand for new Hawaiian shirts diminished somewhat in the 1970s and early 1980s, considered by many to be passé and kitschy. At the same time younger buyers, particularly those embracing the retro, counterculture, and surfing movements, began frequenting thrift stores, buying up older Hawaiian shirts. Thus was rekindled an interest that eventually led to a groundswell in the new millennium, as those buyers matured, acquired more personal wealth, and continued amassing personal shirt collections.

By 1988, there were approximately 150 garment manufacturers in Hawaii, generating $120 million in sales. Their market and margins were eroding, however, based on the influx of big box stores to the islands, the abundance of easily available and less expensive goods manufactured offshore, and the popularity in the islands of swap-meets, where low-cost imported Hawaiian-style shirts were sold by the truckload.[38] The term *swap meet*, commonly used in Hawaii, is something of a misnomer, the equivalent of a mainland flea market in which goods are exchanged for money. Perhaps the best known of these is the swap meet is located at Aloha Stadium, in which even today new Hawaiian shirts—nearly all manufactured offshore—can be had for as little as three dollars.

Among collectors of older pre-owned shirts, as well as buyers of pricier new garments, there has always been a certain cachet to the "Made in Hawaii" label. Much of the time, the Hawaiian appellation is printed on the brand label in large letters, often not the case with offshore-manufacturers' Hawaiian shirts, where the country of origin might be printed instead on a label in the inseam. A similar situation exists within the European luxury garment and accessories market, where legendarily tony manufacturers have gone to great lengths to preserve the image of their brands by either manufacturing goods in the country of their origin or, if manufacturing in a developing nation, hiding it as much as is legally possible. "Perceived quality is more important than real quality," stated the CEO of one European luxury brand. Haute couture houses are aware that they can charge more for a product created with "European craftsmanship" than they can for products made in China, Korea, or Bangladesh.[39] As is the case with Hawaii, it costs more to make a product at home than it does to build it in another country in which labor is less expensive and the workers less prone to—or legally proscribed from—striking for higher wages.

Are the Hawaiian-made shirts of today superior, from a quality perspective, than aloha shirts made in other countries? Not always. One offshore manufacturer typically makes Hawaiian shirts with French seams on plackets, arms, collars, and yokes, an expensive process that adds to the durability of the garment. Many of its shirts are made in Bangladesh. Island manufacturers, on the other hand, quite often eschew that expense and others like it in order to be as price-competitive as possible. In addition to single-sewn seams, other cost-cutting measures include foregoing extra buttons as well as neglecting to match pockets to the surrounding design and front panels to each other, which would allow for a cohesive "face" to the garment.

Offshore manufacturers might also play fast and furious with abstract tropical-inspired designs and colors that initially appear to have little to do with traditional Hawaiian motifs. One garment company might create a shirt based on an abstract, inexact leaf pattern with otherworldly colors, while another would feature a modified Asian script as painted by the Japanese brush, its golden tint aglow on silk against an ebony background.[40] The broadening of themes, colors, and designs by offshore manufacturers has encouraged Hawaii-based manufacturers to move beyond traditional island motifs. The brand now known as Hilo Hattie was founded in 1963 by James S. "Jim" Romig (b. 1938?) as Pomare Ltd. He opened his Kaluna Hawaii Sportswear shop the same year. Two years later, he hired 20 seamstresses and began manufacturing on a larger scale. In 1979, Pomare acquired the Margolis Manufacturing and Retail Co. Its owners, Richard and Evelyn Margolis, had begun a partnership with entertainer Hilo Hattie in 1971 and branded a clothing line using her name. Romig acquired the rights to the name with the purchase and began manufacturing under the Hilo Hattie name.[41] Romig's company was one that evolved its designs to non-representational images, particularly after the mid–1980s. Some of its shirts stretched the boundaries of what could be considered truly Hawaiian, utilizing patterns that appear to be created using wax-resist designs, with abstract fish, coral, and traditional motifs in bright white on black or navy. Another Hilo Hattie design of the era recreated a volcanic fantasy jungle scene on silk with exploding cinder cones surrounded by vegetation, reminiscent of the impressionist work of Paul Cezanne.[42]

Even newer Hawaiian aloha shirts are traded today in used clothing stores specializing in vintage garments. How can a shirt barely 20 years old be classified as vintage? Author Dana Thomas devotes several paragraphs to the term, reflecting on the seasons and years in which clothing now considered vintage was sold originally.[43] In terms of Hawaiian shirts, prints were licensed for varying periods, typically a year. When the run sold out, it was not remade.[44] Hawaiian shirt manufacturers have gone out of business, filed for bankruptcy, and occasionally started up again, with a new ownership and design philosophy. Shirts sold as vintage prints today, therefore, can be as young as 15 years old. The most valuable, though, are the decades-old Hawaiian-made shirts. Shirts from the 1960s are still relatively common, those from the 1950s and earlier less so. Collectors today prize these older garments, focusing on their purity of design, color palette, craftsmanship, and longevity. Provenance can be a factor determining the market value of Hawaiian shirts as well. How much can they be worth today? Honolulu Aloha shirt merchant David Bailey notes several recent high profile sales: "The $5,500 Jimmy [Buffett] spent for a very rare Art Vogue hula girl back panel is our record. Number two, Nick Cage spent $4,200 for a rare purple colored 50's shirt … we understand he paid $17,000 for a dragon themed shirt in London … last month the shirt Patrick Swayze wore in the movie *Ghost* sold at auction for over $11,000."[45]

To a very large extent, however, the boom in internationally manufactured Hawaiian shirt design and manufacturing has benefitted the customer, who can find an incredible array of tropical shirts, available at thousands of retail outlets at affordable prices. Many of them are extremely well crafted. Although they will probably never be the focus of collectors, these shirts, sold in department stores ranging from Macy's and Nordstrom to Kohl's and Target, are more than occasionally as compelling, from a design and manufacturing perspective, as many of the Hawaiian shirts made by the pricier manufacturers of today.[46] But are they truly, from an authenticity perspective, Hawaiian shirts? As Josh Feldman, Tori Richard's VP noted, "The term 'Hawaiian shirt' has come to mean anything that has a bright, colorful, whimsical print on it."[47] Some of the most intriguing Hawaiian shirts today boast abstract floral patterns and non-representational images, done up in an imaginative and nontraditional palette of colors. The art form continues to evolve, further defying any attempt to describe what a Hawaiian shirt is, or isn't.

What hasn't changed is their appeal to all classes of society, reflected in price points for new garments that rarely exceed $100, and in most cases retail new for $50 or less.

Three of the higher-end manufacturers are Tori Richard, Reyn Spooner, and Tommy Bahama, although it might be argued that the latter, with no roots in Hawaii, shouldn't even be in the conversation.[48] But taking Josh Feldman's quote to heart, Bahama, along with Jamaica Jaxx, whose colorful silk and jacquard weave shirts make it a Bahama direct competitor, can be said to fit within the category.[49] Tori Richard, with nine boutiques in the islands and marketing through a retail network as well, is said to be the most prolific high-end manufacturer in the islands, while Reyn Spooner, with seven boutiques, comes in at a close second. Reyn, however, does a significant amount of business with identity apparel, creating shirts for everything from sports teams to resorts to the 453-store Trader Joe's food chain. Although not bearing the Reyn label, the grocery chain's Hawaiian shirts, manufactured with a new design every year through the first part of the new millennium, have become collectible. With logoed Hawaiian shirts worn by grocery store clerks and sports team enthusiasts, Hawaiian shirt manufacturers remain creatively cognizant of new markets expanding beyond tropical leisurewear.

Reyn Spooner shirts have a history as a "power shirt" among influential Hawaiian businessmen. In an essay published in 1992, Professor Albert B. Robillard of the University of Hawaii's Social Science Research Institute wrote: "The aloha shirt for local residents is hierarchically differentiated by class and occupation ... the Honolulu downtown or Bishop Street community, bankers, lawyers, accountants, stockbrokers, corporate executives, advertising agency and public relations people, government agency managers, and those who aspire or pretend to the same social strata, wear a Reyn Spooner aloha shirt, a 100 percent cotton, reverse pattern, pastel-colored, button-down shirt ... worn during business hours with the tails tucked in.... The shirt is the embodiment of ... sensitivity to the local hierarchy, command over resources, intention and aspirations which is, in part, the reflexive, practical achievement of being a member of the Hawaii bourgeoisie and managerial classes."[50]

Hawaiian shirts remain the most persuasively visible argument for the universal pervasiveness of exotica. In warmer mainland states, they're out of the closet the year round. Their designs convey an edenic dream-state that takes the wearer to enchanted isles, lands and waters, carrying images that sometimes seem to exist only in the minds of the print designers. The Hawaiian shirt has morphed into something beyond simple hula girls, ukuleles, hibiscus flowers, and Diamond Head patterns. It's been turned inside out (literally, in reverse-print shirts), shifted 90 degrees and evolved into what some companies refer to as resortwear. The evolution of the Hawaiian shirt has multiple facets, and among the more interesting twists and turns through the eddies of the garment world are the stories of companies that include Reyn Spooner, Tori Richard, and HRH/Kahala, garment executives Tim McCullough and Dale Hope, and a number of island artists that created designs and collections for island-based shirt companies.

Two Tropical Shirt Manufacturers: Tori Richard and Reyn Spooner

Through the years, the fortunes of Hawaiian shirt manufacturers have waxed and waned. Some have gone out of business, others, like Hilo Hattie, have declared bankruptcy, reinvented themselves and survived. Well into the first two decades of the new millennium, two companies in particular have remained profitable. A buyer can find new Reyn Spooner or Tori Richard shirts in their own branded shops, in tony boutiques, in sports stadiums and arenas, or in museum stores. Their pervasiveness is underscored by the fact that retailers of pre-owned clothes almost always have one or more shirts in their inventories made by either of these two manufacturers. As Dale Hope's book *The Aloha Shirt: Spirit of the Islands* attests, most manufacturers have fascinating stories to tell regarding their origins. Reyn and Tori sit at the higher end of the market, price-wise, and largely, their designs are recognizably unique enough that even less-experienced collectors can identify their shirts before they bother looking at the label.

Tori Richard

Tori Richard, Ltd., has been making resort apparel in Honolulu since 1956, when Mort Feldman (1921- 2004) and his soon-to-be wife, Janice Moody (d. 1977), named their new company after one of Mort's sons, Richard, and Janice's daughter Victoria. Joining them in the venture as one of three co-founders was pattern maker Mitsue Aka (b.1921). For nearly two decades, their product line consisted primarily of women's resort fashions. At the behest of Liberty House, one of their department store customers, they began making men's Hawaiian shirts in the 1970s. In one memorable custom project, the company introduced Tegaki handprints from Japan, made by stretching a fabric between two poles, embellished with designs crafted by two active and hardworking painters in motion. In all, more than a million yards of this customized fabric were crafted into men's and women's fashions, with no two pieces being exactly alike. By the end of the 1980s, sales of men's Hawaiian shirts had eclipsed those of their women's fashions and had become the prime focus of the company.

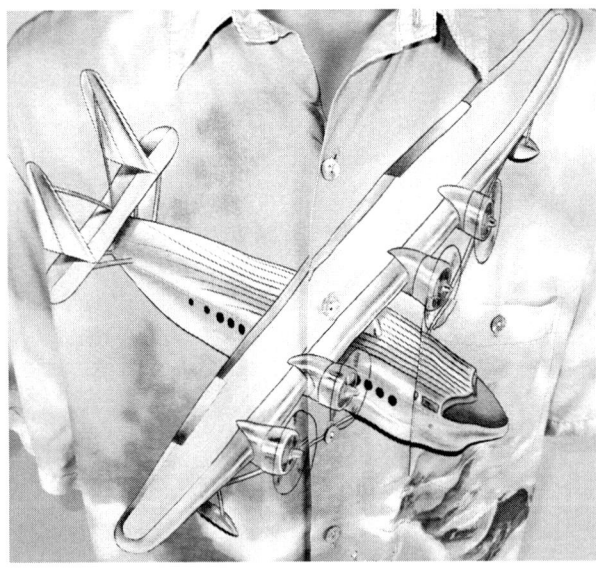

Detail of Sikorsky S-42 flying boat shirt by Tori Richard. Note the exact rendering of propeller wash lines and matching front panels and pocket (author's collection).

One particularly striking shirt from the era consists of an engineered print showing a Sikorsky S-42 flying boat as seen from above, flying over the Hawaiian coastline, with palm trees, islands, and sailboats below. The colors are muted yellows, blues, and greens, the buttons made of mother of pearl with "Tori Richard" printed in tiny, exact lettering.

Following several management changes, Mort Feldman returned in 1994 from retirement, and along with son Josh, whose background included a strong graphic arts influence, re-invented the company. Matching front panels and pockets, French-pressed seams, and large, colorful, and intricate graphics were now notable characteristics of Tori Richard shirts. By the end of the 1990s, the firm was making more than 400 textile designs per year, and in 2002, expanded by re-introducing its women's line of clothing. CEO Josh Feldman is reluctant to characterize Tori Richard as an "aloha shirt" company, feeling that catch-all phrase will diminish and stereotype the breadth of the collection, with its wide variation of prints. "It was always the print, the art of the print, which formed the core of the company," he stated in 2006.[51] Tori Richard's shirts encompass an abundance of styles and motifs, but are universal in the sense that they are stylistically appropriate whether worn under a linen suit, a sports jacket, or with a pair of khaki or denim trousers.

Tori Richard does indeed still sell traditional Hawaiian aloha shirts, though, primarily through its Kahala Sportswear line, having acquired the legendary company in 2006.[52] According to Josh Feldman, Tori Richard and Kahala have always had a number of collaborations with artists (resulting in named collections), brands, and museums. One memorable museum partnership was with the Honolulu Museum of Art, which held its "Art Deco Hawaii" exhibit from July 3, 2014 through Jan. 11, 2015. In celebration of the exhibit, Tori Richard introduced two new shirt designs, "Boat Day" and "FestivAloha," compelling prints made from illustrations drawn from Eugene Savage's vintage 1938 murals made for Matson Navigation.[53]

From a marketing and sales perspective, the company has grown dramatically over the decades. Today, more than 1500 shops carry their shirts and the company has 15 company owned retail stores, spread over four of Hawaii's islands. The company also has licensed concept stores in Cape Cod and Nantucket, Massachusetts.

Reyn Spooner

Reyn Spooner is a premium sportswear brand traditionally associated with the reverse print men's Hawaiian shirt. It is also notable for standard print garments as well as identity apparel and themed aloha shirts made under license for entities including sports teams and colleges. Reyn garments are typically sold in higher-end retail establishments and are prized by collectors, having a resale value on the secondary market that is among the highest for Hawaiian shirt manufacturers.

Having been in the clothing business for more than a decade, Reyn McCullough had probably just about seen it all when his assistant store manager Tom Anderson showed him a rather unique Hawaiian shirt. It was 1961 and it was made by a bartender and it was inside out. Pat Dorian, who tended a bar on Waikiki, had made some shirts for himself in which he recreated the faded, well-worn look prized in the surfing community. Turn the print inside out, he reasoned, and you can have the sun-bleached look without stressing the garment fibers the way that hours in the sun will. He wore them to work and customers liked them so much that they began ordering shirts from him. He began carrying them in his mobile stockroom, the trunk of his car. When Anderson unveiled Dorian's shirt to McCullough, an evolution in the Hawaiian shirt business was about to begin.

Reyn McCullough (1918–1984) was a Californian, raised on Catalina Island, where in 1949, he bought his employer's men's retail clothing operation and renamed it Reyn's Men's Wear. His business grew to six stores, selling resort wear, swimwear, and a selection of Hawaiian shirts manufactured by Pali Hawaiian Style, a California operation run by Clarence Hara and his father in law, Isamu Takabuki. Their enchanting stories of island culture, along with the ever-increasing DC-7 air-traffic flying over Avalon, Catalina Island, to and from Hawaii, influenced Reyn in 1958 to take a trip to Honolulu to investigate the prospects for Reyn's expansion. While there, he was introduced to Donald Houston Graham Jr. (1914–2010), who represented the Dillingham Corporation and was in the process of developing a new shopping center that would be called Ala Moana Center. Graham's goal was to include several Hawaii men's retailers, including Ross Sutherland. Ross, however, no longer wanted the space it had reserved and Reyn took Sutherland's spot. He opened his first Hawaii Reyn's Men's Wear shop at the Ala Moana Center in 1959.

Ironically, Reyn didn't want to sell Hawaiian shirts in his store, as those garments were already well represented by many long-time local retailers. Instead, he introduced to Hawaii shoppers traditional "Ivy League" business clothing, furnishings and leisure apparel, manufactured by old-school garment companies in the Eastern U.S. Additionally, Reyn felt that printed Hawaiian shirts were just too gaudy for his new under-stated haberdashery. Things changed when Tom Anderson walked in the door with Pat Dorian's reverse print shirt.

The subtlety of Dorian's shirt impressed Reyn, who could see a place for it in the store, if done to his standards. It would need to have a "Reyn" feel, notably a combined Hawaiian and Ivy League look. The resulting garment consisted of a pullover shirt with a button-down collar and tails that could be tucked into trousers, all crafted from reverse print fabric, using the single-needle workmanship of early English tailoring. Reyn didn't have to invent the pattern, either. Already selling in his Ala Moana store, he borrowed the "Hugger Body" style from his friends and colleagues, noted New Haven dress-shirt manufacturers, Elliott and Arthur Gant, who graciously provided Reyn with the patterns.

The next step was getting the shirts sewn. Ruth Spooner, who had a Waikiki swimwear sewing business, Spooner's of Waikiki, was already supplying Reyn with custom swimwear to his specifications and was willing to take on the new line of shirts. They combined forces, using fabric purchased from both Eastern mills with early Americana designs, and locally from Alfred Shaheen, noted for making tropical floral prints with a screen printing process that allowed for the superior color penetration needed for reverse prints.[54] In 1962, Reyn acquired Spooner's of Waikiki and moved Ruth and her custom sewing operation into the basement of Reyn's Ala Moana store.[55] It was small, consisting of a four foot by six foot cutting table and two sewing machines, but still took up nearly the entire 600 square foot basement. The new operation was based on efficiency, consolidating retail and manufacturing operations under one roof.

Reyn's first Hawaiian-themed proprietary design was produced in 1968. Called "Lahaina Sailor," and resembling the bandana prints worn by 19th century New England whaling sailors who had frequented the islands, it was configured within a four square geometric layout and represented notable Hawaiian icons: the state flag, the state bird (nene), the state flower (hibiscus) and the state tree (kukui nut). It was intended to be a hybrid, Hawaiian in theme, but with a classic early American look.

Tim McCullough, who had grown-up in the family company, started as a full-time employee at 16 years of age and had enjoyed a career as a surf photographer in the 1960s before becoming president of the company in 1978. He immediately identified ways the manufacturing process could be streamlined and the quality enhanced. To appreciate the significance of those changes, it helps to understand a few of the many different operations it takes to manufacture a Reyn Spooner shirt. McCullough notes that there are an astounding 44 of them.

Some of these processes are made even more complex due to the nature of the garment in question. Reverse prints, mentioned earlier, are one example, referring to printed shirts that are cut, assembled and sewn in reverse. They have been a Reyn Spooner staple since 1962. "By reversing the fabric designs, a water-washed, sun-bleached shirt of subdued colors was created," says Tim, and "this helped to tone down the intensity of the imagery. Our shirts had a reliably conservative make and look."

One of the first things Tim McCullough tackled was the complex issue of manufacturing reverse print shirts to satisfy a growing market. In 1979, he, along with his manufacturing manager, bought Reyn Spooner's manufacturing interests and gave it a new name, No Ka Oi Producers, Inc. An initial issue McCullough faced as a comprehensive designer and now manufacturer was finding a way to create fabric designs in-house in order to assure exclusivity of product and the Reyn Spooner brand.

Reyn had traditionally relied on designs made by artists employed by Eastern U.S. fabric manufacturers where he had been obtaining his fabric. Instead, Tim wanted to create a "Reyn look" series of shirts. But in order to have his designs printed by a domestic fabric manufacturer, he had to commit to an order of 6,000 to 8,000 yards of fabric for each design, good enough for approximately 3,000 to 4,000 shirts. "We didn't have that kind of distribution," says McCullough, "3,000 yards, 1,500 shirts, was max for what we were looking for at the time."

Earlier, Tim had begun working with select free-lance textile artists. The process involved Tim coming up with the original design concept envisioned, and then having the free-lance artist execute it. The completed design art would then be transferred to a silk screen, a specialized task that McCullough refers to both as "an art and a science." A separate screen is made for each motif/color; four motifs/colors equal four screens, for example. The color to fabric transfer process involved a mechanical screen machine. But there was a problem with the domestic U.S. printers McCullough was using. Its application of color to the fabric was inconsistent in terms of rendering an image that could produce a superior reverse print shirt. "The ink has to be infused all the way through the screen, and it has to be monitored so the pressure through the screen is constant for an even penetration of the design imagery," says McCullough, "and we weren't getting that. The images on each shirt might vary from light to dark, which was unacceptable."

The printers were also working with a blended fabric consisting a 50 percent cotton and 50 percent polyester yarn ratio, which resulted in a unique chambray effect visible on the reverse print of a finished garment and, gave the shirt greater durability. The yarn needed to be saturated equally throughout the fabric to provide the consistency required for the refined Reyn look. The color inconsistency problem experienced with Eastern U.S. manufacturers was solved when McCullough found a fabric house in Japan that successfully rendered the colors in equal intensity throughout the fabric's reverse side. In addition to solving the printing issues, smaller print-runs were negotiated with Reyn Spooner's new source in Japan, which promoted a greater diversity of designs to be developed, further enhancing market development. Another significant benefit to the move was that Tim was able to improve on the fabric's composition by specifying a new 60 percent cotton and 40 percent polyester spun-blended yarn construction resulting in superior cool-wearability and washability for the new shirts. Additionally, Tim now began a working relationship with a Japanese design firm to supplement those made by his Hawaii-based freelancers,

McCullough also had to tackle the expensive process of having to go through a "converter," or middleman, when engaging with a printer. To cover the up-front costs to the printer, the converter "fronted" the money in lieu of eventual payment from the shirt manufacturer for which the order was placed. Typically, this would cost out in the range of $3 to $4 per yard of fabric. Figure two yards for each shirt, therefore, and each shirt would have a fabric cost of approximately $6 to $8 (as discussed below, more fabric was added for sizes XL and larger and for shirts requiring front panel matching). Utilizing a converter added middleman costs and time to the manufacturing process and did not always assure quality consistency for the finished fabric and design. McCullough solved this by establishing a direct relationship with a Japanese printing house, thus assuming full control of and responsibility for the supply line to Reyn Spooner's future.

The Japanese printer used an exacting flat-screen process that made flawless prints and was willing to print yardage in the smaller amounts specified by McCullough. The evolution to a new supplier had taken a number of months, but the challenges of design, printing consistency, and amount of fabric allocated per design were solved. The McCullough family of companies, which included Reyn's Men's Wear in retail, Reyn Spooner in design and wholesale marketing, and No Ka Oi Producers in manufacturing, was now a finely tuned vertically integrated operation within their full control.

Some Nuts and Bolts of Shirt Manufacturing

The fascinating elements of garment manufacturing are invisible to the consumer wearing the shirt. A discussion with Reyn Spooner's Tim McCullough opened the door the process of what goes into determining the eventual retail price of the garment.

Initially the fabric, known as grey goods (or greige goods, an industry term derived from the combination of yarn colors grey and beige of post loom-state fabric) is un-dyed, unbleached and un-printed, fresh from the loom. For Reyn Spooner, it was a muslin color pre-bleached to its specifications as an acceptable printed design base-cloth, using a number of different wet solutions and heat process. McCullough made it a point to limit the bleaching processes to ensure the integrity of the fabric strength, thus assuring product longevity.

The fabric is then printed using either flat screens on a flatbed machine or cylinder screens mounted on a rotary press. In Reyn Spooner's "reverse-print" case, this means using a flat screen machine that prints onto massive 400–500 yard lengths, 47 to 49 inches wide. After completion of the printing and finishing processes, these lengths are then cut into 60-yard lengths and rolled on to cardboard bolts for packing and shipping. By doing so, these lengths can be manually swung up onto the cutting table to initiate the manufacturing journey.

On the cutting table, paper patterns are laid out on the fabric and then scribed. They are then cut with a vertical reciprocating knife. Next, the resulting pieces are assembled into a color-shaded "bundle," which is sent to the sewing line to be assembled into shirts. For the pocket to properly match the shirt design, it must arrive at the pocket-positioning operation "overcut" so there is enough fabric to allow the seamstress sufficient allowance to position it onto the left front panel. This ensures exact design alignment on the body. Pattern-matching pockets on Hawaiian shirts did not exist until being introduced with the early manufacture of Reyn Spooner shirts.[56] Pattern-matching front body panels for button-front shirts, an element of higher design that provides a relatively seamless design-art continuity to the face of the shirt when buttoned, increases by 50 percent the total amount of fabric that must be allocated for each shirt. This additional expense explains the shortage in the marketplace of matching panel shirts compared to the overall production of Hawaiian shirts in a given year.

Not every sewing operation requires the same skill set. Experienced sewers tend to get the toughest (and highest paid) jobs, which include adding the collar and crafting a placket, the folded front-face detail through which the buttons are fastened.

Sewing operators are employees that are paid hourly wages, receive standard benefits, and can receive productivity bonuses. Reyn Spooner's daily production output could vary depending on several factors including fabric type, design complexity and color assortment, and McCullough noted that, "A big day in the No Ka Oi plant was the completion of 800 to 1,000 garments." Although print-runs varied, depending on the design, the rule of thumb was that 1,500 shirts of any given design had to sell for the run to be financially successful.

How much cloth does it take to make a shirt? Figure that 600 yards (21,600 inches) will make 290 shirts, more or less, and therefore 74.48 inches per shirt would be used. For sizes XXL and larger, add another yard (at 36 inches, the shirt now totaling 110.48 inches). That's all without front panel matching should the design require it. As mentioned earlier, panel matching adds a 50 percent increase in cloth to the fabric amount (now a total of 165.72 inches). A Hawaiian shirt in large sizes with matching front panels, therefore, will be among the costliest shirts to manufacture, reflected in the retail prices on the rack. In Reyn Spooner's case, it raises the amount of fabric needed to produce a large-size matching panel shirt from the standard 74.48 inches to 165.72 inches of linear print fabric.

Reyn Spooner also began producing the "engineered" shirt, which featured the design running a continual 360 degrees around the shirt. Reyn also initiated aloha shirt designs for major league sports teams, beginning with baseball. As McCullough remembers it, Reyn Spooner's first foray into the sports business resulted from its custom Hawaiian-themed shirt made for expressly for Disney's animated film, *Toy Story*, produced by John Lasseter's Pixar studio. "A Los Angeles Dodger merchandiser had sold Reyn Spooner shirts in retail prior to being associated with the team, and he approached us, that's how it started," McCullough says. Additional MLB teams, including the San Francisco Giants, Los Angeles Angels, Boston Red Sox, Chicago Cubs, Seattle Mariners, and others soon began selling their own Reyn Spooner shirts.

Reyn McCullough passed away in 1984 and Tim McCullough then assumed leadership of the three Reyn companies, a responsibility he maintained over the next 24 years. One of Tim's passions involved incorporating island-inspired art, embodied in the work of artists including Guy Buffet, Miles Mason, Robert Lyn Nelson, Dietrich Varez, and Eddy Y, into the design collections of Reyn Spooner shirts. "We were always looking for new creativity with inspiring direction that we felt would be attractive as 'wearable art,'" McCullough notes. He explained the exacting and often painstaking process of selecting the artists, the art, the printing process, and the marketing logistics of bring island art to Reyn's garment customers:

"Naturally, all of the art ventures were always at great risk at the outset of each artist I chose to want to collaborate with. And, was honored to receive the trust and confidence of each with this pursuit of bringing their hard developed art, to the consumer in a broader venue. Once we could determine the consumer's response, progressing into further development of new works became somewhat easier. Balancing the art angle with the business realities seemed natural to me, as I felt confident in the subject matter I was interested in coupled with the considerable success most of the collaborative artists I worked with had enjoyed and saw opportunity. Why not take this work to a broader audience!

"Determining which work was applicable to wearable art was an art form in its own process! Many, many refined modifications necessary in structural content, of the original image, so as to attain proper placement in textile printing to assure these images could be properly cut on the cutting table and sewn into shirts with strategic placement on the shirt to assure proper placing on the wearer's body, was a very considerable challenge. And, all without compromising the original art itself. Replicating the original imagery within the discipline of textile printing requirements was monumental especially when attempting a complicated subject with extensive color ranges. I was fortunate enough to have the invested collaborative commitment of my Japanese partners who re-interpreted these arts so as to be engravable-to-print-screens, 16 screens/colors in some cases with considerable up-charges that their print machines could produce was one of those behind the scenes challenges [neither] the consumer public nor the artists themselves, ever knew about. Often times I felt more like a sorcerer magician, this process was only hugely rewarding with the resulting accomplishments!"[57]

In 2008, Tim McCullough sold Reyn Spooner to Wedbush Capital Partners, but stayed on-board for another year as Chief Design Officer to help smooth the creative transition. In 2015, the company was sold again to Aloha Brands LLC, chaired by entrepreneur Charles B. Baxter. Today, Tim McCullough can be found leisurely driving the roads around his long-time home, Waimea, on Hawaii's Big Island, in his stock 1951 red Chevy pickup. He maintains a passion for, and waxes eloquently on the industry and company that was his family's prime point of business focus for six decades.[58]

Artists as Hawaiian Shirt Designers

Print designs utilized by specialty or higher-end shirt companies making Hawaiian shirts are typically created by in-house or contracted designers. Some of the most compelling designs in this category are those created by island-based artists working with Hawaiian thematic material. Artists that have cooperated with shirt manufacturers on shirt designs include Guy Buffet, Mike Field, Naoki Hayashi, Miles M. Mason, Robert Lyn Nelson, Dietrich Varez, and Eddie Y, each of whom contributed designs in individually named collections sold by Reyn Spooner. Ron Anderson, Nicholas Black, Michael Cassidy, Yvonne Cheng, Avi Kiraty, Marcia Ray, John Severson, and Mary Spears were artists whose designs were made into shirts by Kahala. Anderson's, Cassidy's, Cheng's, Kiriaty's, and Severson's shirts bore labels and hang tags with the name of the designer.

Dale Hope noted the logistical challenges of making collections specific to an individual artist. "Early on, we had to distinguish between textile artists and fine artists. Fine artists got a custom-designed shirt label and hang tag, textile artists unfortunately didn't. It could be a nightmare for the sewers. In one case, they accidently put one artist's label on a shirt made by another." Kahala's artist runs were typically 1,500 shirts, which divided down by a factor of 12 into what Hope described as a "1–2–5–2–2 breakdown," indicating the percentage of shirts made in S-M-LG-XL-2XL sizes.[59]

Reyn Spooner had been manufacturing "art shirts" since the mid–1960s. "We had a hand-loom, block printed cloth that came from remote villages surrounding Varanasi, India," Tim McCullough recalls. "Each block would be hand-carved from wood, and then the yarn spinning, cloth looming and design-motifs printing were done by many families in different villages. The colors would be from slightly to considerably different in their finished appearance, depending on the village that printed them. This was truly cottage-trade in its purest form! Each year, Mr. Daz would visit us exclusively in Hawaii and share his new design ideas. We created a line, 'India Cotton,' and sold the shirts for about 10 to 15 years."[60] By the latter part of the first decade of the new millennium, Reyn Spooner had created collections comprising seven different island artists. Consisting of what must be more than one million shirts, it may be said that the firm was responsible for one of the most significant undertakings involving well-known living artists and garments in the history of Hawaiian clothing manufacturing.[61]

Ron Anderson

The way Dale Hope tells it, he wasn't sure how Ron Anderson's designs would ever make it onto Kahala shirts. "Dick Braeger had a store in Fashion Island in Newport Beach, Garys Island.[62] He sold a lot of our shirts and Avi Kiriaty even went there to meet customers and discuss his shirts at an event with steel drums and entertainers. Dick kept telling me there was this artist, Ron Anderson, who I had to meet because he'd be perfect for our shirts. So I met Ron and he was doing this crazy 3-D art. I couldn't figure how we could put that on a shirt and sell it successfully. He was a surfer, and I saw something he did with a Woodie station wagon, so I said 'Make a painting with a golden retriever in a woodie, a dog in a backwards baseball cap, and the ocean and tropical flowers, on the road to Hana.' Ron created the design as a 4×8 foot 3-D sculpture, which was then rendered into a repeat design for textile printing. It turned out that Ron was a perfectionist, and it took a long time for him to approve the design, through several iterations when we were converting the art for textiles. After we made the shirt, which we called 'Road to Hana,' I took it to the Men's Apparel Show in Vegas, and everybody went crazy for the shirt. We ended up doing more than 40 Ron Anderson designs from the time he started with us, in the late 1990s, for the 'Ron Anderson by Kahala' collection. Since Local Motion owned Kahala, I convinced them to make a gift to Ron, a longboard with the 'Road to Hana' print laminated on top of the board. We put it in this huge box and mailed it to him."[63]

Born in Los Angeles in 1947, Ron Anderson eventually ended up in Santa Barbara via other Southern California beach towns. Our telephone conversation is interrupted by a blaring series of deafening blasts on a train horn. "Sounds like the Coast Starlight," I say, "you must live right next to the water. That train should make it up to here in San Jose in 10 or 12 hours...."

"Right, I'm overlooking the Pacific. I started surfing in about 1959 and it's been a major part of my life ever since." He reflected on his world of art. "I actually started drawing by doodling on those donation envelopes they have in the back of church pews, and it grew from there. I got serious when I was 13 or 14, and eventually enrolled in art classes at UC Santa Barbara. Dick Braeger was a collector of my art and introduced me to Dale Hope. I think we did close to 40 designs for Kahala, with two to four colorways for each shirt. I was doing crazy stuff with multimedia, too. It started when I raided Renny Yater's garbage can for some board foam, then added wood, resins, and found objects and created a whole new art form."[64] Anderson's work today includes sculpting, painting, and mixed media, about which he says, "My purpose is to uplift people, show them possibilities of creativity, create a conversation and allow the viewer to tell his own story about the work."[65]

Nicholas "Nicky" Black

Island artist Nicky Black's friendship with Dale Hope goes back to when they met as school chums at the age of 12. Born in Washington, D.C., in 1953, Black arrived with his military family in Honolulu at the age of one. He took to the water right away. "You didn't need a babysitter if you lived in Hawaii," Black says, "If a child can swim, he'd always be playing in the water. A few years later I met Dale, and we surfed together at Tongg's Beach. We grew up together in Kahala, right on the other side of Diamond Head." At the prestigious Punahou School, Black confesses that he was a lousy student. "That's how I really got started on art, drawing on the floor and on the desks," he says. He would eventually get bachelor's and master's degrees in fine arts at the University of Hawaii at Manoa, along with a teaching credential, and spent a year taking grad courses at Pasadena's Art Center College of Design. His career as a teacher and an artist coincided. "In 1980, Dale broke his arm on an outrigger one day, challenging a 35 foot wave with Tommy Holmes and Aka Hemmings.[66] I went to work with him to help out doing various things at HRH, which soon became Kahala. I spent four or five years there. Eventually, we started incorporating my designs into aloha shirts, probably 35 in all." Black never wanted his name on a label, which makes his designs impossible to identify unless you know his art. During his time at HRH, his prints were used as designs on shirts made by a fictitious company, Kahala Bay Club, that Hope had developed, and sold in Hawaii's Liberty House department store. Some of Black's better-known designs, used on HRH/Kahala labeled shirts were "Glassballs," "The Schooner Goodwill," and "Olapa Hula."

Dale Hope remembers working with Black on those designs: "For 'Olapa Hula,' Nicky arranged to have some Hula dancers with their handmade Ti leaf traditional outfits come to our factory so that he could photograph them and be accurate with their attire. He shot them with black and white film in our shipping loading dock. With 'Glassballs,' I went to Honolulu Harbor and hopped on the fishing sampan *Marcia*, and photographed large glassball floats tied to bamboo poles, used when fishing. From there Nicky created a masterful design that was hand-printed in Honolulu. With 'Goodwill,' I spent at least four years tracking down sail and hull plans, photos taken in the 53 Transpac Yacht race … we even got the diary from the victorious crossing. We took pride to tell meaningful stories; it was a great design, and many stories followed after the shirts got out, especially around Newport where the boat was from."[67]

When Hope sold his Kahala company, Nicky free-lanced for a short time with Tori Richard, where five of his deigns, including line drawings and an "Ahi" print, were crafted onto shirts. His last Tori Richard shirt appeared in approximately 2007. During his aloha shirt days, Black sold his art in galleries and taught art to middle school students for Hawaii's Department of Education. "It was fun teaching art to the kids … basically, you're just a big kid with all the power, and everyone likes art, just as they do PE and lunch," he said. The locally manufactured shirt business was challenged with tough economic times in those days "The big box stores moved into Hawaii, and U.S. labor costs were high," Black notes. "Making shirts overseas was cheaper. We found it tough to compete. Those big stores could retail an aloha shirt for the same price that local manufacturers charged for wholesale." But he and Dale Hope cooked up yet another idea.

Under Hope's new Hawaiian Style company, Black's designs, including "Ahi," "Aweoweo Hawaii," and "Kagami Hawaii," appeared on T-shirts, which were cheaper to manufacture and easier to sell than button-front aloha shirts. "I've gotta tell you, Dale was a marketing genius," Black says. "He had what we call the 'squid eye,' you know, always being able to find the octopus. I was like the piano player. Everyone puts tips in my jar, but Dale was the composer, cooking up the ideas and making it all happen behind the scenes." Today, Nicky Black exhibits his paintings, woodcuts, and line drawings in galleries all over Hawaii. "I'm done with shirts," he says, "I'm into doing the art."[68]

Guy Buffet

Guy Buffet was born in 1943 in Paris and spent his early years in Montparnasse. His parents owned a small restaurant, with a number of artists among the regular clientele. Conversations often centered around art, and Guy would eagerly listen in. His father also introduced him to cafes that were frequented by the artists Modigliani, Picasso, Chagall, and Braque, and would regale him with stories and discuss their art. On the 12th birthday, his mother gave him a set of colors and brushes, and soon he was hanging his paintings on the restaurant's walls.

Guy painted his first painting at the age of 12. His father having passed away, he moved at the age of 14 to the south of France to a small harbor town of Sanary-sur-Mer, near St. Tropez. Soon, he quit school to concentrate on painting at the Beaux Arts School of Toulon, and developed a fascination for Van Gogh and Gauguin. His mother returned to Paris after a year, but Buffet stayed, helping to pay for his expenses by working in restaurants. He enjoyed the experience to the extent that restaurants, as well as harbors, became themes that he would continually revisit as an artist. He joined the French Navy in 1961 at the age of 18 and was given an assignment to "paint the world."

Buffet fell in love with the South Pacific, and the captain of Buffet's ship gave him permission to mount an exhibition at a gallery in one of its ports. From there, he exhibited in Tahiti and New Caledonia, and the French navy facilitated an exhibition of his at the Royal Hawaiian Art Gallery in Honolulu. In Hawaii, he met Stephen M. Cooke, who wrote Buffet's introduction in the exhibit catalogue, and whose family became his first major patron. At the age of 20, he was out of the Navy and living in Hawaii.[69] Traveling has always been in Buffet's blood and is reflected in his canvases, which include scenes from China, India, Tahiti, and of course Hawaii. He lived in San Francisco for 10 years, raised his children on Maui, and has had numerous commissions, from air carriers, to cruise lines to hotels.[70] Approximately 60 of Buffet's designs appeared on Reyn Spooner shirts.[71] Buffet's relationship with Reyn lasted from the late 1980s to the late 1990s, and approximately 1,500 to 3,000 shirts were made from each design, so therefore a total of 150,000 Buffet garments were probably created. "I left Reyn Spooner because I had so many products," Buffet says. "We created a series of plates for Williams-Sonoma, and in the same time I was working with Reyn, we sold 3 million plates.

I remember wearing one of my shirts on a flight, and this American man came up to me, pronouncing my name with the American pronunciation, 'Guy Buffett.' He said 'I like your work, my wife has your shit all over the kitchen.'" Today, Buffet rides herd over his considerable artistic and licensing enterprises, which include a continuing series of voyages on Paul Gauguin Cruise Lines, where he gives art classes and enjoys the waters of Polynesia.[72]

Tim McCullough was always protective of the Reyn Spooner brand, as he believed the company was no better than its reputation. "Really, our art collection is very conservative," notes McCullough. "Reyn's and Reyn Spooner were driven by what I had learned over many years of growing up around and later on working for and with my Dad in the business and what he instilled in me to be: 'in good taste,' 'of classic style' and what we genuinely wanted to see our customers wear with confidence."[73] The firm's brand-consciousness took precedence in the printing of one of Buffet's designs. "It was my painting, 'A Happy Man,'" Buffet recalls. "There is a man sitting in front of a fireplace, drinking a glass of wine, while a nude woman plays piano in the background. When the shirt was released, she was wearing panties!"[74]

Michael Cassidy

"I discovered Mike through an article written about him in *Surfer's Journal*," Dale Hope says. "I called Steve Pezman, publisher of the *Journal*, got Mike's number. Mike and I became friends and we started traveling together, surfing and snowboarding. I was stoked on his designs, which required special layouts and engineering to create border designs."[75] Hope estimates that seven to ten Cassidy designs were crafted into Kahala shirts. Today, Cassidy is an artist renowned for his paintings of South Pacific, Native American, and Western art.[76]

Yvonne Cheng

Born in 1941 in Surabaya, Java, Indonesia, Yvonne Cheng took private art lessons until she arrived in Honolulu in 1967, whereupon she enrolled in batik courses at the Bishop Museum. She began making paintings and murals, primarily focusing on Hawaiian women and hula dancers. She also made line drawings of women in ink, reminiscent of the work of Aubrey Beardsley. By then a well-known island-based artist, her first line of herringbone silk batik shirt prints was sold for Dale Hope at Kahala in 2002, introducing the "Yvonne Collection by Kahala." Hope had been enamored of her art and had been considering using her batik art on Kahala shirts for a number of years when he serendipitously found her signing her gas receipt ahead of him at a local car wash. "I saw her sign her name," says Hope, "then I walked around to where the customers were picking up their cars. 'Are you Yvonne Cheng, the artist?' I asked her." Several meetings later, she somewhat reluctantly agreed to create designs for Kahala. At the time, she was engaged in painting murals for the Neiman Marcus Mariposa restaurant, and was concerned that her designs wouldn't translate well to fabric. Once she agreed to work with Hope, she went to work on the designs from her studio in the farmlands of Palolo Valley on Oahu, recreating the floral life of Hawaii, surfers, and being a dancer herself, the hula. Her designs were based on the retro look, common to the 1930–1950 era. Each of her designs was based on a palette of 12 or 13 colors, and generally each garment was printed in three different color combinations.[77] When Neiman Marcus saw the finished product, they wanted the line exclusively, but Hope was able to negotiate an agreement by which a limited number of other stores could sell Cheng's line as well. "She was really a phenomenon on the islands. I've attended art exhibitions where women stand in long lines just to meet her. I saw a photograph in a Hawaiian magazine, and many of the executive staff of one bank was wearing her shirts," said Hope. He estimates that she created between 15 to 20 different designs for Kahala Sportswear, with a run of 500 shirts for each design. "Typically, with cotton, we'd make 1,500 shirts," noted Hope, "but with Yvonne's herringbone silk, the run was smaller." Because of the small run and desirability of her shirts, Yvonne Cheng's Kahala shirts are highly difficult to find today on the secondary market.[78]

Mike Field

Born on the island of Guam in 1967, Mike Field is known for his colorful illustrations of Hawaiian beach and water culture. His designs have appeared on shirts made by Kahala, Reyn Spooner (the "M. Field by Reyn Spooner Collection") and Quiksilver. Shortly after Mike's birth, his father became fatality in the Vietnam War, and Mike and his artist mother soon moved to Hawaii. Field was a waterman almost as soon as he could walk, and later attended college at Franklyn Pierce University (Ringe, New Hampshire) and Loyola Marymount University in Los Angeles, where he received his BA in Art and Communication. Returning to Hawaii, he ended up meeting and showing his designs to Dale Hope. "Mike used to house-sit for me," Hope recalls, "and would leave little notes with these watercolor sketches on them. Soon, he was doing all sorts of things at Kahala, working at the factory, shelving and pulling stock, and driving trucks."[79] In the late 1990s, his designs began appearing on Hope's Kahala shirts. Shortly thereafter, Field read an article about Reyn Spooner's Tim McCullough, who mentioned that he'd been giving away quite a few "Mele Kalikimaka" Christmas shirts, but joked that he didn't seem to get many in return. Field went to McCullough's office, and in an aloha moment, left one of his shirts for him, neglecting to mention his name. Several years later, Field's wife Terry had a chance encounter with McCullough's wife in an island frame shop and she recognized Field's work from the shirt he'd left at the Reyn office. "Tim's been looking for you," she said, "but he never knew your name." A beer with Tim McCullough was the result, and the series of "M. Field" Reyn shirts followed, beginning in 2005. Field estimates that seven of his designs were used on Reyn button-front shirts. Four designs that Field remembers being made into Reyn shirts were "Afternoon Sail," "Paddleboarder," "Big Wave Surfer," and "OC-1 Waverider."

Field was also running a storefront shop at the Kukio Golf and Beach Club in Kailua-Kona on the Big Island, where he was designing his own linen aloha shirts. "I was buying new linen shirts from Ross at $20, screening and hand-printing my designs on them, then putting my own labels on the shirts, which I sold in my shop," he said. In 2012, a team from Quiksilver saw the shirts, and soon four or five of Field's designs appeared in the Quiksilver line. Field, however, became a victim of Quiksilver's bankruptcy of 2015.[80] "I tried to buy back my shirts, but no luck," he says. Field good-naturedly takes it all in stride and remains a committed waterman. When he's not in the surf, you'll find him today on the Big Island in his Mike Field Gallery on the Old Mamalahoa Highway, in the village of Holualoa near Kailua-Kona. Run by Mike and Terry, an artist in her own right, the gallery offers M. Field prints, apparel, and unique art pieces.[81]

Naoki Hayashi

Naoki Hayashi specializes in the Japanese art of gyotaku (fish + rubbing), a method developed in the mid–19th century, to capture the image of a fish through direct contact with printing materials. Gyotaku take the form of one of two techniques: one consists of placing a piece of plain paper on top of the fish and then rubbing colors over the paper, bringing out the relief. The other involves coloring the fish first prior to applying and then pressing the paper. Hayashi is a fisherman and diver, and prints only edible fish that will soon be eaten by friends and family. Approximately two dozen of his designs were printed onto shirts by Reyn Spooner for its "Gyotaku by Naoki" collection.

Hayashi was born in Kyoto, Japan, in 1962, and moved to Hilo on the Big Island at the age of six, where he lived with his grandparents. He began making gyotaku prints at the age of 11. He later attended school in New Zealand and England, and received a degree in chemistry at Chapman College in Orange, California. He became a scuba instructor when he returned to Hawaii, teaching in the morning and fishing in the afternoon. His return to Hawaii saw a rekindling of his passion for gyotaku, and one of his products consisted of yearly gyotaku calendars. Reyn Spooner's Tim McCullough received one of these as a Christmas present from one of his workers. "So Tim called me," recalls Hayashi, "and said we should consider working together on a shirt. We had a few meetings, then started our working relationship that went on for five or six years, until Tim sold the company." Asked about some of his more memorable designs that were made into shirts, Naoki says, "In my art, I try to show what nature has shown me. My favorite fish is the ono. It's not the prettiest fish, and not the best recognized, but it's the best eating fish, and it's the logo for my company. My shirts with mahi mahi and ahi were popular on the mainland, because people recognized those fish. And then there was the octopus swimming in its own ink, surrounded by kagami ulua fish, that one was special. I only do gyotaku prints from fish I eat, so there's no kihikihi Moorish idol fish."[82]

About Hayashi, Tim McCullough writes, "Gyotaku artist Naoki Hiyashi was quite prolific with his signature polychromatic fish impressionism on traditional Japanese masa paper. His interpretation of the ancient Japanese custom of recording fish catches was just so progressive, very creative. He transitioned this historic monochromatic art form to contemporary polychromatic with his use of color to replicate the live fish's true colorations. A very complex process in itself, let along the subject matter he worked with. Some of his works involved huge fish weighing considerable poundage and the logistics were complicated. Then he would do smaller subjects with very complex appendages of various color shades. He is a master! And, a lovely artist to have worked with."[83]

After McCullough sold Reyn Spooner, Naoki Hayashi was approached by Dale Hope. "Dale told me he was friends with Tim and respected him, so he would never approach an artist Tim was already working with. Now that Tim had sold the company, Dale asked if I would make designs for Kahala shirts. We agreed, but before we produced the first shirt, Dale sold Kahala. My relationships with Tim and Dale were so special, both of them had such positive energy. All three of us had this in common: we loved nature, we were all watermen, we all loved the healthy surroundings of the water. The positive energy with Tim and Dale was always so wonderful that I really never really considered working with the new people at Reyn or Kahala."[84]

Today, Hayashi is still fishing, diving, and making his gyotaku prints, created in his studio in Kaneohe, Oahu. He sells them through his website and in a number of island galleries as well. His enthusiasm for beauty, island life, and the ocean are catching. His closing words to my conversation with him were "Hey, let's go fishing!"[85]

Avi Kiriaty

Avi Kiriaty's "Avi" Collection for Kahala represented a vibrant element in the company's Hawaiian shirt catalogue from the early 1990s to 2002. He created more than 200 prints for the company. Born in Israel in 1957, he lived a bohemian existence in a number of different places before settling in Hawaii, where he engaged in farming, fishing, and painting. While he lived on Kauai, Hawaii, and Molokai, he eventually made his home and located his studio in Maui. He has worked in many media, including oil painting, linoleum block printing, lava and bronze sculpture, pencil and ink drawing, watercolors, ceramic platters, and serigraphs. For his shirt collection, he created colored and textured works by using the medium of linoleum block prints, in a "reduction" style with overlaid hand printing, done in stages as colors were progressively added. His range of themes is far-reaching, many relating to his own work experiences, with an emphasis on Polynesian culture. The motif on one shirt, for example, features a theme surrounding an inter-island trading schooner, hauling bananas and copra. Another features a café scene on the waterfront of an idyllic village. Multitudes of col-

Detail of shirt design by Avi Kiriaty from the Avi Collection by Kahala (author's collection).

orful fish abound in his prints. Another particularly memorable Avi design consists of a border print shirt with the repeating motif of an indigenous man standing on a beach holding a paddle, adjacent to a longboard, under a tree. Created from a linoleum block, the tree is a vibrant green and brown, the man and board printed in muted earth tones.

Avi is an artist who never seems to stop working, and describes how his relationship with Kahala began and evolved: "The textile designing began when Dale saw some of my artwork around the Islands & approached me to see what we could create. Around 600 designs were used and printed and many more were created that I still have, but they could only use a certain amount since I work long hours every day at my art and am therefore quite prolific. Since some of the designs were requested for certain Kahala marketing areas, including the San Diego Padres baseball team, the San Diego Zoo, the Newport Beach Snowbirds, wineries, Baja California and more, it was interesting to see how different subject matter came out with my style remaining the same."[86]

Avi's contact at Kahala was Dale Hope, who describes their working relationship: "Avi first lived on the Big Island before moving to Maui where he currently lives. I used to fly over to the Big Island with a 30 or 40 pound bag of books with print concepts as references, and we would collaborate at his Puna home, high in rainforest mist, on their outside porch studio. He would hand carve and print linoleum blocks to create what I think was a collection of the most imaginative, Pacific inspired textile art I had seen in my run as a shirt maker."[87]

Floral detail from front of Hawaiian shirt featuring Miles Mason design, from the Miles Collection by Reyn Spooner (**Miles M. Mason**).

Much of the joy derived by Avi Kiriaty's sojourn in the shirt business is in seeing his designs worn by people all around the world. There were a lot to see. Within the first five years of his tenure with Kahala, more than a quarter million shirts were sold. After ten years, he decided to move on to the next project, "to focus more on my fine art." Some of Avi's designs, however, are still being sold by Kahala, while others are available in the preowned market. Today, this prolific and talented artist is marketing his art through various galleries, his website, and by appointment at his current studio on the North Shore of Maui.[88]

Miles M. Mason

Miles M. Mason, whose designs comprised Reyn Spooner's "Miles Collection," is known for his lavishly colored botanical-themed patterns.[89] A visit to his studio today reveals his ongoing interest in varying and inventive color combinations and repeating motifs. Tribal patterns are of great interest to him, and one very large (4 foot × 6 foot) painting reflects in excruciating detail the colors, designs, and minute imperfections in a representational painting of a traditional tapa cloth. Mason is a dreamer and visionary whose personal history reflects a keen interest in the world around him.

After graduating college with a degree in Cultural Anthropology, Mason served in the Peace Corps in the Kingdom of Tonga, taught school in numerous developing nations, and sketched, photographed, and dived all over the Caribbean, Southeast Asia, and the South Pacific. His paintings reflect these youthful dreams of the exotic world: "I spent many childhood hours lost in the romance of the tropics, dreaming of worlds replete with coconut palms, balmy trade winds, and blue lagoons teeming with colorful fish."

He relates his experience in adding shirt design to his artistic portfolio. It started with a chance meeting with Tim McCullough of Reyn Spooner in 1988: "[McCullough] lived in the same town here and came to an art show of mine, and liked what I was doing. He chose the paintings of mine that he liked and thought would look good on his clothing. I don't remember how many paintings were used—maybe about 10. Each design was then printed in perhaps three or four colorways (same design but with different colored backgrounds). I don't know how many of my shirts were sold in total, as I was paid per yards of fabric that was printed using my work. The fabric was made into dresses and other clothing items as well as shirts. It was a privilege to be chosen to be part of this series of items featuring local artists. Though I had no say in what they chose or what they did with it, the association with the company was mutually beneficial. Seeing my signature on the shirt label, my bio on the hang tag, the media ads featuring my designs, the relationship with the owner—it was all good."

Mason noted an additional, though unforeseen benefit of putting his designs on the shirts: "I have seen my shirts on people in many strange places—once in a while in a vintage shirt shop like Bailey's in Honolulu. Once even at the De Anza College (California) monthly flea market.... One time I was riding an elevator in a skyscraper on the mainland and a guy got on wearing one of my shirts. I ended up signing the tail of it for him with a Bic pen while we were going up."[90]

One exceptionally lovely design in the "Miles Collection" was a geometric print shirt with Reyn Spooner's trademark French seams, incorporating six repeating images of anthurium, heliconia flowers, monstera leaves, and areca palm fronds, encased in tapa motif rectilinear borders cornered by tiny palm trees. Although Mason's "Miles Collection" is no longer being sold by Reyn Spooner, his vintage shirts can still be found in stores that sell classic pre-owned Hawaiian wear. But there's another "secret" source, where you might be able to buy one of them, brand new. Miles welcomes visitors to his studio in Kukuihaele, near the Waipio Valley Lookout, on the Big Island. "I still have some of the shirts in their original packaging with tags, unworn—part of my compensation was to receive one of each," he says. "I sell them occasionally to clients who own some of my originals and ask about the shirts." Mason's studio hosts a fascinating array of work, from paintings to prints to hand-painted guitars and ukuleles. His artwork shows up on musical stages as well. At least one well-known rock musician engaged Mason to custom-paint the face of one of her guitars after visiting his studio on a mission to see his shirts. Jane Wiedlin of the Go-Go's' C.F. Martin acoustic guitar now sports a stunning Hawaiian scene with swaying palms, rolling clouds, and surf pounding against volcanic cliffs, painted in siennas and ochres.

Robert Lyn Nelson

Robert Lyn Nelson (b. 1955) is the creator of the "Two Worlds" concept of painting, in which marine life is shown simultaneously above and below the surface of the ocean. Several of his designs were used on shirts created by Reyn Spooner. Nelson, born in Southern California's San Bernardino County, recalls that his passion for art began at the age of three. His father, an artist and architectural draftsman, began teaching his son art techniques at the age of four. He began college at the age of 13, attending art courses at both Mt. San Antonio College (Walnut, California), and Chaffey College (Rancho Cucamonga, California). He came to Hawaii in 1973 with a mission to surf and paint. Hawaii opened up an extraordinarily rich palette of colors and forms for him, and he became particularly enamored of what lay below the surface of the ocean. Seeing a group off whales while surfing off the coast of Lahaina, Maui, inspired him to develop the "Two Worlds' concept. "Two Worlds," his landmark painting of 1979, depicted three whales cavorting below the surface of the sea on the lower two-thirds of the canvas. The upper third consists of the above-surface view of a distant harbor, volcanic peaks, and a cloud-strewn sunset. A whale fluke bisects the biological planes. Nelson refers to the concept as "Two Worlds Environmental Surrealist School of Painting," and indeed it is a school, as a number of other painters have copied it. Nelson, who has exhibited in numerous galleries and museums, works in a number of styles and genres, and his influences include Jongkind, Rembrandt, Picasso, and Hockney. He is a passionate conservationist and co-founded the National Marine Sanctuary Foundation. He has lived in Hawaii for the past 42 years.[91]

John Severson

John Severson (1933–2017) was best known for founding *Surfer* magazine as well as making a number of classic early surf movies. In clothing circles, however, he is known as outstanding artist who, in conjunction with his wife Louise, designed a significant number of Hawaiian shirts sold by Kahala. A successful publisher

Waterman, designer, and publisher John Severson aboard Dale Hope's outrigger canoe off Diamond Head (Dale Hope).

and filmmaker, Severson entered the 1970s by releasing his film *Pacific Vibrations,* sold *Surfer* magazine shortly thereafter, then moved the family to Maui. He was 38 years old. In Maui, he rekindled his passion for painting and photography while Louise began her career in textiles and serigraph design.

In the 1990s, their art was made into prints for Kahala, who developed a "John Severson Collection by Kahala" line utilizing his paintings and block prints and Louise's floral and retro Hawaiiana designs. It was a family affair, with wife Louise and daughter Anna contributing designs to the Kahala line, labeled under John's name. Severson-designed shirts are unique in terms of their use of varied media, ranging from photography to block prints to watercolors, often utilizing mixed media to create a series of abstract designs reflective of surfing culture and tropical landscape and seascape motifs.[92]

Hope's relationship with the Seversons developed after he began the distribution of Kahala's line of shirts with designs created by artist Avi Kiriaty. Hope had kept Louise's phone number for a number of years, hoping one day to translate her tablecloth designs to shirts. He was enthusiastic on the prospect of meeting John again, who he knew from the surfing world. Hope recalls working with the Seversons: "John and Louise had seen a special on TV about six months prior about a Big Island artist, Avi [Kiriaty], who was doing art for us. They were inspired to talk about art too, and said they were getting ready to meet us! John and Louise started doing surf and island-inspired textile designs for us around 1997. John really got into the technical aspects of it, backed off with his golfing, really retrenching himself back with his insanely great art, and started surfing more again. He was in his early 60's at the time, so talented, sharp and smart. He learned fabric repeats and how the computer could assist him with his hand painted original art, and work it in to creative, fresh textile art. He and his wife and daughter Anna all got stoked and started working up creative pieces out of their Maui 'Art Lab.' They were real, uncontrived, and a following for their shirts under Severson's name grew quickly. I'd estimate 200 designs or more were created."[93]

John Severson reflected on the joys of having a family enterprise in an idyllic corner of the world: "Many a long day of design and printing drifted into sunsets, wine, and music as we pursued this new art of Aloha. Kahala always used provocative names, and we were well armed. I served up 'Jungle Jam,' 'Surf Indigo,' 'End of the Road,' 'Fish Jazz,' 'Take Off,' 'Summer Daze,' and so on. Louise offered 'Duke's Ukes,' 'Hapi Shirt,' 'Flying Down to Rio,' 'Papa's Tapa,' 'Reef Madness,' and a hundred more. Anna always hit the jackpot with 'Naughty Nani,' 'Sophisticated Fish,' 'Local Boy Poi,' 'Rubbah Slippah,' etc.

"Pre-computer, we would take photos of the artwork to test the repeat. We'd shoot dupes, drive across the island to get them processed, and back home, cut and tape them to make half-dropped aloha shirt mock-ups. Although primitive and time consuming, it worked. Then we were introduced to the computer where you could automate the half drops, and all the while we were getting smoother with our repeats. There were so many answers in the computer and programs, but I could see that Photoshop was the gem. I was still playing some golf and would take the PS manuals to read between shots.

"Perhaps most challenging element in the textile art is how a design is repeated so the pattern in the shirt is not a series of boxes with white spaces. The repeat is the secret, and the simplest is the half-drop. The top of the design must exactly line up with the bottom. The top right art lines up with the bottom left and the top left with the bottom right, pass the wine. Painting a palm branch top right, and lining it up with a diminishing palm bottom left can be a challenge, pass the wine. In the final print, the design flows with only one palm. You learn to think in half-drop.

"There are many rewarding moments in aloha design, and one of them is [getting] a box of the latest shirts. Another is seeing your design walking toward you, or sitting next to you.... My most successful shirt went in two different directions, before settling into its ultimate groove. 'Vintage Boards,' with direction from Dale, started as a block print; a line-up of early surfboards in brown line. Almost, but not quite. Since I had several prints, I had nothing to lose. I painted in the surfboards, and then painted the background black. That doesn't mean the background has to be black. Enter color ways. A design usually tops out at about 12 to 14 colors, each having its own screen. Change the black screen to blue and leave everything else the same—totally different shirt. Tinker with most of the colors, and the possibilities are endless. Kahala recently rereleased a beach and fishing shirt I designed called 'Hukilau.' By changing a few colors to red and green, they created a Christmas shirt. But I left the background black in 'Vintage Boards,' and it was printed and reprinted in many color possibilities, and they all looked good."[94]

Dietrich Varez

Varez (1939–2018) was born in Berlin. His biological father was Friedrich Donat, an architect and engineer who served under the infamous Nazi industrialist Albert Speer. His father mandated that Dietrich employ exacting standards as a young draftsman, insisting his son's pencil lines were drawn straight. "He was a pretty fussy old bastard. A nasty architect is about as stiff as you can get," Varez would later say. After the war, his father, fleeing allied authorities, left the family. Dietrich's mother soon re-married, to U.S. Army Sgt. Manuel Varez, who adopted both Dietrich and his brother and moved his new family to Oahu. Dietrich eventually earned a master's degree in English at the University of Hawaii. In 1968, Dietrich, his wife, and newly born son moved to the Big Island, and in 1969 bought sight-unseen a nine acre property near Kilauea. The family lived in a tent on their land or in cabins at Hawaii Volcanoes National Park. He applied his woodworking skills, learned during his tenure at Ala Wai Marina boatyard in Waikiki, to craft a sturdy wooden house on his property. Varez supported his family through jobs as a golf course groundskeeper and as a bartender at Volcano House. He began carving images of Pele, the volcano goddess, which he began selling at the bar, and soon was carving woodblocks and making them into prints, which he sold at the Volcano House gift shop for two dollars each.[95] By 1974, he was selling his work at the nonprofit Volcano Art Center, which allowed him to make a career out of art.[96] He published more than 225 wood and linoleum block prints, from which he printed hundreds of thousands of prints, many of which he gave away. He wrote his own books, illustrating them as well as those written by others.

Varez' work encompasses Hawaiian legends and flora, and Hawaiian cultural traditions, including fishing, music and dance, canoe building, and surfing. And he insisted on selling his prints for no more than $20. "I want my work to be affordable and for everyone to have it, so Joe Six-Pack can buy a print if he wants one," he said.[97]

Reyn Spooner's Tim McCullough had been a fan of Varez' art long before he began printing his shirts: "I had been aware of Dietrich's work for decades and had acquired several of his Hawaiiana prints early on. He was a noted Volcano resident-artist and familiar personality at his job behind the bar at the Volcano House Lodge. Was hard not to know who Dietrich was as his hospitality and friendliness at the Lodge was well known. Around the mid 90's I first considered the possibility of reinterpreting his Hawaiian mythological imagery as wearable art on Reyn Spooner shirts. The idea just seemed like a natural fit to me. We met at the Volcano Art Center to discuss the possibility of our collaboration and to determine the depth of Dietrich's interest. He lives pretty much off the grid and rarely travels off the Big Island. Dietrich is a wonderful, friendly personality and, he enjoys his deserved privacy."[98]

How many Dietrich Varez designs were made into Reyn Spooner shirts? McCullough estimates that approximately 80 Reyn shirts carried Varez designs prior to McCullough leaving in 2008. His guess is that perhaps another four to six dozen Varez prints have been made into Reyn shirts since then.

Eddy Y

Tokyo-born Big Island artist Tatsuya "Eddy Y" Yamamoto is renowned for his designs that were developed into "The Art of Eddy Y Collection" Hawaiian shirts by Reyn Spooner, reflecting his interest in Hawaiian themes, vintage cars, guitars, and ukuleles. Eddy came to live in Hawaii at the age of 14 after first visiting Hawaii at the age of 10. "I couldn't believe how beautiful this place was, that kids went to school barefoot, and everyone drove big cars," he remembered. "I never wanted to return to Japan, so when I finished junior high…. I begged my auntie to bring me to Hawaii to learn English." He put himself through the University of Hawaii at Manoa partially by painting posters and signs, then caught a big break in 1976 when he was commissioned to paint a 108-foot-long, 8-foot-high barrier that fronted the Aloha Stadium stage for a Kalapana and Cecilio & Kapono concert (he also designed the cover for Kalapana's second album). Eventually, Eddy moved to Southern California, where he designed T-shirts as a free-lancer for a number of companies, including Disney, Ocean Pacific (OP), and Surfline. In 1979, OP commissioned Eddy to create its Hobie Apparel line. In 1984, he was brought on board as VP of Merchandizing, and Hobie became the nation's second largest surf wear brand, generating more than $60 million in annual sales through the 1980s, primarily in silkscreen T-shirts. Gradually, life in the fast lane lost its appeal. "There was always so much stress, and so little time for relaxation that one day I woke up and asked myself, Why?" he said. He returned to Hawaii to stay in 1992. Since his return, he's become a noted poster designer and painter, specializing in Hawaiian themes, lifestyle images, and portraits. His best-known posters would include the four made for Hilo's Merrie Monarch Festival from 1997 through 2000). His paintings include a 60-foot mural created for Hilo's Lyman Museum & Mission House, housed in its permanent collection. In addition to oil and acrylic, he paints on sand.[99]

Painting on sand is a tedious venture, he noted in a 2001 interview. "You have to wear special gloves and you have to laminate the sand on a board. Then you paint, but after that, it's my trade secret. I experiment a lot with techniques. Took me about five years to get this sand painting thing right."[100]

Tim McCullough remembers his working relationship with Eddy Y. "My introduction to Eddy Yamamoto was also in the mid 90's and had been associated with an image I wanted to develop basing the vintage Sampan buses that had plied Hilo town and plantation destinations on the North Hilo coast in the 1940's to the late 1960's. A Hilo company had recently

Eddy Y design for ENC Kaanapani Classic, 2000 (Eddy Yamamoto).

restored three or four vehicles and had returned them to limited service within Hilo town and out to some Hilo neighborhoods. After working on this project with Eddy I reviewed his portfolio and was so impressed with his work I sought his collaboration with Reyn Spooner and he was excited for the opportunity. [Prior to 2008] I believe we developed somewhere in the region of 60 Reyn Spooner Eddy Y shirt images. He was also prolific in developing many of our Reyn Spooner images in support of our Disney, automotive, MLB, NFL, NBA collections under license with these respective entities."[101]

One of the licensees was General Motors, allowing Eddy to begin making shirts featuring vintage Chevys (one classic shirt shows them cruising below the "Hollywood" sign). "My thing is lifestyle art," Eddy says. Eddy's shirts speak to the cultures of Hawaii and Southern California. They include images of surf villages, tropical seascapes, electric guitars, hot rods, woodies, and vintage cars of several makes. Eddy Y stopped designing for Reyn Spooner in 2015 but retained the copyright to his designs. Currently, his shirts are sold by Island Heritage.

Eddy is a human dynamo who designs seemingly dozens of different lifestyle products. "I probably should retire," he says, "but I can't stop designing." When he's not designing, he's perched somewhere on his 20-acre ranch in Laupahoehoe, on the Hamakua Coast of the Big Island, painting, with an eye on the Pacific Ocean below.[102]

Aloha Shirt Historian/Creator/Executive/Waterman: Meet Dale Hope

The name Dale Hope figures prominently in the reminiscences of every artist who created designs used in shirts that Hope manufactured. He was born in Honolulu in 1953. The son of textile salesman and entrepreneur Howard R. Hope, Dale Hope is a multi-faceted and enthusiastic executive, historian, and writer, author of two of the most comprehensive books on Hawaiian shirts published to date. As his own story shows, through company changes and evolutions, he just can't leave the business: "The year I was born, [my dad] bought a small factory and started a brand called Sun Fashions of Hawaii. In the third grade, I remember ordering shirts from him … he would bring home new shirts when mine got small, and I wore them to school every day. In those days, we all wore Hawaiian shirts to school. As a teenager, I would buy them at the local Goodwill or Salvation Army stores and at our school's thrift shop where my mom volunteered a few days a week.[103]

"I grew up in my parents business, Sun Fashions, and they had two different garment factory locations through my childhood. I worked there in the summers and broke a lot of fabric cases full of printed fabrics from Japan, carrying fabric bolts on my shoulders up the long flight of stairs to our 2nd floor cutting room. Every summer, the view of Diamond Head from the landing was obscured from the growth and rising new concrete buildings. I went away for college for a year, worked a bit on my return, and was on my way back to college when my Dad asked me to come work with him, as he really needed help with sales in the garment company.

"So I began with selling, but the bulk of his line was with Ladies and Missy fashions, which were hard for me to get excited about. I asked if I could give making and selling men's shirts a try. We started slowly and over the years built up a great base with the local retailers, and we grew every year from there. Since I'd left college early, I lacked a formal education, so business was a bit daunting…. I was—and still am—more concerned about making the best shirt, and not how to save five cents on every unit. So we began selling men's shirts under the HRH label, then we did a younger, more active line with T shirts and shorts, called Hawaiian Style.[104] Then we launched a line called Kahala Bay Club, which led to acquiring the name Kahala 1987. Kahala was the first company to make factory made Aloha shirts, back in 1936. The name had been dormant for a long time when we got it, so we changed the name of our HRH label to Kahala. We soon started making our own textile art with our concepts and designs.

"In 1991, we sold Kahala to Local Motion, and I was retained to stay on as the Art Director, which lasted nearly 10 years. I had a great time, working and developing lines with many fabulous fine artists that created fantastic innovative textile designs for us. Around 2001, Patagonia asked if I could come and help with their Pataloha line. We recreated that label and redeveloped the line that had originated with a real special wahine and true ambassador of

Aloha, Rell Sunn.[105] I spent several years working for what had to be one of the best companies on the planet. Several years later, Kahala, which was now under new ownership, asked me to return, so I went back and helped reinvigorate our brand back into the market place, starting with a new look and new retail store in the Ala Moana shopping center.

"In the early 1990s, my friend Tommy Holmes, author of the most definitive book on the Hawaiian Canoe, told me he was writing a book on the Aloha shirt industry, and asked if I would help him with a list of people he could interview, as well as topics that should be covered in the chapters. Holmes was more than a friend: he was a scholar, big wave canoe rider, an original member of the Hokulea Polynesian Voyaging Society, and a big wave body surfer. I gave him a list of people and ideas, and he said, 'You know more about this than I ever will, so let's do this together, at it will be by Hope and Holmes.' Regrettably, Tommy passed away from a heart attack in 1993 while paddling with his canoe crew off Waikiki. That left me with a book project to embark on, which we completed in 2000, naming it *The Aloha Shirt: Spirit of The Islands*, and dedicated to him. It was later printed in Japan, England, and Germany, and updated and printed in Japan again. I believe it's sold more than 40,000 copies so far. This year, Patagonia has revised it and republished it in a much larger edition."[106]

"Today, I'm working on a new vintage shirt line of shirts, a new book on the Tahitian pareo shirt, and a documentary film on the Aloha Shirt story and how it all began. But you know, some things never change. In the early days, when driving to work or on my way home, when I would see a guy wearing one of our shirts, that gave me a great feeling, especially if he was a respected man, an accomplished ocean man, or respectable businessman, a guy had chosen one of our shirts amongst all the choices that were available. To this day, I'm still checking every sleeve in traffic to see what guys are wearing, guess that just doesn't go away."[107]

To paraphrase Dale Hope, it's the Hawaiian shirts, in truth, that just don't seem to go away. Their influence on men's fashion on the mainland is undeniable and long lasting. The brief biographies of designers and manufacturers of Hawaiian shirts show a geographical cross-pollination that trends from Hawaii to the mainland, then back again, as a significant number of those individuals chose Hawaii for their permanent residences. Many of them who originated in the mainland, however, didn't come to Hawaii with the idea of creating Hawaiian shirts. They came for the surf.

NINE

If It Swells, Ride It
A Surfin' Tsunami Surges to the California Coast

In terms of the sheer numbers of mainlanders who have taken to the waves on boards, Hawaii can be said to have influenced American sport as much as any offshore or contiguous territory or country. Surfing's financial influence is cast far wider than simply board sales and includes a multitude of books, magazines, web sites, films, clothing, and music. And surfing music, depending on its sub-genre, may be considered either its heart or its Achilles heel.

I grew up in a town 20 or so miles north of Santa Cruz and Steamer Lane, Northern California's legendary surfing spot. While a number of my extended family members surfed, I didn't, preferring instead to lie naked on the sands of Panther Beach, about seven miles north of Santa Cruz. Over a three-year period during my early 20s, I was at Panther approximately 200 days a year. So I get the surf 'n' sand angle. I just never got surfing. It was because of the Beach Boys. I was mostly into jazz, avant-garde, and ethnic music (as we called it in those days), and the Wilson clan from Southern California was producing probably the most insipidly dreadful pop music I'd ever heard. The strains of the falsetto-charged ballad "Surfer Girl" just curdled my buttermilk, and I wouldn't have any part of a sport or lifestyle that thrived on musical schmaltz. Nudies like me didn't need theme music anyway to go naked and play in the surf. What I wasn't aware of was the hard-charging rock music today known as instrumental surf, with its machine-gun, oud-like repeated motifs, wet-reverb, and whammy-bar vibrato. I had, of course, heard "Pipeline" by the Chantays but never made the surf connection. With its minor key theme, it sounded Middle Eastern enough to me that it evoked an oil pipeline winding its way up, over, and around bleak burning, blistering hot deserts, functionally devoid of water. The tune, of course, is all about water. Let's just say, as I once told John Severson, I missed the wave...

Although wave surfing, which most scholars consider to have originated in Hawaii, is indelibly linked to Southern California, it actually debuted first on the mainland in Santa Cruz, some 300 miles north. In 1885, three Hawaiian princes, attending school in San Mateo, California, fashioned surfboards out of California redwood and paddled into the breakers in Santa Cruz at the mouth of the San Lorenzo River. It is said to be the first time anyone surfed on the mainland.[1]

Wave-riding had been popular in Polynesia for centuries before Westerners became aware of it, but it seems to have appeared first in Hawaii as a communal event with religious and royal connotations. Surfing scholarship continues to be a work in progress, but author

Matt Warshaw cites AD 1200 as the approximate year that Hawaiian adults began standing on their boards, riding the surf into the shore, and making a communal, ceremonial, and recreational activity out of it. There were competitions, betting, and feasts. During the *Makahiki* celebration, of which surfing was an elemental part, warfare and work were banned in honor of the festivities dedicated to the god Lono.[2]

The first Westerners to document its presence were those on Captain James Cook's voyages to the Pacific. Wave-riding was mentioned in a journal entry published in 1777 under Cook's name as *A Voyage to the Pacific Ocean*. Historians have now concluded that ship's botanist Joseph Banks (1743–1820), writing during the years of Cook's first voyage (1768–1771), made the first journal entry pertaining to wave-riding, based on his observations in Matavai Bay, on the north coast of Tahiti. He noted the joy of the "Indians" riding the surf "just as our holiday youth climb the hill in Greenwich park for the pleasure of riding down it."

It comes as little surprise that wave-riding was reviled by the first Calvinist missionaries to arrive in the islands in 1820. Half-clothed native men and women who enjoyed themselves doing virtually anything fun in public view, from hula dancing to wave-riding, earned the moralistic ire of the sanctimonious newcomers, who referred to them as "savages." The Rev. Hiram Bingham arrived on the first missionary ship and wrote of the sexually mixed welcoming party that came out to meet them, swimming or in canoes or on boards. "The appearance of destitution, degradation, and barbarism ... was appalling. Some of our number, with gushing tears, turned away from the spectacle."

Many Westerners who came later felt differently. The first illustration of surfing to reach Western eyes was published in 1831, and others followed, showing joyous Sandwich Islanders of both sexes, half-clad or naked, reveling in the breaking waves that powered their boards toward the shore. Mark Twain was one Western observer who was fascinated by the spectacle, which he'd briefly tried, with limited results, in 1866.

Traditionally, three types of papa hee nalu (surfboards) were used by pre-contact Hawaiians. The grandest of these was the olo, a monstrous board carved from the wiliwili tree (Erythrina sandwicensis), reserved for use by the alii ruling class. It was 20 feet long, two feet wide, and had a rounded top and bottom to create a thickness that might reach eight inches. The board weighed as much as 200 pounds. American surfing champion Tom Blake joined Duke Kahanamoku in making a replica, based on older examples in Honolulu's Bishop Museum. Duke's board was 16 feet long and weighed 130 pounds, a longboard judged exceptional for riding large waves. The second type of traditional board, the alia, was much smaller, six to seven feet long, weighing about 45 pounds, with a round nose, tapered and squared-off tail, and usually less than two inches thick. Unlike the olo, it was easily paddled into the waves and was highly maneuverable, perfect for stand-up riding in lighter surf. The paipo, at three feet long and 16 inches wide, was the smallest of the three, generally used by children, who rode it in a prone position. The adult version of this round-nosed board could be as long as six feet, and riders often rode it kneeling or standing up. None of these boards had stabilizing fins, a later invention that revolutionized the maneuverability of surfboards.[3]

Entering into the 20th century, the wave-riding phenomenon in Hawaii was presented in nickelodeons throughout the U.S. for the first time in public, via "Surf Board Riders" and "Surf Scenes," two of the 30 sequences in the Edison Company's 1906 compilation film, *Hawaiian Islands*. It was filmed by Robert Kates Bonine (1862–1923), sent to Hawaii by Edison for three months to create footage of the islands. Although these segments total fewer than three minutes, they are historically significant, showing standing wave-riders, wipeouts, and paddling techniques.[4]

In 1907, Jack London (b. John Griffith Chaney, 1876–1916) arrived in Honolulu on his 55-foot ketch, the *Snark*, after a harrowing three-week voyage, complicated by the inadequacies in design and construction of the custom-built boat and the errant calculations of his wife's uncle, who served as captain and navigator.[5] From the beachfront of the Moana Hotel, he eagerly watched the surfers at Waikiki, and soon was soon wave-riding himself, tutored by watermen Alexander Hume Ford (1868–1945) and George Douglas Freeth, Jr. (1883–1919). London learned first on the small *paipo* board, then gravitated to the larger *alia* board. Fresh from the stunning successes of his books *The Call of the Wild* (1903) and *The Sea-Wolf* (1904), he penned a 4,000-word essay on surfing at Waikiki, which was first published in the October 1907 issue of *Women's Home Companion* magazine, and later in his biographical travelogue of 1911, *The Cruise of the Snark*. When published, the article was the most detailed description of the art and sport of surfing ever written.[6]

Alexander Ford, a wealthy orphaned son of South Carolina plantation owners, was already an experienced world traveler when he arrived in Hawaii at the age of 39, six months before Jack London. He reportedly learned surfing by spending four hours every day in the water for three straight months. In 1908, Ford founded the men-only Outrigger Canoe and Surfboard Club, the first such organization dedicated to promoting surfing as a sport. He built a clubhouse and dance pavilion on Waikiki beach between the Moana and Seaside hotels in 1910, and the club grew to a membership of 1,500 by the time women were admitted in 1926. Although there were no racial restrictions to joining the club, it was perceived as a whites-only organization by locals, who founded their own Hui Nalu club in 1911, located a hundred yards away. Hui Nalu was smaller, with a talent-based membership, which soon resulted in friendly rivalry between the neighboring clubs. Duke Paoa Kahinu Mokoe Hulikohola Kahanamoku (1890–1968), Olympics star, legendary waterman, character actor, and sheriff of Honolulu, was a founding member of Hui Nalu and also joined the Outrigger Canoe Club in 1915.[7]

Of Jack London's two surfing teachers, Ford, a journalist by trade, continued to enjoy the success of the club, and went on to found the *Mid-Pacific* magazine, which was published from 1911 to 1936.[8] George Freeth, two months after giving the novelist his initial lesson, left Honolulu for the mainland at the behest of railway and property magnate Henry Edwards Huntington (1850–1927).[9] Huntington, who had seen Freeth surfing in Hawaii, wished to promote his seaside holdings in Redondo Beach, California, and hired him to demonstrate the art of surfing twice each weekend day at the Redondo Hotel beachfront, advertising him as "The Man Who Could Walk on Water."[10]

According to surfing historian Matt Warshaw, Freeth was already surfing at Venice Beach when his employment with Huntington began in 1907 or 1908. He commuted between the two beach communities by electric rail, making his living as a lifeguard, swimming instructor, and showman. He also gave free surfing lessons to admiring youth. For the remainder of his short life, he continued to give surfing demonstrations in beach towns along the Los Angeles-San Diego corridor. He left almost no written record of his life and only three photographs of him are known to exist, but he is nonetheless credited—despite the 1885 visit of the Hawaiian princes to Santa Cruz—with introducing surfing to the mainland.[11]

While Freeth was popularizing surfing up and down the Southern California coast, Waikiki Beach on Oahu was becoming an ever more enchanting spot for Hawaiian beachboys to show their surfing technique while making tips from various activities, including teaching surfing and chatting up and having affairs with Western female admirers. The surf at Waikiki was ideal for close-to-shore learners and the intermediates, who surfed a little farther out, and, at 300 yards and beyond, for those proficient enough to handle larger boards and more challenging surf. Currents were mild and the waters shark-free. The beach—mostly man-made—had its sand imported from Manhattan Beach, California, a town originally built on a system of sand dunes that rose up to 60 feet high.[12] At the Royal Hawaiian and Moana hotels, beachboys were invited to intermingle with the guests, although not allowed in the lobbies. Mostly in their 20s and 30s, they were available for hire, particularly as tour guides and surfing instructors. As opposed to the rigidly nonsexual milieu of mainland beaches, visiting Western women on Waikiki could take surfing lessons from men who would—of necessity—have to touch, hold, and coddle them as part of the learning process. Horseplay and fondling in the seas was all part of the fun, and was later often brought to full fruition in hotel room beds. Bedding women for tips was yet another occupation for the beachboys, who, of course, boasted of their conquests and vied for the companionship of each freshly arriving female steamship passenger.[13] Beachboys frequently set up ad hoc musical and comedy entertainment, yet another way to meet tipping customers. They were known as natty casual dressers, sporting silk shirts and nicely pressed khaki slacks. Tips of $100 were not uncommon, and true to the exuberance of youth, were more than occasionally blown in bar bashes, with endless rounds of drinks bought for friends and customers alike. The beachboy scene was a major element of the Waikiki experience for the ensuing decades leading up to the war, and it is said that William "Chick" Daniels (1899–1982), famous for his "pants-dropping dance," was, even during the Depression years, making $1000 or more each week, roughly $15,000 in today's money.[14]

By the end of the 1920s, Southern California beach towns were becoming more populated and increasingly accessible for surfers due to the ongoing advancement of the automobile, which would carry friends, surfboards, and an instant party right down to the water. Surfers could find relatively empty beaches a short distance from LA. Always looking for the endless sunset, a number of California surfers began exporting themselves to Hawaii, back to where it all began.

Growing up on the shores of Lake Superior, Wisconsin-born Thomas Edward "Tom" Blake (1902–1994) took to the water at an early age. He eventually migrated to California, won several distance swimming events, learned to surf, and, in 1924 made his first trip to Hawaii. He returned in 1926 and within a few short years created two revolutions in board design. By drilling holes in a paddleboard and then covering them with laminate, he crafted a board that was lighter and had superior floating capability. He became an expert surfer, organizing and winning the first Pacific Coast Surfriding Championship in 1928, riding one of his new, lightweight boards. By this time, he was shuttling back and forth between Hawaii and the mainland, which he would do almost continually for the next three decades. In 1932, he, along with two friends, made the first successful attempt to paddle the 26 miles between the mainland and Catalina Island. The same year, he patented his hollow board, which he called a "water sled," made prototypes, and licensed several woodworking firms to manufacture them. In 1935 by inserting a stabilizing fin under the board, he created a mechanism that allowed surfer to steer the board by shifting weight and foot positions. It was also the year that Blake published the first comprehensive book on surfing, *Hawaiian Surfboard*. It was 95 pages long, had 46 illustrations, and contained an introduction by Duke Kahanamoku. Yet another major technical innovation attributed to Blake was his creation of a waterproof wooden housing for his Graflex camera that allowed him to take action-packed surfing photos when mounted on his board. Others before had taken photos of surfers, but due to his treatment of it as a specialized photo genre, he is considered to be the first surfing photographer. This banner year for Blake included his successful introduction of a sail and foot rudder attached to a surfboard, and thus, he may be credited with the creation of a craft that led to the sport of windsurfing.[15]

Blake was an ascetic, a vegetarian who lived in shacks while in Hawaii, and in cars and vans for most of his time on the mainland. He wrote books on philosophy and lived the prototype of what would eventually be called the "surfing lifestyle." He seemed never interested in forming a romantic relationship. Feeling that Hawaii had finally become too crowded for him, he left the islands for good, living a peripatetic lifestyle on the mainland that included stops in California's Salton Sea, Boca Raton, Florida, and finally back to Wisconsin. His friend and biographer Gary Lynch reported that he owned one plate, one knife, one fork, one dish, and one chair. His final years were spent in his boyhood town of Washburn, Wisconsin, living in an apartment on Lake Superior. His grave marker notes only his wartime Coast Guard service, and nothing of his other achievements.[16]

Prior to the 1930s, surfboards were primarily handcrafted by their users, bought from individual shapers, or acquired from small shops specializing in board making. Modern industrial manufacturing techniques hit the surfboard business in 1932 with Blake's hollow board, and also with a laminated, mixed wood design built around a balsa wood core developed by Pacific System Homes of Vernon, a small town near Los Angeles. The idea was actualized by Meyers Butte, a son of one of the co-founders, who named the subsidiary the Swastika Surf-Board Company, based on the ancient sign for good luck (Butte wasn't a Nazi supporter and soon changed the name to Waikiki Surf-Boards). The boards were as strong as single-piece wooden boards, and light: their 10-foot board weighed in at 45 pounds. They were sold at department stores, sporting goods stores and beach clubs, and were exported to Hawaii as well. They weren't cheap at a price point around $35 (around $620 in today's money). Concurrently, membership-based surf clubs were springing up all up and down the California coast, perpetuating a surf culture and providing a ready customer base for board manufacturers. They sponsored surfing competitions, offered endless opportunities to talk shop, and served as a meeting ground for like-minded teens and young adults of both sexes.[17]

In Hawaii, board shaping experiments by individuals continued unabated, as surfers planed, cut, laminated, drilled, and trimmed their now-customized boards, seeking a more powerful and refined way to control the breakers.

John Melville Kelly Jr. (1919–2007) came to Hawaii in 1926 with his artist parents John and Katherine. His first surfboard was acquired when he was seven years old, shaped by Duke Kahanamoku's brother David. In 1937, recognizing that his friend Fran Heath's expensive Swastika board lacked maneuverability, Kelly and friend Wally Froiseth chopped the rear of the board with an axe, with Heath's approval. The narrow, streamlined rear end allowed for better control on large waves and this new "hot curl" board became the model for the next iteration in surfboard design. It wasn't the last innovative board design for Kelly. He patented his hydroplane surfboard, with a raised tail, in 1963. Although never achieving commercial success, it served as an example of Kelly's imaginative desire to continue to improve board technology. Kelly was a polymath and larger than life character. He received a bachelor's degree at Julliard in 1950, conducted symphonies and directed the music school at Palama Settlement. His book *Surf and Sea*, a 300-page treatise on surfing was published in 1965. He was a skilled free-style diver and swimmer. He is perhaps best remembered on Oahu for Save Our Surf (SOS), an organization he co-founded in 1961. Through activism, promotion (he designed and printed the organization's posters and leaflets), and media-savvy advocacy, SOS is credited with saving some 140 surfing sites, reefs, and ocean resources from development. A digital collection of ephemera related to Kelly's work with the SOS organization is housed in the Hamilton Library at the University of Hawaii at Manoa.[18] Kelly was injured in approximately 1987 when he was struck on the head by his own surfboard, leading to a decline that led to Alzheimer's disease. An innovator and iconoclast, he was yet another example of the initial wave of Hawaiian influence on mainland surfing that ended up echoing back to Hawaii.[19]

Surfers were as active as any demographic in serving for the military in the war, with an understandable preference for Navy or Coast Guard duty. John Kelly and Fran Heath managed to serve together aboard ship, and their captain allowed them to carry their boards with them, going so far as to let them surf at Christmas Island and Midway during shore leave.

With the end of the war, Southern California boomed in jobs, population, and money. It was home to much of the nation's defense, aerospace, and aircraft industry, with household names including Douglas, Lockheed, Northrup, and Hughes jockeying to grab as many qualified workers as they could. Much of the local economy was driven by the burgeoning commercial airline business, whose continually lowered fares resulted in exponentially more travelers, requiring aircraft deliveries almost as fast as the manufacturers could build them. Orchards were plowed under in droves, and by the time the early 1950s had arrived, Los Angeles County had the largest population in the country. San Diego and Orange counties soon followed in the top five.[20] New roads sprung up everywhere, providing this automobile-driven culture easy access to beaches that were logistically challenging to visit in the pre-war years.

Surfing on Southern California's shores quickly grew to the extent that prime surfing sites, including Malibu, were inundated, forcing many of the earlier surfers to go as far afield as they could to find relatively secluded ocean spots. From the desire to "own" one's surfing spot grew the term "localism," a word that reflected a growing resentment among local surfers that visitors with boards were unwelcome in "their" surf. At its extreme, victims of localism were—and are—subject to hurled rocks, flat tires, broken car windows, and other forms of intimidation. Visiting surfers are finally fighting back through legal action. A class action lawsuit was filed in 2016 against a localist group known as the "Lunada Bay Boys" in Palos Verdes, California.[21] Localism is hardly limited to the California surfing scene. Seaside Point in Oregon, where standard forms of harassment have traditionally included insults scribbled on car windows with difficult-to-remove surf wax and dog excrement applied to door handles, was the home of a fabled incident when a group of well-known surfers arrived from southern California in the early 2000s. Returning to the car, they found a severed deer head mounted atop the roof.[22] One Portland lawyer is actively advertising legal services for those intimidated or attacked on Oregon beaches ranging from Agate Beach to Seaside. Ironically, in a state famous for the bumper sticker "Don't Californicate Oregon," much of the harassment has been directed at out of town fellow Oregonians.[23]

The post-war surf years heralded the era in which teen culture began driving a significant part of the California economy, and beaches became de rigueur gathering spots for parties. "Booze, boards, and broads" was a big part of the draw, and board shapers and manufacturers soon found a ready audience with enough discretionary income to buy their products. A new wave of board design was driven by the action on the Southern California coast. Robert Wilson "Bob" Simmons (1919–1954), with a background in engineering, was one of the first. He'd begun apprenticing informally in 1945 with Gardner "Gard" Chapin (1918?–1957), an expert surfer and boardmaker.[24] Beginning in 1946, Simmons began studying the technical aspects of everything from hull design to wave science. He left Chapin in 1947 and began building boards that used newer materials including fiberglass and resin. The designs were optimized for ultra-fast speed, although sacrificing much in maneuverability. Joe Quigg (b. 1925) and Matt Kivlin (1929–2014) were two other pioneer board designers. After a partnership with Bob Simmons fell apart, they began designing boards themselves, lighter and easier to control and turn. A new board made by Quigg in 1947 was short and light enough that female surfers of lesser physical stature could easily load their boards into the back seats of their convertibles (Darrilyn Zanuck, daughter of producer Darry Zanuck, had been the first recipient). Kivlin's boards, while not as finely crafted as Quigg's were churned out faster. Quigg and Kivlin's "Malibu chip" boards soon became the board of choice among the young men and women riding at Malibu. Surfer Dave Rochlen (b. 1924), who went on to fame as the producer of the Jams line of board shorts, created a series of bright, colorful graphic designs for the boards. The revolutionary boards made by Quigg and Kivlin were light, maneuverable, and allowed novices to experience the thrill of riding waves in a shorter timeframe than the heavier Simmons creations.[25]

Surfing Films

The early 1950s also saw the debut of surfing films made for surfers, filmmakers including Bud Browne and John Severson, predating the Hollywood treatments of surfing themes that would follow later. Browne (1912–2008) is credited with making the first surfing film shown in public, the 45-minute *Hawaiian Surfing Movie* compilation of 1953. Browne was a University of Southern California grad who captained the school's swim team in 1933. He traveled to Hawaii in 1938 on the SS *Matsonia*, meeting up there with Duke Kahanamoku, joining the Waikiki Surf Club, and surfing and shooting surfing footage. Employed by the Navy in the Second World War, he toured Polynesia. After the war, the taught Physical Education and English in Los Angeles schools and continued shooting films, first on 8mm, and later on 16mm. He learned editing at the USC film school. Showing and promoting *Hawaiian Surfing Movie* was essentially a one man effort, with Browne printing up the handbills, nailing them to telephone poles, collecting the 65-cent admission at the door, running the projector, and narrating the film. He created more than a dozen surfing films, making his final movie in 1977. He later contributed camera work for MacGillivray Freeman Films, and worked as a consultant on the feature surfing film *Big Wednesday* (1978, dir. John Milius).[26]

Greg "Da Bull" Noll (b. 1937), who received his nickname from fellow surfer Phil Edwards for the manner in which Noll charged down the face of the wave, began surfing from his Manhattan Beach home when he was seven years old. He made his fame as a big wave rider and board shaper and lent his name to a line of clothing. Noll made surf movies from 1956 to 1961, all called *Search for Surf,* featuring a number of legendary surfers." He developed his own waterproof camera rig and was an exceptional cinematographer. Many of his shots, reproduced on non-fade color film, are breathtaking. Known for his abrupt, but generally good-natured personality, he wasn't exactly an expert in terms of camera mechanics. As related by writer and historian Matt Warshaw, filmmaker Bruce Brown once asked Noll about his f-stop setting and Noll looked puzzled. Brown "then gestured to the numbered ring on Noll's lens and said it adjusted the incoming light. Noll shrugged and said the guy at the store had done all that stuff when he'd bought the camera a few months earlier." Noll and Bruce Brown compiled some of Noll's best shots in an 80-minute film, *Greg Noll Search for Surf.*[27]

Born in Pasadena and raised in San Clemente, John Severson (1933–2017) majored in art and could be found painting scenes at the San Clemente pier in his early twenties. He was drafted into the U.S. Army and was stationed in Hawaii. "I was blown away when I first landed in Hawaii," he says. "It was like seeing in color for the first time."[28] In his off time, he filmed a number of surf sequences that were used in his first film, *Surf* (1958). After leaving the military, he followed with his second film *Surf Safari* (1959). John married his wife Louise during the filming of his third film, *Surf Fever* (1960). The marriage didn't exactly start out on traditional footing. Severson noted, "I really gave her the supreme test when we got to Oahu in 1959. We're heading to Honolulu to get married and the surf was 25 feet at Waimea Bay. 'Honey,' I said, 'This will make the film—maybe our lives.' It was bigger than anything I'd seen or filmed. I capped it with 'We can get married tomorrow but chances are, we won't have the surf tomorrow.' She understood!"[29]

To fund *Surf Fever* film, Severson created a special photo magazine called *The Surfer*, using California and Hawaii stills and 16mm screen shots from his earlier films. Intended as an annual, it quickly evolved into a quarterly version before ending up as a bi-monthly, which was then simply called *Surfer*. Severson also created a typeface that was used in everything from surfing posters to the magazine itself. "I had been looking at album covers, especially Saul Bass and how he distorted fonts, and captured jazz and addiction, beyond typefaces and into art. My typeface evolved, capturing the 'stoke' of surfing, and I called the font 'Surf Fever.'"[30]

Severson bought his first motion picture camera, a Keystone 16mm model, in 1951 at the age of 18, and grew increasingly more proficient as a cinematographer. From 1958 to 1964, he produced one movie a year. None of Severson's early films has apparently survived intact, being lost, destroyed, or cannibalized for footage. His final film, the 90-minute *Pacific Vibrations* (1970) was both an ode to surfing and a hard-edged plea to reconsider the damage to the ocean and the oceanfront environment by everything from oil drilling to garbage. The soundtrack included raga, rock, blues, and folk, and the graphics included a number of optical variations on his color footage. The neo-psychedelic environmental/surf film cost $200,000 to make and lost money at the box office. *Pacific Vibrations* can't be shown commercially due to rights issues pertaining to the music used in the film, but is available online, although the images are not broadcast quality.[31] The film poster was made by old friend and noted underground commix and poster artist Richard Alden "Rick" Griffin (1944–1991). Severson had first become aware of Griffin's art through the graphics the artist was creating for Greg Noll Surfboards at the age of 13. Severson hired him to do freelance artwork for *Surfer* magazine, which included the legendary surf cartoon character "Murphy," for which Griffin retained the copyright.[32] Severson sold *Surfer* magazine shortly after the release of *Pacific Vibrations*, moved to Maui, and, along with wife Louise and their daughters, concentrated on illustration, design, and textiles, including graphics made into aloha shirts made by Kahala, as mentioned in the previous chapter. He took up wind surfing, edited *Wind Surf* magazine, and was still surfing into his 80s. He passed away after a battle with leukemia. His wife Louise noted: "John died here in Napili, in the house he loved, at the surf spot he loved. It was a beautiful sunny morning and four of his girls were around him."[33]

The films of Bud Browne, Greg Knoll, and John Severson typically weren't shown in movie theaters. They were generally one-off shows, screened in school auditoriums, Elks lodges, and any place with affordable rent. In 1959, however, a surfing film did make it to the big screen. The hit film was big enough that it fostered sequels, lookalike films, made stars out of relative unknowns, and is given credit for introducing surfing culture to national and international viewers. Gidget had come to Hollywood. And in a fact that still surprises many, Gidget was a real live person with a real live nickname. Fifteen-year-old Kathy Kohner (b. 1941) was just another teen girl at Malibu in 1956, going gaga over surfers and trading a ride or two on a board in return for homemade peanut butter sandwiches she'd made expressly for the purpose of borrowing a board. Surfer Terry "Tubesteak" Tracy (1935–2012) coined the moniker, a portmanteau of "girl" and "midget," for this girl who stood about 5 feet tall and weighed less than 100 pounds. Kathy told her father, screenwriter Frederick Kohner (1905–1986) that she wanted to write a book about her experiences. He was so excited about her idea that he decided to write it for her, completing the manuscript in six weeks. He was fascinated with the culture and the jargon, which he picked up by listening in on a few of Kathy's phone calls. In 1957, the novel *Gidget: The Little Girl with Big Ideas* was published. The film *Gidget* (1959, dir. Paul Wendkos), based on the book, was an instant hit, starring James Darren, Cliff Robertson (himself a surfer) and Sandra Dee. Noted surfers Mickey Dora and Mickey Munoz (b. 1937) were among the stunt men. It spawned two sequel films and, a later television series (1965) starring Sally Field, and numerous other screen treatments, starring teen heartthrobs that included, most famously, Annette Funicello and Frankie Avalon. The *Gidget* franchise visually introduced the California surf culture—in bowdlerized fashion, to be sure—to millions of Americans from the late 1950s through the 1960s, embodying a sport, a pastime, and a culture, derived from Hawaii.[34] Veteran surfers weren't much impressed with Hollywood films depicting their culture. Bruce Brown's *The Endless Summer* (1964), documenting two California surfers traveling the world in search of the perfect wave, was more their speed.

Born (1937) in San Francisco, Brown grew up in Southern California and began surfing at the age of 11, summarizing his high school years by noting, "I majored in not going to school." He enlisted in the Navy after high school, was stationed in Hawaii, and began making 8mm surfing films there. Brown was sponsored for his first film by board maker Dale Velzy (1927–2005), who bought Brown a Bolex 16mm film camera and editing equipment. He also contributed $5000 in expense money, enough to get Brown and five surfers to Hawaii and back and pay Brown's living expenses for a year. Brown read a book on filmmaking on the flight to Hawaii, and after returning to California, edited directly from his color master rather than paying for a separate work print. *Slippery When Wet* (1958) was the result, shown with a reel-to-reel sound track featuring jazz tenorman Bud Shank and narrated by Brown. Four more surfing short films, *Surf Crazy* (1959), *Barefoot Adventure* (1960), *Surfing Hollow*

Days (1961), and *Water-Logged* (1962), followed. *Hollow Days* is especially notable for its scenes showing Phil Edwards' unprecedented rides at the Banzai Pipeline off Ehukai Beach Park in Pupukea on Oahu's North Shore. Brown used the standard method for making early days surf films: "[I] proceeded according to the guerrilla template of the times—shoot all winter, edit in the spring, run your ass off all summer showing the damn thing (including doing your own live narration) in school auditoriums and small halls, then pack up for another winter on the road and do it all over again."[35]

Brown's next film, *The Endless Summer* was much more ambitious, and costly. The premise of the film was that winter in the Northern hemisphere equaled summer south of the equator, and by following the sun, surfers, Robert August (b. 1945) and Mike Hynson (b. 1942), reveled in the fact that for dedicated surfers, summer never had to end.[36] The film was introduced in 1964 and was showing in major theaters all over the U.S. by 1966. It had taken four months to shoot in places that included New Zealand, Tahiti, Indonesia, Ghana, and South Africa, where they found the "perfect wave" at Cape St. Francis. Brown bankrolled it for $50,000 by completely draining his savings account. The three traveled lightly, one board each for August and Hynson, and less than 100 pounds of film gear for Brown. There was no crew. It wasn't all fun. Four months together on a world tour can drive any three people nuts, and then there were the authorities. In India, their boards and camera gear were impounded until they left.[37]

The film's iconographic poster, created by surfer and art student John Van Hamersveld (b. 1941) for $150, remains the quintessential image of the surfing culture, more than 50 years after its creation. Brown, August, and Hynson are silhouetted against red sands, a purple sky, and an enormous yellow setting sun, inspiring variations that are endlessly replicated on everything from woodie wagons to aloha shirts. Van Hamersveld recalled how he got the job: "It was a 'Hey-could-you-do-this?' thing.... I had designed [Brown's] business card and he liked it."[38] In a sense, the poster was more popular than the film. A wild guess would be that millions of people who recognize the poster have never seen the film. That would be a tribute to Brown's marketing genius. Realizing he had lightning in a bottle, he hustled to find a distributor. Fifty years later, the film has grossed more than $30 million. Brown parlayed the profits from the film into sequels and other film projects. His *On Any Sunday*, a 1970 motorcycle sports film co-produced by his friend Steve McQueen, was nominated for an Academy Award in the Best Documentary Feature category. It must have been tough being Bruce Brown during the final few years of his life. He spent much of his time racing his all-wheel drive, turbo-charged Mazda rally car, and mentioned that he "intends to go surfing" whenever he gazed at the Pacific from his remote ranch somewhere north of Santa Barbara. He passed away at the age of 80 in December 2017.[39]

Back to the Boards

The literature on surfing seems to focus preponderantly on two quests: the perfect wave, and the perfect board on which to ride it. From the early 1950s onward, there was a growing need for more, better, and less expensive surfboards. One issue with custom-made boards was that you couldn't always get a duplicate if yours was dinged or destroyed. On the other hand having a one-off master crafted board was a mark of individuality. Depending on your perspective, the eventuality of mass-marketed boards could be a dream or a nightmare. Some might say that Hobie Alter's approach would make the argument a moot one.

Hobart Laidlaw "Hobie" Alter (1933–2014) began building balsa wood surfboards from his parents' Laguna Beach garage in 1950. Reportedly, he made 80 of them over a three-year period. Alter began quietly scoping out the shop of soon-to-be-competitors Dale Velzy and Hap Jacobs (b. 1930), makers of the so-called "pig" boards, and small but successful board manufacturers and retailers, with shops in Manhattan Beach and Venice Beach. Alter opened his business, Hobie Surfboards, with a production facility at Dana Point on the Pacific Coast Highway in 1954, and sold 1500 boards by early 1958. Facing a waiting list six weeks long, he began hiring shapers that would enable his company to finish five boards a day. Velzy meanwhile, feeling the pinch from his efficient and aggressive competitor, opened a new shop in San Clemente in 1955, five miles south of Alter's, in an attempt to scoop Hobie's potential customers. The rivalry grew, as customers lined up loyally behind either Alter or Velzy. Competitive shops and manufacturers soon dotted the California coastline as well, including Greg Noll's in Manhattan Beach and Jack O'Neill's Surf Shop, with two locations, one of them 300 miles north in Santa Cruz, and another a few miles north of that on the Great Highway in San Francisco. In June 1958, after Alter's seemingly endless series of experimentations with shaper Gordon "Grubby" Clark (b. 1933), they teamed together and began successfully making boards out of polyurethane foam.[40] Alter wasn't the first to use the material to create a surfboard (Dave Sweet, for one, reportedly made his first polyurethane board in 1956), but he was the first to mass-produce and mass-market them. Polyurethane, from a production viewpoint, was a dream. It took hours to carve a balsa blank before it could be made into a board, with weight varying by the amount of wood used. By contrast, poly blanks could be fully crafted in 40 minutes, ready to be made into boards. The ride was different, as poly boards flexed in the water, a characteristic veteran surfers rapidly mastered. Hobie's quickly manufactured polyurethane technology was a boon to the fast-growing mania for surf, whereas balsa wood was seen as facing an uncertain future due to a dwindling supply coming from lumber yards. A number of well-known professional surfers eschewed the new boards for reasons of both look and feel, but times had changed. During the 1959–1960 winter, a slow time of year when most manufacturers had perhaps a dozen boards to sell, Alter turned out 170 of them and put them on sale for $20 off. He sold them all in two days.

By 1966, much of the market for Hobie's boards had shifted east, as 70 percent of his production was being shipped out to Atlantic seaboard dealers. Surfing had been around for decades on the east coast, even if its up swell in popularity had been slower than in the west. Duke Kahanamoku had given demonstrations in Atlantic City in 1912, around the same time that James Matthias "Big Jim" Jordan Jr. had ridden his Hawaii-made board on Virginia Beach. Brothers William Francis "Bill" (1914–2007) and Dudley Allen (1920–2011) Whitman rode their handcrafted belly boards in Florida in the 1930s, and soon were riding boards made by Tom Blake.[41] It took a while, though for eastern surfers to catch as many waves as their counterparts in the west. In 1959, it was estimated that there were only 250 dedicated surfers riding the waves from Miami to Cape Cod. Much of that changed with the excitement surrounding the introduction of surfing films in movie theaters. In 1966, there were about as many surfers in the east as in the west, approximately 200,000 on each coast. Eastern weather could be daunting. Virginia Beach waters might plummet to 39 degrees Fahrenheit in the winter. A friend of the author, surfing off Cape Hatteras during a hurricane, was savagely catapulted to the shore, terrified and happy to be alive. The general agreement that the east's best surfing, with relatively steady waves and a warm climate, was on central Florida oceanfronts between Melbourne and Daytona Beach.[42]

Another innovation attributed to Hobie Alter was his improved skateboard design. The first manufactured skateboards had been made by surf shop owner Bill Richard, who contracted with the Chicago Roller Skate Company to produce sets of skate wheels which they attached to wooden boards. In 1962, Hobie and Tim Richards of the Val Surf shop in the San Fernando Valley combined their talents to produce high performance skateboards with beautiful laminated wood decks that resembled finely crafted surfboards. In 1964, Hobie joined forces with the Vita-Pakt juice company and produced Hobie Skateboards and the Hobie Super Surfer skateboard team of crack riders to promote his line of skateboards.[43] Other manufacturers would continue to make further skateboard improvements in the 1970s, which included steerable trucks, wider decks, and polyurethane wheels.[44]

Surfer Phil Edwards prepares to paddle out for some afternoon surf at Toe's-Niu from Takaberry's house, March 1968 (photograph © Tim McCullough).

Ironically, Hobie Alter's best-known invention, the Hobie Cat catamaran, was more a product of idle tinkering in his off-hours than a planned business enterprise. Essentially a masted double-pontooned surfboard, it was developed as an alternative to surfers—a co-designer was surfer Phil Edwards—for times when the waves were not active enough to do much surfing, but breezes were nonetheless present.[45] The first model, a 14-footer, went on sale in 1968 for $1,200, a little more than $8,000 in today's money. The sail made it perfect for use on lakes, expanding its popularity beyond ocean shores. Culturally, it created a far more diverse mix than did the milieu of traditional sailboats, "like going to a rock concert instead of a regatta," noted one catamaran designer. By the time of Alter's death in 2007, Hobie Cats sold in excess of 200,000 units, fetching upwards of $20,000 for top of the line models.[46]

The Wet Suit Arrives

Hobie Alter changed the face of surfing with his products and marketing, but he couldn't do anything about the water temperature off the mainland Pacific, which was chilly during Southern California's winter months and cold all year around up north. Jack O'Neill was one of several people who decided to do something about it.

Jack O'Neill's memorial in Santa Cruz was something to behold. On July 9, 2017, an estimated 2,000 to 3,000 surfers paddled out into the surf at Pleasure Point and formed a circle, stretching more than half a mile across. Outside the circle were 83 vessels, holding some 700 people. Inside the circle was O'Neill's first boat, a double-master with his family aboard, along with the 65-foot catamaran, the *O'Neill Sea Odyssey*, his research vessel. Thousands viewed the spectacle from the cliffs above. A Coast Guard helicopter made two passes at 11 am, kicking off the event. Jack O'Neill would have loved his celebration. One Santa Cruz resident remembered him, in his old age, sitting on the deck at his cliffside house, gazing at the ocean. "He was looking out to sea," said Jahde Brown, "like where his next surfing spot is going to be, like Valhalla or heaven or something like that."[47]

Jack O'Neill (1923–2017) is credited in some circles as having invented the wetsuit, but more truthfully, he refined it to the point to where it was both secure and comfortable. University of California Berkeley physicist Hugh Bradner (1915–2008) had actually stitched together the first neoprene wetsuit. His scientific career was already formidable before he hit the water. Graduating with a Ph.D. at the California Institute of Technology, he was hired shortly thereafter by Robert Oppenheimer to work on the Manhattan Project and is credited with co-designing the triggering mechanism for the atomic bomb as well as working on the town layout of Los Alamos. His colleagues included Luis Alvarez and John von Neumann, and he married Marjorie Hall, a secretary on the project. Bradner had long been aware of the challenges in fitting theoretically impermeable dry suits to Navy divers, and posited that *neoprene*, a foamed, gas-celled synthetic product developed by DuPont, would provide superior flexibility while insulating by trapping a thin layer of water, warmed by body heat, between the diver's skin and the material. He successfully tested the suit with divers from Scripps Institute, where he was also engaged in testing the new SCUBA regulator designed by Jacques Cousteau and Emile Gagnan. The suit was introduced in 1952, but the navy decided to stick with the dry suit. Bradner marketed the suit through his EDCO company in 1954, the EDCO Sub-Mariner selling for $45 for the short version and $75 for the "full suit" ($412 and $688 respectively in today's money). Bradner's company never gained commercial traction, and he joined the Scripps Institute as a research geophysicist in 1961, staying there until his retirement in 1980.[48]

Beverly "Bev" Morgan (b. 1932), a diver and surfer, discovered Bradner's plans for the construction of the neoprene wetsuit while visiting the library at Scripps in 1952. He and surfboard shaper Hap Jacobs opened their Dive N' Surf shop only a few weeks later, and Morgan began fitting neoprene strips together with nylon thread and sold the suits in the shop. They weren't perfect. The interior surfaces tended to bind when pulled on, stitches could rip, and the neoprene wasn't found to be completely durable. Divers increasingly found the suits to be serviceable, although surfers, believing the suits to be insulting to their macho image, didn't take to them immediately.[49]

In 1953, identical twin brothers Robert "Bob" (1928–2013) and Bill (1928–2006) Meistrell, military veterans, surfers, and Los Angeles County lifeguards, bought out Hap Jacobs' share in the Dive N' Surf shop in 1953, becoming partners with Bev Morgan (Jacobs left to found his own surfboard company). From an early age, the brothers had an active interest in underwater activities. During their childhood in Missouri, they rigged a diving apparatus out of a five-gallon vegetable can, using a bicycle pump and a garden hose to provide air to their primitive diving helmet. After moving to Southern California, the high schoolers bought a diving helmet, inexpensive at $25 because the previous owner had died while using it, and soon were experimenting with it on the waters off Southern California beaches. After their military service ended with the Korean War, the brothers bought into the Dive N' Surf shop, where Morgan and the Meistrell brothers continued refining their neoprene wetsuits. The brothers eventually bought full control of the business from Morgan in 1957, who took an extended sailing trip in the Pacific. By 1962, Morgan had started another company, specializing wetsuits for surfers, which required a significant amount of missionary work, convincing surfers that they could stay in the water much longer if they didn't freeze while doing it. Morgan, who disliked the manufacturing aspect of the business, soon sold his company, again to the Meistrell brothers, who eventually spun off their surfers-only wetsuit line to form their Body Glove International company.[50]

Concurrently with the Meistrell's wetsuit developments in Southern California, Jack O'Neill was working on a similar approach up north. Unlike Southern California, the waters in Northern California, from Monterey northward, are cold the year round, sometimes abysmally.[51] Jack O'Neill had opened his board shop in San Francisco in 1952, and soon was experimenting with a vest made of neoprene as well as testing a dry suit when bodysurfing. Neither kept out the cold during surfing sessions, and the dry suit took in water through the waist cuff during wipeouts. Eventually, O'Neill would build a zip-front jacket and a long john out of the material, which he found far superior to the vest-only neoprene garment. His shop in Santa Cruz soon became a go-to spot for Northern California surfers, and his wetsuit business would eventually, as did Body Glove's, encompass a line of surfwear.[52]

The wetsuit wasn't the last technical innovation associated with the world surfing. Over the next several decades, a multitude of developments occurred in rapid-fire order. Boards might have an additional number of fins. There were the endless arguments: short board vs. long board, toes on the nose vs. traditional riding, my shape vs. your shape, your composition materials vs. mine. Surfers could eventually be towed by watercraft powerful enough to allow 80-foot waves to be surfed. The evolution wasn't only in technology. Aerial surfing, perfected by surfers including Christian Fletcher (b. 1970) and Kelly Slater (b. 1972), involved moves performed in the airspace above the wave, originally derived from skateboard tactics.[53] Ancillary products like skateboards and snowboards enabled surfing to be enjoyed on sidewalks and mountainsides. The surfwear industry, populated with the names Body Glove, Hang Loose, Hobie, Ocean Pacific (OP), Gotcha, Jams/Surf Line, Quiksilver USA, and O'Neill, became a billion dollar industry well before the advent of the new millennium.

A Passion for Big Waves

One element of surfing that never changed was the global fascination with Big Wave riding, a dangerous and potentially deadly pastime involving surf riders, powered by only the sea, attempting to tame waves running anywhere from 20 to approximately 30 feet. Prime big wave spots included Makaha on Oahu's western shore, Waimea Bay and Alligator Rock on Oahu's North Shore, and Mavericks, just north of Half Moon Bay in Northern California. Wiping out on these waves can plunge a surfer 20 to 50 feet below the surface, a depth that can puncture eardrums. To rise to the surface, riders must quickly establish equilibrium and swim to the top, a situation complicated by the possibility of being buried again by a following wave. Surfboard leashes present another potential hazard, as they can get caught on underwater reefs, rocks, or submerged marine junk, trapping the surfer underwater. That, allegedly, is what killed big wave surfer Mark Foo (1958–1994) at Mavericks. Icarine death plunges by big wave surfers evoke the possibility of death-by-philosophy. One questions whether, for certain big wave riders, the urge to continue to ride ever more monstrous waves is, while not necessarily a death wish, perhaps a way to guarantee that death won't come by cancer, ALS, old age, or Alzheimer's. Foo, in a taped interview a year before his death, mentioned that he didn't fear death-by-big wave surfing, but if so, he hoped it would be on a 50-foot wave.[54] Foo's death was reminiscent of an earlier famous, albeit non-surfing instance of a fatal attempt to conquer water, that of powerboat speed demon Donald Campbell (1921–1967). Disappointed at just having set a new speed record of 297.6 mph in his *Bluebird K7* jet-powered craft on Jan. 4 of the year of his death, he made another try at his goal of 300 mph without taking the time to refuel and with wave wake remnants of his previous attempt still present. The boat had been somewhat unstable on the earlier attempt, but he couldn't resist the sea nymphs beckoning ever more boldly from the northern end of Coniston Water, Lancashire, England. Experts still disagree as to what caused the high-powered boat to nose-up, flip over, and cartwheel on the last ride he would ever take. Campbell's boat wasn't recovered until October 2000, and what was left of his body was brought up in 2001.[55]

Alec "Ace Cool" Cooke (1956–2015) was among the world's best-known big wave raiders when he set out alone at Waimea Bay on a late October afternoon in 2015. Possessor of "a stuntman's sense of adventure—and a showboat's out-sized ego," according to writer Sarah Kaplan, he was known for his braggadocio that he backed up by engaging in stunts like being dropped in 1985 at Kaena Point from a helicopter behind a 20-foot wave, riding it more than a mile to shore, then paddling out again for another heat. He duplicated the feat on a 30-footer the following year.[56] As with the earlier helicopter-assisted drop, he ensured that photographers were there to document his successful conquest.[57] No one witnessed Cooke's final big wave ride, though. His truck was found parked on the Kamehameha Highway with the keys still inside. He was reported missing by his girlfriend on Oct. 28 and his board washed up at the mouth of the Waimea River the next day. The Coast Guard gave up looking for Cooke's body in November after nearly a week of searching.[58]

Surf Music Revisited

Instrumental surf music, with its roots in the Middle East rather than Hawaii, was preferred by most surfers to the music of popular vocal groups which would include the Beach Boys and Jan and Dean. Surfer Greg Noll echoed the views of the surfing community in general by saying "We hated that crap. Those record company guys would come around to the surf shops handing out free Beach Boys records, and two seconds after they were gone we'd be tossing the records out the back door into the dumpster."[59] Instrumental surf, though, was another story. The innovator was Dick Dale (b. Richard Anthony Monsour, 1937) whose rapidfire machine-gun like guitar bursts melded a perfect blend of hard-charging rock beat and the sound of the middle-eastern oud stringed instrument. Dale's Lebanese oud-playing uncle, who often performed in family gatherings that included belly-dancing relatives, taught him to play a Middle Eastern drum called the darbuka. Dale, a multi-instrumentalist, incorporated the sound of the oud and the rhythmic qualities of the drum into his guitar playing, his double-picking technique so frenetic that it was said that it "melted his guitar picks."[60] Dale, whose friendship with Leo Fender produced a number of innovations in amplifier design, was also a master of the vibrato-inducing whammy bar. Dale created an avalanche of sounds, including the searing "dive bomb" effect of hard-charging, descending notes. Dale's live version of the song "Misirlou," filmed in 1963 (www.youtube.com/watch?v=ZIU0RMV_II8) is a virtual school of early and elemental surf guitar technique.[61] Dale's breakout album was *Surfers' Choice* of 1962, followed by *King of the Surf Guitar* (1963), a name Dale has been known by ever since. Dale and his Del-Tones featured another song with Middle Eastern roots, "Hava Nagila," on the second recording.

Dale, himself a surfer, described how his music was linked to his passion for surfing: "There was a tremendous amount of power I felt while surfing and that feeling of power was simply transferred into my guitar when I was playing surf music. The style of music I developed, to me at the time, was the feeling I got when I was out there on the waves. It was a good rambling feeling I got when I was locked in a tube with the white water caving in over my head. I was trying to project the power of the ocean to the people."[62]

Dale's music influenced virtually every instrumental surf band that followed, both in its hard-charging sound and its inspiration from different ethnicities. The Bobby Fuller 4's version of "Misirlou," for example, incorporates both "Hava Nagila" and Ernesto Lecuona's "Malagueña" into the pastiche (https://www.youtube.com/watch?v=V5mywpfktQU).

Another guitarist whose technique was frequently incorporated by surf guitarists was Fred Lincoln "Link" Wray, Jr. (1929–2005), whose loud, bent, and flattened notes and pulsating chords can be heard to powerful effect in his version of "Apache" (www.youtube.com/watch?v=t4cArRsnt98). This tune, originally performed by the British band the Shadows in 1960, was prototypical in the sense that it formed part of the basic song set that early surf bands tended to have in their repertoires (www.youtube.com/watch?v=QhIs1k8yuPU). There were roughly a couple of dozen other obligatory instrumental surf tunes, including the Chantays' "Pipeline" https://www.youtube.com/watch?v=omG-hZfN6zk and Richie Allen & the Pacific Surfers' "The Quiet Surf" (both 1963) https://www.youtube.com/watch?v=HnPia9Go70o, both pieces that helped popularize the classic "wet reverb" sound effect. A short list of other repertoire tunes includes "Baja" (The Astronauts), "Mr. Moto" (The Bel-Airs), "Penetration" (The Pyramids), "Walk, Don't Run" (The Ventures), and "Wipe Out" (The Surfaris).

Instrumental surf has evolved to encompass surf punk bands Agent Orange and the Surf Punks, and has brought international surf bands into the breakers as well, including The Atlantics (Australia), Sir Bald Diddley and His Right Honourable Big Wigs, and The Sid Presley Experience (England) and Finland's Laika and the Cosmonauts, who recorded from 1988 through 2008 and whose version of the "Theme from Endless Summer" (www.youtube.com/watch?v=gyFfntitB2k) is considered by critics to be among the most evocative versions ever recorded. Surf has even gone Jewish with Mel Waldorf's band Meshugga Beach Party, who dress in orthodox fashion on stage and lace their sets with traditional and modern Jewish tunes in surf mode (https://www.youtube.com/watch?v=ylKmC4EiFWE).[63]

From an international music perspective on the influence of instrumental surf, it shouldn't be surprising that perhaps the last word in surf exoticism emanates from Santa Cruz, California. It's instrumental surf played on the sitar. Ashwin Batish's "Bombay Boogie" is a sitar-driven, double-picking laden inferno that combines elements of raga and surf, and has achieved a fair amount of play on surf radio programs https://www.youtube.com/watch?v=bbJErA_DAI4).

Instrumental surf's ongoing legacy includes a number of later-era bands writing their own tunes as well as playing the standards, which would include the Aqua Velvets, the Insect Surfers, Jon & the Nightriders, the Woodies, and San Francisco's psychedelic surf band, The Mermen.[64]

Instrumental surf music has traveled to other genres, having an unmistakable influence, for example, on Spaghetti Western composer Ennio Morricone, particularly in his minor key themes to Sergio Leone's western films *A Fistful of Dollars* (1964), and *For a Few Dollars More* (1965) (www.youtube.com/watch?v=mLXQltR7vUQ). Morricone may have been influenced by the 1959 hit recording of "The Enchanted Sea" by The Islanders, incorporating whistling in the lead, with tremolo guitar in the background (https://www.youtube.com/watch?v=n_7jtgTjmjE).[65] Although today classified by critics as "one hit wonders," the band's 1960 LP, *The Enchanted Sound of the Islanders,* also delved into musical Exotica with the tune "Paradise Lost," adding bird cries that appear to be created on guitar strings and Martin Denny–like piano voicings to the whistling melody and tremolo guitar (www.youtube.com/watch?v=fN6vETN0mU4).

Surfing culture has evolved to have many tendrils, emerging in the waves of Hawaii and greater Polynesia, engendering a culture that first found immense success in Southern California, then spread through the mainland to distant international shores through the sport itself, surfboard crafting, surfwear and fashion, and through a genre of music as well, that, although having no direct relationship with Hawaii, is evocative of the ocean waves that surround it. Surfing also was the genesis for skateboarding and snowboarding, sports that allowed participants to enjoy the surfing experience without the presence of an ocean.[66]

Surfing, from its early days on Waikiki in the 20th century, was an interracial experience in which haoles and natives surfed and socialized together. For the most part, serious cultural and racial conflict was non-existent in the surfing community. From today's perspective, surfing represented was an early racial icebreaker in an island environment that had struggled mightily in terms of engendering an environment of equality and racial harmony.

Ten

Breeding a Hope for the Future
Interracial Romance Embarks for the Mainland

One of the most compelling arguments to counter the notion of exotica being little more than a fad is the role played by Hawaii in helping to erode mainland racial stereotypes by providing a model suggesting that interracial romantic relationships were the norm, rather than a taboo. Hawaii's struggle to form a successfully working interracial society was not an easy one, but the islands succeeded in showing mainlanders how individuals from differing ethnic origins could live, love, and thrive together. It was, and still is, a laboratory of social interaction within a multi-racial framework, with questions posed, hypotheses offered and tested, results analyzed, and questions posed anew. The fact that the laboratory was 3,000 miles from the mainland would have been a simple blip on the radar screen had Hawaii not been a magnet, first as an agricultural draw, second as an exotic travel destination, and third as a war zone. Hawaii's impact as a successful, promotable, and accessible environment for interracial interaction can be seen, felt, and heard today in the contiguous mainland states and Alaska, cemented by qualitative and quantitative data relating to the ever-increasing social surge toward interracial dating and marriage.

The interactions among differing racial groups, fed or forced by the Pacific War, heralded the beginning of an evolution in racial attitudes on the part of a significant number of mainlanders. For the first time in the history of the United States, the cognitive and affective elements inherent in the construct of exotica made it socially cool and hip for whites to enjoy hanging out with darker-skinned (or "other-skinned") people over a large geographical area. In the post war era, Hawaiian natives of both genders and a number of ethnicities were advertised by the travel industry as being fun, friendly, and accessible. While the major societal impact on the mainland resulted from relationships encountered as a result of war postings and relocation, the seeds of interracial social interaction had been sown long before.

Stateside men had been attracted to women of the Pacific islands for as long as ships had sailed those waters. Pre-20th century women coming from the mainland were primarily wives, missionaries, or schoolteachers. The 20th century, however, brought a different class of mainland woman to the islands, vacationers who had no intention of staying. With the implementation of the Nineteenth amendment in 1920, establishing women's right to vote, many mainland women exercised options relating to personal independence that had heretofore been considered masculine pursuits. Mainland women visiting Hawaii for the holidays were relatively monied (steamship passage would be too expensive for middle class budgets). Many were not adverse to exotic romantic adventures, far removed from judgmental eyes at home. It wasn't difficult for them to meet Hawaiian men. In the years immediately predating the Second World War, it was acceptable and even fashionable for mainland women of just about any age to seek out and obtain a massage at the tropical seashore from a friendly Hawaiian beach boy.

"Waikiki was the first beach where bathing attire went modern, and women adopted bathing suits that revealed necks, arms, legs, and even waistlines and cleavage," writes social historian Christine Skwiot. "They cultivated suntans, outwardly changing races from Caucasian to Polynesian and enhancing their sensuality with the assistance of a beach boy." She quotes from a book written in 1937 by travel writer Clifford Gessler: "Here an eastern lady of fashion lies prone beneath the sun while a smiling Hawaiian youth anoints her back and legs with coconut oil to encourage protective and ornamental tan ... another bronze boy kneels over another fair visitor, kneading and manipulating the muscles in smoothing and relaxing massage."[1]

Although beach boys were not allowed in the lobbies of the Moana and Royal Hawaiian hotels, Skwiot notes that liaisons were easy to achieve in hotel rooms facilitated by a tip to appropriate hotel personnel.[2] It went both ways: island men would check out the mainland women coming off the boat, determining who the most attractive were and trying to meet them as quickly as they could. Author David Stannard cites several references in noting, "Beach boys would ... recall how they met arriving ships and 'sized up the girls that came in,' telling one another 'that one up there with the blue dress, that's mine, okay?'"[3]

For vacationing mainlanders, it was easy to see the lure, take the bait, and enjoy the meal. The disposability of young Hawaiian "vacation dates" of both sexes made them exotically attractive. Meet a Hawaiian gal or guy on holiday, have some fun, then go home. You didn't have to pack them in your suitcase for the return voyage. They didn't live in your neighborhood, eat at your lunch counter, or try to marry your son or daughter. These dark-skinned folks were easy to love. They sang, they danced, made merry (or made love), and were at the same time both accessible on the beach and optionally avoidable in the hotel. While the reality of an island romance was fraught with misunderstandings, missed signals, and cultural missteps, the fantasy of it could be encased in memory, the occasional rough edges worn down by time and distance, becoming a romance remembered, as beautiful and fleeting as a warm afternoon trade wind blowing through the fronds of Hawaii's gracefully bowing palms.

There was a degree of political expediency to embrace the multi-racial aspect of Hawaii in the mid–20th century push to make the island territory a state. Skwiot, in her book *The Purposes of Paradise: U.S. Tourism and Empire in Cuba and Hawaii*, demonstrates the importance of the islands as a post-war cultural component to the U.S. foreign policy goal of promoting racial inclusion as a fundamental element of its democratic system of government. It wasn't difficult to find skeptics, internally and internationally. The United States, particularly during the immediate post–World War II era, had made methodical work of eroding or democratic governments in a number of countries. Back home, racial inequality, and the increasingly fervent opposition to it, was most often reported in the southern United States, but was a factor north of the Mason-Dixon line as well. With frequently violent outcomes, the ugly reality of racial strife on the mainland made world headlines.

The multiculturalism of Hawaii was viewed as a powerful arrow in the Cold War quiver of the United States. Skwiot continues, "The United States needed multiracial Hawaii to demonstrate to the people of the world, especially those in the decolonizing and developing world, that it was capable of accepting persons of color as equals and first-class citizens."[4] In Hawaii, there was a growing corporate movement to openly embrace multiple cultures as a good business practice. Industrialist Henry J. Kaiser, in building his new Hawaiian Village Hotel in 1955, intended the polyglot of architectural styles—Polynesian, Asian, and Caucasian—to foster international and interracial friendship, cooperation, and understanding among vacationers and business guests. On the philosophical aspects of conducting commerce at the hotel, Skwiot quotes business mogul and author W. Clement Stone: "At the Hawaiian Village you feel the brotherhood of man a reality and not a theory. Europeans, Americans, Polynesians and Orientals meet on a plane of equality."[5] The Shell Bar at the Hawaiian Village was a favorite watering hole for the international crowd, featuring musical headliners including as Arthur Lyman, himself a product of multiracial bloodlines.

Hawaii: A Mixing Bowl or a Melting Pot?

Hawaii became a mixed-race society principally because of the need to import agricultural workers to plant, harvest, process, and ship Hawaiian agricultural crops including sugar, coffee, and later pineapple, which wasn't significantly harvested as a crop until the 20th century. Sugar cane grew abundantly in all the islands, but the modern-day industry is said to have started at a plantation in Kaloa, Kauai in 1835. The first mill was set up there in 1837, and soon there were operations on other islands, most notably Oahu and Maui. By 1850, Hawaii was exporting 750,000 pounds of sugar annually. The industry boomed, with Hawaiian sugar sold all over the world. In 1873, more than a third of the production was being shipped to Australia, New Zealand, and British Columbia. Importers in the United States were told that the entire crop of 1875–1876 would be sold to British colonies. The United States government was beginning to fear that Hawaii would be increasingly pulled into the British Empire's sphere of influence. As a result, a reciprocal act was established with the United States that would guarantee the availability of Hawaiian sugar to American interests. With the advent of the treaty, new capital from the mainland began flowing into the Hawaiian sugar industry. By 1890, more than 250 million pounds of sugar were exported.[6]

Coffee trees were originally brought to Hawaii from Brazil and the Philippines. Coffee was first grown in Kona by missionaries in the late 1820s, and soon plantations were set up in Hilo on the Big Island, Hanalei on Kauai, and in the Manoa Valley on Oahu. By 1854, 91,090 pounds of coffee were exported. The cattle industry was growing as well, thriving from stock left behind by early voyagers. In Hawaii's lush environment, cattle and goats multiplied rapidly, and the worldwide desire for beef prompted the development of large cattle ranches. By the end of the reign of Kamehameha III (1825–1854) it was estimated that there were 40,000 head, including 12,000 wild cattle, whose killing was banned in 1840. Other agrarian industries, cotton, silk, wheat, and potatoes, among them, were initiated in the 19th century, with mixed results. But agriculture and animal husbandry were now big businesses in the islands. And there were not enough native Hawaiians available to handle the workload. Haoles refused to do farm labor, as viewed as demeaning in terms of their social status and educational level.[7]

By the second decade of the 19th century, ill health and disease were already decimating the native population of Hawaii. During Kamehameha III's reign, Hawaii's native population had diminished by 50 percent. In 1850, a law was passed to allow foreign workers into the territory, and beginning in 1851, Chinese laborers arrived on five-year contracts to augment native agricultural workers.[8]

Hawaii's native population had been further decimated by 1875, reaching its lowest point in recorded history up until that time. Several years later, the smallpox epidemic of 1881 lowered the native population even further. The importing of foreign workers accelerated. In 1876, a successful effort was made, despite the significant transportation costs, to bring Portuguese laborers from its Atlantic islands of Madeira and the Azores. Between 1877 and 1890, more than 55,000 immigrant workers arrived in Hawaii. Roughly half were Chinese, 8,000 of whom came via California to seek a new life after laboring on railroads and in gold fields. As Hawaiian agricultural interests soon discovered, the Chinese weren't a completely satisfying answer to the farm labor crisis. Many Chinese immigrants had the entrepreneurial spirit and built their own farms, started stores, or engaged in other non-farming activities, often preferring to live and work in cities, away from the crops. The territorial government soon placed restrictions on Chinese immigration, a nod to the inexorable influence of Washington, D.C., which signed the Chinese Exclusion Act (described below) into law in 1882.

In 1886, a treaty was reached with Japan allowing for the importation of Japanese labor into Hawaii. Westerners were brought in as well, primarily to fill management and skilled labor positions. By 1890, Hawaii's population of 90,000 was made up of 41,000 Hawaiians, 15,000 Chinese, 12,000 Japanese, 9,000 Portuguese, 2,000 Americans, 1,300 British, and 1,000 Germans. Hawaii's melting pot continued to swell over the next decade to the extent that her census in the year 1900 showed a total population of 154,000, with the largest ethnic groups consisting of 61,111 Japanese, 39,656 Hawaiians and part-Hawaiians, 25,767 Chinese, and 18,000 Portuguese. With the increased activity in the pineapple industry, additional workers were brought in during the first decade of the 20th century, including 5,000 Koreans and several thousand Puerto Ricans.[9] To increase interest on the part of potential immigrants, a number of plantations sweetened the deal by offering immigrating labor families an acre of land and a house, with the potential of eventually receiving the title to the property. Filipinos began arriving in 1907, invited by sugar planters. Their population in Hawaii would increase to 53,000 by 1948.[10]

To be sure, there were many instances of overt bigotry along the way. In one notable example, the haole-prepared constitution drawn up for the emergence of the Republic of Hawaii on July 4, 1894, denied citizenship to "Orientals" not born in Hawaii, and required English proficiency in order to be eligible to vote. After the annexation of Hawaii to the United States in 1898, wrote Ralph Kuykendall and A. Grove Day in their book *Hawaii: A History from Polynesian Kingdom to American Commonwealth*, "much stress was laid on the importance of bringing in American settlers and Europeans who could become American citizens, in order to prevent the Orientalizing of Hawaii."[11]

Much of the desire to limit non-white immigration to the United States and Hawaii was driven by a fear that racial mixing might occur, thus eroding Caucasian bloodlines. The popular term was "eugenics," which can be defined as "the science of improving a population by controlled breeding to increase the occurrence of desirable heritable characteristics."[12] On a political level, it encompassed a belief system suggesting an open immigration policy would result in a degradation of control over interracial relationships believed to be a consequence of a fully integrated racial environment.

Two pieces of legislation, in particular, were fundamental elements in the attempts of white mainland legislators to keep non–Caucasians out of the United States. On May 6, 1882, President Chester A. Arthur signed the Chinese Exclusion Act, prohibiting the immigration of Chinese laborers. It was amended in 1884 to clarify the point that ethnic Chinese laborers from any country were prohibited. Originally intended to have a limit of 10 years, the Act became permanent law in 1902. It was the first law prohibiting the immigration of a specific ethnicity to the United States.[13] The Immigration Act of 1924, signed into law by Calvin Coolidge on May 24 of that year went even further, placing a complete ban on immigration to the United States from a number of Asia-Pacific countries, including Burma, Ceylon, the Dutch East Indies, French Indochina, India, Japan, Korea, Malaya, the Philippines, Siam, and Singapore. The chief architects of the Act, Congressman Albert Johnson (R-WA) and Senator David Reed (R-PA), might be termed equal opportunity haters. Southern and Eastern Europeans, particularly Italians and Eastern European Jews were faced with significant immigration restrictions, as were Africans. Arabs and Asians were essentially banned.[14]

The mainland-fueled fear of racial mixing extended to like-minded, financially powerful and politically influential Caucasians in Hawaii. One such individual was U.S. Navy Rear Admiral Yates Stirling Jr. (1872–1948), Commandant of the 14th Naval District, which included Hawaii, from September 1931 through June 1933. Yates figured prominently in the decision to charge five innocent Hawaiian men of the crime of raping a white woman in the infamous Massie Affair of 1931.[15]

For locals, the presence of the Navy was a mixed bag. The infusion of money into local economies was counterbalanced by a significant social cost. One famous brawl involving hundreds of locals and sailors occurred in 1919 outside the Hotel Blaisdell in Honolulu. It was precipitated, it was said, by sailors referring to two local ukulele players as "niggers." Having the strength of numbers, emboldened sailors on shore were at liberty to insult local men and women without fear of reprisal. Writing the *New York Herald Tribune* in January 1932, a former Honolulu newspaper editor, in describing Naval personnel behavior in Hawaii, noted: "I have seen naval officers, in their colorful evening clothes, swaggering about the public rooms of the Royal Hawaiian Hotel as if they were in an occupied country … and have heard innumerable references to 'the niggers' from these soldiers, sailors, and their officers … a large percentage of whom originate in our so-called Southern states."[16] The blame couldn't be fully charged to those originating in the South, however. Admiral Stirling, born in California and educated at the United States Naval Academy, was quoted in Assistant Attorney General Seth W. Richardson's 1932 report, *Law Enforcement In The Territory of Hawaii*, as saying mixed-race peoples "are of a lower moral and mental caliber than the pure-blooded types of each race." He also cautioned that continued interbreeding would lead to "lower intellect and increasing degeneracy."[17]

The precariously balanced cauldron of racial discord in Hawaii finally boiled over with the Massie Affair. On Sept. 12, 1931, Thalia Massie, a mainlander married to a sailor in the U.S. Navy stationed in Honolulu, drunkenly flagged down a car after a party one evening. She appeared to have suffered facial wounds and claimed that five island men had beaten and raped her. Admiral Stirling was incensed upon hearing the accusation, suggesting that an appropriate response would be "to seize the brutes and string them up on trees."[18] Despite the fact that police could find no concrete evidence linking them to the alleged crime, five local men were charged. A mistrial was declared when the jury was unable to reach a verdict. If the men had been found guilty, it would have been a first, as the historical record showed no instance of a Hawaiian man ever raping a white woman. To the contrary, there were numerous instances over the previous hundred years of white men raping Hawaiian women. If ever captured, the perpetrators were often given a judicial slap on the wrist.[19]

The mistrial, however, lit the fuse that exploded the event into a worldwide news story. Furious that her daughter's name had become tarnished through information made public at the trial, Thalia's mother, Grace Fortescue, convinced Thalia's husband, Thomas Massie, and two Navy men, Albert O. Jones and Edward J. Lord, to abduct Joe Kahahawai, one of the five previous defendants. He was kidnapped on Jan. 8, 1932. Kahahawai's murdered body was found a short time later in the back seat of a car stopped by police and occupied by Fortescue, Tommie Massie, and Lord. On April 29, 1932, in the case of *Territory of Hawaii v. Fortescue et al.,* Fortescue and her three co-defendants were convicted of manslaughter in the death of Kahahawai. In angered response, the Navy organized a boycott against any firm employing any of the jurors in the case, and threatened to terminate all contracts with those companies.[20] In a session before Judge Charles S. Davis beginning at 10 a.m. on May 3, the guilty parties were each sentenced to hard labor for a period of not more than 10 years. At an 11 a.m. news conference the same day, Hawaii governor Lawrence M. Judd, under pressure from the Navy and mainland and local haole interests, reduced the sentences of the guilty conspirators to one hour each, to be "served" in the presence of the judge in chambers. The sentences had been effectively commuted. Four days later, the Massies and Fortescue prudently left the islands on the *Malolo,* bound for San Francisco.[21]

The case represented a telling example of how little native Hawaiian lives were valued by the Navy as well as many of the privileged whites that had ruled Hawaii since Queen Liliuokalani lost her throne with the annexation of the territory to the United States in 1898. What comes as something of a surprise to those discovering the Massie case for the first time is that lawyer Clarence Darrow, famous for his defense of teacher John Thomas Scopes and well-known for his public speeches on behalf of African Americans, agreed to take on the defense of Grace Fortescue and her conspirators. He reportedly took on the case because his retirement funds had been wiped out in the stock market crash. Author David Stannard reported that sometime later, Darrow discussed the reason he had taken on the job, "He says, later on, 'There were a couple of reasons. One, I needed the money. Two, I'd never been to Hawaii and I always wanted to go.' So he took the case."[22]

The racial attitudes evidenced by much of the white establishment, exemplified in newspaper headlines associated with the Massie trial as well as numerous racially charged opinions written in local newspapers, proved that a move toward greater racial harmony and integration was going to have to proceed as a continual "start and stop" process, rather than an enlightened and forceful forward movement. Commonly agreed upon, by the non-white population of Hawaii of course, was the need to equalize the rights of everyone, haole, native, and immigrant.

In the fields and factories, laborers of all ethnicities had historically worked and lived side-by-side. Moving into the 20th century, many within Hawaii's ethnic communities integrated socially and matrimonially. People of Polynesian, Caucasian, Chinese, and, to a lesser extent, Japanese blood freely intermarried. During the 1920s, for example, nearly 50 percent of native Hawaiians intermarried, compared with 20 percent for haoles and Chinese, and fewer than 3 percent for Japanese.[23] A middle class emerged in the 1930s, many of whom were descendants of families brought to Hawaii as laborers. They found financial success through a number of different avenues, including opening successful shops, managing factories, and owning property.

As Hawaii gained prominence as the center of U.S. Navy operations in the Pacific, military personnel became increasingly confronted with the fact that the territory's economy was based on an interracial social and business model. By 1940, concerned with increasing Japanese belligerence, the U.S had increased its military population, including dependents, in Hawaii to 29,831 individuals, a six-fold increase over the 5,942 that were stationed there in 1920.[24] For newly arriving mainlanders not used to socializing in a mixed-race environment, it could be odd, uncomfortable, or exhilarating. Back at home, many Americans of European extraction had never even spoken to an African American, a Latino, or Asian American. They'd never gone into a business run by persons of color, attended the same church, or socialized with them. That's not to say, though, that they'd never seen a Hawaiian.

The Allure of Romanticism in Polynesia

The mainland hula circuit had been established as early as the late 1890s, with Hawaiian dancers and musicians appearing in vaudeville, dime museum shows, and fairs all over the country well into the 20th century. Hula dancers were ballyhooed by barkers as an exotic treat to play up the sexual image of the dance and sell tickets. The temptation was real, the audience sitting or standing a few scant feet away. The women were accessible, all right, but as is the case with female circuit performers since time immemorial, they were, to a large extent, romantically unattainable.

The iconic images associated with beautiful Polynesian women as a lure for male travelers dated from the early 20th century. They were seen in everything from tourism advertisements to covers of sheet music, and were a favorite subject of artists. Western scholars and critics have had a field day in describing typical illustrations of the Hawaiian native woman, smiling, seemingly servile, waiting breathlessly to perform or be kissed, eyes held aloft, arms raised in supplication, and often bare-breasted. And if not entirely topless, tantalizingly semi-clothed. This is the vision that countless mainland men carried with them when destined for Hawaii. It was one of the many misconceptions partial to mainlanders who never had the opportunity to step outside of their own social stratum.

Not only were most military personnel landing in Hawaii not used to socializing outside of their own races, many even had trouble communicating to others within their own racial groups, unfamiliar with the customs, preferences, and accents of others born in distant parts of the United States. The military was now bringing them together in a far-off land, where, over military chow, they puzzled over religious differences, moral attitudes, confusing accents and dialects, and conflicting senses of humor.

In addition to those serving in the military, civilian war workers—an estimated 82,000 of them—came to Hawaii from the mainland. The civilian population in Oahu soared from 258,000 in 1940 to 348,000 in 1945. A large percentage of this increase comprised defense workers, typically white males, between 20 and 40 years old and without families, facing the same social challenges in this new environment as their military counterparts.[25]

Given the limited social commerce between large numbers of Caucasian men, be they servicemen or defense workers, and people of different racial backgrounds, it's reasonable to suggest that these same individuals never had sex previously with a woman of color either. The reasons would have spanned the spectrum from lack of interest to lack of availability. At home, the prospect of having sex at all was, in a large number of cases, limited to what was available under the bonds of matrimony. Although prostitution was illegal in every state of the union, it existed as an underground activity, easily accessible in most large cities as well in many rural areas. It was a standard form of entertainment in private men's social clubs, where the upper crust could participate in a clandestine activity, winked at by the law (politicians and law enforcement officials were commonly club members), that was, as such, legally denied to lower income individuals.

For those Caucasians whose fantasies included having sex with people of color, a posting or a visit to Hawaii would provide opportunities that could be unimaginable on the mainland. Judging by the numbers of men that spent time in Hawaii during the World War II years and considering the sexual opportunities available there, it's reasonable to infer that any man who desired sex with a woman of another race easily had the opportunity to do so. And just as importantly, men who hadn't the slightest thought about having sex with a woman of color back home now had the opportunity to have the experience. To do so, it took a small amount of money and the patience to do what GIs have done since time immemorial: wait in a very long line.

During the war era, there were other, less sexually overt ways for Caucasian servicemen to meet interracial women as well. The Hui Menehune, for instance, was a group of Hawaiian American, Japanese American, Chinese American, and Korean American women who hosted dances at the USO. The Flying Squadron was another, featuring Caucasian women on Oahu, but interracial females on other Hawaiian islands.[26]

In Hawaii, interracial romantic and sensual fantasies could be made real. GIs and war workers could satisfy them without telling their buddies aboard ship about what they did and whom they did it with.[27] The neighbors back home would never know about these racially ambitious adventures, nor would parents or fellow church-goers. Doubtlessly, many servicemen and defense workers began questioning their own beliefs and prejudices regarding race. Sexual intimacy can be a potent equalizer, and it's not far-fetched to suppose that some Caucasian mainlanders questioned the value of disliking or distrusting people of other races when one was dancing with them, making love to them, perhaps even shacking up with them. Others doubtless considered or fully realized the ultimate fantasy of marrying a Hawaiian, starting their own genetic tribes, reveling in the joy of living in bamboo huts with ocean views, and wasting the rest of their precious time by drinking, fishing, sailing, surfing, and eating pineapples, coconuts, luau pork, and sea food.[28]

How many servicemen from the mainland filtered through Hawaii during the war? Troop numbers were a matter of top security, but after the battle of Midway, which ended on June 7, 1942, Hawaii became a significant staging ground for military operations in the Pacific. Military strength in Hawaii soared, fell, and leapt upward again as ships departed for one battle and returned after another. U.S. Marine personnel numbers in Hawaii fluctuated between a low of fewer than 7,400 in 1943, to 79,000 in January 1945, to 116,000 in August of that year. Naval personnel in Oahu peaked at 137,200 in December 1944, but that number didn't include men at sea. Around 550,000 men were afloat in the Pacific during the spring of 1945, prior to the battle of Okinawa. Almost all returned to port at least once for brief R&R. It is estimated that as many as 35,000 could have been on Oahu at any one time. In 1944, there were 442,160 active military personnel stationed in Hawaii.[29] Soldiers, being based in Hawaii, were typically the largest group of servicemen represented in the islands. Before the expected invasion of Japan in June 1945, 253,000 soldiers were quartered on Oahu, which had 50 army bases and 26 navy stations. During the immense Pacific offensive, more than a million Army men passed through Oahu's Schofield Barracks.[30]

Not surprisingly, the men were young. In terms of U.S. Navy personnel alone, 80 percent were under the age of 30, 98 percent under the age of 40.[31]

Enlisted men were paid $21 a week, roughly $278 in today's currency, still enough to go out to a bar or two or meet a few women at USO dances. The USO operated 51 clubs in the islands. The Breakers, a navy recreation center, served up to 4,000 men daily, while the Army's Maluhia Club, reported to have the best dance floor in the islands, sometimes drew 10,000 men a day. The money spent by the GIs provided needed revenue to the local economy, spent in bars, shops, and on individuals. "Shack jobs" weren't uncommon, mostly involving men with Hawaiian and Filipino women. The high male-to-female ratio was a common GI complaint, as numbers were estimated to range from as low as 150 men to one woman, and as high as 1,000 to one (according to the 1940 census, there were 56,227 women in Hawaii between the ages of 15 and 29, many of whom were married). For many servicemen, brothels were a ready solution to the general unavailability of women. An estimated 250,000 GIs a month walked through their doors, many of them on Honolulu's Hotel Street.[32]

It was in the pleasure houses that many Caucasian servicemen and defense workers had their first opportunities to have sex with a woman of a different racial background. One brothel, The Bronx, was particularly noted for its women of color. Half of its team of approximately 24 women were non–Caucasian, including five women who were Hawaiian or part Hawaiian, two Puerto-Ricans, and six Japanese. The mama-san, Tomi Abe, was Japanese American. Another Hotel Street dark-skinned woman, said to be black, was said to be one of the most requested women on the street.[33]

Fifteen brothels opened for business in the Hotel Street area of Honolulu during the war years, but the prostitution trade had been a thriving business in the port city of Honolulu since the 1920s. Many in Hawaii's mixed race society did not view prostitution as a social evil. In fact, it was viewed by more than a few members of Honolulu's establishment elite as a way of keeping lower class white sailors and dark-skinned plantation workers away from "respectable women," who, in their view, were predominantly white.[34] The statistics involving prostitution are substantial, although inexact. Men began lining up at the Hotel Street brothels as early as 9 a.m. and stood in line until their turns arrived. When they did, they entered a "bullpen," as it was called, consisting of four small rooms. This was akin to an assembly line, and each brothel had several bullpens in separate enclosures. In the last room of the four, the man who had just finished was dressing—after he and his woman washed up—and would soon depart. His woman was in the third room, already entertaining her new customer. In the second room, an awaiting man waited undressed and ready for the moment when the previous customer was finished and he was called. In the first room, the fourth and last customer in this sequence was undressing. It was said that a woman could handle 12 or more men per hour in this fashion, and when a woman became exhausted, another woman took her place. The assembly line was efficient, but not easy for all men, especially first-timers.

Some men, who may never have seen a disrobed woman in their lives, became so excited that they ejaculated on first touch, while others could not perform within the allotted time. In either instance, men were given "rain checks" so they could return without paying.[35]

The commonly stated price for servicemen was "three dollars for three minutes" (though locals paid only two), roughly $40 in today's money. Although 12 men per hour has been stated as the standard run rate, it's more likely that the number was closer to 10, which would allow the woman six minutes to have sex, wash up, and perhaps throw on a robe. If that were the case, figuring in ablutions and replacing (or rearranging) bed linen, a woman was realistically capable of serving 10 men an hour. If she worked a 12-hour shift, allowing an hour or two for exhaustion breaks, a few bites to eat and bathroom calls, she'd therefore service 100 men in that time.[36] Of the three-dollar fee, she earned two, therefore she'd make $120 in a 10-hour shift, or about $1,627 in today's money. Estimating a six-day work week, she'd be making $720 a week ($9,762 in today's money). If she worked an entire year, she would have an income, in today's buying power, of $507,624. Before taxes, of course. These numbers are calculated based on the year 1944, the last year the war brothels operated, and are an estimate, but probably a very close one. Some women worked seven days out of eight, some probably worked six or fewer out of every seven. Brothel hours might vary. Brothel women had their expenses, too, including room and board (about $100 per month), tips for the maids, and laundry service.[37]

Madams, who controlled all activities at the brothels, were highly paid for their services. The going rate for their salaries was said to be $150,000 a year, the equivalent for more than $2 million in today's currency. One madam paid taxes on an income of $383,000 (more than $5 million today) in 1943. It was estimated that many prostitutes made $30,000 to $40,000 a year ($434,548 to $579,397 today). It wasn't difficult for any attractive woman to make good money in Hawaii during the war years. Due to the comparative dearth of women in the islands, any woman who wasn't in the paid sex business but was nevertheless engaged in some form of entertainment, did well, financially. Daily tips for bar waitresses ranged from $25 to $50 (the equivalent of $341 to $682 today), while "hula girls," who wore leis and cellophane skirts, posed for 75-cent photographs (about $10 today) with military men and war workers, and were paid a weekly salary of $100 ($1,364 today). In Hotel Street bars, the price for a photo was a bit more, at $5, but with the added feature that the woman was topless.[38] Men often tipped them generously, and women could pose for as many as 150 men a day. Estimating a six-day work week over 52 weeks a year, or 312 working days, "hula girls" would earn—at minimum and disregarding tips—$70,928, while high earning bar waitresses earned a somewhat astounding $212,784, the latter two figures in today's money. It was, of course, a case of easy come, easy go for many of them, and lots of that income was spent on entertainment, food, liquor, and tobacco. Nevertheless, the U.S. Office of Price Administration estimated that no economy in the world during the wars years represented a greater per capita income than Hawaii. While countless numbers of GIs sent money home, they also knew they might never return from their next combat mission. As the statistics relate, they spent much of their money on women.[39]

As prostitution was illegal, part of the madam's job was to take care of the needs of the vice squad. Operating under Honolulu police chief William Gabrielson, the vice officers would be responsible for closing down brothels that had violated various edicts (drug use was one of them) and using strong-arm discipline if necessary to keep the women in line.

Each house was responsible for payments of $50 per woman per month to vice officers. It would not be unthinkable to suggest that vice officers were "comped" sexually as well.[40]

Women had to pay for their own weekly gynecological exams, VD tests, and hospitalization costs. In 1943 alone, 120 prostitutes were hospitalized a total of 166 times for venereal disease (there were an estimated 250 women—licensed as "entertainers" because prostitution, of course, was illegal in Hawaii—working in the profession at the time). They were hospitalized, treated, and cleared by a doctor before returning to work.[41]

The women working on Honolulu's Hotel Street were free agents who could change houses or choose to leave the territory. They were not slaves, although it was undoubtedly a fatiguing job for these women, many of whom, like the GIs and war workers they entertained, came from the mainland. But one fact is indisputable: if a woman could handle the volume, she could make a lot of money in wartime Oahu. Some of the women rebelled against the over-regulation of their houses and activities, including engaging in what they called "stand-up strikes," one of which lasted three weeks. Some women set up shop in private houses, most of which, it appears, were eventually shut down by the vice squad. During the final months of the war, military and civil authorities decided that open prostitution was more bother than it was worth. On Sept. 21, 1944, territorial governor Ingram Stainback officially ended the previously recognized and nominally illegal brothel business. Not surprisingly, it continued to thrive as an underground activity.[42]

The wartime commercial sex trade is worthy of investigating as an element of the exotic world of Hawaii and the Pacific as it potentially impacted life on the mainland. Without the easy availably of Hawaiian brothels, countless men coming from the mainland wouldn't have had sexual access to women of other races. This availability gave many of these individuals the opportunity to break through racial barriers may have served to modify their social and racial ideas and preferences. Their evolving attitudes, deriving from Hawaii's mixed race society, were eventually relocated to the mainland via the ships that returned them from the war.

The Beginnings of a Racial Revolution?

The door to interracial sex, dating, and marriage was thus unlocked for GIs and defense workers, and it would remain open in the decades to come. Some 3,000 to 7,000 of these people enjoyed the weather and culture enough to stay on in Hawaii after the war. In Hawaii, interracial marriage statistics had increased with the war years. In 1939, 22 percent of all Hawaiian marriages were of mixed-race couples. For the fiscal year ending in June 1944, the figure rose to 32 percent. Caucasian men represented the highest rate of "out of race" marriages. In June 1941, 20.3 percent of Caucasian grooms in Hawaii married non–Caucasian women. By 1944, the figure had risen to 40.6 percent (Caucasian women, on the other hand, married outside their race only 9 percent of the time). Effectively, therefore, mixed-race marriages involving Caucasian men had doubled, with most grooms in that number marrying part-Hawaiians or women of Japanese ancestry.[43]

With millions of U.S. military personnel passing through Hawaii during World War II, the free association of races in the islands, anathema in many states of the union, was embraced by many newly minted freethinking GIs who had rarely or never experienced such a culture at home. As the marriage statistics attest, for many of them, interracial relationships were not just merely accepted. They were preferred.

In the immediate post-war era, the romance of the Pacific was popularized by the writing of James A. Michener, whose fictional *Tales of the South Pacific* won the Pulitzer Prize of 1948, and was followed by *Return to Paradise*, a collection of short stories published in 1951. His quasi-autobiographical novel *Sayonara*, published in 1954, focused on an interracial relationship between a Caucasian man and a Japanese woman. Another popular novel of the era, Chinese-born Han Suyin's *A Many-Splendored Thing*, published in 1952, fictionalized the true story of her relationship with a Caucasian reporter.[44] As with the adaptation of Michener's *South Pacific* (1958, dir. Joshua Logan), Suyin's book was made into a popular film, *Love is a Many-Splendored Thing* (dir. Henry King), released in 1955.[45]

How did the Hawaiian interracial experience affect the thoughts, words, and deeds of those men who didn't stay, but instead elected to return home to the mainland? Many returned to wives and families while others brought their overseas relationships back to the mainland.

Japanese war brides were a big part of the story. With the passage of the McCarren-Walter Act of 1952, eliminating race as a barrier to immigration, the population of Japanese war brides soared on the mainland. There were fewer than 900 of these prior to the Act, but 4,220 by the end of 1953. The uptick in war bride marriages prompted *Life* magazine to commission James Michener to write a story about it, "Pursuit of Happiness by a GI and a Japanese," which appeared in the February 21, 1955 issue.[46] Michener profiled the journey of Frank and Sachiko Pfeiffer of Melrose Park, Illinois, documenting their meeting and courtship in Japan, their challenges in gaining acceptance from Frank's mother, and racial intolerance from their neighbors. Eventually they moved to another neighborhood, where they were accepted by their new neighbors, two of whom also fought the Japanese in the war. They and their wives became close friends of the Pfeiffers.[47] War brides represented the largest group of Asian women to migrate to the United States for several decades following World War II, numbering, from 1947 to 1964, nearly 73,000, including 46,000 Japanese, 14,000 Filipinas, and 6,000 each from Korea and China. The trend surged upward in the ensuing decade. From 1964 to 1975, Asian war brides numbered approximately 166,000, including 67,000 Japanese, 52,000 from the Philippines, 28,000 from Korea, more than 11,000 from Thailand, and 8,000 from Vietnam.[48]

The men returning from World War II and the Korean War soon started families. Within a few short years, the baby boomers, children of these GIs and war workers, became a major force in changing the face of America, in terms of not only their openness to other racial groups, but their demand for their social and political inclusion on a national level as well. The more liberal racial philosophies that the parents of many of the boomers instilled in their children may very well have been engendered by their days in the interracial society of Hawaii.

The reality of engaging in a racially mixed marriage in the United States wasn't a great comfort to men who wanted to bring their interracial girlfriends over to meet the parents. Hawaii, they discovered in a philosophical sense, was indeed a long way from home. Interracial sexual relations, which included both dating and marriage, were barred in many states throughout the first half of the 20th century. The Expatriation Act of 1907, sections 3 and 4, mandated that a woman who was a U.S. citizen would lose her citizenship if she married a foreigner, although men who married foreign nationals were allowed to keep their citizenships. The law was partially repealed by the Cable Act of 1922 (ch. 411, 42 Stat. 1021), under which only women citizens marrying Asian men would lose their citizenship. In 1931, the Naturalization Act of 1906 was finally amended to discard the Asian racial bias.[49]

In 1948, the Supreme Court of the state of California declared, in the Perez v. Sharp case, that California's anti-miscegenation statute was unconstitutional. The plaintiff, Andrea Perez, of Mexican ancestry, had listed herself as "white" on her marriage application with the County Clerk of Los Angeles, allowable under extant California law which considered Mexican Americans as Caucasians due to their Spanish ancestry. Her fiancé was Sylvester Davis, an African American. Both Catholics, they had wanted a marriage in church with an accompanying mass. Clerk W.G. Sharp had denied their application, citing, among other things, California Civil Code Section 69, which stated "no license may be issued authorizing the marriage of a white person with a Negro, mulatto, Mongolian or member of the Malay race." The court, in a 4:3 decision, ruled Section 69 to be in violation of the Fourteenth Amendment, with Justice Douglas Edmonds adding that in denying them the right of marriage, Perez and Davis were thereby unable to participate fully in the sacraments of their religion. The California Supreme Court was therefore the first U.S. court to find anti-miscegenation laws to be in violation of the U.S. Constitution.[50] It wasn't until 19 years later that the historic *Loving v. Virginia* case, brought before the United States Supreme Court in a decision reached in 1967, finally invalidated all state laws banning marriages between people of different races.[51]

While the interracial laws were changing, school systems weren't exactly quick on the uptake. The concept of interracial dating certainly was not a topic freely discussed or taught in many mainland schools, and there was an almost total lack of curricular materials on the subject. Throughout much of the latter half of the 20th century, in addition to textbooks, Caucasian-biased educational materials, including textbooks and films, reflected a segregated, ethnically stratified society. Through the early 1960s, educational film companies remained largely opposed to making films showing African American and Caucasian children in the same frame, reacting to threats by predominantly Southern school districts that such films would not be purchased. The first such film introducing a white and a black man as social peers was director John Barnes' *Sir Francis Drake: The Rise of English Sea Power*, released in 1957 by Encyclopaedia Britannica Films.[52] Until President Lyndon B. Johnson signed the Civil Rights Act in 1964, segregated schools were eligible to receive federal funding for curricular materials that eschewed images of dark-skinned individuals or racially mixed groups. The idea of interracial dating being shown in school films was so taboo that possibly the first film dealing with the subject to be distributed in U.S. wasn't even made in the United States. It wasn't an English language film, either. *Vacances en Bretagne* was a French language instruction film made in France in 1970, distributed by Scholastic. The film, directed by Pierre Sisser, suggests an active mutual interest on the part of an African girl from Senegal and a French youth, in an interaction considered acceptable and normal by the boy's French parents.[53]

Despite such struggles, the door to Pandora's Box, unlocked by GIs and war workers in wartime Hawaii, would continue to open wider. In the more than 50 years since the *Loving v. Virginia* decision, interracial marriage trends have been driven sharply upward. According to U.S. census data analyzed by the Pew Research Center, by 2015, 17 percent of all U.S. newlyweds had a spouse of a different race or ethnicity, a five-fold increase since 1967, when the figure was 3 percent. On a broader scope, 10 percent of all married people had an interracial spouse.[54] This trend appears to be rising, based on the preference for many of meeting potential spouses on online dating sites. In their paper *The Strength of Absent Ties: Social Integration via Online Dating*, published in September 2017, Josué Ortega and Philipp Hergovich suggest that online dating, which expands the universe of available marriage candidates beyond one's immediate social sphere, was responsible for a 4 percent spike in interracial marriages for newlyweds over a general rising trend from the years 1967 to 1994, the latter year being given for the emergence of the dating site Match.com. They suggest that additional sites, including OkCupid and Tinder, will continue driving interracial marriage trends upward in the United States.[55]

I suggested earlier that baby boomers, the children of the 1960s and 1970s, were apt to be even more liberal than their parents regarding interracial dating and marriage. The boomers apparently aren't as embracing of interracial romance as their own children, however. According to a survey taken in 2014, 85 percent of Americans between the age of 18 and 29 responded that they would accept a family member marrying a person of a different race or ethnicity, compared to just 38 percent of those 65 or over.[56]

This chapter proposes that the growing acceptance of interracial dating and marriage on the mainland evolved—albeit slowly—largely from the experiences of GIs and war workers stationed in or traveling through Hawaii during World War II. It was underscored by the growing acceptance of Asia-Pacific war brides in the years following World War II and the Korean War.

We have seen that Hawaii and the Pacific islands profoundly influenced the mainland, and continue to do so, in music and dance, popular culture, furniture, apparel, and water sports. The adoption of those elements has enriched the United States, disseminating a greater sense of diversity, inclusion, and multiculturalism. Perhaps Hawaii's greatest gift to the mainland was her interracial aloha. That particular genie had struggled stateside, but had been at last let out of the bottle in Hawaii, beginning in the latter half of the 19th century. Once freed, it soared and resonated over the islands, to be seen, heard, and felt by Hawaii's visitors, experienced on a personal level by each of them. In a racial sense, it was a case of the tail wagging the dog, while ridding it of some of its most troublesome fleas in the process. From a social standpoint, the mixed race environment of Hawaii as an exemplar of successful integration may be her most significant and lasting contribution to mainland culture.

Afterword

It's irresistible to question how the stories in this book might have unfolded had Hawaii remained an independent country from its annexation date of 1898 onward, never becoming a territory or a state. Given the promotional machine that existed in the islands from the earliest part of the 20th century, the chapters on shipping and flight might have remained much the same. Mainlanders were enamored of the increasingly accessible "Paradise of the Pacific" a land that didn't require facility with a foreign language to enjoy. Likewise, the hula and Hawaiian music were on a trajectory that began in the late 19th century, as did the sport of surfing. Donn Beach and Vic Bergeron would have certainly still gone to this island nation and brought tiki culture back to the mainland with them. What's questionable is whether this island realm would have forged stronger ties with Japan, potentially becoming a protectorate, and thus ceding control of Pearl Harbor to the Japanese prior to the advent of the Second World War. If that were the case, would millions of American GIs been exposed, to the extent they were, to aloha shirts and rattan furniture? Would so many temporary and permanent romantic relationships been formed?

Queen Liliuokalani lost her throne in 1893, refusing to issue a call to arms that would have subjected her people to a war with the United States that she knew would decimate her population. By her death in 1917, she would have noted both that her nation was a rapidly expanding tourist destination and that it was also having an impact on mainland culture. She would have been aware that hula was taking the mainland by storm and that Hawaiian musicians were active and popular in the states. It would be surprising if she didn't own some of the earliest Edison recordings of Hawaiian music. She was aware of Duke Kahanamoku's Olympic victories in 1912 and may have known he was giving surfing demonstrations on the mainland that same year. What she couldn't have foreseen is the extent of how air travel would open Hawaii to mainlanders in unprecedented numbers. Aloha shirts hadn't been "invented" yet and Polynesian-themed mainland bars and restaurants were still a couple of decades into the future.

It's tempting to wonder how she would have felt if she could have gazed into a crystal ball and witnessed the World War II years and their aftermath, particularly concerning Hawaiian culture's significant impact on and contributions to daily life on the mainland. Whether her emotions would have reflected bitterness, resignation, elation, or perhaps a mixture of all three, no one will ever know. One would like to think that to somehow mitigate the disappointment of her own political sunset, she would have recognized that through her nation's remarkable and far-reaching cultural dissemination, she had achieved an unpredictable but strongly enduring victory.

APPENDIX A

Bigger, Better and Braver

Why the World's Largest Flying Boat Ever Made Never Flew a Commercial Route to Hawaii

Despite the innovations and carrying capacity associated with the big Boeing 314 Clipper, it wasn't an aircraft large enough, many thought in those pre-war years, to handle the anticipated increase of visitor traffic to Hawaii and the Far East. The dearth of land runways throughout the Pacific in that era necessitated improving flying boat technology and capacity, thought two entrepreneurial giants. To meet the challenge, a celebrity airman and a legendary industrialist combined their efforts and personnel to produce not just the biggest flying boat, but the most gargantuan aircraft ever made. That the airman was looking beyond military uses, to post-war transoceanic passenger flights, is undeniable. Unfortunately, although it was built, no commercial passenger ever had the luxury of flying on it.

The HK-1 sprouted from an idea that a huge flying boat could deliver men and materiel faster than ocean-going freighters while avoiding the privations of German U-Boats. During one week in May 1942, for instance, German submarines cost the U.S. losses of 300,000 deadweight in shipping, carrying 200,000 tons of cargo. On May 22 of that year, F.H. Hoge, Jr., of the War Production Board recommended that a massive flying boat be put into production. Such a craft could make multiple ocean crossings in the time it would take a freighter to make one voyage. The submarine menace would no longer exist, and the payload numbers would be significantly higher as the aircraft grew larger. Hoge reported that current cargo aircraft devoted 38 percent of takeoff weight to fuel and oil, while a 300,000-pound craft would use only 19 percent to 20 percent for that purpose. Landing gear, which contributed 15 percent of the total weight of an airplane, would not be necessary for the gargantuan flying boat, thus making further improvement in carrying capacity. In addition, landing strips would not have to be built, as harbors were everywhere.[1]

The idea captured the imagination of industrialist Henry John Kaiser (1882–1967), who surmised he could build one in days, rather than weeks or months (Liberty ships, after all, took a week to complete), but he *would* have to find a talented aircraft designer good enough and with vision enough to make it work. He chose Howard Hughes, aircraft builder, air racing record holder, and movie mogul. The decision was made to name the plane the Hughes-Kaiser 1(HK-1). By March 1944, Kaiser, frustrated by the challenges of working with the mercurial Hughes, was out of the picture. The craft's new name was the *Hughes H-4 Hercules*. When finished, its wingspan would be, at 320 feet, greater than a football field and both end zones, its surface area, at 11,460 square feet, more than three times that of any aircraft in existence. The length of the fuselage was 200 feet, about the size of a 20-story building. Its tail was seven stories high. Its hull was 24 feet, or approximately two stories, in diameter. It had a gross weight of 400,000 pounds and had eight of the largest engines in production, each rated at 3,000 horsepower. World War II would end before its completion in 1947. Howard Hughes and a small crew took the Hughes Hercules up on a test flight in Long Beach, California, on Nov. 2, 1947. It was airborne for about one mile at an altitude of 70 feet. It was the one and only time it ever flew. Today, most people know this colossal aircraft as the "Spruce Goose."

What's significant about this plane is that in all probability, Hughes considered this the next evolution in overseas passenger craft, a fact he was often reticent to state publicly, due to accusations, particularly those made by Senator Ralph Owen Brewster, that he was squandering public money on a military aircraft that would never fly. Hughes admitted that Duramold, a birch-based plywood that formed the skin of the plane, was a poor substitute for metal, which was unavailable to him during the war years. "Now this … is not an airplane that can be used to haul excursion passengers … this is not an airplane which as one article can ever be used in a commercial sense."[2] Clearly, Hughes was deflecting potential criticism that he was using government money to fund a commercially viable passenger plane. On the day the giant flying boat went aloft, however, Hughes had switched gears, proudly stating that the craft would be capable of carrying 700 passengers.[3] The reason for including this craft in this appendix is because it evokes a wonder of fantasy and speculation. Under different circumstances, might the HK-4 have been the first wide-bodied aircraft to allow passengers the luxury of low-cost travel to the Hawaiian Islands?

By 1947, though, trans-Pacific air carriers had no need for flying boats. The military had built landing strips everywhere, capable of handling large aircraft, from bombers to large passenger airliners. The days of the large flying boat as viable commercial long-distance passenger carriers were numbered. The U.S. military's influence on Pacific commercial air travel wasn't limited to just building runways, either. There were surplus B-29 bombers in the hangar, waiting to be remodeled and repurposed. And the "Spruce Goose," settled into its own hangar, mothballed to an uncertain oblivion, never to fly again.

I'm here in the HK-1's mausoleum in McMinnville, Oregon. I settle into the cockpit of the HK-1, impressed by the multitude of instruments that lie before me, then gazing backward at the enormous flight deck, larger than the combined living and dining rooms of my home. How could anyone fly this thing, I ask myself. It's like flying a skyscraper. I look out the windows and get a view of western Oregon. I try to imagine the rumble of its eight enormous engines, thinking that it would be capable of rattling the bolts loose of the building that houses it. Below me are dozens of smaller aircraft sitting in its shadow. For years, the enormous aircraft sat next to the *Queen Mary* in Long Beach as a tourist attraction until it wore out its welcome, no longer bringing in enough revenue for the Walt Disney Company, owner of the property on which is sat, to deem it a viable draw. The final winning bid to save its life came from Oregon. On Oct. 13, 1992, the shrink-wrapped fuselage and wings began a five-day barge voyage up the Pacific Coast to Portland. The massive cargo was then floated down the Willamette River at low tide, ducking under bridges. It was then offloaded to three 475 horsepower movers, each with 104 forward gears, pulling the 181 hydraulic dolly on which it reposed, followed by the tail sections, 39 feet long and 62 feet high. The convoy traveled the back roads of Yamhill County, nodding to its fields and vineyards, finally coming to rest at the new Evergreen Aviation and Space Museum, after a 1,005 mile, 138 day trip.[4]

"Go ahead, try on the fedora," says Bob Deacon, the former Vietnam war pilot and FBI agent who's taken me into the cockpit of the HK-1. I think no, that would be foolish, then realize it would be more foolish not to. Deacon snaps a photo, and suddenly I'm immortalized, if only in my own mind. I gaze out the cockpit windows, then look back at the struts and braces exposed in the flight deck. I can't help but think of Jane Russell's underwire bra, also designed by Hughes, that might have utilized similar design principles. I mention this to Bob, who brings a card out of his wallet, showing the names of A-List female Hollywood stars who Hughes was said to have entertained. I turn the card over, and there are more than I have the time to count, all household names. I'm basking in the fantasy of being Howard Hughes for five minutes, at the time when he was a star aviator, aircraft designer, and celebrity, decades before the reclusive genius decided cutting his fingernails was no longer worthwhile.

Appendix B

The Zenith Trans-Oceanic

*Bringing Hawaii to
Your Living Room via Shortwave*

For most of the long life of the *Hawaii Calls* radio program, listeners could only hear the program via shortwave radio. For many, it meant tuning it in on the Zenith Trans-Oceanic, probably the most popular portable shortwave radio ever made. Its immediate predecessor was the Zenith Companion, was tested on an Arctic expedition by Commander Donald Baxter MacMillan (1874–1970) in 1923 and marketed to the public in 1924.[1] While a number of early radios were advertised as portable, the Companion was the first that could be carried while listening, with the tuning and volume controls on the exterior of the cabinet and the antenna inside.

It was the size of a small suitcase, leading to continued experiments in miniaturization. Battery life was short, and tubes easily became loose as the set was moved. In 1938, the Loktal tube mount was introduced, with its spring clip fastener ensuring consistent tube contact when the radio was jostled. In 1939, the 1.5-volt filament tube was made available, providing decreased battery drain and improved sound quality. Commander Eugene Francis McDonald (1886–1958), co-founder and president of Zenith Radio Corporation and a frequent world traveler, asked his engineers to design and build a radio that allowed him to hear world news in any of his ports of call. He asked that it be rugged and as small and light as possible.

In 1942, after experimenting with

The *Hawaii Calls* shortwave radio program could be received virtually anywhere in the world on the Zenith G500 Trans-Oceanic portable shortwave radio (author's collection).

more than 20 prototypes, the Zenith 7G605 Trans-Oceanic Clipper was introduced. It was considered to be the first all-band, truly transportable consumer radio ever produced. World War II interrupted Zenith's consumer assembly line in 1942, resulting in a short three-month civilian life for the 7G605. It was the first Trans-Oceanic model and the genesis for all that followed.[2]

The Trans-Oceanic's durability became legendary in the war years, as a number of military men were able to carry them overseas. During the war, Zenith received numerous letters from military personnel requesting radios, but the company, now geared up to produce electronic devices for military use only, could not supply them. Zenith published newspaper advertisements apologizing to American military personnel, headlined "A thousand letters Which Break Our Hearts." In the March 1945 issue of *The Zenith Radiorgan*, the company boasted about the Trans-Oceanic's durability in an article entitled "Zeniths Fight On All Fronts: Vets of Two Theaters Take It ... Ask for More." Two Trans-Oceanics are pictured, and still working, labeled "This One Was Bombed in the Pacific" and "This One Fell Into the Mediterranean."[3]

Between the end of the war and 1953, Zenith produced the 8G0057 series and the G500 and H500 Trans-Oceanics. They weren't cheap. The G500 retailed for about $100 in 1951 (roughly $922 in today's currency) and the H500 for about $124 ($1,100 today) in 1953. In spite of the relatively high prices, the Trans-Oceanics were extremely popular. The G500 had a three-year production run of 89,681 units, while the H500 line produced 245,544 radios in its four-year production cycle. The mass popularity of the Trans-Oceanic tube radio peaked with the 600 series (L600, R600, T&Y 600, A & B 600), totaling 269,099 sets manufactured between the years of 1953 and 1962.[4]

Commander McDonald passed away in 1958. By 1960, Zenith dramatically reduced its advertising for the Trans-Oceanic line while increasing its production of television sets. New Zenith Trans-Oceanics were made using solid-state technology, but the glory days of Zenith portable shortwave radios were at an end. The last Trans-Oceanic, the R7000, was offered in 1981. Only 25,000 units were manufactured that year. In the same year, Sony announced its ICF-2001. For the same price as the R7000, it offered digital frequency, a numerical keypad, and was one-quarter the size and weight of the Zenith.[5]

Like vintage Hawaiian shirts, Zenith Trans-Oceanics, particularly the pre–1962 tube models in good condition, are highly collectible today, but those without significant cabinet damage are relatively rare. These shortwave radios evoke the nostalgic times of the pre-television era, when *Hawaii Calls* could be heard but not seen, luring listeners guided only by their imaginations to the sights and sounds of the far-off isles of romance.

Chapter Notes

Of Hawaiian Words and a Note on Money

1. For more on Eliasen's methodology, visit https://frinklang.org/#HistoricalUSPriceData. For historical currency conversions pegged to the U.S. dollar, see https://frinklang.org/fsp/dollar.fsp.

Introduction

1. For the sake of brevity, I use the term "America" in this book to describe the United States. The influence of exotica reached Canada as well, but less into Mexico or any other of the countries of the Americas, whose indigenous and mestizo lifestyles encompassed for centuries the core elements that are inherent in the term "exotic."
2. The phrase "under God" was incorporated into the Pledge of Allegiance on June 14, 1954, by a Joint Resolution of Congress. "In God We Trust" first appeared on U.S. money in 1957 as a result of a Joint Resolution by the 84th Congress (P.L. 84–140) and approved by President Dwight Eisenhower on July 30, 1956. The first car I ever owned was repaired in a shop with a sign reading "In God We Trust. All Others Pay Cash."
3. Naval History and Heritage Command "U.S. Navy Personnel in World War II: Service and Casualty Statistics," https://www.history.navy.mil/research/library/online-reading-room/title-list-alphabetically/u/us-navy-personnel-in-world-war-ii-service-and-casualty-statistics.html.
4. All definitions in this section may be found at http://www.websters-online-dictionary.org.
5. Lebanese microtonal pianist Abdallah Chahine's recording *Oriental Bouquet*, featuring his amazing quarter-tone piano, is just one example. https://www.youtube.com/watch?v=s2MXGYmOs2M.
6. Rebecca Laydon in Hayward, Philip (Editor). *Widening the Horizon: Exoticism in Post-War Popular Music*, pp. 46–47.
7. Said, Edward W. *Orientalism*, p. 63.
8. Lofgren, Orvar. *On Holiday: A History of Vacationing*, p. 148. He credits the term "imagined reality" to Arjun Appadurai from his book *Modernity at Large: Cultural Dimensions of Globalization* (1996).
9. http://www.ohadatabook.com/QT-P9_United%20States.pdf.

Chapter One

1. "Art Deco in Hawaii: Modernity and Tradition in Commercial Art." Papanikolas, Theresa, with Brown, DeSoto, in the book *Art Deco Hawaii*, p. 25. A number of classic Art Deco images of Hawaiian themes were displayed in the Honolulu Museum of Art's "Art Deco Hawaii" exhibition held from July 3, 2014, to Jan. 11, 2015.
2. There's an amusing story concerning O'Keeffe's work for Dole. N.W. Ayer & Son advertising executive Charles T. Coiner pioneered the use of fine art paintings in advertisements, thereby associating his ad client companies as collectors and patrons of the arts. In the summer of 1938, Coiner funded O'Keefe's trip to Hawaii in exchange for two paintings to be used in a Dole promotional campaign. She agreed with the stipulation that she could paint anything she wanted. She stayed nine weeks, painting valleys, waterfalls, and flowers. Returning to the mainland, she presented Coiner with two paintings, one of a heliconia, the other of papaya trees. She hadn't painted a pineapple, as the one sent to her by Dole was processed and sliced. Coiner then convinced Dole to send her a fresh one, which was convincing enough that she painted a stunning work, called "Pineapple Bud." That, and a heliconia painting called "Crab's Claw Ginger, Hawaii," were then used in Dole's print advertising. Lynes, Russell. *The Tastemakers: The Shaping of American Popular Taste*, pp. 293–295. Sibley, Gail. "Georgia O'Keeffe in Hawaii ... Really???" April 12, 2013. http://www.gailsibley.com/2013/04/12/georgia-okeeffe-in-hawaii-really.
3. A number of artists became renowned through their sheet music covers, and the romance of Hawaii was the subject of many of them. Notable illustrators active in the genre included Albert Barbelle (1887–1957), John Frew (1875–1955), Andre De Takacs (1880–1919), Frederick Stewart Manning (1874–1960), Edward Taylor Paull (1858–1924), Edward Henry Pfeiffer (1868–1932), "RS" Rosebud, Morris Rosenbaum Studios, and William (1872–1955) and Frederick (1878–1962) Starmer, http://researchguides.gonzaga.edu/c.php?g=67703&p=436859. Yet another noted illustrator known for his sheet music covers was Leland Stanford "Le Morgan" Morgan (1886–1981), https://en.wikipedia.org/wiki/Leland_Stanford_Morgan.
4. "The Exotics of Leisure: Art Deco in Hawaii." Theresa Papanikolas in Papanikolas, Theresa, with Brown, DeSoto, *Art Deco Hawaii*, p. 11.
5. Lofgren, Orvar. *On Holiday: A History of Vacationing*, pp. 20–21.
6. Souhami, Diana. *Selkirk's Island: The True and*

Strange Adventures of the Real Robinson Crusoe, p. 107. Author Tim Severin posits that while Selkirk was perhaps an inspiration for Defoe, the actual model for Crusoe was probably ship's surgeon Henry Pitman, whose experiences included being "a white slave, a runaway, and a maroon among pirates." Severin, Tim. *In Search of Robinson Crusoe.*

7. Brooke, James, Sir. *The Private Letters of Sir James Brooke, K.C.B., Rajah of Sarawak: Narrating the Events of His Life, from 1838 to the Present Time, Vol. 1,* p. 244.

8. Heimann, Judith M. *The Airmen and the Headhunters,* p. 198.

9. Headquartered in Kuching, Sarawak, Borneo, journalist and author James Ritchie has written three outstanding essays on the subject: "How Headhunting Originated in Sarawak," "An Iban Veteran Tells How Heads are Smoked," and "The Religious Basis for Headhunting." These are published online under the headline "James Ritchie's Headhunting How-Tos," http://www.wowasis.com/travelblog/?p=1198.

10. Marryat, Frank S. *Borneo and the Indian Archipelago,* p. 15.

11. https://en.wikipedia.org/wiki/Paul_Gauguin.

12. Stephens, Harold. *Painted in the Tropics: The Life and Times of Swiss Artist Theo Meier,* p. 165.

13. Princess Miriam Likelike Kekauluohi Keahelapalapa Kapili was 19 years old when she married the 35-year-old Cleghorn (1835–1910). She died at the age of 36.

14. Linnéa, Sharon. *Princess Ka'iulani: Hope of a Nation, Heart of a People,* pp. 147–151. Webb, Nancy, and Jean Francis. *Ka'iulani: Crown Princess of Hawaii,* pp. 119–120.

15. Webb, Nancy, and Jean Francis. *Kaiulani: Crown Princess of Hawaii,* pp. 208–209. The estate of Ainahau was cleared of all buildings in 1953 and the hotel, named the *Princess Kaiulani,* was constructed by Matson Navigation and opened in 1955.

16. Hopkins, Jerry. "Hula City: It's Probably the Most Recognizable Dance on Earth, and Probably the Most Misunderstood." *Los Angeles Times,* Oct. 17, 1993, http://articles.latimes.com/1993-10-17/magazine/tm-46603_1_hula-dancer.

17. Day, A. Grove (editor). *Mark Twain's Letters from Honolulu,* p. xiv.

18. Webb, pp. 62–67.

19. As an example, records show that the *Comet,* an American bark, made the voyage from Honolulu to San Francisco in 1861 in 10 days, 20 hours. McCarty, Louis P. (editor). *The Statistician and Economist, 1905–1906,* p. 642.

20. More than a century after the Panama Canal has been in operation, few bother to give a thought to the travails of Cape Horn passage. Cape Horn isn't part of the mainland, but rather the southern tip of an island called Isla Hornos, now part of Chile. Cape Horn is the home of massive winds, large waves, powerful currents, and icebergs. It rains 278 days a year, and snows another 70. Average temperature is about 40 degrees Fahrenheit. Sixty mile-an-hour squalls occur the year round. Gale force winds and seasonal fog add to its treacherous nature. The Straights of Magellan, to the north and between the mainland and Tierra Del Fuego, is a shorter but much more dangerous route, where the unpredictable and tempestuous williwaw winds, air masses descending from higher elevations, imperiled ships sailing too close to the rocks. At 56 degrees south latitude, Cape Horn lies well below the famed "roaring forties" and halfway through the "furious fifties." Rounding the horn prompted the intrepid Charles Darwin to write "One sight of such a coast is enough to make a landsman dream for a week about shipwrecks, peril and death." Prior to the transcontinental railroad in the United States, Hawaii was, from a practical perspective, off-limits to American easterners, excepting the most seasoned and courageous seamen. https://en.wikipedia.org/wiki/Cape_Horn.

21. The Pacific Mail Steamship Company initiated the first regularly scheduled steamship service on Pacific routes in 1867, to the ports of San Francisco, Hong Kong, Yokohama, and Shanghai. It added a San Francisco-to-Hawaii route on the steamship *Costa Rica* in 1873, a service that was ended when she was damaged in a shore incident. A lucrative element of Pacific Mail's business was its San Francisco to Australia/New Zealand run on its ships *Dakota, Nebraska,* and *Nevada.* Worden, William L. *Cargoes: Matson's First Century in the Pacific,* p.12.

22. McCarty, Louis P. (editor). *The Statistician and Economist, 1905–1906,* p. 642.

23. Things weren't always rosy within the Spreckels family. In 1894 Claus Spreckels was sued, along with his son Claus August (Gus), by yet another son, Rudolph (1872–1958), accusing them of financial irregularities. The same year, Gus sued his father and brothers over shares of company stock. In 1895, the first suit was settled and the second was cancelled. The same, year, Gus sued his father again, this time for slander. With the elder Spreckels' death in 1908, all sons engaged in a massive court battle over their inheritance. The Spreckels family can be thanked for adding a much-used term to the English lexicon. After Claus Spreckels death, son Adolph became president of the family business. He married Alma de Bretteville (1881–1968), 24 years his junior. Because of their difference in years and the source of the family fortune, she referred to him as her "sugar daddy." Kim, Alice. "The Sugar Daddies: The Spreckels Family Feud." Hawaii Digital Newspaper Project, https://sites.google.com/a/hawaii.edu/ndnp-hawaii/Home/historical-feature-articles/the-sugar-daddies-the-spreckels-family-feud. Alma was a story unto herself. At six feet tall, she was a renowned nude model for San Francisco painters, and met Adolph Spreckels while modeling—presumable clothed—for the Dewey Memorial *Winged Victory* statue, erected atop a 79-foot Corinthian column over San Francisco's Union Square in 1902. She married Spreckels at the age of 22, after five years as his mistress. "I'd rather be an old man's darling than a young man's slave," she said. When Adolph Spreckels died in 1924, she was bequeathed the equivalent today of more than $100 million, making her the wealthiest women in the western United States. She was a noted philanthropist, an early patron of sculptor Auguste Rodin, and both used her own money and successfully cajoled others to fund much of the art that exists today in San Francisco's Palace of the Legion of Honor museum. A colorful, mercurial character, Alma was known for smoking heavily, drinking martinis by the pitcherful, and a biting tongue spiced with swear words that would be the envy of any sailor. Carroll, Jerry. "The Palace That Alma Built / Philanthropist Spreckels Almost Single-Handedly Brought Legion into Being." *San Francisco Chronicle,* Oct. 29, 1995, http://www.sfgate.com/entertainment/article/The-Palace-That-Alma-Built-Philanthropist-3020125.php.

24. Mak, James. *Creating "Paradise of the Pacific": How Tourism Began in Hawaii,* pp. 10–11.

25. Worden, William L. *Cargoes: Matson's First Century in the Pacific*, pp. 5–6.
26. Mak, pp. 16–17.
27. Worden, pp. 36–37.
28. Matson sold his share in the first *Lurline* in 1896. In 1915, she collided with the *Panaman* of the American-Hawaiian line in 1915 off Salina Cruz, Mexico, drifted crewless to the Magellan Straits and ran aground, a total loss. Lyman, John. "Pacific Coast Built Sailers, 1850–1905." *The Marine Digest*. June 14, 1941, p. 2. Krantz, Lynn Blocker, Krantz, Nick, and Fobian, Mary Thiele. *To Honolulu in Five Days: Cruising Aboard Matson's S.S. Lurline.*, p. 8. The second *Lurline* was sold by Matson Navigation in 1928, renamed twice by subsequent owners, and scrapped in 1953. Worden, William L. *Cargoes: Matson's First Century in the Pacific*, pp. 161–162.
29. Four of Matson's white-hulled ships, the *Malolo* (1925), *Monterey* and *Mariposa* (1931), and the *Lurline* (1932) were designed by the noted naval architects and brothers William Francis (1886–1967) and Frederic Herbert (unknown birth and death dates) Gibbs.
30. Imada, Adria L. *Aloha America: Hula Circuits Through the U.S. Empire*, p. 172. Mossman was also a charter hula dancer as one of Ray Kinney's "Aloha Maids," dancing in the Hotel Lexington's Hawaiian Room in 1937. Gee, Pat. "'Gift of aloha' Was Face of Matson: Pualani Mossman / 1916–2006" *Honolulu Star-Bulletin*, May 10, 2006, http://archives.starbulletin.com/2006/05/10/news/story07.html. For more on Notley, see Hopkins, Jerry. *The Hula (1982)*, pp. 164–165.
31. Hopkins, Jerry. *The Hula (1982)*, p. 159.
32. Brown, DeSoto. "Beautiful, Romantic Hawaii: How the Fantasy Image Came to Be." *The Journal of Decorative and Propaganda Arts*, Vol. 20, 1994, p. 252.
33. Burlingame, Burl. "Prints of the Sea." *Honolulu Star-Bulletin*, Feb. 5, 2007.
34. Richard C. Moore, email to the author, July 7, 2015. Moore's website is http://www.ship-paintings.com.
35. John Kelly, Jr. (1919–2007) was a noted surfer, board shaper (designer of the "hot curl" surfboard), and environmentalist. For more on John Jr., see the chapter on surfing in this book.
36. Forbes, p. 262.
37. "Art Deco in Hawaii: Modernity and Tradition in Commercial Art." Papanikolas, Theresa, with Brown, DeSoto. *Art Deco Hawaii*, p. 44. The books were Frances Elizabeth Crichton's *Peep-in-the-World*; *Magic Gold; A Story of the Time of Roger Bacon* by Marion Florence Lansing; *Canute Whistlewinks and Other Stories* by Zacharias Topelius. Mahony, Bertha, Latimer, Louise P., Folmsbee, Beulah. *Illustrators of Children's Books: 1744–1945*, p. 337, 422.
38. Hope, Dale, with Tozian, Gregory. *The Aloha Shirt: Spirit of the Islands* (2nd revised edition, 2016), p. 303.
39. Hope (2016), pp. 131–135. Meigs, a well-regarded designer of Hawaiian shirts, lived from 1916 to 2003. https://www.findagrave.com/cgi-bin/fg.cgi?page=gr&GRid=79650069.
40. To view the murals online, visit http://www.artnews.com/2015/07/10/eugene-savage-the-matson-murals-at-honolulu-museum-of-art.
41. The Pacific Mail Steamship Line operated as a subsidiary of W.R. Grace and Company from 1916 to 1925. The Dollar Steamship Line lasted until 1938, when the Federal Maritime Commission took control of the financially failing concern in return for cancelling its debts, and renamed it American President Lines, Ltd. "Dollar SS Company." *The Ships List*. S. Swiggum & M. Kohli. 2008–07–01. http://www.theshipslist.com/ships/lines/dollar.shtml.
42. The Territorial Hotel Company, the hotel's owners, and Territorial Properties, Ltd., were liquidated in 1934, their assets transferred to Hawaii Properties, Ltd. That company was liquidated in 1941 and taken over by Matson's hotel division. Worden, William L. *Cargoes: Matson's First Century in the Pacific*, pp. 59–60, 72.
43. Hopkins (1982), pp. 164–168.
44. Worden, p. 61.
45. Skwiot, Christine. *The Purposes of Paradise: U.S. Tourism and Empire in Cuba and Hawaii*, pp. 110, 114.
46. Forbes, David W. *Encounters with Paradise: Views of Hawaii and its People, 1778–1941*, pp. 255–256. In 1929, Manookian had his only one-man show at Gump's Gallery in Honolulu. His paintings are rarely seen in public today, but up until 2010, several were on display at the Hotel Hana-Maui. Art professor John Seed later determined that a number of these were actually painted by artist Larry Mayo, who created Manookian lookalikes at the request of the hotels' owners in the 1950s. Seed, John. "Rare Manookian Paintings Removed from the Hotel Hana-Maui." HuffPost, July 14, 2010, https://www.huffingtonpost.com/john-seed/rare-manookian-paintings_b_643357.html.
47. Krantz, Lynn Blocker, Krantz, Nick, and Fobian, Mary Thiele. *To Honolulu in Five Days: Cruising Aboard Matson's S.S. Lurline*, p. 14.
48. Worden, pp. 86, 98.
49. Seventy-six percent of the stock of the company was owned by the Inter-Island Steam Navigation Company, Ltd., which obtained an airmail contract in 1934 and soon added Sikorsky S-43 aircraft to its fleet. It changed its name to Hawaiian Airlines in October 1941 and the same year acquired three DC-3s and in 1942 started an inter-island freight service. Davies, R.E.G. *Airlines of the United States Since 1914*, pp. 315–316.
50. Worden, p. 84.
51. *Ibid.*, pp. 84, 101–104. Author R.E.G. Davies notes the CAB's overall philosophy toward the nonscheduled carriers of the era: "The CAB interpreted the letter of the law and confined scheduled operations to the appropriate certified carriers. But many saw in its action a denial of justice and poor reward for the spirit of enterprise which has traditionally been a cornerstone of the American Society." Davies, R.E.G. *Airlines of the United States Since 1914*, p. 338.
52. Kuykendall, Ralph S., and Day, A. Grove. *Hawaii: A History from Polynesian Kingdom to American Commonwealth*, p 272. The Big Five were Castle & Cooke, Alexander & Baldwin, C. Brewer & Co., American Factors, and Theo H. Davies & Co. Alexander & Baldwin and C. Brewer & Company had also invested in Matson's shipping empire. Worden, William L. *Cargoes: Matson's First Century in the Pacific*, p. 36.
53. Worden, p. 126.
54. Krantz, p. 17. For more on the *Britanis*, visit www.ssmaritime.com/britanis.htm.

Chapter Two

1. Pacific Aviation Museum, http://www.pacificaviationmuseum.org/pearl-harbor-blog/pan-ams-pacific-clippers.

2. By comparison, the Atlantic route is longer, a distance of 3,470 miles from New York to London—or 3,071 miles from New York to Foynes, Ireland, the westernmost fueling stop for inbound flights to the U.K. The Boeing 314 was the first passenger airline to fly across the Atlantic, on June 24, 1939, traveling from New York to Marseilles via Horta and Lisbon. http://www.flyingclippers.com/transoceanic.html http://www.clipperflyingboats.com/transatlantic-airline-service.

3. You can fly on this spectacular anachronism too: http://www.eaa.org/en/eaa/flight-experiences/fly-the-ford-eaa-ford-tri-motor-airplane-tour.

4. Larkins, William T. *The Ford Tri-Motor 1926–1992*, pp. 72–76.

5. Larkins, p. 75.

6. Van der Linden, F. Robert. *The Boeing 247: The First Modern Airliner*, p.xi.

7. Larkins, p. 62.

8. Larkins, pp. 62–76.

9. https://en.wikipedia.org/wiki/Ford_Trimotor.

10. Larkins, p. 59.

11. Van der Linden, pp. 123–125, 137–139, 142–144, 164–165.

12. Jones, Geoff. *Douglas DC-3: 80 Glorious Years*, p. 40.

13. At the start of World War II, a total of 332 aircraft in the U.S. were flying on scheduled runs, and 260 of these were DC-3s. The Nakajima/Shōwa L2D and the Russian Lisunov Li-2, passenger airliners built under license from Douglas, are included in the total number of DC-3s sold, as are the military iterations. C-47 military aircraft differed from commercial DC-3s with strengthened floors and larger doors, and were generally outfitted with 14-cylinder Pratt & Whitney R-1830 Twin Wasp engines, superior in power to the 9-cylinder Wright Cylone of the DC-3B. Jones, Geoff. *Douglas DC-3: 80 Glorious Years*, p. 12, 43, 105.

14. Jones, pp. 114–120.

15. Horvat, William J. *Above the Pacific*, pp. 52–53.

16. *Ibid.*, pp. 54–56.

17. *Ibid.*, pp. 56–61. Rodgers was killed a year later on Aug. 27, 1926, when his single-engine aircraft crashed in the Delaware River. A full-length feature screenplay, *Hawaii Calls*, depicting these historic events was created by Rick Helin, a California screenwriter, but has yet to be optioned.

18. *Ibid.*, pp. 64–65.

19. *Ibid.*, pp. 55–69, 71–79. The first private citizens to accomplish the non-stop flight were Ernie Smith and Emory B. Bronte in their plane *City of Oakland*. After getting a debriefing from Maitland and Hegenberger, who had returned by ship from their successful California to Hawaii non-stop air crossing, they took off for the islands on July 14, 1927. They crash landed, in a cluster of keawe trees, on Molokai a day later, both surviving. The Dole Air Derby finally took place on Aug. 16, 1927, with eight aircraft participating. The winner was the *Wolleroc*, piloted by Arthur C. Goebel and navigated by Navy Lieutenant William V. Davis. They arrived after a flight of just over 26 hours.

20. Davies, pp. 6–12.

21. http://aviation.hawaii.gov/pioneer-airlines/pan-american-airways. Noonan and Musick both perished or disappeared in separate and well-known tragedies. Noonan's craft, piloted by Amelia Earhart, was last heard from on July 3, 1937. Musick was killed piloting the S-42B on a survey flight near Pago Pago, Samoa, on Jan. 11, 1938, when a fuel fire erupted as the aircraft was over water.

22. Davies, pp. 250–251, 254–255, 315–316. Pan Am ultimately purchased ten Sikorsky S-42Bs, an updated version of the original craft. It would continue to be used by Pan American on a once a week flight between Hong Kong and Manila, connecting with the Martin M-130 flight arriving at Manila, and was used in the Caribbean as well.

23. http://www.historynet.com/martin-m-130-flying-boat-china-clippers-trans-pacific-flights.htm.

24. Hopkins, Jerry. *The Hula* (1982), p. 165.

25. Allen, Roy. *The Pan Am Clipper: The History of Pan American's Flying Boats 1931 to 1946*, pp. 57–60, 66.

26. http://www.historynet.com/martin-m-130-flying-boat-china-clippers-trans-pacific-flights.htm https://en.wikipedia.org/wiki/Pan_Am_Flight_1104.

27. Allen, pp.70–71, 84, 90.

28. The story is documented in a five minute film, *The Long Way Home: The Flight of the Pacific Clipper*: https://www.youtube.com/embed/Ms84WfJwall. It is also the subject of a book, Ed Dover's *The Long Way Home: A Journey Into History with Captain Robert Ford* (2008).

29. Allen, p.107.

30. http://www.northwestartmall.com/view-by-artist/mike-rangner/mr-1718-pacific-flyways or http://rangnerfineart.com/about.

31. United Douglas DC-6—"San Francisco & Honolulu"—1948 https://www.youtube.com/watch?v=pc9ULGsb4nk.

32. Francillon, Rene J. *Skyleaders DC-1 through DC-7: The Douglas Propliners*, pp. 226, 254–256, 258, 260, 264, 319–320.

33. *Ibid.*, pp. 137–139. The Lindbergh letter may have contributed to the demise of Douglas Aircraft's prototype DF-151, a 32 passenger twin engine flying boat that first flew in September 1936. Pan Am expressed no interest, and the DF-151 never went into full-time production.

34. The Stratocruiser's two biggest piston-driven competitors were the smaller Douglas DC-6 and Lockheed Constellation. The DC-6 series had a wingspan of 117 feet and a maximum takeoff weight of approximately 107,000 lbs.; the Lockheed Super Constellation, which superseded the smaller Constellation, had a wingspan of 126 feet with a maximum takeoff weight of 137,500 lbs.

35. Veronico, Nicholas A. *Boeing 377 Stratocruiser*, p. 11.

36. Veronico, p. 64. The aircraft set the record for a flight from San Francisco to Wasington, DC, on March 5, 1949, in 6 hours, 12 minutes, p. 51.

37. Del Giudice designed the interiors of each succeeding generation of Boeing passenger craft through at least the late 1960s, including the radical new interior for the Boeing 707. He became president and chief executive of the Dorwin firm in 1972. Veronico, Nicholas A. *Boeing 377 Stratocruiser*, pp. 40–42. Lambert, Bruce. "Frank J. Del Giudice Dies at 77; Designed Generations of Airliners." *New York Times*, Oct. 24, 1993. http://www.nytimes.com/1993/10/24/obituaries/frank-j-del-giudice-dies-at-77-designed-generations-of-airliners.html.

38. Zay Smith was a polymath who flew airplanes, was an inventor and designer, and architect. He flew the Boeing 247 for United Airlines and eventually became chief of United's design department. His responsibilities included designing terminals, stewardess uniforms, the corporate logo, and minutiae including sugar cube covers. He invented the world's first flight calculator. He designed

the arrow pen clasp on Parker Pens as a favor to a friend. As a civic leader, he founded a community theatrical troupe and a dancing school. Kogan, Rick. "Pioneer Aviator, Civic Leader Zay Smith." *Chicago Tribune*, May 2, 1995. http://articles.chicagotribune.com/1995-05-02/news/9505020331_1_eagle-scout-mr-smith-amelia-earhart

39. Hope, Dale, with Tozian, Gregory. *The Aloha Shirt: Spirit of the Islands* (2nd revised edition), pp. 66, 110. The United shirt was manufactured by Made in California.

40. Joseph Feher (1908–1987) was an outstanding watercolorist whose work is often reminiscent of that of Frank McIntosh. Born in Hungary, he came to the United States in 1928, studied art, and embarked on a career of commercial design, portraiture, landscape, and teaching. His first visit to Hawaii was in 1934 and he became a permanent Hawaiian resident in 1947. His life in Hawaii involved numerous art projects and illustrations, writing a book (*Hawaii: A Pictorial History*, 1969) and teaching. http://www.josephfeher.com.

41. Veronico, pp. 85–88.

42. *Ibid*., pp. 85–90.

43. Veronico, p. 57.

44. The $278 one way fare was provided by http://aviation.hawaii.gov/events/chronology/1940-1949. Houses prices are found at https://www.census.gov/hhes/www/housing/census/historic/values.html.

45. Income statistics by year can be found at https://www.irs.gov/pub/irs-soi/16-05intax.pdf.

46. Veronico, pp. 64, 104. United Airlines' last 377 flight was in 1954 and Northwest's final 377 flight was in September 1960. https://en.wikipedia.org/wiki/Boeing_377_Stratocruiser.

47. Veronico, pp. 75–80.

48. Mansdorf's estate was an element of a notorious trial that occurred in the Los Angeles Superior Court, involving allegations of elder abuse and fraud, MANSDORF v. GIACOMAZZA. https://www.leagle.com/decision/incaco20110318019, also http://articles.latimes.com/2009/aug/07/local/me-seaside-malibu7.

49. Veronico, pp. 80–83.

50. Birtles, Philip J. *De Havilland Comet*, pp. 8, 14, 20.

51. Francillon, Rene J. *Boeing 707: Pioneer Jetliner*, p. 20.

52. Birtles, pp.37–38.

53. *Ibid*., pp. 42–43.

54. Francillon, p. 22.

55. "De Havilland Comet Crash." Aerospace Engineering Blog, June 9, 2012. http://aerospaceengineeringblog.com/dehavilland-comet-crash.

56. Francillon, p. 25.

57. Birtles, pp. 83, 96, 110–111. http://www.dehavillandmuseum.co.uk/aircraft/de-havilland-dh106-comet-1a.

58. Davies, p. 510.

59. *Ibid*., pp. 510–511.

60. Francillon, pp. 47, 70–71, 75.

61. Waddington, Terry. *Douglas DC-8*, p. 32.

62. Both airlines had been superseded by Qantas, which flew from the U.S. to Australia with a stopover in Honolulu beginning June 30, 1959. Hawaii Aviation: An Archive of Historic Photos and Facts, http://aviation.hawaii.gov.

63. Waddington, pp. 42–43.

64. *Ibid*., pp. 18, 20, 32, 109–111. See Rick Rojatt's performance at https://vintageairliners.com/the-human-fly.

65. http://www.dc8.org/library/unusual.

66. Francillon, p. 84.

67. Horvat, p.188.

68. Schmitt, Robert C. *Historical Statistics of Hawaii*. Honolulu: University Press of Hawaii, 1977. Table 11.6, "Mode and Direction of Travel and Visitor Status of Passengers Arriving in Hawaii, 1951 to 1976: Visitor Status of Westbound Passengers," p. 272.

69. *Ibid*., Table 11.8, "Characteristics of Westbound Visitors to Hawaii, 1951 to 1976: Visitor Status of Westbound Passengers," p. 276.

Chapter Three

1. Halau Hula (Hula Schools, a list of hula schools throughout the world), http://www.mele.com/resources/hula.html.

2. Of that total, 949 are considered native Hawaiian alone, 1,117 are mixed Hawaiian-Pacific Islander, and the remainder consists of individuals with Hawaiian mixed with non-Pacific ethnicities. http://www.ohadatabook.com/QT-P9_United%20States.pdf.

3. The Hawaii Promotion Committee changed its name to the Hawaii Tourist Bureau in 1919. In 1944, the Hawaii Chamber of Commerce created the Hawaii Travel Bureau. The Hawaii Visitors Bureau was launched in 1945 and its name was changed to the Hawaii Visitor and Convention Bureau in 1966. Hawaii Convention and Visitors Bureau (History of) http://www.hvcb.org/corporate/history.htm.

4. Lynes, Russell. *The Tastemakers: The Shaping of American Popular Taste*, p. 11.

5. Imada, Adria L. *Aloha America: Hula Circuits Through the U.S. Empire*, pp. 11, 39.

6. Stone, Scott C.S. *Yesterday in Hawaii: A Voyage Through Time*, pp. 28–29.

7. Hopkins, Jerry. *The Hula* (1982), pp. 43–45.

8. Kuykendall, Ralph S., and Day, A. Grove. *Hawaii: A History from Polynesian Kingdom to American Commonwealth*, pp. 43–45, 49, 76–77. For Hawaiian population statistics for 1853, see http://totakeresponsibility.blogspot.com/2013/07/hawaii-population-distribution-1853.html.

9. Sanburn, Curt. "The Mahu and Aikane Traditions in Old Hawaii." *Honolulu Weekly*, July 20, 2011. http://kumuhina.tumblr.com/post/26465852292/the-mahu-and-aikane-traditions-in-old-hawaii, http://honoluluweekly.com/story-continued/2011/07/the-aikane-tradition-homosexuality-in-old-hawaii, https://en.wikipedia.org/wiki/Aikāne.

10. Hopkins (1982), pp. 42–43. See also "Missionaries and the Decline of Hula," HawaiiHistory.org, http://www.hawaiihistory.org/index.cfm?fuseaction=ig.page&CategoryID=253.

11. Hopkins (1982), pp. 43–45.

12. Twain, Mark (Samuel L. Clemens). *Roughing It*, p. 476.

13. Kamehiro, Stacy L. *The Arts of Kingship: Hawaiian Art and National Culture of the Kalākaua Era*, pp. 24–25, 59.

14. *Ibid*., p.24.

15. Hopkins (1982), p. 57.

16. *Ibid*., p. 57.

17. Skwiot, Christine. *The Purposes of Paradise: U.S. Tourism and Empire in Cuba and Hawaii*, pp. 34–35.

18. Hopkins (1982), pp. 160–161, 166.

19. Imada, pp. 29–30. Hopkins (1982), p. 170.
20. Kamehiro, p. 19. See also http://totakeresponsibility.blogspot.com/2012/09/hale-naua-society.html.
21. Imada, pp. 35–37.
22. *Ibid.*, pp. 59–60, 75, 294 n. 77. Imada notes that the working contractual conditions for the troupe were unfair. The Hawaiians' contract was canceled when one member broke her leg in a stunt demanded by the manager. They had to appeal to the Hawaiian consulate to get the funds to return to the islands (Ibid., pp. 75–76).
23. *Ibid.*, pp. 59–60.
24. https://en.wikipedia.org/wiki/World%27s_Columbian_Exposition.
25. Imada, p. 71.
26. *Ibid.*, pp.174–175.
27. *Ibid.*, p. 293 n. 57.
28. *Ibid.*, p. 96.
29. *Ibid.*, pp. 14, 73, 94, 146–147. As Imada notes, hula remains a controversial topic within the islands. Performers today are still criticized for "selling out" by those who insist that only traditional hula be performed, and then only by Hawaiian performers.
30. *Ibid.*, pp. 144–145.
31. The Hawaiian cyclorama was probably painted by Walter Wilcox Burridge, a noted panoramic artist and set designer. The cyclorama itself was commissioned by Honolulu businessman and annexation advocate Lorrin Andrews Thurston. It was introduced at the Chicago Exposition of 1893, and also erected for San Francisco's California Midwinter International Exposition of 1894, and at a fair in Boston in 1895, prior to the Buffalo Exposition. Meier, Gene. "Kilauea Volcano Cyclorama" Aug.12, 2012. http://www.genealogy.com/forum/surnames/topics/thurston/1570, The Cyclorama was purchased by showman E. W. McConnell prior to its appearance in Buffalo. Imada, Adria L. *Aloha America: Hula Circuits Through the U.S. Empire*, pp. 129, 307 n. 98.
32. Imada, p. 130.
33. *Ibid.*, pp. 112–114.
34. *Ibid.*, p. 145.
35. *Ibid.*, pp. 103, 116.
36. Hopkins (1982), pp. 59, 170.
37. Imada, pp. 101–102, 117, 124, 300 n. 178, 30 n. 6. Bana Lahui comprised Hawaiian musician of several ethnic backgrounds. Known as the Royal Hawaiian Band during the time of King David Kalākaua, its members refused to sign a loyalty oath to the provisional government that had overthrown Queen Liliuokalani. The date of Kini's marriage to Johnny is generally given as May 8, 1909.
38. For more on Wilson's political career, see https://en.wikipedia.org/wiki/John_H._Wilson_(Hawaii).
39. Hope (2016), p. 112.
40. Hopkins (1982), p. 170.
41. Adria Imada's essay on Kini Kapahu reports fascinating details of her tours and life. Of particular interest were the ongoing and insistent requests that the dancers remove their clothes. Imada, Adria L. "Transnational Hula as Colonial Culture." *The Journal of Pacific History*. Vol. 46 (September 2011), http://www.tandfonline.com/doi/full/10.1080/00223344.2011.607260
42. Toots and July were married on Oct. 21, 1903, in Chicago, Marjean Workman, posting on https://www.ancestry.com/boards/thread.aspx?mv=flat&m=1247&p=localities.northam.usa.states.hawaii.counties.honolulu. As of the 1940 census, July, age 65, and Toots, age 69, were living in Santa Monica, https://www.ancestry.com/1940-census/usa/California/July-Paka_2hnd4j. Hannah Toots Jones may have been born in Michigan Jan. 18, 1871. Historically, she remains something of a mystery and is deserving of further scholarly research, https://www.wikitree.com/wiki/McCauliff-4.
43. None of these recordings is known to exist today. Paka and fellow steel guitarist Tom Hennessy are believed to be the first Hawaiian steel guitarists to travel to the mainland. Ruymar, Lorene (Editor). *The Hawaiian Steel Guitar and its Great Hawaiian Musicians*, pp. 27, 88.
44. Hopkins (1982), pp. 68–70.
45. "Yaaka Hula Hickey Dula" was sung by mainland entertainers from Al Jolson to Bing Crosby. A well-known version was performed by British bandleader Felix Mendelssohn and his Hawaiian Serenaders, who always managed to have Hawaiians in his band, including the well-known Tau Moe and his family. Ruymar, Lorene (Editor). *The Hawaiian Steel Guitar and its Great Hawaiian Musicians*, p. 36.
46. Hawaiian Quintette (1913), "Tomi Tomi," https://www.youtube.com/watch?v=28DPLvY1wuE. The group recorded 24 sides in 1913 for the Victor Talking Machine Company.
47. Skwiot, pp. 82–83. Also see Kim, Alice. "The Bird of Paradise: A Broadway Show," Hawaii Digital Newspaper Project, https://sites.google.com/a/hawaii.edu/ndnp-hawaii/Home/historical-feature-articles/bird-of-paradise. The reference to Blanding is from Hopkins, Jerry. *The Hula* (1982), p. 70.
48. Stannard, David E. *Honor Killing: How the Infamous "Massie Affair" Transformed Hawaii*, p. 24.
49. Hopkins, Jerry. *The Hula: A Revised Edition* (2011), pp. 69–75, 163. The documentary films are *Hoolauea* (dir. Francis Haar, 1950) and *'Iolani Luahine* (dir. Tip Davis, 1979). The Shawn quote is from Hopkins, Jerry. *The Hula* (1982), p. 104.
50. Aggie Auld is the lead dancer in a clip from *Mona Koora*, at https://www.youtube.com/watch?v=8c8Fzpr8djA.
51. Details of Aggie Auld's life are difficult to come by, and not always in agreement. One source of information on her is Todaro, Tony. *The Golden Years of Hawaiian Entertainment, 1874–1974*. See also Hopkins *The Hula* (1982), p. 148.
52. For more on Love and Brown, see Wright, Renee. "Mementos of a Royal Hawaiian Love Story," March 30, 2011, http://www.worthpoint.com/blog-entry/mementos-royal-hawaiian-love-story *The Blonde Captive* can be viewed at https://www.youtube.com/watch?v=Q5z08fjXGvE. For more details of Love's life, see Hopkins, Jerry. *The Hula* (1982), pp. 161–162.
53. Hilo Hattie, "The Cockeyed Mayor of Kaunakakai" (from the television series *Hawaii Calls*), https://www.youtube.com/watch?v=mCcfn5gTaQk.
54. Hilo Hattie (with Betty Grable), "Down on Ami Ami Oni Oni Isle" from the film *Song of the Islands* (1942), https://www.youtube.com/watch?v=lhyrgOjpQUs.
55. The clothing firm was founded on Kauai in 1962 by James Romig as Kaluna Hawaii Sportswear, and renamed after Hilo Hattie following her death in 1979.
56. Hopkins, *The Hula* (1982), p. 152.
57. Enid Markey will be forever remembered as Tarzan's first Jane, appearing opposite Elmo Lincoln in *Tarzan of the Apes* (1918, dir. Scott Sidney). Fraser, G. Gerald. "Enid Markey, Actress, Dead; Starred In First Tarzan Film." *New York Times*, Nov. 16, 1981, http://www.nytimes.com/1981/

11/16/obituaries/enid-markey-actress-dead-starred-in-first-tarzan-film.html.
58. Hopkins, *The Hula* (1982), p.88. An uncredited Duke Kahanamoku also appeared in the film.
59. Hopkins, *The Hula* (1982), p.89, 176–178. Hopkins' filmography includes valuable information on Hawaiian dancers and musicians who performed in Hollywood productions of the era. Powell's *Honolulu* dances can be seen at Powell, Eleanor. "Hula" (from the film *Honolulu*, 1939), https://www.youtube.com/watch?v=ks2fHGt68TI. Powell, Eleanor. "Hula Tap" (from the film *Honolulu*, 1939) https://www.youtube.com/watch?v=9KDMy5w2JB4.
60. Napoleon, Nanette Naioma. "Dancing with Fame: Alice Kealoha Holt's Hula Skills Brought Statewide Acclaim and a Small Film Role." *Honolulu Star-Advertiser*, April 2, 2015, http://merriemonarch.staradvertiser.com/dancing-with-fame.
61. The Lexington Hotel closed in 1966 due to the expense associated with renovations needed to conform to fire safety regulations. http://www.honolulumagazine.com/Honolulu-Magazine/August-2012/75th-Anniversary-of-the-Hawaiian-Room-in-NYC.
62. Kanahele, George S. (Editor), Berger, John (Revision). *Hawaiian Music and Musicians: An Encyclopedic History*, p. 282.
63. *Ibid.*, p. 421.
64. Imada, pp. 168–172, 224. Mossman, the daughter of Honolulu entrepreneur George Mossman, was most widely known as the "Matson Girl" with the red hibiscus in her hair, who appeared in the shipping line's ubiquitous advertisements. Gee, Pat. "'Gift of aloha' Was Face of Matson: Pualani Mossman / 1916–2006" *Honolulu Star-Bulletin*, May 10, 2006, http://archives.starbulletin.com/2006/05/10/news/story07.html.
65. *Ibid.*, pp. 177, 191, 320 n129, n130.
66. Kanahele, pp. 282–283.
67. McIntyre, Lani. "King Kamehameha" (1947), https://archive.org/details/KingKamehameha. "Holo Holo Kaa" https://archive.org/details/HoloHoloKaa.
68. Imada, pp. 172–174, 176–177, 179–181.
69. Glazner, Tim "Swanky." *Mai-Kai: History and Mystery of the Iconic Tiki Restaurant*, p. 127. Pualani Mossman's shop in Florida reportedly sold more Alfred Shaheen Hawaiian apparel than any other mainland retailer.
70. Imada, pp. 207–209. http://www.squareone.org/Hapa/becker.html. Eleanor Leilehua Becker. Furtado is a member of the Desha/Beamer clan, http://www.hulapreservation.org/kupuna.asp?ID=23.
71. Reynolds, Karyl. "The Legacy of Lalani Village." *Waikiki Magazine*, Sept. 5, 2013, http://www.waikikivisitor.com/2013/ilove-waikiki/the-legacy-of-lalani-village. Imada, Adria L. *Aloha America: Hula Circuits Through the U.S. Empire*, p. 159. Tucker, Terry. "George Paele Mossman, Part I—The Ukulele Builder" UkuZoo, Feb. 14, 2011, http://ukuzoo.com/Blogs/post/George-Paele-Mossman-Part-I-The-Ukulele-Builder.aspx.
72. Hopkins, *The Hula* (2011), pp. 94–97. See also https://newsroom.byuh.edu/node/2136.
73. Hopkins, *The Hula* (1982), p. 153.
74. Reynolds, Karyl. "The Legacy of Lalani Village." *Waikiki Magazine*, Sept. 5, 2013, http://www.waikikivisitor.com/2013/ilove-waikiki/the-legacy-of-lalani-village. Imada, pp. 160, 162.
75. Reynolds
76. Hopkins, *The Hula* (1982), p.103. The Calvinist antipathy toward the hula was still apparent as late as 1958, Hopkins notes, when Nona Beamer's dance to Pele, performed at the Kona Inn, was chastised by the minister of the Mokuaikaua Congregational Church in his sermon the following morning (if he were there himself, one wonders if he found his "research" gratifying on any level).
77. Britsch, R. Lanier. *Moramona: The Mormons in Hawaii (Mormons in the Pacific Series) 1st Edition*, p. 119.
78. Imada, p.313 n32.
79. *Ibid.*, pp. 163, 313 n32, n33. The informal melding of traditional beliefs with successor eastern and western religions is common to many cultures. In Thailand, for example, traditional animist beliefs are commonly practiced in conjunction with Theravada Buddhism.
80. *Ibid.*, p.313 n31.
81. Hopkins (1982), pp. 76–78.
82. Essayist and professor Albert B. Robillard is critical of the Polynesian Cultural Center, noting, "the supposedly authentic Marquesan and Tahitian villages are at times staffed by Samoans. Pacific islanders are used interchangeably. The ethnic villages are sanitized versions of the real island locales, without the smells of farm animals, turned earth, crops, fish, sewage, and the ever present flies." Robillard, Albert B. (Editor). *Social Change in the Pacific Islands*, pp. 389–390.
83. Hopkins, *The Hula* (1982), pp. 78, 104. The LDS church is not the only religious body responsible for preserving traditional Pacific cultures. The Jehovah's Witnesses are mandated to print religious literature in as many languages as possible, including those for which language fonts have not yet been developed. In conjunction with Stanford University linguists, they document the language, produce the fonts, and print literature, which now appears in more than 750 languages. This process was explained to me in 1985 by an individual working on the font creation team at Watchtower Farms in New York. This was confirmed in a discussion with a linguist participating in the project at Stanford. For more about the language translation program, visit https://www.jw.org/en/publications/books/jehovahs-will/literature-written-and-translated
84. *Ibid.*,, p. 154.
85. *Ibid.*, pp. 148–150, 171.
86. Imada, pp. 217, 324 n16. 75 years have passed since then, but the Aloha message still resonates. The Hawaii Tourism Authority today touts "Sharing Aloha," http://www.sharingaloha.com.
87. Hopkins, *The Hula* (1982), pp. 168, 171.
88. Allen, Gwenfread. *Hawaii During the War Years: 1941–1945*, pp. 274, 278.
89. *Ibid.*, pp. 275, 279–280, 284.
90. Krauss, Bob. "Memoirs of a Very Old Soldier." *Honolulu Advertiser*, March 2, 2005, http://the.honoluluadvertiser.com/article/2005/Mar/02/ln/ln54pbob.html
91. Imada, pp. 241, 329 n105.
92. Hopkins, *The Hula* (1982), p. 109. Director Daves had a fascinating career and was a remarkable individual. In his essay on Delmer Daves, film director and critic Bertrand Tavernier notes Daves' use of stark nature shots to recreate the mood of his characters as well as other notable elements of his filmmaking technique. Daves could also apparently mimic the handwriting of anyone, and delighted in painting the signs for the inns in is historical films. Tavernier, Bertrand. "The Ethical Romantic," *Film Comment*, January/February 2003, https://www.filmcomment.com/article/delmer-daves-bertrand-tavernier.

93. Presley made three Hawaii-themed films, all shot on location in the islands. The theme song "Blue Hawaii," sung in the first film, became a hit and, as Jerry Hopkins notes, delivering "Hawaii's quintessential promise: 'Dreams come true/In blue Hawaii.'" The song was first sung in film by Bing Crosby in the 1937 picture *Hawaiian Wedding*. Presley's first two Hawaiian films, *Blue Hawaii* (1961) and *Girls! Girls! Girls!* (1962), were directed by Norman Taurog. Michael (Micky) Moore directed the final film, *Paradise, Hawaiian Style* (1966). Each flm generated a soundtrack album of the same name. Hopkins, Jerry. *Elvis in Hawaii*, pp. 31–56.

94. Horvat, p. 186. It's doubtful whether we'll ever again see dancing flight attendants on United States carriers. This is not the case with Filipino carriers, where Cebu Pacific Airlines' discoing flight attendants energetically demonstrate safety devices prior to take-off, http://www.wowasis.com/travelblog/?p=4223.

95. Hopkins, *The Hula* (1982), p. 99.

96. *Ibid.*, pp. 99–100.

97. The firm, founded by Domenico Ghirardelli, was incorporated in 1852 and is one of the oldest chocolate companies operating in the United States. The family would have voyaged on a Matson ship. Decades later, William Matson Roth built the famous Ghirardelli Square complex on San Francisco's waterfront.

98. Marguerite Kuuipolani Duane (Hunkin) published her book *The Hawaiian Hula: Authentic Techniques for Teachers and Students* in 1970.

99. Hopkins, *The Hula* (1982), pp. 100–103, 109.

100. *Ibid.*, p. 124. For a review of the embezzlement case, see "Henry Taylor, Appellant, v. United States of America, Appellee, 320 F.2d 843 (9th Cir. 1963)," http://law.justia.com/cases/federal/appellate-courts/F2/320/843/38674.

101. http://merriemonarch.com/history-merriemonarch-festival and http://merriemonarch.com/2017-miss-aloha-hula-participants.

102. Hopkins, *The Hula* (1982), pp. 131–132.

103. Kanahele, George S. "Haw'n Renaissance Grips, Changes Island History." From a lecture delivered in May 1979 as part of Kamehameha Schools' Hawaiian Culture Lecture Series. Reproduced in the Hawaiian Music Foundation's *Hailono Mele* newsletter, Volume V, number 7, July 1979. http://ulukau.org/gsdl2.80/collect/hailono/cgi-bin/hailono?a=pdf&d=DHMN005007.1.1&dl=1&sim=Screen2Image.

104. https://en.wikipedia.org/wiki/H%C5%8Dk%C5%ABle%CA%BBa.

105. Kanahele, pp. 4–5. The world, of course, was already well aware of Thor Heyerdahl's epic Pacific voyage aboard the raft *Kon-Tiki*. She was made of balsa wood logs and other native materials. After a 101-day, 5,000 mile journey beginning in Peru, she smshed up on a reef in the Tuomotu islands of Fench Polynesia on August 7, 1947. Heyerdahl documented the journey by publishing a book in 1948, reprinted in English in 1950 as *Kon-Tiki: Across the Pacific in a Raft*, which became a best seller. The *Kon-Tiki* is on exhibit today in Oslo's Kon-Tiki Museum. https://en.wikipedia.org/wiki/Kon-Tiki_expedition.

106. http://www.paifoundation.org/more-exciting-mamo-2016-events/about-2.

107. Imada, pp. 258–259, 265–266.

108. http://hawaiianfestivalpnw.com.

109. Hula encompasses the movement of hands, arms, feet, and hips. There are at least 26 basic hand movements in hula, describing geological features, weather, body parts, flora, and emotions. There are also at least 10 basic foot movements: http://halauokanoelani.com/hula-basics.

110. Hopkins, *The Hula* (1982), p. 137.

111. Hopkins, email to the author, April 26, 2017.

112. Hopkins, *The Hula* (1982), p.138. Hopkins is acutely aware that as a haole, his credentials will be always under suspicion when writing on Hawaiian subject matter. As he told the *Honolulu Weekly* in 2012, "The artistry of dance, along with the joy that accompanies performance, often has been countered by jealousy and a certain—well, let's be frank—bitchiness. Hula is not exempt from this. Surely, there were some in hula who were not thrilled that a haole was writing their history." Adams, Wanda A. "A Complicated Dance." *Honolulu Weekly*, May 30, 2012, http://honoluluweekly.com/story-continued/2012/05/a-complicated-dance.

113. Traditional Tahitian dance is also taught in many hula schools on the mainland.

114. This photo may be viewed at https://commons.wikimedia.org/wiki/File:Japanese_American_women_doing_hula,_Santa_Anita_Assembly_Ctr_cph.3c33814.j pg. Operating as an internment center from March to October 1942, Santa Anita held more than 18,000 people of Japanese descent under arduous conditions. The population was transferred to a number of relocation camps when the center was closed in October 1942. Santa Anita then became Camp Santa Anita, a training center for 20,000 army ordinance personnel. A total of 100,000 were trained there until November 1944, when it then became a holding facility for German POWs. "Santa Anita (detention facility)" Densho Encyclopedia http://encyclopedia.densho.org/Santa_Anita_%28detention_facility%29.

115. Halau Hula (Hula Schools, a list of hula schools throughout the world), http://www.mele.com/resources/hula.html.

116. Aguiar, Eloise. "Japan Hooked on Hula and the Ukulele" *Honolulu Advertiser*, July 11, 2005, http://the.honoluluadvertiser.com/article/2005/Jul/11/ln/507110329.html.

Chapter Four

1. http://bb.steelguitarforum.com/viewtopic.php?t=299717&sid=63bc5b831bb43a287c1af3e626112316.

2. Ruymar, Lorene (Editor). *The Hawaiian Steel Guitar and its Great Hawaiian Musicians*, p. 21.

3. Tosches, Nick. *Country: Living Legends and Dying Metaphors in America's Biggest Music* (Revised), pp. 173–174.

4. Kanahele, George S. (Editor), Berger, John (Revision). *Hawaiian Music and Musicians: An Encyclopedic History*, p. 131. Henessey and Paka were accompanied and recorded with fellow Hawaiian musicians Tony Zablan, Tommy Silva, and David Makuakane.

5. Kolomoku also appeared in director D.W. Griffith's film *The Idol Dancer* (1920), playing the role of a native musician, https://en.wikipedia.org/wiki/The_Idol_Dancer.

6. Kanahele, pp. 567–569.

7. Blecha, Peter. "Seattle's Star Hawaiian Guitarist, Helen Louise Ferera, Mysteriously Disappears from a Steamship on December 12, 1919." Nov. 8, 2009, historylink.org, http://www.historylink.org/File/9201. Blecha's

essay includes additional historical information on Ferera's life. See also Ruymar, Lorene (Editor). *The Hawaiian Steel Guitar and its Great Hawaiian Musicians*, p. 86.

8. Kanahele, p. 152.

9. Ruymar, p. 99. Listen to Lua and Kaili's "Kohala March" (1914) at https://www.youtube.com/watch?v=PjwYtsZUdBc. "Hilo-Hawaiian March" (1914), by the Irene West Royal Hawaiians, features the melody and improvisation presumably by Lua, accompanied by ukulele https://archive.org/details/78_hilo_irene-west-royal-hawaiians_gbia0000293a/Hilo+-+Irene+West+Royal+Hawaiians.flac. Irene West (b. 1882) was a noted Texas-born dancer, vaudeville performer, manager, booking agent, and journalist. Kanahele, pp. 870–872.

10. Ruymar, pp. 27, 98. The individual recording titles are listed at http://adp.library.ucsb.edu/index.php/talent/detail/53995/Hawaiian_Quintette_Vocal_group. Although Kolomoku's steel guitar can barely be heard, A. Kiwala's extraordinary vocals should be noted on the Quintette's 1913 recording of "Tomi Tomi," Hawaiian Quintette (1913), "Tomi Tomi," https://www.youtube.com/watch?v=28DPLvY1wuE.

11. Kanahele, pp. 633–634. Musicians and hula dancers weren't the only Hawaiians of the era making an impact on mainland entertainment. "Honolulu Johnny" Williams gained brief notoriety as the first Hawaiian to play major league baseball, with the Detroit Tigers in 1914. Costello, Rory. "Johnny Williams," https://sabr.org/bioproj/person/7a544ac1.

12. http://chroniclingamerica.loc.gov/lccn/sn83030214/1917-02-21/ed-1/seq-5.

13. Ruymar, p. 55.

14. *Ibid.*, pp. 90, 120.

15. Kanahele, p. 323.

16. *Betty Boop's Isle* may be seen at: https://www.youtube.com/watch?v=3DODcdtA8U8.

17. Kanahele, pp. 322, 324.

18. Hoopii, Sol. "Musical Moments with Sol Hoopii and His Hawaiian Guitar," (1942) from *The Scriptures Visualized*. The C.O. Baptista Films, Chicago, https://www.youtube.com/watch?v=gb0A2RLE32U.

19. Ruymar, p. 83.

20. *Ibid.*, p. 82.

21. *Ibid.*, p. 108.

22. Kanahele, pp. 872–876.

23. *Ibid.*, pp. 577–578.

24. *Ibid.*, pp. 88, 546–548.

25. In Van Eps' case, xylophones were used as a contrapuntal gimmick in his quartet's 1920 recording of "The Hula Blues," https://www.youtube.com/watch?v=cBNGB56neis. Reid's Hawaiian Serenaders eventually included the vibraphone, used harmonically and as a solo instrument on his recording of "Rhythm of the Waves." Although I was unable to date the recording, stylistically it would appear to have been made in the 1930s, fitting easily into the Hawaiian Swing category. https://www.youtube.com/watch?v=cBNGB56neis.

26. Kanahele, pp. 85–87. For more on latter-day Canadian electric steel guitar players, see Kanahele, pp. 88–93.

27. Felske, Lorry, and Rasporich, Beverly (Editors). *Challenging Frontiers: The Canadian West*, pp. 194–195. See also https://en.wikipedia.org/wiki/Hank_Snow

28. Ruymar, p.49.

29. Tosches, p. 175.

30. Ruymar, p.67. Kanahele, p. 655.

31. https://en.wikipedia.org/wiki/Roy_Smeck

32. Kanahele, p. 797.

33. Ruymar, p. 120. Ruymer also makes mention of the electric guitar built by the Stromberg-Voisinet Company's Hank Kuhrmeyer in approximately 1928. Its amplification was based on the vibrating guitar body, rather than the Beauchamp invention, which was based on amplifying the strings.

34. "The Earliest Days of the Electric Guitar." Rickenbacker International Corporation, http://www.rickenbacker.com/history_early.asp.

35. Blecha, Peter. "Los Angeles-Based Orville Knapp Orchestra Performs a Seattle Concert—Featuring What Is Almost Certainly the Local Public Debut of the Electric Guitar—on Sept. 13, 1934." Oct. 12, 2016, historylink.org http://historylink.org/File/20161. The Knapp band also played at the Beverly Wilshire Hotel during roughly the same timeframe it appeared at the Grand Hotel. Smith, Richard. *Rickenbacker*, p.11.

36. Ruymar, p. 120.

37. *Ibid.*, pp. 120–121, 131. Snibbe, Kurt. "Getting Plugged In: The Next Time You Hear an electric Guitar, Remember that the First Was Built in California." *San Jose Mercury News*, Aug. 13, 2017. Oliver, Myrna. "Francis Hall; Helped Fender, Rickenbacker Guitar Firms." *Los Angeles Times*, Aug. 30, 1999, http://articles.latimes.com/1999/aug/30/news/mn-5096.

38. Leo Fender: https://www.findagrave.com/cgi-bin/fg.cgi?page=gr&GRid=3045. Francis C. Hall: https://www.findagrave.com/cgi-bin/fg.cgi?page=gr&GRid=7323457.

39. Vale, p. 99.

40. Kanahele, p. 793.

41. Tosches, pp. 180–184.

42. *Ibid.*, p. 189.

43. *Ibid.*, p.190.

44. Kanahele, p. 798.

45. Hopkins, Jerry (Editor) "Another Category of Hawaiian Music: 'Haole Hawaiian.'" *Hailono Mele*, March, 1979, pp. 1–3. Hopkins, Jerry (Editor) "'Haole Hawaiian' Music Revisited—Auwe & Oh Boy!" *Hailono Mele*, October 1979, pp. 8–9.

46. Ejiri, Masakazu. *The Development of Waikiki, 1900–1949: The Formative Period of an American Resort Paradise*, p. 195.

47. *Ibid.*, pp. 197–201. Hopkins, Jerry. *The Hula: A Revised Edition*, pp. 80–81.

48. "I Went to Hilo." *Johnny Noble and his Hawaiian Music featuring Sam Alama*, recorded 1928. Words and music copyright Sam Alama.

49. McIntire's name is misspelled in the film as "McIntyre."

50. Reportedly, Kamehamaha's last words were "e 'oni wale no 'oukou i ku'u pono 'a'ole e pau," which Ted Fio Rito may have been trying to convey. These words have been translated in a number of ways, from "endless is the good that I have given you to enjoy" (http://www.greenbankhawaii.com/kamehameha.html) to "You need only act in my righteousness" (Kamehiro, Stacy L. *The Arts of Kingship: Hawaiian Art and National Culture of the Kalākaua Era*, pp. 46–47). Noble noted that "King Kamehameha" was published by Miller Music, Inc., a subsidiary of the Robbins Music Corp. "Unpublished [Johnny] Noble Manuscript Found In Gift to HMF." Originally published in the *Hailono Mele* newsletter, September 1979, http://ulukau.org/gsdl2.80/collect/hailono/cgi-bin/hailono?e=11off—1-v——101025-10-1-0—0-0-1&a=

d&cl=CL1&dl=DHMN005009.1.5&gpl=5&d= DHMN005009.1.5.

51. Severson, John. *John Severson's Surf.*

52. Lanza, Joseph. *Elevator Music: A Surreal History of Muzak, Easy-Listening, and Other Moodsong*, p. 32.

53. Owens also is credited with writing the delightfully double-entendre "Princess Poopooly Has Plenty Papaya (And She Loves to Give it Away)." He and his Royal Hawaiians recorded a memorable version with vocalist Hilo Hattie: https://www.youtube.com/watch?v=GMq_zXfXLIA. According to Don McDiarmid, Jr., however, his father, Don senior, actually wrote the tune along with Doug Renolds. Owens published it, then was sued by Renolds, who won the suit and ended up selling the rights to Owens anyway. Lyrics and back story at http://www.squareone.org/Hapa/p5.html.

54. Hopkins, Jerry. The Hula (1982), pp. 168–169.

55. Webley Edwards hosted the show until he suffered a heart attack in 1972 and was replaced by Danny Kaleikini for the program's remaining years. Al Kealoha Perry took over from Harry Owens as musical director in 1937 and Benny Kalama replaced the retiring Perry in 1967. Ruymar, pp. 46–47.

56. Godfrey met singer Haleloke Kahauolopua (1923–2004) while appearing on *Hawaii Calls*, then hired her to perform on his *Arthur Godfrey and His Friends* television show. He fired her, along with several other cast members, in 1955, but hired her to manage one of his hotels in Miami. A rumor persists that Haleloke was Godfrey's mistress. https://en.wikipedia.org/wiki/Arthur_Godfrey, http://people-vs-drchilledair.blogspot.com/2005/02/haleloke-est-morte_06.html.

57. Ejiri, pp. 202–205.

58. Ruymar, p. 47.

59. Rampell, Ed. "'Hawaii Calls' Again On Two Audiences." *Chicago Tribune*, Feb. 28, 1993, http://articles.chicagotribune.com/1993-02-28/travel/9303185744_1_hilton-hawaiian-village-hawaii–visitors-hawaii-calls.

Chapter Five

1. Vale, V., and Juno, Andrea (Editors). *Incredibly Strange Music, Volume I*, p. 142.

2. https://en.wikipedia.org/wiki/Eden_ahbez.

3. Hedley is discussed in the tiki chapter of this book.

4. "Russell Garcia (composer)," https://en.wikipedia.org/wiki/Russell_Garcia_(composer).

5. A portmanteau of the words "volcano" and "fog," vog is a mixture of sulphur dioxide and other volcanic gases blended with oxygen, humidity, and sunlight. Vog is blown by winds to various parts of the Big Island, creating a blanket that can last for days: http://www.konaweb.com/vog/index.shtml.

6. Hawaiian "slack key" guitar music is popular today in the islands and on the mainland. Its best-known players include Atta Isaacs, Ray Kane, Sonny Lim, and Gabby Pahinui. Slack key, however, refers to a tuning, rather than a musical style in itself. The strings of the guitar are loosened, or "slackened" and, traditionally, these tunings were developed by an individual player, passed down through generations, and kept as family secrets. It is therefore primarily an island-based technique, rather than being a transformational stylistic influence on mainland-based American guitarists. Kanahele, George S. (Editor), Berger, John (Revision). *Hawaiian Music and Musicians: An Encyclopedic History*, p. 751.

7. From Shuhei Hosokawa's essay "Martin Denny and the Development of Musical Exotica" in Hayward, Philip (editor). *Widening the Horizon: Exoticism in Post-War Popular Music*, pp. 83–84.

8. Sandy Warner is a member of a lengthy conga-line of beautiful women gracing the covers of phonograph albums, mostly in the pre-psychedelic era. That particular marketing technique was used to halt mostly male buyers in the act of hastily flipping through stacks of albums in record store bins, settling on the album photo of a comely lass, whose picture might entice them to buy the album. My own personal sexy cover ballot would be cast in favor of the unnamed woman in the fetching leopard-print dress, lying atop a set of vibes on Dave Pike's *Manhattan Latin* LP. I met Pike in Savannah, Georgia, in August 1992, and asked him about the woman. "Oh, you mean the hooker," he said. The story he related was that the photographer, Hal Buksbaum, had looked out the window and saw her walking past the recording studio. He invited her up, asked her to pose atop Dave Pike's vibes, and the photo was selected for the cover. Pike wrote me a short note on August 13 of that year, adding, "The hooker on the cover I never did meet, but she coincidentally looked extremely like my first wife."

In Martin Denny's case, he never met Sandy Warner until, as Dana Countryman documented in his 1997 interview, she sat in his audience one day: "I finally did get to see her. She came to Hawaii and sat in the audience right in front of the stage. After my performance, she sort of waved at me to come over. I walked over to her table, and it turned out that she was on her honeymoon. But I didn't know who she was. Then she said 'You and I have a lot in common.' And I said 'Oh, really? What's that?' She said, 'Well, I'm the girl on your album covers!' I looked at her, and said 'My God, you're right!' (Laughs) But that's the one and only time I ever met her." Countryman, Dana. "The Ultimate Martin Denny Interview." July 4, 1997.

9. I like Philip Hayward's more precise definition and differentiation of these terms. "World Music," he suggests, is best understood as "the recording and/or packaging of non-western musics for the western music market," while "World Beat" may be understood as "a syncretic/fusion practice involving musicians and/or musical styles from the West and 'non-West.'" Hayward, Philip (editor). *Widening the Horizon: Exoticism in Post-War Popular Music*, p. 17, nn. 38, 39.

10. McCoy Tyner: "African Village. https://www.youtube.com/watch?v=KMaya5Xef34. A live performance of this piece can be found at https://www.youtube.com/watch?v=XxXfhCvHTM8. Tyner also dabbled in exotica in his opening to the Antonio Carlos Jobim song "Once I Loved—O Amor Em Paz" from his *Trident* album of 1975, playing the celeste over an ostinato bass line, https://www.youtube.com/watch?v=WsKwRIHihYA.

11. Stix Hooper: "Jasmine Breeze." https://www.youtube.com/watch?v=tacsVgv3ZTE.

12. The remarkable breadth of this instrument, as played by Oswaldinho, can be seen at "A Cuica tem Voz nas mãos de OSWALDINHO": https://www.youtube.com/watch?v=t9xlRJbIfmk.

13. Examples would include the Fleetwood Mac 1968 single "Albatross" (https://www.youtube.com/watch?v=2KLvy9__xMg); Focus (1972): "Love Remembered" from the album *Focus 3* (https://www.youtube.com/

watch?v=g6-9OSABCOA); Jade Warrior's (1974) *Floating World* album (https://www.youtube.com/watch?v=iePV2WXMsq8), in particular the tune running from 6:10 to 8:40.

14. https://en.wikipedia.org/wiki/Quiet_Village.
15. Kraft, David, and Bohn, Ronald. "A Conversation with Les Baxter." *Soundtrack Magazine* No. 26, 1981.
16. Hayward, Philip (Editor). *Widening the Horizon: Exoticism in Post-War Popular Music*, pp. 57–59.
17. Spencer, James. *Les Baxter*, pp. 42–61.
18. Spencer, pp. 87–127, 148–151, 153–154.
19. https://en.wikipedia.org/wiki/Freddie_Slack.
20. Spencer, pp. 156–171, 176–177. The Les Baxter Trio recorded a four-song album for Discovery Records in 1951.
21. *Ibid.*, p. 192.
22. Hayward, p. 66.
23. The liner notes to the original album credit two songs to Baxter, the others to Sumac's husband, Moisés Vivanco. In 1992, Baxter refuted this: "Finally, to get them both off my ass, I wrote what I wanted which was a completely original collection of eight songs in an orchestral tonal poem similar to works of Ravel ... together we agreed upon titles and descriptions, once I was able to keep Moisés out of my hair." Spencer, James. *Les Baxter*, pp. 239–240.
24. Call, James, and Huestis, Peter. "Les Baxter Interviewed at His Palm Springs Home, Jan. 24, 1995."
25. Spencer, pp. 238–240.
26. A prime example of Baxter's artistic fall from grace would be his 1967 album *The Colors of Brazil*. Despite having a stellar lineup of jazz and Brazilian musicians, including flautist Paul Horn, guitarist John Pisano, keyboardist Clare Fischer, bassist Sebastiao Neto, and percussionist Paulinho Magalhães (the latter two of whom were playing in guitarist Bola Sete's group at the time), the music is overwhelmed by a mawkish "doo-doo" chorus. It's doubtful if any of those musicians would be thrilled with listing this LP on their resumés.
27. Spencer, pp. 288–289, 582.
28. Hayward, p. 57.
29. Countryman, Dana. "The Ultimate Martin Denny Interview," http://www.danacountryman.com/denny/denny1.html.
30. Hayward, p. 63.
31. The hotel opened in 1955, and management was taken over by Westin Hotels in May 1956 (in February 1961, Hilton Hotels assumed management). In 1957, Kaiser erected a Buckminster Fuller-designed 145-foot diameter geodesic dome on the property. It was aluminum-skinned, built in Kaiser's Oakland shipyard, shipped to Honolulu, and assembled in 20 hours. At the Hawaiian Village, it was used for concerts, events, and to record music—including several of Lyman's records—due to its unique acoustical properties. Lyman's group recorded the album *Pele* there, recording nightly from 1 to 6 a.m. after its shows ended at the Shell Bar. The dome was torn down in 1999 to make room for Hilton's Kalia Tower hotel addition. https://en.wikipedia.org/wiki/Hilton_Hawaiian_Village.
32. Denny would later produce and arrange Colón's Liberty Records albums *Sophisticated Savage* (1959) and *Chant of the Jungle* (1960).
33. Countryman, 1997.
34. Vale, p. 150.
35. Wechter formed the Baja Marimba Band in 1962.
36. Vale, p. 151. By 1959, Kaiser was busy building the 6,000-acre Hawaii Kai model city 12 miles north of Honolulu. He sold 50 percent of his interest in the Hawaiian Village Hotel to Conrad Hilton in 1961. "Henry J. Kaiser, Hawaiian Booster," The Antiplanner: http://ti.org/antiplanner/?p=552.
37. Adinolfi, Francesco. *Mondo Exotica: Sounds, Visions, Obsessions of the Cocktail Generation*, p. 7.
38. http://tikilagoon.blogspot.com/2012/09.
39. Byrnes, Kerry J. "Arthur Hunt Lyman (2/2/32–2/24/02)" http://www.okemosalumni.org/Arthur-Lyman.htm.
40. Vale, p. 151. Kramer's obituary can be found at http://obits.staradvertiser.com/2014/09/30/john-burnett-kramer.
41. From the liner notes of *The Exotic Sounds of Arthur Lyman at the Crecendo*. The notes omit the name of Augie Colón, but Colón's participation as co-originator has been confirmed by several sources.
42. Vale, p. 143.
43. *Ibid.*, p. 146.
44. *Ibid.*, p. 144.
45. Countryman, 1997.
46. Sources have mentioned that the instrument was a vibraphone or mariba, but daughter Kapiolani Lyman confirms that her dad told her it was a xylophone. Lyman, email to the author, Dec. 9, 2016.
47. Years later he would meet Hampton, who was flattered by Lyman's story. They would remain friends until their deaths, which occurred a few months apart in 2002. From a Harold Chang interview, filmed by Robert Joyce, at https://www.youtube.com/watch?v=opmsCShAum8.
48. Chinen, Nate. "Carrying a Tiki Torch for Band Leader Arthur Lyman." *Honolulu Star-Bulletin*, March 4, 2002.
49. Carroll, Rick. "The Mood Merchant of Exotic Music Casts His Spell Again in Waikiki." http://www.kevdo.com/exotica/arthurlyman-profile.html.
50. Chinen, 2002.
51. Severson, email to the author, Oct. 5, 2016.
52. Vale, pp. 150–151.
53. Kapiloani Lyman, email to the author, August 24, 2016.
54. Byrnes, Kerry J. "Arthur Hunt Lyman (2/2/32–2/24/02)."
55. Chinen, 2002.
56. "The Magic of the Exotica Lyman Years and More with Harold Chang" (interviewed by Leo Hura), https://www.youtube.com/watch?v=J8RDJiQXUzI, Dec. 4, 2014.
57. Kapiolani Lyman, email to the author, August 24, 2106.
58. Carroll.
59. "The Magic of the Exotica Lyman Years and more with Harold Chang" (interviewed by Leo Hura), https://www.youtube.com/watch?v=J8RDJiQXUzI, Dec. 4, 2014.
60. Carroll.
61. Byrnes.
62. Hyatt, Wesley, *A Critical History of Television's The Red Skelton Show, 1951–1971*, p. 167.
63. http://atvaudio.com/ata_search.php (search for "Lyman"); Chenault, Jeff. "Arthur Lyman: King of the Jungle Vibes." *Cool and Strange Music! Magazine*, Issue #25, May 2002—August 2002.
64. Chenault, Jeff, email to the author, Aug. 3, 2017.
65. Chenault, Jeff. "Arthur Lyman: King of the Jungle Vibes." *Cool and Strange Music! Magazine*, Issue #25, May 2002—August 2002.

66. Chinen.
67. Hayward, pp. 100–104.
68. Byrnes, Kerry J. "Paul Kenton Conrad (6/5/32–present)," http://www.okemosalumni.org/Paul-Conrad.htm.
69. Chenault, Jeff. "Arthur Lyman: King of the Jungle Vibes." *Cool and Strange Music! Magazine*, Issue #25, May 2002–August 2002.
70. Hayward, p. 97.
71. Marty Wilson, like Gene Rains, has disappeared from standard musical references, yet his recording will always have a place among aficionados of album cover art. *Jun'gala's* cover was extraordinarily racy, considering the era.
72. At the time of the recording, the genre of jazz alternately known as West Coast jazz, Chamber jazz, or Third Stream jazz, was riding a wave of popularity led by notables including the Modern Jazz Quartet, Chico Hamilton, Jimmy Giuffre, and Gunther Schuller, among others. Milt Jackson's vibes work with the MJQ would certainly have been known to Lyman.
73. Chenault, Jeff. "Arthur Lyman: King of the Jungle Vibes." *Cool and Strange Music! Magazine*, Issue #25, May 2002–August 2002.
74. Byrnes, Kerry J. "Paul Kenton Conrad (6/5/32–present)," http://www.okemosalumni.org/Paul-Conrad.htm.
75. http://www.tikiroom.com/tikicentral/bb/viewtopic.php?topic=8362&forum=11&39. Several of Stordahl's exotica-inspired pieces can be heard online. "Paradise," from *The Magic Islands Revisited*, opens with vibes and birdcalls (https://www.youtube.com/watch?v=aOBJfKkEWHw). The album *Jasmine and Jade* is replete with Les Baxter-inspired orchestrations and vibes. Especially notable is the tune "Lotus Land," heard at 31:35 (https://www.youtube.com/watch?v=pDEkU7IkAP4).
76. Byrnes, Kerry J. "Paul Kenton Conrad (6/5/32–present)." The lack of biographical information begs the question as to what Gene Rains' full name was, or whether, by some chance, it was a pseudonym. An Arthur Gene Rains did live in the United States during the musician's lifetime. Further details on the life of this mysterious and talented performer will be left to the investigative work of future historians.
77. "Robert Drasnin." https://en.wikipedia.org/wiki/Robert_Drasnin.
78. Raskin, who was best known for his studio, film, and television work, apparently recorded only one album. His *Exotic Percussion* album of 1960 is a renamed version of *Kapu*.
79. It's difficult to know where to start with Magne, although somewhat easier to end it. Riddled with debts and having suffered several nervous breakdowns, he died by his own hand via a drug overdose in a Novotel hotel in Cergy-Pontoise, France, on Dec. 19, 1984. He initially became known for his film scores, the most famous of which was probably the one he orchestrated for Jackie Gleason, *Gigot* (1962, dir. Gene Kelly). There were more than 100 others. His fame soared in 1969 when he built the residential Strawberry Recording Studio in his sprawling Le Château d'Hérouville, originally constructed in 1740, with its five-acre park an hour north of Paris. Among other amenities, it had 20 bedrooms and multiple kitchens and dining rooms. The legends who recorded there, including Pink Floyd, T. Rex, and Elton John, along with stories of their times at the chateau, could fill a very long book. You'd have to include the time Magne got the entire local fire department stoned on LSD. In 1970, at the age of 40, He picked up a 16-year-old hitch-hiking schoolgirl, Marie-Claude Calvet, and married her two years later, in November 1972. Christian Vander's Carl Orff-inspired rock group Magma played at the wedding. By 1973, he was out of the studio business, which had essentially bankrupted him (the studio, under different hands, continued to function until 1985). His now out-of-print autobiography, *"L'Amour de Vivre" (Love of Life)*, was published in 1980. Ernould, Franck. "Michel MAGNE: An Outstanding Man, a Visionnaire Composer," http://ernould.com/Artigrou/magneengl.html. As of 2017, a movement's afoot to restore the chateau and open a recording studio there again. See Schofield, Hugh. "The Return of the Honky Chateau." BBC News, Dec. 17, 2015. http://www.bbc.com/news/magazine-35152716. The chateau's website is http://honkychateau.fr.

80. For an idea of how far ranging the interpretations of, and personnel making exotica recordings were, two online discographies have an abundance of information. Virtually any recording referenced in either discography may be accessed online through *YouTube*. http://www.hipwax.com/music/exotica.html, https://en.wikipedia.org/wiki/Exotica.

81. Von Falkenhausen, Lothar. *Suspended Music: Chime-Bells in the Culture of Bronze Age China*, p. 114, 158–164. Von Falkenhausen's important text, written before the discovery of Marquis Yi's bells, is an extraordinary treatise on Bronze Age Chinese bells, with elaborate passages on everything from the construction of the bells to how—and why—they were played.

82. Major, John S., and So, Jenny F., in So, Jenny F. (Editor). *Music in the Age of Confucius*, pp. 15–19.

83. Marquis Yi's bianzhong instrument has been replicated and played, along with other replicated instruments found in the tomb, utilizing the music of today's composers. One example recorded at the Hubei Museum may be heard at https://www.youtube.com/watch?v=ZXEDv8bJ27M.

84. Bagley, Robert, in So, Jenny F. (Editor). *Music in the Age of Confucius*, p. 35.

85. Hear audio samples of these Thai instruments at: http://www.seasite.niu.edu/Thai/music/classical/instruments/khryang_tii2.htm.

86. "Victor-Charles Mahillon," https://en.wikipedia.org/wiki/Victor-Charles_Mahillon.

87. "Hornbostel–Sachs": https://en.wikipedia.org/wiki/Hornbostel%E2%80%93Sachs.

88. A somewhat dizzying list of instruments commonly appearing in percussion ensembles, including non-Hornbostel-Sachs classified whistles and Australian wobble boards, may be found at "List of percussion instruments": https://ipfs.io/ipfs/QmXoypizjW3WknFiJnKLwHCnL72vedxjQkDDP1mXWo6uco/wiki/List_of_percussion_instruments.html.

89. As cited above, Tyner's exotic celeste intro to "Once I Loved" from his *Trident* album of 1975 was an exception.

90. *Forbidden Island* (1958), https://www.google.com/search?q=forbidden+island+martin+denny&ie=utf-8&oe=utf-8.

91. For more on Leedy, visit http://www.leedydrum.com/since1895.html and https://www.findagrave.com/cgi-bin/fg.cgi?page=gr&GRid=33009903.

92. The words tremolo and vibrato are often inter-

changed. They create much the same harmonic effect, but through different technologies. Vibrato refers to rapid variance in pitch, which can be accomplished mechanically through devices including vibes resonator butterfly fans, spinning Leslie speakers in Hammond organ cabinets, and "whammy bars" on guitars. Tremolo, on the other hand, produces a similar aural effect through changes in electrical amplitude. https://www.sweetwater.com/insync/what-is-the-difference-between-vibrato-and-tremolo.

93. Goreing, Andrew. "Thank you, Herman E Winterhoff." http://www.hopestreetmarimba.com/thank-you-herman-e-winterhoff.

94. A noted percussionist, Gladstone was also a tireless inventor. In addition to the vibes dampener, he invented hollow vibes mallets, a double-action bass drum pedal, and a lighted baton, among other musical devices. Reed, Ted. "A Tribute to Billy Gladstone." *Modern Drummer* magazine, https://www.moderndrummer.com/article/october-1981-a-tribute-to-billy-gladstone.

95. "Thank you, Herman E Winterhoff." http://www.hopestreetmarimba.com/thank-you-herman-e-winterhoff.

96. Deagan's reputation as a tuned bell manufacturer was underscored by a period color postcard showing the Deagan Building, with its prominent clock tower, and a description, "The Home of Deagan Musical Bells, Chicago, U.S.A." http://www.hopestreetmarimba.com/thank-you-herman-e-winterhoff.

97. "Deagan Vibraharps," http://www.malletshop.com/deagan.cfm?id=51, http://www.deaganresource.com/vibraphones.html.

98. "All Girl" bands seemed to be a novelty that continued to draw crowds throughout the ensuing several decades. One of the more memorable was "Tipsy's Topless Band," consisting of two separate bands, the Ladybirds and the Hummingbirds, who performed at Tipsy's lounge in San Francisco's North Beach in the mid-to-late 1960s (http://allgirltoplessbands.weebly.com). The Ladybirds's topless act was documented for posterity with their performance in film *The Wild, Wild World of Jayne Mansfield* (1968, dir. Charles W. Broun Jr., Joel Holt, Arthur Knight), https://xhamster.com/videos/the-ladybirds-the-wild-wild-world-of-jayne-mansfield-4964530.

99. http://120years.net/musser-maestro-marimba-metron-clair-omar-musser-usa-1949.

100. http://rhythmdiscoverycenter.org/online collection/mussers-celestaphone.

101. https://library.ucsd.edu/dc/object/bb3687295j/_2.pdf.

102. http://www.conn-selmer.com/en-us/about/history/our-brands/musser.

103. http://amhistory.si.edu/archives/ac0188.pdf. Leedy brand drums, owned by Slingerland, however, were sold until 1965. As of 2003, Fred Gretsch owns the Leedy name, trademark, patents, and parts. http://www.leedydrum.com/since1895_3.html.

104. Goodman's was actually the fourth group to integrate a black player in live performances, preceded by bands led by Jimmy Durante (1918), Arthur Hand (1922), and Ben Bernie (1925). https://en.wikipedia.org/wiki/Charlie_Christian.

105. Watrous, Peter. "Lionel Hampton, Who Put Swing in The Vibraphone, Is Dead at 94." *New York Times*, Sept. 1, 2002.

Chapter Six

1. That's more than twice the number for "aloha shirt" at about 30,000, about 14,000 for "rattan furniture," and 50,000 for "hula."

2. Hukilau, Fort Lauderdale: https://thehukilau.com; Ohana, Lake George: http://www.fraternalorderofmoai.org/ohana; Tiki Oasis, San Diego: http://tikioasis.com.

3. http://www.fraternalorderofmoai.org.

4. von Busack, Richard. "Tiki It to The Limit." *Metro* (San Jose, CA), Jan. 4–10, 1996. http://www.metroactive.com/papers/metro/01.04.96/tiki-9601.html.

5. Covarrubias, enchanted by the exotic, was no stranger to lush Pacific islands, having sailed to Bali with his wife Rosa in 1930 and 1933. He published his book *Island of Bali* in 1937, illustrated by his paintings, sketches, and line drawings, and Rosa's photographs.

6. http://www.tikiroom.com/tikicentral/bb/about.php.

7. Bitner, Arnold. *Scrounging the Islands with the Legendary Don the Beachcomber*, pp. 15–17, 22.

8. Ibid., p. 27. Based on 365 days a year, Beach would spend about $374 a day on leis alone. A "Zombie" cost $32 in today's money, meaning he'd only have to sell 11 of them to even out the cost of the leis. It can be easily imagined, though, that Donn's high-flying male patrons would be eager to buy one for their female companions of the evening, further lowering the cost of the investment.

9. Ibid., p. 24. Antonio Cornero (1899–1955) was born in Lequio Tanaro, Italy. He and his family migrated to the United States in 1904. By 1926, he was bootlegging under the cover of a shrimping business. Over a storied career, he was also heavily involved in offshore vessels operating as floating casinos, illegal liquor manufacturing, and Las Vegas casinos and restaurants. In 1948, he survived four shots in the stomach, apparently delivered by influential people not wanting him to take his business to Baja California. He met his demise in 1955 over a game of craps in Las Vegas. Reportedly, his drink had been poisoned. It was said that Cary Grant's role as Joe Adams in the film *Mr. Lucky* (1943, dir. H.C. Potter) was based on Cornero, https://en.wikipedia.org/wiki/Anthony_Cornero http://www.americanmafia.com/Feature_Articles_26.html. Before settling on "Donn Beach," Gantt had experimented with at least two other names, "Donn Beach-Comber" and "Donn Beachcomber."

10. Glazner, Tim "Swanky." *Mai-Kai: History and Mystery of the Iconic Tiki Restaurant*, p. 13.

11. Berry, Jeff, in Kirsten, Sven A. *The Book of Tiki: The Cult of Polynesian Pop in Fifties America*, pp. 160–166.

12. Glazner, pp. 15–16, 27.

13. Bitner, pp. 25–26, 41.

14. Ibid., p. 27.

15. Berry, Jeff, in Kirsten, Sven A. *The Book of Tiki: The Cult of Polynesian Pop in Fifties America*, pp. 162–166.

16. Kirsten, Sven A. *The Book of Tiki: The Cult of Polynesian Pop in Fifties America*, p. 99.

17. Bitner, p. 28.

18. Torrence, Bruce. "Hollywood's Don the Beachcomber Restaurant." Hollywoodphotographs.com, Aug. 21, 2011.

19. Bitner, pp. 48–74.

20. Glazner, p. 19. "The Bronze Star Medal is awarded to any person who, after December 6, 1941, while serving in any capacity with the Armed Forces of the United

States, distinguishes himself or herself by heroic or meritorious achievement or service, not involving participation in aerial flight," http://www.americanwarlibrary.com/personnel/bronze.htm. "The Purple Heart is awarded to members of the armed forces of the U.S. who are wounded by an instrument of war in the hands of the enemy and posthumously to the next of kin in the name of those who are killed in action or die of wounds received in action. It is specifically a combat decoration," http://www.purpleheart.org/HistoryOrder.aspx.

21. Kirsten, p. 74.
22. Bitner, pp. 78–79.
23. Ibid., pp. 94–95.
24. Ibid., pp. 112–113, 115–144.
25. Sanburn, Curt. "The Way We Were: His Buildings Set the Tone for Waikiki. Maybe We Should Take Another Look at What Peter Wimberly Built." *Honolulu Weekly*, Dec. 20, 2000.
26. Ibid.
27. Kelly, Jim. "Last of '50s 'Tiki-Style' Hotels to Disappear from Waikiki." *Pacific Business News*, Feb. 27, 2005.
28. Kelly, 2005.
29. Kirsten, pp. 84–85.
30. Bitner, pp. 27–28.
31. Anderson, Susan Heller. "A Social Institution Called Trader Vic's." *New York Times*, Oct. 17, 1979.
32. Bergeron, Victor. "Trader Vic." *Frankly Speaking: Trader Vic's Own Story*, pp. xvii–xviii. As an aside, wooden legs were extremely tricky in that era, and those wearing them were often bound to their makers and fitters for a lifetime. The hardware, which consisted of nuts, bolts, and braces, would occasionally break down, leaving the bearer immobile. A friend with a prosthetic leg told me of a harrowing story that occurred in front of the State House on Beacon Street in Boston. "My wooden leg broke and I fell to the sidewalk. I couldn't qualify for an ambulance, because I wasn't hurt. A taxi wouldn't take me anywhere, because I'm 200 pounds and we couldn't get me in a cab. Plus, when I got home, I wouldn't be able to make it up the stairs. My leg guy was in Quincy and I got someone to call him. Fortunately, he was home, and drove into town to meet me so he could make a repair on the spot. The worst part of it was when a woman, seeing me lying on the sidewalk and feeling sorry for me, gave me a dollar bill. Totally humiliating."
33. http://www.sfgate.com/bayarea/article/1984-Victor-J-Trader-Vic-Bergeron-dies-3283926.php.
34. http://www.docomomo-wewa.org/architects_detail.php?id=149.Today, there are 19 Trader Vic's restaurants operting internationally, 11 of them in Arab countries.
35. http://www.oaklandmomma.com/2016/08/04/tropical-dreamin-hinky-dinks-mai-tai-roa-ae-one-legged-trader/.
36. "Frances Langford's Outrigger, Jensen Beach, FL (restaurant)," http://www.tikiroom.com/tikicentral/bb/viewtopic.php?topic=13970&forum=2.
37. One of Langford's best known roles was Blanche Bickerson, playing opposite Don Ameche's John Bickerson, in the radio and recording comedy, *The Bickersons*: https://www.youtube.com/watch?v=d2B2W4Ga2uc.
38. Glazner, pp.24–26.
39. Ibid., p. 63.
40. More about architect Charles F. McKirahan can be found at http://www.tropicfl.com/features/april4_2015-2.html. His son, Charles "Chuck" McKirahan, Jr., was also an architect, who, like his father, died at a relatively young age: http://articles.sun-sentinel.com/2007-07-19/news/0707190133_1_cindi-hutchinson-health-problems-broward-county.
41. Glazner, pp.27–29, 38–39.
42. Ibid., pp. 29–30, 45.
43. Ibid., pp. 49–60, 155, 160. The hair color code was eventually relaxed for red-haired server Ann Campbell. In the day, each girl had to weigh in, and those judged to be overweight were sent home. Weigh-ins were fairly normal in that era for female servers working in male-oriented dining and entertainment venues. It was also true for airline flight attendants, who were weighed weekly, given warnings if overweight, and had notes entered into their personnel files for violations. Glazner has a selection of Mai-Kai calendar girls on his website at www.swankpad.org/maikaical.
44. Sid Latham's book, *A Guide To Available Light Photography*, was published in 1956.
45. http://www.maikaihistory.com/2016/01/30/rare-mai-kai-8mm-movie.
46. Hartz-Seeley, Deborah S. "Looking to Own a Piece of Mai-Kai History?" *Miami Herald*, Aug. 1, 2010. Kirsten, Sven A. *The Book of Tiki: The Cult of Polynesian Pop in Fifties America*, pp. 138–139. The mystery girl in the film was Ann Campbell. Glazner, pp. 157–158.
47. Glazner, pp. 160–161.
48. Ibid., pp. 78–88.
49. Ibid., p. 134.
50. Ibid., pp. 127–133. Both Mossman and Lee eventually left after the Mai-Kai changed their initial financial arrangements.
51. Skelley, Steven. "Mai-Kai Restaurant and Polynesian Islander Revue." EDGE Media Network, Mar 2, 2012, https://www.edgemedianetwork.com/index.php?ch=entertainment&sc=theatre&sc2=reviews&sc3=performance&id=130561.
52. Glazner, pp. 89–92, 151.
53. Ibid., pp. 147–148, 151–152, 159.
54. http://maikai.com/images/stories/articlePDFS/MAI%20KAI%20HISTORY%2009.pdf.
55. https://thehukilau.com/about.
56. Perhaps Kientz's best-knowns design was of the horse on the Rolling Rock Beer bottle. Schmidt, Karen. "A New Book Revisits Columbus' Storied Tiki Temple, Gone but Not Forgotten." *Columbus Monthly*, Dec. 9, 2014.
57. Altenbach is often confused with his father, Bernard C. Altenbach (1904–1995), also an architect, http://www.tikiroom.com/tikicentral/bb/viewtopic.php?topic=18136&forum=5&start=450&hilite=kona.
58. Meyers, David, Walker, Elise Meyers, Chenault, Jeff, Motz, Doug. *Kahiki Supper Club: A Polynesian Paradise in Columbus*.
59. Whitaker, Jan. "Ohio + Tahiti = Kahiki." May 28, 2013, https://restaurant-ingthroughhistory.com/tag/coburn-morgan/.
60. Meyers, p.42.
61. Curtis, Wayne. "The Tiki Wars: How Do We Distinguish the Historic from the Sentimental?" *The Atlantic*, February 2001, https://www.theatlantic.com/magazine/archive/2001/02/the-tiki-wars/302084.
62. Meyers, p.139.
63. Ibid., pp. 71–72.
64. A 1965 recording, *Beachcomber Trio Live at the Kahiki*, was released on vinyl in 2010 by Jeff Chenault and Lee Joseph of Dionysus Records. Meyers, David, Walker,

Elise Meyers, Chenault, Jeff, Motz, Doug. *Kahiki Supper Club: A Polynesian Paradise in Columbus*, pp.48–49.

65. Other Kenley Players cities included Dayton and Akron, Ohio. Impresario John Kenley (1906–2009), who once danced with Martha Graham and died at the age of 103.

66. *Ibid.*, pp.126–129.

67. Motz, Doug. "History Lesson: The History of Columbus' Most Famed 'Lost' Restaurant—The Kahiki." Columbus Underground, Sept.11, 2012. http://www.columbusunderground.com/history-lesson-the-history-of-columbus-most-famed-lost-restaurant-the-kahiki.

68. Crane, Cheryl L., and Jahr, Chris. *Detour: A Hollywood Story*, pp.70–71.

69. *Ibid.*, pp.71–72, 89–90, 128.

70. *Ibid.*, pp. 155–156. Cheryl Crane famously stabbed to death mobster Johnny Stompanato in defense of her mother, actress Lana Turner, who had an ongoing, abusive relationship with him.

71. Meyers, p. 35.

72. Crawfordsville (Indiana) District Public Library, https://web.archive.org/web/20120331140535/http://www.cdpl.lib.in.us/lh/crane/index.html.

73. Crane, pp. 317, 323.

74. *Ibid.*, p. 330.

75. Now located in the White Point Royal Palms Beach Park, today the only vestige of Hedley's house is its foundation.

76. Hedley, Marilyn. *How Daddy Became a Beachcomber*, p. 60.

77. *Ibid.*, pp. 62–64, 70–72, 135–137.

78. Eugene Gustavovitch Berman (1899–1972) was born in St. Petersburg, Russia. He was a Surrealist and Neo-Romantic painter who studied with Pierre Bonnard and Edouard Vuillard. He moved to the United States in 1935. With his love for architecture, he designed sets for the New York's Metropolitan Opera, Igor Stravinsky, and George Ballanchine, among others. Brand-Fisher, Sonia. "Eugene Berman (1899–1972)," Caldwell Gallery, http://www.caldwellgallery.com/bios/berman_biography.html.

79. Hedley, p. 138.

80. Kirsten, pp. 74–77. See also: http://www.enterthetiki.com/content/eli-hedley.

81. Glazner, p.148.

82. The Down Under closed in 1996 and Casa Vecchia in 1994.

83. Lisa Kocab Meade (Kocab's former wife) provided important details of Kocab's life in an email to the author on July 17, 2017. See also: Williams, Mary C. "Al Kocab, Part Owner of La Vieille Maison, the Down Under." *Sun-Sentinel*, Feb. 19, 1994. Hartz-Seeley, Deborah S. "Looking to Own a Piece of Mai-Kai History?" *Miami Herald*, Aug. 1, 2010. For more on Kocab's business partner Leonce Picot, see Tanasychuk, John, and Yee, Ivette M. "Landmark Restaurant to Bid Au Revoir." *Sun-Sentinel*, May 25, 2006, http://articles.sun-sentinel.com/2006-05-25/news/0605250133_1_restaurant-la-vieille-maison-fort-lauderdale.

84. http://www.tikiroom.com/tikicentral/bb/viewtopic.php?topic=133&forum=1.

85. http://ngc-heritage.com/ngc-sixty.htm.

86. Whitaker, Jan. "Ohio + Tahiti = Kahiki." May 28, 2013, https://restaurant-ingthroughhistory.com/tag/coburn-morgan.

87. Oceanic Arts: http://www.oceanicarts.net/oa_about.htm#oahistory.

88. http://www.legacy.com/obituaries/skagitvalleyherald/obituary.aspx?page=lifestory&pid=183535508.

89. Many Witco pieces, particularly its wall art, are pedestrian. Its carved poodles, cats, and Don Quixote figures would go perfectly next to a velvet bullfight or "big eye" Keane painting.

90. http://www.enterthetiki.com/content/william-westenhaver.

91. https://en.wikipedia.org/wiki/Adventures_in_Paradise_(TV_series).

92. https://en.wikipedia.org/wiki/Hawaiian_Eye, "Henry J. Kaiser, Hawaiian Booster," The Antiplanner, http://ti.org/antiplanner/?p=552.

93. https://en.wikipedia.org/wiki/Hawaii_Five-O_(1968_TV_series).

94. Hopkins, note to the author, February 12, 2018.

95. https://en.wikipedia.org/wiki/Magnum,_P.I.

96. https://web.archive.org/web/20031207015023/http://www.indianajones.com/raiders/bts/news/news20030923.html.

97. https://en.wikipedia.org/wiki/Jake_and_the_Fatman.

98. https://en.wikipedia.org/wiki/Island_Son, http://www.afana.org/slatelane.htm.

99. Dooley, James. *Sunny Skies, Shady Characters: Cops, Killers, and Corruption in the Aloha State*, pp. 81–82, 167–171.

100. https://en.wikipedia.org/wiki/One_West_Waikiki.

101. Hopkins, Jerry. *Romancing the East*, pp. 129–137. https://en.wikipedia.org/wiki/Chang_Apana.

102. Huang Yunte. *Charlie Chan: The Untold Story of the Honorable Detective and His Rendezvous with American History*. https://www.npr.org/templates/story/story.php?storyId=129260913.

Chapter Seven

1. Pineapple Upside Down Cake probably wouldn't have been as pervasive without the invention of the Ginaca Machine, invented by Henry Gabriel Ginaca (1876–1918). In 1911, the Hawaii Pineapple Company's James Dole hired Ginaca to design a machine that would automatically trim off the tops and bottoms, and then core the pineapple. The machine increased pineapple production from 15 to 50 pineapples per minute (later versions would core 100 per minute), and required only three to five operators. Dole shipped its first million-case shipment in 1912. Dole, who loved sponsoring contests, took out an ad in nine women's magazines in 1925, asking for recipes using pineapple. One hundred winning entries would be published in a book, *Pineapple as 100 Good Cooks Serve It* (1926). Each recipe chosen earned the winner $50 (roughly $685 in today's money). Of the 60,000 entries, 2,500 were for Pineapple Upside Down Cake, which Dole proceeded to promote through additional advertising. Mrs. Robert Davis of Norfolk, Virginia, had the honor of having her Upside Down Cake recipe chosen as the ultimate winner. https://www.asme.org/about-asme/who-we-are/engineering-history/landmarks/167-ginaca-pineapple-processing-machine, http://feedmethat.com/recipe.php?id=54826%20Who%20Invented%20Pineapple%20Upside%20Down%20Cake?.html.

2. Schwartz, Harvey. *Rattan: Tropical Comfort Throughout the House*, pp. 12, 42, 93.

3. Levine, Bettijane. "Modern, Inside-Out: Paul T. Frankl's Sleek Simplicity Gave Rise to a California Look." *Los Angeles Times*, Aug. 16, 2007, http://articles.latimes.com/2007/aug/16/home/hm-frankl16.

4. Long, Christopher, *Paul T. Frankl and Modern American Design*, p. 103.

5. Long, pp. 115–123.

6. Hale's holdings were confiscated by Japan's military government at the outset of the Pacific war, to be used to manufacture goods for the Japanese war effort. Hale was interned in Santo Thomas. After the war, he rebuilt his businesses on a smaller scale, and died in 1952. "Frank H. Hale, Old Timer, Industrialist, and Friend of the *Filipino* People." Ateneo de Manila University, American Historical Collection, Rizal Library, http://rizal.lib.admu.edu.ph/ahc/exhibit/FrankHale.pdf.

7. Long, pp. 123–125.

8. Long, p. 139. It's not difficult to imagine the communication challenges in the Frankl-Puyat dynamic. Frankl undoubtedly was dealing with significant back orders, and his revenue stream would have been severely impacted by the gap between Hale's bankruptcy and his agreement to begin manufacturing with Puyat. Frankl would have needed the product as quickly as possible, a situation easily leading to misunderstandings in terms of quality control, a difficult situation to quickly resolve in the days when communication was usually by telegram and letter. Puyat, under his House of Puyat brand, had been making furniture and wood-related products, including billiard tables and bowling alleys, since the 1920s. By the 1960s, with approximately 350 woodworkers, it was estimated to be the largest furniture manufacturer in the East. Castro, Alex R. "The House that Puyats Built." Views from the Pampang, May 27, 2009. http://viewsfromthepampang.blogspot.com/2009/05/151-house-that-puyats-built.html.

9. Harvey Schwartz, conversation with the author, March 29, 2017.

10. Long, pp. 153, 164. Ficks Reed, founded in 1885 by Louis Ficks as the National Carriage and Reed Company, made furniture from materials including rattan, wicker, bamboo, and a number of hardwoods. In addition to Frankl, other designers crafting rattan furniture for Ficks included Paul László (1900–1993) and John B. Wisner (1913?–2007). https://www.justcollecting.com/miscellania/ficks-reed-furniture-company.

11. This is no exaggeration; several pieces of rattan in the author's collection were found lying in state in neighborhood gutters, waiting for the trash folks. Like many another appreciator of the decorative arts, I'm not adverse to dumpster diving for vintage rattan.

12. Harvey Schwartz, conversation with the author, March 12, 2017.

13. Ibid.

14. Ibid.

15. Ibid.

16. Schwartz undoubtedly still wishes he had the Allard. They're selling for more than $100,000 these days.

17. Harvey Schwartz, conversation with the author, March 12, 2017.

18. Ibid.

19. Shirley Ritts assisted on the set designs for Elvis Presley's *Blue Hawaii* film (1961, dir. Norman Taurog). She and husband Herb were the parents of photographer Herb Ritts. Shirley Ritts' fascinating obituary can be read at: http://articles.latimes.com/2008/mar/01/local/me-passings1.S2.

20. Harvey Schwartz, conversation with the author, March 12, 2017.

21. Schwartz, March 12, 2017. Tobi Smith, conversation with the author, March 15, 2017.

22. Smith, conversation with the author, March 15, 2017. Her "Aloha Spirit" exhibition resulted in the Schiffer book *Aloha Spirit: Hawaiian Art and Popular Design* (1998), with author's credit being given to photographer Douglas Congdon-Martin.

23. Schiffer, Nancy N. *Hawaiian Shirt Designs*, 1997.

24. Schwartz, p. 8.

25. Harvey Schwartz, conversation with the author, March 12, 2017.

26. Barnes, Brooks. "Dress the Set with Tears: It's a Wrap." *New York Times*, June 17, 2009. http://www.nytimes.com/2009/06/18/movies/18props.html.

27. Verrier, Richard. "20th Century Props Reopens Amid Production Rebound in L.A." *Los Angeles Times*, Aug. 18, 2015. http://www.latimes.com/entertainment/envelope/cotown/la-et-ct-20th-century-props-20150819-story.html.

28. Sika (known as sega in Indonesia) is a Tagalog term that includes Calamus caesius and other rattan species that are flexible and less than 1.5 cm in diameter. Buri is a term with Philippine origins, describing the splits made from the Corypha utan palm. Johnson, Dennis V., and Sunderland, Terry C.H. *Rattan Glossary and Compendium Glossary with Emphasis on Africa*.

29. Mehitabel today remains a family business, supplying a number of international furniture companies (http://www.mehitabel.com.ph/our-history). The island of Cebu is noted for its rattan manufacturing tradition. Other rattaners of the immediate post-war era would include Guillermo M. Figueroa, whose Rattan Arts (later Rattan Orginals) sold its own furniture and supplied others as well, including Mehitabel. Anticipating a shortage in rattan materials, he founded Casa Cebuana Incorporada in 1986, focusing on wooden furniture (http://www.casacebuana.com/aboutus.html). Two other rattan makers of the era were Florentino Atillo's (d. 1969) of Atillo's Rattan and Wood Industries and Rattan Pacifica, owned by a man named Nazareno. In the early 1970s, with Cebu's rattan forests being depleted, her five major suppliers, Mindanao Rattan, Standard Rattan, Alenter, Pacific Traders, and Norkis Trading, elected to sell what they had overseas. In 1976, rattan poles were banned for export, and the five companies instead became rattan furniture manufacturers themselves (http://www.cebu-philippines.net/furniture-manufacturers-cebu.html). With island rattan supplies continuing to dwindle, Cebu manufacturers began importing poles from Indonesia and Malaysia, but soon these countries banned the export of rattan poles. Today, Cebu's rattan manufacturers obtain their poles from neighboring islands, Burma (Myanmar), and Papua New Guinea. For more on the state of Cebu's furniture industry, see Zosa, Victoria. *Local Cooperation and Upgrading in Response to Globalization: The Case of Cebu's Furniture Industry*. De La Salle University, Manila. http://www.dlsu.edu.ph/research/centers/aki/_pdf/_concludedprojects/_volumei/zosa.pdf.

30. "John C. McGuire May 6, 1920—December 21, 2013." *San Francisco Chronicle*, Jan. 18, 2014. http://www.legacy.com/obituaries/sfgate/obituary.aspx?pid=169148700.

31. http://www.demischdanant.com/designers/jacques-dumond/biography.

32. In the era, a number of other designers crafted furniture that made extensive use of wicker and hardwoods or metal. Among these designers were John Eero Aarnio (b. 1932), John Risley, and Arthur Umanoff. Hotz, Alexa. "Trend Alert: Rattan Furniture Made Modern (Plus 15 to Buy)." July 22, 2016, Remodelista: https://www.remodelista.com/posts/trend-alert-rattan-furniture-made-modern-with-15-to-buy.

33. Johnson, Dennis V., and Sunderland, Terry C.H. *Rattan Glossary and Compendium Glossary with Emphasis on Africa*, 2004, p. v. See also Alth, Max, and Alth, Charlotte. *Rattan Furniture: A Home Craftsman's Guide*, p. 4.

34. Siebert, Stephen F. *The Nature and Culture of Rattan: Reflections on Vanishing Life in the Forests of Southeast Asia*, p. 23.

35. Alth, Max, and Alth, Charlotte. *Rattan Furniture: A Home Craftsman's Guide*, p. 3. In his book *The Nature and Culture of Rattan*, Stephen F. Siebert lists a number of larger diameter rattans that are also used for rattan furniture frames. These would include Calamus manan, C. oranatus, C.scipionum, C.peregrinus, and C. subinermis, none of which regenerate when cut. By the mid-1980s, the unregulated harvesting of *C. manan* had completely exhausted its supply in Peninsular Malaysia, Sumatra, and Borneo. Another large-diameter rattan used for furniture frames, C. zollengeri, like C. merrillii, does regenerate. Siebert, Stephen F. *The Nature and Culture of Rattan: Reflections on Vanishing Life in the Forests of Southeast Asia*, 2012, pp. 13, 63, 95–96.

36. Sanding off the silica outer layer is performed by large industrial sanders and the solution used to destroy fungus and insects, and prevent discoloration, is typically diesel or palm oil. Siebert, Stephen F. *The Nature and Culture of Rattan: Reflections on Vanishing Life in the Forests of Southeast Asia*, pp. 48, 72.

37. http://www.furniturecebu.com/cfif-ic/cfifFront/viewMaterial.php?mid=54.

38. *Design and Manufacture of Bamboo and Rattan Furniture*. United Nations Industrial Development Organization, 1976, p. 99.

39. *Ibid.*, pp. 63–65.

40. One may question how rigidly these rules are enforced. I own 20 or so pieces of rattan furniture made over the course of several decades. Judging by their durability and construction, it wouldn't surprise me if every one of them adhered to the rigorous Philippine Standard.

41. *Design and Manufacture of Bamboo and Rattan Furniture*. United Nations Industrial Development Organization, 1976, p. 67.

42. Alth, Max, and Alth, Charlotte. *Rattan Furniture: A Home Craftsman's Guide*. New York: Hawthorn, 1979. Barrett, Neil. "Back to Rattan: A Guide to Fabricating Furniture with This Versatile Building Material." *Popular Mechanics*, July 1986, pp. 92–97. https://books.google.com/books?id=GeMDAAAAMBAJ&printsec=frontcover&source=gbs_ge_summary_r&cad=0#v=onepage&q&f=false.

43. Siebert, Stephen F. *The Nature and Culture of Rattan: Reflections on Vanishing Life in the Forests of Southeast Asia*, pp. 21, 63.

44. Cebu's primacy as a source for larger diameter rattan seems to have been diminished in the post World War II years due to overharvesting and deforestation. According to Stephen Siebert, "Calamus merrillii cane … could still be found and was collected for domestic furniture from the few, small forest remnants on Leyte in 1983–84 and likely from a few other regions of the Philippines. However, it was not available in sufficient quantities to meet Filipino rattan furniture manufacturing needs, much less producers in other countries. I do not know when cane was depleted in Cebu, [a source that] was deforested quite early (see David M. Kummer *Deforestation in the Postwar Philippines*, University of Chicago Press, 1992). I suspect Cebu lost its forests and rattan shortly after World War II. Filipino and other rattan furniture manufacturers began shifting to Indonesia and Malaysia for C. manan, which many consider the highest quality cane for furniture framing and which had been harvested in Malaysia and Sumatra since English and Dutch colonial times, when Marcos and [his] cronies increased uncontrolled Dipterocarp harvesting in the 1960s—1970s. The process of logging/deforestation/conversion to oil palm plantations, and over-harvesting in Sumatra, Kalimantan and Malaysia eliminated wild cane supplies in those areas and resulted in large diameter rattan harvesting shifting to new species (e.g., C. zollingeri) in eastern Indonesia (esp. Sulawesi and Papua) and to other species where forests remained in other areas of SEA [Southeast Asia] (e.g., Myanmar)." Siebert, email to the author, Nov. 30, 2017. For more on contemporary rattan growing and harvesting practices, visit World Wildlife Fund rattan resources, http://wwf.panda.org/index.cfm?uGlobalSearch=rattan.

45. Cotter, Holland. "Cambodian Rattan: The Sculptures of Sopheap Pich." *New York Times*, May 2, 2013.

46. Photographs of the work of these designers may be seen at Hotz, Alexa. "Trend Alert: Rattan Furniture Made Modern (Plus 15 to Buy)." July 22, 2016. Remodelista: https://www.remodelista.com/posts/trend-alert-rattan-furniture-made-modern-with-15-to-buy.

47. Frank's Cane and Rush Supply, Huntington Beach, CA, http://www.franksupply.com/bamboo. H.H. Perkins Co., North Haven, CT, https://hhperkins.com/product-category/rattan-swords.

Chapter Eight

1. There is also a "lesbian chic" factor at play regarding men's Hawaiian shirts. A lesbian friend of mine favored Hawaiian shirts (along with motorcycles), and she mostly preferred men's aloha shirts to women's blouses because of the greater variety of patterns, especially in her larger size. She wasn't the type of person to care about which side the buttons faced. (Aloha, Sheila Rone, we'll always miss you).

2. Hawaiian shirts depicting military airplanes are the staple of numerous shops in the air and military museums of the United States. They are a staple of the Kalaheo label, made by RJC Ltd., founded by World War II veteran Robert J. Clancey in 1953. Reyn Spooner pioneered sports-themed Hawaiian style shirts beginning with those they created for the Los Angeles Dodgers.

3. Two Pacific island countries are also notable for their ethnically inspired garments. Indonesia is a leader in batik fashions and Fiji's manufacturers create an amazing array of Fijian fashions, often sporting abstract designs based on tribal and floral motifs. Country-labeled tropical shirts are made and sold in other islands as well, including Samoa and Rapa Nui (Easter Island). In Fiji's case, clothing manufacturing began on a mass scale after the coup in

1987, and the garment business has experienced highs and lows since then. For an analysis of Fiji's garment industry, see Donovan Storey's "End of the Line? Globalisation and Fiji's Garment Industry" (2006) essay from the book *Globalisation and Governance in the Pacific Islands: State, Society and Governance in Melanesia* at http://www.jstor.org/stable/j.ctt2jbj6w.15?seq=1#page_scan_tab_contents.

4. Agins, Teri. *The End of Fashion: The Mass Marketing of the Clothing Business*, p. 7.

5. The size Large of 1970 will usually—but not always—fit today's wearer as a size Medium. Shirts of a given era commonly reflect fashion trends popular on the mainland. Floral patterns of the late '60s and early '70s ranged from traditional, to op art, to abstract, to psychedelic.

6. Malihini and Tropicana were two of the companies that sold shirts with cloth-over-metal buttons.

7. Hope, Dale, with Tozian, Gregory. *The Aloha Shirt: Spirit of the Islands* (2000), pp. 12–13. In addition to being the co-author of the book, Hope, whose own story can be found later in this chapter, served in positions in the garment industry ranging from a laborer to an executive.

8. Brown, DeSoto, and Arthur, Linda. *The Art of the Aloha Shirt*, pp. 10–11. Kapa was traditional clothing made by pounding the bark of the wauke mulberry tree into cloth, then dye-transferring rectilinear and floral woodblock designs to the print. Kapa cloth was valued as a trade item and had a multitude of uses in addition to clothing. Because it lost adhesion when wet, it was supplanted as a clothing fabric with the arrival of westerners and their more durable manufactured materials. DeSoto Brown and Linda Arthur point out that similar cloth was known as tapa in other parts of Oceania, and many of the modern era's Hawaiian shirts consisting of woodblock patterns actually derive from Samoan culture. Bishop Street and Hilo Hattie were two of many companies offering cotton bark cloth tapa-patterned Hawaiian shirts.

9. Arthur, Linda B. *Aloha Attire: Hawaiian Dress in the Twentieth Century*, pp. 23, 28.

10. Chun, a master marketer, brought home a degree in economics from Yale. He eventually closed his profitable shop, became a bank director, and passed away at the age of 91 in 2006. Martin, Douglas. "Ellery Chun, 91, Popularizer of the Shirt that Won Hawaii." *New York Times*, June 8, 2000.

11. Brown and Arthur, pp. 28, 30, 34.

12. Hope (2000), pp. 16, 19, 21, 55.

13. Arthur, p. 26

14. Hope, Dale, with Tozian, Gregory. *The Aloha Shirt: Spirit of the Islands* (2nd revised edition, 2016), pp. 94, 103.

15. "Blind Woman Is Expert Button Maker," *Honolulu Advertiser*, Nov. 13, 1961, Section B, p. 9, quoted in Schiffer, Nancy N. *Hawaiian Shirt Designs*, p. 178.

16. Rath, Paula. "Beyond Island Wear." *Humanities, The Magazine of the National Endowment for the Humanities*, March/April 2013.

17. Hope (2000), pp. 38, 46.

18. Arthur, p. 66.

19. Thomas, Dana. *Deluxe: How Luxury Lost its Luster*, p. 104. Adrian Adolph Greenberg (1903–1959), known as "Adrian," was perhaps best known for his costuming for the film *The Wizard of Oz* (1939, dir. Victor Fleming, et al.).

20. Brown and Arthur, pp. 5, 30. Musa-Shiya sold shirts for the lesser amount in the 1930s, while the latter figure pertains to Hilo sales & Surplus in 1952.

21. Hope (2016), pp. 215–216.

22. *Ibid.*, p. 224.

23. *Ibid.*, pp. 108, 111.

24. Brown and Arthur (p. 55) note that Hawaiian motifs increased from 57 percent in the 1940s to 67 percent in the 1950s, while Japanese themes dropped from 18 to 9 percent in the same period.

25. Hope (2000), pp. 49–53.

26. *Ibid.*, pp. 106–107. Dale Hope credits merchandise manager Jeanette LeVine, who began working at Sears' Honolulu location in 1941, as being the first person to display Hawaiian shirts on hangers, rather than in stacks. As Brown and Arthur note, J.C. Penney opened its first island store in 1966 (p. 57).

27. The store, originally named for its founder, Heinrich Hackfeld, changed its name to Liberty House in 1918 as a response to anti-German rhetoric associated with World War I. It declared bankruptcy in the late 1990s and was purchased by Federated Department Stores, which changed the name of the stores to Macy's.

28. Gobindram "Goma" Watumull, born in Hyderabad, India, was the first person of Indian birth to be allowed to become a U.S. citizen. His wife, Ellen Jensen Watumull, was involved with the League of Women Voters in Hawaii and worked to rescind the Cable Act of 1922, which mandated that American-born women citizens lose their U.S. citizenship when marrying Asian non-citizens. https://www.saada.org/item/20140604-3590. See also Dye, Robert P. (Editor). *Hawaii Chronicles II: Contemporary Island History from the Pages of Honolulu Magazine*, pp. 208–210. For more on the Cable Act, see the chapter on race relations later in this book.

29. Clarke was a legend who is deserving of a biographical book. In addition to his other talents, he wrote a gossip column called "Hawaiian Holidays" that was carried in a number of large metropolitan stateside newspapers. Clarke married Gretchen Mary Klaus in 1954, who became his chief designer and ran the company with him until they folded the business in 2001. Waltah died a year later at the age of 89. McLellan, Dennis. "Waltah Clarke, 89; Brought Style of Hawaii to Mainland Fashion." *Los Angeles Times*, May 11, 2002. http://articles.latimes.com/2002/may/11/local/me-clarke11. Gretchen Clarke passed away in 2011 at the age of 78. For more on Clarke, see Hope (2016), pp. 192–193.

30. Camille Shaheen and Bill Tunberg, conversation with the author, May 14, 2017.

31. Hope (2016), p.159.

32. *Ibid.*, p.166

33. Camille Shaheen and Bill Tunberg, conversation with the author, May 14, 2017. Shaheen's shirts and cocktail dresses formed the core of the exhibit "Hawaii's Alfred Shaheen: Fabric to Fashion," held from May 18 to Aug. 8, 2010, at the San Jose, California-based Museum of Quilts and Textiles. From San Jose, the show traveled to the Arab American National Museum in Dearborn, Michigan, Washington State University in Pullman, and to the Maui Arts & Cultural Center in Kahului, where it closed on Oct. 29, 2011. Another exhibition, "Hi Fashion: The Legacy of Alfred Shaheen," was hosted by Honolulu's Bishop Museum from Nov. 12, 2012, to Feb. 4, 2013. http://www.alfredshaheen.com/museumexhibits.htm.

34. Arthur, p. 64.

35. Hope (2000), pp. 92–97.

36. Hope (2016) p. 120.

37. Camille Shaheen and Bill Tunberg contributed

greatly to ensure that the Alfred Shaheen story was historically accurate.

38. Arthur, p. 135. She also notes that by 1999, the Hawaiian garment industry had sales of $500,000 per year, exporting 30 percent ($165,000) of it to the mainland and other countries.

39. Thomas, pp. 200, 221.

40. The former was crafted by Colore Italiana, silk, made in China, the latter by Al Alvin, also silk and made in China. A similar shirt of the era was crafted of rayon in Indonesia by Ikan.

41. Dinger, Ed. "Pomare Ltd." International Directory of Company Histories. Retrieved May 14, 2017, from Encyclopedia.com: http://www.encyclopedia.com/books/politics-and-business-magazines/pomare-ltd.

42. For more on Romig, see Rath, Paula. "A Fashion Success Story that Began by Accident." *Honolulu Advertiser*, Nov. 6, 2003. http://the.honoluluadvertiser.com/article/2003/Nov/06/il/il02a.html.

43. Thomas, p. 324.

44. When the design did not sell out, remaining shirts might be sold through an in-house or separate retailer, with labels changed to reflect the name of the new seller.

45. Bailey, email to the author, Feb. 6, 2018. What's interesting about the Swayze shirt, which was an item auctioned from his estate and knocked down for $11,250, was that the auction catalogue was listed as having no manufacturer's label (https://www.julienslive.com/view-auctions/catalog/id/212/lot/88649). The film was made in 1990 and therefore the shirt was not exceptionally old by vintage standards. Bailey goes on to state: "We believe the record paid for an aloha shirt was $25,000 paid by Los Angeles dealer Brian Cohen (Snappy Gabs)... but that sale I think was part trade." Bailey's website is www.alohashirts.com.

46. Three examples are: a lily pond themed rayon shirt by Campia Moda (made in Korea, sold in Macy's), an abstract pineapple design cotton shirt by Croft & Barrow (made in Bangladesh, sold in Kohl's), and a cotton desert island-themed shirt by Massimo Supply Co. (sold in Target).

47. Paula Rath, from an article in the *Honolulu Advertiser*, 10/14/97, pp. C1–3, as quoted in Arthur, p. 164.

48. Minnesota, the home of Tommy Bahama cofounder (and namer) Bob Emfield, is a long way from Maui. Tommy Bahama was born in the late 1980s as a fictional character of leisure created by Emfield and his Generra Sportswear associate, sales exec Tony Margolis. They imaged everything from what he ate, drank, and smoked (Rocky Patel cigars, BTW), to how he looked and who he dated. Designer Lucio Dalla Gasperina was brought in as the third partner, who helped define the clothing Tommy Bahama wore. They came up with colorful silk tropical shirts with pattern-matching front panels and pockets, and coconut buttons, with two extra sewn to a tag on the inside seam. One critical fashion aspect of their shirts was vanity sizing, with shirts cut on the big side to allow men to wear a size smaller than they typically wear. Tommy, after all, was a bit on the paunchy side. The original store was located in Naples, Florida, and the trio eventually built the brand into a $500 million business before selling to Oxford Industries in 2003. Today, Bahama markets through department stores and its own channel of approximately 160 boutiques, two of which are in Honolulu, where it also has an outlet store. Ewoldt, John. "Tommy Bahama Menswear Brand Had its Roots in Minnesota 20 Years Ago." *Star Tribune*, Aug. 19, 2013.

49. Jamaica Jaxx is a trademark of Wellmax Apparel Limited, based in Kowloon, China. The similarity of Jaxx shirts to Tommy Bahama shirts can be remarkable. Typically, both are made of silk, with pattern-matching panels and pockets, and two extra buttons sewn into a tag on the inside seam. Each brand is predominantly made in China, but Jaxx silk shirts retail for well less than Bahama on the mainland. Without a brand tag and logo buttons, even experts might have a hard time telling them apart. So are these brands competitors or business partners? If the former, did Jaxx simply do a remarkable job of capturing the look and feel of the Bahama shirt? If the latter, might the Jaxx factory also be making the Bahama line under a separate label? For now, these questions will remain unanswered. Neither company took the opportunity to respond to inquiries.

50. Robillard, Albert B. (Editor). *Social Change in the Pacific Islands*, from the chapter "Where Is Social Change in Hawaii? The Reyn's Aloha Shirt," pp. 377–378. Robillard's Marxist-oriented analysis requires some degree of fortitude on the part of the reader to get through the abundance of scholarly jargon. His use of the word "discourse" seven times over six consecutive sentences may be unequaled.

51. Fujii, Jocelyn. *Tori Richard: The First Fifty Years*, p. 94.

52. Kahala Sportswear has a rich and varied history. The company was founded by George Brangier (1901–1987) and Nat Norfleet, Sr., in 1936 as Branfleet. A year earlier, Brangier had founded, along with partner Neil Miller, the Miller-Brangier men's shop. Soon, Miller returned to the mainland, Brangier sold the store, and then opened Branfleet with Norfleet. They began manufacturing shirts under the names Kahala and Duke Kahanamoku and changed the name of the company to Kahala Sportswear in 1937. The firm declared bankruptcy in the 1970s and the name was purchased by Dale Hope (son of Howard Hope) in 1987. Hope sold the company in 1991 to Local Motion, and stayed on as art director for several years. Hope returned as art director for Kalaha after the company was acquired by Tori Richard in 2006. Kahala is notable for its well-crafted designs and artists' collections.

53. Thanks to Josh Feldman and Jason Zaputo of Tori Richard for their contributions regarding the company history and philosophy.

54. Thanks also to Dale Hope for proving much of the historical information on the early days of Reyn Spooner. More can be found at Hope, Dale. "The Reyn Spooner Story: From Catalina to the Hawaiian Islands." The Museum of Hawaiian Shirts http://www.themohs.org/Reyn_Spooner.html.

55. According to Reyn's son Tim McCullough, Ruth Spooner, who was some 20 years older than Reyn McCullough, had no interest in running a larger business and sold her share to Reyn. She remained with the company in an advisory capacity for several more years. McCullough, conversation with the author, Feb. 22, 2016.

56. Earlier manufacturers often used welt pockets, providing a small slit to a pocket sewn onto the inside of the shirt.

57. McCullough is exact in stating his perspective on artists' shirts within the larger parameter of the entirety of Reyn's offerings: "During the 17-plus years Reyn

Spooner embraced this work within its three annual collections we developed and introduced under my development, I was strategic in disciplining the artist imagery so as to not exceed 25 percent of our offerings. We developed very considerable wearable images/designs from our core internal collective trust with absolutely no association to an external fine artist as this was the very 'soul' of our visual direction. The artist collection was valued 'plus' momentum for us yet, not the core of our own identity." Tim McCullough, email to the author, Sept. 25, 2017.

58. Reyn Spooner's post-1975 history and the discussion of shirt manufacturing processes were derived from the author's interview with Tim McCullough on Feb. 22, 2016, and updated Oct. 10, 2016.

59. Dale Hope, conversation with the author, Oct. 5, 2017. Hope also ensured that the hang tag write-ups were engaging. John Severson's were written by Steve Pezman, Yvonne Cheng's by Jocelyn Fujii, and Mike Cassidy's by Rell Sunn.

60. Tim McCullough, conversation with the author, Oct. 3, 2017. McCullough also remembers Reyn creating a line of shirts in the 1960s featuring designs created by artist Diego Varges. I have not been able to find any biographical data or work by this artist.

61. Reyn also produced at least one line of shirts addressing the surf culture, in its Phil Edwards Collection, honoring the surfing legend. About Edwards, known for being the first to successfully ride the Banzai Pipeline, Reyn's CEO Tim McCullough said: "I selected Phil because he is the closest fit to what Reyn Spooner represents, as a world class surfer, an ambassador of and for surfing, and a real gentleman." McCullough, email to the author, Oct. 15, 2017.

62. Braeger (d. 1974) was a legendary Southern California apparel retailer. See more at http://www.newportbeachindy.com/dick-braeger-garys-owner-cole.

63. Dale Hope, conversation with the author, Oct. 5, 2017.

64. Ron Anderson, conversation with the author, Oct. 6, 2017. Reynolds "Renny" Yater (b. 1932) is a noted surfboard builder whose shop remains continues to thrive in Santa Barbara. http://www.yater.com/history.html.

65. http://www.ronandersonart.com.

66. This was no mere spill. It was perhaps the most famous outrigger canoe wipeout in history. That day in 1980, watermen Tommy Holmes (1946–1993), Aka Hemmings (1953?–2012) and Hope attempted to ride a 20 foot canoe down a wave estimated at 25 to 35 feet at Avalanche, on Oahu's north shore. It left Holmes and Hemmings shaken, and Hope with a broken arm, fractured by an encounter with the iako, the spar that connects the hull with the float. Hope remembers sitting in a room waiting for his doctor and friend Lawrence Gordon to show up. Not wanting to risk giving a general anesthetic to a patient that might have also had a brain concussion, Gordon wrapped Hope's head in a towel, blocked the arm, and then performed the procedure while Hope was conscious. Hope spent the next four days in the hospital. Dale Hope, conversation with the author, Oct. 15, 2017. Without Hope able to continue as a member of the outrigger threesome, Holmes and Hemmings finished their day as a duo, their legendary wipeout documented at https://www.youtube.com/watch?v=DTkRNIVz2s4. More on Hemmings at http://www.staradvertiser.com/2012/03/31/breaking-news/waterman-aka-hemmings-dies-at-age-59-from-illness.

67. Dale Hope, email to the author, Oct. 15, 2017.

68. Nicky Black, conversations with the author, Oct. 9 and 11, 2017, and email to the author, Oct. 10, 2017. Nicky Black's mother, Cobey Black (1922–2014), was a noted journalist and author: Her book *Hawaii Scandal* (2002) chronicled the notorious Massie Case of 1932: http://obits.staradvertiser.com/2014/03/31/cobey-black-1922-2014.

69. Ronn Ronck in Buffet, Guy, and Ronck, Ronn. *The World of Guy Buffet*, pp. 15–17.

70. http://guybuffet.photoshelter.com/about.

71. Reyn's Tim McCullough recalls meeting Buffet: "My introduction was through Jim Killett of Lahaina Gallery, which was Guy's primary benefactor and outlet of his work. Jim's Gallery was a neighbor of ours at Reyn's at the Kapalua Bay Resort in the 1980's and a good friend. Guy and I discussed his work and we determined together where to start with his extensive collection. I would estimate we interpreted five dozen images combined of his noted Hawaiiana, culinary Cinematic as well as a few of his European inspired works." Email to the author, Sept. 25, 2017.

72. Guy Buffet, conversation with the author, Sept. 25, 2017.

73. Tim McCullough, email to the author, Oct. 15, 2017.

74. Guy Buffet, conversation with the author, Sept. 25, 2017.

75. Dale Hope, conversation with the author, Oct. 5, 2017.

76. http://michaelcassidyfineart.com.

77. Rath, Paula. "Local Artists Work Magic on Silk Clothing Lines." *Honolulu Advertiser*, April 8, 2002. http://the.honoluluadvertiser.com/article/2002/Apr/08/il/il01a.html.

78. Dale Hope, conversation with the author, Oct. 5, 2017.

79. Dale Hope, conversation with the author, Oct. 5, 2017.

80. Skindrud, Erik. "How Quiksilver Lost Its Soul and Ended Up in Bankruptcy Court." *OC Weekly*, Jan. 21, 2016. http://www.ocweekly.com/news/how-quiksilver-lost-its-soul-and-ended-up-in-bankruptcy-court-6910851.

81. Mike Field, conversation with the author, Oct. 3, 2017. Field's prints are displayed on his website at http://www.mfield.com/product-category/fine-art/art-prints.

82. Naoki Hayashi, conversation with the author, Oct. 12, 2017.

83. Tim McCullough, email to the author, Sept. 25, 2017.

84. Naoki Hayashi, conversation with the author, Oct. 12, 2017. Also referenced were O'Connor, Christina. "Very Fishy Art." MidWeek magazine, *Honolulu Star-Advertiser*, Dec. 17, 2013 http://www.midweek.com/naoki-hayashi and http://www.hawaiibeachcombers.com/hawaii-etc/hawaii-artists/naoki-hayashi.

85. Naoki Hayashi's website is http://www.gyotaku.com.

86. Avi Kiriaty, email to the author, June 12, 2015.

87. Dale Hope, email to the author, Sept. 9, 2016.

88. http://www.avikiriaty.com.

89. Miles' stylized signature on the shirt label has confused a number of collectors who mistakenly refer to his shirts as the "Miley" collection.

90. Miles Mason, emails to the author, May 20–21, 2015.

91. http://robertlynnelson.com/about-rln. About Robert Lyn Nelson, Tim McCullough writes: "Lovely guy to work with. We met in 1991 or so as I was so impressed with his exceptionally unique 'Two Worlds' style of aquatic painting, which was truly the very beginning of this perspective. Splitting the view-plane with the under and above water vision which naturally provides a double reality of our world and is very unique. And, unfortunately, his work has been broadly copied yet, not in any way near the realism and authenticity Robert captures in his work. He is the real god-father of the 'Two Worlds' style and I think we interpreted three or four of his works into wearable art at Reyn Spooner." Email to the author, Sept. 24, 2017.

92. Kampion, Drew. "John Severson (December 12, 1933-), http://www.surfline.com/surfing-a-to-z/john-severson-biography-and-photos_905.

93. Dale Hope, email to the author, Sept. 9, 2016.

94. John Severson's comments are from emails to the author dated from Sept. 30 to Oct. 7, 2016. John passed away on May 26, 2017. He was among the most enthusiastic contributors to this book. A short film on his life made was made in conjunction with his receipt of a Lifetime Achievement Award in 2011 from *Surfer Magazine*, which, of course, he founded. The video may be viewed at http://23breaths.blogspot.com/2011/12. See also http://www.ocregister.com/2017/05/28/surfer-magazine-founder-john-severson-dies-at-83.

95. Thomas, Paula. "Dietrich Varez: A Malihini's Legacy of Illuminating Hawaiian Culture and Legend." *Keola Magazine*, May–June 2017. https://keolamagazine.com/hawaii–island/hawaii–island-2017-may-june/dietrich-varez.

96. A collection of Varez' woodblock prints may be seen at http://volcanoartcenter.org/?s=Dietrich+Varez.

97. Thomas.

98. Tim McCullough, email to the author, Sept. 20, 2017. Varez and his wife live a no-frills, traditional rural lifestyle. Their property had no electricity for 30 years, they capture rainwater to supply their needs, and the road to their housed has been deemed "barely passable." https://en.wikipedia.org/wiki/Dietrich_Varez.

99. Ryan, Tim. "Big Island Artist Eddie Y Likes to Cut to the Chase." *Honolulu Star-Bulletin*, April 27, 2001 http://archives.starbulletin.com/2001/04/27/features/story3.html.

100. Harada, Wayne. "Painting in the Sand." *Honolulu Advertiser*—Island Life, April 26, 2001.

101. Tim McCullough, email to the author, Sept. 20, 2017. McCullough, a Big Island resident, particularly enjoyed working with Dietrich Varez and Eddy Y, who also reside on the island: "Both artists became good personal friends as we worked together through this period exchanging ideas for new shirt design concepts envisioned from the artists, as well as from myself. And as we all lived here on the Island of Hawaii we shared common interests and experiences as well as we knew some of the same people. It was an enriching process and I have only the highest level of respect for both artists as well as appreciation for their investment of their time and their talent in developing the beautiful Reyn Spooner shirt designs these collaborations brought to our devoted customers."

102. Eddy Y, conversation with the author, Sept. 19, 2017. Eddy's website is www.artofeddyy.com.

103. Hope (2016), p. 35.

104. HRH was named after Dale's father Howard R. Hope, and was also marketed as the His Royal Highness line.

105. Known as "The Queen of Makaha," Rell Kapoliokaehukai Sunn (1950–1998) was a pioneer in the world of women's surfing and a much-loved Hawaiian figure. More than 3,000 people attended her memorial, where her ashes were scattered over the water at Makaha, Oahu.

106. Hope, Dale, with Tozian, Gregory. *The Aloha Shirt: Spirit of the Islands* (2nd revised edition), 2016.

107. Hope, email to the author, Oct. 17, 2016.

Chapter Nine

1. Warshaw, Matt. *The History of Surfing*, p. 48. Warshaw's book remains the most comprehensive history of the sport, an invaluable resource. Young members of Hawaiian royalty were routinely sent to St. Mathew's Hall, also known as St. Matthew's Military Academy, in San Mateo, founded in 1865 by the Rev. Alfred Brewer. It closed in 1915. Horgan, John. "Hawaiian Connection in San Mateo Rooted in Education." *Mercury News*, Jan 18, 2018. https://www.mercurynews.com/2018/01/18/horgan-hawaiian-connection-in-san-mateo-rooted-in-education/.

2. Warshaw, pp. 23–24.

3. *Ibid.*, pp. 25–26.

4. The film clips may be seen at https://www.youtube.com/watch?v=dz32fG3Y2dY. For more on Bonine, see Lafrance, Adrienne. "Thomas Edison and the Origins of Surf Filmography." *The Atlantic*, Feb. 23, 2017, "Everything You Need to Know about Thomas Edison's 1906 Surf Film." Surfertoday.com, March 16, 2017, and http://www.victorian-cinema.net/bonine.php.

5. Newlin, Keith. "Jack London: Sailor." *BoatU.S.*, Dec. 2016.

6. Warshaw, pp. 43–44, 47.

7. *Ibid.*, pp. 45, 47.

8. The Outrigger Canoe Club today has more than 4,000 members. https://www.outriggercanoeclub.com/history.

9. Huntington was the nephew of Collis P. Huntington, one of the "Big Four" of transcontinental railroad fame. Some years after his uncle's death, Henry married his widow, Arabella Yarrington Huntington (1850?–1924). Arabella, an art collector, philanthropist, and real estate tycoon in her own right, was essential in building the art collection for the Huntington Library in San Marino, California. Born in a hardscrabble environment, she remained steadfastly private her entire life, and mandated that her private papers be burned at her death. She is worthy of a biography, although she left few clues of her origins and younger years. Slipek, Edwin. "Beyond the Boudoir: How Richmond Courtesan Arabella Huntington Became the Richest Woman in the World." *Style Weekly*, Jan. 10, 2012. https://www.styleweekly.com/richmond/beyond-the-boudoir/Content?oid=1653029.

10. Megowan, Maureen. "History of Redondo Beach." http://www.maureenmegowan.com/Pages/History-of-Redondo-Beach.aspx.

11. Warshaw, pp. 47–52.

12. Masters, Nathan. "Manhattan Beach: The City Built on Sand Dunes Celebrates Its Centennial." KCET, December 13, 2012. Dalton, Rex. "Manhattan: Isle's Sandman." *Daily Breeze*, Oct. 13, 1973.

13. Overtly playing with visiting women and drinking

didn't exactly fit into the book of rules at some establishments. Edward Kenneth Kaleleihealani "Dude" Miller, a champion swimmer and accomplished musician, ran the beach concession at the Moana Hotel for a number of years, and invited fellow members of the Hui Nalu club to join him there. His established code of conduct for them included no drinking, gambling, or "hands straying over female tourists." http://www.hawaiihistory.org/index.cfm?PageID=394.

14. Warshaw, pp. 52–53.
15. *Ibid.*, pp. 61–65, 72. See also "Tom Blake (surfer)." Wikipedia. https://en.wikipedia.org/wiki/Tom_Blake_(surfer).
16. "Tom Blake (surfer)." Wikipedia. https://en.wikipedia.org/wiki/Tom_Blake_(surfer). Much of the information in the Wikipedia article is derived from Lynch, Gary. *Tom Blake: The Uncommon Journey of a Pioneer Waterman.*
17. Warshaw, pp. 71–79.
18. http://digicoll.manoa.hawaii.edu/sos/index.php.
19. Toth, Catherine E. "Hawaii Surf Activist John Kelly Dies." *Honolulu Advertiser*, Oct. 5, 2007.
20. Warshaw, pp. 88, 95–96.
21. Therolf, Garrett. "Lunada Bay Surfer Gang Targeted by Class-Action Lawsuit." *Los Angeles Times*, March 29, 2016. http://www.latimes.com/local/lanow/la-me-ln-surfer-gang-class-action-20160329-story.html.
22. Despite this incident, Seaside Point surfers are surprisingly more amenable to Californians—who they know will be departing soon—than to Portlanders, whom they fear will become regular visitors. (Conversation between a Seaside surfer and the author, July 29, 2017.)
23. "Visitors Fed Up with Localism Use the Law to Fight Back." Ross Law, April 4, 2016, http://www.rosslawpdx.com/law-blog/2016/4/4/visitors-fed-up-with-localism-use-the-law-to-fight-back.
24. Chapin was also stepfather to the equally mercurial legendary surfer Miklos Sandor "Mickey Da Cat" Dora (1934–2002). McLellan, Dennis. "Miklos 'Miki' Dora, 67; Rebel Surfer." Jan. 5, 2002.
25. Warshaw, pp. 98–108.
26. Warshaw, Matt. *The History of Surfing*, pp. 137–138. Much of the information written on Bud Browne is contradictory. Among other sources referenced were http://www.budbrownefilmarchives.com/about and http://www.ocregister.com/2008/03/21/filmmaker-browne-won-surfers-respect.
27. Greg Noll. *Search for Surf*: https://www.youtube.com/watch?v=jsnDNkObXJg. See also Warshaw, Matt. *The History of Surfing*, p. 138.
28. Severson, interview with Nathan Howe, in Severson, John. *John Severson's Surf.* Bologna, Italy: Damiani, 2014.
29. *Ibid.*
30. *Ibid.* Two examples of Bass's fonts can be seen in posters for the films *The Man with the Golden Arm* (1955), and *Anatomy of a Murder* (1959). http://illusion.scene360.com/design/49712/saul-bass-anatomy-of-a-poster.
31. *Pacific Vibrations* can be seen at https://www.youtube.com/watch?v=CzhKDusI9as. Hosted by Robert Weaver, *The Surfer's Journal: 50 Years of Surfing on Film— John Severson* (2014? dir. Ira Opper) is an important 23-minute film that features Severson discussing his films and includes numerous clips: https://www.youtube.com/watch?v=7NiTmjo1kek.
32. Griffin, who died in a motorcycle accident, would be best known for his rock posters and edgy comics, produced in magazines including *Zap Comix* and *Snatch Comix*. He also did work for artist and car designer Ed "Big Daddy" Roth. Rick Griffin (USA): http://www.christiancomicsinternational.org/griffin_pioneer.html.
33. Kampion, Drew. "John Severson 1933–2017" https://surferart.com.
34. Warshaw, pp. 157–158. See also https://en.wikipedia.org/wiki/Gidget.
35. "Bruce Brown—'The Pioneer of Narrated Lifestyle Documentaries.'" http://www.brucebrownfilms.com/about/bruce-brown.
36. The career trajectories of the protagonists have followed radically different paths. August has been creating custom boards and promoting surfing events since 1974, https://robertaugust.com. Hynson has led a more peripatetic life, including spending significant amounts of time with counterculture communities. Schou, Nick. "Mike Hynson, Co-Star of 'The Endless Summer,' Resurfaces with Tales of the Brotherhood." *OC Weekly*, July 9, 2009. http://www.ocweekly.com/news/mike-hynson-co-star-of-the-endless-summer-resurfaces-with-tales-of-the-brotherhood-6413929.
37. Warshaw, pp. 228–229.
38. Berg, Tom. "The Poster that Changed Orange County." *Orange County Register*, Jan. 13, 2009. http://www.ocregister.com/2009/01/13/the-poster-that-changed-orange-county. Van Hamersveld went on to a storied career as an illustrator, especially noted for his rock posters and album covers, which included the Beatles' *Magical Mystery Tour* and the Rolling Stones' *Exile on Main Street*.
39. "Bruce Brown—'The Pioneer of Narrated Lifestyle Documentaries,'" http://www.brucebrownfilms.com/about/bruce-brown http://www.latimes.com/local/obituaries/la-me-bruce-brown-20171211-story.html.
40. Clark, who founded Clark Foam in 1961, graduated from Pomona College with degrees in math and physics. The firm was worth approximately $40 million when Clark abruptly closed it in 2005, destroying its molds and equipment in the process. At the time, it was estimated that 90 percent of all surfboards in the U.S. and 60 percent of those in the entire world used Clark's surfboard blank molds. Clark cited increasing pressure from the EPA over its choice of chemicals and equipment as well as lawsuits filed by former employees as the reasons for terminating his Laguna Niguel-based business. At its height, his catalogue offered some 70 different board blanks and he was shipping an estimated 1,000 blanks a day. Finnegan, William. "Blank Monday." *The New Yorker*, Aug. 21, 2006. http://www.newyorker.com/magazine/2006/08/21/blank-monday. For more on the aftermath of Clark's closing up shop, see Housman, Justin. "Clark Foam's Demise, 10 Years Later: A Decade after 'Blank Monday,' It's a Great Time to Be a Surfboard Customer." *Surfer*, Dec. 11, 2015. http://www.surfer.com/blogs/culture/clark-foams-demise-10-years-later-grubby-clark.
41. Bill Whitman, who surfed well into his 80s, gained later fame as a self-taught horticulturist, specializing in tropical fruits. He is credited as being the first person to grow mangosteen fruit outdoors in the United States. With brother Dudley, he built and patented an underwater camera that was used in several films, including *The Sea Around Us* (dir. Irwin Allen), winner of an Oscar for Best Documentary Feature Film in 1952. Karp, David. "Bill Whitman, 92, Is Dead, Scoured the Earth for Rare Fruit." *New*

York Times, June 4, 2007. http://www.nytimes.com/2007/06/04/us/04whitman.html?mcubz=3. For more on the Whitman brothers, see http://www.floridasurfmuseum.org/kahunas/east-west-william-francis-whitman-family and http://www.legendarysurfers.com/2011/09.

42. Warshaw, pp. 162–168, 212–215.
43. Snyder, Craig. "Hobie Alter: Industry Pioneer and Innovator." Skateboarding Heritage Foundation, http://www.skateboardingheritage.org/programsmenu/skateboardingheritagehalloffame/hobiealter.
44. https://en.wikipedia.org/wiki/Skateboarding.
45. Tim McCullough mentioned Phil Edwards as the Hobie Cat's co-designer. Email to the author, Sept. 30, 2017.
46. Hevesi, Dennis. "Hobie Alter, Innovator of Sailing and Surfing, Dies at 80." *New York Times*, March 31, 2014.
47. Guzman, Kara. "Thousands Paddle Out in Santa Cruz for Jack O'Neill." *Santa Cruz Sentinel*, July 9, 2017.
48. Taylor, Michael. "Hugh Bradner, UC's Inventor of Wetsuit, Dies." *San Francisco Chronicle*, May 11, 2008. http://www.sfgate.com/bayarea/article/Hugh-Bradner-UC-s-inventor-of-wetsuit-dies-3214987.php. See also "Obituary Notice Renowned Physicist and Inventor of Wetsuit: Hugh Bradner." Scripps Institute, May 8, 2008. https://scripps.ucsd.edu/news/2462.
49. Warshaw, p. 170.
50. Agostini, Kristin S. "Body Glove Co-Founder Bob Meistrell Dies on Boat during Catalina Paddleboard Race." *Daily Breeze*, June 17, 2013. http://www.dailybreeze.com/article/zz/20130617/NEWS/130618746, https://bodyglove.com/pages/company-history. The Meistrells were also scuba instructors whose students included Lloyd Bridges, Gary Cooper, Charlton Heston, and Richard Harris. They made customized suits for Bridges (which he wore in his television series *Sea Hunt*), and basketball star Kareem Abdul-Jabbar. Bob Meistrell also co-designed a number of one-man submarines, each named *Snooper*, which aided in searches for shipwrecks, downed aircraft, and municipal water pipe leakage. He expressed surprise that more people weren't enamored of plumbing ocean depths in a small cramped submersible."I can't believe anybody doesn't want to do it," was his response. He celebrated his 81st birthday by diving 81 feet, and then doubled it in remembrance of brother Bill. Chawkins, Steve. "Bob Meistrell Dies at 84; Co-Founder of Surfwear Firm Body Glove," *Los Angeles Times*, June 17, 2013, http://articles.latimes.com/2013/jun/17/local/la-me-bob-meistrell-20130618. Additional information on the Meistrells was sourced from Eisenstadt, Dave. "Famed Waterman Bill Meistrell, 1928–2006," *The Beach Reporter*, July 27, 2006, http://tbrnews.com/news/redondo_beach/famed-waterman-bill-meistrell/article_bfa0aa98-ad90-5828-b90a-b78b3fabc1a6.html.
51. I dived off Carmel's Monastery Beach on a cold December day in order to qualify for my PADI Advanced Underwater rating. In addition to the frigid temperatures, the surge was enormous. Six of us clung to a wildly seesawing rope 40 feet down with nearly zero visibility. Thirty minutes later, the divemaster gave us the thumbs-up sign, and we ascended, keeping an elbow hooked around the rope the whole time. "Worst conditions I've ever dived in," he said. "You guys all get your advanced rating by virtue of the fact that you didn't end up somewhere out in the Pacific."
52. Warshaw, pp. 170–171.
53. http://www.theinertia.com/oakley/christian-fletcher-wins-1989-surf-bout-opens-door-for-aerial-surfing. https://www.surfertoday.com/surfing/8016-how-to-do-an-aerial-in-surfing.
54. Warshaw, p. 436.
55. Donald Campbell's last ride may be witnessed at https://www.youtube.com/watch?v=4xemKc2In5Y.
56. Kaplan, Sarah. "Alec Cooke, the 'Evel Knievel' of the Dangerous Sport of Big Wave Surfing, Has Disappeared." *Washington Post*, Oct. 30, 2015. https://www.washingtonpost.com/news/morning-mix/wp/2015/10/30/alec-cooke-the-evel-knievel-of-the-dangerous-sport-of-big-wave-surfing-has-disappeared/?utm_term=.bb8f3e476dd3.
57. Warshaw, p. 409.
58. Kaplan. See also "Search for Surfer Alec "Ace Cool" Cooke Ends, Coast Guard Assumes the Worst." The Inertia, Nov. 3, 2015. http://www.theinertia.com/surf/search-for-surfer-alec-ace-cool-cooke-ends-coast-guard-assumes-the-worst.
59. Warshaw, p. 194.
60. Sherwood Ball, as quoted in Crowley, Kent. *Surf Beat: Rock'N'Roll's Forgotten Revolution*, p. 213.
61. Still playing today, the fiery Dale has lost none of his riotous technique. A 1995 version of "Misirlou" is a testament to the ageless and powerful performer: https://www.youtube.com/watch?v=lRH_70_Foow.
62. Szatmary, David P. *Rockin' in Time*, 8th edition, p. 73.
63. About the exotic musical scales that have found their place in Meshugga's music, Waldorf writes: "I think the 'Middle Eastern' scales come into surf music from several directions. Exotic melodies had been a part of popular music since at least the big band era—think Duke Ellington's 'Caravan'—plus the Latin music craze (mambo, bossa nova) and the popularity of Polka music all had made elements of the Middle Eastern/Eastern European scales familiar. That's the background when Dick Dale recorded 'Misirlou' in 1962 and I think that opened a lot of eyes to the expressiveness of the scales, particularly helpful for instrumental music! It was Dick Dale's 1963 recording of 'Hava Nagila' that inspired me to start Meshugga Beach Party. There were so many great Jewish melodies that hadn't been given the surf instro treatment, so it was an opportunity to combine my love of Jewish music with Surf Guitar!" Waldorf, email to the author, Aug. 2, 2017.
64. For more on the instrumental surf music phenomenon, the reader is directed to Kent Crowley's excellent history of the movement, *Surf Beat: Rock'N'Roll's Forgotten Revolution*.
65. The whistling on the two Ennio Morricone soundtracks was done by Alessandro Alessandroni (1925–2017), a veteran Italian musician and composer who first whistled on a film recording for composer Nino Rota. Morricone called upon Alessandroni to whistle on his Western film soundtracks. "It was a whistle that defined an era," Alessandroni said. "Everyone was imitating me; every western had a whistle like mine." Adinolfi, Francesco. *Mondo Exotica: Sounds, Visions, Obsessions of the Cocktail Generation*, pp. 200–201.
66. *Surfer* magazine founder John Severson introduced *The Quarterly Skateboarder*, the first magazine dedicated to the sport of skateboarding, in 1964. By the third issue, its name had changed to *Skateboarder Magazine*.

Chapter Ten

1. Gessler, Clifford. *Hawaii: Isles of Enchantment*, pp. 148, 150.
2. Skwiot, Christine. *The Purposes of Paradise: U.S. Tourism and Empire in Cuba and Hawaii.*, pp. 110–112.
3. Stannard, David E. *Honor Killing: How the Infamous "Massie Affair" Transformed Hawaii*, p. 27, n. 434.
4. Skwiot, 213.
5. Ibid., pp. 185–186. She cites W. Clement Stone, "The Man Whose Work Will Never End" in *Success Unlimited*, August 1957, p. 8.
6. Kuykendall, Ralph S., and Day, A. Grove. *Hawaii: A History from Polynesian Kingdom to American Commonwealth*, pp. 151–152, 235–237.
7. Ibid., pp. 92–96.
8. Ibid., pp. 96–97.
9. The pineapple, traditionally brought back to their home countries by visitors to Hawaii, was essentially a 20th century crop. Not indigenous to Hawaii, it is believed to have been brought to Hawaii by Spanish explorers. Unlike sugarcane, it can be grown at high elevations and is less dependent on irrigation. During the 1880s, several varieties were imported, including the Smooth Cayenne (Ananas comosus), which has a high sugar content and is well adapted to canning for export. James Drummond Dole (whose father's cousin was Sanford Ballard Dole, first president of the Republic of Hawaii) founded the Hawaiian Pineapple Company in 1901 and pineapples, originally harvested on Oahu, were planted the islands of Kauai, Hawaii and Maui. In 1922, the company bought almost the entire island of Lanai for pineapple production. It built docks, imported harvesting and processing equipment, and created housing for its workers. Kuykendall, pp.235–236.
10. Ibid., pp. 156–157, 210–212.
11. Ibid., p. 210.
12. https://en.oxforddictionaries.com/definition/eugenics.
13. https://en.wikipedia.org/wiki/Chinese_Exclusion_Act. A number of people judged to be "non-laborers" managed to live in the United States anyway. Writer Leslie Charteris, creator of *The Saint* series of novels, was one of them, while working as a Hollywood screenwriter for Paramount Pictures in 1932. Born Leslie Charles Bowyer-Lin in Singapore, Charteris' father was a Chinese physician, his mother was English. Because Charteris had "50 percent or greater Chinese blood," he was denied permanent residency and had to renew his temporary visitor's visa every six months. https://en.wikipedia.org/wiki/Leslie_Charteris. In 1947, U.S.-born actor Dean Jagger (1903–1991) was denied permission to marry his fiancée, New Yorker Gloria Lin, in California because her father was Chinese-born. State law at the time forbade "unions between Caucasians and Mongolians." "Film Actor, Secretary, Denied License to Wed." *Pottstown Mercury*, Jan. 25, 1947, p. 8. https://www.newspapers.com/clip/1321624/dean_jagger_encounters_prejudice_in_the.

The Chinese Exclusion Act was repealed by the Magnusen Act of 1943, by which time China had become a U.S. ally in World War II. It, however, did not repeal the prohibition of ethnic Chinese owning property or businesses, as was the law in a number of states. https://en.wikipedia.org/wiki/Magnuson_Act.

14. https://en.wikipedia.org/wiki/Immigration_Act_of_1924.
15. https://en.wikipedia.org/wiki/Yates_Stirling_Jr.
16. Stannard, pp.152, 441.
17. Ibid., pp. 321–322.
18. Ibid., p. 104.
19. Ibid., p. 153.
20. *American Experience: The Massie Affair* (2005, dir. Mark Zwonitzer) PBS, at the 47:00 minute mark: https://www.youtube.com/watch?v=pLgZzHtbPQ0.
21. Information in this paragraph was referenced in Stannard.
22. David Stannard, interviewed at the 39:19 minute mark at *American Experience: The Massie Affair* (2005, dir. Mark Zwonitzer). PBS: https://www.youtube.com/watch?v=pLgZzHtbPQ0.
23. Stannard, p.78. Such statistics would never have been kept on the mainland. As discussed later, it wasn't until 1947, when California struck down its anti-miscegenation statute, that any state legally allowed interracial couples to marry.
24. Schmitt, Robert C. *Historical Statistics of Hawaii*. Honolulu: University Press of Hawaii, 1977, p. 660. http://files.hawaii.gov/dbedt/economic/data_reports/Historical-Statistics-of-Hawaii.pdf.
25. Bailey, Beth, and Farber, David. *The First Strange Place: The Alchemy of Race and Sex in World War II Hawaii*, pp. 22, 23. Allen, Gwenfread. *Hawaii During the War Years: 1941–1945*, pp. 249, 381.
26. Bailey, p. 179. Allen, p.278.
27. More than 30,000 black servicemen and defense workers visited or were posted in Hawaii during World War II. Bailey and Farber provide a cogent and poignant discussion of both their challenges in coping with both Hawaii and the military in their chapter "Strangers in a Strange Land" (pp. 133–166). Significant numbers of Latinos and Asian Americans served as well. Because part of my focus is to illustrate the role of exotica—which includes interracial interactions—in challenging racial discrimination practices in the mainland United States, the examples in this chapter relate largely to interactions between Caucasian men and women of color. A more complete analysis would include a larger color, gender, and gender identity spectrum. Such subjects might include men of color and Caucasian women, intra and inter-color relationships, and critical but probably anecdotal dynamics relating to the lesbian, gay, and transgender world. Gay and lesbian relationships remain an under-documented facet of the mainlander-islander dynamic. So were experiences with mahu, third gender persons who filled a traditional spiritual and social role within Hawaiian culture. This role was paralleled in other parts of Polynesia and the Pacific, and included maohi in Tahiti, fakaleiti in Tonga, and faafafine in Samoa. Native transgender relations with mainland-origin GIs and war workers, as well others within the greater LGBT stratum, are worthy of further scholarly exploration. For more on the subject, see Sanburn, Curt. "The Mahu and Aikane Traditions in Old Hawaii." *Honolulu Weekly*, July 20, 2011. http://kumuhina.tumblr.com/post/26465852292/the-mahu-and-aikane-traditions-in-old-hawaii.
28. I'm reminded of the quote from footballer George Best (1946–2005), in summing up his career: "I spent a lot of money on booze, birds [women] and fast cars—the rest I just squandered."
29. Schmitt, p. 661.

30. Allen, pp. 231–232, 235, 240.

31. Naval History and Heritage Command "U.S. Navy Personnel in World War II: Service and Casualty Statistics." https://www.history.navy.mil/research/library/online-reading-room/title-list-alphabetically/u/us-navy-personnel-in-world-war-ii-service-and-casualty-statistics.html.

32. Bailey, p. 43, 50, 95, 191–192.

33. *Ibid.*, pp. 235–236 n19, 237 n24.

34. "Gender Histories and Heresies." *Radical History Review*, Issue 52, Winter 1992, pp. 57, 60. The traditional Western concept of sexuality is just one of the many of its moral precepts that are often far-removed from or in direct conflict with those of the East and Oceania. Others are worth noting as well. Particularly in the United States, the individual social constructs of contrarianism and confrontation can be highly valued. Conflict, as a means of striving for or achieving a social or political goal, is suggestive of a narrative that evokes the concept as practically a reward in itself. Such endemic Yankee traits were powerful elements in the movement that led to the conquest of the continental United States. They enabled the nation to win battles, wars, and territories. Contrarianism, confrontation, and conflict were a big part of the story in how businesses were unionized, how women got the right to vote, and how racial groups carried on the struggle for equality, on the streets and in the courts. They are as American as applejack. Another perception trades on the alleged docility of Asian and Pacific peoples. Westerners often equate the traditional Asian and Oceanic customs of politeness and civility with docility, subservience, and submission. Historically, it may be argued, the United States was blind-sided by the Japanese war machine on December 7, 1941, at least partly by the failure to recognize the underlying intelligence and social and political awareness of its adversary. These were cloaked from Western eyes by the Eastern and Oceanic physical bearing and tactful language that fairly, it seemed, screamed subservience to a major world power. This public demeanor was misread by a number of American interests as a philosophy based on submission, Nanking notwithstanding. It was a lesson that Westerners would learn again decades later in a nation called Vietnam.

35. Chernin, Ted. "My Experiences in the Honolulu Chinatown Red-Light District." *The Hawaiian Journal of History*, vol. 34, 2000, pp. 212–213.

36. I've not been able to determine closing time for brothels. During the war, blackout hours were determined by sunset, varying from 6:30 p.m. to 8:30 p.m. It was extended to 9 p.m. in Feb. 1942, and 10 p.m. in May of that year. Allen, p. 126.

37. Bailey and Farber state that the women worked at least 20 days out of every month. They cite several accounts that state that each prostitute serviced 100 men a day. Bailey, pp. 98–101, 234 n12.

38. The figure of 75 cents per photo is from Imada, Adria L. *Aloha America: Hula Circuits Through the U.S. Empire*, pp. 220, 325 n29. Hopkins, Jerry *The Hula* (1982), p. 99, notes the figure for topless photos.

39. Bailey, p. 131. Allen, pp. 349–350, 388.

40. *Ibid.*, p. 112.

41. *Ibid.*, p. 100.

42. Allen, p. 268. For more on the prostitutes' strike, see Bailey, pp. 123–124, 240–241, n. 37.

43. Allen, p. 403, lists the number of post-war GIs settling in Hawaii. See also Bailey, pp. 46, 194, 252–253 n. 57.

44. Born Rosalie Matilda Kuanghu Chou, Han Suyin (1916–2012) was the Eurasian daughter of a Chinese father and Flemish mother.

45. The role of Dr. Han Suyin, the Eurasian female protagonist, was given to Jennifer Jones, a Caucasian. Things really came full circle with director Lewis Milestone's *Mutiny on the Bounty* (1962). The interracial romance portrayed in the film famously evolved into reality when co-stars Marlon Brando and Tarita Teriipaia married each other.

46. Michener's article, which appears on pages 124 through 141 of the February 21, 1955 issue of *Life* magazine, can be read at https://books.google.com/books?id=LFQEAAAAMBAJ&pg=PA124&lpg=PA124&dq=Pursuit+of+Happiness+by+a+GI+and+a+Japanese+Michener&source=bl&ots=BkxzaO1Kgk&sig=xHEotzoMPlzWs1fE3m4FdDMxkno&hl=en&sa=X&ved=0ahUKEwiCkK6s4dbZAhUZ3YMKHY2ACmYQ6AEIJzAA#v=onepage&q=Pursuit%20of%20Happiness%20by%20a%20GI%20and%20a%20Japanese%20Michener&f=false.

47. The Pfeiffers' story is documented in Shibusawa, Naoko. *America's Geisha Ally: Reimagining the Japanese Enemy*, p.48.

48. The statistics are from Hopkins, Jerry. *Romancing the East*, pp. 142–146.

49. Gobindram "Goma" Watumull, born in Hyderabad, India, was the first person of Indian birth to be allowed to become a U.S. citizen. He is briefly discussed in this book's chapter on the Hawaiian shirt. For more on the Cable Act, see https://en.wikipedia.org/wiki/Cable_Act.

50. https://en.wikipedia.org/wiki/Perez_v._Sharp.

51. https://en.wikipedia.org/wiki/Loving_v._Virginia. Stolberg, Sheryl Gray. "50 Years After Loving v. Virginia." *New York Times*, June 11, 2017. https://www.nytimes.com/2017/06/11/us/50-years-after-loving-v-virginia.html.

52. Initially, the film was banned in the state of Georgia. It was later accepted when Barnes, history textbook in hand, convinced state school authorities to the veracity of the peer relationship. Alexander, Geoff. *Films You Saw in School: A Critical Review of 1,153 Classroom Educational Films (1958–1985) in 74 Subject Categories*, pp. 143–144.

53. Alexander, Geoff. *Films You Saw in School: A Critical Review of 1,153 Classroom Educational Films (1958–1985) in 74 Subject Categories*, p. 246. *Vacances en Bretagne* (1970, dir. Pierre Sisser) may be viewed at https://archive.org/details/TouteLaBandeVacancesEnBretagne.

54. The five-page Pew study, in its entirety, makes for fascinating reading. Livingston, Gretchen, and Brown, Anna. "Intermarriage in the U.S. 50 Years After Loving v. Virginia: One-in-Six Newlyweds Are Married to Someone of a Different Race or Ethnicity." Pew research Center, May 18, 2017. http://www.pewsocialtrends.org/2017/05/18/intermarriage-in-the-u-s-50-years-after-loving-v-virginia.

55. Ortega, Josuém and Hergovich, Philipp. "The Strength of Absent Ties: Social Integration via Online Dating." Oct. 2, 2017, pp. 21–23. https://arxiv.org/pdf/1709.10478v1.pdf.

56. Kopf, Dan. "Why Is Interracial Marriage on the Rise?" Priceonomics, Sept. 1, 2016, https://priceonomics.com/why-is-interracial-marriage-on-the-rise.

Afterword

1. Barton, Charles. *Howard Hughes and His Flying Boat* (Rev.), p. 13.
2. Hughes, testimony before the Senate Special Committee to investigate the national defense hearings, Aug. 7, 1947, as quoted in Barton, p. 190.
3. Barton, p. 217.
4. *Ibid.*, pp. 233–234.

Appendix B

1. MacMillan made more than 30 expeditions to the arctic. Among his many achievements was compiling and Inuktitut dictionary. https://en.wikipedia.org/wiki/Donald_Baxter_MacMillan.
2. Bryant, John H., and Cones, Harold N. *Zenith Trans-Oceanic: The Royalty of Radios* (2nd ed.), pp. 8–9.
3. *Ibid.*, p. 12.
4. *Ibid.*, pp. 72, 80, 153. The B600 is widely considered the last tube portable radio ever manufactured in the United States.
5. *Ibid.*, p. 120.

Bibliography

Books

Adamson, Jeremy. *American Wicker: Woven Furniture from 1850 to 1930*. Washington, D.C.: Smithsonian Institution, 1993.
Adinolfi, Francesco. *Mondo Exotica: Sounds, Visions, Obsessions of the Cocktail Generation*. Durham, NC: Duke University Press, 2008.
Agins, Teri. *The End of Fashion: The Mass Marketing of the Clothing Business*. New York: William Morrow, 1999.
Alexander, Geoff. *Academic Films for the Classroom: A History*. Jefferson, NC: McFarland, 2010.
Alexander, Geoff. *Films You Saw in School: A Critical Review of 1,153 Classroom Educational Films (1958–1985) in 74 Subject Categories*. Jefferson, NC: McFarland, 2014.
Allen, Gwenfread. *Hawaii During the War Years: 1941–1945*. Kailua, Hawaii: Pacific Monograph, 1999. Originally published in Honolulu: University of Hawaii Press, 1950.
Allen, Jim, and James Austin. *Hulaland: The Golden Age of Hawaiian Music*. Sherman Oaks, CA: Rock Beat Records, 2015.
Allen, Roy. *The Pan Am Clipper: The History of Pan American's Flying Boats, 1931 to 1946*. London: Amber, 2000.
Alth, Max, and Charlotte Alth. *Rattan Furniture: A Home Craftsman's Guide*. New York: Hawthorn, 1979.
Arthur, Linda B. *Aloha Attire: Hawaiian Dress in the Twentieth Century*. Atglen, PA: Schiffer, 2000.
Augustin, Laura Maria. *Sex at the Margins: Migration, Labour, Markets, and the Rescue Industry*. London: Zed, 2007.
Bailey, Beth, and David Farber. *The First Strange Place: The Alchemy of Race and Sex in World War II Hawaii*. New York: Free, 1992.
Barley, Nigel. *White Rajah: A Biography of Sir James Brooke*. London: Little, Brown, 2003.
Barton, Charles. *Howard Hughes and His Flying Boat* (rev. ed.). Vienna, VA: Charles Barton, 1998.
Bergeron, Victor "Trader Vic." *Frankly Speaking: Trader Vic's Own Story*. New York: Doubleday, 1973.
Birtles, Philip J. *De Havilland Comet*. London: Ian Allan, 1990.
Bitner, Arnold. *Scrounging the Islands with the Legendary Don the Beachcomber*. Lincoln, NE: iUniverse, 2007.
Britsch, R. Lanier. *Moramona: The Mormons in Hawaii (Mormons in the Pacific Series)*. Laie, HI: Institute for Polynesian Studies, Brigham Young University, Hawaii, 1989.
Brooke, James, Sir. *The Private Letters of Sir James Brooke, K.C.B., Rajah of Sarawak: Narrating the Events of His Life, from 1838 to the Present Time, Vol.1*. London: Richard Bentley, 1853.
Brown, DeSoto, and Linda Arthur. *The Art of the Aloha Shirt*. Honolulu: Island Heritage, 2002.
Bryant, John H., and Harold N. Cones. *Zenith Trans-Oceanic: The Royalty of Radios* (2nd ed.). Atglen, PA: Schiffer, 2008.
Buffet, Guy, and Ronn Ronck. *The World of Guy Buffet*. San Francisco: Cameron, 1999.
Congdon-Martin. Douglas. *Aloha Spirit: Hawaiian Art and Popular Design*. Atglen, PA: Schiffer, 1998.
Covarrubias, Miguel. *Island of Bali*. New York: Alfred A. Knopf, 1946.
Crane, Cheryl L. and Chris Jahr. *Detour: A Hollywood Story*. New York: Arbor House, 1988.
Crowley, Kent. *Surf Beat: Rock'N'Roll's Forgotten Revolution*. New York: Backbeat, 2011.
Davies, R.E.G. *Airlines of the United States since 1914*. Washington, D.C.: Smithsonian Institution Press, 1972.
Day, A. Grove (Editor.). *Mark Twain's Letters from Honolulu*. Honolulu: University of Hawaii Press, 1975.
Design and Manufacture of Bamboo and Rattan Furniture. Vienna, Austria: United Nations Industrial Development Organization, 1976.
Dooley, James. *Sunny Skies, Shady Characters: Cops, Killers, and Corruption in the Aloha State*. Honolulu: University of Hawaii Press, 2015.
Dover, Ed. *The Long Way Home: A Journey Into History with Captain Robert Ford* (Revised). Albuquerque, NM: Ed Dover, 2008.
Dye, Robert P. (Editor). *Hawaii Chronicles II: Contemporary Island History from the Pages of Honolulu Magazine*. Honolulu: University of Hawaii Press, 1997.

Eastwood, A.B., and J. Roach. *Piston Engined Airliner Production List*. West Drayton, England: AJ Aviation, 2007.
Ejiri, Masakazu. *The Development of Waikiki, 1900–1949: The Formative Period of an American Resort Paradise*. May 1996. University of Hawaii at Manoa Ph.D. Thesis. http://hdl.handle.net/10125/9303.
Evans, Tom D., et al. *A Field Guide to the Rattans of Lao PDR*. Kew, England: Royal Botanic Garden, 2001.
Feather, Leonard. *The Encyclopedia of Jazz*. New York: Crown, 1960.
Felske, Lorry, and Beverly Rasporich (Editors). *Challenging Frontiers: The Canadian West*. Calgary: University of Calgary Press, 2005.
Forbes, David W. *Encounters with Paradise: Views of Hawaii and its People, 1778–1941*. Honolulu: Honolulu Academy of Arts, 1992.
Francillon, Rene J. *Boeing 707: Pioneer Jetliner*. Osceola, WI: MBI, 1999.
Francillon, Rene J. *Skyleaders DC-1 through DC-7: The Douglas Propliners*. Newbury Park, CA: Haynes North America, 2011.
Fujii, Jocelyn. *Tori Richard: The First Fifty Years*. Honolulu: TR, 2006.
Gauguin, Paul. *Noa Noa*. San Francisco: Chronicle, 1994.
Germain, Scott E. *Lockheed Constellation & Super Constellation*. North Branch, MN: Specialty, 1998.
Gessler, Clifford. *Hawaii: Isles of Enchantment*. New York: D. Appleton-Century, 1937.
Glazner, Tim "Swanky." *Mai-Kai: History and Mystery of the Iconic Tiki Restaurant*. Atglen, PA: Schiffer, 2016.
Hayward, Philip (Editor). *Widening the Horizon: Exoticism in Post-War Popular Music*. Sydney, Australia: John Libbey, 1999.
Hedley, Marilyn. *How Daddy Became a Beachcomber*. Bloomington, IN: Author House, 2006.
Heimann, Judith M. *The Airmen and the Headhunters*. Orlando, FL: Harcourt, 2007.
Hope, Dale, with Gregory Tozian. *The Aloha Shirt: Spirit of the Islands*. Hillsboro, OR: Beyond Words, 2000.
Hope, Dale, with Gregory Tozian. *The Aloha Shirt: Spirit of the Islands* (2nd revised edition). Ventura, CA: Patagonia, 2016.
Hopkins, Jerry. *Elvis in Hawaii*. Honolulu: Bess, 2005.
Hopkins, Jerry. *The Hula*. Hong Kong: Apa Productions, 1982. Hopkins' first edition contains an abundance of hula lore. The second edition (see below), revised by another writer, had a number of unfortunate shortcomings, including reduced text and biographies, bowdlerized photography, no filmography, and an uncorrected index, much to Hopkins' chagrin.
Hopkins, Jerry. *The Hula: A Revised Edition*. Honolulu: Bess, 2011. (See notes to the first edition, above).
Hopkins, Jerry. *Romancing the East*. Hong Kong: Tuttle, 2013.
Horvat, William J. *Above the Pacific*. Fallbrook, CA: Aero, 1966. https://aviation.hawaii.gov/wp-content/uploads/2017/02/Above-the-Pacific-by-William-J.-Horvat-1966.pdf.
Huang Yunte. *Charlie Chan: The Untold Story of the Honorable Detective and His Rendezvous with American History*. New York: W.W. Norton, 2011.
Imada, Adria L. *Aloha America: Hula Circuits Through the U.S. Empire*. Durham, NC: Duke University Press, 2012.
Johnson, Dennis V., and Terry C.H. Sunderland. *Rattan Glossary and Compendium Glossary with Emphasis on Africa*. Rome, Italy: Food and Agriculture Organization of the United Nations, 2004.
Jones, Geoff. *Douglas DC-3: 80 Glorious Years*. Stroud, England: Fonthill, 2015.
Kamehiro, Stacy L. *The Arts of Kingship: Hawaiian Art and National Culture of the Kalākaua Era*. Honolulu: University of Hawaii Press, 2009.
Kanahele, George S. (Editor), John Berger (Revision). *Hawaiian Music and Musicians: An Encyclopedic History*. Honolulu: Mutual, 2012.
Kirsten, Sven A. *The Book of Tiki: The Cult of Polynesian Pop in Fifties America*. Köln, Germany, Taschen, 2000.
Krantz, Lynn Blocker, Nick Krantz and Mary Thiele Fobian. *To Honolulu in Five Days: Cruising Aboard Matson's S.S. Lurline*. Berkeley: Ten Speed, 2001.
Kuykendall, Ralph S., and A. Grove Day. *Hawaii: A History from Polynesian Kingdom to American Commonwealth*. New York: Prentice-Hall, 1948.
Lanza, Joseph. *Elevator Music: A Surreal History of Muzak, Easy-Listening, and Other Moodsong*. New York: St. Martin's, 1994.
Larkins, William T. *The Ford Tri-Motor, 1926–1992*. West Chester, PA: Schiffer, 1992.
Linnéa, Sharon. *Princess Ka'iulani: Hope of a Nation, Heart of a People*. Cambridge, England: Wm. B. Eerdmans, 1999.
Lofgren, Orvar. *On Holiday: A History of Vacationing*. Berkeley: University of California Press, 1999.
Long, Christopher. *Paul T. Frankl and Modern American Design*. New Haven, CT: Yale University Press, 2007.
Long, Christopher. In Kaplan, Wendy (Editor). *California Design, 1930—1965: Living in a Modern Way*. Cambridge, MA: MIT, 2011.
Lynch, Gary. *Tom Blake: The Uncommon Journey of a Pioneer Waterman*. Corona del Mar, CA: Croul, 2001.
Lynes, Russell. *The Tastemakers: The Shaping of American Popular Taste*. New Yok: Dover, 1980 (originally published 1955).
Mahony, Bertha, Louise P. Latimer and Beulah Folmsbee. *Illustrations of Children's Books: 1744–1945*. Boston: Horn, 1947.
Marryat, Frank S. *Borneo and the Indian Archipelago with Drawings of Costume and Scenery*. London: Longman, Brown, Green, and Longmans, 1848.
McCarty, Louis P. (Editor). *The Statistician and Economist, Volume 23, 1905–1906*. San Francisco: L.P. McCarty, 1906.

McWilliams, Peter. *Ain't Nobody's Business If You Do: The Absurdity of Consensual Crime in a Free Society.* Los Angeles: Prelude, 1993.
Meyers, David, Elise Meyers Walker, Jeff Chenault and Doug Motz. *Kahiki Supper Club: A Polynesian Paradise in Columbus.* Mt. Pleasant, SC: Arcadia, 2014.
Papanikolas, Theresa, with DeSoto Brown. *Art Deco Hawaii.* Honolulu: Honolulu Museum of Art, 2014.
Robillard, Albert B. (Editor). *Social Change in the Pacific Islands.* London: Kegan Paul International, 1992.
Ruymar, Lorene (Editor). *The Hawaiian Steel Guitar and its Great Hawaiian Musicians.* Anaheim Hills, CA: Centerstream, 1996.
Said, Edward W. *Orientalism.* New York: Vintage, 1979.
Schiffer, Nancy N. *Hawaiian Shirt Designs.* Atglen, Pennsylvania: Schiffer, 1997.
Schmitt, Robert C. *Historical Statistics of Hawaii.* Honolulu: University Press of Hawaii, 1977. http://files.hawaii.gov/dbedt/economic/data_reports/Historical-Statistics-of-Hawaii.pdf.
Schwartz, Harvey. *Rattan: Tropical Comfort Throughout the House.* Atglen, PA: Schiffer, 1999.
Severin, Tim. *In Search of Robinson Crusoe.* New York: Basic, 2002.
Severson, John. *John Severson's Surf.* Bologna, Italy: Damiani, 2014.
Shibusawa, Naoko. *America's Geisha Ally: Reimagining the Japanese Enemy.* Cambridge, MA: Harvard University Press, 2010.
Siebert, Stephen F. *The Nature and Culture of Rattan: Reflections on Vanishing Life in the Forests of Southeast Asia.* Honolulu: University of Hawaii Press, 2012.
Skwiot, Christine. *The Purposes of Paradise: U.S. Tourism and Empire in Cuba and Hawaii.* Philadelphia: University of Pennsylvania Press, 2010.
Smith, Richard. *Rickenbacker.* Anaheim Hills, CA: Centerstream, 1987.
So, Jenny F. (Editor). *Music in the Age of Confucius.* Washington, D.C.: Smithsonian Institution, 2000.
Souhami, Diana. *Selkirk's Island: The True and Strange Adventures of the Real Robinson Crusoe.* New York: Harcourt, 2005.
Spencer, James. *Les Baxter.* Huntington Beach, CA: James Spencer, 2016.
Stannard, David E. *Honor Killing: How the Infamous "Massie Affair" Transformed Hawaii.* New York: Viking, 2005.
Stephens, Harold. *Painted in the Tropics: The Life and Times of Swiss Artist Theo Meier.* Garberville, CA: Wolfenden, 2013.
Stevenson, Robert Louis. *South Sea Tales.* Oxford, England: Oxford University Press, 1996.
Stindt, Fred A. *Matson's Century of Ships.* Kelseyville, CA: Fred A. Stindt, 1982.
Stone, Scott C.S. *Yesterday in Hawaii: A Voyage Through Time.* Waipahu, Hawaii: Island Heritage, 2003.
Szatmary, David P. *Rockin' in Time,* 8th ed. Upper Saddle River, NJ: Pearson, 2014.
Thomas, Dana. *Deluxe: How Luxury Lost its Luster.* New York: Penguin, 2007.
Todaro, Tony. *The Golden Years of Hawaiian Entertainment, 1874–1974.* T. Todaro, 1974.
Tosches, Nick. *Country: Living Legends and Dying Metaphors in America's Biggest Music* (Revised). New York: Charles Scribner's Sons, 1985.
Twain, Mark (Samuel L. Clemens). *Roughing It.* Chicago: American Publishing Company, 1872.
Vale, V., and Andrea Juno (Editors). *Incredibly Strange Music, Volume I.* San Francisco: Re/Search, 1993.
Vale, V., and Andrea Juno (Editors). *Incredibly Strange Music, Volume II.* San Francisco: Re/Search, 1994.
Van der Linden, F. Robert. *The Boeing 247: The First Modern Airliner.* Seattle: University of Washington Press, 1991
Veronico, Nicholas A. *Boeing 377 Stratocruiser.* North Branch, MN: Specialty, 2002.
Von Falkenhausen, Lothar. *Suspended Music: Chime-Bells in the Culture of Bronze Age China.* Berkeley: University of California Press, 1993.
Waddington, Terry. *Douglas DC-8.* Miami: World Transport, 1996.
Warshaw, Matt. *The History of Surfing.* San Francisco: Chronicle, 2010.
Webb, Nancy, and Jean Francis. *Kaiulani: Crown Princess of Hawaii.* New York: Viking, 1962.
Willmott, H.P. *B-17 Flying Fortress.* New York: Gallery, 1980.
Worden, William L. *Cargoes: Matson's First Century in the Pacific.* Honolulu: University of Hawaii Press, 1981.
Yellin, Emily. *Our Mothers' War: American Women at Home and at the Front During World War II.* New York: Free, 2004.

Articles

Adams, Wanda A. "A Complicated Dance." *Honolulu Weekly,* May 30, 2012. http://honoluluweekly.com/story-continued/2012/05/a-complicated-dance.
Agostini, Kristin S. "Body Glove Co-Founder Bob Meistrell Dies on Boat during Catalina Paddleboard Race." *Daily Breeze,* June 17, 2013. http://www.dailybreeze.com/article/zz/20130617/NEWS/130618746.
Aguiar, Eloise. "Japan Hooked on Hula and the Ukulele." *Honolulu Advertiser,* July 11, 2005. http://the.honoluluadvertiser.com/article/2005/Jul/11/ln/507110329.html.
Anderson, Susan Heller. "A Social Institution Called Trader Vic's." *New York Times,* Oct. 17, 1979. http://www.nytimes.com/1979/10/17/archives/a-social-institution-called-trader-vics-mai-tai-cocktail.html.
Barnes, Brooks. "Dress the Set with Tears: It's a Wrap." *New York Times,* June 17, 2009. http://www.nytimes.com/2009/06/18/movies/18props.html.

Barrett, Neil. "Back to Rattan: A Guide to Fabricating Furniture with This Versatile Building Material." *Popular Mechanics*, July, 1986, pp.92–97. https://books.google.com/books?id=GeMDAAAAMBAJ&printsec=frontcover&source=gbs_ge_summary_r&cad=0#v=onepage&q&f=false.

Berg, Tom. "The Poster That Changed Orange County." *Orange County Register*, Jan. 13, 2009. http://www.ocregister.com/2009/01/13/the-poster-that-changed-orange-county.

Brown, DeSoto. "Beautiful, Romantic Hawaii: How the Fantasy Image Came to Be." *The Journal of Decorative and Propaganda Arts*, vol. 20, 1994, p. 252.

Burlingame, Burl. "Prints of the Sea." *Honolulu Star-Bulletin*, Feb. 5, 2007. http://archives.starbulletin.com/2007/02/05/features/story01.html.

Call, James, and Peter Huestis. "Les Baxter Interviewed at His Palm Springs Home, Jan. 24, 1995." *Hypno Magazine*, Spring 1995. http://www.tamboo.com/baxter/baxinterview/index.html.

Carroll, Jerry. "The Palace That Alma Built / Philanthropist Spreckels Almost Single-Handedly Brought Legion into Being." *San Francisco Chronicle*, Oct. 29, 1995. http://www.sfgate.com/entertainment/article/The-Palace-That-Alma-Built-Philanthropist-3020125.php.

Chawkins, Steve. "Bob Meistrell Dies at 84; Co-Founder of Surfwear Firm Body Glove." *Los Angeles Times*, June 17, 2013. http://articles.latimes.com/2013/jun/17/local/la-me-bob-meistrell-20130618.

Chenault, Jeff. "Arthur Lyman: King of the Jungle Vibes." *Cool and Strange Music! Magazine*, Issue 25, May–August 2002.

Chernin, Ted. "My Experiences in the Honolulu Chinatown Red-Light District." *The Hawaiian Journal of History*, vol. 34, 2000. https://evols.library.manoa.hawaii.edu/bitstream/10524/228/2/JL34209.pdf.

Chinen, Nate. "Carrying a Tiki Torch for Band Leader Arthur Lyman." *Honolulu Star-Bulletin*, March 4, 2002. http://archives.starbulletin.com/2002/03/04/features/index.html.

Cotter, Holland. "Cambodian Rattan: The Sculptures of Sopheap Pich." *New York Times*, May 2, 2013. http://www.nytimes.com/2013/05/03/arts/design/cambodian-rattan-the-sculptures-of-sopheap-pich.html.

Dalton, Rex. "Manhattan: Isle's Sandman." *Daily Breeze*, Oct. 13, 1973. http://manhattanbeachhistorical.org/mb-sand-to-waikiki.

Downes, Lawrence. "Arthur Lyman, 70, King of the Jungle Vibraphone." *New York Times*, March 3, 2002. http://www.nytimes.com/2002/03/03/nyregion/arthur-lyman-70-of-hawaii-king-of-the-jungle-vibraphone.html.

Eisenstadt, Dave. "Famed Waterman Bill Meistrell, 1928–2006." *The Beach Reporter*, July 27, 2006. http://tbrnews.com/news/redondo_beach/famed-waterman-bill-meistrell/article_bfa0aa98-ad90–5828-b90a-b78b3fabc1a6.html.

Ewoldt, John. "Tommy Bahama Menswear Brand had Its Roots in Minnesota 20 Years Ago." *Star Tribune*, Aug. 19, 2013. http://www.startribune.com/tommy-bahama-menswear-brand-had-its-roots-in-minn-20-years-ago/220288151.

Finnegan, William. "Blank Monday." *The New Yorker*, Aug. 21, 2006. http://www.newyorker.com/magazine/2006/08/21/blank-monday.

Fraser, G. Gerald. "Enid Markey, Actress, Dead; Starred In First Tarzan Film." *New York Times*, Nov. 16, 1981. http://www.nytimes.com/1981/11/16/obituaries/enid-markey-actress-dead-starred-in-first-tarzan-film.html.

Gee, Pat. "'Gift of aloha' Was Face of Matson: Pualani Mossman / 1916–2006." *Honolulu Star-Bulletin*, May 10, 2006. http://archives.starbulletin.com/2006/05/10/news/story07.html.

"Gender Histories and Heresies." *Radical History Review*, 52, Winter 1992.

Guzman, Kara. "Thousands Paddle Out in Santa Cruz for Jack O'Neill." *Santa Cruz Sentinel*, July 9, 2017. http://www.santacruzsentinel.com/article/NE/20170709/NEWS/170709720.

Harada, Wayne. "Painting in the Sand." *Honolulu Advertiser*, Island Life, April 26, 2001.

Hartz-Seeley, Deborah S. "Looking to Own a Piece of Mai-Kai History?" *Miami Herald*, Aug. 1, 2010. http://maikai.com/images/stories/articlePDFS/chairarticle_080910.pdf.

Hevesi, Dennis. "Hobie Alter, Innovator of Sailing and Surfing, Dies at 80." *New York Times*, March 31, 2014. https://www.nytimes.com/2014/04/01/sports/hobie-alter-surfboard-and-sailboat-innovator-dies-at-80.html.

Hopkins, Jerry. "Hula City: It's Probably the Most Recognizable Dance on Earth, and Probably the Most Misunderstood." *Los Angeles Times*, Oct.17, 1993. http://articles.latimes.com/1993–10-17/magazine/tm-46603_1_hula-dancer.

Housman, Justin. "Clark Foam's Demise, 10 Years Later: A Decade after 'Blank Monday,' It's a Great Time to be a Surfboard Customer." *Surfer*, Dec. 11, 2015. http://www.surfer.com/blogs/culture/clark-foams-demise-10-years-later-grubby-clark.

Imada, Adria L. "Transnational Hula as Colonial Culture." *The Journal of Pacific History*, Vol. 46, September 2011. http://www.tandfonline.com/doi/full/10.1080/00223344.2011.607260.

"John C. McGuire May 6, 1920–December 21, 2013." *San Francisco Chronicle*, Jan. 18, 2014. http://www.legacy.com/obituaries/sfgate/obituary.aspx?pid=169148700.

Kanahele, George S. "Haw'n Renaissance Grips, Changes Island History." From a lecture delivered in May 1979 as part of Kamehameha Schools' Hawaiian Culture Lecture Series. Reproduced in the Hawaiian Music Foundation's *Hailono Mele* newsletter, Volume V, number 7, July 1979. http://ulukau.org/gsdl2.80/collect/hailono/cgi-bin/hailono?a=pdf&d=DHMN005007.1.1&dl=1&sim=Screen2Image.

Kaplan, Sarah. "Alec Cooke, the 'Evel Knievel' of the Dangerous Sport of Big Wave Surfing, Has Disappeared." *Washington Post*, Oct. 30, 2015. https://www.washingtonpost.com/news/morning-mix/wp/2015/10/30/alec-cooke-the-evel-knievel-of-the-dangerous-sport-of-big-wave-surfing-has-disappeared/?utm_term=.821ba084ad25.

Karp, David. "Bill Whitman, 92, Is Dead, Scoured the Earth for Rare Fruit." *New York Times,* June 4, 2007. http://www.nytimes.com/2007/06/04/us/04whitman.html?mcubz=3.

Kelly, Jim. "Last of '50s 'Tiki-Style' Hotels to Disappear from Waikiki." *Pacific Business News,* Feb. 27, 2005. http://www.bizjournals.com/pacific/stories/2005/02/28/focus2.html.

Kogan, Rick. "Pioneer Aviator, Civic Leader Zay Smith." *Chicago Tribune,* May 2, 1995. http://articles.chicagotribune.com/1995-05-02/news/9505020331_1_eagle-scout-mr-smith-amelia-earhart.

Kraft, David, and Ronald Bohn. "A Conversation with Les Baxter." *Soundtrack Magazine* 26, 1981. https://www.runmovies.eu/les-baxter.

Krauss, Bob. "Memoirs of a Very Old Soldier." *Honolulu Advertiser,* March 2, 2005. http://the.honoluluadvertiser.com/article/2005/Mar/02/ln/ln54pbob.html.

Lafrance, Adrienne. "Thomas Edison and the Origins of Surf Filmography." *The Atlantic,* Feb. 23, 2017. https://www.theatlantic.com/technology/archive/2017/02/thomas-edison-and-the-origins-of-surf-filmography/517614.

Lambert, Bruce. "Frank J. Del Giudice Dies at 77; Designed Generations of Airliners." *New York Times,* Oct. 24, 1993. http://www.nytimes.com/1993/10/24/obituaries/frank-j-del-giudice-dies-at-77-designed-generations-of-airliners.html.

Levine, Bettijane. "Modern, Inside-Out: Paul T. Frankl's Sleek Simplicity Gave Rise to a California Look." *Los Angeles Times,* Aug. 16, 2007. http://articles.latimes.com/2007/aug/16/home/hm-frankl16.

Lyman, John. "Pacific Coast Built Sailers, 1850–1905." *The Marine Digest.* June 14, 1941.

Martin, Douglas. "Ellery Chun, 91, Popularizer of the Shirt That Won Hawaii." *New York Times,* June 8, 2000.

McLellan, Dennis. "Miklos 'Miki' Dora, 67; Rebel Surfer." *Los Angeles Times,* Jan. 5, 2002. http://articles.latimes.com/2002/jan/05/local/me-20528.

McLellan, Dennis. "Waltah Clarke, 89; Brought Style of Hawaii to Mainland Fashion." *Los Angeles Times,* May 11, 2002. http://articles.latimes.com/2002/may/11/local/me-clarke11.

Napoleon, Nanette Naioma "Dancing with Fame: Alice Kealoha Holt's Hula Skills Brought Statewide Acclaim and a Small Film Role." *Honolulu Star-Advertiser,* April 2, 2015. http://merriemonarch.staradvertiser.com/dancing-with-fame.

Newlin, Keith. "Jack London: Sailor." *BoatU.S.,* December 2016. http://www.boatus.com/magazine/2016/december/jack-london-sailor.asp.

O'Connor, Christina. "Very Fishy Art." MidWeek magazine, *Honolulu Star-Advertiser,* Dec. 17, 2013. http://www.midweek.com/naoki-hayashi.

Oliver, Myrna. "Francis Hall; Helped Fender, Rickenbacker Guitar Firms." *Los Angeles Times,* Aug. 30, 1999. http://articles.latimes.com/1999/aug/30/news/mn-5096.

Rampell, Ed. "'Hawaii Calls' Again on Two Audiences." *Chicago Tribune,* Feb. 28, 1993. http://articles.chicagotribune.com/1993-02-28/travel/9303185744_1_hilton-hawaiian-village-hawaii-visitors-hawaii-calls.

Rath, Paula. "A Fashion Success Story That Began by Accident." *Honolulu Advertiser,* Nov. 6, 2003. http://the.honoluluadvertiser.com/article/2003/Nov/06/il/il02a.html.

Rath, Paula. "Local Artists Work Magic on Silk Clothing Lines." *Honolulu Advertiser,* April 8, 2002. http://the.honoluluadvertiser.com/article/2002/Apr/08/il/il01a.html.

Reed, Ted. "A Tribute to Billy Gladstone." *Modern Drummer.* https://www.moderndrummer.com/article/october-1981-a-tribute-to-billy-gladstone.

Reynolds, Karyl. "The Legacy of Lalani Village." *Waikiki Magazine,* Sept. 5, 2013. http://www.waikikivisitor.com/2013/ilove-waikiki/the-legacy-of-lalani-village.

Ryan, Tim. "Big Island Artist Eddie Y Likes to Cut to the Chase." *Honolulu Star-Bulletin,* April 27, 2001. http://archives.starbulletin.com/2001/04/27/features/story3.html.

Ryan, Tim. "Sellin' the Sway: Hula Instructor Kent Ghirard, 86, Will Be Honored at the Waikiki Shell for his Contributions to Hawaiian Dance." *Honolulu Star-Bulletin,* Nov. 11, 2004. http://archives.starbulletin.com/2004/11/11/features/index.html.

Ryan, Tim. "Surfer Dude, Surfer Duds: Phil Edwards Is Credited as Being the First to Ride the Banzai Pipeline." *Honolulu Star-Bulletin,* April 15, 1997. http://archives.starbulletin.com/97/04/15/features/story2.html.

Sanburn, Curt. "The Mahu and Aikane Traditions in Old Hawaii." *Honolulu Weekly,* July 20, 2011. http://kumuhina.tumblr.com/post/26465852292/the-mahu-and-aikane-traditions-in-old-hawaii http://honoluluweekly.com/story-continued/2011/07/the-aikane-tradition-homosexuality-in-old-hawaii.

Sanburn, Curt. "The Way We Were: His Buildings Set the Tone for Waikiki. Maybe We Should Take Another Look at What Peter Wimberly Built." *Honolulu Weekly,* Dec. 20, 2000. https://archive.li/9Y7F3#selection-215.0-227.103.

Schou, Nick. "Mike Hynson, Co-Star of 'The Endless Summer,' Resurfaces with Tales of the Brotherhood." *OC Weekly,* July 9, 2009. http://www.ocweekly.com/news/mike-hynson-co-star-of-the-endless-summer-resurfaces-with-tales-of-the-brotherhood-6413929.

Skindrud, Erik. "How Quiksilver Lost Its Soul and Ended Up in Bankruptcy Court." *OC Weekly,* Jan. 21, 2016. http://www.ocweekly.com/news/how-quiksilver-lost-its-soul-and-ended-up-in-bankruptcy-court-6910851.

Slipek, Edwin. "Beyond the Boudoir: How Richmond Courtesan Arabella Huntington Became the Richest Woman in the World." *Style Weekly,* Jan. 10, 2012. https://www.styleweekly.com/richmond/beyond-the-boudoir/Content?oid=1653029.

Snibbe, Kurt. "Getting Plugged In: The Next Time You Hear an Electric Guitar, Remember That the First was Built in California." *San Jose Mercury News,* Aug. 13, 2017.

Stolberg, Sheryl Gray. "50 Years after Loving v. Virginia." *New York Times*, June 11, 2017. https://www.nytimes.com/2017/06/11/us/50-years-after-loving-v-virginia.html.

Tanasychuk, John, and Ivette M. Yee. "Landmark Restaurant to Bid Au Revoir." *Sun-Sentinel*, May 25, 2006. http://articles.Sun-Sentinel.com/2006–05-25/news/0605250133_1_restaurant-la-vieille-maison-fort-lauderdale.

Tavernier, Bertrand. "The Ethical Romantic." *Film Comment*, January/February 2003. https://www.filmcomment.com/article/delmer-daves-bertrand-tavernier.

Taylor, Michael. "Hugh Bradner, UC's Inventor of Wetsuit, Dies." *San Francisco Chronicle*, May 11, 2008. http://www.sfgate.com/bayarea/article/Hugh-Bradner-UC-s-inventor-of-wetsuit-dies-3214987.php.

Therolf, Garrett. "Lunada Bay Surfer Gang Targeted by Class-Action Lawsuit." *Los Angeles Times*, March 29, 2016. http://www.latimes.com/local/lanow/la-me-ln-surfer-gang-class-action-20160329-story.html.

Thomas, Paula. "Dietrich Varez: A Malihini's Legacy of Illuminating Hawaiian Culture and Legend." *Keola Magazine*, May-June 2017. https://keolamagazine.com/hawaii-island/hawaii-island-2017-may-june/dietrich-varez.

Thursby, Keith. "Gretchen Clarke Dies at 78; Waltah Clarke's Hawaiian Shops Executive." *Los Angeles Times*, Jan. 31, 2011. http://articles.latimes.com/2011/jan/31/local/la-me-gretchen-clarke-20110131.

Toth, Catherine E. "Hawaii Surf Activist John Kelly Dies." *Honolulu Advertiser*, Oct. 5, 2007. http://the.honoluluadvertiser.com/article/2007/Oct/05/ln/hawaii710050375.html.

Verrier, Richard. "20th Century Props Reopens Amid Production Rebound in L.A." *Los Angeles Times*, Aug. 18, 2015. http://www.latimes.com/entertainment/envelope/cotown/la-et-ct-20th-century-props-20150819-story.html.

von Busack, Richard. "Tiki It to the Limit." *Metro* (San Jose, CA), Jan. 4–10, 1996. http://www.metroactive.com/papers/metro/01.04.96/tiki-9601.html.

Watrous, Peter. "Lionel Hampton, Who Put Swing in the Vibraphone, Is Dead at 94." *New York Times*, Sept. 1, 2002. http://www.nytimes.com/2002/09/01/nyregion/lionel-hampton-who-put-swing-in-the-vibraphone-is-dead-at-94.html?mcubz=3.

Williams, Mary C. "Al Kocab, Part Owner of La Vieille Maison, the Down Under." *Sun-Sentinel*, Feb. 19, 1994. http://articles.Sun-Sentinel.com/1994–02-19/news/9402190518_1_mobil-travel-guide-la-vieille-maison-waterway-restaurants.

Online Sources, Newsletters and Working Papers

Alfred Shaheen. http://www.alfredshaheen.com.

Avi Kiriaty's Art-Pacifica Prints, Inc. http://www.avikiriaty.com.

Blecha, Peter. "Los Angeles-Based Orville Knapp Orchestra Performs a Seattle Concert—Featuring What Is Almost Certainly the Local Public Debut of the Electric Guitar—on Sept. 13, 1934." Oct. 12, 2016, historylink.org http://historylink.org/File/20161.

Blecha, Peter. "Seattle's Star Hawaiian Guitarist, Helen Louise Ferera, Mysteriously Disappears from a Steamship on Dec. 12, 1919." Nov. 8, 2009, historylink.org http://www.historylink.org/File/9201.

Boyle, Alexander. "Seminole Dreams of Florida Past: Paintings by Eugene Francis Savage (1883–1978)." http://www.hamiltonauctiongalleries.com/Eugene-Savage.htm.

Brand-Fisher, Sonia. "Eugene Berman (1899–1973)." Caldwell Gallery. http://www.caldwellgallery.com/bios/berman_biography.html.

"Bruce Brown—'The Pioneer of Narrated Lifestyle Documentaries.'" http://www.brucebrownfilms.com/about/bruce-brown.

Byrnes, Kerry J. "Arthur Hunt Lyman (2/2/32–2/24/02)." http://www.okemosalumni.org/Arthur-Lyman.htm.

Byrnes, Kerry J. "Paul Kenton Conrad (6/5/32 - present)." http://www.okemosalumni.org/Paul-Conrad.htm.

Carroll, Rick. "The Mood Merchant of Exotic Music Casts His Spell Again in Waikiki." http://www.kevdo.com/exotica/arthurlyman-profile.html.

Castro, Alex R. "The House that Puyats Built." Views from the Pampang, May 27, 2009. http://viewsfromthepampang.blogspot.com/2009/05/151-house-that-puyats-built.html.

Cebu Furniture Industries Foundation. http://www.furniturecebu.com/cfif-ic/cfifFront/viewMaterial.php?mid=54.

"Clair Omar Musser." https://en.wikipedia.org/wiki/Clair_Omar_Musser.

Cook, Lynn. "The Print Master." *Hanahou Magazine*. http://www.kellyarthawaii.com/Hawaiian_Idyll_Exhibit_2005_files/Hanahou%20Magazine.pdf.

Costello, Rory. "Johnny Williams." https://sabr.org/bioproj/person/7a544ac1.

Countryman, Dana. "The Ultimate Martin Denny Interview." July 4, 1997 (Originally published in *Cool and Strange Music! Magazine*, issue 7. http://www.danacountryman.com/denny/denny1.html.

Curtis, Wayne. "The Tiki Wars: How Do We Distinguish the Historic from the Sentimental?" *The Atlantic*, February 2001 https://www.theatlantic.com/magazine/archive/2001/02/the-tiki-wars/302084.

"Deagan Vibraharps." http://www.malletshop.com/deagan.cfm?id=51.

"De Havilland Comet Crash." Aerospace Engineering Blog, June 9, 2012. http://aerospaceengineeringblog.com/dehavilland-comet-crash.

Dinger, Ed. "Pomare Ltd." International Directory of Company Histories. Retrieved May 14, 2017 from Encyclopedia.com, http://www.encyclopedia.com/books/politics-and-business-magazines/pomare-ltd.

"The Earliest Days of the Electric Guitar." Rickenbacker International Corporation. http://www.rickenbacker.com/history_early.asp.
Eddy Y. www.artofeddyy.com.
"Eden Ahbez." https://en.wikipedia.org/wiki/Eden_ahbez.
Enter the Tiki: A Celebration of Polynesian Pop. http://www.enterthetiki.com.
Ernould, Franck. "Michel MAGNE: An Outstanding Man, a Visionnaire Composer." http://ernould.com/Artigrou/magneengl.html.
"Everything You Need to Know about Thomas Edison's 1906 Surf Film." Surfertoday.com, March 16, 2017. https://www.surfertoday.com/surfing/13506-everything-you-need-to-know-about-thomas-edison-1906-surf-film.
"Exotica." http://www.hipwax.com/music/exotica.html.
Farmer, David C. "John Kelly, Visionary of Old Hawaii." Oct. 2, 2005. The *Honolulu Advertiser*: http://the.honoluluadvertiser.com/article/2005/Oct/02/il/FP510020307.html.
"Ford Trimotor." https://en.wikipedia.org/wiki/Ford_Trimotor.
"Frances Langford's Outrigger, Jensen Beach, FL (restaurant)." http://www.tikiroom.com/tikicentral/bb/viewtopic.php?topic=13970&forum=2.
"Frank H. Hale, Old Timer, Industrialist, and Friend of the Filipino People." Ateneo de Manila University, American Historical Collection, Rizal Library. http://rizal.lib.admu.edu.ph/ahc/exhibit/FrankHale.pdf.
Frank's Cane and Rush Supply, Huntington Beach, California. http://www.franksupply.com/bamboo.
Goossens, Reuben. "Matson/Chandris Lines SS Monterey / RHMS Britanis." http://www.ssmaritime.com/britanis.htm.
Goreing, Andrew. "Thank You, Herman E Winterhoff." http://www.hopestreetmarimba.com/thank-you-herman-e-winterhoff.
Green, Maj. Gen. Thomas H. "Martial Law in Hawaii December 7, 1941 –April 4, 1943." http://www.loc.gov/rr/frd/Military_Law/pdf/Martial-Law_Green.pdf.
Halau Hula (Hula Schools, a list of hula schools throughout the world). http://www.mele.com/resources/hula.html.
Hawaii Aviation: An Archive of Historic Photos and Facts. http://aviation.hawaii.gov.
Hawaii Convention and Visitors Bureau (History of). http://www.hvcb.org/corporate/history.htm.
Hawaiian Place Name Spellings. http://manoa.hawaii.edu/hpicesu/DPW/2010_YER/011.pdf.
"Henry J. Kaiser, Hawaiian Booster." The Antiplanner. http://ti.org/antiplanner/?p=552.
"Henry Taylor, Appellant, v. United States of America, Appellee, 320 F.2d 843 (9th Cir. 1963)." http://law.justia.com/cases/federal/appellate-courts/F2/320/843/38674.
H.H. Perkins Co., North Haven, CT. https://hhperkins.com/product-category/rattan-swords.
Historical Currency Conversions (Alan Eliasen). https://frinklang.org/fsp/dollar.fsp.
Hope, Dale. "The Reyn Spooner Story: From Catalina to the Hawaiian Islands." The Museum of Hawaiian Shirts. http://www.themohs.org/Reyn_Spooner.html.
Hopkins, Jerry (Editor). "Another Category of Hawaiian Music: 'Haole Hawaiian.'" *Hailono Mele,* March 1979. http://ulukau.org/gsdl2.80/collect/hailono/cgi-bin/hailono?e=11off—0-v——101025-10-1-0—0-0-1&a=d&cl=CL1.3&d=DHMN005003.
Hopkins, Jerry (Editor). "'Haole Hawaiian' Music Revisited — Auwe & Oh Boy!" *Hailono Mele,* October 1979, pp. 8–9. http://ulukau.org/gsdl2.80/collect/hailono/cgi-bin/hailono?e=11off—0-v——101025-10-1-0—0-0-1&a=d&cl=CL1.3&dl=DHMN005010.1.8&gpl=8&d=DHMN005010.1.8.
"Hornbostel–Sachs." https://en.wikipedia.org/wiki/Hornbostel%E2%80%93Sachs.
Hotz, Alexa. "Trend Alert: Rattan Furniture Made Modern (Plus 15 to Buy)." July 22, 2016. Remodelista. https://www.remodelista.com/posts/trend-alert-rattan-furniture-made-modern-with-15-to-buy.
Hula Preservation Society. http://www.hulapreservation.org.
Kampion, Drew. "John Severson (December 12, 1933-)." http://www.surfline.com/surfing-a-to-z/john-severson-biography-and-photos_905.
Kampion, Drew. "John Severson 1933–2017." https://surferart.com.
Kanoa-Martin, Kaiulani. "Huapala: Hawaiian Music and Hula Archives" (offers lyrics to many Hawaiian songs). http://www.huapala.org.
Kim, Alice. "The Bird of Paradise: A Broadway Show." Hawaii Digital Newspaper Project. https://sites.google.com/a/hawaii.edu/ndnp-hawaii/Home/historical-feature-articles/bird-of-paradise.
Kim, Alice. "The Sugar Daddies: The Spreckels Family Feud." Hawaii Digital Newspaper Project. https://sites.google.com/a/hawaii.edu/ndnp-hawaii/Home/historical-feature-articles/the-sugar-daddies-the-spreckels-family-feud.
Kopf, Dan. "Why Is Interracial Marriage on the Rise?" Priceonomics, Sept. 1, 2016. https://priceonomics.com/why-is-interracial-marriage-on-the-rise.
"List of Percussion Instruments." https://ipfs.io/ipfs/QmXoypizjW3WknFiJnKLwHCnL72vedxjQkDDP1mXWo6uco/wiki/List_of_percussion_instruments.html.
Livingston, Gretchen, and Anna Brown. "Intermarriage in the U.S. 50 Years after Loving v. Virginia: One-in-Six Newlyweds Are Married to Someone of a Different Race or ethnicity." Pew Research Center, May 18, 2017. http://www.pewsocialtrends.org/2017/05/18/intermarriage-in-the-u-s-50-years-after-loving-v-virginia.
Long, Tony. "June 17, 1947: Pan Am Launches 'Round-the-World Service." *Wired Magazine,* May 17, 2009. https://www.wired.com/2009/06/dayintech_0617.
Mak, James. *Creating "Paradise of the Pacific": How Tourism Began in Hawaii.* Honolulu: UHERO: The Economic

Research Organization at the University of Hawaii. (Working Paper No. 2015–1, Feb. 3, 2015). http://www.uhero.hawaii.edu/RePEc/hae/wpaper/WP_2015–1.pdf.

Masters, Nathan. "Manhattan Beach: The City Built on Sand Dunes Celebrates Its Centennial." KCET, Dec. 13, 2012. https://www.kcet.org/shows/lost-la/manhattan-beach-the-city-built-on-sand-dunes-celebrates-its-centennial.

Megowan, Maureen. "History of Redondo Beach." http://www.maureenmegowan.com/Pages/History-of-Redondo-Beach.aspx.

Merrie Monarch Festival. http://merriemonarch.com.

"Missionaries and the Decline of Hula." HawaiiHistory.org. http://www.hawaiihistory.org/index.cfm?fuseaction=ig.page&CategoryID=253.

Motz, Doug. "History Lesson: The History of Columbus' Most Famed 'Lost' Restaurant—The Kahiki." Columbus Underground, Sept. 11, 2012. http://www.columbusunderground.com/history-lesson-the-history-of-columbus-most-famed-lost-restaurant-the-kahiki.

Museum of Hawaiian Shirts. http://www.themohs.org.

Naval History and Heritage Command. "US Navy Personnel in World War II: Service and Casualty Statistics." https://www.history.navy.mil/research/library/online-reading-room/title-list-alphabetically/u/us-navy-personnel-in-world-war-ii-service-and-casualty-statistics.html.

Oceanic Arts. http://www.oceanicarts.net/oa_about.htm#oahistory.

Office of Hawaiian Affairs: 2010 United States Census. http://www.ohadatabook.com/cen2010.html http://www.oha-databook.com/QT-P9_United%20States.pdf.

Ortega, Josué, and Philipp Hergovich. "The Strength of Absent Ties: Social Integration via Online Dating." Oct. 2, 2017. https://arxiv.org/pdf/1709.10478v1.pdf.

Pacific Aviation Museum. http://www.pacificaviationmuseum.org/pearl-harbor-blog/pan-ams-pacific-clippers.

Rath, Paula. "Beyond Island Wear." *Humanities, the Magazine of the National Endowment for the Humanities,* March/April 2013.

"Rick Griffin (USA)." Christian Comics International. http://www.christiancomicsinternational.org/griffin_pioneer.html.

Ritchie, James. "James Ritchie's Borneo Headhunting "How-Tos." WoWasis.com, June 7, 2010. http://www.wowasis.com/travelblog/?p=1198.

"Robert Drasnin." https://en.wikipedia.org/wiki/Robert_Drasnin.

"Russell Garcia (composer)." https://en.wikipedia.org/wiki/Russell_Garcia_(composer).

"Santa Anita (detention facility)." Densho Encyclopedia. http://encyclopedia.densho.org/Santa_Anita_%28detention_facility%29.

Schmidt, Karen. "A New Book Revisits Columbus' Storied Tiki Temple, Gone but Not Forgotten." Columbus Monthly, Dec. 9, 2014. http://www.columbusmonthly.com/content/stories/2014/12/book-excerpt-back-to-the-kahiki.html.

Schofield, Hugh. "The Return of the Honky Chateau." BBC News, Dec. 17, 2015. http://www.bbc.com/news/magazine-35152716.

"Search for Surfer Alec 'Ace Cool' Cooke Ends, Coast Guard Assumes the Worst." The Inertia, Nov. 3, 2015. http://www.theinertia.com/surf/search-for-surfer-alec-ace-cool-cooke-ends-coast-guard-assumes-the-worst.

Seed, John. "Rare Manookian Paintings Removed from the Hotel Hana-Maui." HuffPost, July 14, 2010. https://www.huffingtonpost.com/john-seed/rare-manookian-paintings_b_643357.html.

Sibley, Gail. "Georgia O'Keeffe in Hawaii……Really???" April 12, 2013. http://www.gailsibley.com/2013/04/12/georgia-okeeffe-in-hawaii-really.

Skelley, Steven. "Mai-Kai Restaurant and Polynesian Islander Revue." EDGE Media Network, March 2, 2012. https://www.edgemedianetwork.com/index.php?ch=entertainment&sc=theatre&sc2=reviews&sc3=performance&id=130561.

Snyder, Craig. "Hobie Alter: Industry Pioneer and Innovator." Skateboarding Heritage Foundation. http://www.skateboardingheritage.org/programsmenu/skateboardingheritagehalloffame/hobiealter.

Snyder, Midori. "Dreamy Art Deco Magazine Covers for Asia Magazine by Frank McIntosh." May 14, 2009. http://www.midorisnyder.com/the_labyrinth/2009/05/dreamy-art-deco-magazine-covers-by-frank-mcintosh.html.

Swank Pad (Tim Glazner). www.swankpad.org.

Swiggum, S., and M. Kohli. "Dollar SS Company." The Ships List: 2008–07–01. http://www.theshipslist.com/ships/lines/dollar.shtml.

Tiki Central. http://www.tikiroom.com.

"Tom Blake (surfer)." Wikipedia. https://en.wikipedia.org/wiki/Tom_Blake_(surfer).

Torrence, Bruce. "Hollywood's Don the Beachcomber Restaurant." Hollywoodphotographs.com, Aug. 21, 2011. http://hollywoodphotographs.com/blog/hollywoods-don-the-beachcomber-restaurant.

Tropical Sun Rattan Company. http://www.tropicalsunrattan.com.

Tucker, Terry. "George Paele Mossman, Part I: The Ukulele Builder." UkuZoo, Feb. 14, 2011. http://ukuzoo.com/Blogs/post/George-Paele-Mossman-Part-I-The-Ukulele-Builder.aspx.

United States Census Bureau. Census of Housing, historical home values. https://www.census.gov/hhes/www/housing/census/historic/values.html.

United States Internal Revenue Service. "Ninety Years of Individual Income and Tax Statistics, 1916–2005." https://www.irs.gov/pub/irs-soi/16–05intax.pdf.

"Unpublished [Johnny] Noble Manuscript Found in Gift to HMF." Originally published in the *Hailono Mele* newsletter, September 1979, p. 7. http://ulukau.org/gsdl2.80/collect/hailono/cgi-bin/hailono?e=11off—1-v——101025-10-1-0—0-0-1&a=d&cl=CL1&dl=DHMN005009.1.5&gpl=5&d=DHMN005009.1.5.

"Victor-Charles Mahillon." https://en.wikipedia.org/wiki/Victor-Charles_Mahillon.

"Visitors Fed Up with Localism Use the Law to Fight Back." Ross Law, April 4, 2016. http://www.rosslawpdx.com/law-blog/2016/4/4/visitors-fed-up-with-localism-use-the-law-to-fight-back.

"Waikiki Beachboys." http://www.hawaiihistory.org/index.cfm?PageID=394.

Whitaker, Jan. "Ohio + Tahiti = Kahiki." May 28, 2013. https://restaurant-ingthroughhistory.com/tag/coburn-morgan.

Wright, Renee. "Mementos of a Royal Hawaiian Love Story." March 30, 2011. http://www.worthpoint.com/blog-entry/mementos-royal-hawaiian-love-story.

Zosa, Victoria. *Local Cooperation and Upgrading in Response to Globalization: The Case of Cebu's Furniture Industry.* De La Salle University, Manila. http://www.dlsu.edu.ph/research/centers/aki/_pdf/_concludedprojects/_volumei/zosa.pdf.

Online Films and Video Clips

American Experience: The Massie Affair. Dir. Mark Zwonitzer, PBS, 2005. https://www.youtube.com/watch?v=pLgZzHtbPQ0.

Bianzhong Concert at Hubei Museum. https://www.youtube.com/watch?v=ZXEDv8bJ27M.

China Clipper Inaugural Passenger Flight 1936, Part 1. https://www.youtube.com/watch?v=XR0K6HfDe4w.

China Clipper Inaugural Passenger Flight 1936, Part 2. https://www.youtube.com/watch?v=FBLP3VKnZcQ.

China Clipper Inaugural Passenger Flight 1936, Part 3 https://www.youtube.com/watch?v=362cfVEyu0s.

China Clipper Inaugural Passenger Flight 1936, Part 4 https://www.youtube.com/watch?v=XMMTuKDDfcM.

Coniston: Fate Stepped In. British Pathé. https://www.youtube.com/watch?v=4xemKc2In5Y.

Flying with Arthur Godfrey/ Prod. Jerry Fairbank, 1953. An Eastern Airlines Lockheed L-1049 Super Constellation Promo Film. Here, Arthur Godfrey discusses the history of passenger flight, the Super Constellation's role, and pilots it on a flight from New York to Miami. https://www.youtube.com/watch?v=U6VfkKjlhXs.

Giants, the Flying Boats. (History of the Martin Mars flying boat). https://www.youtube.com/watch?v=Y22F9O3A0EM.

"Greg Noll Search for Surf." https://www.youtube.com/watch?v=jsnDNkObXJg.

"Harold Chang-Hawaii's Living Legend." Filmed by Robert Joyce. https://www.youtube.com/watch?v=opmsCShAum8.

"The Human Fly." Vintage Airliners.com. June 22, 2014. https://vintageairliners.com/the-human-fly.

"John M. Kelly, Artist in Hawaii." https://www.youtube.com/watch?v=ImQ_chwKv-8.

Lyman, Arthur. "Arthur Lyman at the Makai Bar." https://www.youtube.com/watch?v=_nrP0GcZRTw.

Lyman, Arthur. "On the Town, Pt. 2, Taboo." https://www.youtube.com/watch?v=72jr7VAn29s.

The Magic of the Exotica Lyman Years and More with Harold Chang. https://www.youtube.com/watch?v=J8RDJiQXUzI.

Pan Am Boeing 377 Stratocruiser Promo Film, 1950. https://www.youtube.com/watch?v=v92U2F9gbUo.

Powell, Eleanor. "Hula" (from the film *Honolulu*, 1939). https://www.youtube.com/watch?v=ks2fHGt68TI.

Powell, Eleanor. "Hula Tap" (from the film *Honolulu*, 1939). https://www.youtube.com/watch?v=9KDMy5w2JB4.

Severson, John. *Pacific Vibrations* (1969). https://www.youtube.com/watch?v=CzhKDusI9ashttps://www.youtube.com/watch?v=CzhKDusI9as.

"Surf Board Riders" and "Surf Scenes," two of the 30 sequences in the Edison Company's 1906 compilation film, *Hawaiian Islands*, filmed by Robert Kates Bonine. https://www.youtube.com/watch?v=dz32fG3Y2dY.

"The Surfer's Journal: 50 Years of Surfing on Film—John Severson." Dir. Ira Opper, 2014? https://www.youtube.com/watch?v=7NiTmjo1kek.

(Thai musical instruments) Khryang Tii: Hit Instruments (Made of Metal). http://www.seasite.niu.edu/Thai/music/classical/instruments/khryang_tii2.htm.

"Thomas A. Edison's 'Hawaiian Islands'": The Surf Scenes Shot in 1906. https://www.youtube.com/watch?v=dz32fG3Y2dY.

"Tribute to Harold Chang: Harold Chang and Arthur Lyman — 18 Years of Making Music Together." https://www.youtube.com/watch?v=G9PslwssoVk.

Vacances en Bretagne. Dir. Pierre Sisser, 1970. https://archive.org/details/TouteLaBandeVacancesEnBretagne.

Index

Numbers in **_bold italics_** indicate pages with illustrations

Abe, Tomi 218
Aberle, George *see* ahbez, eden
Abraham, Janine 152
Adventures in Paradise (television series) 68, 139
AeroSpacelines, Inc. 46–47
African-American service and defense personnel in WW II Hawaii 253n27
Agent Orange (rock band) 208
Agins, Terry 158
ahbez, eden 95
Air France 47
aircraft disasters 40–41, 45, 48
Aiu, Margaret 71
Aka, Mitsue (Tori Richard) 170
Akea, Keoki 86
Aku Aku Restaurant (Stardust Casino, Las Vegas) 126, 136
Alama, Sam 92
Albini, Franco 152
Alessandroni, Alessandro 252n65
Alitalia 49
"all girl" bands 118, 242n98
Allan, Kirby (Sidney Allen Pittman) 110
Allen, Richie and the Pacific Surfers 208
Allen, Steve 108
Allman, Duane 90
Aloha Airlines 73
Aloha Hawaii 65
Aloha Maids (Hawaiian Room, Hotel Lexington) 67–69
Aloha Oe 66
aloha shirt *see* Hawaiian shirt
Aloha Week 73–74, 162
Aloma, Hal (Harold David Alama) 69, 84–85, 93
Aloma of the South Seas 66
Altenbach, Bernard 133
Alter, Hobart "Hobie" 203–204
Alth, Charlotte 156
Alth, Max 156
Anderson, Ron ix, 176–178
Anderson, Tom 171–172
Andrade apparel 164, 166

Anzac Clipper (Boeing 314) 42
Apaka, Alfred 93, 103, 112, 126
Apana, Det. Chang 141
Apollo space program 46
The Aqua Velvets 209
Arago, Jacques 53, **_53_**
Archer, George Tautu 73
Armstrong, Louis 90, 117–118
Army Air Corps *see* U.S. Army Air Corps
USS *Aroostook* 38
Around the World in Eighty Days 65
Art Vogue apparel 168
Arthur, Pres. Chester A. 214
Arthur, Linda 160–162
Asia magazine 26
the Astronauts 208
ATA (Air Transport Association of America) 48
Atillo's Rattan and Wood Industries 245n29
The Atlantics 208
August, Robert 202, 251n36
Auld, Agnes "Aggie" 65–66, 71, 235n51
Auletta, Ted 113
Avalon, Frankie 201
The Aviator 148
Awai, George "Keoki" 83, 87

Bailey, David (Bailey's Antiques and Aloha Shirts, Honolulu) 168, 185, 248n45
Bain, Barbara 139
Bali 21, 116, 242n98
Bana Lahui (Hawaiian National Band) 62, 235n37
The Banjo Barons 91
Banks, Joseph 14–15
Banner Records 85
Barbelle, Albert 230ch1n3
Barefoot Adventure 201
Barnes, Brooks 150
Barnes, John 222
Barrett, Neil 156
Barrymore, Ethel 63
Barrymore, John 161

Barrymore, Lionel 63
baseball team Hawaiian shirts 184, 189, 246n2
Bass, Saul 200, 251n30
Batish, Ashwin 209
Baughman Furniture Factory 143, 149
Baxter, Les ix, 12–13, 95–101, 104, 111, 113, 240n23, 240n26
Beach, Donn (Ernest Gantt) 124–126, 129 , 136, 224, 242n8, 242n9; *see also* Don the Beachcomber Restaurant
The Beach Boys 193, 307
beach boys of Waikiki 196, 211
Beamer, Harriet, Helen Desha, and Winona 66, 71
Beauchamp, George 88
Becker, Leilehua "Lei" 68–69
The Bel-Airs 208
Bel Geddes, Norman 26
bells, tuned musical *see* Chinese bianzhong bells
Berger, John 84
Bergeron, Victor Jules 127–129, 224, 243n32; *see also* Trader Vic's Restaurant
Berle, Milton 134
Berman, Eugene 136, 244n78
Betty Boop 84
Betty's Bamboo Isle 84
"Big Five" sugar monopolies 31, 232n52
Big Jim McLain 74
big wave surfing 206–207
Big Wednesday 199
Bigard, Albany "Barney" 100
Bigelow, Bill 94
Biggers, Earl Derr 141
Bingham, the Rev. Hiram 54, 194
bird calls and animal cries in exotica music 103–104
Bird of Paradise (airplane) 39
Bird of Paradise (Broadway musical) 64, 83
Bird of Paradise (film) 66, 73, 84
Bishaw, Mapuana Mossman 67

265

Bishop Museum (Honolulu) 69, 71, 180
Black, Cobey 249n68
Black, Nicholas "Nicky" ix, 176, 178–179
Blake, Thomas Edward "Tom" 194, 196–197, 203
Blanco, Antonio 21
Blanding, Donald Benson 64
The Blonde Captive 65
Blue Hawaii 66, 73, 245n19
BOAC (British Overseas Airway Corporation) 42, 47–48
Body Glove International wetsuits and apparel 206
Boeing Airplane Company 12, 30, **32**, 33–34, 36, **41**, 40–47, 46–50
Boeing flying boats requisitioned by U.S. military, WWII 42, 161
Boeing B-29 Superfortress bomber 44, 226
Boeing B-47 turbojet bomber 49
Boeing B-52 Stratofortress bomber 49
Boeing 247 36, 233–234n38
Boeing 314 Clipper flying boat **32**, 33–34, 40–44, **41**, 46, 124, 160, 225, 233n2
Boeing 367–80 demonstrator 49
Boeing 377 Stratocruiser 12, 34, 43–47, 50, 234n46
Boeing 707 jet 46–50, 233n37
Boeing XC-97 44
Bogart, Humphrey 135
Bonine, Robert Kates 194–195
Bonnet, Rudolf 21
Borneo 20–21, 122, **122**, 231n9
Borzage, Frank 84
Bow, Clara 66
Bowes, Edward "Major" 118
Boyd, Bill and His Cowboy Ramblers 81, 89
Boyer, Charles 145
Brabazon Committee 47
Bradner, Hugh 205
Braeger, Dick (Garys Island) 177
Brando, Marlon 254n45
Branfleet/Kahala apparel, 248n52
Brangier, George 248n52
Braniff Airlines 49
Bray, David "Daddy" 70–71, 73, 92
Bray, Lydia "Mama" 70–71, 73, 92
Brewster, Sen. Ralph Owen 226
Bridges, Lloyd 252n50
Bright, Solomon Kekipi "Sol K" 84–85
Briner, Herbert "Herb" 161, 164
The Bronx (brothel) 218
Brooke, James (Rajah of Sarawak) 20
brothels 15, 218–220, 254n36; *see also* prostitution
Brown, Bruce 200–202
Brown, DeSoto ix, 25, 160
Brown, Francis Hyde II 65, 103, 235n52

Brown, Milton and His Musical Brownies 81, 89
Browne, Bud 199–201
Buffet, Guy 14, 175–176, 179–180, 249n71
Buffett, Jimmy 123, 168
Burgi, Richard 141
Burke, Sonny 112
Burr, Henry 86
Burr, Raymond 134
Burridge, Walter 235n31
Butte, Meyers 197
Byrd, Gerald "Jerry" 90
Byrnes, Kerry J. 113

C & H Sugar jingle 75
Cable Act of 1922 221–222, 247n28
Caen, Herb 129
Cage, Nicolas 168
Calatrava, Santiago 156
Calder, Alexander 49
California Gold Rush 54
California Heritage Museum 149
California Supreme Court 222
Cambra, George 141
Campbell, Al 86
Campbell, Donald (death) 207
Canada, Hawaiian music and hula performances in 76, 86–87
Canadian Pacific Air Lines 47, 49
Candy, John 149
Capitol Records 100–101, 105
Carlisle, Cliff 87, 90
Carter, Pres. Jimmy 166
Casa Cebuana Incorporada 245n29
Cassidy, Michael 176, 180, 249n59
Castle & Cooke 31, 232n52
cattle industry 212
Cebu Furniture Industries Foundation 153
Cecilio & Kapono 189
celeste 117
Chamberlain, Richard 140–141
Chang, Harold 106–107
The Chantays 193, 208
Chapin, Gardner "Gard" 199, 251n24
Chaplin, Charlie 124, 145
Charlie Chan at Treasure Island 84
Charlie Chan films 84, 141–142
Charteris, Leslie (Leslie Charles Bowyer-Lin) 131, 253n13
Chenault, Jeff ix, 108
Cheng, Yvonne 176, 180–181, 249n59
Cherry, Don 110–111
Chiha, Signor Lou "Friscoe" 118
China Clipper (Martin M-130) 41
Chinese-Americans 217, 221
Chinese bianzhong bells 13, 114–116, **115**, 241n81, 241n83
Chinese Exclusion Act of 1882 213–214, 253n13
Chinese-Hawaiians 15, 72, 142, 213, 215–216

Chinese war brides 221
Choris, Louis 53, **54**
Chun, Ellery 160–161, 247n10
Church of Jesus Christ of Latter-day Saints *see* LDS Church
City of Wichita Ford Tri-Motor 34–35
Civil Aeronautics Board (CAB) or Administration 30–31, 49
Civil Rights Act of 1964 222
Clancey, Robert J. 246n2
Clark, Gordon "Grubby" 203, 251n40
Clark, Virginia 100
Clarke, Walter "Waltah" 164, 166, 247n29
Clark's Royal Hawaiians *see* Hokea, Ben
Cleghorn, Archibald Scott 21–22
Cleghorn, Victoria Kaiulani *see* Princess Kaiulani
Clemens, Samuel *see* Twain, Mark|
Cleopatra (film, 1934) 148
Clift, Montgomery 162–163
Clipper Good Hope (Pan American) 45
Clipper Mayflower (Pan American) 45
Clipper Southern Cross (Pan American) 45
Club House Party see Smeck, Roy
Cobonpue, Kenneth 156
coffee industry 212
Coiner, Charles T. (N.W. Ayer & Son) 230ch1n2
Colbert, Claudette 148
Cole, Nat King 96
Collette, Buddy 110
Collins, Cryin' Sam 87
Colman, Ronald 145
Colón, August "Augie" 97, 102–104, 240n41
Coltrane, John 109–111
Como, Perry 85
Connell, Lt. B.J. 38
Conniff, Ray 91
Conrad, James 140
Conrad, Paul Kenton 109, 112–113
Conrad, William 140
Conroy, John M. "Jack" 46
Consolidated PBY Catalina flying boat 43
Contino, Dick 91
Cooder, Ry 90
Cook, Captain James 11, 15, 20, 22, 194
Cooke, Alec "Ace Cool" (death) 207
Coolidge, Pres. Calvin 214
Cooper-Hewitt Museum 151
Cornero, Tony (Anthony Cornero Stralla) 125, 242n9
cost of transpacific air travel 34, 40, 43, 45–46, 50, 123
cost of transpacific passenger ship passage 24

Index

Countryman, Dana 105
Cousteau, Jacques 205
Covarrubias, Miguel 18, 21, 122–123, 242n5
Cover Girl 136
Crane, Cheryl 135–136, 244n70
Crane, Stephen 14, 124, 134–136
Crawford, Joan 162
Crosby, Bing 65, 73, 91, 124, 163, 235n45
Cugat, Xavier 104
Cunha, Albert Richard "Sonny" 63, 92
Curly Top 66
currency conversion to modern figures 7
Curtis, Wayne 133–134

Daffan, Theron "Tad" and the Blue Islanders 89
Dale, Dick (Richard Anthony Monsour) 15, 207–208, 252n63
Dana, Bill "Jose Jimenez" 91
Dana, Charles Henry 63
Daniels, William "Chick" 196
Darren, James 201
Darrow, Clarence 215
Daves, Delmer 73, 236n92
Davidson, Wayne 130
Davis, Bette 65
Davis, Judge Charles S. 215
Davis, Miles 109
Day, A. Grove 213
Deagan, J.C., Inc. (John Calhoun Deagan) 118
Dean, Don 102
DeCarlo, Yvonne 139
Decca Records *see* Burke, Sonny
Dee, Sandra 201
Defoe, Daniel *see* Robinson Crusoe
de Havilland, Sir Geoffrey 47
de Havilland Comet 47–48
Del Giudice, Frank J. 44, 233n37
Del Rio, Dolores 65
Delta Air Lines 49
Denny, Martin 12–13, 95–98, 101–106, 111–112, 117, 120, 126, 209, 239n8
Derby, Charles 53–54
Desha, Helen 66
Desha, Isabella 66
De Tackacs, Andre 230ch1n3
Diddley, Sir Bald and His Right Honourable Big Wigs 208
Dietrich, Marlene 124
Dillingham Corporation 171
Disney apparel 189–190
Disney World Polynesian Village 85, 138
Disneyland Adventureland 137
Disneyland Enchanted Tiki Room 123
Divorced Sweethearts 84
Dobro Manufacturing Company 82

Dr. Kanahele's Hawaiian Music and Musicians 82
Dole, Sanford Ballard 253n9
Dole Air Derby 87, 233n19
Dole Pineapple Company (James Drummond Dole) 18, 38, 230ch1n2, 233n19, 244n1, 253n9
Dollar Line 27, 232n41
Don Juan 87
Don the Beachcomber Restaurant 11, 73–74, 102–103, 122, 124–130, 137, 164
Doohan, James 140
Dooley, James 141
Doolittle, Gen. James "Jimmy" 126
Dora, Miklos "Mickey Da Cat" 201, 251n24
Dorian, Pat 171–172
Dorsey Brothers 68, 85
Douglas, Donald 41
Douglas Aircraft Company 30–31, 37, 40–41, 43–44, 47–50 198, 233n33
Douglas DC-2 40
Douglas DC-3 37, 73, 233n13
Douglas DC-4 30–31
Douglas DC-6 43–44, 233n33
Douglas DC-8 jet 47–50
Douglas Sleeper Transport (DST) 37
Dowsett, Queenie Ventura 126
Drasnin, Robert 112–113
Duane, Marguerite 74
Dulles, Allen 8
Dumond, Jacques 152
Dunn, Bob 13, 81, 88–89

Earhart, Amelia 35, 39, **163**, 233n21
East India Store *see* Watumull's
Eastern Airlines 48
Eden, Barbara 139
Edison Company, films and recordings 82, 118, 194–195, 224, 250n4
Edwards, Phil 199, 202, **204**, 204, 249n61, 252n45
Edwards, Webley 93–94, 103, 239n55
Eek, Piet Hein 156
Ejiri, Masakazu 91
Electro String Instrument Company *see* Rickenbacker Manufacturing Company
Ellington, Edward "Duke" 100, 252n63
Ellis, William Kalii Sumner 82
Emma Claudina (Matson) 24
Endless Summer 201–202
English, Rear Adm. Robert Henry 41
SS *Enterprise* (Matson, 1901) 24
eugenics (fear of interracial breeding) 213–214
Evergreen Aviation and Space Museum 227

Evinrude, Ralph 129
exotica music: elements 97, 239n55; rock bands influence by 97, 239–240n13; sexy album covers 96–97, **97**, **109**, 109–110, 241n71
exoticism 9–11, 17–19, 210, 229
Expatriation Act of 1907 221

Fairbanks, Douglas 161
Fairmont Hotel, San Francisco *see* Tonga Room
Family Affair (television series) 68
Feher, Joseph 45, 234n40
Feldman, Josh (Tori Richard) ix, 168–171
Feldman, Mort (Tori Richard) ix, 168–171
Fender, Clarence "Leo" and Fender Guitars 88, 208
Ferreira, Helen Louise Geenus 82–83, 86
Ferreira, Palikiko "Frank Ferera" 82–83, 86
Ficks Reed Furniture Company 146, 245n10
Field, Mike ix, 176, 181
Field, Sally 201
Fijian shirts 246–247n3
Filipina war brides 221
Filipino-Americans 221
Filipino-Hawaiians 15, 213
Fio Rito, Ted 93
A Fistful of Dollars 209, 252n65
Fitzgerald, Jon 108–110
Fleetwood Mac *see* Green, Peter
Fleischer, Dave 84
Fleming, Victor 66
Fletcher, Christian 206
Flirtation Walk 84
Flying Squadron (female USO entertainers) 217
Focus (rock band) 97
Foersom, Johannes 156
Fokker C-2-3 airplane 39
Foo, Mark (death) 207
For a Few Dollars More 209, 252n65
Forbidden Island 103
Ford, Alexander Hume 195
Ford Tri-Motor airplane 12, 34–37
Fortescue, Grace 215
Foster, Harry W. 58–59
Foster, John 8
Foynes Flying Boat Museum 33
Franchini, Anthony J. 83
Frankl, Paul Theodor 14, 143–146, 148, 151, 245n8
Fraternal Order of Moai 121
Frazier, Charles 25
Freeth, George, Jr. 195
French Polynesia *see* Polynesia
Frew, John 230ch1n3
From Here to Eternity 162
Frontiere, Dominic 113
Fujii, Jocelyn 249n59

Fuller, Buckminster 240n31
Funicello, Annette 201

Gabor, Zsa Zsa 134
Gabriel, Florian 135
Gabrielson, Honolulu Police Chief William 219–220
Gagnan, Emile 295
gamelan orchestra 116
Gant, Arthur 172
Gant, Elliot 172
Gantt, Ernest *see* Don the Beachcomber Restaurant
Garbo, Greta 124
Garcia, Russ 96
Gardner, Ava 135
Gauguin, Paul 12, 21–22, 26, 179
Gennett Records 85
Gessler, Clifford 211
Ghirard, Kent 74, 112, 126
Ghirardelli Chocolate Company 74, 237n97
Gibbs, Frederic 231n29
Gibbs, William 231n29
Gibson, Edmund "Hoot" and the Hawaiian Foursome 84, 87
Gidget 201
Gigot 241n79
Gilliom, Lloyd 68
GIs and war workers in Hawaii and the Pacific 8–9, 13, 15, 17, 50, 72–73, 146, 216–224, 229, 253n27
Gladstone, William "Billy" 118, 242n94
Gleason, Jackie 241n79
Glenn L. Martin Company *see* Martin, Glenn Luther
Godfrey, Arthur 73, 85, 93–94, 163, 239n56
Golden Gate International Exposition (San Francisco, 1939), 77, 85, 122
The Golden Girls (television series) 148
Goodman, Benny 106, 119, 242n104
Gotcha apparel 206
Gould, Morton 113
Goulet, Robert 134
Grable, Betty 66–67
Graham, Donald Houston, Jr. 172
Grant, Archie 107, 112
Grauman's Chinese Theater (Sid Grauman) 86, 88
Green, Lloyd 89
Green, Peter 90, 97
Greg Noll Search for Surf 200; *see also* Noll, Greg
Griffin, Richard "Rick" 200–201, 251n32

Haaheo, Sam Pua 70
Hailono Mele newsletter *see* Hawaiian Music Foundation
Halau Na Wai Ola (Island Moves) *see* Isa-Kahaku, Kaui

Hale, Frank 144–149, 245n6, 245n8
Hale, Helen 74
Hale Hawaii apparel 161
Hall, Edmond Celeste Quartet 117
Hall, Francis C. 88
Hall, Litheia 26
Hamilton, Forestorn "Chico" 110, 110, 241n72
Hampton, Lionel 106, 118–120, 240n47
Hana Like Club 72
Hang Loose apparel 206
"Haole Hawaiian" music 90–91
Hapa Haole Hula Competition (Vancouver, BC, Canada) 76
hapa haole music 63–64, 76, 82, 86, 90–94
Hapa Haole Music Festival (Honolulu) 76
Hara, Clarence 171
Harrison, Charles 86
Hawaii Calls (film) 65
Hawaii Calls (radio program) 13, 15, 82, 93–94, 228–229, 239n55, 239n56
Hawaii Clipper (Martin M-130) 41–42
Hawaii Five-0 (television series) 66, 113, 140–141
Hawaii Teamsters Union Local 996, interference with film crews 141
Hawaii Tourist Bureau 18, 72, 234n3
Hawaiian Airlines 39, 232n49; *see also* Inter-Island Airways, Ltd.
Hawaiian Annual 65
Hawaiian Bureau of Information *see* Hawaiian Promotion Committee
Hawaiian Casuals apparel 164
Hawaiian Eye (television series) 13, 68, 107–108, 139–140
Hawaiian fashion industry sales 162–164, 167, 248n38, 248n44
Hawaiian Guitar Duet *see* Ferreira, Palikiko "Frank Ferera"
Hawaiian interracial marriage statistics 215–216
Hawaiian Islands (film) 194–195
Hawaiian language 7, 54
Hawaiian music and song, traditional forms 91
Hawaiian Music Foundation viii, 75, 91
Hawaiian musical instruments, traditional 92
Hawaiian National Band *see* Bana Lahui
Hawaiian Nights 84
Hawaiian Novelty Five *see* Nawahi, "King Bennie"
Hawaiian Pineapple Company *see* Dole Pineapple Company
Hawaiian population statistics 213, 216, 218, 234n8

Hawaiian Promotion Committee (HPC) 52, 64
Hawaiian Quintette 64, 82–83
Hawaiian Renaissance 75–76
Hawaiian Republic *see* Republic of Hawaii
Hawaiian Room (Hotel Lexington, New York) 13, 67–69, 73, 85, 92–93, 122
Hawaiian shirt: artists 175–191, 248–249n57, 249n59; classifications and elements 158–160, 174–175, 247n5, 247n8, 248n56; costs and pricing 174–175, 179; history 160–192; manufacturing 164–168, 172–177, 187–188; prices 168
Hawaiian Style apparel 191
Hawaiian Surfing Movie 199
Hawaiian-themed television series 139–141
Hawaiian Village Hotel 140, 212, 240n31; *see also* Kaiser, Henry J.
Hawkins, Coleman 100
Hayashi, Naoki ix, 176, 182–183
Hayon, Jaime 156
Hayward, Philip 108–110
Hayworth, Rita 135
headhunting 20, 231n9
Heath, Fran 197–198
Hedley, Eli 14, 96, 136–137, 244n75
Hedley, Marilyn 14, 96, 136–137, 244n75
Hefner, Hugh 139
Hegenberger, Lt. Albert Francis 39, 233n19
Hell's Half Acre 74, 126
Helzapoppin' (Broadway musical) 68
Hemmings, Aka 178, 249n66
Henie, Sonja 65
Hennessey, Tom 82, 235n43
Henry, Leland "Lee" (Kahiki Supper Club) 133–134
Heyerdahl, Thor 135, 237n105
Heywood Bros. & Company 152
HiFi records *see* Vaughn, Richard
High Tension 84
Hilo Hattie (Clara Inter) 66, 90, 162, 168
Hilo Hattie apparel 168–169, 247n8
Hilo Hawaiian Orchestra *see* Ferreira, Palikiko "Frank Ferera"
Hines, Earl "Fatha" 117
Hiort-Lorenzen, Peter 156
Hiram, Eleanor Leilehua 70–71
His Jazz Bride 84
His Pastimes see Smeck, Roy
Hite, Les (Sebastian's Cotton Club Orchestra) 119
HK-1 (Hughes-Kaiser 1 flying boat) *see* "Spruce Goose"
Hobie apparel 189, 206
Hobie Cat catamaran 204, 252n45

Index

Hobie skateboards 204
Hobie surfboards 203–204
Hoge, F.H., Jr. 225
Hokea, Ben 86
Hokulea (seafaring canoe) 76
Holland, Milt 113
Holmes, Tommy 178, 192, 249n66
Holo-Holo apparel 161
Holt, Alice Kealoha 67
Holt, Meymo Ululani 67–68
"Honky Chateau" 241n79
Honolulu (film) 67
Honolulu Chamber of Commerce 61–62
Honolulu Lu 67
Honolulu Magazine 75
Honolulu Museum of Art 171, 230ch1n1
Honolulu Star-Bulletin 29, 160
Hooper, Stix 97
Hoopii, Sol 7, 13, 77, 84–85, 87, 89
Hoover, Herbert C. (president) 62
Hope, Bob 100
Hope, Dale ix, 14, 160–161, 169, 176–182, 184, **186**, 187–188, 191–192, 248n52, 248n54, 249n59, 249n66, **C7**
Hope, Howard R. 161, 191, 250n104
Hopkins, Jerry viii, 63, 66–67, 74, 76–77, 90–91, 140–142
Hornbostel-Sachs system of musical instrument classification 116–117, 241n88
USS *Hornet* 106
Hotel Street (Honolulu) 218–220
House, Eddie "Son" 87
Howell, Bill 102
HRH apparel (Howard Hope) 178, 191, 250n91
Huang, Yunte 142
Hughes H-4 Hercules see "Spruce Goose"
Hughes, Howard and Hughes Aircraft 15, 148, 198, 225–227
Hui Menehue 217
Hui Nalu Club 195, 250–251n13
Hukilau Festival (Fort Lauderdale, FL) 121
Hula (film) 66
hula: banned in Hawaii 54–55, 236n76; basic movements 79, 237n109; schools 12, 51–52, 68, 71–72, 74, 76–80
Hula Nani Girls *see* Ghirard, Kent
Huntington, Henry Edwards 195, 250n9
Huntington Library (Arabella Yarrington Hntington) 250n9
Hurricane 83
Husokawa, Shuhei 96
Hutcherson, Bobby 13, 97, 119
Hynson, Mike 202, 251n36

idiophones *see* vibraphone history
Imada, Adria 53, 62, 73
Immigration Act of 1924 214
Ince, John 66
Ince, Thomas 66
Indonesian shirts 246n3
Inka Taky Trio 101
The Insect Surfers 209
Inter, Clara *see* Hilo Hattie
Inter-Island Airways Ltd. 30, 39, 232n49
interracial dating-themed literature and film 221–222
interracial marriages *see* Hawaiian interracial marriage statistics; marriages, interracial
Iolani apparel 161, 164
Iona, Andy 67, 84, 90
Irene West Royal Hawaiians *see* West, Irene Royal Hawaiians
Isa-Kahaku, Kaui ix, 51–52, 77–80, **78**
Isaacs, Alvin "Barney" 94
Isaacs, Bud 89
Island Son (television series) 140–141
Island Trade Store *see* Hedley, Ed
The Islanders 209
Isle of Tabu 68
Israeli Air Force 46
Ives, Burl 91

Jackson, Milt 119, 241n71
Jacobs, Hap 203, 205
Jacobsen, Arne 152
Jade Warrior 97
Jake and the Fat Man (television series) 140–141
Jamaica Jaxx apparel 169, 248n49
James, Elmore 90
Jams apparel 199, 206
Jan and Dean 307
Japanese-Americans 77–79, **79**, 217, 221, 237n114
Japanese-Hawaiians 15, 77–79, 164, 213, 215–216
Japanese war brides 221
J.C. Penney apparel 164, 166, 247n26
Jefferson, Lemon "Blind Lemon" 87
Johnson, Rep. Albert 214
Johnson, Leon "Chaino" 110
Johnson, Pres. Lyndon B. 222
Johnson, Robert 87
Jolson, Al 93–94, 235n45
Jon & the Nightriders 209
Jones, Albert O. 215
Jordan, James "Big Jim" 203
Judd, Gov. Lawrence M. 215
Jungle Jim (film series) 136

K & F Manufacturing Corporation *see* Fender, Clarence "Leo"
Kaahumanu (queen) 54, 65
Kahahawai, Joe 215
Kahala Bay Club apparel 178, 191
Kahala Sportswear 171, 176–177–178, 180–184, 186–188, 191–192, 201, 248n52, **C7**
Kahalewei, Haunani 126
Kahanamoku, Duke 15, 161, 163, **163**, 194–195, 197, 199, 203, 224
Kahananui, Dorothy M. 66
Kahauolopua, Haleloke 239n56
Kahiki Supper Club, Columbus, Ohio) 124, 133–134, 137–138
Kaili, David 82–83
Kainapau, George 67
Kaipualani 107
Kaiser, Henry J. 102–193, 106, 108, 140, 212, 240n31, 240n36
Kalaheo apparel 246n2
Kalakaua, David (king) 7, 13, 21, 23, 55–58, **56**, 61–62, 75
Kalakiela, 'Too Bad' Jack 22
Kalapana 189
Kamehameha I 54, 162
Kamehameha II (Liholiho) 54
Kamehameha III (Kauikeaouliu) 54, 93, 212–213, 238–239n50
Kamehameha IV (Alexander Liholiho) 55
Kamehameha V (Lot Kapuaiwa) 55
Kamehameha Garment Company 27, 161, 164
Kamuca, Richie 139
Kanahele, George S. 75–76, 84
Kanahele, Katherine "Keaka" 65, 71
Kanakole, Edith 71
kapa cloth 247n8
Kapahu, Kini (Jennie Wilson) 13, **57**, **59**, 57–63, 67, 235n22
Kapiolani (queen) 58
Kapuaiwa, Lot (king) *see* Kamehameha V
Kauffman, Clayton "Doc" 88
Kauikeaouliu (king) *see* Kahehameha III
Kawananakoa, Abigail (princess) 74
Kaye, Sammy 68
Kekahuna, Pauline 25, 74, 126
Kekaula, Katie (Kakalina Nakaula) 71
Kekuku, Joseph 82–83
Kelii, David 93
Kelly, John Melville 25–26, 197
Kelly, John Melville, Jr. 25–26, 197–198
Kelly, Katherine "Kate" 25–26, 197
Kelly, Marion 26
Kenley Players 134, 244n65
Kientz, Philip E. 133
Kilauea Volcano Cyclorama 61–62, 235n31
Kingdom of Hawaii 24; *see also* Kalakaua, David (king); Liliuokalani (queen)
King-Smith apparel shop *see* Chun, Ellery

Kinney, Ray 67
Kiriaty, Avi ix, 176–177, **183**, 183–184, 187, **C7**
Kirsten, Sven 121–123, 126
Kivlin, Matt 199
Kiwala, A. 64, 238*n*10
Knapp, Orville and Orchestra 88
Kocab, Al ix, 131, **132**, 133–134, 137, **137–138**, **C4**, **C5**
Kohner, Frederick 201
Kohner, Kathy 201
Kolomoku, Walter 64, 82–83, 89, 237*n*5
Kon-Tiki raft *see* Heyerdahl, Thor
Kon-Tiki Restaurants 135
Korean-Americans 217, 221
Korean-Hawaiians 15, 213
Korean war brides 221
Kramer, John Burnett 102–103, 106
Krauss, Bob 73
Kumulipo chant 77
Kuykendall, Ralph 213

La Belle Irene and the Royal Hawaiians *see* West, Irene Royal Hawaiians
Lacy, Clay 46, 49
Ladd, Cheryl 141
Laika and the Cosmonauts 208
Lalani Hawaiian Village *see* Mossman, George Paele
Lamour, Dorothy 65–66, 90
Langford, Frances 90, 124, 129, 137, 243*n*37
USS *Langley* 38
László, Paul 245*n*10
Latham, Sid 131, **C5**
Laughton, Charles 145
Lauhala apparel 161
Lawrence, Ed 129, 137
laws against interracial marriage 221–222, 247*n*28
LDS Church 70–71
Lee, Alvin 90
Lee, Kuiokalani "Kui" 132
Leedy Manufacturing Company (Ulysses Grant "Lys" Leedy) 118
The Legend of Pele (album cover) **109**, 109–110
Lei, Betty Hula Studio 74
Leilani, Prince 65
Leone, Sergio 209
Leslie, Glenwood 84
Letty Lynton 162
Levy, David (Mai-Kai Restaurant) 131–133
Levy, Mireille (Mai-Kai Restaurant) 131–133
Lewis, Max 164
Lewis, Meade "Lux" 117
Leydon, Rebecca 99, 101–102
Liberty House apparel 164, 170, 178, 247*n*27
Liberty Records **97**, 102–104
Life Magazine 162, 221

Light, Enoch 108
Light Crust Doughboys 89
Liholiho (king) *see* Kamehameha II
Lihoiliho, Alexander (king) *see* Kamehameha IV
Likelike (princess) 21, 23
Liliuokalani (queen) 21, 23, 62, 215, 224, 235*n*37
Lincoln, "Bill" 71
Lindbergh, Charles 35, 38, 43, 233*n*33
Linn's apparel 164
"Little Egypt" 59–60
Local Motion apparel 177, 191, 248*n*52
Lock, Julia Tong 71
Lockheed Constellation 233*n*33
Lockheed Corporation 46, 148, 198, 233*n*33
Lockheed L-188 Electra 46
Loewy, Raymond 31–32
Lofgren, Orvar 11, 19, 230Intro.*n*8
Logan, Eldridge 25
London, Jack 12, 15, 195
Lord, Edward J. 215
Lord, Jack 140
Los Angeles Mirror 148
Los Angeles Steamship Company 18
Love, Winona Nancy 65–66, 71, 103
Love Is a Many-Splendored Thing 221
Lovegren, Lloyd 129
Loving v. Virginia 222
Low, Clem 107
Lua, Pale 82–83, 86
Luahine, Iolani 65, 71, 73, 126
Lunalilo, William Charles (king) 55
Lurline (1887) 24, 232*n*28
SS *Lurline* (Matson, 1908) 24, 232*n*28
SS *Lurline* (Matson, 1932) 12, 25–26, **28**, **29**, 29–32, 107, 232*n*28
SS Lurline (Matson, 1963) 32
Lyman, Arthur Hunt 5, 12–13, 95–98, 102–112, **105**, **109**, 120, 126, 140, 212, 240*n*31, 240*n*46, 240*n*47
Lyman, Kapiolani 107
Lynde, Paul 134
Lynes, Russell 52

MacGillivray Freeman Films 199
Machado, Lena 77–78
Machell, Thomas 117
Mack, Norman Edward 63
MacLeod, Gavin 140
MacMillan, Cdr. Donald Baxter 228
Macnee, Patrick 140
Macouillard, Louis 25
Mader, Vivienne 71

Magma (rock band) 241*n*79
Magne, Michel 114, 241*n*79
Magnum, P.I. (television series) 140–141
Magnusen Act of 1943 253*n*9
Mahillon, Victor Charles 117
mahu transgender dancers 53–54, 253*n*27
Mai-Kai (film) 131
Mai-Kai Restaurant (Fort Lauderdale, Florida) ix, 14, 113, 121, 124, 127, 129–133, **132**, 137, **138**, 243*n*43, **C4**, **C5**
Maitland, Lt. Lester James 39, 233*n*19
Makai Bar 107
Malibu beach 198–199
Malihini apparel 161, 164, 247*n*6
Mallinson Company 27
SS *Malolo* 12, 26, 28–29, 215
Mangelsdorff, Albert 111
Manhattan Project 205
Mann, Herbie 97
Manning, Frederick 230ch1*n*3
Manookian, Armand Tateos **18**, 29, 232*n*46
Mansdorf, Lee 46, 234*n*48
Maoris 122
Margolis Manufacturing and Retail Co. (Richard and Evelyn Margolis) *see* Hilo Hattie apparel
marimba orchestras 118
SS *Mariposa* (Matson, 1931) 12, 25–26, 30
SS *Mariposa* (Oceanic, 1883) 24
Markey, Enid 66, 235–236*n*57
Marquis Yi of Zeng (Zeng Hou Yi) *see* Chinese bianzhong bells
marriages, interracial 215–216, 220–223, 254*n*45
Marryat, Frank 20
Martin, Glenn Luther 30, 34, 39–43, 45, 233*n*22
Martin, Paula *see* Becker, Leilehua "Lei"
Martin, Ross 140
Martin Company *see* Martin, Glenn Luther
Martin guitars 84, 185
Martin M-130 flying boat 34, 39–43, 45, 233*n*22
Marx Brothers 124
Mason, Miles M. ix, 175–176, **184**, 184–185, 249*n*89, **C7**
Massie (Thalia) Affair of 1931 214–215, 249*n*68
Matson, William 12, 24, 27
Matson liners converted to troop carriers during WWII 27, 30–31, 161
Matson Navigation Company 12, 17–18, 24–32, **28**, **29**, 39–32, 41, 69, 72, 92, 160, **163**, 171, 232*n*28, 232*n*29, **C1**, **C2**
SS *Matsonia* 26, 31, 84–85, 94, 163, 199

Index

Maurin, Nicolas Eustache 53, **53**
Maynard, Amie and Her Royal Hawaiians 85
McAuliffe, Leon 13, 81, 88–89
McCarthy, Sen. Joseph 8
McColgan, John N. 62
McCullough, Reyn 171–172, 175
McCullough, Tim viii-ix, 14, 169, 172–174, 180–182, 184–185, 188–189, **204**, 248n55, 248–249n57, 249n60, 249n61, 249n71, 250n91, **C6**; *see also* Reyn Spooner
McConnell, E.W. 62, 235n31
McDonald, Cdr. Eugene Francis 228–229
McDowell, Mississippi Fred 90
McGuire, Allan 86
McGuire, John (McGuire Furniture Company) 151–152
McInerny's apparel 164, 166
McIntire, Dick 84, 90
McIntire, Lani 67–68, 84–85, 92–93
McIntosh, Frank 12, 17, 25–26, 30, **C2**
McKay, Gardner 139
McKirahan, Charles F. (Mai-Kai Restaurant) 127, 130
McPherson, Aimee Semple 84
McQueen, Steve 202
Mehitabel Furniture Company 151–152
Meier, Theo 21
Meigs, John Keoni 27
Meistrell, Bill 205–206, 252n50
Meistrell, "Bob" 205–206, 252n50
Melanesia 122, 127
Memphis Slim 17
Merman, Ethel 90
The Mermen 209
Merrie Monarch Festival (Hilo) 58, 74–75, 189
Meshugga Beach Party 208, 252n63
metallophones *see* vibraphone history
Metro-Goldwyn-Mayer *see* MGM
Metropolitan Museum of Art (New York) 156
MGM 67, 145
Michener, James A. 95, 139, 221
Micronesia 123
Mid-Pacific magazine 195
MidWinter Fair (California Midwinter International Exposition, San Francisco, 1894) 62, 235n31
Miles, William 86
Milius, John 199
Miller, Edward "Dude" 250–251n13
Miller, Jack 84, 88
Million Dollar Weekend 43
Mills, Arnold 102
Mills Brothers 90

Mitchum, Robert 135
Miyamoto, Koichiro 160–161
Moana Hotel 25, 65, 74, 92–93, 195–196, 211, 250–251n13
Monk, Thelonious 117
Montalbán, Ricardo 140
Montenegro-Aboitiz, Doña Maria *see* Mehitabel Furniture Company
SS *Monterey* 12, 25, 30–31
Montgomery, Rosalie Lokalia 73
Montgomery, Tim 73
Montgomery Ward 164
Moody, Janice (Tori Richard) 170
The Moon of Mona Koora 65
Moore, Richard C. 25
Moore-Brabazon, Lord John Theodore Cuthbert 47
"Le Morgan" *see* Morgan, Leland Stanford
Morgan, Beverly "Bev" 205–206
Morgan, Coburn 133, 137–138
Morgan, Leland Stanford "Le Morgan" 230ch1n3, **C3**
Mormons *see* LDS Church
Morricone, Ennio 209, 252n65
Morse, Ella Mae 100
Mossman, George Paele 69–70
Mossman, Leilani 70
Mossman, Piilani 68, 70
Mossman, Pualani 13, 25, 67–70, 132, 236n64, 236n69
Mossman, Sterling and His Barefoot Bar Gang 140
MPS Records (Germany) 110–111
Munoz, Mickey 201
Munson, Lucy Logan 71
Murray, Arthur 101
"Musa-Shiya the Shirtmaker" *see* Miyamoto, Koichiro
Musick, Edwin Charles 39 233n21
Musser Marimba Company (Clair Omar Musser) 118–119
Mustel, Auguste 117
Mustel, Victor 117
Mutiny on the Bounty (1935 film) 83
Mutiny on the Bounty (1962 film) 254n45
My Three Sons (television series) 68

Nainoa, Eugenia 82
Nainoa, Samuel 82
Nakashima, George 130, 133, 135
Namekalua, Alice 71
Naope, George 74–75
National String Instrument Corporation 82, 85, 88
Native Hawaiian population statistics 213
Naturalization Act of 1906 222
Nawahi, Joe 84–86
Nawahi, "King Bennie" 84–86
Nelson, Robert Lyn ix, 14, 175–176, 186, 250n91

Never So Few 104
New Guinea 123, 133
New York Herald Tribune 214
New York Times 150
New York Tribune 83–84
Nieman Marcus 180–181
No Ka Oi Producers, Inc. (Reyn Spooner) 173–175
Noble, Johnny, 28, 63, 65, 84, 91–93
Noelani Hawaiian Orchestra 88
Noll, Greg "Da Bull" 199–200, 203, 207
Noonan, Frederick Joseph 39, 233n21
Norfleet, Nat, Sr. 248n52
SS *North Haven* 39
Northwest Orient Airlines 44–45
Norvo, Red 119
Notley, Tootsie 25, 40, 72–73

Oahu Publishing Company 89
Ocean Pacific (OP) apparel 189, 206
Oceanic Arts 138–139
Oceanic Steamship Company 23–24, 27
Ohana: The Luau at the Lake (Lake George, NY) 121
O'Keeffe, Georgia 18, 230ch1n2
Oland, Warner 141
Olko, Henry 152
O'Loughlin, Alex 140
On Any Sunday 202
On Mark Engineering 46
101 Strings 91, 101
One West Waikiki (television series) 141
O'Neill, Jack 203, 205–206
Oni Oni E 68
Oppenheimer, Robert 205
Orbison, Roy 139
Orientalism 10–11
Owens, Harry 66, 92–93, 162, 239n53

Pa, Solomon 73
Pacific Clipper (Boeing 314) 42, 233n28
Pacific Commercial Advertiser 55
Pacific Mail Steamship Company 23, 27, 83, 232n41
Pacific Sportswear apparel 161, 164
Pacific System Homes 197
Pacific Vibrations 187, 200–201
Padilla, Marcel "Marsh" and Beachcomber Trio 134, 243–244n64
Page, Bettie 130
Pahinui, Philip "Gabby" 93, 239n6
Pahonu Estate (Oahu) 140
Paka, July Kealoha 63, 82, 235n42, 235n43
Paka, Toots 63–65, 82, 235n42
Palea, James Kuluwaimaka 69
Pali Hawaiian Style apparel 171

Pan American Airways 12, 30–34, 39–46, 49, 73, 160–161, 233n22
Pan-American Exposition (Buffalo, 1901) 61–62, 235n31
Panama-Pacific International Exposition (San Francisco, 1915) 64–65, 83
Papanikolas, Theresa 19
Paradise of the Pacific magazine 29
Paramount Pictures 145
Passion Fruit 66
Patagonia apparel (Pataloha) 191–192
Patterson, Pat (Champion Rep Riders) 87
Paull, Edward 230ch1n3
Penny, Joe 140
Perez v. Sharp 222
Perkins, Wilson "Lefty" 81, 89
Perry, Al Kealoha and Singing Surfriders 93, 239n55
Peterson, Byron L. 112
Peterson, Oscar 117
Pezman, Steve 180, 249n59
Pfeiffer, Edward 230ch1n3
Pfeiffer, Frank 221
Pfeiffer, Sachiko 221
Philippine Clipper (Martin M-130) 41
Philippine Islands 143–146
Pich, Sopheap 156
Pickford, Mary 161
Picot, Leonce 137
Picture Island 65
pineapple industry 164, 244n1, 253n9, **C8**
Pleshette, Suzanne 139
Plum, Mette Munk 156
PN-9 flying boat (U.S. Navy) 38
Polynesia 21, 122–123
Polynesian architecture 123, 126–127, 130, 133, 212
Polynesian-themed bars and restaurants 123–124, 126–127, 134–138, 224; *see also* Crane, Stephen; Don the Beachcomber; Kahiki Supper Club; Mai-Kai; Trader Vic's; Wimberly, George "Pete"
Polynesian-themed décor 134–138, 146–156
Polynesian women, allure of 20–22, **53**, **109**, **128**, 216–217, 235n41, **C5**
Pomare apparel 168
Popular Mechanics magazine 156
Portuguese-Hawaiians 83, 213
Post, Robert, Jr. 139
Powell, Eleanor 67, 236n59
"Pregnant Guppy" (AeroSpacelines B-377PG) *see* AeroSpacelines, Inc.
SS President (Pacific Steamship) 83
Presley, Elvis 66, 73, 139, 163, 237n93
primitivism 9–10

Princess Kaiulani 21–23, **22**
prostitution 135, 217–220, 254n37; fees and salaries during the war 219; *see also* brothels
Puerto Rican Hawaiians 213
Pukui, Mary Kawena 71
Punahou School (Honolulu) 178
Puuhonua o Honaunau National Park, Hawaii 122
Puyat, Gonzalo 145, 245n8
The Pyramids 208

Quigg, Joe 199
Quiksilver apparel 181, 206

USS R-4 submarine 38
Ragsdale, Harvey 103
Rain 129, 137
Rains, Gene 112–113, 241n76
Rangner, Mike 42–43
Raskin, Milt 113, 241n78
rattan: buying recommendations 150; depletion of forests 245n29, 246n44; furniture manufacturing 145, 153–156, **154**, 246n36; furniture terms 151–152, **154**, 245n28; harvesting and varieties 152–153, 246n35; stress-testing, Philippine Standard 153–155
Rattan: A Home Craftsman's Guide 156
Rattan Art & Decorations (furniture retailer) 143
Rattan Arts (Rattan Originals) 245n29
Rattan Pacifica 245n29
Rattan: Tropical Comfort Throughout the House 150
Rawitzer, William S. 151; *see also* Vogue Rattan Manufacturing Company
Ray, Marcia 176
Reed, Sen. David 214
Reid, Willis "Billy" 86
Remington, Herb 88–89
Republic of Hawaii 23, 58, 213, 215, 224, 253n9
Revel, Harry 100
Reyn Spooner apparel 14, 43, 169–174, 179–182, 184–186, 188–190, 248–249n57, 249n60, 249n61, **C6**, **C7**
Richard, Bill 204
Richards, Tim 204
Richardson, Asst. Atty. Gen. Seth W. 214
Rickenbacher, Adolph 88
Rickenbacker, Eddie 48, 88
Rickenbacker Manufacturing Company 84, 88
Ritts Furniture Company (Herb and Shirley) 146, 149, 245n19; *see also* Blue Hawaii
RJC apparel 246n2
Ro-Pat-In A-22 "Frying Pan" guitar 88

Road to Singapore 66
Robertson, Cliff 201
Robillard, Albert B. 169
Robinson Crusoe 19–20, 230–231ch1n3
Rochester, Charles E. 67–68
Rochlen, Dave 199
Roderick Dhu (Matson, 1896) 24
Rodgers, Jimmy 87, 90
Rodgers, John 38, 233n17
Rojatt, Rick "The Human Fly" 49, 234n64
Rol, Dirk Jan 152
Rollini, Adrian 119
Romig, James S. "Jim" 168
Rooke, Emma (queen consort) 55
Roosevelt, Pres. Franklin D. 87
Rosenbaum, Morris Studios 230ch1n3
Ross Sutherland apparel 164, 172
Roth, Ed "Big Daddy" 251n32
Roth, William Matson 27
Roth, William P. 27
Rousseau, Henri 21
Roy, Pierre 18
Royal Hawaiian apparel 161, 164
Royal Hawaiian Band 119
Royal Hawaiian Girls Glee Club *see* Silva, Louise Akeo
Royal Hawaiian Glee Club 83
Royal Hawaiian Hotel 25, 28–29, 65, 71–72, 74, 92–93, 102, 127, 196, 211, 214
Royal Hawaiian Orchestra 29, 92–93
Royal Hawaiian Quartet *see* Awai, George "Keoki"
"RS" Rosebud 230ch1n3
rum drinks 125, 128–129, 131
Russell, Jane 227

Sacramento Union 22, 55
Said, Edward W. 10–11
sailing passage to Hawaii 23–24, 231n19, 231n20
St. Denis, Ruth 71
San Francisco Chronicle 127,129
San Francisco Examiner 151
San Jose Giants Hawaiian Night 51–52, 77–78, **78**
Sanburn, Curt 127
Sandwich Islands 20, 194
Santa Cruz, California 193, 195, 203, 205–206, 209
Santa Monica Heritage Museum 149
Santamaria, Mongo 110
Sapp, Bill (Kahiki Supper Club) 133–134
Savage, Eugene 12, 25–27, 171, **C1**
Save Our Surf (SOS) 198
Schiffer, Nancy (Schiffer Publishing) 149–150, 162
Schiffer, Peter (Schiffer Publishing) 149–150, 162
Schluter, Henry J. 118

Index

Schmaltz, LeRoy *see* Oceanic Arts
Schofield Barracks (Oahu) 218
Schroder, Andrew "Andy" 81, 89
Schwartz, Harvey ix, 143, **144**, 147, 146–151, 156, **C4**
Scott, Cyril 112
The Sea Around Us 251–252n41
Sea Hunt (television series) 252n50
Search for Surf 200
Sears, Roebuck and Company 164, 247n26
Selkirk, Alexander 19–20, 230–231ch1n3
Selleck, Tom 140–141
Selznick, David O. 65
Sennett, Mack 84
Severson, John viii-ix, 14, 106, 176, **186**, 186–188, 193, 199–201, 249n59, 250n94, 252n66
The Shadows 208
Shaheen, Alfred Ltd. ix, 162, 164–166, 172, 236n69, 247n33
Shaheen Tunberg, Camille ix, 164, 166
Shank, Bud 201
Sharpe, Emma Kapiolani Farden 65, 72
Shawn, Ted 65, 71
Shearing, George 102, 106
sheet music covers 19, 230ch1n3, **C3**
Shell Bar (Hawaiian Village Hotel) 12, 102–103, 106–108, 112, 140, 212, 240n31
The Sid Presley Experience 208
Sikorsky S-38 flying boat 30, 39
Sikorsky S-41 flying boat 43
Sikorsky S-42 flying boat 34, 39, **42**, 42, 170, **170**, 233n22, **C7**
Sikorsky S-43 flying boat 39
Silva, Louise Akeo 28, 93
Simmons, Robert "Bob" 199
Sinatra, Frank 140, 162
Sir Francis Drake: The Rise of English Sea Power 222
Sitz, Ken 88–89
Skateboarder Magazine 252n66
skateboarding 204
Skelton, Red 108
Skwiot, Christine 64, 211–212
Slack, Frederick "Freddie" 100
slack key guitar 96, 239n6
Slate, Lane 141
Slater, Kelly 206
Slippery When Wet 201
Smeck, Roy 87
Smith, Tobi 149
Smith, Zay & Associates 44, 233–234n38
Snow, Hank 87
Snow, Maude Marie 87
Soares, Alan 106–108
Song of the Islands 66
South African Airlines 48
South of Pago Pago 83

South Pacific (film) 221
South Seas Adventure 126
Spaatz, Gen. Carl 126
Spaghetti Westerns 209, 252n65
Spears, Mary 176
Speer, Albert 188
Spencer, James ix, 99, 101
Spooner, Ruth 172, 248n55
Spreckels, Adolph Bernard 23, 231n23
Spreckels, Alma de Bretteville 231n23
Spreckels, Claus 12, 23–24, 62, 231n23
Spreckels, John Dietrich 23
Spreckels family dissention 231n23
"Spruce Goose" 225–227
Stafford, Jo 90
Stainback, Gov. Ingram 220
Stannard, David 64, 211, 215
Steer, Col. Frank 72–73
Steichen, Edward 25
Stein, Ralph of Hudson (New York) 150
Sterling, Rear Adm. Yates, Jr. 214
Stetson apparel 166
Stevens, Connie 107, 140
Stevens, Dave 137
Stevens, Harriet Daisy "Napua" 65, 71, 93
Stevens, Inger 139
Stevens, R.T. 28
Stevenson, Elinor (McGuire Furniture Company) 151–152
Stevenson, Robert Louis 12, 23, 56, 58
Stevenson, Rosalie 126
Stone, Sharon 140
Stone, W. Clement 212
Stordahl, Axel 112, 241n75
Streisand, Barbra 149
Sturges, John Eliot 104
sugar industry 24, 31, 164, 212–213, 232n52
Sugarman, Harry M. (The Tropics club) 125, 135
Sullivan Ed 85
Sumac, Yma (Zoila del Castillo Vivanco) 100–101, 240n23
Sund, Cora Irene "Sunny" 126, 130
Sunn, Rell 192, 249n59, 250n105
"Super Guppy" (AeroSpacelines B-377SG) *see* AeroSpacelines, Inc.
Surf 200
Surf Crazy 201
Surf Fever 200
surf music, instrumental 207–209
The Surf Punks 208
Surf Safari 200
The Surfaris 208
surfboard technology 202–204, 206

surfboards, traditional Hawaiian classifications 194
Surfer magazine 186–187, 200–201
Surfer's Journal 180
surfing films 199–202
Surfing Hollow Days 201–202
Surfline apparel 189, 206
Surf'n'Sand Hand Prints *see* Shaheen, Alfred
Surfriders apparel 161
surfwear apparel and industry 189, 206
Sutherland, Ross 172
Suyin, Han 221, 254n45
Swastika Surf-Board Company 197
Swayze, Patrick 168, 248n45
Sweet, Dave 203

Tahiti 21, 127, 179, 194
Tahiti Nights 162
Takabuke, Isamu 171
Takamine, Vicky Holt 76
Takeshige, Robert 161
Tales of the South Pacific 221
Tampa Red 87
tapa cloth *see* kapa cloth
Tatum, Art 117
Taylor, Hound Dog 90
Tchicai, John 111
Teague, Walter Dorwin Associates 44
Temple, Shirley 66
Tenney, Edward Davies 27
Terorotua, Sizou 131
Terorotua, Toti 131
Terri, Salli 113
Territory of Hawaii v. Fortescue (1932) 215
Thai war brides 221
Thomas, Dana 162, 168
Thornhill, Claude 69
Thornton, Jack R. 129–133; *see also* Mai-Kai Restaurant
Thornton, Robert F. "Bob" 129–133; *see also* Mai-Kai Restaurant
Thrum, Thomas George 65
Thurston, Asa 54
Thurston, Lorrin Andrews 52, 235n31
Tiki Central 123
tiki: culture 14, 114, 139, 142, 224; images **122**, 122–123, 133, 136–137, **138**, 139
Tiki Oasis (San Diego, CA) 121
Tjader, Cal 110, 119
Tommy Bahama apparel 169, 248n48
Tonga Room (Fairmont Hotel, San Francisco) 68, 85
Tori Richard Ltd. apparel ix, 27, 43, 164, **170**, 168–171, 178, 248n52, **C7**
Tormé, Melvin "Mel" and the Mel-Tones 100
Towncraft apparel *see* J.C. Penney
Toy Story 175

Tracy, Terry "Tubesteak" 201
Trade Winds Trading Company (Donn Beach) 125
Trader Joe's (grocery retailer) 169
Trader Vic's Restaurant 11, 103, 124, 126–129, *128*, 134, 164, 243*n*34
Transcontinental Air Transport (TAT) 35–36
Transcontinental and Western Air, Inc. *see* TWA
Trans-Mississippi Exposition (Omaha, 1898) 61–62
Trans-Pacific Airlines *see* Aloha Airlines
Treaty of Reciprocity 24, 212
Trippe, Juan Terry 39, 41, 43–44; *see also* Pan American Airways
Tropical Sun Rattan Company *see* Schwartz, Harvey
Tropicana apparel 164, 247*n*6
Tropicraft Corporation *see* Hale, Frank
Tropitan *see* Ritts Furniture Company
Truman, Pres. Harry S 162
Tsao, Alice (Kahiki Supper Club) 134
Tsao, Michael (Kahiki Supper Club) 134
Turner, Ike 90
Turner, Lana 135, 244*n*70
TWA 36
Twain, Mark 12, 21–22, 55, 77, 194
20th Century-Fox 150
20th Century Props *see* Schwartz, Harvey
Tyner, McCoy 13, 97, 111, 117

UAT (Union Aéromaritime de Transport) airlines 47
Uggams, Leslie 140
ukulele craze on the mainland 64–65, 82, 86, 96
United Air Lines 31, 37, 43–45, 49, 73
USO (United Service Organizations) 15, 72–73, 106, 217–218
U.S. Army 72, 200, 218
U.S. Air Force 49, 112
U.S. Army Air Corps and Forces 38–39, 42, 102, 126, 165
U.S. Marines 217
U.S. Navy 38–39, 42, 106, 127, 151, 199, 201, 205, 214–218, 230Intro.*n*3
U.S. Supreme Court 222

van der Linden, Robert F. 35
Van Dorpe, Robert "Bob" 130–131
Van Eps, Fred 86
Van Hamersveld, John 201, 251*n*38

Van Oosting, Robert *see* Oceanic Arts
Varez, Dietrich 175–176, 188–189, 250*n*98
Varges, Diego 249*n*60
Vaughn, Richard 108–109
Velez, Lupe 67
Velzy, Dale 201, 203
The Ventures 208
vibraharp *see* vibraphone history
vibraphone history 114, 117–120, 241–242*n*92
Victor Talking Machine Company (Victor Records) 83–85, 88, 235*n*46
Vidor, King 65, 84
Vietnamese war brides 221
visitor statistics from mainland to Hawaii 23, 50, 163–164, 234*n*68
Vivanco, Moisés 101, 240*n*23
Vogue Rattan Manufacturing Company 146, 149, 151
Von Busack, Richard 121
von Neumann, John 205
von Stroheim, Otto 107
Von Tempski, Armine 66

Waikiki sand imported from Manhattan Beach, California 196
Waikiki Surf-Board Company 197
Waikiki Wedding 84
Wakefield Rattan Company 152
Waldorf, Mel *see* Meshugga Beach Party
Walker, Aaron "T-Bone" 100
Waller, Thomas "Fats" 117
war brides 221, 223
Warner, Sandy Faye 96, **97**, 239*n*8
Waronker, Simon "Si" 95, 102–103
Warshaw, Matt ix, 194, 200
Watanabe, Alan 112
Waters, Bruce M. 149–150
Waters, Muddy (McKinley Morganfield) 90
Watumull's (Jhmandas and Gobindram J. "Goma" and Ellen Jensen Watumull) 164, 247*n*28, 254*n*45
Webb, Jean Francis 22
Webb, Nancy 22
Weber, Myrna 130
Webster, Benjamin "Ben" 100
Wechter, Julius 103
Wells, Pat 133
West, Irene Royal Hawaiians 83, 85–86
West, Mae 124
West, Sam Ku 84–85
West, Wesley "Speedy" 89
West Coast jazz 110, 241*n*72
Westenhaver, William 139
wet suit invention and technology 204–206

Wheeler Field (Honolulu) 39
The White Flower 66
Whitford, Hannah Toots Jones *see* Paka, Toots
Whitman, "Bill" 203, 251–252*n*32
Whitman, Dudley 203, 251–252*n*32
Whitman, Ottis "Slim" 90
Whitney, Henry Martyn 55
Whitney, Samuel 55
Wiedlin, Jane ix, 185
William and Frederick (illustrators) 230ch1*n*3
Williams, Andy 91, 108, 134
Williams, John 113
Willow and Reed *see* Olko, Henry
Wills, Bob and His Texas Playboys 81, 89
Wilson, Charles 62
Wilson, Jennie *see* Kaphau, Kini
Wilson, John Henry "Johnny" 61–63
Wilson, Marty 110, 113–114, 241*n*71
Wilson, Stanley 114
Wimberly, George "Pete" 14, 124, 126–127, 130
Wind Surf magazine 201
Winter, Johnny 90
Winterhalter, Hugo 91
Winterhoff, Herman E. 118
Wisner, John 245*n*10
Witco Décor 139
women of the South Seas (early travelers' descriptions) 20–22
Wood, Ronnie 90
Wood, Sally 71–72
Woodd, Jennie "Napua" 67–69
the Woodies 209
Worden, William L. 28
Works Progress Administration (WPA) 26
world music and world beat 96–97, 239*n*9
World's Columbian Exposition (Chicago, 1893) 59–60, 235*n*31
Wray, Fred Lincoln "Link" 208

Y, Eddy (Tatsuya Yamamoto) ix, 14, 175–176, **190**, 189–191, **C6**
Yankee Clipper (Boeing 314) 33, **41**
Yater, Reynolds "Renny" 178, 249*n*64
Yeager, Linnea "Bunny" 130
yodeling cowboy singers 90
Young, Gordon S. 160
Young, Lester 100

Zanuck, Darrilyn 199
Zaputo, Jason ix
Zenith Transoceanic radio 15, **228**, 228–229